W9-CDX-567

Sources of

Twentieth-Century
Global History

Sources of

Twentieth-Century Global History

James H. Overfield
University of Vermont

HOUGHTON MIFFLIN COMPANY   BOSTON   NEW YORK

◆ *To Andrew, Jane Ellen,*
and Kathleen, all children
of the twentieth century

Editor-in-Chief: Jean Woy
Sponsoring Editor: Nancy Blaine
Associate Editor: Julie Dunn
Senior Project Editor: Bob Greiner
Senior Production Coordinator: Jodi O'Rourke
Senior Manufacturing Coordinator: Marie Barnes
Senior Marketing Manager: Sandra McGuire

Source and photo credits appear on pages 453–456, which constitute an extension of the copyright page.

Copyright © 2002 by Houghton Mifflin Company. All rights reserved.

No part of this book may be reproduced or transmitted in any form or by any means, electronic or mechanical, including photocopying and recording, or by any information storage or retrieval system without the prior written permission of Houghton Mifflin Company unless such copying is expressly permitted by federal copyright law. Address inquiries to College Permissions, Houghton Mifflin Company, 222 Berkeley Street, Boston, MA 02116-3764.

Printed in the U.S.A.

Library of Congress Catalog Card Number: 2001092363

ISBN: 0-395-90407-2

5 6 7 8 9 FFG 08 07 06 05 04

Contents

Contents

Preface

Several goals and principles have guided the writing of *Sources of Twentieth Century Global History.* Primary among them is the conviction that students of history at any level need to meet the challenge of analyzing primary sources, thereby becoming active inquirers into the past. Involvement with primary-source evidence accomplishes what is beyond the capacity of even the best textbooks and the most stirring lectures: It reveals to students that historical scholarship is more than memorizing facts and someone else's conclusions; it is an intellectual process of drawing inferences and discovering patterns from clues — primary sources — yielded by the past.

Structure and Themes

At a time when this project was just getting started, an outside reviewer of a very preliminary outline of the proposed book stated that the author would undoubtedly find it an "interesting" challenge to choose just one hundred or so sources that would capture the richness and complexity of twentieth century global history. Several years and many outlines later, I can state unequivocally that this outside reviewer was correct. Choosing what sources should comprise *Sources of Twentieth Century Global History* has been interesting . . . and frequently frustrating, humbling, and at times overwhelming.

From start to finish, however, my decisions were guided by a number of considerations:

- First, I wanted to produce a book that was truly global in scope. Without an understanding and appreciation of the experiences of *all* the world's major regions and peoples, no true understanding of the twentieth century is possible.

- Second, I wanted the book to cover the whole twentieth century, not just the "short twentieth century" from 1914 to 1991.

- Third, I wished to show the book's student readers that history is more than the study of past wars, politics, and diplomacy. Although these topics are amply covered in *Sources of Twentieth-Century Global History,* the arts, popular culture, social change, intellectual developments, economics, technology, and the environment also are represented. Special efforts were made to include sources pertaining to the experiences of women in the twentieth century.

- Fourth, I was interested in introducing students to a variety of sources, both written and nonwritten. The collection contains speeches, private letters, treaties, poems, memoirs, advertisements, magazine illustrations, government documents, newspaper accounts, and diplomatic correspondence.

- Fifth, I never lost sight of the fact that the book's ultimate test would be its classroom effectiveness. I have tried to include sources that will capture and hold students' interests, while at the same time providing instructors with material that can be woven into lectures and can serve as the basis for class discussions and a variety of written assignments.

The result is a book of more than one hundred sources, divided into four parts.

Part I, which consists of two chapters, takes the story of the twentieth century back to its roots in the late nineteenth century and ends in 1914. Chapter 1 focuses on the growing interaction among the world's peoples and the extent and effect of the West's economic and political power throughout the world. Chapter 2 concentrates on forces of change in the years before World War I — political revolution, feminism, and new intellectual currents.

Part II, the longest section in the book, begins with a chapter on World War I. This is followed by four chapters on the Western world and the Soviet Union (Chapter 4), Latin America (Chapter 5), Africa (Chapter 6), and Asia (Chapter 7) in the 1920s and 1930s.

Part III covers the period from World War II to the early 1970s. Chapter 8, on World War II and the origins of the Cold War, is followed by chapters on the industrialized, capitalistic West (Chapter 9), the Soviet bloc and Communist China (Chapter 10), and Latin America, Africa, and those parts of Asia emerging from colonialism (Chapter 11). In other words, this section is organized around the concept of the "three worlds," first, second, and third, a way of viewing the world that originated and gained wide currency in the 1950s, 1960s, and 1970s.

Part IV deals with the period from the 1970s through the 1990s. It consists of two chapters, both of which are global in scope. This final section of the book reflects the degree to which by century's end globalization had broken down the world's traditional ideological and geo-political divisions.

I have chosen and organized the sources so that each one of them is connected thematically with others in the book. No source exists in isolation. Each chapter is divided into several smaller sections in which two or three sources that center on a common theme are grouped together. In some cases the sources in these sections complement one another, and in other cases they present different perspectives on the same phenomenon. Many sources, especially those dealing with key topics such as nationalism, colonialism, gender relations, race, war and peace, and migration, are linked with sources in other chapters. Such linkages give students a sense of change and development, and provide opportunities to make cross-cultural comparisons.

Learning Aids

Analysis of primary sources can be a daunting challenge for any student. With this in mind, every effort has been made to make these sources as accessible as possible by providing the student-reader with a variety of aids.

- The *Prologue* defines primary sources, discusses their importance, and provides guidelines for their analysis.

- Extensive *part, chapter, section, and individual source introductions* help the reader place each selection in historical context and understand the source's historical significance.

- Suggested *Questions for Analysis* precede each source. Their purpose is to help students make sense of each piece of evidence and wrest from it as much insight as possible. They are also intended to resemble the historian's approach to source analysis and to help students make historical and cross-cultural comparisons. Some questions are quite specific and are intended to assist the reader in picking out important pieces of information. Questions of this type require the student to address two issues: What does the document or artifact say, and what meaningful facts can I garner from it? Addressing concrete questions of this sort prepares the student for the next, more important level of analysis: drawing inferences. Questions that require inferential conclusions follow the fact-oriented questions. Finally, whenever possible, we have included questions that require students to make comparisons between two or more sources.

- Many of the sources have *extensive footnotes*. These explain words and allusions that most college students cannot reasonably be expected to know.

In summary, the goal of *Sources of Twentieth-Century Global History* has been to prepare the student-reader for success — success being defined as comfort with historical analysis, proficiency in critical thinking, greater understanding of twentieth century global history, and a greater awareness of the rich varieties, as well as shared characteristics, of the world's peoples.

Feedback

If you have questions or comments about the book, please address them to James.Overfield@uvm.edu.

Acknowledgments

I am in debt to many individuals who provided help, assistance, and encouragement during the preparation of *Sources of Twentieth-Century Global History*. They include editors at Houghton Mifflin, especially Julie Dunn and Nancy Blaine; many reference and circulation librarians at the University of Vermont; and scholars and colleagues at the University of Vermont including Abbas Alnasrawi, Robert V. Daniels, Denise J. Youngblood, Sean Stilwell, Peter Seybolt, Walter Hawthorn, and Mark Stoler. I owe a special debt to my colleague, co-author, and friend, Alfred J. Andrea, who provided much of the inspiration for the Prologue to *Sources of Twentieth Century Global History*.

I would also like to thank the following historians who read and commented on the book at various stages in its development: Tyra Benoit, *Butte Community College;* Donald N. Clark, *Trinity University;* Joel S. Cleland, *Lander University;* Kenneth P. Czech, *St. Cloud State University;* Hal M. Friedman, *Henry Ford Community College;* Robert

Irwin, *University of Alaska, Fairbanks;* Thomas W. Judd, *SUNY Oswego;* John F. Lyons, *Joliet Junior College;* Nicholas C. J. Pappas, *Sam Houston State University;* David Prochaska, *University of Illinois, Urbana-Champaign;* Kenneth Pomeranz, *University of California at Irvine;* Barbara Reinfeld, *N.Y. Institute of Technology;* James C. Riley, *Indiana University;* Arthur Schmidt, *Temple University;* Jutta K. Scott, *South Carolina State University;* John Snetsinger, *Cal Poly San Luis Obispo;* and Bruce B. Solnick, *SUNY Albany.*

Thanks, finally, to Susan, for her constant support on this project and much else.

James H. Overfield
Essex Center, Vermont
June, 2001

PROLOGUE

Primary Sources and
How to Read Them

Imagine a course in organic chemistry in which students never set foot in a laboratory; or a literature course in which they read commentaries on Shakespeare's plays
but none of the plays themselves; or a course on the history of jazz in which they
never listen to a note of music. Most students would consider such courses both
strange and deficient, and many would soon be beating a path to the door of their
academic advisor or college dean with complaints about flawed teaching methods
and wasted tuition payments. One simply cannot understand chemistry without
doing experiments. Nor can one understand literature without reading plays,
poetry, and fiction; or music without listening to performances.

In much the same way, one cannot truly understand history without reading and
analyzing *primary sources*. Primary sources are historical records produced at a
time that is contemporary with the event or period that is being studied. They are
distinct from *secondary sources* — books, articles, television documentaries, and
even historical films — that were produced after the events they describe have
already occurred. Secondary sources — "histories" in the conventional sense of the
term — organize the jumble of past events into understandable narratives; provide
interpretations; make comparisons; and discuss questions of motive and causation.
When well done, they provide pleasure and insight to their readers. But such works
are still *secondary,* in that they are written after the fact and, more importantly,
derive their evidence and information from primary sources.

History is an ambitious discipline that deals with all aspects of past human activity
and belief. This means that the primary sources historians use to recreate the past
are equally wide-ranging and diverse. Most of the primary sources they use are
written sources — government records, law codes, private correspondence, literary
works, religious texts, merchants' account books, memoirs, and an almost endless
list of others. So important are written records to the study of history that past
societies with no alphabet or system of writing are called "prehistoric" — not
because they lacked a history but because there is no way of retrieving their history due to the lack of records. Nonwritten records can also be primary sources
for historians. Important insights about the past have been derived from humble
objects that are part of everyday life — fabrics, tools, kitchen implements, weapons,
farm equipment, jewelry, pieces of furniture — as well as from paintings, buildings,
sculpture, musical compositions, photographs, and film.

To be a historian is to work with primary sources. But to do so effectively is not easy. Each source provides only one glimpse of reality, and no single source by itself gives us the whole picture of past events and developments. Many sources are difficult to understand, and can be interpreted accurately only after the precise meaning of their words have been deciphered and their backgrounds thoroughly investigated. Many sources contain distortions and errors that can be discovered only by rigorous internal analysis and comparison with evidence from other sources. Only after all these source-related difficulties have been overcome can a historian hope to achieve a coherent and accurate understanding of the past.

To illustrate some of the challenges of working with primary sources, let us imagine a time in the mid-twenty-first century when a historian decides to write a history of your college class in connection with its fiftieth reunion. Since no previous books or articles about your class have been written, our historian has no secondary sources to consult, and must rely entirely on primary sources. What primary sources might he or she use? The list would be a long one: the school catalogue, class lists, academic transcripts, yearbooks, college rules and regulations, and similar official documents; lecture notes, syllabi, examinations, term papers, and textbooks; diaries and private letters; articles from the campus newspaper and programs for sporting events, concerts, and plays; posters and handbills; and recollections written down or otherwise recorded by some of your classmates long after they graduated. With a bit of thought you could add other items to the list, among them some unwritten sources, such as recordings of music popular at the time and photographs and video-tapes of student life and activity.

Even with this imposing list of sources our future historian will only have an incomplete record of the events that made up your class's experiences. Many of these events — telephone conversations, discussions between students and professors, and gossip exchanged at the student union — never made it into any written records. Also, consider the fact that those sources that will be available to our future historian in the mid twentieth century will be fortunate survivors. They will represent only a small percentage of the vast amount of material generated by you, your classmates, professors, and administrators over a two- or four-year period. Wastebaskets and recycling bins will have claimed much written material; the "delete key" and inevitable changes in computer technology may make it impossible to retrieve basic sources such as your university's website, email, and a vast amount of other online materials. It is also probable that it will be difficult to find information about certain groups within your class. Fewer records might have been generated and preserved regarding the experiences of part-time students, non-traditional students, and commuters.

For all these reasons, the evidence available to our future historian will be fragmentary at best. This is always the case when doing historical research. The records of the past cannot be retained in their totality, not even those pertaining to the recent past.

How will our future historian utilize the many individual pieces of surviving documentary evidence about your class? As he or she reviews the list, it will quickly become apparent that no single primary source provides a complete or unbiased picture. Each source has its perspective, value, and limitations. Imagine that the personal essays submitted by applicants for admission were a historian's only sources of information about the student body. On reading them, would it not be reasonable for this researcher to conclude that your school attracted only the most gifted, talented, interesting, and intellectually committed students imaginable?

Despite their flaws, however, essays composed by applicants for admission can still be important pieces of historical evidence. They certainly reflect the would-be students' perceptions of the school's cultural values and the types of people it hopes to attract, and usually the applicants are right on the mark because they have read the school's catalogue and the brochures prepared for prospective students by the admissions office. Admissions office materials and, to a degree, even the catalogue, are forms of creative advertizing, and both present an idealized picture of campus life. But such publications have value for the careful researcher because they reflect the values of the faculty and administrators who composed them. The catalogue also provides useful information regarding rules and regulations, courses, instructors, school organizations, and similar items. Such factual information, however, is the raw material of history, not history itself, and certainly it does not reflect anything close to the full historical reality of your class's collective experience.

What is true of the catalogue is equally true of the student newspaper and every other piece of evidence pertinent to your class. Each primary source is a part of a larger whole, but as we have already seen, we do not have all the pieces. Think of historical evidence in terms of a jigsaw puzzle. Many of the pieces are missing, but it is possible to put most, though probably not all, of the remaining pieces together in a fashion to form a fairly accurate and coherent picture. The picture that emerges will not be complete, but it is useful and valid. The keys to fitting these pieces together are hard work and imagination. Each is absolutely necessary.

Examining Primary Sources

Hard work speaks for itself, but students are often unaware that historians also need imagination to reconstruct the past. After all, many students ask, doesn't history consist of strictly defined and irrefutable dates, names, and facts? Where does imagination enter into the process of learning these facts? Again, let us consider your class's history and its documentary sources. Many of those documents provide factual data — dates, names, grades, statistics. While these data are important, individually and collectively they have no historical meaning until they have been *interpreted.* Your college class is more than a collection of statistics and facts. It is a group of individuals who, despite their differences, share and help mold a collective experience. It is a community evolving within a particular time and place. Any valid or useful history must reach beyond dates, names, and facts and interpret the historical characteristics and role of your class. What were its values? How did it change and why? What impact did it have? These are some of the important questions a historian asks of the evidence.

To arrive at answers, the historian must examine each and every piece of relevant evidence in its full context and wring from that evidence as many *inferences* as possible. *An inference is a logical conclusion drawn from evidence, and it is the heart and soul of historical inquiry.* Facts are the raw materials of history, but inferences are its finished products.

By the time you complete your course on twentieth-century global history you will have learned many historical facts: for example, that on June 28, 1914, Gavrilo Princip assassinated the archduke and archduchess of Austria-Hungary in the Bosnian city of Sarajevo; that on March 6, 1957, the former British colony of the Gold Coast became the independent state of Ghana; and that in 1962 and 1963 Rachel Carson's book about insecticides, *Silent Spring,* topped the bestseller charts in the United States. Knowing these facts will be of little value, however, unless it contributes to your understanding of twentieth-century global history. What motivated Princip, and why did his murder of the archduke and archduchess bring about World War I? What caused Ghanian independence and what was its significance in African history? Why did Carson's book become a bestseller, and what was its role in inspiring the environmental movement in the United States? Finding answers to questions such as these are the historian's ultimate goal, and these answers can be found in primary sources.

One noted historian, Robin Winks, has written a book entitled *The Historian as Detective,* and the image is appropriate although inexact. Like a detective, the historian examines evidence to reconstruct events. Like a detective, the historian is interested in discovering what happened, who did it and why. Like a detective interrogating witnesses, *the historian also must carefully examine the testimony of sources.*

First and foremost, the historian must evaluate the *validity* of the source. Is it what it purports to be? Artful forgeries have misled many historians. Even authentic sources still can be misleading if the author lied or deliberately misrepresented reality. In addition, the historian can easily be led astray by not fully understanding the *perspective* reflected in the document. As is soon learned by any detective who has examined eyewitnesses to an event, witnesses' accounts often differ widely. The detective has the opportunity to reexamine witnesses and offer them the opportunity to change their testimony in the light of new evidence and deeper reflection. The historian is not so fortunate. Even when the historian compares a piece of documentary evidence with other evidence in order to uncover its flaws, there is no way to cross-examine its author. Given this fact, it is absolutely necessary for the historian to understand as fully as possible the source's perspective. Thus, the historian must ask several key questions — all of which share the letter W.

- *What* kind of document is this?

- *Who* wrote it?

- For *whom* and *why?*

- *Where* was it composed and *when?*

What is important because understanding the nature of a source will give the historian an idea of what kind of information he or she can expect to find in it. Many sources simply do not address the questions a historian would like to ask of them, and knowing this can save a great deal of frustration. Your class's historian would be foolish to try to learn much about the academic quality of your school's courses from a study of the registrar's class lists and grade sheets. Student and faculty class notes, copies of syllabi, examinations, student papers, and textbooks would be far more useful.

Who, for whom, and *why* are equally important questions. The school catalogue and publicity materials prepared by the admissions office undoubtedly address some issues pertaining to student social life. But should documents like these — designed to attract potential students and to place the school in the best possible light — be read and accepted uncritically? Obviously not. They must be tested against student testimony, which is discovered in such sources as private letters, memoirs, posters, the student newspaper, and the yearbook.

Where and *when* are also important questions to ask of any primary source. As a rule, distance from an event in space and time colors perceptions and can diminish the reliability of a source's testimony. Recollections of a person celebrating a twenty-fifth class reunion could be an insightful and valuable source of information for your class's historian. Conceivably this graduate would have a perspective and information that he or she lacked a quarter of a century earlier. Just as conceivably, however, that person's memory of what college was like might have faded to the point where his recollections have little value.

You and the Sources

This book will actively involve you in the work of historical inquiry by asking you to draw inferences based on your analysis of primary source evidence. This may prove difficult at first, but it is well within your capability.

You will analyze two types of evidence: documents and artifacts. Each source will be authentic, so you do not have to worry about validating it. Editorial material in this book also supplies you with the information necessary to place each piece of evidence into its proper context and will suggest questions you legitimately can and should ask of each source.

It is important to keep in mind that historians approach each source they consider with questions, even though they might be vaguely formulated. Like detectives, historians want to discover some particular truth or shed light on a particular issue. This requires asking specific questions of the witnesses or, in the historian's case, of the evidence. These questions should not be prejudgments. One of the worst errors a historian can make is setting out to prove a point or to defend an ideological position. Questions are simply starting points, nothing else, but they are essential. Therefore, as you approach a source, have your question or questions fixed in your mind and constantly remind yourself as you work your way through a source what issue or issues you are investigating. Each source in this anthology is preceded by a number of suggested Questions for Analysis. You or your professor may want to ask other questions. Whatever the case, keep focused on your questions and issues, and take notes as you read a source. Never rely on unaided memory; it will almost inevitably lead you astray.

Above all else, you must be honest and thorough as you study a source. Read each explanatory footnote carefully to avoid misunderstanding a word or allusion. Try to understand exactly what the source is saying and what its author's perspective is. Be careful not to wrench items, words, or ideas out of context, thereby distorting them. Above all, read the entire source so that you understand as fully as possible what it says and does not say.

This is not as difficult as it sounds. But it does take concentration and work. And do not let the word "work" mislead you. True, primary source analysis demands attention to detail and some hard thought, but it is also rewarding. There is great satisfaction in developing a deeper and truer understanding of the past based on a careful exploration of the evidence.

Good luck, and have fun!

Sources of

Twentieth-Century
Global History

PART ONE

The World in an Era of Transformation and Western Dominance, 1880–1914

To gain a sense of the direction of late-nineteenth- and early-twentieth-century history, one needs only to consider the following events:

- In 1881 the sultan of the Ottoman Empire, Abdul Hamid II, agreed to the formation of the Ottoman Public Debt Administration, whose seven-member board assumed oversight over tax collection, budget planning, and expenditures for the sultan's government and control of the empire's overall economic development, including railroad construction. Only two board members were to be Ottoman subjects, one chosen by the sultan and one nominated by the European-controlled Ottoman bank. The rest were European financiers representing European banks and bondholders.

- In November 1884 representatives of fourteen European nations and the United States met in Berlin to decide a number of questions relating to Africa. After several months of discussions, they accepted freedom of trade and navigation on the Congo and Niger Rivers and gave control of the territory in the Congo Basin to the International Association of the Congo, a self-styled philanthropic organization founded by King Leopold II of Belgium. They also established certain rules that European nations would have to follow when annexing African territory. No one thought it strange that no Africans attended the conference and that no effort was made to solicit their opinions.

- In 1901, a year after a mostly European-U.S. force of forty-five thousand troops quelled an antiforeign uprising in China known as the Boxer Rebellion, the victors forced the Chinese to accept the Boxer Protocol, which required them to execute ten high government officials and imprison hundreds more, destroy forts, allow foreign troops to guard railway stations, and pay an indemnity of $333,990,000.

- In 1898 British and British-trained Indian troops invaded Sudan from Egypt to make good Great Britain's claim to Sudanese territory. They met a Sudanese army at the Battle of Omdurman, which resulted in approximately eleven thousand casualties for the Sudanese and a mere forty dead for the British and Indians.

After the battle, English troops dug up the grave of the Sudanese charismatic religious leader known as the Mahdi, who had died in 1885, and used his skull for a soccer game. Sudan became Anglo-Egyptian Sudan, a British colony.

• In 1903, with the aid of the U.S. Navy and the U.S. State Department, Panamanian rebels won their independence from Colombia and established an independent Panamanian state on the thin link of land connecting North and South America. Within two weeks the new government agreed to the Hay-Bunau-Varilla Treaty, in which in return for $10,000,000 it granted the United States authority over the land where it planned to build a canal linking the Atlantic and Pacific Oceans. Here, in the Canal Zone, the U.S. government established its own postal service, custom houses, and commissaries. In Panama itself, the United States disbanded the local army, stationed Marines throughout the country, and established a virtual protectorate over the newly "independent" state. The Panama Canal opened in 1914.

All of these episodes reveal the gap that by 1900 had opened up between "the West" — essentially the states of Europe and a small group of European offshoots such as the United States — and the people of Africa, Asia, and Latin America. Better armed, more efficiently governed, immeasurably wealthier, and confident of their moral and technological superiority, Europeans conquered and colonized Africa and much of Asia, manipulated the foreign policy and finances of dozens of "sovereign" Asian and Latin American states, and turned the world into a market for their manufactures, a supplier of their food, and a source of raw materials for their factories. Throughout the world they built railroads and telegraph systems, used steam-driven machinery to dig harbors and canals, introduced new political and economic concepts, and undermined centuries-old customs and values. At an ever-accelerating rate, the people and governments of the West were transforming the globe.

Such an outcome would have surprised an observer of world affairs as late as the eighteenth century, even though Europe's importance had been growing for some two hundred years. In the 1500s and 1600s Europeans used their maritime skills and gunpowder weapons to take control of the Americas and establish a commercial presence in Africa and Asia. Even after two centuries of economic growth, however, in the mid-eighteenth-century Europeans were on average no wealthier than the people in China, Japan, and parts of India, and still paid for coveted Asian silks and porcelain with silver because their own products were of little interest to sophisticated Asian buyers. Aside from the Philippines and some islands in the East Indies, they had established their political authority only in the Americas; even here the descendants of European settlers were about to throw off European rule in a series of anticolonial revolts between the 1770s and 1810s.

By 1900, however, Europeans held sway over much of the world. This dramatic development resulted from two revolutions, one economic and one political, that began in the late eighteenth century. Europe's economic transformation, known as the industrial revolution, resulted from the application of new machines and energy sources to the tasks of manufacturing, transportation, and communications. It began in the 1760s in England, where the manufacture of cotton textiles was transformed by the use of new spinning, carding, and weaving machines that were driven first by water power and from the 1780s onward by coal-burning steam engines. In the 1800s industrialization spread to the European continent and the United States, and at the end of the century entered a new phase of innovation and growth. In this so-called second industrial revolution, new industries based on discoveries in chemistry and the utilization of electricity were created, and steel production boomed. Utilizing steamships, railroads, and the telegraph, and drawing on its vast financial resources, Europe became the center of an international trade network through which industrialized nations exported textiles, chemicals, tools, weapons, machines, ceramics, and hardware to every corner of the globe. In return they imported beef, wheat, and bananas from Latin America; diamonds, gold, and palm oil from Africa; cotton from India and Egypt; tin from Malaya; and countless other agricultural products and raw materials from around the world.

Far-reaching political changes accompanied Europe's economic transformation. Beginning in the late eighteenth century with the American (1776–1783) and French (1789–1799) Revolutions, Americans and Europeans rejected the principles of absolutism, divine right monarchy, and aristocratic privilege and sought to establish popularly elected governments based on the rule of law, individual freedom, and legal equality. By 1900, after a century of experimentation and upheaval, most European states were still monarchies, but they were now constitutional monarchies, in which popularly elected parliaments made laws, approved budgets, held ministers accountable for their actions, and exerted at least some influence on foreign policy. Citizens of these states closely identified their own interests with those of their governments, prided themselves on their nations' traditions and accomplishments, and developed a strong emotional attachment to their compatriots. Nationalism had become a potent political force.

The people of Asia, Africa, and Latin America had little choice but to acquiesce to Western dominance. Those who lived in European colonies had no meaningful say in their affairs whatsoever. Leaders of states that still had a measure of sovereignty drew up plans for economic modernization and military reform but faced formidable obstacles in carrying them out. In the opening years of the twentieth century, there was every reason to believe that the West's domination of the world would continue indefinitely.

In retrospect, however, the foundations of Western dominance were being undermined in those very years when they seemed so secure. Beginning in 1868, Japan transformed itself from a preindustrial society, vulnerable to Western aggression, into a modern industrial state with a formidable army and navy. In 1905 the world took notice when Japan defeated Russia, one of the "great powers" of Europe, in the Russo-Japanese War. In 1885 Indian professionals and civil servants, most with European-style educations and some with degrees from Oxford or Cambridge, founded the Indian National Congress, dedicated to expanding Indian participation in political decision-making and the Indianization of the Indian Civil Service. This organization spearheaded the drive for Indian independence in the first half of the twentieth century. In the early 1900s several states — Persia in 1905, the Ottoman Empire in 1908, China and Mexico in 1911 — experienced political revolutions. In the short run none of them was successful; all led to further turmoil and, in the case of China, complete political collapse. Even in their failure, however, they indicated that non-Western peoples were breaking with their pasts and moving along paths previously followed only by Europeans.

Meanwhile nationalism intensified and diplomatic tensions grew in Europe. Newly united Germany maintained Europe's most powerful army, built a formidable navy, sought colonies in Africa and Asia, and aggressively competed with Great Britain for control of world markets. France brooded over its defeat by Germany in the Franco-Prussian War (1870–1871), and, while waiting for revenge, sought to bolster its status as a great power by building an overseas empire second in size only to that of Great Britain. Great Britain resented Germany's economic success, military power, and diplomatic bluster, but until the early 1900s also competed with Russia and France for territories in Africa and Asia. Statesmen worried about Russian expansion into the Balkans and Asia Minor, should the Hapsburg Empire of Austria-Hungary disintegrate or should Ottoman military power continue to decline.

As tensions grew, statesmen sought security through alliance systems, and politicians approved huge military budgets to pay for new weapons and ever-expanding armies and navies. Generals developed strategies and drew up timetables to fight the major war that everyone expected. In 1914 that war — World War I — finally came, setting in motion events that dramatically altered the course of twentieth-century history.

CHAPTER 1

Global Interaction in an Era of Imperialism and Migration

The level of global interaction among the world's peoples began to increase in the fifteenth and sixteenth centuries after European mariners sailed around Africa to reach Asia and, more importantly, crossed the Atlantic and discovered the Americas. These voyages inaugurated a new era in world commerce in which Europeans traded directly with India, Southeast Asia, and China, and turned the Atlantic into a thoroughfare of international exchange linking Europe, Africa, and the Americas. The European discoveries also led to the increased movement of people. Between the fifteenth and eighteenth centuries, millions of Africans, who went as slaves, and millions of Europeans, who went voluntarily, migrated to the Americas, where they repopulated a hemisphere whose native inhabitants had been ravaged by the introduction of Old World diseases. The Old World pathogens that caused the American epidemics are just one example of the many biological exchanges that took place from the fifteenth century onward. Cattle, horses, swine, fruit trees, and grain crops were introduced to the Americas, while New World crops such as maize, tobacco, and the potato spread to Africa and Eurasia.

These developments set the stage for the rapid acceleration of global integration that took place in the nineteenth century. The amount of international trade, for example, tripled between 1780 and 1840, quadrupled between 1840 and 1870, and doubled again between 1870 and 1910. The types of goods traded also changed. No longer was international commerce dominated by luxuries such as silks and porcelains from China and nonessentials such as sugar, cocoa, tobacco from the Americas. Increasingly, world trade shifted to necessities. By 1900 Europe could not have fed itself without importing Canadian wheat and Argentinean beef; nor would Canadian farmers and Argentinean ranchers have had a market for their products without European buyers.

In addition, in the nineteenth century Europe's industries became dependent on raw materials imported from around the world: rubber from the Congo and Amazon River Basins; palm oil from Africa; cotton from the United States, India, and Egypt; jute from India and Africa; tin from the Malay Peninsula; copper from Chile, Peru, and Central Africa; and gutta-percha, a plastic derived from tree sap and used to coat undersea telegraph cables, from Malaya. During the century, Asians and Africans stopped making many of the articles needed for daily living and bought them from industrialized nations. India, the world's leading exporter of cotton textiles in the eighteenth century, imported most of its cotton cloth from Great Britain by the end of the 1800s.

These changes in world trade would not have occurred without revolutionary developments in transportation. The first commercial railroad began hauling coal to the English North Sea port of Stockton in 1820. By 1900 close to 300,000 miles of track had been laid around the world, on which more than one hundred thousand steam locomotives pulled almost a million freight and passenger cars that carried unprecedented quantities of goods and people. Steam engines also revolutionized ocean travel. The first oceangoing steamship, the *Savannah,* had a wooden hull and side-wheels powered by a steam engine so inefficient that it relied on sails for twenty-three of the twenty-seven days it took to reach England from the United States in 1819. By 1900 steamships had steel hulls, efficient compound engines that drove propellers, rather than side-wheels, and refrigerators if they carried perishable foodstuffs. After 1869, when making the passage between Asia and Europe, navigators reduced the length of their voyage almost 50 percent by using the Suez Canal rather than making the long voyage around Africa.

Changing trends in international trade, along with advances in steamship and railroad technology, contributed to another dimension of increasing global interchange in the nineteenth century — namely, the rising tide of migration. From the mid 1800s to the early twentieth century, approximately a million Indians left the Asian subcontinent to seek economic opportunities in South America, the Caribbean, Malaya, and Africa, and large numbers of Chinese immigrated to Pacific islands, Malaya, Singapore, Peru, Canada, and the United States. As large as it was, the number of Asian immigrants was dwarfed by the swarm of Europeans who migrated to the United States, Canada, Argentina, Australia, and New Zealand. In the 1830s and 1840s between 300,000 and 400,000 emigrants left Europe every year; by the early twentieth century, between 1,000,000 and 1,400,000 European immigrants arrived each year in the United States alone.

While railroads and steamships revolutionized travel, the electric telegraph revolutionized international communications. Introduced in England in 1837 and the United States in 1844, the telegraph was useful only on land until the 1860s when the placement of effective, durable telegraph wires at the bottom of the world's oceans became possible. Soon several hundred thousand miles of cables undersea and on land linked every continent in a communication network that carried millions of messages a year. In 1800 it might have taken a letter ten months to two years to reach England from China. By 1900 a telegram from China to England arrived in a matter of minutes.

Trade, technology, and migration all played a role in integrating the world's peoples and regions in the 1800s, but so too did military conquest. The late nineteenth century was an age of imperialism, in which a small number of states, predominantly European, used their superior weaponry — repeating rifles, light machine guns, and dum-dum bullets that exploded on contact — to conquer or simply annex all of Africa except Liberia and Ethiopia, much of Southeast Asia, and hundreds of Pacific islands. Surpassing the conquests of legendary figures such as Alexander the Great and Ghengis Khan, imperialism was a monument to the West's political, economic, and military ascendancy and a powerful expression of the world's growing integration.

◆

Imperialism: Western Justifications

In the late nineteenth and early twentieth centuries — the era of imperialism — the long history of Western expansion culminated in a land-grab unprecedented in human history. The amount of territory and the numbers of human beings added to European empires between 1871 and 1900 are astounding: Great Britain, 4.25 million square miles and 66 million people; France, 3.5 million square miles and 26 million people; Germany, 1 million square miles and 13 million people; Belgium, 900,000 square miles and 13 million people; Italy, 900,000 square miles and just under a million people. Portugal expanded its holdings in Africa, and Spain, although it lost Cuba and the Philippines, annexed Morocco and some sparsely populated lands in the Western Sahara. The only non-European imperialist nations were the United States, which took over Cuba, the Philippines, and a few Pacific islands, and Japan, which acquired Korea and Taiwan.

Late-nineteenth-century imperialism was made possible by a number of key technological developments. The replacement of sailing vessels by steel-hulled steamships reduced two-month ocean voyages to two weeks; undersea telegraph lines enabled government officials and business owners to communicate in seconds, not weeks or months; medical advances and new drugs protected Europeans from tropical diseases such as malaria; rapid-fire rifles and machine guns gave Western troops an insurmountable advantage over Africans or Asians who offered resistance.

But technological capability alone cannot explain the expansionist fever that swept through the West in the late 1800s. As the sources in this section reveal, anticipated economic gains, national rivalries, missionary fervor, a strong sense of racial superiority, and faith in the West's civilizing mission all contributed to the psychological and political atmosphere that led to this final chapter of Western expansion.

A Defense of French Imperialism

❖

1 ❖ Jules Ferry,
SPEECH BEFORE THE FRENCH CHAMBER OF DEPUTIES, 1883

Jules Ferry (1832–1893) was a French politician who twice served as premier during the Third Republic, the name of the French government from 1871 until 1940. Ferry was an ardent imperialist, and during his premierships France annexed Tunisia and parts of Indochina and began exploring Africa. He frequently defended his policies in debates in the French Chamber of Deputies against both socialist and conservative critics, who for different reasons were anti-imperialist. The following selection from his speech on July 28, 1883, summarizes Ferry's reasons for supporting French expansionism and also sheds light on his opponents' views.

QUESTIONS FOR ANALYSIS

1. According to Ferry, what recent developments in world trade have made it urgent for France to have colonies?
2. What ideological arguments against imperialism have been raised by Ferry's critics? How does Ferry counter them?
3. Aside from providing markets for French goods, what other economic advantages do colonies offer, according to Ferry?
4. What noneconomic arguments does Ferry offer in favor of patriotism?

M. Jules Ferry. . . . It is as strenuous for me as for you, but I believe that there is some benefit in summarizing and condensing, in the form of arguments, the principles, the motives, and the various interests by which a policy of colonial expansion may be justified; it goes without saying that I will try to remain reasonable, moderate, and never lose sight of the major continental interests which are the primary concern of this country. What I wish to say . . . is that . . . the policy of colonial expansion is a political and economic system; I wish to say that one can relate this system to three orders of ideas: economic ideas, ideas of civilization in its highest sense, and ideas of politics and patriotism.

In the area of economics, I will allow myself to place before you, with the support of some figures, the considerations which justify a policy of colonial expansion from the point of view of that need, felt more and more strongly by the industrial populations of Europe and particularly those of our own rich and hard working country: the need for export markets. . . . I will formulate only in a general way what each of you, in the different parts of France, is in a position to confirm. Yes, what is lacking for our great industry, drawn irrevocably on to the path of exportation by the . . . treaties of 1860,[1] what it lacks more and more is export markets. Why? Because next door to us Germany is surrounded by barriers, because beyond the ocean, the United States of America has become protectionist, protectionist in the most extreme sense, because not only have these great markets, I will not say closed but shrunk, and thus become more difficult of access for our industrial products, but also these great states are beginning to pour products not seen heretofore onto our own markets. . . . It is not necessary to pursue this demonstration any farther. . . .

. . . Gentlemen, there is a second point, a second order of ideas to which I have to give equal attention, but as quickly as possible, believe me; it is the humanitarian and civilizing side of the question. On this point the honorable M. Camille Pelletan[2] has jeered in his own refined and clever manner; he jeers, he condemns, and he says "What is this civilization which you impose with cannon-balls? What is it but another form of barbarism? Don't these populations, these inferior races, have the same rights as you? Aren't they masters of their own houses? Have they called upon you? You come to them against their will, you offer them violence, but not civilization." There, gentlemen, is the thesis; I do not hesitate to say that this is not politics, nor is it history: it is political metaphysics. ("Ah, Ah" *on far left*.)[3]

. . . Gentlemen, I must speak from a higher and more truthful plane. It must be stated openly that, in effect, superior races have rights over inferior races. (*Movement on many benches on the far left.*)

M. Jules Maigne.[4] Oh! You dare to say this in the country which has proclaimed the rights of man!

M. de Guilloutet. This is a justification of slavery and the slave trade!

M. Jules Ferry. If M. Maigne is right, if the declaration of the rights of man was written for the blacks of equatorial Africa, then by what right do you impose regular commerce upon them? They have not called upon you.

M. Raoul Duval. We do not want to impose anything upon them. It is you who wish to do so! . . .

M. Jules Ferry. I repeat that superior races have a right, because they have a duty. They have the duty to civilize inferior races. . . .

That is what I have to answer M. Pelletan in regard to the second point upon which he touched.

He then touched upon a third point, more delicate, more serious, and upon which I ask your permission to express myself quite frankly. It is the political side of the question. . . .

"It is a system," he says, "which consists of seeking out compensations in the Orient with a circumspect and peaceful seclusion which is actually imposed upon us in Europe."

I would like to explain myself in regard to this. I do not like this word "compensation," and, in effect, not here but elsewhere it has often been used in a treacherous way. If what is being said or insinuated is that a republican minister could possibly believe that there are in any part of the world compensations for the disasters which we have experienced,[5] an injury is being inflicted . . . and an injury undeserved by that government. (*Applause at the center and*

---

[1]These agreements with Great Britain lowered tariffs between the two nations.
[2]Pelletan (1815–1846) was a radical republican politician and an ardent patriot.
[3]Going back to a tradition begun in the legislative assemblies of the French Revolution, democrats sat on the left, moderates in the center, and conservatives and monarchists on the right. By the 1880s, the "left" also included socialists.
[4]Maigne and the speakers who follow, Guilloutet and Duval, were members of the Chamber of Deputies.
[5]The reference is to France's defeat by Prussia and other German states in the Franco-Prussian War of 1870–1871.

left.) I will ward off this injury with all the force of my patriotism! (*New applause and bravos from the same benches.*)

Gentlemen, there are certain considerations which merit the attention of all patriots. The conditions of naval warfare have been profoundly altered. ("Very true! Very true!")

At this time, as you know, a warship cannot carry more than fourteen days' worth of coal, no matter how perfectly it is organized, and a ship which is out of coal is a derelict on the surface of the sea, abandoned to the first person who comes along. Thence the necessity of having on the oceans provision stations, shelters, ports for defense and revictualing. (*Applause at the center and left. Various interruptions.*) And it is for this that we needed Tunisia, for this that we needed Saigon and the Mekong Delta, for this that we need Madagascar, that we are at Diégo-Suarez and Vohemar[6] and will never leave them! (*Applause from a great number of benches.*) Gentlemen, in Europe as it is today, in this competition of so many rivals which we see growing around us, some by perfecting their military or maritime forces, others by the prodigious development of an ever growing population; in a Europe, or rather in a universe of this sort, a policy of peaceful seclusion or abstention is simply the highway to decadence! Nations are great in our times only by means of the activities which they develop; it is not simply "by the peaceful shining forth of institutions" that they are great at this hour. . . .

The Republican Party has shown that it is quite aware that one cannot impose upon France a political ideal conforming to that of nations like independent Belgium and the Swiss Republic; that something else is needed for France: that she cannot be merely a free country, that she must also be a great country, exercising all of her rightful influence over the destiny of Europe, that she ought to propagate this influence throughout the world and carry everywhere that she can her language, her customs, her flag, her arms, and her genius. (*Applause at center and left.*)

---

[6]Madagascar port cities.

Imperialism and the Life of Manly Courage

◆

2 ◆ *Theodore Roosevelt, THE STRENUOUS LIFE*

The expanding role of the United States in world affairs is one of the twentieth century's momentous developments. As late as the 1890s, the United States was on no one's list of "great powers" despite its growing population, resources, and industrial expansion. It had no colonies, a tiny army, a "washtub" navy, and a diplomatic corps notorious for its unprofessionalism. The United States had played a key role in opening Japan to foreign trade in the 1850s and 1860s, and although it intervened frequently in Latin American affairs, the U.S. government and the American people showed little interest in the affairs of Europe or Asia.

This changed in the late 1890s. Motivated by nationalism, anticipated economic gains, a sense of national mission, and fears that European imperialism might spill over into the Caribbean and Latin American, the United States built up its navy, annexed Hawaii in 1898, assumed a more aggressive role in China, and, after the Spanish American War (1898), became an imperialist power when it took over Cuba, the Philippines, Guam, and Puerto Rico.

Among the advocates of an expanded international role for the United States, none was more enthusiastic and vociferous than Theodore Roosevelt. Born in 1858 in New York and a graduate of Harvard, Roosevelt was an author, rancher, state assemblyman, New York City police commissioner, and undersecretary of the navy before being elected vice-president on the Republican ticket in 1900. He became president in 1901 after the assassination of President McKinley, and was reelected in 1904. As president, Roosevelt directed the construction of the Panama Canal, helped broker an end to the Russo-Japanese War in 1905, sent the Navy on a world cruise to "show the flag," and announced the "Roosevelt Corollary" to the Monroe Doctrine, by which the United States proclaimed the right to intervene in the political affairs of Latin American states.

Roosevelt delivered the following speech in early 1899 during the heated national debate following the U.S. victory over Spain in the Spanish American War. According to the armistice agreement of August 12, 1898, Spain ceded to the United States Puerto Rico, Cuba, and Guam. In December the two sides negotiated the Treaty of Paris, by which the United States would receive the Philippines in return for twenty million dollars. Senate ratification of the treaty was bitterly opposed by most Democrats and members of the Anti-Imperialism League, who believed that annexing the Philippines clashed with the nation's commitment to liberty and freedom. In his Chicago speech, "The Strenuous Life," and in many other statements, Roosevelt vigorously opposed the anti-imperialists' arguments. He and other supporters of the new U.S. imperial role won the day when the Senate narrowly approved the Treaty of Paris in February 1899.

QUESTIONS FOR ANALYSIS

1. According to Roosevelt, what lessons does the example of China offer for the United States?
2. In Roosevelt's view, what is the ultimate purpose of colonialism?
3. Roosevelt often refers to "duty" in his speech. What does he mean by the term?
4. What are Roosevelt's views of the people of Cuba and the Philippines? How do these views resemble his views of Native Americans?
5. How does Roosevelt characterize the opponents to increased U.S. military spending and expansion?

We of this generation do not have to face a task such as that our fathers faced, but we have our tasks, and woe to us if we fail to perform them! We cannot, if we would, play the part of China, and be content to rot by inches in ignoble ease within our borders, taking no interest in what goes on beyond them, sunk in a scrambling commercialism; heedless of the higher life, the life of aspiration, of toil and risk, busying ourselves only with the wants of our bodies for the day, until suddenly we should find, beyond a shadow of question, what China has already found, that in this world the nation that has trained itself to a career of unwarlike and isolated ease is bound, in the end, to go down before other nations which have not lost the manly and adventurous qualities. If we are to be a really great people, we must strive in good faith to play a great part in the world. We cannot avoid meeting great issues. All that we can determine for ourselves is whether we shall meet them well or ill. In 1898 we could not help being brought face to face with the problem of war with Spain. All we could decide was whether we should shrink like cowards from the contest, or enter into it as be-seemed a brave and high-spirited people; and, once in, whether failure or success should crown our banners. So it is now. We cannot avoid the responsibilities that confront us in Hawaii,[1] Cuba, [Puerto] Rico, and the Philippines. All we can decide is whether we shall meet them in a way that will redound to the national credit, or whether we shall make of our dealings with these new problems a dark and shameful page in our history. . . .

. . . The timid man, the lazy man, the man who distrusts his country, the over-civilized man, who has lost the great fighting, masterful virtues, the ignorant man, and the man of dull mind, whose soul is incapable of feeling the mighty lift that thrills "stern men with empires in their brains" — all these, of course, shrink from seeing the nation undertake its new duties; shrink from seeing us build a navy and an army adequate to our needs; shrink from seeing us do our share of the world's work, by bringing order out of chaos in the great, fair tropic islands from which the valor of our soldiers and sailors has driven the Spanish flag. . . .

. . . The guns that thundered off Manila and Santiago[2] left us echoes of glory, but they also left us a legacy of duty. If we drove out a me-dieval tyranny[3] only to make room for savage anarchy, we had better not have begun the task at all. It is worse than idle to say that we have no duty to perform, and can leave to their fates the islands we have conquered. Such a course

would be the course of infamy. It would be followed at once by utter chaos in the wretched islands themselves. Some stronger, manlier power would have to step in and do the work, and we would have shown ourselves weaklings, unable to carry to successful completion the labors that great and high-spirited nations are eager to undertake. . . .

The problems are different for the different islands. [Puerto] Rico is not large enough to stand alone. We must govern it wisely and well, primarily in the interest of its own people. Cuba is, in my judgment, entitled ultimately to settle for itself whether it shall be an independent state or an integral portion of the mightiest of republics. But until order and stable liberty are secured, we must remain in the island to insure them, and infinite tact, judgment, moderation, and courage must be shown by our keeping the island pacified, in relentlessly stamping out brigandage, in protecting all alike, and yet in showing proper recognition to the men who have fought for Cuban liberty. The Philippines offer a yet graver problem. Their population includes half-caste and native Christians, warlike Moslems, and wild pagans. Many of their people are utterly unfit for self-government, and show no signs of becoming fit. Others may in time become fit but at least can only take part in self-government under a wise supervision, at once firm and beneficent. We have driven Spanish tyranny from the island. If we now let it be re-placed by savage anarchy, our work has been for harm and not for good. I have scant patience with those who fear to undertake the task of gov-erning the Philippines, . . . or that they shrink from it because of the expense and trouble; but I have even scanter patience with those who make a pretense of humanitarianism to hide and cover their timidity, and who cant about "liberty" and the "consent of the governed," in order to excuse

---

[1]The United States annexed Hawaii in 1898 after almost a century of economic penetration and missionary activity.
[2]The naval battles of Manila Bay, in the Philippines, and

Santiago, in Cuba, were major U.S. victories in the Spanish American War.
[3]This is a disparaging reference to Spain.

themselves for their unwillingness to play the part of men. Their doctrines, if carried out, would make it incumbent upon us to leave the Apaches of Arizona to work out their own salvation, and to decline to interfere in a single Indian reservation. Their doctrines condemn your forefathers and mine for ever having settled in these United States. . . .

I preach to you, then, my countrymen, that our country calls not for the life of ease but for the life of strenuous endeavor. The twentieth century looms before us big with the fate of many nations. If we stand idly by, if we seek merely swollen, slothful ease and ignoble peace, if we shrink from the hard contests where men must win at hazard of their lives and at the risk of all they hold dear, then the bolder and stronger peoples will pass us by, and will win for themselves the domination of the world. Let us therefore boldly face the life of strife, resolute to do our duty well and manfully; resolute to uphold righteousness by deed and by word; resolute to be both honest and brave, to serve high ideals, yet to use practical methods. Above all, let us shrink from no strife, moral or physical, within or without the nation, provided we are certain that the strife is justified, for it is only through strife, through hard and dangerous endeavor, that we shall ultimately win the goal of true national greatness.

◆

The Economics of Imperialism

Throughout history, imperialism has meant not just political subordination but also economic exploitation in the form of land confiscation, plunder of wealth and resources, new taxes, and forced labor. Western imperialism before World War I had its share of outright plunder, but its economic ramifications went well beyond simple exploitation. In Africa and Asia, the imperialists built railroads, deepened harbors, strung telegraph lines, brought in machines to extract minerals and metals from deep in the earth, and mandated the cultivation of crops they needed to feed their people and supply their factories. They transformed isolated agrarian economies into component parts of a single world economy driven by Western industrialization and capitalism.

Furthermore, late nineteenth-century imperialism involved more than newly drawn boundaries and direct political control by colonial administrators. For many states that remained theoretically sovereign, imperialism meant economic, not political, subordination. Latin America became a vast area of U.S. and European investment, with a country such as Nicaragua becoming almost a private fiefdom of the United Fruit Company, the Boston-based corporation that supplied Europe and North America with bananas. The Ottoman Empire and Persia acquiesced to extensive foreign control of their finances and economic development. China by 1900 was divided into "spheres of influence," in which Britain, Germany, France, Japan, Russia, and to a degree the United States enjoyed exclusive trading rights and favorable tariffs, leased large tracts of land, and held concessions to build railroads, exploit mines, and establish banks. Such examples of Western economic penetration are just as much a part of the history of imperialism as the political takeover of Africa and Asia.

Cotton Growing and Rebellion in German East Africa

◆

3 ◆ RECORDS OF THE MAJI-MAJI UPRISING

The Germans were latecomers to imperialism, but after they gained control of territories in Africa and Oceania, they were quick to adopt the view that colonies exist to serve the economic interests of the colonial master. This was their philosophy in German East Africa, a large and politically diverse region on Africa's east coast, surrounded by Kenya to the north, the Belgian Congo to the west, and Northern Rhodesia and Mozambique to the south.

German economic policy lacked direction in the 1880s and 1890s as the Germans struggled to overcome resistance and experimented with various plans to coerce Africans into growing crops such as cotton that the Germans needed for their home industries. In 1902 the Germans implemented a plan to cultivate cotton in the coastal and southern sections of the colony according to which each village was compelled to provide workers to grow cotton a certain number of days a year on government estates, settler plantations, and especially village fields. To force Africans to accept these low-paying jobs, the Germans instituted a head tax payable only in cash.

Opposition to the German plan led to rebellion in 1905. Encouraged by religious leaders who supplied the rebels with *maji,* a supposedly magic water that would protect warriors from bullets, the rebellion spread throughout the colony's central and southern regions. The Germans fought back with maxim guns, mass executions, and the burning of villages. The rebellion ended in 1907, at a cost of seventy-five thousand African deaths, many caused by famine.

The following testimony concerning the Maji-Maji revolt was gathered and published in 1967 in a book by two Tanzanian historians, G. C. K. Gwassa and John Iffle. Most of the information deals with the experiences of the Matumbi, highlanders who lived in the southeastern part of the colony.

QUESTIONS FOR ANALYSIS

1. What do these records and testimonies reveal about the German approach to administering its colony?
2. Why did the Africans object so strongly to German agricultural policy?
3. What other aspects of German rule did the Africans find objectionable?
4. What does the source reveal about German views of Africans and of their African colonies?
5. What information does the source provide about the role of women in the African village?

[RECOLLECTION OF AMBROSE NGOMBALE MWIRU CONCERNING THE ARRIVAL OF A GERMAN AGENT IN 1897]

Then when that European arrived he asked, "Why did you not answer the call by drum to pay tax?" And they said, "We do not owe you anything. We have no debt to you. If you as a stranger want to stay in this country, then you will have to ask us. Then we will ask of you an offering to propitiate the gods. You will offer something and we will propitiate the gods on your behalf; we will give you land and you will get a place to stay in. But it is not for us as hosts to give you the offering. That is quite impossible."

[RECOLLECTIONS OF NDUNDULE MANGAYA]

The cultivation of cotton was done by turns. Every village was allotted days on which to cultivate at Samanga Ndumbo[1] and at the Jumbe's[2] plantation. One person came from each homestead, unless there were very many people. Thus you might be told to work for five or ten days at Samanga. So a person would go. Then after half the number of days another man came from home to relieve him. If the new man did not feel pity for him, the same person would stay on until he finished. It was also like this at the Jumbe's. If you returned from Samanga then your turn at the Jumbe's remained, or if you began at the Jumbe's you waited for the turn at Samanga after you had finished. No woman went unless her husband ran away; then they would say she had hidden him. Then the woman would go. When in a village a former clan head was seized to go to cultivate he would offer his slave in his stead. Then after arriving there you all suffered very greatly. Your back and your buttocks were whipped, and there was no rising up once you stooped to dig. The good thing about the Germans was that all people were the same before the whip. If a jumbe or akida[3] made a mistake he received the whip as well. Thus there were people whose job was to clear the land of trees and undergrowth; others tilled the land; others would smooth the field and plant; another group would do the weeding and yet another the picking; and lastly others carried the bales of cotton to the coast . . . for shipping. Thus we did not know where it was taken. Then if that European gave out some bakshishi[4] to the akida or jumbe they kept it. We did not get anything. In addition, people suffered much from the cotton, which took three months to ripen and was picked in the fourth. Now digging and planting were in the months of Ntandatu and Nchimbi, and this was the time of very many wild pigs in this country.[5] If you left the chasing of the pigs to the women she could not manage well at night. In addition, the pigs are very stubborn at that period and will not move even if you go within very close range. Only very few women can assist their husbands at night and these are the ones with very strong hearts. There were just as many birds, and if you did not have children it was necessary to help your wife drive away the birds, while at the same time you cleared a piece of land for the second maize crop, because your wife would not have time. And during this very period they still wanted you to leave your home and go to Samanga or to work on the jumbe's plantation. This was why people became furious and angry. The work was astonishingly hard and full of grave suffering, but its wages were the whip on one's back and buttocks. And yet he [the

---

[1]A coastal town.
[2]A chief or headman given low-level administrative responsibilities by the Germans.
[3]An official appointed by the Germans with functions similar to those of jumbes; akidas, however, were recruited from coastal towns and were usually Muslims.
[4]A bribe or, in this case, a payment.
[5]A threat to cultivated crops.

German] still wanted us to pay him the tax. Were we not human beings? And Wamatumbi . . . since the days of old, did not want to be troubled or ruled by any person. They were really fierce, ah! Given such grave suffering they thought it better for a man to die rather than live in such torment.

Thus they hated the rule which was too cruel. It was not because of agriculture, not at all. If it had been good agriculture which had meaning and profit, who would have given himself up to die? Earlier they had made troubles as well, but when he began to cause us to cultivate cotton for him and to dig roads and so on, then people said, "This [man] has now become an absolute ruler. Destroy him."

[RECOLLECTION OF NDULI NJIMBWI CONCERNING WORK ON A PLANTATION OWNED BY A GERMAN SETTLER NAMED STEINHAGEN].

During the cultivation there was much suffering. We, the labor conscripts, stayed in the front line cultivating. Then behind us was an overseer whose work it was to whip us. Behind the overseer there was a jumbe, and every jumbe stood behind his fifty men. Behind the line of jumbes stood Bwana Kinoo[6] himself. . . . The overseer had a whip, and he was extremely cruel. His work was to whip the conscripts if they rose up or tried to rest, or if they left a trail of their footprints behind them.[7] Ah, brothers, God is great — that we have lived like this is God's Providence! And on the other side Bwana Kinoo had a bamboo stick. If the men of a certain jumbe left their footprints behind them, that jumbe would be boxed on the ears and Kinoo would beat him with the bamboo stick using both hands, while at the same time the overseer lashed out at us laborers.

[EXCERPTS FROM AN INTERVIEW WITH A GERMAN OFFICIAL VON GEIBLER CONCERNING THE COMMUNAL PLOTS]

Village plots were set up in each akida's and headman's area early in 1902 (September–October). Bushland was mainly chosen. The people were consulted in choosing the post. Each headman made a plot for his area in the neighborhood of his headquarters. The principle was that every 30–50 men were to cultivate 2½ acres. . . . Where possible, the advice of the natives was obtained as to the crop to be grown. So far as possible, one crop was to be grown on each plot, according to the type of soil. Some 2,000 acres were cleared and cultivated. The size varied from 2½ to 35 acres; the average was about 12½ acres.

In 1903–04 it was ordered that each village plot should be extended by at least a quarter. The total area in that year came to 3,215 acres. Maize, millet, simsim,[8] groundnuts, rice, and coconut palms were grown during 1902–03. Cotton was added in 1903–04.

No extension took place in 1904–05, but the cultivation of other crops was abandoned in favor of cotton.

What was the labor situation and the supervision?

. . . According to returns by the headmen, the number of able-bodied men amounted to:

1902–03	c. 25,000 men
1903–04	c. 26,000 men
1904–05	c. 25,000 men

During the last year, women and children had to be brought in to help, since the men frequently refused to work.

In Herr von Geibler's opinion, two days' work a week, as proposed by the District Office

---

[6]The Matumbi's name for Steinhagen.
[7]Such a trail would mean that the person had walked away from his or her assigned work.

[8]Sesame.

order, was insufficient from the start; 50–100 per cent more had to be worked from the first. When cotton became a main crop, continuous work was sometimes necessary. . . .

The akidas were relied upon to report on the condition of the plots, and they were also responsible for punishing those whom the headmen reported as refractory workers. There was no European control of this — who among the natives worked, and for how many days — although agricultural students (some of them children) were sent out, each with a note-book, to judge the condition of the plots and the work performed, and to report to the District Officer. Only once a year did a European visit the plots, to measure them out and select the land. No lists of workers were kept anywhere; the profits were distributed only according to the total numbers.

Work on most of the plots was *flatly* refused during 1904–05. The headmen complained that they no longer had the people in hand. The officials of the Commune believed at the time that they could detect a state of ferment.

Were refractory workers punished, and by whom?

Last year (1904–05), following reports from the akidas and from Sergeant Holzhausen, who was sent to inspect the headmen, numerous headmen were punished by the District Office with imprisonment in chains or solitary confinement for totally neglecting their village plots as a result of the natives' refusal to work. The last, in June, was headman Kibasila, who got one month in chains.

Indian Railroads and the People's Welfare

❖

4 ❖ G. V. Joshi, THE ECONOMIC RESULTS OF FREE TRADE AND RAILWAY EXTENSION

An enduring monument to British imperialism in India is the railway system, which at the time of independence in 1947 was the fourth largest in the world in terms of track mileage, following only that of the United States, Canada, and the Soviet Union. The first railway was built in India in 1850, and by 1915 India had over forty thousand miles of track and approximately one hundred million railroad passengers per year. Railway construction was supported by several powerful groups: British cotton manufacturers, for whom railways were a cheap and efficient way to get cotton to the coast for shipment to England; British manufacturers, who supplied India with most of its rails, locomotives, moving stock, and equipment; colonial officials, who saw railroads as a means of quickly moving troops to trouble spots and as an essential part of the Indian postal system; and millions of Indians, who took to rail travel with great enthusiasm.

But was India's new railway system a good investment? Did it contribute to India's overall economic development? Did it justify its enormous costs? Among those who answered "no" to these questions, few were as eloquent or persistent in their criticisms of British economic policy as G. V. Joshi (1851–1911), a teacher and schoolmaster who also was one of India's leading economic writers. His essay on public works and free trade was published in 1884.

QUESTIONS FOR ANALYSIS

1. What benefits for the Indian people does Joshi see in the program of railroad construction?
2. Why is it wrong in Joshi's view to base Indian economic policy on the model of the United States?
3. According to Joshi, what were Lord Dalhousie's motives for building India's railway system?
4. What long-term effects has India's railway system had on India's economic situation, according to Joshi?
5. If Joshi had been given an opportunity to draw a blueprint for India's economic development, what would it have looked like?

ECONOMIC REALITIES

In this country, which is economically in such a primitive and backward condition, a too exclusive policy of pushing on Railways at American speed, beyond the resources of Indian finance, will, unless accompanied by other economic measures of far greater importance, only end in national impoverishment. We are not opposed to the growth of Railways *per se.* They are good in their own way as providing cheap transit, and promoting national solidarity, and facilitating trade-movements, but when their extension is made the ultimate goal of State action on its economic side, their tendency to prevent, in a country like India, a healthy material advance on *normal lines* must be duly taken into account; for, unless they are accompanied by other and more important measures conducive to a better organisation of national industries, they do not add to the intensive strength of the country, which alone furnishes a firm foundation to its expansive greatness. . . .

Every consideration, therefore, of prudence and justice alike dictate that the action of Government,[1] in such circumstances, shall be thoroughly national in its aims, purposes, and principles of execution. It might employ foreign talent for the prosecution of such works; it might borrow foreign capital for the purpose. But it is on no grounds justified in bringing the foreigner with his talent and capital into the country, and suffering him to appropriate permanently the national field of improvement, to the exclusion of the native element, and forming the nucleus of a domineering foreign aristocracy in the land with purposes and interests adverse to those of the nation — a result which cannot but be regarded as at once a serious political danger, and a great economic evil. . . .

THE EFFECTS OF FREE TRADE

The Public Works policy of the Government of India was first formulated by Lord Dalhousie,[2] under whose administration the proposal of a separate Department for the promotion of Public Works undertaken on Government account, or with Government guarantee,[3] was carried out.

---

[1]The "Government," or the "Government of India," consisted of a British governor-general, his six-man Executive Council, and a Legislative Council consisting of the Executive Council and six to twelve additional members. All these various Councils were dominated by the British.

[2]The Marquis of Dalhousie had been head of the Railway Department of the English Board of Trade before serving as governor-general of India between 1848 and 1856. He was a strong advocate of India's economic modernization

and sponsored a host of public works projects, including railroads, canals, roads, and irrigation systems. He created the Department of Public Works to oversee the many new undertakings.

[3]The "guarantee" was a policy by which railroad companies were guaranteed a 5 percent profit on their investment and were reimbursed by the government if profits fell below that percentage.

. . . It was Lord Dalhousie's dream to strengthen the domination not only of English rule, but of English trade and commerce in India, and the permanent interests of this country were subordinated to this all-engrossing ambition. The contemporaneous rise of the school of Free Trade[4] in England, and the great reputation which its apostles enjoyed, furnished the metaphysical ground-work for this essentially selfish and grasping policy. The value of India to the British nation was measured by the quantity of raw material which the resources of Indian agriculture enabled it to export for the feeding and maintenance of the Lancashire manufactures.[5] India was to devote all its energies to raise the raw exports; and canals, Railroads and improved communications were to be pushed on at any cost to facilitate the export of raw articles and the import of English manufactures. India's own industrial needs were of comparatively no consequence. . . . So far as this result was inevitably due to natural conditions, we have no fault to find with Government. But surely it was not a legitimate exercise of the State's parental functions to help with Indian resources the one country which needed no such help, at the cost of paralyzing its great unfortunate dependency, whose salvation from its depression of ages depends upon its industrial growth in all directions. . . .

The extent of the mischief that has been worked already is admitted by the more keen-sighted of English statesmen, and is witnessed to by the ghastly spectacle so recently witnessed of a condition of things when six millions of people died during a single year of scanty rainfall, . . . and one-third of the population lives from hand to mouth on a single meal a day. And yet Government professes itself to be powerless to raise its little finger to stop the drain,[6] or divert it into less exhaustive channels. It cannot

undertake to subsidize native industrial growth, or stimulate local manufactures without exposing itself to the fire of Free-Trade fanatics, and the opposition of the vested foreign interests which it has created. . . . The abolition of these duties [on imports to India] has worked mischief in that it has exposed to the unrestricted competition of the world the rude and undeveloped industries of the country. These duties were not, as in England, levied upon raw products, but upon finished articles such as cotton, silk and woollen manufactured goods, and wrought metal. These imported articles were all of them machine-made, and necessarily displaced the hand-made products of native skill. This displacement was to a certain extent inevitable, but Government, as the protector of national Indian interests, should not have gone out of its way to stimulate this process of the violent disintegration of important industries in this country. . . . People point out with pride to the fact that, in the course of fifty years, the imports have risen from six to sixty crores of Rupees.[7] To enable our readers to understand the true character of these figures, we append below a table showing the growth in the import of manufactured goods during the last 25 years.

Articles	1859–60	1870–71	1881–82
	£	£	£
Woollen goods	358,557	582,330	1,276,263
Cotton goods	11,698,928	19,044,869	24,000,237
Metal	454,457	850,319	2,772,178
Sugar	220,270	555,801	1,243,758
Umbrellas	136,670	Not available	209,572

These figures show what displacement has occurred in the consumption of the chief manufactured goods of home production. It cannot be maintained for one moment that India did not

---

[4]Advocates of free trade espoused the teachings of Adam Smith in the *Wealth of Nations* (1776). They called for the abolition of all tariffs on imports and exports. In England such doctrines were popular among industrialists who believed the lowering or end of tariffs would ensure markets for British manufactured goods and keep down the price of imported foodstuffs.

[5]The region of England where cotton manufacturing was concentrated.
[6]A term used by critics of British colonialism to describe the loss of Indian wealth to Britain through taxes and trade.
[7]The rupee was the basic coin in the Indian currency system; one crore equaled ten million rupees.

clothe itself in cotton or other fabrics in times past. As a matter of fact, India did not only clothe itself, but even so late as the first quarter of this century, it exported its fine muslims[8] to Europe in large quantities, and even to this day the raw material of cotton and wool is exported in larger quantities than the imported goods. . . .

NATIVE VERSUS FOREIGN MANAGEMENT

. . . Even where native capitalists have embarked their capital in such [manufacturing] enterprises, they are not able to command native skill of management, but find it necessary to import foreign talent and skill. With a partial exception in Bombay, these new industries are all managed throughout by European skill, thus giving the foreigners a monopoly of the advantages reaped, over and above their natural monopoly as shippers, and carriers and insurers. Even in those departments of money dealings where the native has a natural claim to succeed, European enterprise has driven out native talent. We refer here to the banking enterprise of the country. As many as 323 banking companies have been established in this country since 1861, and 140 of these establishments are in active operation to this day. All these are managed by Europeans, though their dealings are for the most part with native customers, and their funds are derived to a large extent from native depositors.

RAILWAYS AND TECHNICAL TRAINING

Notwithstanding this financially burdensome and economically ruinous policy of the Government . . . the people of India would have had good reason to welcome this diversion of public funds by the State, if the vast expenditure incurred for railway construction had the effect of training the nation by suitable arrangements for their technical education, and liberal association in the management, to take up in course of time in their own hands the new sphere of industrial activity represented by railway enterprise. . . . The people of India needed above all things a technical training in mechanical arts and manufacturing processes, and pecuniary aid in the shape of State subsidies in starting new enterprises. Above all, they had to be protected from the predominance of a foreign plutocracy, with vested interests opposed to those of the Native producer. None of these considerations have attracted the attention of Government as they deserved. The system of public education, . . . is mainly intended to qualify native youths for inferior service in the State departments. The scientific branches of the service are all but sealed to the natives by reason of their education not fitting them to take their natural place in mechanical and engineering enterprises. . . . The result is that, after 25 years of continuous State direction, the natives of the country are as unfitted to take up this work of railway construction or management, as ever they were when Lord Dalhousie first sanctioned the proposal of covering India with a network of railway lines. The railway establishments in all the higher grades are a close[d] preserve for the foreigner and even the lower duties of collecting or clipping tickets are entrusted to other hands than those of the natives of the country. A few native guards and drivers and fitters are all that the companies can show in the way of training natives for higher work, and the position and status of these people are anything but comfortable. . . . Everything for the people, and nothing by the people, this was the maxim of the great Napoleon, and in no country in the world has it been more vigorously carried out than in India, where the foreigner does everything for the people, who look upon all that is done with rustic amazement.

---

[8]A term for a number of types of plain, finely woven cotton textiles.

Responses to Western Domination

Africans who saw their communal lands turned into European-owned plantations; Indians offended by the racism of British colonial officials; Chinese humiliated by their empire's military impotence; Persians who saw their country partitioned between Great Britain and Russia in 1907; Filipinos who in 1898 shed one colonial master, Spain, only to be claimed by a new one, the United States; and countless others in Asia, Africa, and Latin America — all faced the same question in the years around 1900: How should we respond to the economic strength, military power, and ever-increasing political ascendancy of the West?

For many Asians and Africans whose independence was under attack, the first response to this question was often "Fight back!" Africans fiercely resisted the European takeover of their continent, and European troops had to engage in hundreds of battles and skirmishes before securing their rule. It took the Germans twenty-five years of fighting before they finally pacified their colony, German East Africa, in 1907. In Asia the Burmese, Filipinos, and Vietnamese fought against the British, Americans, and French, respectively, before they succumbed to colonial rule.

By the early twentieth century, however, it was clear that fighting back was futile. Only Ethiopia, whose King Menelik had equipped his soldiers with modern weapons in the 1890s, successfully repulsed the European imperialists when its army defeated Italy, the least great of the great powers, at the Battle of Aduwa in 1896.

Once armed resistance ended and colonial administrations were in place, asking how to respond to the West became a meaningless exercise for the colonized. "Natives" might have low-echelon jobs as clerks, policemen, or soldiers, but they had no voice in making policy. Acquiescence, at least for the time, was the only reasonable option for people under direct European rule.

India was an exception. Having been under British rule for better than a century and with a sizable number of educated Indians who had studied in British-sponsored schools, India experienced the first stirrings of nationalism in the late nineteenth century. A key step was taken in 1885 with the founding of the Indian National Congress, an organization dedicated to improving the prospects of Indians in the colonial administration and ultimately to winning Indian independence.

Debates about how to respond to the West were most intense and meaningful in those states in which Western imperialism fell short of outright political control. In China and the Ottoman Empire, for example, there were ardent Westernizers, who believed that progress and survival depended on making a clean break with the past and embracing Western values, practices, and institutions. At the opposite extreme were those who hated Western values and sought to preserve their society's unique traditions. Between these two extremes were those who represented every form of compromise between unbending traditionalism and single-minded zeal for Westernization.

China and the Foreign Devils

◈

5 ◆ *TWO PROCLAMATIONS OF THE BOXER REBELLION*

No country was more deeply humiliated by its inability to prevent Western aggression in the nineteenth century than China. Despite its great size, long imperial tradition, and centuries of achievement in the arts, scholarship, and technology, China experienced military defeat, punitive treaties, territorial losses, foreign political interference, and an influx of missionaries and traders from nations the Chinese had always viewed as barbaric and inferior.

The Boxer Rebellion of 1898 was partly an expression of Chinese rage over almost a century of foreign exploitation. It was also the culmination of a decades-long struggle within the imperial administration between reformers and conservatives. Reformers were convinced that only radical changes could rescue China from its domestic morass and prevent its dismemberment by foreigners. They rejected much of China's Confucian heritage, and called for the introduction of Western-style military training, industrialization, and educational reforms. Conservatives affirmed China's inherent superiority to the West, and sought to preserve the emperor's power, Confucianism's intellectual ascendancy, and China's traditional agrarian economy.

The deadlock ended in 1898 when Emperor Guangxu (r. 1875–1908) initiated the Hundred Days' Reform. With the guidance of reform-minded advisors, he issued dozens of decrees to weed out corrupt officials, streamline the government, stimulate education, reform the military, and introduce Chinese-owned banks, railroads, and newspapers. Opposition coalesced around the emperor's aunt, Empress Dowager Cixi, who in September 1898, with the help of generals and threatened officeholders, placed the emperor under house arrest and annulled his reforms. To further their conservative, antiforeign agenda, in 1899 Cixi and her supporters encouraged the popular movement led by a Chinese secret society known as the "Righteous and Harmonious Fists." The result was the Boxer Rebellion, another sad chapter in the history of Chinese-Western relations.

The Society of Righteous and Harmonious Fists, known to Westerners as Boxers because their formal exercises resembled boxing, was one of many secret societies that flourished in late imperial China. The Boxers believed that foreigners, especially foreign missionaries, were the cause of China's problems. In 1899 they launched a murder campaign against foreign missionaries and business owners, many of whom fled to Beijing for protection in the foreign legation quarter. The Boxers pursued them and, encouraged by Cixi and her followers, placed the legation quarter under siege. A force of European, Japanese, and U.S. troops easily lifted the siege, and in 1901 China was forced to sign another humiliating treaty, the Boxer Protocol, which among other things required an indemnity payment of $333,900,000.

As the Boxer movement gathered strength in 1900, the Boxers posted and distributed thousands of proclamations in the hope of gaining followers. The two following selections are representative samples.

QUESTIONS FOR ANALYSIS

1. What do these proclamations reveal about the Boxers' vision of China's future?
2. What is the Boxer attitude toward Western technology?
3. According to the Boxers, what evils have resulted from the foreign presence in China?
4. Why were the Boxers confident of their ultimate victory?

The Gods assist the Boxers,
The Patriotic Harmonious corps,
It is because the "Foreign Devils" disturb
   the "Middle Kingdom."
Urging the people to join their religion,
To turn their backs on Heaven,
Venerate not the Gods and forget the
   ancestors.

Men violate the human obligations,
Women commit adultery,
"Foreign Devils" are not produced by
   mankind,
If you do not believe,
Look at them carefully.

The eyes of all the "Foreign Devils" are
   bluish,
No rain falls,
The earth is getting dry,
This is because the churches stop
   Heaven,
The Gods are angry;
The Genii[1] are vexed;
Both come down from the mountain to
   deliver the doctrine.

This is no hearsay,

The practices of boxing will not be in
   vain;

Reciting incantations and pronouncing
   magic words,
Burn up yellow written prayers,
Light incense sticks
To invite the Gods and Genii of all the
   grottoes.

The Gods come out from grottoes,
The Genii come down from mountains,
Support the human bodies to practice the
   boxing.

When all the military accomplishments or
   tactics
Are fully learned,
It will not be difficult to exterminate the
   "Foreign Devils" then.

Push aside the railway tracks,
Pull out the telegraph poles,
Immediately after this destroy the
   steamers.

The great France
Will grow cold and downhearted.
The English and Russians will certainly
   disperse.

Let the various "Foreign Devils" all be
   killed.
May the whole Elegant Empire of the
   Great Qing Dynasty be ever
   prosperous!

---

[1]Minor spirits.

Attention: all people in markets and villages of all provinces in China — now, owing to the fact that Catholics and Protestants have vilified our gods and sages, have deceived our emperors and ministers above, and oppressed the Chinese people below, both our gods and our people are angry at them, yet we have to keep silent. This forces us to practise the Yike[2] magic boxing so as to protect our country, expel the foreign bandits and kill Christian converts, in order to save our people from miserable suffering. After this notice is issued to instruct you villagers, no matter which village you are living in, if there are Christian converts, you ought to get rid of them quickly. The churches which belong to them should be unreservedly burned down. Everyone who intends to spare someone, or to disobey our order by concealing Christian converts, will be punished according to the regulation when we come to his place, and he will be burned to death to prevent his impeding our program. We especially do not want to punish anyone by death without warning him first. We cannot bear to see you suffer innocently. Don't disobey this special notice!

---

[2]Yike means "United in Righteousness." It identifies the type of martial arts (yikequan) practiced by the boxers.

"Freedom Is My Birthright"

◆

6 ◆ *Bal Gangadhar Tilak,* SPEECH TO THE INDIAN NATIONAL CONGRESS, 1907

Living in a country that had seen many conquerors, most Indians greeted the increase of British authority on the subcontinent from the 1770s onward with indifference. Some, who anticipated benefits from Western science and law, even greeted it with approval. By the end of the nineteenth century, however, disillusionment with the British and opposition to colonialism were growing. Such feelings were strongest among middle-class Hindus, especially those who had been educated in British-sponsored schools and held posts in the Indian Civil Service. They resented the colonial administration's economic policies and its failure to give Indians anything but menial government jobs. In 1885 dissatisfied Indians formed the Indian National Congress, a moderate group dedicated to achieving a greater Indian voice in government and ultimately independence.

In 1906, however, the annual meeting of the Congress was rocked by a bitter conflict precipitated by a split between the Moderates, who endorsed the Congress's policy of cooperation with the British and gradual reform, and the Extremists, who sought the immediate expulsion of the British — if necessary, through violence. Frustration with British rule had earlier reached a flash point when in 1905 the British announced the partition of the province of Bengal, with one part to be predominantly Hindu and the other predominantly Muslim. The British claimed that administrative efficiency dictated the change, but the Indians considered it another example of British high-handedness and an effort to weaken Indian nationalism by encouraging religious antagonism. Support grew for the Extremists, who formed a new organization within the Congress called the New Party.

The leading spokesman of the New Party was Bal Gangadhar Tilak (1856–1920), a scholar and religious philosopher who, as the editor of a widely read Marathi-language newspaper, thundered against the evils of British rule and defended Hindu traditions. His mottos — "Militancy not Mendicancy" and "Freedom Is My Birthright, and I Shall Have It" — spread throughout India. The British considered him a rabble-rouser and imprisoned him in 1897 and 1908 for sedition. He delivered the following speech to the 1906 meeting of the Indian National Congress at which the Moderate-Extremist split surfaced. In it he outlines the New Party's beliefs and expresses his support for the newly organized boycott movement.

QUESTIONS FOR ANALYSIS

1. According to Tilak, what are the major differences between the Moderates and the Extremists?
2. In Tilak's view, why were many Indians at first convinced that British rule was a good thing?
3. Why, according to Tilak, have most Indians become disillusioned with British rule?
4. What does Tilak mean by "boycott?" Does it mean an economic boycott only?
5. What is Tilak's ultimate goal for India?

. . . One thing is granted, namely, that this government does not suit us. As has been said by an eminent statesman — the government of one country by another can never be a successful, and therefore, a permanent government. There is no difference of opinion about this fundamental proposition between the old and new schools. One fact is that this alien government has ruined the country. In the beginning, all of us were taken by surprise. We were almost dazed. We thought that everything that the rulers did was for our good and that this English government has descended from the clouds to save us from the invasions of Tamerlane and Genghis Khan,[1] and, as they say, not only from foreign invasions but from internecine warfare, or the internal or external invasions, as they call it. We felt happy for a time, but it soon came to light that the peace which was established in this country did this . . . — that we were prevented from going at each other's throats, so that a foreigner might go at the throat of us all. *Pax Britannica* has been established in this country in order that a foreign government may exploit the country. That this is the effect of this *Pax Britannica* is being gradually realized in these days. It was an unhappy circumstance that it was not realized sooner. We believed in the benevolent intentions of the government, but in politics there is no benevolence. Benevolence is used to sugarcoat the declarations of self-interest and we were in those days deceived by the apparent benevolent intentions under which rampant self-interest was concealed. That was our state then. But soon a change came over us. English education, growing poverty, and better familiarity with our rulers, opened our eyes and our

[1]Genghis (also Chingis or Jenghis) Khan (ca. 1167–1277) was the Mongol conqueror who founded the largest land empire in history. By the time of his death he ruled an area that stretched from the Pacific to the Black Sea and from Siberia to Southeast Asia. Tamerlane, or Timur the Lame (1336–1405), of Turco-Mongol descent, was another famous conqueror who invaded India and took Delhi in 1398.

leaders'; especially, the venerable leader[2] who presided over the recent Congress was the first to tell us that the drain from the country was ruining it, and if the drain was to continue, there was some great disaster awaiting us. So terribly convinced was he of this that he went over from here to England and spent twenty-five years of his life in trying to convince the English people of the injustice that is being done to us. He worked very hard. He had conversations and interviews with secretaries of state, with members of Parliament — and with what result?

He has come here at the age of eighty-two to tell us that he is bitterly disappointed. . . .

You can now understand the difference between the old and the new parties. Appeals to the bureaucracy are hopeless. On this point both the new and old parties are agreed. The old party believes in appealing to the British nation and we do not. That being our position, it logically follows we must have some other method. There is another alternative. We are not going to sit down quiet. We shall have some other method by which to achieve what we want. We are not disappointed, we are not pessimists. It is the hope of achieving the goal by our own efforts that has brought into existence this new party. . . .

We have come forward with a scheme which if you accept [it], shall better enable you to remedy this state of things than the scheme of the old school. Your industries are ruined utterly, ruined by foreign rule; your wealth is going out of the country and you are reduced to the lowest level which no human being can occupy. In this state of things, is there any other remedy by which you can help yourself? The remedy is not petitioning but boycott. We say prepare your forces, organize your power, and then go to work so that they cannot refuse you what you

demand. . . . We are not armed, and there is no necessity for arms either. We have a stronger weapon, a political weapon, in boycott. We have perceived one fact, that the whole of this administration, which is carried on by a handful of Englishmen, is carried on with our assistance. We are all in subordinate service. This whole government is carried on with our assistance and they try to keep us in ignorance of our power of cooperation between ourselves by which that which is in our own hands at present can be claimed by us and administrated by us. The point is to have the entire control in our hands. I want to have the key of my house, and not merely one stranger turned out of it. Self-government is our goal; we want a control over our administrative machinery. We don't want to become clerks and remain clerks. At present, we are clerks and willing instruments of our own oppression in the hands of an alien government, and that government is ruling over us not by its innate strength but by keeping us in ignorance and blindness to the perception of this fact. . . . What the new party wants you to do is to realize the fact that your future rests entirely in your own hands. If you mean to be free, you can be free; if you do not mean to be free, you will fall and be for ever fallen. So many of you need not like arms; but if you have not the power of active resistance, have you not the power of self-denial and self-abstinence in such a way as not to assist this foreign government to rule over you? This is boycott and this is what is meant when we say, boycott is a political weapon. We shall not give them assistance to collect revenue and keep peace. We shall not assist them in fighting beyond the frontiers or outside India with Indian blood and money. We shall not assist them in carrying on the administration of justice. We shall have our own courts, and when time comes we shall not pay taxes. Can

---

[2]A reference to Dadabhai Naoroji (1825–1917), founder and, at the time of Tilak's speech, president of the Indian National Congress. Born into a prominent Hindu family, Naoroji abandoned a career as a mathematician to live in England, where he tried to convince the government to

improve conditions in India. While in England he was elected to Parliament in 1892. Naoroji formulated the concept of the "drain," the process by which Britain systematically depleted Indian wealth and resources.

you do that by your united efforts? If you can, you are free from tomorrow. . . . This is a lesson of progress, a lesson of helping yourself as much as possible, and if you really perceive the force of it, if you are convinced by these arguments, then and then only is it possible for you to effect your salvation from the alien rule under which you labor at this moment.

There are many other points but it is impossible to exhaust them all in an hour's speech. If you carry any wrong impression come and get your doubts solved. We are prepared to answer every objection, solve every doubt, and prove every statement. We want your cooperation; without your help we cannot do anything singlehanded. We beg of you, we appeal to you, to think over the question, to see the situation, and realize it, and after realizing it to come to our assistance, and by our joint assistance to help in the salvation of the country.

A Blueprint for Japanese Military Modernization

❖

7 ❖ *Yamagata Aritomo,* *OPINION ON MILITARY AFFAIRS AND CONSCRIPTION*

Japan's response to the West had no parallels anywhere else in the world. Under the government of the Tokugawa shoguns, who took power in the early 1600s, Japan had pursued a policy of commercial and cultural isolation until Commodore Perry arrived on behalf of the U.S. government in 1853 and forced Japan to open its ports to foreign trade. Dreading the prospect of foreign domination and disillusioned with the ineffectual response of the Tokugawa government, in 1868 aristocrats led by the Satsuma and Chosu clans seized power and reinstated the emperor, until then a figurehead living in seclusion in Kyoto, as head of the Japanese state. The emperor took Meiji as his reign name, and hence the events of 1868 are known as the Meiji Restoration.

During the Meiji Era (1878–1912), a small group of aristocratic reformers, claiming to act on behalf of the emperor, embarked upon a vigorous program of Westernization in keeping with their motto "Enrich the Nation, Strengthen the Army." In short order, they abolished the shogunate, stripped the feudal aristocrats, or samurai, of their privileges, and plunged headlong into modernizing the economy. Railroads, steamships, factories, the telegraph, and silk mills along with Western dress and even baseball became part of Japanese life. The ultimate goal, however, was to build a strong army and navy to keep the Westerners at bay and make Japan a power to be reckoned with in Asia. The Meiji reformers were spectacularly successful, as victories over China in 1895 and Russia in 1905 amply proved.

Few individuals played a more important role in the history of Meiji Japan than did Yamagata Aritomo (1838–1922), best known as the architect of the Japanese army, but also a statesman who influenced economic policy, education, and the writing of Japan's constitution. Born into a low-ranking samurai family, he committed himself to the antiforeign, antishogun movements of the 1860s and was a supporter of the imperial restoration. The new regime immediately assigned him its most pressing task, the modernization of Japan's military. After an eighteen-month trip to Europe to observe military practices, he submitted the following memorandum to Japan's leaders on the nation's military needs. One year later, in 1873, he framed the imperial decree that established Japan's conscript army.

QUESTIONS FOR ANALYSIS

1. According to Yamagata, why is it necessary for Japan to strengthen its army and navy?
2. What are some of the lessons Yamagata learned from his observations of Western military practices?
3. In his view, what lessons should Japan learn specifically from the example of Belgium and the Netherlands?
4. What can you infer from this document about the arguments being made by opponents to a military build-up?
5. On the basis of Yamagata's proposals, what might you conclude about the ways Japan's new military affected Japanese society as a whole?

. . . The status of our armed forces today is as follows: We have the so-called Imperial Guards whose functions are nothing more than to protect the sacred person of His Majesty and to guard the Imperial Palace. We have altogether more than twenty battalions manning the four military garrisons who are deployed to maintain domestic tranquility, and are not equipped to fight against any foreign threat. As to our navy, we have a few battleships yet to be completed. How can they be sufficient to counteract foreign threats? . . .

The first concern of the Ministry of Military Affairs is to set up a system to defend our homeland. For this purpose two categories of soldiers are required: a standing army and those on the reserve list. The number of troops differ from country to country. Of the major countries, Russia maintains the largest number of troops and the United States the smallest. The reason for this discrepancy comes from the fact that the governmental system differs from one country to another. Consequently the regulations governing each of the countries also differ. The Netherlands and Belgium are among the smallest countries, but they are located between large countries, and in order to avoid contempt and scorn from their neighbors, they diligently go about the business of defending their countries. Even though one of these countries has a total area not exceeding one-third of the area of our country, it maintains a standing army numbering not less than forty to fifty thousand. If we apply the existing standards prevailing in our country to judge these two countries, they may appear to be concerned only with military affairs to the neglect of other matters. However, they do attend to hundreds of other affairs of state and do not abandon them. This is possible because their national goals are already set, and they can act accordingly to implement them.

At a time like this it is very clear where the priority of this country must lie. We must now have a well-trained standing army supplemented by a large number of reservists. We must build warships and construct batteries. We must train officers and soldiers. We must manufacture and store weapons and ammunitions. The nation may consider that it cannot bear the expenses. However, even if we wish to ignore it, this important matter cannot disappear from us. . . .

Therefore the creation of a standing army for our country is a task which cannot be delayed. It is recommended that a certain number of strong and courageous young men be selected from each of the prefectures in accordance with the size of the prefectures, and that such young men be trained in the Western-type military science and placed under rigorous drills, so that they may by deployed as occasion demands. . . . All of the countries in Europe have reservists, and amongst them Prussia has most of them. There is not a single able-bodied man in Prussia who is not trained in military affairs. Recently Prussia and France fought each other and the former won handily.[1] This is due in large measure to the strength of its reservists.

It is recommended that our country adopt a system under which any able-bodied man twenty years of age be drafted into military service, unless his absence from home will create undue hardship for his family. There shall be no distinction made between the common man and those who are of the samurai class. They shall all be formed into ranks, and after completion of a period of service, they shall be returned to their homes.[2] In this way every man will become a soldier, and not a single region in the country will be without defense. Thus our defense will become complete.

The second concern of the Ministry is coastal defense. This includes building of warships and constructing coastal batteries. . . . Our country has thousands of miles of coastline, and any mobile corner of our country can become the advance post of our enemy. However, since it is not possible to construct batteries along the coastline everywhere, it is imperative to expand our navy and construct the largest warships. . . .

The third concern of the Military is to create resources for the navy and the army. There are three items under consideration, namely military academics, a bureau of military supplies, and a bureau of munitions depots. It is not difficult to have one million soldiers in a short time, but it is difficult to gain one good officer during the same span of time. Military academies are intended to train officers for these two services. If we pay little attention to this need today, we shall not be able to have the services of capable officers for another day. Therefore, without delay military academies must be created and be allowed to prosper. Students shall be adequately trained by the faculty consisting of experts from several countries. . . . The bureau of military supplies shall be in charge of procuring military provisions and manufacturing weapons of war for the two services. The bureau of munitions depots shall store such provisions and munitions. If we lack military provisions and weapons and our munitions depots are empty, what good will the million soldiers in the army or thousands of warships do? Therefore, well-qualified craftsmen from various countries must be hired to make necessary machines and build strong storage houses. We must make our own weapons and store them, and must become self-sufficient without relying on foreign countries. The goal is to create a sufficient amount and if there is any surplus it may be sold to other countries.

Some people may argue that while they are aware of the urgency in the need for the Ministry of Military Affairs, they cannot permit the entire national resources to be committed to the need of one ministry alone. . . . This argument fails to discern the fundamental issues. The recommendations herein presented by the Ministry of Military Affairs in no way asks for the stoppage of all governmental activities or for the monopolization of all government revenues. But in a national emergency, a new set of priorities must be established. Those of us who are given the task of governing must learn from the past, discern the present, and weigh all matters carefully.

---

[1]A reference to the Franco-Prussian War (1870–1871), in which the German states under the leadership of Prussia defeated the French.

[2]This means they will become reservists.

In the past there was Emperor Peter[3] who was determined to make his country a great nation. He went overseas and studied naval sciences. After his return he built many battleships and constructed St. Petersburg. He created a standing army numbering several million, and was able to engage in the art of international politics against five or six of the strongest nations. . . . It is to him that the credit is due for making Russia a great nation.

Those of us who govern must first of all discern the conditions prevailing in the world, set up priorities and take appropriate measures. In our opinion Russia has been acting very arrogantly. Previously, contrary to the provisions of the Treaty of Sevastopol[4] she placed her warships in the Black Sea. Southward, she has shown her aggressive intent toward Muslim countries and toward India. Westward, she has crossed the borders of Manchuria and has been navigating the Amur River. Her intents being thus, it is inevitable that she will move eastward sooner or later by sending troops to Hokkaido,[5] and then taking advantage of the seasonal wind move to the warmer areas.

---

[3]A reference to Peter the Great, tsar of Russia from 1689 to 1725, famous for his efforts to Westernize Russia. Much of what Yamagata claims about Peter is exaggerated, either because he received false information or because he intentionally distorted the facts. His statements that Peter constructed "many battleships," recruited an army of "several million," and fought "five or six" strong nations are inaccurate.

[4]Yamagata seems to be referring to the 1858 Treaty of Paris, which ended the Crimean War; it denied the defeated Russians access to the Black Sea. Sevastopol is a city on the Black Sea.

[5]A Japanese island north of Honshu.

◆

Migrants and Their Experiences

Migration — over land and water, by laborers and conquerors, hunters and herdsmen, farmers and traders — has always been a part of human history. In the years around 1900, however, people were on the move in unprecedented numbers. Southern blacks were moving to northern cities in the United States; rural Europeans were moving to new industrial centers; Indians left for Southeast Asia, the Caribbean, Africa, and South America; Chinese were moving to Malaya, Singapore, and the Americas. Most dramatically of all, millions of Europeans were migrating to the United States, Argentina, Australia, New Zealand, and Canada.

As in the past, population pressure was an incentive to move. China's population increased from approximately 142 million in the mid eighteenth century to 432 million around 1850, and to better than 450 million in 1900. India's population increased from approximately 150 million in 1850 to 250 million in 1881, while the population of Europe grew from 187 million in 1800 to 266 million by midcentury, and 435 million by 1914. This demographic surge ruined the economic prospects of many peasants and agricultural workers, who faced land shortages at a time when rural unemployment was growing as a result of the commercialization and mechanization of agriculture.

Economic necessity drove millions of Europeans and smaller numbers of Asians to seek new lives in Australia, New Zealand, and especially the Americas. Steamships made long-distance travel across the world's oceans cheaper, more reliable, and quicker than in the age of sailing ships. By the end of the nine-teenth century, crossing the Atlantic was so inexpensive that it made economic sense for Italian workers known as "swallows" to travel to Argentina every year to harvest the wheat crop, then return home.

How were immigrants greeted in their new homelands? What experiences did they have? The documents in this section provide some answers to these questions.

Indian Merchants in South Africa and Their Problems

◈

8 ◆ *Abdool Rehman,*
MEMORANDUM TO LORD SELBORNE, HIGH COMMISSIONER OF TRANSVAAL, OCTOBER 1905

Although Indians had traded on the east African coast for centuries, only in the nineteenth century did they begin to settle in Africa's interior. In the 1880s and 1890s approximately thirty-two thousand indentured Indian laborers worked on the construction of the East Africa Railway, which on its completion stretched from the Kenyan port of Mombasa all the way to Lake Victoria in Uganda. Else-where in Africa most Indian immigrants were indentured farm laborers, im-ported to work five-year stints on European-owned plantations. Approximately a quarter of these laborers remained in Africa after their five years of required service, and they were joined by increasing numbers of "passenger Indians" who paid their own way. Among these was Mohandas Gandhi, later the leader of the Indian independence movement, who practiced law in South Africa between 1893 and 1914.

By 1900 approximately one hundred thousand Indians lived in Natal, a British territory on the east coast of South Africa. Smaller numbers lived in Transvaal, a republic to the north of Natal that for several decades had been a source of conflict between the British, who had annexed the territory in 1877, and the Dutch-speaking Boers, who had rebelled against British rule in 1880–1881 and won back their independence. After the defeat of the Boers in the Boer, or South African, War (1899–1902), Transvaal again came under British rule. In Natal and Transvaal Indians were laborers, small farmers, cooks, waiters, clerks, masons, and carpenters, but most were merchants who sold their wares in small shops, on street corners as hawkers, or door-to-door. Indian mer-chants encountered intense opposition from white competitors, who success-fully pressured officials in Natal and Transvaal to withhold licenses from Indian merchants or charge them prohibitive licensing fees. The Indians responded by hiring lawyers, forming political organizations, and deluging government offi-cials with letters and petitions.

The following letter was written by Abdool Rehman, an Indian merchant who was secretary of the Indian Association in the Transvaal town of Potchefstroom.

He sent the letter to the highest-ranking British official in South Africa, High Commissioner Lord Selborne, to answer criticisms of Indian merchants made by a white merchants' association, the Anti-Asiatic Vigilance Society.

QUESTIONS FOR ANALYSIS

1. What allegations against the Indian merchant community have been made by the Anti-Asiatic Vigilance Society?
2. How would you characterize Rehman's response to these allegations?
3. What can be learned about the characteristics of Indian trade in Transvaal from Rehman's letter?
4. Aside from the difficulties experienced by the merchants, what other forms of discrimination were encountered by Indians in Transvaal?
5. What does the source reveal about general attitudes toward Indians on the part of Transvaal's white population?

Did we not know that what has been called the Anti-Asiatic Vigilance Society is to make representations to Your Excellency with reference to the British Indians, so far as regards Potchefstroom, we would not have given any trouble whatsoever to Your Excellency, especially as we are aware that Your Excellency is to meet very shortly a deputation of the British Indian Association at Johannesburg.[1]

Mr. Loveday it was who stated that Potchefstroom was being inundated with indentured Indians from Natal. To this we beg to give an empathic contradiction. Some of us know the Natal laws, and we know that [it] is next to impossible for an indentured Indian to escape. In any case not a single instance has been brought forward to prove the statement above referred to.

Another statement was made by the mayor of Johannesburg when he was here. He is reported to have said that, whereas there were nineteen licences issued to Asiatics before the war,[2] now there were ninety-six traders' licences and thirty-seven hawkers'[3] licences. This statement, so far as

traders are concerned, is not true. We supplied before the war a list of British Indian traders in the town of Potchefstroom to the British Agent, and there were twenty-two British Indian stores in the town of Potchefstroom, as distinguished from the district. We have a true copy of the list that was sent to the British Agent, and we are today in a position, not only to give the names, but to locate each of the store-keepers. Seeing that Mr. Goch[4] mentions ninety-six traders' licences in connection with the nineteen before the war, we take it that he refers to ninety-six traders' licences for the town of Potchefstroom. If so, this is grossly untrue. There are only twenty-four British Indian stores in this town at the present day. We state this with a full sense of responsibility and knowledge, and we challenge our detractors to prove the contrary.

A third statement that has been made against us in Potchefstroom is with reference to the so-called insanitary condition of our dwellings and shops. These, indeed, speak for themselves, but when the charge was made, we took the

---

[1]Apparently a member of the Anti-Asiatic Vigilance Society.
[2]The South African War (1899–1902), also known as the Boer War, resulted in a hard-fought British victory over South Africans of Dutch descent who sought independence from British rule.

[3]Street vendors.
[4]The mayor of Johannesburg.

opportunity of showing our places to the district surgeon of Potchefstroom, and the following is the report that [he] gave:

In going through the various premises, I am pleased to say I was greatly impressed with the general condition of each place I visited, both internally as well as externally. Taking all things into consideration, the backyards are all perfectly clean and sanitary. I saw no accumulation of rubbish, this I understand being carried away daily by the contractor. The bucket system is enforced as in other parts of the town, which is also attended to by the Sanitary Department, and I can find no fault from what I saw. There appears to me to be no overcrowding as regards sleeping accommodation. At the back of each business premise, in addition, I noticed a kind of mess room capable of seating about five to eight persons, and each has its own kitchen; these are also well kept.

We mention these things to show under what disadvantages, we have to labour, and what misrepresentations are made against us. We have no hesitation in saying that the whole of the anti-Asiatic agitation is due to trade jealousy. Nothing can be further from our wish than to enter into an unfair competition with the white store-keepers.

Much has been said against our mode of life. We are proud to think that we are sober and simple in our habits, and if thereby we have an advantage over the rival white traders, we hardly think that it should be brought up against us in order to traduce and degrade us. It is totally forgotten, in this connection, by those who denounce us, that the white traders have other advantages which we cannot dream of having, namely their European connection, their knowledge of the English language, and their better organising powers. Moreover, we are able to carry on our trade only because of the goodwill of the poor whites, and our ability to please the poorest class of customers; also, we have the support of wholesale European houses.

It has been said that our competition resulted in many European shops being closed. We deny this. In the first instance, some of the shops that have been closed were not shops with which we could possibly enter into competition, for instance hairdressers and others. Some general goods stores have undoubtedly closed, but to connect their closing with Asiatic competition would be [as] unfair as to connect the closing of several Asiatic shops with European competition in this town. There is trade depression all over South Africa, and it has only resulted in getting rid of overtrading that was indulged in soon after the war, based, as it was, on high expectations which have never been fulfilled.

May we also, in this connection, state that much of the agitation against us is kept up not by bona-fide British subjects but by aliens who can have very little indeed to complain of against us. The policy adopted to drive us out of the township is a policy of irritation and insults which, though petty in themselves, are galling enough to be very much felt by us.

Without the slightest occasion, we are now served at special counters in the Post Office. We are debarred from having a breath of fresh air in a park which is called a 'public' park, and which is kept up from rates which we are called upon to pay in common with other citizens. We mention these instances to draw Your Excellency's attention to the awkward position in which we are placed without any fault of ours. No opportunity is missed of degrading us and humiliating us. We do not wish to burden Your Excellency with such other instances. We have a right, we submit, to expect the British Government to protect us from such humiliation, and insure for us that freedom to which, as loyal British subjects, we are entitled wherever the Union Jack flies.

We beg to thank Your Excellency for giving us a patient hearing, and in conclusion hope that, as a result of Your Excellency's visit to this township, there will be an amelioration in our condition.

"The Gates Should No Longer Be Left Unguarded"

◆

9 ◆ Henry Cabot Lodge, SPEECH TO THE UNITED STATES SENATE, MARCH 16, 1896

In the decades following the Civil War, immigration to the United States reached new heights, with more than twenty million new arrivals between 1870 and 1910. Although these millions included appreciable numbers of Japanese and Chinese, close to 98 percent of them came from Europe. Unlike previous European migrants, who mostly had come from England, Germany, and, beginning in the 1840s, Ireland, migrants of the late nineteenth century mainly were from Italy, the Austro-Hungarian Empire, Russia, and Poland (which was mostly under Russian rule). Most were Roman Catholics or, in the case of many of the emigrants from Poland and Russia, Jews.

Anti-immigrant sentiment, or nativism, which had flared up in the 1840s and 1850s in response to the influx of the Irish, again became a powerful force in American life. Workers and small business owners worried about competition from the new immigrants; many Protestants were troubled by the growing numbers of Catholics and Jews; and Americans in general wondered if the republic could survive if the country was overrun by people unfamiliar with democracy and constitutional government. Anti-immigrant prejudice was given a "scientific" justification by contemporary racial theories, which ranked the world's races in a hierarchy with northern Europeans (except the Irish) at the top. Although there was some disagreement about other peoples' exact "ranking," most experts agreed that among Europeans, Italians, Slavs, and Jews were at the bottom, but at least were superior to Asians and Africans.

Anti-immigrant groups had some legislative success. In 1870 Congress passed the Naturalization Act, which barred the Chinese from citizenship. This was followed in 1882 by the Chinese Exclusion Act, which barred Chinese immigration altogether. Then in the 1890s the Immigration Restriction League (IRL), founded in 1894, proposed legislation to require new immigrants to pass a literacy test, which, IRL members hoped, the least desirable would fail.

A leader in the fight for immigration restriction was Henry Cabot Lodge, a member of a distinguished Boston family who served in the House of Representatives from 1887 to 1893 and the Senate from 1893 until his death in 1924. He presented the following remarks to the Senate in support of anti-immigration legislation under consideration in 1896. The bill failed to pass, and millions of immigrants continued to pour into the United States until Congress passed a series of restrictive laws in the 1920s.

QUESTIONS FOR ANALYSIS

1. What, according to Lodge, distinguishes "desirable" and "undesirable" immigrants?
2. What fears does Lodge entertain about the future of the United States unless immigration is restricted?
3. What are Lodge's views of race, and how do they affect his attitude toward immigration? According to Lodge, what are the qualities of the various "races" he discusses?
4. The bill Lodge supported was defeated in the Senate. What arguments against immigration restriction do you think were made by the bill's opponents?

. . . The question before the committee was . . . by what method the largest number of undesirable immigrants and the smallest possible number of desirable immigrants could be shut out. Three methods of obtaining this further restriction have been widely discussed of late years and in various forms have been brought to the attention of Congress. The first was the imposition of a capitation tax on all immigrants. . . .

The second scheme was to restrict immigration by requiring consular certification of immigrants. . . .[1]

The third method was to exclude all immigrants who could neither read nor write, and this is the plan which was adopted by the committee and which is embodied in this bill. . . . It is found, in the first place, that the illiteracy test will bear most heavily upon the Italians, Russians, Poles, Hungarians, Greeks, and Asiatics, and very lightly, or not at all, upon English-speaking emigrants or Germans, Scandinavians, and French. In other words, the races most affected by the illiteracy test are those whose emigration to this country has begun within the last twenty years and swelled rapidly to enormous proportions, races with which the English-speaking people have never hitherto assimilated, and who are most alien to the great body of the people of the United States.

On the other hand, immigrants from the United Kingdom and of those races which are most closely related to the English-speaking people, and who with the English-speaking people themselves founded the American colonies and built up the United States, are affected but little by the proposed test. . . . These kindred races also are those who alone go to the Western and Southern states, where immigrants are desired, and take up our unoccupied lands. The races which would suffer most seriously . . . furnish the immigrants who do not go to the West or South, where immigration is needed, but who remain on the Atlantic seaboard, where immigration is not needed and where their presence is most injurious and undesirable. . . .

It now remains for me to discuss the second and larger question, as to the advisability of restricting immigration at all. . . . It has two sides, the economic and the social. As to the former, but few words are necessary. There is no one thing which does so much to bring about a reduction of wages and to injure the American wage earner as the unlimited introduction of cheap foreign labor through unrestricted immigration. Statistics show that the change in the race character of our immigration has been accompanied by a corresponding decline in its

---

[1]U.S. consuls in overseas cities would judge immigration eligibility.

quality. The number of skilled mechanics and of persons trained to some occupation or pursuit has fallen off, while the number of those without occupation or training, that is, who are totally unskilled, has risen in our recent immigration to enormous proportions. This low, unskilled labor is the most deadly enemy of the American wage earner, and does more than anything else toward lowering his wages and forcing down his standard of living. . . .

. . . There is no danger, at present at all events, to our workingmen from the coming of skilled mechanics or of trained and educated men with a settled occupation or pursuit, for immigrants of this class will never seek to lower the American standard of life and wages. On the contrary, they desire the same standard for themselves. . . .

I now come to the aspect of this question which is greater and more serious than any other. . . . That which it concerns us to know and that which is more vital to us as a people than all possible questions of tariff or currency is whether the quality of our citizenship is endangered by the present course and character of immigration to the United States. To determine this question intelligently we must look into the history of our race. . . .

The English-speaking race . . . has been made slowly during the centuries. Nothing has happened thus far to radically change it here. In the United States, after allowing for the variations produced by new climatic influences and changed conditions of life and of political institutions, it is still in the great essentials fundamentally the same race. . . . Analysis shows that the actual mixture of blood in the English-speaking race is very small, and that while the English-speaking people are derived through different channels, no doubt, there is among them nonetheless an overwhelming preponderance of the same race stock, that of the great Germanic tribes who reached from Norway to the Alps. They have been welded together by more than a thousand years of wars, conquests, migrations, and struggles, both at home and abroad, and in so doing they have attained a fixity and definiteness of national character unknown to any other people. . . .

When we speak of a race, then, we do not mean its expressions in art or in language, or its achievements in knowledge. We mean the moral and intellectual characters, which in their association make the soul of a race and which represent the product of all its past, the inheritance of all its ancestors, and the motives of all its conduct. The men of each race possess an indestructible stock of ideas, traditions, sentiments, modes of thought, an unconscious inheritance from their ancestors, upon which argument has no effect. . . . These are the qualities which determine their social efficiency as a people, which make one race rise and another fall. . . .

Those qualities are moral far more than intellectual, and its is on the moral qualities of the English-speaking race that our history, our victories, and all our future rest. There is only one way in which you can lower those qualities or weaken those characteristics and that is by breeding them out. If a lower race mixes with a higher in sufficient numbers, history teaches us that the lower race will prevail. The lower race will absorb the higher, not the higher the lower, when the two strains approach equality in numbers. In other words, there is a limit to the capacity of any race for assimilating and elevating an inferior race, and when you begin to pour in unlimited numbers people of alien or lower races of less social efficiency and less moral force, you are running the most frightful risk that any people can run. The lowering of a great race means not only its own decline but that of human civilization. . . .

The time has certainly come, if not to stop at least to check, to sift, and to restrict those immigrants. In careless strength, with generous hand, we have kept our gates wide open to all the world. If we do not close them, we should at least place sentinels beside them to challenge those who would pass through. The gates which admit men to United States and to citizenship in the great republic should no longer be left unguarded.

CHAPTER 2

Seeds of Change: Politics, Society, and Culture

It is a truism that every historical era carries within it the seeds of future change. This was never more the case than in the forty years that preceded the outbreak of World War I in 1914. Those living through these decades experienced remarkable changes themselves — the colonization of Africa and Asia; the ongoing shrinkage of time and space through railroads, steamships, and the telegraph; industrial growth and rapid urbanization; and in Western nations, the steady advance of democracy and liberalism accompanied by the broad acceptance of middle-class values and culture. Those of the prewar generation who lived into the 1920s and 1930s were stunned by how much of their pre-1914 world was swept away in the onrush of postwar revolution, cultural change, and social conflict, and by their realization of the extent to which these upheavals had been anticipated by events and developments before the war.

This was especially true in Europe and the rest of the Western world. The years before World War I had seen the triumph of the railroad, steamship, and telegraph, but also inventions that would relegate them to secondary importance — the telephone in 1876, the automobile in the 1890s, and the airplane in 1903. The prewar years had seen the almost universal acceptance of liberal, parliamentary governments, but also the emergence of antidemocratic philosophies that in the 1920s and 1930s brought many liberal democracies to ruin. The years before World War I had seen the ascendancy of middle-class, "Victorian" values of patriarchy, religion, and morality, but also the appearance of militant feminism and the emergence of a cultural and artistic avant-garde committed to the demolition of bourgeois taste and sensibilities. The late nineteenth and early twentieth centuries had been years of peace, but also of growing nationalist fervor and militarism, the two prime causes of World War I.

Seeds of future change were also apparent in the non-Western world before World War I. The founding of the moderate Indian National Congress in 1885 and the emergence just twenty years later of an aggressive "Extremist" faction within it were indications of nationalism's explosive power among the victims of colonialism. Japan's successful modernization and subsequent aggression in East Asia revealed that neither industrialization nor imperialist expansion would remain Western monopolies. More fundamentally, revolutions in the Ottoman Empire, Iran, and China revealed that some Asian societies were discarding centuries-old traditions that had rendered their early response to the West so ineffectual. There also were signs — primarily the Mexican Revolution of 1911 — that some Latin Americans were prepared to seek broader and more sweeping solutions to their problems of poverty, dictatorship, and inequality. In all these ways, the decades before World War I prepared the way for the momentous transformations that were to follow.

◆

Revolutionaries and Revolutions in the Early 1900s

Because revolutions occur in societies already undergoing intellectual, economic, and social transformations, until the twentieth century they took place mainly in Western Europe and the Americas, where economic and intellectual changes undermined traditional notions of aristocratic privilege, ecclesiastical power, and authoritarian government. England's seventeenth-century revolutions blocked royal absolutism, preserved and expanded the powers of Parliament, and strengthened the principle of constitutionalism. Revolutions in Britain's Thirteen Colonies and in Latin America between the 1770s and the 1810s affirmed the principle of freedom from colonial domination and, in the case of the United States, created a new type of government based on personal liberty and limited democracy.

Of all the West's revolutions, the French Revolution (1789–1799) was by far the most significant. It involved more social groups, was more violent and more democratic in its outcome, and inspired Europe's first nationalist movements. Its memory helped spark revolutionary movements across Europe in 1820, 1830, and 1848, and convinced the founder of communism, Karl Marx, that an earth-shaking, apocalyptic revolution pitting the proletariat against the bourgeoisie would destroy capitalism and usher in a classless society.

After the bloody suppression of the Paris Commune in 1871, however, for the next several decades revolutions ceased in Western and Central Europe, and revolutionary activity shifted to Russia (1905), Persia (1905), the Ottoman Empire (1908), Mexico (1910), and China (1911). All of these revolutions were directed against governments and leaders that were corrupt, incompetent, out of touch with their subjects, and out of their depth in dealing with their country's momentous problems. Since the 1890s China had been ruled indirectly by Empress Dowager Cixi, who had scuttled the reforms of her nephew, Emperor Guangxu, in 1898, had encouraged the disastrous Boxer Rebellion in 1900, and had used funds for the navy to build a handsome marble boat that sat in a lake on the grounds of the imperial summer palace and was a fine place for picnics. Iran's shahs since the 1880s eagerly turned over much of their country's economy to foreigners in return for large personal bribes and modest payments to the treasury. Bored and overwhelmed by the perplexities of politics and finance, they escaped whenever possible to Europe's spas and capitals. Russia's Tsar Nicholas II was well-meaning but indecisive; the Ottoman sultan Abdul Hamid II was inflexible in his conservatism; and Mexico's aging dictator Porfirio Díaz showed utter indifference to his people's poverty while enriching himself and his cronies.

When intellectuals, politicians, despairing ministers, and dedicated revolutionaries considered alternatives to such regimes, they drew inspiration from both their own past and from Western models. Most reformers sought at minimum to establish Western-style liberal governments with elected parliaments, protection of individuals' rights, and constitutions. In Russia, China, and Mexico, revolutionaries had more ambitious dreams of redistributing land, helping impoverished factory workers, and ending the privileges of the rich. Marxists and anarchists dreamed of getting rid of the rich altogether. In ever-greater numbers, those who were dissatisfied saw revolution as their best hope for achieving their goals. This too was something they had learned from the political experience of the West.

A Revolutionary Formula for China's Revival

❖

10 ❖ *Sun Yat-sen,*
THE THREE PEOPLE'S PRINCIPLES AND THE FUTURE OF THE CHINESE PEOPLE

By 1900 the prognosis for China's imperial regime had deteriorated from poor to critical. Plagued throughout the nineteenth century by peasant revolts, military defeats, foreign exploitation, and failed reforms, China in the 1890s and early 1900s reached a low point. Its humiliating defeat in 1895 by Japan in the Sino-Japanese War set off a struggle between conservatives and reformers, with conservatives ascendant after the suppression of the One Hundred Days reform movement by Empress Dowager Cixi in 1898. Reformers regained the upper hand after the failure of the Boxer Rebellion in 1900. Their New Policy Reforms encouraged Chinese youths to study abroad; introduced science, mathematics, and foreign languages to schools; established military academies; sought to foster Chinese-owned businesses; and changed the system of recruiting government officials when the ancient civil service examinations were abolished in 1905. The reforms backfired. They burdened the peasantry with higher taxes; alienated large landowners; and failed to satisfy the generals, business people, and intellectuals who were convinced that China's only hope lay in ousting the Qing Dynasty and rebuilding China from its foundations.

China's leading revolutionary was Sun Yat-sen (1866–1925), a man far different from previous Chinese reformers. Born to a poor rural family from the Guangzhou region and educated in Hawaii and missionary schools in China, he developed a worldview more Western than Confucian. Galled by China's military impotence and Qing ineptitude, in 1894 he founded the secret Revive China Society, which in 1895 made plans to overthrow the Guangzhou provincial government. The plot was uncovered, and Sun was forced into exile. After sixteen years of traveling, planning, writing, and organizing, his hopes were realized when revolution broke out in 1911 and ended the Qing Era in 1912.

On his return to China from the United States (he had read about the revolution in a Denver newspaper while on a train to Kansas City), he was elected provisional president of the United Provinces of China on December 30, 1911. Sun's moment of glory, however, was short-lived. Without an army or organized political party to back him up, he resigned as president in 1912 in favor of the military strongman Yuan Shikai, who in 1913 exiled Sun as part of his plan to establish a dictatorship. Sun returned to Guangzhou in 1917 and attempted to establish a parliamentary government, but by then China had begun to descend into the chaos of warlord rule. When Sun died in 1925, the prospects of national unity and orderly government for China were still dim, but for his efforts Sun was viewed even then as the "father of modern China."

In the following selection Sun presents an early formulation of his "three people's principles," which served as the ideology of the United League, an organization he founded in 1905 in Tokyo that combined secret societies from China, overseas Chinese groups, and Chinese students in Japan. When the United League joined several other groups to form the Guomindang, or Nationalist, Party in 1912, Sun's three principles provided its platform. Sun presented the following analysis of his three principles in a speech to the United League in Tokyo in 1906 to help celebrate the first anniversary of the League's publication, *Min Pao* (the People's Journal).

QUESTIONS FOR ANALYSIS

1. What is meant by Sun's principle of nationalism? Against whom is nationalism directed?
2. What does he mean by the principle of democracy, and why does he consider it so important to the future of China?
3. What, according to Sun, have been the good and bad effects of the "advances of civilization"? Why have the benefits of these advances been so poorly distributed?
4. Briefly describe Sun's "land valuation procedure" and its relation to the principle of livelihood. What are its strengths and flaws?
5. What is Sun's attitude toward the West? How and in what ways will the future government and society of China be superior to those of the West?
6. To what extent are Sun's ideas inspired by Western ideologies and to what extent do they draw on Chinese thought and practice?

Let us pause to consider for a moment: Where is the nation? Where is the political power? Actually, we are already a people without a nation! The population of the globe is only one billion, several hundred million; we Han,[1] being 400 million, comprise one-fourth of that population.

Our nation is the most populous, most ancient, and most civilized in the world, yet today we are a lost nation. Isn't that enormously bizarre? The African nation of the Transvaal has a population of only 200,000, yet when Britain tried to destroy it, the fighting lasted three years.[2] The Philippines have a population of only several million, but when America tried to subdue it, hostilities persisted for several years.[3] Is it possible that the Han will gladly be a lost nation?

We Han are now swiftly being caught up in a tidal wave of nationalist revolution, yet the Manchus continue to discriminate against the Han. They boast that their forefathers conquered the Han because of their superior unity and military strength and that they intend to retain these qualities so as to dominate the Han forever. . . . Certainly, once we Han unite, our power will be thousands of times greater than theirs, and the success of the nationalist revolution will be assured.

As for the Principle of Democracy, it is the foundation of the political revolution. . . . For several thousand years China has been a monarchical autocracy, a type of political system intolerable to those living in freedom and equality. A nationalist revolution is not itself sufficient to get rid of such a system. Think for a moment: When the founder of the Ming dynasty expelled the Mongols and restored Chinese rule, the nationalist revolution triumphed, but his political

system was only too similar to those of the Han, Tang, and Song dynasties.[4] Consequently, after another three hundred years, foreigners again began to invade China. This is the result of the inadequacy of the political system, so that a political revolution is an absolute necessity. . . . The aim of the political revolution is to create a constitutional, democratic political system. . . .

◆　◆

Now, let me begin by discussing the origins of the Principle of the People's Livelihood, a principle that began to flourish only in the latter part of the nineteenth century. . . . As civilization advanced, people relied less on physical labor and more on natural forces, since electricity and steam could accomplish things a thousand times faster than human physical strength. For example, in antiquity a single man tilling the land could harvest at best enough grain to feed a few people, notwithstanding his toil and trouble. Now, however, as a result of the development of scientific agriculture, one man can grow more than enough to feed a thousand people because he can use machinery instead of his limbs, with a consequent increase in efficiency. . . .

In view of this, everyone in Europe and America should be living in a state of plenty and happiness undreamed of in antiquity. If we look around, however, we see that conditions in those countries are precisely the opposite. Statistically, Britain's wealth has increased more than several thousandfold over the previous generation, yet poverty of the people has also increased several thousandfold over the previous generation. Moreover, the rich are extremely few, and the poor extremely numerous. This is because the power of human labor is no match for the power

---

[1]*Han* in the Chinese language means "the Chinese people." Essentially it applies to those who speak Chinese and share a common Chinese culture and history.

[2]A reference to the South African War, or Boer War (1899–1902), fought between Great Britain and the two Afrikaner, or Boer, states in south Africa – Transvaal and the Orange Free State. Cultural friction and political conflict between the British settlers and administrators in the region and the Dutch residents of the two states caused the war.

[3]Between 1899 and 1901, Filipinos under the leadership of Emilio Aguinalado fought against their new colonial master, the United States, after the United States took over the Philippines from Spain at the conclusion of the Spanish American War.

[4]The Ming Dynasty ruled from 1368 to 1644 C.E. The Han (202 B.C.E.–220 C.E.), Tang (618–906 C.E.), and Song (960–1279 C.E.) were Chinese dynasties.

of capital. In antiquity, agriculture and industry depended completely on human labor; but now, with the development of natural forces that human labor cannot match, agriculture and industry have fallen completely into the hands of capitalists. The greater the amount of capital, the more abundant the resources that can be utilized. Unable to compete, the poor have naturally been reduced to destitution. . . .

Indeed, this constitutes a lesson for China. . . . Civilization yields both good and bad fruits, and we should embrace the good and reject the bad. In the countries of Europe and America, the rich monopolize the good fruits of civilization, while the poor suffer from its evil fruits. . . . Our current revolution will create a nation that not only belongs to the citizenry but is socially responsible. Certainly, there will be nothing comparable to it in Europe or America.

Why have Europe and America failed to solve their social problems? Because they have not solved their land problem. Generally speaking, wherever civilization is advanced, the price of land increases with each passing day. . . . In China capitalists have not yet emerged, so that for several thousand years there has been no increase in land prices. . . . After the revolution, however, conditions in China will be different. For example, land prices in Hong Kong and Shanghai are currently as much as several hundred times higher than those in the interior. This increment is the result of the advance of civilization and the development of communications. It is inevitable that, as the entire nation advances, land prices everywhere will rise accordingly. . . . Fifty years ago, land along the banks of the Huangpu River in Shanghai was worth up to a million dollars a *mou*.[5] This is evidence of the clearest sort, from which we can see that in the future the rich will get richer every day, and the poor poorer. . . . Consequently, we must come up with a solution now. . . .

With respect to a solution, although the socialists have different opinions, the procedure I most favor is land valuation. For example, if a landlord has land worth 1,000 dollars, its price can be set at 1,000 or even 2,000 dollars. Perhaps in the future, after communications have been developed, the value of his land will rise to 10,000 dollars; the owner should receive 2,000, which entails a profit and no loss, and the 8,000 increment will go to the state. Such an arrangement will greatly benefit both the state and the people's livelihood. Naturally, it will also eliminate the shortcomings that have permitted a few rich people to monopolize wealth. This is the simplest, most convenient, and most feasible method. . . .

Once we adopt this method, the more civilization advances, the greater the wealth of the nation, and then we can be sure our financial problems will not become difficult to handle. After the excessive taxes of the present have been abolished, the price of consumer goods will gradually fall and the people will become increasingly prosperous. We will forever abolish the vicious taxation policies that have prevailed for several thousand years. . . . After China's social revolution is accomplished, private individuals will never again have to pay taxes. The collection of land revenues alone will make China the richest nation on earth. . . .

Obviously, . . . it is necessary to give considerable attention to what the constitution of the Republic of China should be. . . . The British constitution embodies the so-called separation of powers into executive, legislative, and judicial, all mutually independent. . . . The Frenchman [Montesquieu][6] later embraced the British system and melded it with his own ideals to create his own school of thought. The American constitution was based on Montesquieu's theories

---

[5]A *mou* equals 1.5 acres.
[6]Montesquieu (1689–1755) was a French political philosopher, best known for his *The Spirit of the Laws* (1748), in which he argues that individual freedom is safest in a state in which the three powers of government, the judicial, executive, and legislative, are kept separate.

but went further in clearly demarcating the separation of powers. . . . As to the future constitution of the Republic of China, I propose that we introduce a new principle, that of the "five separate powers."

Under this system, there will be two other powers in addition to the three powers just discussed. One is the examination power. . . . American officials are either elected or appointed. . . .

With respect to elections, those endowed with eloquence ingratiated themselves with the public and won elections, while those who had learning and ideals but lacked eloquence were ignored. Consequently, members of America's House of Representatives have often been foolish and ignorant people who have made its history quite ridiculous. As for appointees, they all come and go with the president. The Democratic and Republican parties have consistently taken turns holding power, and whenever a president is replaced, cabinet members and other officials, comprising no fewer than 60,000–70,000 people, including the postmaster general, are also replaced. As a result, the corruption and laxity of American politics are unparalleled among the nations of the world. . . . Therefore, the future constitution of the Republic of China must provide for an independent branch expressly

responsible for civil service examinations. Furthermore, all officials, however high their rank, must undergo examinations in order to determine their qualifications. Whether elected or appointed, officials must pass those examinations before assuming office. This procedure will eliminate such evils as blind obedience, electoral abuses, and favoritism. . . .

The other power is the supervisory power, responsible for monitoring matters involving impeachment. For reasons that should be evident to all, such a branch is indispensable to any nation. The future constitution of the Republic of China must provide for an independent branch. Since ancient times, China had a supervisory organization, the Censorate,[7] to monitor the traditional social order. Inasmuch as it was merely a servant of the monarchy, however, it was ineffectual. . . .

With this added to the four powers already discussed, there will be five separate powers. That constitution will form the basis of the sound government of a nation that belongs to its own race, to its own citizens, and to its own society. This will be the greatest good fortune for our 400 million Han people. I presume that you gentlemen are willing to undertake and complete this task. It is my greatest hope.

---

[7]The Censorate, or Board of Censors, was a unique feature of Chinese government during the Ming and Qing Eras. Members of the board were responsible for reviewing the conduct of officials and reporting to the emperor when they discovered dereliction of duty. They were considered the "eyes and ears" of the emperors.

A Marxist Blueprint for Russia

◆

11 ◆ *PLATFORM OF THE RUSSIAN SOCIAL DEMOCRATIC PARTY, 1903*

Russia was full of discontent around 1900. Its two hundred million peasants, having been emancipated by Tsar Alexander II in 1861, were no longer serfs, but they were still bound to the land, abysmally poor, illiterate, and taxed to their capacity and beyond. Its urban working class, a product of Russia's recent and ongoing industrialization, experienced poverty and squalor in the slums of St. Petersburg and Moscow that rivaled the poverty and squalor in the peasant villages from which most workers had come. Its intellectuals, students, professionals, business owners, and some members of the landed gentry were disgusted with their inefficient and arbitrary government and troubled by the enormous gap between rich and poor. For decades these alienated Russians espoused political causes ranging from anarchism to constitutional monarchy. With the fervor of religious zealots, they argued, organized, hatched plots, planned revolutions, assassinated government officials, and tried, not always successfully, to stay a step ahead of the secret police.

By 1921, after the dust had settled on years of war, revolution, and civil war, one group of revolutionaries, a faction of the Social Democratic Party known as the Bolsheviks, gained power. They changed the course of Russian and global history by establishing the world's first Marxist government.

When the Social Democratic Party was founded in 1898 in the city of Minsk, it joined numerous other parties and organizations dedicated to overthrowing the tsarist autocracy. In the 1890s the two most prominent of these organizations were the Constitutional Democrats, moderates who sought to turn Russia into a constitutional monarchy, and the Social Revolutionaries, who sought a rural-based insurrection that would end the inequalities in Russian society. The Social Democrats also sought a revolution, but, as followers of Karl Marx, they believed it would be a revolution of the urban working class, or proletariat, which would eliminate capitalism and class exploitation.

In 1903 the Social Democrats, with most of their leaders in exile, split into two factions during their second party congress in London and Brussels. The Mensheviks, following orthodox Marxist doctrine, believed Russia was not ready for a communist revolution. It first had to fully industrialize and eliminate tsarist autocracy. The Bolsheviks, led by Lenin (Vladimir Ilyich Ulyanov, 1870–1924), believed that revolution was possible immediately if planned and organized by a small core of dedicated party members.

Despite the split, the two factions managed to agree on a platform in 1903, excerpts from which follow. The first part summarizes Marxist views of the class struggle, capitalism, and revolution. The second part outlines the party's short-term goals for Russia before the achievement of true communism.

QUESTIONS FOR ANALYSIS

1. What views of capitalism are expressed in the first part of the party platform? What implications does capitalism have for class relationships?
2. The document speaks of "contradictions in bourgeois society." What are these contradictions, and how will they affect capitalism's future?
3. To what extent does the state envisioned by the Social Democrats embrace the liberal principles of freedom and representative government?
4. To what extent does the statement show particular concern on the part of the Social Democrats for women and peasants?
5. What does the document reveal about the condition of the Russian working class?

Considering itself one of the detachments of the universal army of the proletariat, Russian social democracy is pursuing the same ultimate goal, as that for which the social democrats in other countries are striving. This ultimate goal is determined by the nature of contemporary bourgeois society and by the course of its development. The main characteristic of such a society is production for the market on the basis of capitalist production relations, whereby the largest and most important part of the means of production and exchange of commodities belongs to a numerically small class of people, while the overwhelming majority of the population consists of proletarians and semi-proletarians who, by their economic conditions, are forced either continuously or periodically to sell their labor power; that is, to hire themselves out to the capitalists, and by their toil to create the incomes of the upper classes of society.

The expansion of the capitalist system of production runs parallel to technical progress, which, by increasing the economic importance of large enterprises, tends to eliminate the small independent producers, to convert some of them into proletarians, to reduce the socio-economic role of others and, in some localities, to place them in more or less complete, more or less open, more or less onerous dependence on capital.

Moreover, the same technical progress enables the entrepreneurs to utilize to an ever greater extent woman and child labor in the process of production and exchange commodities. And since, on the other hand, technical improvements lead to a decrease in the entrepreneur's demand for human labor power, the demand for labor power necessarily lags behind the supply, and there is in consequence greater dependence of hired labor upon capital, and increased exploitation of the former by the latter.

Such a state of affairs in the bourgeois countries, as well as the ever growing competition among those countries on the world market, render the sale of goods which are produced in greater and greater quantities ever more difficult. Overproduction, which manifests itself in more or less acute industrial crises . . . is the inevitable consequence of the development of the productive forces in bourgeois society. Crises and periods of industrial stagnation, in their turn, tend to impoverish still further the small producers, to increase still further the dependence of hired labor upon capital and to accelerate still further the . . . deterioration of the condition of the working class.

Thus, technical progress, signifying increased productivity of labor and the growth of social wealth, becomes in bourgeois society the cause of increased social inequalities, of wider gulfs between the wealthy and the poor, of greater insecurity of existence, of unemployment, and of numerous privations for ever larger and larger masses of toilers.

But together with the growth and development of all these contradictions inherent in bourgeois society, there grows simultaneously dissatisfaction with the present order among the toiling and exploited masses; the number and solidarity of the proletarians increases, and their struggle against the exploiters sharpens. At the same time, technical progress . . . creates more and more rapidly the material possibility for replacing capitalist production relations by socialist ones; that is, the possibility for social revolution, which is the ultimate aim of all the activities of international social democracy as the class-conscious expression of the proletarian movement.

By replacing private with public ownership of the means of production and exchange, . . . the social revolution of the proletariat will abolish the division of society into classes and thus emancipate all oppressed humanity, and will terminate all forms of exploitation of one part of society by another. . . .

In Russia, where capitalism has already become the dominant mode of production, there are still preserved numerous vestiges of the old pre-capitalist order, when the toiling masses were serfs of the landowners, the state, or the sovereign. . . .

The most outstanding among these relics of the past, the mightiest bulwark of all this barbarism, is the tsarist autocracy. By its very name it is bound to be hostile to any social movement, and cannot but be bitterly opposed to all the aspirations of the proletariat toward freedom.

By reason of the above, the first and immediate task put before itself by the Russian Social Democratic Workers' Party is to overthrow the tsarist authority and to replace it with a democratic republic whose constitution would guarantee the following:

1. The sovereignty of the people; that is, the concentration of all supreme state power in the hands of a legislative assembly. . . .
2. Universal, equal, and direct suffrage for all male and female citizens, twenty years old or over, at all elections . . .; biennial parliaments; salaries to be paid to the people's representatives.
3. Broad local self-government. . . .
5. Unlimited freedom of religion, speech, press, assembly, strikes, and unions.
6. Freedom of movement and occupation.
7. Abolition of classes; equal rights for all citizens, irrespective of sex, religion, race, or nationality.
8. The right of any people to receive instruction in its own language, to be secured by creating schools at the expense of the state and the local organs of self-government. . . .
12. Replacement of the standing army by a general armament of the people. . . .
14. Free and compulsory general and professional education for all children of both sexes up to the age of sixteen; provision by the state of food, clothing, and school supplies for poor children. . . .

In order to *safeguard the working class* against physical and moral degeneration, as well as to insure the development of its power to carry on the struggle for freedom, the party demands the following:

1. Eight-hour working day for all hired labor.
2. A law providing a weekly uninterrupted forty-two-hour respite for all hired labor, of both sexes, in all branches of the national economy.
3. Complete prohibition of overtime work.
4. Prohibition of night work (from 9 p.m. to 6 a.m.) in all branches of the national economy, with the exception of those in which this is absolutely necessary because of technical considerations approved by labor organizations.
5. Prohibition of the employment of children of school age (up to sixteen) and restriction of the working day of minors (from sixteen to eighteen) to six hours.
6. Prohibition of female labor in those branches of industry which are injurious to women's health; relief from work four weeks before and six weeks after childbirth, with regular wages paid during all this period.
7. Establishment of nurseries for infants and children in all shops, factories, and other enterprises that employ women; permission for freedom of at least a half-hour's duration to be granted at three-hour intervals to all nursing mothers.
8. Old-age state insurance, and insurance against total or partial disability. . . .
11. Appointment of an adequate number of factory inspectors in all branches of the national economy . . .; participation of representatives, elected by the workers and paid by the state, in supervising the enforcement of the factory laws, the fixing of wage scales, and in accepting or rejecting the finished products and other results of labor.
12. Control by organs of local self-government, together with representatives elected by the workers, over sanitation in the dwellings assigned to the workers by the employers, as well as over internal arrangements in those dwellings and the renting conditions. . . .
13. Establishment of properly organized sanitary control over all establishments employing hired labor . . .; in times of illness, free medical aid to be rendered to the

workers at the expense of the employers, with the workers retaining their wages. . . .

In order to *remove the vestiges of serfdom* that fall directly and heavily upon the peasants, and to encourage the free development of the class struggle in the *village,* the party demands above all:

1. Abolition of redemption payments and quit rents as well as all obligations which presently fall on the peasantry, the tax-paying class.[1]
2. Repeal of all laws which restrict the peasant in disposing of his land.
3. Return to peasants of money collected from them in the form of redemption payments and quit rents; confiscation of monastery

and church properties as well as property belonging to princes, government agencies, and members of the royal family. . . .

To attain its immediate goals, the Russian Social Democratic Workers' Party will support every opposition and revolutionary movement directed against the existing social and political system in Russia. . . .

On its own part, the Russian Social Democratic Workers' Party is firmly convinced that a full, consistent, and thorough realization of the indicated political and social changes can only be attained by the overthrow of autocracy and by the convocation of a Constituent Assembly freely elected by the entire people.

---

[1]After serfdom was ended in 1861, emancipated peasants still had to pay redemption fees to reimburse the gentry for lands they had lost. They also paid landowners special fees and quitrents for the use of woodlands and pastureland.

Agrarian Reform and Revolution in Mexico

◈

12 ◆ THE PLAN OF AYALA

When Porfirio Díaz was elected president in 1876, Mexico had no railroads, factories, or significant foreign investment; it had a capital, Mexico City, notorious for floods and epidemics, an outdated silver industry, farms without modern equipment or fertilizers, and a desperately poor population that was 85 percent illiterate. When he left office in 1911, Mexico had an oil industry; fifteen thousand miles of railroads; improved harbors; factories making cement, textiles, furniture, brick, and glass; a modernized silver industry; and a capital, Mexico City, that had a drainage system, electric trams, a new municipal palace, and a splendid national theater. It still had a desperately poor population that was 85 percent illiterate.

Díaz's almost total disregard for the Mexican people's poverty was one reason why a small but articulate group of Mexicans turned against him in the opening years of the twentieth century. Another reason was his flouting of the 1857 constitution through censorship, manipulation of elections, and the packing of the judiciary and provincial administration with favorites. Around 1900 Díaz's opponents, some of whom were in exile, began to demand an end to the dictatorship and its replacement with a constitutional government dedicated to social reform. Their expectations were heightened in 1908 when Díaz announced he would not stand for reelection as president, then dashed in 1910 when he reversed himself and decided to run. In June 1910, with his main rival Francisco I. Madero and thousands of his opponents in jail, Díaz was reelected. Madero called on the Mexican people to rise up against Díaz, and even named a date, November 20, 1910, when it should happen. On cue, rebellions erupted throughout the country, and when federal troops were unable to quell them, Díaz resigned, paving the way for Madero's election as president in October 1911.

By this time, however, divisions had appeared among the revolutionaries. No less than six rebellions against the Madero presidency took place within a year, and turmoil plagued Mexico until 1920. The first faction to break from Madero was led by Emiliano Zapata (1879–1919), a small landowner, muleteer, horse trainer, and stable master who had led a small rebel army against pro-Díaz troops in 1911 in his native state of Morelos, just to the south of Mexico City. His followers were mainly poor villagers, many of whom had lost their land to wealthy hacienda owners during the Díaz regime. In late 1911 Zapata turned against Madero after he became convinced that the new president was not committed to social reform.

In November 1911 Zapata and his followers officially broke from the president by issuing their Plan of Ayala. Although its exact authorship is uncertain, its importance in Mexican history is indisputable. It served as a bible for Zapata's followers during the civil war of the 1910s and remained a symbol of the Mexican Revolution's commitment to rural social reform long after Zapata was murdered by federal troops in 1919.

QUESTIONS FOR ANALYSIS

1. According to the document, what caused Zapata and his followers to break from Madero?
2. According to Zapata's followers, aside from Madero, what individuals and groups in Mexico are responsible for holding back the revolution?
3. What solutions does the document propose to the problem of Mexico's rural poverty?
4. What is there about the Plan of Ayala that accounts for its popularity?

Taking into consideration that the Mexican people led by Don Francisco I. Madero went to shed their blood to reconquer liberties and recover their rights which had been trampled on, and not for a man to take possession of power, violating the sacred principles which he took an oath to defend . . . taking into consideration that that man to whom we refer is Don Francisco I. Madero, . . . who . . . having no in-tentions other than satisfying his personal ambitions, his boundless instincts as a tyrant, and his profound disrespect for the fulfillment of the preexisting laws emanating from the immortal code of '57, written with the revolutionary blood of Ayutla;[1]

Taking into account that the so-called Chief of the Liberating Revolution of Mexico, Don Francisco I. Madero, through lack of integrity

---

[1]The Revolution of Ayutla, which took place in 1855, deposed General Santa Anna and led to the Constitution of 1857, which placed authority in a unicameral legislature and included extensive protections of individual freedoms.

and the highest weakness, did not carry to a happy end the revolution which gloriously he initiated with the help of God and the people, since he left standing most of the governing powers and corrupted elements of oppression of the dictatorial government of Porfirio Díaz . . . ; taking also into account that the aforementioned Sr. Francisco I. Madero, present President of the Republic, tries to avoid the fulfillment of the promises which he made to the Nation . . . by means of false promises and numerous intrigues against the Nation nullifying, pursuing, jailing, or killing revolutionary elements who helped him to occupy the high post of President of the Republic;

Taking into consideration that the so-often-repeated Francisco I. Madero has tried with the brute force of bayonets to shut up and to drown in blood the pueblos[2] who ask, solicit, or demand from him the fulfillment of the promises of the revolution, calling them bandits and rebels, condemning them to a war of extermination without conceding or granting a single one of the guarantees which reason, justice, and the law prescribe; taking equally into consideration that the President of the Republic Francisco I. Madero has made of Effective Suffrage a bloody trick on the people, . . . entering into scandalous cooperation with the científico[3] party, feudal landlords, and oppressive bosses, enemies of the revolution proclaimed by him, so as to forge new chains and follow the pattern of a new dictatorship more shameful and more terrible than that of Porfirio Díaz. . . .

For these considerations we declare the aforementioned Francisco I. Madero inept at realizing the promises of the revolution of which he was the author, because he has betrayed the principles with which he tricked the will of the people and was able to get into power: incapable of governing, because he has no respect for the law and justice of the pueblos, and a traitor to the fatherland, because he is humiliating in blood and fire Mexicans who want liberties, so as to please the científicos, landlords, and bosses who enslave us, and from today on we begin to continue the revolution begun by him, until we achieve the overthrow of the dictatorial powers which exist. . . .

The Revolutionary Junta of the State of Morelos manifests to the Nation under formal oath: that it makes its own the plan of San Luis Potosí,[4] with the additions which are expressed below in benefit of the oppressed pueblos, and it will make itself the defender of the principles it defends until victory or death. . . .

As an additional part of the plan we invoke, we give notice: that [regarding] the fields, timber, and water which the landlords, científicos, or bosses have usurped, the pueblos or citizens who have the titles corresponding to those properties will immediately enter into possession of that real estate of which they have been despoiled by the bad faith of our oppressors, maintaining at any cost with arms in hand the mentioned possession. . . .

In virtue of the fact that the immense majority of Mexican pueblos and citizens are owners of no more than the land they walk on, suffering the horrors of poverty without being able to improve their social condition in any way or to dedicate themselves to Industry or Agriculture, because lands, timber, and water are monopolized in a few hands, for this cause there will be expropriated the third part of those monopolies

---

[2]*Pueblo* in Spanish means "village"; in this context *pueblos* refers to villagers as collective owners of property.

[3]*Científico* means "scientific." *Científicos* were advisors and confidants of Díaz who prided themselves on being pragmatic and scientific in their approach to Mexico's economic and social problems. The term was used broadly to refer to the Díaz political establishment.

[4]Madero's Plan of San Luis Potosí was written in San Antonio, Texas, in the middle of October 1910. In order to avoid complications with the U.S. government, however, Madero dated it October 5, the last day he spent in prison in San Luis Potosí, Mexico, after his arrest by federal police. It was an appeal to the Mexican people to overthrow Díaz and establish a constitutional state, but contained only a few references to social reform.

from the powerful proprietors of them, with prior indemnization, in order that the pueblos and citizens of Mexico may obtain . . . foundations for pueblos or fields for sowing or laboring, and the Mexicans' lack of prosperity and well-being may improve in all and for all.

Regarding the landlords, científicos, or bosses who oppose the present plan directly or indirectly, their goods will be nationalized and the two third parts which [otherwise would] belong to them will go for indemnizations of war pensions for widows and orphans of the victims who succumb in the struggle for the present plan.

In order to execute the procedures regarding the properties aforementioned, the laws of disamortization[5] and nationalization will be applied as they fit, for serving us as norm and example can be those laws put in force by the immortal Juárez on ecclesiastical properties,[6] which punished the despots and conservatives who in every time have tried to impose on us the ignominious yoke of oppression and backwardness. . . .

Once triumphant the revolution which we carry into the path of reality, a Junta of the principal revolutionary chiefs from the different States will name or designate an interim President of the Republic, who will convoke elections for the organization of the federal powers. . . .

Mexicans: consider that the cunning and bad faith of one man is shedding blood in a scandalous manner, because he is incapable of governing; consider that his system of government is choking the fatherland and trampling with the brute force of bayonets on our institutions; and thus, as we raised up our weapons to elevate him to power, we again raise them up against him for defaulting on his promises to the Mexican people and for having betrayed the revolution initiated by him, we are not personalists, we are partisans of principles and not of men!

Mexican People, support this plan with arms in hand and you will make the prosperity and well-being of the fatherland.

Ayala, November 25, 1911

[5]In this context this means the return of lands that had been confiscated from the pueblos.
[6]Benito Juárez, secretary of justice following the Revolution of Ayutla, sponsored laws that limited Catholic clerics'

immunity from trial in nonecclesiastical courts. Later, the government passed laws forbidding the Church to own property other than churches, monasteries, and seminaries.

◆

The New Voice of Women in the Early Twentieth Century

At the start of the twentieth century, feminism was already an important force in Western societies. Drawing on the natural rights philosophy of the eighteenth-century Enlightenment and the democratic principles of the French Revolution, nineteenth-century women had campaigned to achieve political and legal rights, greater vocational opportunities, and equal access to education. By century's end these feminists had made modest gains. In Europe, the United States, Canada, Australia, and New Zealand, girls had access to primary and secondary education, and small numbers of women were able to attend universities and enter professions such as medicine and journalism. As a result of industrialization, urbanization, and the growth of government and private businesses, more women also were entering the paid work force as teachers, white-collar workers, factory workers, and nurses. Legal changes gave married women greater control of their property and easier access to divorce.

Nowhere, however, could women vote in national elections. To change this, women around 1900, especially in England and the United States, campaigned energetically to win the vote. When World War I began in 1914, feminists had achieved their goal in only Norway, Finland, and a few western states in the United States. But feminism had emerged as a powerful political and social force in Western societies.

Women's lives and expectations were also changing in non-Western societies around 1900, in many cases as a result of contacts with the West. Colonialism, for example, had brought an end to the practice of *sati* in India after British administrators banned this custom of ritual suicide expected of widows of certain castes. Colonialism had also altered the legal status of women in Algeria, Tunisia, and Libya, where European legal systems superseded Islamic law, including family law.

Both in colonies and semicolonial areas such as China and the Ottoman Empire, foreign missionary schools created new opportunities for female education. They made primary and secondary schooling available to girls on a more or less equal footing with boys, and introduced students of both genders to Western concepts of equality and individualism. In Egypt, India, and Southeast Asia, increasing numbers of upper-class city dwellers hired tutors to teach their daughters European languages and culture as part of their efforts to emulate Europeans. Around 1900 the growing number of women authors and many of their readers were products of these new educational experiences.

In addition to colonialism, nationalism in non-Western lands encouraged an interest in women's issues. Nationalist reformers in Ottoman Turkey, Arab lands, India, China, and Japan came to see the oppression and abuse of women as an impediment to modernization and a source of national embarrassment. They supported greater freedom, education, and vocational opportunities for women, and sought to end perceived symbols of their society's backwardness such as foot-binding in China and the veiling and seclusion of women in Islamic lands.

Advocates of women's rights outside the West faced formidable obstacles. Their audience was small, and their views were bitterly opposed by conservatives who considered their demands subversive to religion and morals. Patriarchal values remained strong despite the mounting feminist critique. Even in Meiji Japan, which sought universal literacy for boys and girls alike through a system of state-supported elementary schools, girls were barred from advanced academic high schools, technical schools, and universities. But new issues had been raised, positions staked out, and agendas clarified. As much as in Europe and the United States, the efforts of Arab, Chinese, Indian, and Japanese feminists before World War I prepared the way for the profound changes in women's status and opportunities that occurred during the rest of the twentieth century.

An Early Voice of Arab Feminism

◈

13 ◆ *Bahithat al-Badiya,* A LECTURE IN THE CLUB OF THE UMMA PARTY, 1909

Malak Hifni Nasif, better known by her pen name, Bahithat al-Badiya (Arabic for "Seeker in the Desert"), was an early Egyptian feminist. Born into a prosperous Cairo family, she was educated at home and then at the Saniyya School in Cairo, a school for women. On graduating she became a teacher at the school, and a regular contributor of essays and poems to Cairo literary journals. Her life abruptly changed in 1911 when at the age of twenty-four she moved to an oasis west of Cairo following an arranged marriage to a Bedouin chief. To her chagrin she discovered that the chief already had a wife and a daughter, whom she was expected to tutor. Despite disappointment and anger, she remained with her husband until she died of influenza in 1918.

In her writings and speeches, which were published in 1910 under the title *Al-Nisaiyat* (Feminist Pieces), Bahithat addressed a wide range of issues pertaining to Egyptian women, including education, paid work, and especially proper public attire. The following remarks were delivered in 1909 as part of a weekly lecture series that catered to well-to-do Cairo women. It was held in the hall of the Umma Party, a moderate Egyptian nationalist party founded in 1906.

QUESTIONS FOR ANALYSIS

1. What does the source tell us about the arguments being made by opponents of women entering the paid work force? How does the author counter these arguments?
2. What does the source reveal about relations between males and females in Egypt in the early 1900s?
3. What are the shortcomings of upper-class Egyptian women, according to Bahithat?
4. How does she view European women? Why does she consider them poor role models for Egyptian women?
5. How much of what the author says relates to the experiences of lower- and middle-class Egyptian women?
6. If the provisions of the author's program had been carried out, how would Egyptian women's lives have changed?

Men say when we become educated we shall push them out of work and abandon the role for which God has created us. But, isn't it rather men who have pushed women out of work? Be-fore, women used to spin and to weave cloth for clothes for themselves and their children, but men invented machines for spinning and weaving and put women out of work. In the past, women sewed clothes for themselves and their households but men invented the sewing machine. . . . Then men took up the profession of tailoring and began to make clothes for our men and children. Before women winnowed the wheat and ground flour on grinding stones for the bread they used to make with their own hands, sifting flour and kneading dough. Then men established bakeries employing men. They gave us rest but at the same time pushed us out of work. . . .

The question of monopolizing the workplace comes down to individual freedom. One man wishes to become a doctor, another a merchant. Is it right to tell a doctor he must quit his profession and become a merchant or vice versa? No. Each has the freedom to do as he wishes. . . . Work at home now does not occupy more than half the day. We must pursue an education in order to occupy the other half of the day but that is what men wish to prevent us from doing under the pretext of taking their jobs away. . . .

The division of labor is merely a human creation. We still witness people like the Nubians[1] whose men sew clothes for themselves and the household while the women work in the fields. Some women even climb palm trees to harvest the dates. Women in villages in both Upper and Lower Egypt help their men till the land and plant crops. Some women do the fertilizing, haul crops, lead animals, draw water for irrigation, and other chores. You may have observed that women in the villages work as hard as the strongest men and we see that their children are strong and healthy.

Specialised work for each sex is a matter of convention. It is not mandatory. We women are now unable to do hard work because we have not been accustomed to it. . . . After long centuries of enslavement by men, our minds rusted and our bodies weakened. Is it right that they accuse us of being created weaker than them in mind and body?

Men criticize the way we dress in the street. They have a point because we have exceeded the bounds of custom and propriety. We claim we are veiling but we are neither properly covered nor unveiled. I do not advocate a return to the veils of our grandmother because it can rightly be called being buried alive, not *hijab,*[2] correct covering. The woman used to spend her whole life within the walls of her house not going out into the street except when she was carried to her grave. I do not, on the other hand, advocate unveiling, like Europeans, and mixing with men, because they can be harmful to us. . . .

If we had been raised from childhood to go unveiled and if our men were ready for it I would approve of unveiling for those who want it. But the nation is not ready for it now. Some of our prudent women do not fear to mix with men, but we have to place limits on those who are less prudent because we are quick to imitate and seldom find our authenticity in the veil. . . .

If the change that some women have made in the *izar*[3] is in order to shed it when they go out that would be all right if these women would only uncover their faces but keep their hair and figures concealed. I think the most appropriate way to dress outside is to cover the head and wear a coat with long sleeves which touches the ground the way the European women do. I am told this is the way women in Istanbul[4] dress when they go out shopping. . . .

On the subject of customs and veiling I would like to remind you of something that causes us

---

[1]A Negroid people who inhabit the region in southern Egypt and northern Sudan between the Nile and the Red Sea.
[2]*Hijab* in Arabic literally means "veil" or "partition"; it also means adherence to certain standards of modest dress for women.

[3]A loose-fitting shawl, usually made of white calico.
[4]The largest city in Turkey and the seat of Ottoman government.

great unhappiness — the question of engagement and marriage. Most sensible people in Egypt believe it is necessary for fiancés to meet and speak with each other before their marriage. It is wise and the Prophet[5] himself, peace be upon him and his followers, did not do otherwise. . . .

By not allowing men to see their prospective wives following their engagement we cause Egyptian men to seek European women in marriage. They marry European servants and working class women thinking they would be happy with them rather than daughters of pashas and beys[6] hidden away in 'a box of chance'. If we do not solve this problem we shall become subject to occupation by women of the West. We shall suffer double occupation, one by men and the other by women. The second will be worse than the first because the first occurred against our will but we shall have invited the second by our own actions. . . . Most Egyptian men who have married European women suffer from the foreign habits and extravagance of their wives. The European woman thinks she is of a superior race to the Egyptian and bosses her husband around after marriage. When the European woman marries an Egyptian she becomes a spend-thrift while she would be thrifty if she were married to a westerner. . . .

Our beliefs and actions have been a great cause of the lesser respect that men accord us. How can a sensible man respect a woman who believes in magic, superstition, and the blessing of the dead and who allows women peddlars and washerwomen, or even devils, to have authority over her? Can he respect a woman who speaks only about the clothes of her neighbor and the jewellery of her friend and the furniture of a bride? This is added to the notion imprinted in

a man's mind that woman is weaker and less intelligent than he is. . . .

We shall advance when we give up idleness. The work of most of us at home is lounging on cushions all day or going out to visit other women. . . . Being given over to idleness or luxury has given us weak constitutions and pale complexions. We have to find work to do at home. At a first glance one can see that the working classes have better health and more energy and more intelligent children. The children of the middle and lower classes are, almost all of them, in good health and have a strong constitution, while most of the children of the elite are sick or frail and prone to illness despite the care lavished on them by their parents. . . .

Now I shall turn to the path we should follow. If I had the right to legislate I would decree:

1. Teaching girls the Quran and the correct Sunna.[7]
2. Primary and secondary school education for girls, and compulsory prepatory school education for all.
3. Instruction for girls on the theory and practice of home economics, health, first aid, and childcare.
4. Setting a quota for females in medicine and education so they can serve the women of Egypt.
5. Allowing women to study any other advanced subjects they wish without restriction.
6. Upbringing for girls from infancy stressing patience, honesty, work and other virtues.
7. Adhering to the *Sharia*[8] concerning betrothal and marriage, and not permitting any woman and man to marry without first meeting each other in the presence of the father or male relative of the bride.
8. Adopting the veil and outdoor dress of the Turkish women of Istanbul.

---

[5]Islam's greatest prophet and founder, Muhammad lived from 570 to 632 C.E. God's revelations to him comprise Islam's most holy book, the Quran, or Koran.
[6]Courtesy titles for Egyptian gentlemen of high rank.

[7]*Sunna* refers to the customs and traditions of the Islamic community.
[8]Literally, the "right path," or Islamic law.

9. Maintaining the best interests of the country and dispensing with foreign goods and people as much as possible.

10. Make it encumbent upon our brothers, the men of Egypt, to implement this program.

"Race Decadence" and the U.S. Women's Movement

❖

14 ❖ *Anna Howard Shaw,* *PRESIDENTIAL ADDRESSES AT THE CONVENTIONS OF NATIONAL AMERICAN WOMAN SUFFRAGE ASSOCIATION, 1905, 1906*

For many opponents of feminism in Europe and the United States, its most disturbing figure was not Elizabeth Cady Stanton, a founder of the U.S. women's rights movement who insisted that "obey" be left out of her marriage vows; it was not Margaret Sanger, who pioneered the birth control movement in the United States; it was not even Emmeline Pankhurst and her daughters, E. Sylvia and Christabel, who led the militant fight for women's suffrage in England. It was not a real woman at all. It was Nora, the fictional heroine of the Norwegian playwright Henrik Ibsen's *A Doll's House*, which was performed throughout Europe and the United States after its premiere in 1880. Having endured a childhood dominated by a stifling father and eight years of an empty marriage, Nora abandons her husband and three children to begin a quest for self-enlightenment and fulfillment.

To opponents of women's rights, Nora's rejection of domesticity epitomized the unhealthy individualism and egotism that underlay women's search for equality, meaningful work, and independence. Such egotism, they feared, threatened to consign woman's traditional role as wife and mother to oblivion. Anxieties over the incompatibility of motherhood and female emancipation were deepened in the 1880s by declining birth rates in industrialized nations, especially for the middle class. This troubled European nationalists, who feared manpower shortages for the military. It also worried many Americans of northern European stock, who feared inundation by the millions of new immigrants from southern and eastern Europe.

Never one to skirt such issues, U.S. President Theodore Roosevelt (1858–1919) discussed women's true calling and duties in a speech to the National Congress of Mothers in Washington, D.C., in 1905. Although a supporter of women's suffrage and equal rights, Roosevelt was an advocate of "equality in difference." In his view, men should run the government, manage businesses, and earn a living; women should marry, become mothers, and raise children. In his speech he expressed contempt for women who out of "viciousness, coldness, shallowheartedness, or self-indulgence" neglected their duty to raise families. He further stated that "the existence of women of this type was one of the most unpleasant and unwholesome features of modern life."

The president's remarks gained a quick response from Anna Howard Shaw (1847–1919), president of the National American Woman Suffrage Association from 1904 to 1915. Born in England and raised in Michigan, she obtained degrees in divinity and medicine from Boston University. She chose a life of political action, however, first through the Women's Christian Temperance Union, and then on behalf of women's suffrage. She remained single to better accomplish her life's work.

The following excerpts come from her presidential addresses to the annual meetings of the National American Woman Suffrage Association in 1905 and 1906. In both excerpts she discusses women's work and its relationship to motherhood and the family.

QUESTIONS FOR ANALYSIS

1. What evidence is there that Shaw accepts Roosevelt's premise that "race decadence" is a problem in the United States? How does her view of its causes differ from that of the president?
2. What ulterior motives does she ascribe to those who blame women for "race-suicide"? What are the flaws in their arguments?
3. How does Shaw link the problems she describes in U.S. society to women's lack of political rights?
4. What similarities, if any, do you see between the points made in Shaw's speech and those made by Bahithat al-Badiya in her 1909 lecture in the club of the Umma Party?

[1905]

When the cry of race-suicide is heard, and men arraign women for race decadence, it would be well for them to examine conditions and causes, and base their attacks upon firmer foundations of fact. Instead of attacking women for their interest in public affairs and relegating them to their children, their kitchen, and their church, they will learn that the kitchen is in politics; that the children's physical, intellectual, and moral well-being is controlled and regulated by law; that the real cause of race decadence is not the fact that fewer children are born, but to the more fearful fact that, of those born, so few live, not primarily because of the neglect of the mother, but because men themselves neglect their duty as citizens and public officials. If men honestly desire to prevent the causes of race decadence, let them examine the accounts of food adulteration, and learn that from the effect of impure milk alone, in one city 5,600 babies

died in a single year. Let them examine the water supply, so impregnated with disease that in some cities there is continual epidemic of typhoid fever. Let them gaze upon the filthy streets, from which perpetually arises contagion of scarlet fever and diphtheria. Let them examine the plots of our great cities, and find city after city with no play places for children, except the streets, alleys, and lanes. Let them examine the school buildings, many of them badly lighted, unsanitary, and without yards. Let them turn to the same cities, and learn that from five to a score or thousand children secure only half-day tuition because there are not adequate schoolhouse facilities. Let them watch these half-day children playing in the streets and alleys and viler places, until they have learned the lessons which take them to ever-growing numbers of reformatories, whose inmates are increasing four times as rapidly as the population. Let them follow the children who survive all these ills of early childhood, until they enter the sweat-shops and factories, and behold there the maimed, dwarfed, and blighted little ones, 500,000 of whom under 14 years of age are employed in these pestilential places. Let them behold the legalized saloons and the dens of iniquity where so many of the voting population spend the money that should be used in feeding, housing, and caring for their children. Then, if these mentors of women's clubs and mothers' meetings do not find sufficient cause for race degeneracy where they have power to control conditions, let them turn to lecturing women. . . . That which is desirable is not that the greatest possible number of children should be born into the world; the need is for more intelligent motherhood and fatherhood, and for better born and better educated children. . . .

The great fear that the participation of women in public affairs will impair the quality and character of home service is irrational and contrary to the tests of experience. Does an intelligent interest in the education of a child render a woman less a mother? Does the housekeeping instinct of woman, manifested in a desire for clean streets, pure water, and unadulterated food, destroy her efficiency as a home-maker? Does a desire for an environment of moral and civic purity show neglect of the highest good of the family? It is the "men must fight and women must weep" theory of life which makes men fear that the larger service of women will impair the high ideal of home. The newer ideal, that men must cease fighting and thus remove one prolific cause for women's weeping, and that they shall together build up a more perfect home and a more ideal government, is infinitely more sane and desirable. . . .

[1906]

. . . To draw sweeping and universal conclusions in regard to a matter upon which there is an "almost complete dearth of data" is never wise. While it is true that marriage and the birth-rate have decreased within recent years, before the results are charged to the participation of women in industry, one must answer many questions.

Is it true that there is more "domestic infelicity" to-day than in times past? Is it true that there is greater "domestic infelicity" in homes where women are engaged in gainful pursuits than in those homes in which the strength of women is never taxed by toil, even to the extent of self-service? Is it true that there is a lower birth-rate among working women than among those of the wealthy class? Are not the effects of over-work and long hours in the household as great as are those of the factory or of the office?

. . . Is the birth-rate less among women who are engaged in the new pursuits or occupations unknown to women of the past? Or is the decline alike marked among those who are pursuing the ancient occupations which women have followed from time immemorial, but under different conditions? . . .

Woman as an industrial factor and wage-earner is not new. But woman as an industrial competitor and wage-collector with man is new, not because of woman's revolt against her own industrial slavery, but because changed economic conditions through inventive genius and industrial centralization have laid their hands upon the isolated labors and products of woman's toil, and brought them forth from the tent, the cottage, and the farm house, to the shop, the factory, and the marketplace.

If conditions surrounding their employment are such as to make it a "social question of the first importance" it is unfortunate the President had not seen that women, the most deeply interested factor in the problem, should constitute at least a part of any commission authorized to investigate it. No body of men, unaided by women, can be qualified to do so "in a sane and scientific spirit." . . .

But if the required investigations were made, even with women upon the committee, what power would the five millions of disfranchised women possess to enact beneficent laws or enforce needed reform?

One can not but wish that with his recognized desire for "fair play" and his policy of "a square deal," it had occurred to the President that, if five millions of American women are employed in gainful occupations, every principle of justice known to a Republic would demand that these five millions of toiling women should be enfranchised to enable them to secure enforced legislation for their own protection.

An Attack on Foot-binding in China

❖

15 ❖ *Qiu Jin,*
AN ADDRESS TO TWO HUNDRED MILLION FELLOW COUNTRYWOMEN

Beginning in the late ninth and tenth centuries C.E., and continuing until the twentieth century, millions of Chinese girls between the ages of five and nine had their feet tightly wrapped and gradually bent until the arch was broken and all the toes except the big toe, were turned under. With feet growing to only half their normal size, these girls were condemned to lives as semicripples. Originally, foot-binding was limited to wealthy families who wanted to demonstrate that their women did not have to work. Gradually, however, the practice spread to all levels of society, and small feet began to have a strong erotic attraction for Chinese males. Girls with "big feet" were considered unmarriageable.

Although foot-binding always had its opponents, only at the end of the nineteenth century did the practice come under widespread criticism. Many reformers and intellectuals considered foot-binding, along with opium smoking, one of the social customs that underlay the country's backwardness. Protestant missionaries, many of them women, also denounced the practice, and one of their number, Mrs. Archibald Little, founded the Natural Foot Society in 1895. Also in the 1890s, anti-foot-binding societies, whose members agreed to arrange marriages for their daughters with unbound feet, were founded in major cities. In 1902 Empress Dowager Cixi outlawed foot-binding, but it took decades for the practice to die out completely.

Among the Chinese women writers who attacked foot-binding, the most outspoken was Qiu Jin (1875–1907), who devoted her life to women's liberation and the overthrow of the Qing Dynasty. Raised in a moderately wealthy family and well-educated, Qiu was married to an older man at age twenty-one, but left him in 1903 to study in Japan. On her return in 1906 she founded a women's magazine and became principal of a girls' school. In 1907 she and her cousin were arrested and beheaded for revolutionary activity. In the following speech, delivered probably in 1906, she denounces foot-binding and other examples of women's oppression in China.

QUESTIONS FOR ANALYSIS

1. As described by Qiu, what kind of relationship did most Chinese girls have with their parents?

2. What can be learned from the source concerning Chinese marriage customs and the relationship between husbands and wives?
3. What were the motives, according to Qiu, for subjecting women to foot-binding and preventing them from learning how to read?
4. In Qiu's view, what share of the blame for their oppression must be assumed by women themselves?
5. What are Qiu's solutions for China's problems?
6. What similarities do you see between the views of Qiu Jin and those of Bahithat al-Badiya?

Alas! The greatest injustice in this world must be the injustice suffered by our female population of two hundred million. If a girl is lucky enough to have a good father, then her childhood is at least tolerable. But if by chance her father is an ill-tempered and unreasonable man, he may curse her birth: "What rotten luck: another useless thing." Some men go as far as killing baby girls while most hold the opinion that "girls are eventually someone else's property" and treat them with coldness and disdain. In a few years, without thinking about whether it is right or wrong, he[1] forcibly binds his daughter's soft, white feet with white cloth so that even in her sleep she cannot find comfort and relief until the flesh becomes rotten and the bones broken. What is all this misery for? Is it just so that on the girl's wedding day friends and neighbors will compliment him, saying, "Your daughter's feet are really small"? Is that what the pain is for?

But that is not the worst of it. When the time for marriage comes, a girl's future life is placed in the hands of a couple of shameless match-makers and a family seeking rich and powerful in-laws. A match can be made without anyone ever inquiring whether the prospective bridegroom is honest, kind, or educated. On the day of the marriage the girl is forced into a red and green bridal sedan chair, and all this time she is not allowed to breathe one word about her future. After her marriage, if the man doesn't do her any harm, she is told that she should thank Heaven for her good fortune. But if the man is bad or he ill-treats her, she is told that her marriage is retribution for some sin committed in her previous existence. If she complains at all or tries to reason with her husband, he may get angry and beat her. When other people find out they will criticize, saying, "That woman is bad; she doesn't know how to behave like a wife." What can she do? When a man dies, his wife must mourn him for three years and never re-marry. But if the woman dies, her husband only needs to tie his queue[2] with blue thread. Some men consider this to be ugly and don't even do it. In some cases, three days after his wife's death, a man will go out for some "entertainment." Sometimes, before seven weeks have passed, a new bride has already arrived at the door. . . . Why is there no justice for women? We constantly hear men say, "The human mind is just and we must treat people with fairness and equality." Then why do they greet women like black slaves from Africa? How did inequality and injustice reach this state?

Dear sisters, you must know that you'll get nothing if you rely upon others. You must go out and get things for yourselves. In ancient times when decadent scholars came out with such nonsense as "men are exalted, women are lowly," "a virtuous woman is one without talent," and

---

[1]Despite Qiu's use of the male pronoun, the actual work of binding feet was performed by female members of the girls' families, usually mothers.

[2]The braid of hair worn at the back of the head by Chinese men.

"the husband guides the wife," ambitious and spirited women should have organized and opposed them. . . . Men feared that if women were educated they would become superior to men, so they did not allow us to be educated. Couldn't the women have challenged the men and refused to submit? It seems clear now that it was we women who abandoned our responsibilities to ourselves and felt content to let men do everything for us. As long as we could live in comfort and leisure, we let men make all the decisions for us. When men said we were useless, we became useless; when they said we were incapable, we stopped questioning them even when our entire female sex had reached slave status. At the same time we were insecure in our good fortune and our physical comfort, so we did everything to please men. When we heard that men liked small feet, we immediately bound them just to please them, just to keep our free meal tickets. As for their forbidding us to read and write, well, that was only too good to be true. We readily agreed. . . . It was only natural that men, with their knowledge, wisdom, and hard work, received the right to freedom while we became their slaves. And as slaves, how can we escape repression? Whom

can we blame but ourselves since we have brought this on ourselves? . . .

. . . Let us all put aside our former selves and be resurrected as complete human beings. Those of you who are old, do not call yourselves old and useless. If your husbands want to open schools, don't stop them; if your good sons want to study abroad, don't hold them back. Those among us who are middle-aged, don't hold back your husbands lest they lose their ambition and spirit and fail in their work. After your sons are born, send them to schools. You must do the same for your daughters and, whatever you do, don't bind their feet. As for you young girls among us, go to school if you can. If not, read and study at home. Those of you who are rich, persuade your husbands to open schools, build factories, and contribute to charitable organizations. Those of you who are poor, work hard and help your husbands. . . . You must know that when a country is near destruction, women cannot rely on the men any more because they aren't even able to protect themselves. If we don't take heart now and shape up, it will be too late when China is destroyed.

Sisters, we must follow through on these ideas!

◆

New Trends in Western Culture and Thought

Beginning in earnest during the era of imperialism, and continuing even after the dissolution of Europe's empires following World War II, Western science, literature, political ideologies, educational theories, art, and architecture have affected non-Western thought and expression profoundly and, in doing so, have created a culture more truly global than at any time in human history. Paradoxically, this export of Western ideas and artistic taste began at time when many of the age-old certainties of Western thought and culture were being challenged and discarded.

The fundamentals of European thought had taken shape between the Renaissance of the fourteenth and fifteenth centuries and the Enlightenment of the eighteenth century. Its basic premise was that nature was orderly, reasonable, and operated according to universal physical laws. Human beings, creatures of reason and capable of moral improvement through education, could understand this natural order through scientific inquiry and could improve the human condition through increased understanding of nature and society. Furthermore, being rational, human beings were capable of governing themselves and could do so most effectively when their freedom of self-expression was protected. Such beliefs were the foundation for the nineteenth century's faith in liberalism and parliamentary government. Western views of art, music, and literature also embodied many of these assumptions about nature and humanity. Since the Late Middle Ages and Renaissance, naturalism — the effort to accurately represent nature in paintings and sculpture — had been the central feature of Western art, and the achievement of harmony and beauty was the goal of composers.

Every one of these beliefs was being challenged around 1900. Scientists discarded old assumptions about motion, light, matter, and the universe. Atoms were not tiny, solid spheres of matter, as had been imagined, but complexes of electrically charged particles; light and other forms of radiant energy were emitted not in a steady stream, but in discrete units, or quanta; mathematics had a realm in which theories capable of rational proof contradicted what the senses apprehended in the "real" world. Most disturbing of all were the theories of Albert Einstein (1879–1955), who in papers published between 1905 and 1916 proposed that matter and energy were a single entity, and that absolute time and distance did not exist but were dependent on the speed and position of the observer.

Although the implications of this "second scientific revolution" were at first only dimly perceived by the European and American publics, changes in philosophy, psychology, and the arts were more conspicuous. Painters, composers, and writers provided one shock after another. Considering themselves to be in the forefront of artistic creativity (like the small group of soldiers trained to attack in front of the main body of troops — an avant-garde), these artists, writers, and composers defied convention and seemed bent on upsetting and insulting their audiences. Painters filled their canvases with barely recognizable images often painted in bright, unnatural colors, with little attention to detail or traditional drawing; architects rejected the classical and Gothic styles for a severe "modern" idiom more attuned to the Machine Age; poets filled their works with arcane symbols and abstruse meanings but rarely with rhymes or, in some cases, even punctuation; composers wrote atonal music and abandoned traditional rhythms; choreographers produced ballets that horrified devotees of the classical repertoire.

Fundamentally disturbing questions were also being raised by philosophers, psychologists, and anthropologists. What if the West's ethical values were enslaving and debilitating humanity? What if the West's moral teachings were no better than those of the "primitive" peoples of Africa and the Pacific islands? What if all human behavior could be reduced to a series of physical responses, thus calling into question the concepts of mind and consciousness? What if, as the Viennese psychiatrist Sigmund Freud suggested, human behavior was not controlled by reason but was instead driven by deep unconscious drives, most of them sexual, that were barely perceptible to the individual?

These were just a few of the questions confronting Westerners as the optimism and confidence of the nineteenth century gave way to the uncertainties and anxieties of the twentieth century.

"God Is Dead ... We Have Killed Him"

❖

16 ◆ *Friedrich Nietzsche,* THE GAY SCIENCE *and* ON THE GENEALOGY OF MORALS

Among the philosophers of the late nineteenth century, none offered a more trenchant and piercing rejection of rationalism, democracy, Christianity, and traditional Western morality than the German philosopher Friedrich Nietzsche (1844–1900). Born into the family of a Lutheran minister, Nietzsche studied the Greek and Roman classics at the universities of Bonn and Leipzig, and then accepted a professorship at the University of Basel, Switzerland, in 1872. Forced to resign for reasons of health in 1879, he spent the last two decades of his life in Switzerland, Italy, and Germany seeking a cure for his deteriorating mental and emotional state. Before he lapsed into insanity in 1889, he published a series of provocative treatises in which he denounced Judaism, Christianity, and democratic egalitarianism as obstacles to the evolutionary development of a new race of superior human beings who would rule through the "will to power." His ideas influenced countless twentieth-century thinkers and movements, including existentialism and Nazism.

The first excerpt is taken from *The Gay Science* (sometimes translated as *The Joyful Wisdom*), a collection of aphorisms on diverse topics written in 1882 after Nietzsche had recovered from a period of illness. The second excerpt is taken from *On the Genealogy of Morals*, published in 1887.

QUESTIONS FOR ANALYSIS

1. What does Nietzsche mean by the "death of God" and his assertion that "we have killed him"?
2. Is the death of God good or bad for humanity, according to Nietzsche?
3. What distinctions does Nietzsche draw between "slave morality" and "noble morality"? How does the "pioneer" called for in the passage from *The Gay Science* embody the ideal of "noble morality"?
4. What implications do Nietzsche's ideas on morality have for democratic theory?
5. Overall, would you characterize Nietzsche's philosophy as optimistic or pessimistic?

[THE GAY SCIENCE]

The Madman — Have you ever heard of the madman who on a bright morning lighted a lantern and ran to the market-place calling out unceasingly: "I seek God! I seek God!" — As there were many people standing about who did not believe in God, he caused a great deal of amusement. Why! is he lost? said one. Has he strayed away like a child? said another. Or does he keep himself hidden? Is he afraid of us? Has he taken a sea-voyage? Has he emigrated? — the people cried out laughingly, all in a hubbub. The insane man jumped into their midst and transfixed them with his glances. "Where is God gone?" he called out. "I mean to tell you! *We have killed him,* — you and I! We are all his murderers! But how have we done it? How were we able to drink up the sea? Who gave us the sponge to wipe away the whole horizon? What did we do when we loosened this earth from its sun? Whither does it now move? Whither do we move? Away from all suns? Do we not dash on unceasingly? Backwards, sideways, forewards, in all directions? Is there still an above and below? Do we not stray, as through infinite nothingness? Does not empty space breathe upon us? Has it not become colder? Does not night come on continually, darker and darker? Shall we not have to light lanterns in the morning? Do we not hear the noise of the grave-diggers who are burying God? Do we not smell the divine putrefaction? — for even Gods putrefy! God is dead! God remains dead! And we have killed him! How shall we console ourselves, the most murderous of all murderers? The holiest and the mightiest that the world has hitherto possessed, has bled to death under our knife, — who will wipe the blood from us? . . . There never was a greater event, — and on account of it, all who are born after us belong to a higher history than any history hitherto!" — Here the madman was silent and looked again at his hearers; they also were silent and looked at him in surprise. At last he threw his lantern on the ground, so that it broke in pieces and was extinguished. . . . It is further stated that the madman made his way into different churches on the same day, and there intoned his *Requiem aeternam deo.*[1] When led out and called to account, he always gave the reply: "What are these churches now, if they are not the tombs and monuments of God?" —

Pioneers. — I greet all the signs indicating that a more manly and warlike age is commencing, which will, above all, bring heroism again into honour! For it has to prepare the way for a yet higher age, and gather the force which the latter will one day require, — the age which will carry heroism into knowledge, and *wage war* for the sake of ideas and their consequences. For that end many brave pioneers are now needed, who, however, cannot originate out of nothing, — and just a little out of the sand and slime of present-day civilisation and the culture of great cities: men silent, solitary and resolute, who know how to be content and persistent in invisible activity: men who with innate disposition seek in all things that which is *to be overcome* in them: men to whom cheerfulness, patience, simplicity, and contempt of the great vanities belong just as much as do magnanimity in victory and indulgence to the trivial vanities of all the vanquished: . . . men with their own holidays, their own work-days, and their own periods of mourning; accustomed to command with perfect assurance, and equally ready, if need be, to obey, proud in the one case as in the other, equally serving their own interests: men more imperiled, more productive, more happy! For believe me! — the secret of realising the largest productivity and the greatest enjoyment of existence is *to live in danger!* Build your cities on the slope of Vesuvius![2] Send your ships into unexplored seas! Live in war with your equals and with yourselves! Be robbers and spoilers, ye knowing ones, as long as ye cannot be rulers and possessors! The time will soon pass when you can be satisfied to live like timorous deer concealed in the forests. . . .

[ON THE GENEALOGY OF MORALS]

— "But what is all this talk about nobler values? Let us face facts: the people have triumphed — or the slaves, the mob, the herd, whatever you wish to call them — and if the Jews brought it

---

[1] Latin meaning requiem (a solemn chant for the dead) to the eternal god.

[2] A volcano in southern Italy.

about, then no nation ever had a more universal mission on this earth. The lords are a thing of the past, and the ethics of the common man is completely triumphant. . . . The 'redemption' of the human race (from the lords, that is) is well under way; everything is rapidly becoming Judaized, or Christianized, or mob-ized — the word makes no difference. The progress of this poison throughout the body of mankind cannot be stayed; . . .

The slave revolt in morals begins by rancor turning creative and giving birth to values — the rancor of beings who, deprived of the direct outlet of action, compensate by an imaginary vengeance. All truly noble morality grows out of triumphant self-affirmation. Slave ethics, on the other hand, begins by saying *no* to an "outside," and "other," a non-self, and that *no* is its creative act. . . . Slave ethics requires for its inception a sphere different from and hostile to its own. Physiologically speaking, it requires an outside stimulus in order to act at all; all its action is reaction. The opposite is true of aristocratic valuations: such values grow and act spontaneously, seeking out their contraries only in order to affirm themselves even more gratefully and delightedly. Here the negative concepts, *humble, base, bad,* are late, pallid counterparts of the positive, intense and passionate credo, "We noble, good, beautiful, happy ones." . . .

All this stands in utter contrast to what is called happiness among the impotent and oppressed, who are full of bottled-up aggressions. Their happiness is purely passive and takes the form of drugged tranquility, stretching and yawning, peace, "sabbath," emotional slackness. Whereas the noble lives before his own conscience with confidence and frankness. . . . Among the noble, mental acuteness always tends slightly to suggest luxury and overrefinement. The fact is that with them it is much less

important than is the perfect functioning of the ruling, unconscious instincts or even a certain temerity to follow sudden impulses, court danger, or indulge spurts of violent rage, love, worship, gratitude, or vengeance. . . .

Here I want to give vent to a sigh and a last hope. Exactly what is it that I, especially, find intolerable; that I am unable to cope with; that asphyxiates me? A bad smell. The smell of failure, of a soul that has gone stale. God knows it is possible to endure all kinds of misery — vile weather, sickness, trouble, isolation. All this can be coped with, if one is born to a life of anonymity and battle. There will always be moments of re-emergence into the light, when one tastes the golden hour of victory and once again stands foursquare, unshakable, ready to face even harder things, like a bowstring drawn taut against new perils. But, you divine patronesses — if there are any such in the realm beyond good and evil — grant me now and again the sight of something perfect, wholly achieved, happy, magnificently triumphant, something still capable of inspiring fear! Of a man who will justify the existence of mankind, for whose sake one may continue to believe in mankind! . . . The leveling and diminution of European man is our greatest danger; because the sight of him makes us despond. . . . We no longer see anything these days that aspires to grow greater; instead, we have a suspicion that things will continue to go downhill, becoming ever thinner, more placid, smarter, cosier, more ordinary, more indifferent, more Chinese, more Christian — without doubt man is getting "better" all the time. . . . This is Europe's true predicament: together with the fear of man we have also lost the love of man, reverence for man, confidence in man, indeed the *will to man.* Now the sight of man makes us despond.

Aesthetics for the Machine Age

❖

17 ❖ *EXCERPTS FROM FUTURIST MANIFESTOS, 1909–1914*

The late nineteenth and early twentieth centuries witnessed an eruption of new artistic movements, all seeking liberation from the dead hand of the past. *Impressionists* left exact copying to photographers and sought to depict momentary sense impressions before they could be fully apprehended and studied by the brain; *pointillists* painted canvases in which color was broken down into thousands of tiny individual dots of pigment; *postimpressionists,* or *expressionists,* were less interested in depicting what they saw than in revealing the inner worlds of their imagination and feelings; *les fauves* ("wild beasts," a name given them by a shocked Parisian critic in 1905) painted pictures made up of color, line, and form, but no real objects; *cubists* dismantled objects and figures and reassembled them in sharp, flat, distorted geometrical patterns. Within a few decades, perspective, realistic color, detail, and narrative all had been abandoned for an art that was abstract, personal — and modern.

Futurism, which burst on the scene in 1909, was the last new artistic movement in prewar Europe and in many ways the most outrageous and iconoclastic. It proposed new standards not just for painting and sculpture but for poetry, music, architecture, and even fashion. Carried away by the cult of youth, the power and dynamism of the airplane and automobile, the wild energies of urban life, and the heroic possibilities of warfare, futurists called for an unequivocal break with the past and a new aesthetic consonant with the age of machines.

The movement began in February 1909 when Tomasso Marinetti published his "futurist manifesto" in the Parisian newspaper, *Le Figaro.* Italian painters and sculptors Gino Severini, Umberto Boccioni, Giacomo Balla, Luigi Russolo, and Carlo Carra identified themselves with the movement and sought in their works to capture the speed, energy, and dynamism of modern life through a style reminiscent of cubism. A number of other young Italians with interests in music, literature, and fashion also adopted the futurist label. They, like futurist painters and sculptors, were quick to issue manifestos that proclaimed their views.

Futurism ended abruptly during World War I when most of its adherents volunteered to fight in Italy's army. In its brief life, however, it was a prime example of the restlessness, unfocused energy, and appetite for innovation that affected many Europeans as they moved fully into the Machine Age and ever closer to the dark abyss of World War I.

The following excerpts are taken from three manifestos issued by futurists between 1909 and 1913. They begin with Marinetti's 1909 manifesto from *Le Figaro,* and continue with later manifestos on painting (issued by Boccioni, Carra, Russolo, Balla, and Severini in 1910), and music (issued by Russolo in 1913).

QUESTIONS FOR ANALYSIS

1. What symbolic attraction do modern machines have for the futurists? How do the characteristics of machines affect the futurists' views?
2. What are the weaknesses and flaws of past artistic styles, according to the futurists?
3. How do you explain the futurists' self-proclaimed veneration of warfare?
4. What might explain the futurists' stated opposition to feminism (see article 9 in Marinetti's manifesto)?
5. What common features or views can be seen in all three futurist manifestos?
6. What similarities, if any, do you see between the views of the futurists and those of Nietzsche?

MANIFESTO OF FUTURISM (1909)

1. We intend to sing the love of danger, the habit of energy and fearlessness.
2. Courage, audacity, and revolt will be essential elements of our poetry.
3. Up to now literature has exalted a pensive immobility, ecstasy, and sleep. We intend to exalt aggressive action, a feverish insomnia, the racer's stride, the mortal leap, the punch and the slap.
4. We affirm that the world's magnificence has been enriched by a new beauty: the beauty of speed. A racing car whose hood is adorned with great pipes, like serpents of explosive breath — a roaring car that seems to ride on grapeshot is more beautiful than the *Victory of Samothrace.*
5. We want to hymn the man at the wheel, who hurls the lance of his spirit across the Earth, along the circle of its orbit.
6. The poet must spend himself with ardour, splendour, and generosity, to swell the enthusiastic fervour of the primordial elements.
7. Except in struggle, there is no more beauty. No work without an aggressive character can be a masterpiece. Poetry must be conceived as a violent attack on unknown forces, to reduce and prostrate them before man.
8. We stand on the last promontory of the centuries! . . . Why should we look back, when what we want is to break down the mysterious doors of the Impossible? Time and Space died yesterday. We already live in the absolute, becaue we have created eternal, omnipresent speed.
9. We will glorify war — the world's only hygiene — militarism, patriotism, the destructive gesture of freedom-bringers, beautiful ideas worth dying for, and scorn for woman.
10. We will destroy the museums, libraries, academies of every kind, will fight moralism, feminism, every opportunistic or utilitarian cowardice.
11. We will sing of great crowds excited by work, by pleasure, and by riot; we will sing of the multicoloured, polyphonic tides of revolution in the modern capitals; we will sing of the vibrant nightly fervour of arsenals and shipyards blazing with violent electric moons; greedy railway stations that devour smoke-plumed serpents; factories hung on clouds by the crooked lines of their smoke; bridges that stride the rivers like giant gymnasts, flashing in the sun with a glitter of knives; adventurous steamers that sniff the horizon; deep-chested locomotives whose wheels paw the tracks like the hooves of enormous steel horses bridled

by tubing; and the sleek flight of planes whose propellers chatter in the wind like banners and seem to cheer like an enthusiastic crowd.

It is from Italy that we launch through the world this violently upsetting incendiary manifesto of ours. With it, today, we establish *Futurism,* because we want to free this land from its smelly gangrene of professors, archaeologists, *ciceroni* and antiquarians. For too long has Italy been a dealer in second-hand clothes. We mean to free her from the numberless museums that cover her like so many graveyards.

MANIFESTO OF THE FUTURIST PAINTERS 1910

TO THE YOUNG ARTISTS OF ITALY!

The cry of rebellion which we utter associates our ideals with those of the Futurist poets. These ideals were not invented by some aesthetic clique. They are the expression of a violent desire which boils in the veins of every creative artist today.

We will fight with all our might the fanatical, senseless and snobbish religion of the past, a religion encouraged by the vicious existence of museums. We rebel against that spineless worshipping of old canvases, old statues and old bric-a-brac, against everything which is filthy and worm-ridden and corroded by time. We consider the habitual contempt for everything which is young, new and burning with life to be unjust and even criminal. . . .

These are our final CONCLUSIONS:

With our enthusiastic adherence to Futurism, we will:

1. Destroy the cult of the past, the obsession with the ancients, pedantry and academic formalism.
2. Totally invalidate all kinds of imitation.
3. Elevate all attempts at originality, however daring, however violent.
4. Bear bravely and proudly the smear of 'madness' with which they try to gag all innovators.
5. Regard art critics as useless and dangerous.
6. Rebel against the tyranny of words: 'Harmony' and 'good taste' and other loose expressions which can be used to destroy the works of Rembrandt, Goya, Rodin. . . .
7. Sweep the whole field of art clean of all themes and subjects which have been used in the past.
8. Support and glory in our day-to-day world, a world which is going to be continually and splendidly transformed by victorious Science.

THE ART OF NOISES (EXTRACTS) 1913

We cannot see that enormous apparatus of force that the modern orchestra represents without feeling the most profound and total disillusion at the paltry acoustic results. Do you know of any sight more ridiculous than that of twenty men furiously bent on redoubling the mewing of a violin? All this will naturally make the music-lovers scream, and will perhaps enliven the sleepy atmosphere of concert halls. Let us now, as Futurists, enter one of these hospitals for anaemic sounds. There: the first bar brings the boredom of familiarity to your ear and anticipates the boredom of the bar to follow. Let us relish, from bar to bar, two or three varieties of genuine boredom, waiting all the while for the extraordinary sensation that never comes.

Meanwhile a repugnant mixture is concocted from monotonous sensations and the idiotic religious emotion of listeners buddhistically drunk with repeating for the nth time their more or less snobbish or second-hand ecstasy.

Away! Let us break out since we cannot much longer restrain our desire to create finally a new musical reality, with a generous distribution of resonant slaps in the face, discarding violins, pianos, double-basses and plaintive organs. Let us break out! . . .

Let us cross a great modern capital with our ears more alert than our eyes, and we will get enjoyment from distinguishing the eddying of water, air and gas in metal pipes, the grumbling of noises that breathe and pulse with indisputable animality, the palpitation of valves, the coming and going of pistons, the howl of mechanical saws, the jolting of a tram on its rails, the cracking of whips, the flapping of curtains and flags. We enjoy creating mental orchestrations of the crashing down of metal shop blinds, slamming doors, the hubbub and shuffling of crowds, the variety of din, from stations, railways, iron foundries, spinning mills, printing works, electric power stations and underground railways. . . .

Here are the 6 *families of noises* of the Futurist orchestra which we will soon set in motion mechanically:

1	2	3
Rumbles	Whistles	Whispers
Roars	Hisses	Murmurs
Explosions	Snorts	Mumbles
Crashes		Grumbles
Splashes		Gurgles
Booms		

4	5	6
Screeches	Noises	Voices of
Creaks	obtained	animals
Rustles	by	and men:
Buzzes	percussion	Shouts
Crackles	on metal,	Screams
Scrapes	wood,	Groans
	skin,	Shrieks
	stone,	Howls
	terracotta,	Laughs
	etc.	Wheezes
		Sobs

PART TWO

Decades of War, Economic Upheaval, and Revolution, 1914–1939

In early August 1914, to the sounds of cheering crowds and military bands, the European-dominated world of the nineteenth and early twentieth centuries began to unravel. On June 28, bullets fired by a Serbian nationalist had killed the future emperor and empress of Austria-Hungary in Sarajevo, setting off a diplomatic crisis that soon escalated beyond the crises that European statesmen had managed to settle peacefully in the previous decade and a half. This time diplomacy failed, and in August what came to be known at first as the Great War, and later as World War I, began.

Many welcomed the conflict. Politicians hoped it would provide a respite from strikes, class antagonisms, socialist agitation, and suffragist demands. Nationalists dreamed of winning glorious victories and settling old scores. Young men with humdrum jobs in shops or offices envisioned excitement, heroism, and being part of a great cause. Not a few philosophers and poets maintained that the war would rouse men from apathy, ennoble them, and inspire them to acts of self-sacrifice and courage; it would weed out the unfit, ensure a place for the strong, and thus contribute to human progress.

Those who hoped for war got their wish, but as they soon learned, it was not what they wanted at all. The short war promised by leaders became an unendurable four-year struggle in which the cheers, rousing marches, resplendent uniforms, and gleaming weapons of the first few weeks gave way to a reality of rat-infested trenches, land mines, shell shock, poison gas, barbed wire, suicide charges against machine-gun nests, massive battles that changed nothing, and unbearably long casualty lists. By the end of 1914, German and French forces had combined casualties of 300,000 dead and 600,000 wounded, and this was only a foretaste of the war's final toll: 65 to 75 million men mobilized; approximately 9 million killed; 22 million wounded, of whom 7 million were permanently disabled. Costs were immense. In the 1920s the Carnegie Endowment for International Peace put the war's cost, including government expenditure, property damage, and the value of lives lost, at $338 billion, a figure so high that errors of plus or minus several billions of dollars are insignificant.

Such sacrifice might have been bearable if the war had settled anything, if it had "made the world safe for democracy," or at least had enabled the belligerents to return to prewar "normalcy" once it was over. Instead, it was the first act of a two-decade tragedy that ended with the onset of another, even more terrible catastrophe, World War II.

The post–World War I treaties, dictated by the winners at the Paris Peace Conference, were censured for being too harsh or too lenient, too idealistic or too hard-headed. In any case, they failed. They fed old grievances, created new probelms, and within fifteen years generally were being ignored. Economic disaster struck winners and losers alike. War debts and reparations entangled international finance; inflation ruined much of the middle class in Germany and Austria; sagging prices plagued farmers; unemployment remained high, even during the "Roaring Twenties." Then the Great Depression struck in 1929, and with international trade halved and unemployment at all-time highs, capitalism's demise seemed imminent. The future of democracy and liberalism looked no brighter. Dictators replaced parliaments in much of Europe, and surviving democracies seemed flabby and weak compared to the dynamic new fascist and totalitarian regimes. Such was the sorry record of a civilization that only a few years earlier regarded its institutions and values as the pinnacle of human achievement and expected a future of continuing progress.

While the industrialized nations lurched from one crisis to another, Asians, Africans, and Latin Americans continued to struggle with problems of colonialism, economic dependency, and political instability. World War I and its aftermath redefined these problems and encouraged new perspectives. The war itself had a wide-ranging impact. It spurred industrialization in Japan, India, and South America when European factories could no longer supply overseas markets. Its senseless slaughter weakened colonialism by undermining the West's claim of moral superiority. The postwar treaties redrew the map of the Middle East by demolishing the Ottoman Empire, and angered Africans, Arabs, and especially Indians by ignoring their interests despite wartime contributions as soldiers and taxpayers.

The Great Depression was a calamity for the nonindustrialized world. As factories closed in Europe and the United States, demand for raw materials plummeted. By 1932 cotton was selling at one-third, and raw rubber at one-fourth, their pre-1929 prices. Prices for Malayan tin, Chilean copper, Japanese silk, and South African diamonds all plunged. Agricultural prices, which had been falling worldwide before 1929, also were hard hit. The price of basic grains sank to historic lows, with Burmese rice farmers and Argentinean wheat growers suffering alike. The price of Brazilian coffee slumped from 22.5 cents per pound in 1929 to 8 cents in 1931, at which point coffee growers began burning coffee beans to keep up prices. With their export-based economies in tatters, unemployment grew, poverty deepened, and demand for European manufactured goods slumped, accelerating the downward cycle of an imploding world economy.

Reaction to the Great Depression varied in the non-Western world. In Japan economic catastrophe strengthened hard-line nationalists, who trumpeted the benefits of imperialist expansion. In Latin America it elicited a variety of political responses, mostly authoritarian, and inspired efforts to end the region's dependency on foreign manufactures. Throughout colonial Africa and Asia, it strengthened nationalism. It unified educated elites, peasants, and factory workers in opposition to colonial regimes that had created the system of export dependency and did nothing to fix it when it collapsed between 1929 and 1933. From the East Indies to Africa, strikes, mass demonstrations, the emergence of popular nationalist leaders, and even revolutions were signs of increasingly restive colonial populations.

Many nationalist leaders, especially in Asia, were now also communists. This link between anticolonialism and Marxism in Latin America, Asia, and even parts of Africa is another example of how events in Europe — in this case the Russian Revolution of 1917 — influenced non-Western politics. Impressed by a revolution that had taken place in a backward agrarian society and by the success of Soviet economic development strategies in the 1930s, increasing numbers of Africans, Asians, and Latin Americans saw Marxism/Leninism as a two-edged weapon to end capitalism and colonialism alike. The strongest communist movement was in China, where in the 1930s the Communist Party under Mao Zedong battled Chiang Kai-shek's Nationalists in China's civil war.

The communists ultimately won the civil war in China, and nationalists throughout Asia and Africa won the struggle for freedom and independence. In each case, World War II played a key role. But without World War I and the tumultuous events of the 1920s and 1930, neither victory would have been possible.

CHAPTER 3

World War I and Its Global Significance

What if the Serb nationalist Gavrilo Princip had failed to assassinate Archduke Ferdinand of Austria-Hungary on June 28, 1914, in Sarajevo? What if German diplomats had discouraged their ally Austria-Hungary from its plan to invade Serbia for its alleged part in the crime? What if the Austro-Hungarians had abandoned their war plans when the Serbs accepted almost all the terms of the Austro-Hungarian ultimatum on July 25? What if Great Britain had made its proposal for a Great Power conference to mediate the crisis early in July, and not on July 26, when chances of success were minimal? What if European statesman had better understood what modern war was like and had worked harder to prevent it?

What if World War I had never happened?

Definitive answers to such questions are impossible, but one thing is certain. Without World War I, twentieth-century history would have been different, profoundly so. World War I has been described as a turning point, a watershed, and a great divide between two eras. All of these descriptions are true. Between 1914 and 1918 the war killed or wounded almost thirty million human beings. After the killing stopped, it continued to put its stamp on all that followed.

In Europe World War I was a prelude to political disaster. In the short run, it triggered the Russian Revolution of 1917, which in turn raised the specter of communism in the rest of Europe and played into the hands of right-wing dictators who promised to smash the "red menace." In the long run, it raised doubts about the wisdom of elected officials, eroded support for parliamentary governments, and thus contributed to the demise of liberalism and democracy in much of Europe in the 1920s and 1930s. The war fostered regimentation, encouraged the use of propaganda, made demands for total obedience and total commitment for soldiers and civilians alike, and transformed politics into a moral crusade. It created new grievances and resentments, and stirred unresolved hatreds that played into the hands of demagogues with seductive and simplistic solutions to their nations' problems. In all these ways it prepared the ground for fascism and totalitarianism.

World War I also contributed to the economic catastrophes of the 1920s and 1930s. Without the massive borrowing by governments to pay for the war, the inflation of the early 1920s might have been avoided. Without reparations and war debts, international financial markets might have avoided the unhealthy dependence on U.S. loans and capital in the 1920s, a situation that spelled disaster after the U.S. stock market crash of 1929. Without the expansion of agricultural production outside of Europe during the war, the surpluses of the 1920s might have been avoided, and with them the slump in farm incomes.

The war's impact stretched well beyond Europe. It encouraged colonized peoples to question the superiority and invulnerability of their European masters. It also planted seeds of doubt among Europeans about their capacity to rule. The war aroused nationalism by drafting colonial subjects from Africa and Asia into the fighting and then, due to the provisions of the postwar treaties, by dashing their hopes for greater self-rule.

But Gavrilo Princip did assassinate Archduke Ferdinand; Germany offered Austria-Hungary a "blank check," not words of restraint; Austria-Hungary disregarded Serbia's response to its ultimatum; Great Britain's proposal for a Great Powers conference came too late. Statesmen could not prevent the Sarajevo crisis from becoming a war. The world was forever changed.

The Trauma of the Trenches

Wars by their very nature are unpredictable, but rarely was the gap between expectations and reality greater than in World War I. Generals and politicians alike promised a short war. A few quick campaigns and a few decisive victories would "bring the boys home by Christmas," perhaps even by the fall. These victories would be won by tactics still inspired by the French commander Napoléon Bonaparte (1769–1821), whose legendary victories had taught that rapid troop movement, surprise, massive artillery fire, and huge infantry and cavalry charges were the keys to battlefield success. Elan and spirit would conquer all obstacles.

This was the war that soldiers anticipated as they marched off to what they imagined would be glorious adventure — an opportunity to fight for the flag or kaiser or queen, to wear colorful uniforms, and to win glory in battles that would decided by spirit and bravery. The war they fought was nothing like the war they envisioned. After the Germans had almost taken Paris early in the fighting, the Western front became the scene of a stalemate that lasted until the armistice on November 11, 1918. Along a four-hundred-mile line stretching from the English Channel through Belgium and France to the Swiss border, defense — a combination of trenches, barbed wire, land mines, poison gas, and machine guns — proved superior to offense — massive artillery barrages followed by charges of troops across no man's land to overrun enemy lines. Such attacks resulted in numbingly long casualty lists, but gains of territory that were measured in yards not miles.

There are many reasons why Europeans found World War I so demoralizing, so unsettling, and so devoid of any aspect or outcome that might have justified its costs. The disparity between expectations and reality — the theme of the sources in this section — is one of them.

The Romance of War

❖

18 ◆ POPULAR ART AND POSTER ART FROM GERMANY, ENGLAND, AUSTRALIA, AND FRANCE

By December 1914, the muddy reality of stalemate had replaced bright dreams of quick victory, and as casualties mounted, shock replaced enthusiasm. Governments no longer could rely on that early burst of patriotic fervor to ensure that men would volunteer, soldiers would reenlist, and citizens would buy war bonds and stoically endure food and fuel shortages. All sides therefore tried to prop up morale through censorship and propaganda. Press reports distorted casualty statistics, misrepresented troop morale, downplayed the hardships of trench warfare, and even described nonexistent victories in which troops overran enemy lines while brandishing swords. Ministries of propaganda churned out broadsheets and circulars describing the enemy's unreasonable war aims and atrocities. They also covered walls with thousands of posters, which with their bright colors, catchy designs, and positive messages encouraged citizens to enlist, buy bonds, save fuel, start vegetable plots, and donate money to care for wounded veterans. Casualty lists and stories from soldiers on leave belied the messages of the broadsheets and posters, and as people came to recognize them for what they were — government-sponsored lies — cynicism about the war deepened.

The four illustrations in this section portray the positive attitudes toward the war that all belligerents shared at the outset and which governments sought to perpetuate as the war dragged on. The first, entitled *The Departure,* shows a German troop train departing for the front. Printed originally in the German periodical *Simplicissimus* in August 1914, it is the work of B. Hennerberg, a Swedish artist and a regular contributor to the magazine. That *Simplicissimus* published such an illustration shows the strength of nationalism at the war's start. Noted before the war for its irreverent satire and criticism of German militarism, *Simplicissimus,* on a decision by its editors, abandoned its antiestablishment stance and lent full support to the war effort.

The second illustration is from a series of cards included by the Mitchell Tobacco Company in its packs of Golden Dawn cigarettes early in the war. It shows a sergeant offering smokes to his soldiers before battle. Tobacco advertising with military themes reached a saturation point in England during the war.

The third illustration is an Australian recruitment poster issued in 1915. Although Australia controlled its domestic affairs, its foreign policy was still managed by Great Britain, and hence when Great Britain went to war, so did Australia. The Australian parliament refused to approve conscription, however, so the government had to work hard to encourage volunteers. This poster appeared in 1915, when Australian troops were heavily involved in the Gallipoli campaign, the Allied effort to knock the Ottoman Empire out of the war. Appealing to members of sports clubs, it promised young men the opportunity to enlist in a battalion made up entirely of fellow sportsmen.

The fourth illustration, a poster from France, was designed to encourage the purchase of war bonds, which were sold by all major belligerents to finance the war. It appeared in 1916 during the German offensive at Verdun, which lasted from February to November and resulted in more than five hundred thousand French casualties. The French soldier shouts, "On les aura!" or "We'll get them!" — words ascribed to General Henri-Philippe Pétain, who was in charge of the Verdun defense until he was given command of all French armies in the field in the summer of 1916.

QUESTIONS FOR ANALYSIS

1. What messages about the war does each of the four illustrations communicate?
2. In what specific ways does each of them romanticize war and the life of a soldier?
3. What impressions of combat do the English tobacco card and the French war bond poster communicate?
4. What does Hennerberg's painting suggest about women's anticipated role in the war?

Advertisement card from Golden Dawn cigarettes

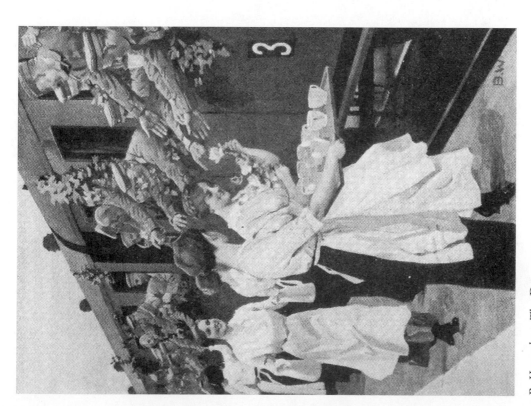

B. Hennerberg, The Departure

French poster encouraging purchase of war bonds (1916)

Australian recruitment poster (1915)

The Reality of War in Verse

◈

19 ◆ *Wilfred Owen,*
DULCE ET DECORUM EST and DISABLED

So great was the carnage of World War I that no historian has captured its horror as vividly as have the poets and novelists who experienced it. Every major belligerent nation had writers who evoked the desolation and inhumanity of trench warfare. Among the most powerful was the British poet Wilfred Owen (1893–1918), who enlisted in the British army in 1915 at the age of 22. Wounded in 1917, he was hospitalized, released, and sent back to the trenches, where he was killed on November 4, 1918, one week before the armistice. His poem, "Dulce et Decorum Est," written in 1915, takes its title from a line by the ancient Roman poet Horace: "It is sweet and fitting to die for one's country." Its subject is a poison gas attack. The Germans launched the first large-scale gas attack in April 1915 when they released chlorine gas from cylinders and let the wind carry it toward French and Canadian troops in the vicinity of Ypres. Subsequently, both sides used poison gas, with phosgene and mustard gas being delivered by artillery shells by 1918. "Disabled," also written in 1915, describes a badly mutilated Scottish soldier who enlisted before he was eighteen, and now sits in a wheelchair in an institution where he survives, but barely.

QUESTIONS FOR ANALYSIS

1. How in "Dulce et Decorum Est" does Owen describe the mental and physical condition of the foot soldiers?
2. What imagery does he apply to the body of the gas victim?
3. Why does Owen find the plight of the young Scottish soldier so compelling?
4. In what specific ways do Owen's poems attempt to dispel the illusions about war represented in the art in the previous section?

DULCE ET DECORUM EST

Bent double, like old beggars under sacks,
Knock-kneed, coughing like hags, we cursed
   through sludge,
Till on the haunting flares we turned our backs
And towards our distant rest began the trudge.
Men marched asleep. Many had lost their boots
But limped on, blood-shod. All went lame; all
   blind;

Drunk with fatigue; deaf even to the hoots
Of tired, outstripped Five-Nines[1] that dropped
   behind.

Gas! GAS! Quick, boys! — An ecstasy of
   fumbling,
Fitting the clumsy helmets just in time;
But someone still was yelling out and
   stumbling,
And flound'ring like a man in fire or lime . . .

---

[1]Slang for artillery shells used by the Germans.

Dim, through the misty panes and thick green
      light,
As under a green sea, I saw him drowning.
In all my dreams, before my helpless sight,
He plunges at me, guttering, choking,
      drowning.

If in some smothering dreams you too could
      pace
Behind the wagon that we flung him in,
And watch the white eyes writhing in his face,
His hanging face, like a devil's sick of sin;
If you could hear, at every jolt, the blood
Come gargling from the froth-corrupted lungs,
Obscene as cancer, bitter as the cud
Of vile, incurable sores on innocent tongues, —
My friend, you would not tell with such high
      zest,
To children ardent for some desperate glory,
The old Lie: Dulce et decorum est
Pro patria mori.

DISABLED

He sat in a wheeled chair, waiting for dark,
And shivered in his ghastly suit of grey,
Legless, sewn short at elbow. Through the park
Voices of boys rang saddening like a hymn,
Voices of play and pleasure after day,
Till gathering sleep had mothered them from
      him.

About this time Town used to swing so gay
When glow-lamps budded in the light blue
      trees,
And girls glanced lovelier as the air grew
      dim, —
In the old times, before he threw away his
      knees.
Now he will never feel again how slim
Girls' waists are, or how warm their subtle
      hands.
All of them touch him like some queer
      disease.

There was an artist silly for his face,
For it was younger than his youth, last year.
Now, he is old; his back will never brace;
He's lost his colour very far from here,
Poured it down shell-holes till the veins ran
      dry,
And half his lifetime lapsed in the hot race
And leap of purple spurted from his thigh.

One time he liked a bloodsmear down his leg,
After the matches, carried shoulder-high.
It was after football, when he'd drunk a peg,
He thought he'd better join. — He wonders
      why.
Someone had said he'd look a god in kilts.
That's why; and maybe, too, to please his Meg,
Aye, that was it, to please the giddy jilts[2]
He asked to join. He didn't have to beg;
Smiling they wrote his lie; aged nineteen
      years.
Germans he scarcely thought of; all their guilt
And Austria's, did not move him. And no fears
Of Fear came yet. He thought of jewelled hilts
For daggers in plaid socks; of smart salutes;
And care of arms; and leave, and pay arrears;
Esprit de corps; and hints for young recruits.
And soon, he was drafted out with drums and
      cheers.

Some cheered him home, but not as crowds
      cheer Goal.
Only a solemn man who brought him fruits
Thanked him; and then inquired about his
      soul.

Now, he will spend a few sick years in insti-
      tutes,
And do what things the rules consider wise,
And take whatever pity they may dole.
Tonight he noticed how the women's eyes
Passed from him to the strong men that were
      whole.
How cold and late it is! Why don't they come
And put him to bed? Why don't they come?

---

[2]Scottish slang for young girls.

The Reality of War in Art

◈

20 ◆ *Christopher Nevinson, THE HARVEST OF BATTLE*
and
Otto Dix, STORM TROOP ADVANCING UNDER GAS

Many European artists fought in World War I or were sent to the front to serve as official painters. During the war itself, their subject matter was carefully monitored by their governments. In England, for example, it was illegal to display a painting that portrayed a dead English soldier. Thus most of the paintings that expressed disillusionment with the war appeared only after hostilities ended. Such was the case with the two works in this section.

The first painting, *The Harvest of Battle,* was completed by the English painter Christopher Nevinson in 1919. Born is 1889, Nevinson was an art student in France when the war started. He served in the Red Cross and the Royal Army Medical Corps before rheumatic fever forced him out of active service in 1916. He returned to the war zone as an official painter in late 1917. On his return to England in early 1918, he exhibited large numbers of war-related paintings and drawings that expressed his deep emotions about the war's human costs. He found little demand for his war-related paintings in the 1920s, and the rest of his career was devoted to townscapes and flower pictures. While serving as a war artist in World War II, he suffered a stroke and died in 1946.

Otto Dix (1891–1969), who created the etching *Storm Troop Advancing Under Gas,* was one of Germany's most important twentieth-century artists. He was on active duty throughout the war, serving as machine gunner, artilleryman, and aerial observer on both the Eastern and Western fronts. Deeply disillusioned with postwar society and its failure to appreciate the sacrifices of veterans, Dix became an ardent pacifist, whose powerful antiwar drawings and paintings contributed to his condemnation and arrest by the Nazis. Only in the desperate closing days of World War II was he drafted into the army.

Storm Troop Advancing Under Gas is one of a series of fifty etchings Dix produced in 1923 and 1924, collectively entitled *War.* Storm troops were highly trained soldiers armed with machine guns, mortars, and flamethrowers whose job was to attack rear areas and artillery positions before direct, large-scale infantry assaults were launched on enemy trenches.

QUESTIONS FOR ANALYSIS

1. What statements about war is each artist attempting to make in his work?
2. What specific details help the artist put his message across?
3. Why do you suppose Nevinson chose the title *The Harvest of Battle* for his work?

C. R. W. Nevinson, The Harvest of Battle

Otto Dix, Storm Troop Advancing Under Gas Attack

The Century's First Genocide

"A coordinated plan of different actions aiming at the destruction of the essential foundations of the life of national groups, with the aim of annihilating the groups themselves." This was the chilling definition of a new word coined in 1944 by the American jurist Raphael Lemkin. The new word was *genocide,* and Lemkin used it to describe the Nazis' systematic extermination of Gypsies, Poles, Russians, and especially Jews during World War II. Sadly, Lemkin's new word applies equally well to dozens of other episodes in the twentieth century, most recently to ethnic cleansing in Bosnia and the mass murder of Tutsis by the Hutus of Rwanda.

The century's first genocide took place in eastern Turkey in 1915, three decades before Lemkin coined a word to describe it. Its victims, numbering from six hundred thousand to one million, were Armenians, a people who since the seventh century B.C.E. had lived in the region south of the Caucasus Mountains and between the Black and Caspian Seas. They became Christians around 300 C.E., and over time developed a distinctive Armenian Apostolic Church close to the Eastern Orthodox Church in most respects. The Armenian heartland was captured by the Ottoman Turks in the sixteenth century and, except for a portion conquered by Persia and taken over by Russia in 1828, remained under Ottoman rule until the empire's demise after World War I. Numbering slightly more than two million, the Armenians, like Jews and other Christian minorities in the Ottoman Empire, were allowed to practice their religion and maintain their distinctive culture. However, they paid special taxes, could not own weapons, and were excluded from government positions.

During the nineteenth century, tensions worsened between the Armenians and Ottoman officials on the one hand and the general Muslim population on the other. Many Muslims were deeply resentful that the Armenian community was experiencing a cultural and economic renaissance while the Ottoman Empire itself was falling apart. Dozens of Armenian schools were founded during the nineteenth century, many by missionaries from the United States and Europe, and increasing numbers of Armenians went abroad to study at Russian or European universities. New Armenian-language newspapers were founded, and Armenian literature flourished. Although most Armenians remained small farmers, many became successful in trade, industry, and banking. Muslim-Armenian relations deteriorated even further when Armenian leaders began to call for greater autonomy and fairer treatment within the empire, although not for total independence.

Against this background, attacks on Armenians grew in the late 1800s, culminating in the massacre of as many as one hundred thousand Armenians by Ottoman troops between 1894 and 1896. The sultan who ordered these massacres (or, according to some interpretations, stood by idly while they occurred), Abdul Hamid II, was overthrown in the Revolution of 1908, which brought to power the Young Turks, or the Committee of Union and Progress. The party controlled Turkey during World War I and was responsible for the genocide of

1915. To jealousy, religious antagonism, and political fears, the Young Turks added another deadly ingredient to the anti-Armenian mix — nationalism. Rejecting the ethnic and religious pluralism of the Ottoman Empire, they favored an exclusively Turkish state. Some even dreamed of extending Turkey's borders to the east to include other Turkic peoples in Russian Central Asia. In neither scenario was there a place for two million Armenians.

World War I, in which Turkey was allied with Germany, offered the Young Turks a pretext and opportunity to deal with the "Armenian problem." By early 1915 the Turkish offensive against Russia in the Caucasus had failed, and the Allies had begun their campaign to take the Dardanelles. Young Turk extremists, specifically Minister of Internal Affairs Talaat Pasha and Minister of War Enver Pasha, sought to make the Armenians scapegoats for military defeats and settle the Armenian issue once and for all. On the night of April 23–24, 1915, scores of Armenian churchmen, intellectuals, educators, and businessmen were arrested in Istanbul, sent to the countryside, and executed. The century's first genocide had begun.

Caravans of Death

◆

21 ◆ *Mary L. Graffam,* *LETTER FROM TURKEY, SUMMER 1915*

Like the Nazi effort to exterminate Europe's Jews, the Turkish attempt to obliterate the Armenians took place under the cover of a world war, thus minimizing the chance of outside intervention. In the case of the Nazis, the outside world was unable to grasp the enormity of their crimes until the closing stages of the war. This was not the case in Turkey. With the United States still neutral in 1915, thousands of American missionaries, diplomats, and businessmen resided in Turkey, and as a result, newspaper accounts, reports to the U.S. ambassador, Henry Morgenthau, and hundreds of personal letters detailed the massacres. Germans and visitors from other neutral nations also provided testimony.

Witnesses described how in the weeks following the arrests of April 23–24, Armenians serving in the Turkish army were disarmed, placed in labor battalions, or simply shot. The general Armenian population faced deportation. Forced from their homes, men were executed by Turkish troops, police, or local Turks and Kurds, while women, children, and old men were driven for weeks over mountains and deserts in caravans that were preyed upon by bandits and local people. Those who reached the Syrian Desert or the swampy regions of the upper Euphrates River were left to die from heat, starvation, or disease. Further atrocities against the Armenians were perpetrated at the war's close when the Turkish army reoccupied portions of eastern Anatolia that had been abandoned by the Russians.

The following is typical of the many letters written by foreign eyewitnesses and later published in newspapers, missionary journals, or Armenian-language publications outside of Turkey. The author is Mary L. Graffam, a Protestant missionary from Massachusetts who was principal of a girls' school in Sivas, a city in north-central Turkey. It reveals the confusion and disbelief that attended the early deportations. Although the letter is undated, the events it describes took place in July 1915.

QUESTIONS FOR ANALYSIS

1. What can be learned from Graffam's letter about the motives of those who attacked the Armenians?
2. What evidence does the letter provide about the ways different groups of Armenians were treated?
3. The author is uncertain about the government's responsibility for ordering the massacres. What experiences did she have that help explain her uncertainty?
4. What do you make of the efforts of government officials to separate Graffam from the Armenian deportees? How does your answer relate to the issue raised in question 3?

When we were ready to leave Sivas, the Government gave forty-five ox-carts for the Protestant townspeople and eighty horses, but none at all for our pupils and teachers; so we bought ten ox-carts, two horse arabas [wagons], and five or six donkeys, and started out. In the company were all our teachers in the college, about twenty boys from the college and about thirty of the girls'-school. It was as a special favour to the Sivas people, who had not done anything revolutionary, that the Vali[1] allowed the men who were not yet in prison to go with their families.

The first night we were so tired that we just ate a piece of bread and slept on the ground wherever we could find a place to spread a yorgan [blanket]. It was after dark when we stopped, anyway. We were so near Sivas that the gendarmes[2] protected us, and no special harm was done; but the second night we began to see what was before us. The gendarmes would go ahead and have long conversations with the villagers, and then stand back and let

them rob and trouble the people until we all began to scream, and then they would come and drive them away. Yorgans [Blankets] and rugs, and all such things, disappeared by the dozen, and donkeys were sure to be lost. Many had brought cows; but from the first day those were carried off, one by one, until not a single one remained.

We got accustomed to being robbed, but the third day a new fear took possession of us, and that was that the men were to be separated from us at Kangal. . . . Our teacher from Mandjaluk was there, with his mother and sisters. They had left the village with the rest of the women and children, and when they saw that the men were being taken off to be killed the teacher fled to another village, four hours away, where he was found by the police and brought safely with his family to Kangal, because the tchaoush [officer] who had taken them from Mandjaluk wanted his sister. I found them confined in one room. I went to the Kaimakam[3] and got an order for them all to come with us.

---

[1]A provincial governor.
[2]Armed rural police representing the Ottoman government.

[3]A district official.

At Kangal some Armenians had become Mo-hammedans, and had not left the village, but the others were all gone. . . . They said that a valley near there was full of corpses. At Kangal we also began to see exiles from Tokat. The sight was one to strike horror to any heart; they were a company of old women, who had been robbed of absolutely everything. At Tokat the Government had first imprisoned the men, and from the prison had taken them on the road. . . . After the men had gone, they arrested the old women and the older brides, perhaps about thirty or thirty-five years old. There were very few young women or children. All the younger women and children were left in Tokat. . . .

When we looked at them we could not imag-ine that even the sprinkling of men that were with us would be allowed to remain. We did not long remain in doubt; the next day we . . . had come to Hassan Tehelebi . . . and it was with terror in our hearts that we passed through that village about noon. But we encamped and ate our supper in peace, and even began to think that perhaps it was not so, when the Mudir [the official in charge] came round with gendarmes and began to collect the men. . . .

The night passed, and only one man came back to tell the story of how every man was compelled to give up all his money, and all were taken to prison. The next morning they col-lected the men who had escaped the night be-fore and extorted forty-five liras from our company, on the promise that they would give us gendarmes to protect us. One " company" is supposed to be from 1,000 to 3,000 persons. Ours was perhaps 2,000, and the greatest num-ber of gendarmes would be five or six. In addi-tion to these they sewed a red rag on the arm of a Kurdish villager[4] and gave him a gun, and he had the right to rob and bully us all he pleased.

Broken-hearted, the women continued their journey. . . .

As soon as the men left us, the Turkish drivers began to rob the women, saying: "You are all going to be thrown into the Tokma Su,[5] so you might as well give your things to us, and then we will stay by you and try to protect you." Every Turkish woman that we met said the same thing. The worst were the gendarmes, who really did more or less bad things. One of our schoolgirls was carried off by the Kurds twice, but her companions made so much fuss that she was brought back. . . .

As we approached the bridge over the Tokma Su, it was certainly a fearful sight. As far as the eye could see over the plain was this slow-moving line of ox-carts. For hours there was not a drop of water on the road, and the sun poured down its very hottest. As we went on we began to see the dead from yesterday's company, and the weak began to fall by the way. The Kurds working in the fields made attacks continually, and we were half-distracted. I piled as many as I could on our wagons, and our pupils, both boys and girls, worked like heroes. One girl took a baby from its dead mother and carried it until evening. Another carried a dying woman until she died. We bought water from the Kurds, not minding the beating that the boys were sure to get with it. I counted forty-nine deaths, but there must have been many more. One naked body of a woman was covered with bruises. I saw the Kurds robbing the bodies of those not yet entirely dead. . . .

The hills on each side were white with Kurds, who were throwing stones on the Arme-nians, who were slowly wending their way to the bridge. I ran ahead and stood on the bridge in the midst of a crowd of Kurds, until I was used up [exhausted]. I did not see anyone thrown into the water, but they said, and I be-lieve it, that a certain Elmas, who has done handwork for me for years, was thrown over the bridge by a Kurd. Our Badvelli's wife was

---

[4]Kurds were a Sunni Muslim people who lived in territory that today makes up parts of southeastern Turkey, north-west Iraq, and northeast Syria; the "red rag" was an arm band that gave the Kurds special status.

[5]A local river.

riding on a horse with a baby in her arms, and a Kurd took hold of her to throw her over, when another Kurd said: "She has a baby in her arms," and they let her go. . . .

The police for the first time began to interfere with me here, and it was evident that something was decided about me. The next morning after we arrived at this bridge, they wanted me to go to Malatia; but I insisted that I had permission to stay with the Armenians. During the day, however, they said that [I had been ordered] to come to Malatia, and that the others were going to Kiakhta. Soon after we heard that they were going to Ourfa, there to build villages and cities, &c.

In Malatia I went at once to the commandant, a captain who they say has made a fortune out of these exiles. I told him how I had gone to Erzeroum last winter, and how we pitied these women and children and wished to help them, and finally he sent me to the Mutessarif.[6] The latter is a Kurd, apparently anxious to do the right thing; but he has been sick most of the time since he came, and the "beys"[7] here have had things more or less

their own way, and certainly horrors have been committed. . . .

My friends here are very glad to have me with them, for they have a very difficult problem on their hands and are nearly crazy with the horrors they have been through here. The Mutessarif and other officials here and at Sivas have read me orders from Constantinople[8] again and again to the effect that the lives of these exiles are to be protected, and from their actions I should judge that they must have received such orders; but they certainly have murdered a great many in every city. Here there were great trenches dug by the soldiers for drilling purposes. Now these trenches are all filled up, and our friends saw carts going back from the city by night. A man I know told me that when he was out to inspect some work he was having done, he saw a dead body which had evidently been pulled out of one of these trenches, probably by dogs. . . . The Beledia Reis [village chief] here says that every male over ten years old is being murdered, that not one is to live, and no woman over fifteen. The truth seems to be somewhere between these two extremes. . . .

---

[6]A district official.
[7]Kurdish chiefs.
[8]Founded in 660 B.C.E. as Byzantium, the city was renamed Constantinople in 330 C.E. by Constantine the Great, and

served as the seat of the Ottoman government from the thirteenth century until after World War I. In 1930 Istanbul became the city's official name.

An Official Version of the Deportations

◈

22 ◆ *Talaat Pasha, POSTHUMOUS MEMOIRS*

At the conclusion of the war, foreign diplomats and officials of the Ottoman government and Great Britain declared their intention to punish the perpetrators of the Armenian genocide. Ottoman courts ordered the execution of two minor officials and one police officer, but other guilty parties were given prison sentences or convicted in absentia. Judicial proceedings were halted and all prisoners released when the Ottoman government was replaced by a new Turkish government under Mustafa Kemal in 1921. In that same year British efforts to try Turkish officials in British military courts, already bogged down by legal and political difficulties, also were abandoned. Throughout the process, efforts to punish those responsible were weakened by the fact that in November 1918 Turkey's wartime leaders fled the country with German help and hence could not be tried in person.

Among those who fled was Talaat Pasha (1874–1921), the Ottoman minister of the interior during the war. A former postal clerk and telegraph operator, he had risen rapidly in the Ottoman administration after the Young Turk Revolution of 1908. Although the precise lines of authority in the Ottoman government are murky, there is little question that Talaat Pahsa along with Enver Pasha (minister of war) and Kemal Pasha (navy minister and military governor of Syria) were the three key figures in the wartime administration. There is also little doubt that Talaat and Enver were mainly responsible for the government's Armenian policy. After he fled Turkey in 1918, Talaat lived in Europe until he was assassinated by an Armenian student in a Berlin suburb in 1921. The assassin was acquitted when a German court ruled that his act was justifiable homicide in view of Talaat's role in the 1915 massacres.

Before his death, Talaat had written a memoir that was unpublished at the time of his assassination. After his assassin's acquittal, Talaat's wife released the memoir to a Turkish newspaper. It was published in 1921 with the enigmatic opening words, "I do not tell all the truth, but all I tell is truth." In the following section he gives his perspective on the Armenian Question.

QUESTIONS FOR ANALYSIS

1. In what ways were the Armenians responsible for their deportation, according to Talaat Pasha?
2. How credible do you find Talaat's arguments about the Armenians' responsibility for their fate?
3. How would you characterize Talaat's portrayal of his role in the massacres? Does he admit any personal responsibility for the massacres?
4. Why in Talaat's view have the numbers of victims been exaggerated?
5. How and in what ways are Talaat's assertions confirmed or refuted by evidence provided in Graffam's letter?

The deportation of the Armenians, in some localities of the Greeks, and in Syria of some of the Arabs, was used inside and outside the empire as a source of attack on the Turkish Government. First of all, I wish to inform the public that the rumors of deportation and assassination were exceedingly exaggerated. The Greeks and the Armenians, taking advantage of the ignorance of the American and European public of the Near Eastern situation and of the character of the Turks, used the deportation as a means for propaganda, and painted it as best suited their

aim. In saying this, I do not mean to deny the facts. I desire only to eliminate the exaggerations and to relate the facts as they occurred.

I admit that we deported many Armenians from our eastern provinces, but we never acted in this matter upon a previously prepared scheme. The responsibility for these acts falls first of all upon the deported people themselves. Russia, in order to lay hand on our eastern provinces, had armed and equipped the Armenian inhabitants of this district, and had organized strong Armenian bandit forces in the said area. When we entered the great war, these bandits began their destructive activities in the rear of the Turkish Army on the Caucasus front, blowing up the bridges, setting fire to the Turkish towns and villages and killing the innocent Mohammedan[1] inhabitants, regardless of age and sex. They spread death and terror all over the eastern provinces, and endangered the Turkish Army's line of retreat. All these Armenian bandits were helped by the native Armenians. When they were pursued by the Turkish gendarmes, the Armenian villages were a refuge for them. When they needed help, the Armenian peasants around them, taking their arms hidden in their churches, ran to their aid. Every Armenian church, it was later discovered, was a depot of ammunition. In this disloyal way they killed more than 300,000 Mohammedans, and destroyed the communication of the Turkish Army with its bases.[2]

The information that we were receiving from the administrators of these provinces and from the commander of the Caucasian Army gave us details of the most revolting and barbarous activities of the Armenian bandits. It was impossible to shut our eyes to the treacherous acts of the Armenians, at a time when we were engaged in a war which would determine the fate of our country. Even if these actrocities had occurred in a time of peace, our Government would have been obliged to quell such outbreaks. The Porte,[3] acting under the same obligation, and wishing to secure the safety of its army and its citizens, took energetic measures to check these uprisings. The deportation of the Armenians was one of these preventive measures.

I admit also that the deportation was not carried out lawfully everywhere. In some places unlawful acts were committed. The already existing hatred among the Armenians and Mohammedans, intensified by the barbarous activities of the former, had created many tragic consequences. Some of the officials abused their authority, and in many places people took preventive measures into their own hands and innocent people were molested. I confess it. I confess, also, that the duty of the Government was to prevent these abuses and atrocities, or at least to hunt down and punish their perpetrators severely. In many places, where the property and goods of the deported people were looted, and the Armenians molested, we did arrest those who were responsible and punished them according to the law. I confess, however, that we ought to have acted more sternly, opened up a general investigation for the purpose of finding out all the promoters and looters and punished them severely. . . .

But we could not do that. Although we punished many of the guilty, most of them were untouched. These people, whom we might call outlaws, because of their unlawful attitude in disregarding the order of the Central Government, were divided into two classes. Some of them were acting under personal hatred, or for individual profit. Those who looted the goods of the deported Armenians were easily punishable and we punished them. But there was another group, who sincerely believed that the general interest of the community necessitated the punishment alike of those Armenians who massacred the guiltless Mohammedans and those who helped the Armenian bandits to endanger our national life. The Turkish elements here referred to were short-sighted, fanatic, and yet sincere in their belief. The public encouraged them, and they had the general approval behind them. They were numerous and strong. Their

---

[1]Muslim.

[2]That Armenians served in the Russian army is hardly remarkable because many Armenians were Russian subjects. Although it is true some Armenians sympathized with the Allies and hoped for Turkey's defeat, many thousands of Armenians fought in the Ottoman army. It is also true that many Armenians were armed, but this was mainly before the war and for self-defense. Blaming the Armenians for the death of three hundred thousand Turks is a wild exaggeration.

[3]The Porte, or Sublime Porte, is a term for the Ottoman government. It refers to the building that housed the high officials of the Ottoman state.

open and immediate punishment would have aroused great discontent among the people, who favored their acts. An endeavor to arrest and to punish all these promoters would have created anarchy in Anatolia at a time when we greatly needed unity. It would have been dangerous to divide the nation into two camps, when we needed strength to fight outside enemies. We did all that we could, but we preferred to post-pone the solution of our internal difficulties until after the defeat of our external enemies. . . .

These preventive measures were taken in every country during the war, but, while the regrettable results were passed over in silence in the other countries, the echo of our acts was heard the world over, because everybody's eyes were upon us.

◆

The Russian Revolution and the Beginnings of the Soviet State

Among the results of World War I, the downfall of Russia's tsarist regime and its replacement by a Marxist-inspired Bolshevik dictatorship is one of the most important. Tsar Nicholas II (r. 1894–1917), facing military defeat, defections within the army, and rioting in Petrograd, abdicated in March 1917, and the tsarist autocracy was replaced by a provisional government that would govern Russia until a constituent assembly could meet and devise a new constitution. Seven months later, the Bolsheviks wrested power from the Provisional Government and, after three years of civil war, established the world's first communist state.

Discontent had plagued Tsar Nicholas's reign from the start, but it intensified after 1905 when Russia's defeat in the Russo-Japanese War sparked a wave of strikes, rural violence, and demands for constitutional reform. The tsar responded with his October Manifesto, in which he promised a democratically elected parliament, or duma, and freedom of the press. Russians soon realized, however, that the tsar had no intention of abandoning control of such crucial areas as finance, defense, and ministerial appointment. Nor did he have any interest in working with recalcitrant parliaments. He dissolved the first two dumas and then changed the election rules in 1907 to disenfranchise workers, peasants, and his non-Russian subjects. His chief minister Peter Stolypin sought to hold things together by cracking down on dissidents and implementing modest reforms. Meanwhile Constitutional Democrats, Social Revolutionaries, Mensheviks, and Bolsheviks, although deeply divided on tactics and goals, plotted to achieve their one common purpose — the overthrow of the tsar's government.

It was a weak and tottering tsarist Russia that entered World War I in August 1914. Less than three years later it became the war's most significant political casualty.

Lenin's Call for Revolution

◆

23 ◆ Lenin, APRIL THESES

After Tsar Nicholas II's abdication on March 2, 1917 (according to the Russian calendar, which was thirteen days behind the Western calendar), an awkward political situation developed in which power was divided between the Provisional Government, backed mainly by Constitutional Democrats, and the Petrograd Soviet of Workers' Deputies, a council representing the Petrograd workers and soldiers. With its membership divided among Mensheviks, Social Revolutionaries, and a few Bolsheviks, the Petrograd Soviet exercised no political authority as such, but its broad support among workers meant that the Provisional Government could take no significant action without its support. With one agency of government, the Soviet, unwilling to rule, and the other, the Provisional Government, unable to, a *"dual power"* resulted in which effective government was impossible.

This was just the type of situation in which an intense, persuasive, ruthless, and single-minded revolutionary might be able to take control of events and achieve an outcome that matched his personal vision. Such a man was Vladimir Ilyich Ulyanov (1870–1924), better known by his adopted revolutionary name, Lenin. The son of a government official and a law school graduate, Lenin dedicated himself to revolution at an early age and was exiled to Siberia with other Marxists in 1895. After his release he left Russia and became a member of the Russian Social Democratic Labor Party. In 1903 he became the leader of the "majority men," or Bolsheviks, who, in opposition to the "minority men," or Mensheviks, demanded highly centralized party leadership, noncooperation with bourgeois liberals, and single-minded devotion to revolution.

Having spent World War I in exile in Switzerland, Lenin returned to Russia on April 3, 1917, with the help of the German army. He immediately sought to convince his fellow Bolsheviks to reject compromise with the Provisional Government and press forward toward a true socialist revolution. His rationale and goals were outlined in two Bolshevik Party meetings on April 4, and then printed on April 7 in the Bolshevik newspaper, *Pravda.* Officially titled " On the Tasks of the Proletariat in the Present Revolution," his proposals are better known as the "April Theses."

Although viewed as unrealistic by many Bolsheviks, Lenin's proposals were soon adopted by the Party. Seven months later Lenin achieved his goal when the Bolsheviks took power in late October and created the world's first Marxist state.

QUESTION FOR ANALYSIS

1. What is Lenin's attitude toward World War I? Under what circumstances would it be possible for him to support Russia's continuing involvement?
2. What unique circumstances exist in Russia, according to Lenin, that make it possible to envision a successful Bolshevik revolution?

3. What does Lenin see as the alternative to the Provisional Government?

4. How does Lenin hope to win over the peasants and greater numbers of workers to the Bolshevik side? What role will the Party play in this process?

1. In our attitude towards the war, which under the new government of Lvov[1] and Co. unquestionably remains on Russia's part a predatory imperialist war owing to the capitalist nature of that government, not the slightest concession to " revolutionary defencism"[2] is permissible. . . .

In view of the undoubted honesty of those broad sections of the mass believers in revolutionary defencism who accept the war only as a necessity, and not as a means of conquest, in view of the fact that they are being deceived by the bourgeoisie, it is necessary with particular thoroughness, persistence and patience to explain their error to them, to explain the inseparable connection existing between capital and the imperialist war, and to prove that without overthrowing capital *it is impossible* to end the war by a truly democratic peace, a peace not imposed by violence. . . .

The most widespread campaign for this view must be organised in the army at the front. . . .

2. The specific feature of the present situation in Russia is that the country is *passing* from the first stage of the revolution — which, owing to the insufficient class-consciousness and organization of the proletariat, placed power in the hands of the bourgeoisie — to its *second* stage which must place power in the hands of the proletariat and the poorest sections of the peasants. . . .

This peculiar situation demands of us an ability to adapt ourselves to the *special* conditions of Party work among unprecedentedly large masses of proletarians who have just awakened to political life.

3. No support for the Provisional Government; the utter falsity of all its promises should be made clear, particularly of those relating to the renunciation of annexations.[3] Exposure in place of the impermissible, illusion-breeding "demand" that *this* government, a government of capitalists, should *cease* to be an imperialist government. . . .

4. . . . The masses must be made to see that the Soviets of Workers' Deputies are the *only possible* form of revolutionary government, and that therefore our task is, as long as *this* government yields to the influence of the bourgeoisie, to present a patient, systematic, and persistent *explanation* of the errors of their tactics, an explanation especially adapted to the practical needs of the masses.

As long as we[4] are in the minority we carry on the work of criticizing and exposing errors and at the same time we preach the necessity of transferring the entire state power to the Soviets of Workers' Deputies, so that the people may overcome their mistakes by experience.

5. Not a parliamentary republic . . . — but a republic of Soviets of Workers', Agricultural Laborers' and Peasants' Deputies throughout the country, from top to bottom.

Abolition of the police, the army and the bureaucracy.

The salaries of all officials, all of whom are elective and displaceable at any time, not to exceed the average wage of a competent worker.

6. The weight of emphasis in the agrarian program to be shifted to the Soviets of Agricultural Laborers' Deputies.

Confiscation of all landed estates.

---

[1]Prince Georg Lvov (1861–1925) was a liberal aristocrat who served as prime minister of the Provisional Government until July 1917, when he was succeeded by Alexandr Kerensky.

[2]Lenin's phrase to describe the position of revolutionaries who supported Russia's involvement in the war.
[3]Territories conquered by Russia during World War I.
[4]The Bolsheviks.

Nationalization of *all* lands in the country, the land to be disposed of by the local Soviets of Agricultural Laborers' and Peasants' Deputies. The organization of separate Soviets of Deputies of Poor Peasants. The setting up of a model farm on each of the large estates . . . under the control of the Soviets of Agricultural Laborers' Deputies and for the public account.

7. The immediate amalgamation of all banks in the country into a single national bank, and the institution of control over it by the Soviet of Workers' Deputies.

8. It is not our *immediate* task to "introduce" socialism, but only to bring social production and the distribution of products at once under the *control* of the Soviets of Workers' Deputies.

9. Party tasks:
   a) Immediate convocation of a Party congress;
   b) Alteration of the Party Program, mainly:
      1) On the question of imperialism and the imperialist war;
      2) On our attitude towards the state and *our* demand for a "commune state";[5]
      3) Amendment of our out-of-date minimum program.[6]
   c) Change of the Party's name.[7]
10. A new International.[8]

We must take the initiative in creating a revolutionary International, an International against the *social-chauvinists* and against the "Centre." . . .

---

[5]In the wake of France's defeat in the Franco-Prussian War (1870–1871), a coalition of republicans, anarchists, socialists, and anticlericals proclaimed Paris a commune in March following national elections that returned a large majority of conservatives and monarchists to the French National Assembly. Government troops crushed the Commune in May, killing approximately twenty-five thousand. To Lenin the Commune was a precursor of proletarian revolution.
[6]A "minimum statement" that set forth the Party's short-term goals.
[7]Lenin believed that the name *Social Democrat* had been besmirched by the European Social Democratic parties that

had supported the war. His proposal that the Bolshevik Social Democrats should call themselves Communists was accepted in 1918.
[8]The International Workingmen's Association, or First International, was an organization founded in 1864 dedicated to the spread of socialism among workers' organizations. The Second International Workingmen's Association, founded in Paris in 1889, was a loose association of national socialist groups. Its annual meetings ceased when war broke out in 1914.

Forging the Soviet State

❖

24 ◆ *COMMUNIST DECREES AND LEGISLATION, 1917–1918*

On October 25, 1917, with the Bolsheviks in control of public buildings and other key points in Petrograd, Lenin confidently opened the Second Congress of Soviets with the words, "We shall now proceed to construct the Socialist order." As Lenin soon found out, building that new socialist order proved difficult. For one thing, while the Bolsheviks had a broad set of revolutionary aspirations for Russia, they had no blueprint for how to govern the country or how to restructure Russian society. Furthermore, the Bolsheviks were a minority party, as shown by the results of the elections for the Constituent Assembly in November 1917, which gave the Bolsheviks only 29 percent of the vote, as opposed to 58 percent for the

Social Revolutionaries. Finally, they faced formidable problems — a ruined economy, continuing involvement in World War I until March 1918, and civil war from 1918 to 1921.

Despite these challenges, the Bolsheviks had no choice but to plunge ahead. In their first year in power they issued hundreds of decrees that touched every aspect of Russian life and government, and initiated programs and policies that in some cases lasted until the Soviet Union's demise in 1991.

The following is a sample of the decrees issued by the Bolsheviks in 1917 and 1918. The *Decree on Land,* issued on October 26 by the Second Congress of Soviets only hours after the Bolsheviks seized power, recognized land seizures that peasants had already carried out.

The *Decree on Suppression of Hostile Newspapers* and the *Decree Dissolving the Constituent Assembly* were two important steps toward one-party dictatorship. The Bolsheviks, both before and after seizing power, had supported convening a popularly elected Constituent Assembly. But the election of November 1917 resulted in only 168 Bolshevik deputies out of 703 and a clear Social Revolutionary majority. The Assembly convened on January 5, 1918, only to be dissolved by the Bolsheviks on January 7. It was the Soviet Union's last democratically elected parliament until 1989.

The *Edict on Child Welfare,* issued in January 1918, was the brainchild of Alexandra Kollontai (1873–1952), a leading Social Democrat who fled Russia in 1908 to escape arrest and, like Lenin, returned to Petrograd after the downfall of the tsar's government. She became a member of the executive committee of the Petrograd Soviet and played a leading role in the events leading up to the Bolshevik coup. As commissioner of social welfare under the Bolsheviks, she was responsible for laws that legalized abortion, liberalized marriage and divorce, and granted women equal standing with men.

The *Decree on Nationalization of Large-Scale Industries* was issued in June 1918 after the beginning of the civil war. Until then, industry had remained under private ownership, supposedly subject to "workers' control." Now it was nationalized without compensation to the owners.

QUESTION FOR ANALYSIS

1. What rationale is provided in these documents for the "undemocratic" steps taken by the Bolsheviks to dissolve the Constituent Assembly and close down hostile newspapers?
2. What are the economic ramifications of the decrees on land use and nationalization of industry? Who benefits and who is hurt?
3. How will these decrees change essential features of Russian society and social relationships?
4. How do the policies outlined in these decrees compare to the platform adopted by the Russian Social Democrats in 1903 (see "A Marxist Blueprint for Russia" on page 43)?
5. In what specific ways do these decrees increase the role of the state? What implications might this have for the Soviet Union's future?

DECREE ON LAND, OCTOBER 26, 1917

"1) *Private ownership of land shall be abolished forever* . . .

   All land . . . *shall be alienated without compensation* and become the property of the whole people, and pass into the use of all those who cultivate it. . . .

2) All mineral wealth, e.g., ore, oil, coal, salt, etc., as well as all forests and waters of state importance, shall pass into the exclusive use of the state. All the small streams, lakes, woods, etc., shall pass into the use of the communities, to be administered by the local self-government bodies.

3) Lands on which *high-level scientific* farming is practised, e.g., orchards, plantations, seed plots, nurseries, hot-houses, etc. *shall not be divided up, but shall be converted into model farms,* to be turned over for exclusive use *to the state or to the communities,* depending on the size and importance of such lands. . . .

6) The right to use the land shall be accorded to all citizens of the Russian state (without distinction of sex) desiring to cultivate it by their own labor, with the help of their families, or in partnership, but only as long as they are able to cultivate it. . . .

DECREE ON SUPPRESSION OF HOSTILE NEWSPAPERS, OCTOBER 27, 1917

Everyone knows that the bourgeois press is one of the most powerful weapons of the bourgeoisie. Especially in this critical moment when the new authority, that of the workers and peasants, is in process of consolidation, it was impossible to leave this weapon in the hands of the enemy at a time when it is not less dangerous than bombs and machine guns. This is why temporary and extraordinary measures have been adopted for the purpose of cutting off the stream of mire and calumny in which the . . . press would be glad to drown the young victory of the people.

As soon as the new order will be consolidated, all administrative measures against the press will be suspended; full liberty will be given it within the limits of responsibility before the laws, in accordance with the broadest and most progressive regulations in this respect. . . .

DECREE DISSOLVING THE CONSTITUENT ASSEMBLY, JANUARY 7, 1918

The October Revolution, by giving the power to the Soviets, and through the Soviets to the toiling and exploited classes, aroused the desperate resistance of the exploiters, and in the crushing of this resistance it fully revealed itself as the beginning of the socialist revolution. The toiling classes learnt by experience that the old bourgeois parliamentarism had outlived its purpose and was absolutely incompatible with the aim of achieving Socialism, and that not national institutions, but only class institutions (such as the soviets), were capable of overcoming the resistance of the propertied classes and of laying the foundations of a socialist society. To relinquish the sovereign power of the soviets, to relinquish the Soviet republic won by the people, for the sake of bourgeois parliamentarism and the Constituent Assembly, would now be a retrograde step and cause the collapse of the October workers' and peasants' revolution. . . .

   The Right Socialist Revolutionary and Menshevik parties are in fact waging outside the walls of the Constituent Assembly a most desperate struggle against the Soviet power, calling openly in their press for its overthrow and characterizing as arbitrary and unlawful the crushing by force of the resistance of the exploiters by the toiling classes, which is essential in the interests of emancipation from exploitation. They are defending the saboteurs, the servitors of capital, and are going to the length of undisguised calls to terrorism, which certain "unidentified groups" have already begun to practice. It is obvious that under such circumstances the remaining part of the Constituent Assembly could only serve as a screen for the struggle of the counterrevolutionaries to overthrow the Soviet power.

Accordingly, the Central Executive Committee resolves: The Constituent Assembly is hereby dissolved.

EDICT ON CHILD WELFARE, JANUARY 1918

After a search that has lasted centuries, human thought has at last discovered the radiant epoch where the working class, with its own hands, can freely construct that form of maternity protection which will preserve the child for the mother and the mother for the child. . . .

The new Soviet Russia calls all you working women, you working mothers with your sensitive hearts, you bold builders of a new social life, you teachers of the new attitudes, you children's doctors and midwives, to devote your minds and emotions to building the great edifice that will provide social protection for future generations. From the date of publication of this decree, all large and small institutions under the commissariat of social welfare that serve the child, from the children's home in the capital to the modest village creche,[1] shall be merged into one government organization and placed under the department for the protection of maternity and childhood. As an integral part of the total number of institutions connected with pregnancy and maternity, they shall continue to fulfil the single common task of creating citizens who are strong both mentally and physically. . . .

For the rapid elaboration and introduction of the reforms necessary for the protection of childhood in Russia, commissions are being organized under the auspices of the departments of maternity and childhood. . . . The commissions must base their work on the following main principles:

1. The preservation of the mother for the child: milk from the mother's breast is invaluable for the child.
2. The child must be brought up in the enlightened and understanding atmosphere provided by the socialist family.
3. Conditions must be created which permit the development of the child's physical and mental powers and the child's keen comprehension of life.

DECREE ON NATIONALIZATION OF LARGE-SCALE INDUSTRIES, JUNE 28, 1918

For the purpose of combating decisively the economic disorganization and the breakdown of the food supply, and of establishing more firmly the dictatorship of the working class and the village poor, the Soviet of People's Commissars has resolved:

1. To declare all of the following industrial and commercial enterprises which are located in the Soviet Republic, with all their capital and property, whatever they may consist of, the property of the Russian Socialist Federated Soviet Republic. [A long list of mines, mills, and factories follows.]
2. The administration of the nationalized industries shall be organized . . . by the different departments of the Supreme Council of National Economy. . . .
4. Beginning with the promulgation of this decree, the members of the administration, the directors, and other responsible officers of the nationalized industries will be held responsible to the Soviet Republic both for the intactness and upkeep of the business and for its proper functioning. . . .
5. The entire personnel of every enterprise — technicians, workers, members of the board of directors, and foremen — shall be considered employees of the Russian Socialist

---

[1] A day nursery.

Federated Soviet Republic; their wages shall be fixed in accordance with the scales existing at the time of nationalization and shall be paid out of the funds of the respective enterprises. . . .

6. All private capital belonging to members of the boards of directors, stockholders, and

owners of the nationalized enterprises will be attached pending the determination of the relation of such capital to the turnover capital and resources of the enterprises in question. . . .

◆

The Peace That Failed

On January 19, 1919, thousands of diplomats, ministers, journalist, and observers gathered in Paris for the first session of the peace conference that was to reorder the world after World War I. Participants included delegates from the thirty-two nations that had been on the winning side, observers from the defeated Central Powers, and spokespersons of numerous religious and ethnic groups — Arabs, Egyptians, Kurds, Irish, Zionists, Persians, Indians, Vietnamese, Africans, African-Americans, and Armenians. Women's organizations and even supporters of the tsarist cause in Russia also were represented.

By May the Paris Peace Conference had completed the treaty dealing with Germany, the Treaty of Versailles, which the Germans grudgingly signed on June 28, 1919. The Conference also produced broad outlines of treaties to be completed later for Austria, Hungary, Bulgaria, and Ottoman Turkey. No one was entirely happy, and many were deeply angry, with the results. Negative feelings intensified in the 1920s and 1930s as the world stumbled toward another, more terrible world war, the prevention of which had been one of the treaty writers' major goals.

The postwar treaties were largely the work of just three leaders: Prime Minister Georges Clemenceau of France, Lloyd George of Great Britain, and President Woodrow Wilson of the United States. A year earlier, in January 1918, Wilson had issued his famous Fourteen Points, a document that many assumed would be the basis of the postwar treaties. Wilson called for open diplomacy, free trade, reduced armies, and national self-determination in Europe. Although Germany would be required to return Alsace-Lorraine to France and abandon conquered territories in Russia and Belgium, there was no talk of harshly punishing Germany or blocking "in any way her legitimate influence and power." Colonial claims were to be "readjusted," in a process in which "the interests of the populations concerned must have equal weight with the equitable claims of the government whose title is being determined." Finally, Wilson called for the founding of a "general association of nations" whose purpose was to preserve peace and guarantee the political integrity of great and small nations alike.

Lloyd George and especially Clemenceau had different agendas. Clemenceau wanted to protect French security by weakening and punishing Germany. Lloyd George was more flexible, but whatever moderate inclinations he might have had were outweighed by his recent election promises to "hang the emperor" and "squeeze the German lemon until the pips squeak." Neither leader was interested in considering the opinions of Africans and Asians in "readjusting colonial claims."

Divided by personal and philosophical conflicts, saddled by conflicting claims and promises, and subject to intense political pressures, the peacemakers faced issues of daunting complexity. In just a few months they were expected to solve political problems around the globe, which had they been addressed one by one without undue pressure still would have taxed fully their wisdom and foresight. Mistakes and blunders were made, and it is easy to understand why. Understanding them makes them no less tragic.

The Allies' "Last Horrible Triumph"

❖

25 ◆ COMMENTS OF THE GERMAN DELEGATION TO THE PARIS PEACE CONFERENCE ON THE CONDITIONS OF PEACE, OCTOBER 1919

The Germans had expected to win the Great War but had lost. In defeat they had expected to be treated with justice and moderation, and again they were bitterly disappointed. The new democratic German government was excluded from the Paris Peace Conference, and when it received a draft of the treaty in late April, 1919, it responded with a list of complaints and counterproposals. All but a few of them were rejected. Germany's chancellor Philip Scheidemann resigned, saying, "What hand would not wither when it signed such a treaty?" The German National Assembly voted in June to accept the treaty but with two reservations: It rejected the claim that Germany was solely responsible for the war and the provision that the kaiser and other high officials were to be tried as war criminals. The Allies dismissed their complaints, and demanded a positive reply in twenty-four hours. Threatened with invasion, the assembly accepted the treaty as written. It was signed on June 28, 1919, and German humiliation was complete.

Germany lost all of its colonies, 13 percent of its land, and 10 percent of its population. Alsace and Lorraine, won from France in 1871, were returned to France. Northern Schleswig went to Denmark, parts of Posen and West Prussia went to Poland, while smaller bits of territory went to Belgium and Czechoslovakia. The coal mines of the Saar Basin were given to France for fifteen years, at which time the German government could buy them back; the Saar region itself was to be administered by the League of Nations. East Prussia was cut off from the rest of Germany by territory ceded to Poland, and the largely German port of Danzig on the Baltic Sea came under Polish economic control. The Germans were permitted to have no air force, a navy of approximately two dozen ships, and a volunteer army of no more than one hundred thousand officers and men. Article 231, the "war-guilt" clause, held Germany and its allies responsible for causing the war. On the basis of this claim, Germany was held accountable for all Allied losses and damages, and would be required to pay reparations. In 1921 the sum was set at $33 billion.

On the day the treaty was signed, the nationalist newspaper *Deutsche Zeitung* published the following statement on its front page:

> Vengeance! German nation! Today in the Hall of Mirrors the disgraceful treaty is being signed. Do not forget it! . . . The German people will with unceasing labor, press forward to reconquer the place among nations to which it is entitled. Then will come vengeance for the shame of 1919!

Few Germans did not harbor such sentiments somewhere in their hearts during the 1920s. Nationalist and antidemocratic politicians learned how to play on these resentments, and in so doing undermined the democratic government that had signed the treaty. Of those politicians, the most successful was Adolf Hitler, whose Nazis took power in 1933 and immediately set out to destroy the Versailles settlement.

The reasons for German resentment are spelled out in the following comments and observations. They were submitted in October 1919 by the German delegation to the Paris Peace Conference, which continued to meet after the signing of the Versailles Treaty until January 21, 1920.

QUESTIONS FOR ANALYSIS

1. In Germany's view, how would the country have been treated differently if the principles they attribute to President Wilson had been applied?
2. What does the document reveal about the difficulty of applying the principle of ethnic self-determination in Europe?
3. To what higher "fundamental" laws does the document appeal to in order to strengthen German assertions?
4. What view of colonialism is expressed in the document? Why do the authors claim that Germany has a right to its colonies?
5. According to the authors of the German complaint, how will various provisions of the treaty hurt Germany's economy?
6. Do you agree with the authors of the document that Germany was being poorly treated? What response to their complaints might defenders of the treaty have made?

Although President Wilson, in his speech of October 20th, 1916, has acknowledged that "no single fact caused the war, but that in the last analysis the whole European system is in a deeper sense responsible for the war, with its combination of alliances and understandings, a complicated texture of intrigues and espionage that unfailingly caught the whole family of nations in its meshes," . . . Germany is to acknowledge that Germany and her allies are responsible for all damages which the enemy Governments or their subjects have incurred by her and her allies' aggression. . . . Apart from the consideration that there is no incontestable legal foundation for the obligation for reparation imposed upon Germany, the amount of such compensation is to be determined by a commission nominated solely by Germany's enemies, Germany taking no part. . . . The commission is plainly to have power to administer Germany like the estate of a bankrupt.[1]

As there are innate rights of man, so there are innate rights of nations. The inalienable fundamental right of every state is the right of self-preservation and self-determination. With this fundamental right the demand here made upon Germany is incompatible. Germany must promise to pay an indemnity, the amount of which at present is not even stated. The German rivers are to be placed under the control of an international body upon which Germany's delegates are always to be but the smallest minority. Canals and railroads are to be built on German territory at the discretion of foreign authorities.

These few instances show that that is not the just peace we were promised, not the peace "the very principle of which," according to a word of President Wilson, "is equality and the common participation in a common benefit. . . ."

In such a peace the solidarity of human interests, which was to find its expression in a League of Nations, would have been respected. How often Germany has been given the promise that this League of Nations would unite the belligerents, conquerors as well as conquered, in a permanent system of common rights! . . .

. . . But in contradiction to them, the Covenant of the League of Nations has been framed without the cooperation of Germany. Nay, still more. Germany does not even stand on the list of those States that have been invited to join the League of Nations. . . . What the treaty of peace proposes to establish, is rather a continuance of the present hostile coalition which does not deserve the name of "League of Nations." . . . The old political system based on force and with its tricks and rivalries will thus continue to thrive!

Again and again the enemies of Germany have assured the whole world that they did not aim at the destruction of Germany. . . .

In contradiction to this, the peace document shows that Germany's position as a world power is to be utterly destroyed. The Germans abroad are deprived of the possibility of keeping up their old relations in foreign countries and of regaining for Germany a share in world commerce, while their property, which has up to the present been confiscated and liquidated, is being used for reparation instead of being restored to them. . . .

In this war, a new fundamental law has arisen which the statesmen of all belligerent peoples have again and again acknowledged to be their aim: the right of self-determination. To make it possible for all nations to put this privilege into practice was intended to be one achievement of the war. . . .

Neither the treatment described above of the inhabitants of the Saar[2] region as accessories to the [coal] pits nor the public form of consulting the population in the districts of Eupen, Malmédy and Prussian Moresnet[3] — which, moreover, shall not take place before they have been put under Belgian sovereignty — comply in the least with such a solemn recognition of the right of self-determination.

The same is also true with regard to Alsace-Lorraine. If Germany has pledged herself "to right the wrong of 1871," this does not mean any renunciation of the right of self-determination of the inhabitants of Alsace-Lorraine. A cession of the country without consulting the population

---

[1]A Reparations Commission appointed by the Peace Conference set the final sum at $33 billion in 1921. In the meantime Germany was required to make an interim payment of $5 billion.

[2]After fifteen years, the people of the Saar would have a plebiscite to decide if they would remain under the administration of a League of Nations commission or become part of France or Germany. In 1935 they voted to become part of Germany.

[3]Moresnet, an area of some fourteen hundred acres and the site of a valuable zinc mine, was annexed outright by Belgium. In Eupen and Malmédy, those who objected to the transfer of the areas to Belgium could sign their names in a public registry. On the basis of this "plebiscite," both areas became Belgian.

would be a new wrong, if for no other reason, because it would be inconsistent with a recognized principle of peace.

On the other hand, it is incompatible with the idea of national self-determination for two and one-half million Germans to be torn away from their native land against their own will. By the proposed demarcation of the boundary, unmistakably German territories are disposed of in favor of their Polish neighbors. Thus, from the Central Silesian districts of Guhrau and Militsch certain portions are to be wrenched away, in which, beside 44,900 Germans, reside at the utmost 3,700 Poles. . . .

This disrespect of the right of self-determination is shown most grossly in the fact that Danzig[4] is to be separated from the German Empire and made a free state. Neither historical rights nor the present ethnographical conditions of ownership of the Polish people can have any weight as compared with the German past and the German character of that city. . . . Likewise the cession of the commercial town of Memel, which is to be exacted from Germany, is in no way consistent with the right of self-determination. The same may be said with reference to the fact that millions of Germans in German-Austria are to be denied the union with Germany which they desire and that, further, millions of Germans dwelling along our frontiers are to be forced to remain part of the newly created Czecho-Slovakian State.

Even as regards that part of the national territory that is to be left to Germany, the promised right of self-determination is not observed. A Commission for the execution of the indem-

nity[5] shall be the highest instance for the whole State. Our enemies claim to have fought for the great aim of the democratization of Germany. To be sure, the outcome of the war has delivered us from our former authorities, but instead of them we shall have in exchange a foreign, dictatorial power whose aim can and must be only to exploit the working power of the German people for the benefit of the creditor states. . . .

The fact that this is an age in which economic relations are on a world scale, requires the political organization of the civilized world. The German Government agrees with the Governments of the Allied and Associated Powers in the conviction that the horrible devastation caused by this war requires the establishment of a new world order, an order which shall insure the "effective authority of the principles of international law," and "just and honorable relations between the nations." . . .

There is no evidence of these principles in the peace document which has been laid before us. Expiring world theories, emanating from imperialistic and capitalistic tendencies, celebrate in it their last horrible triumph. As opposed to these views, which have brought unspeakable disaster upon the world, we appeal to the innate sense of right of men and nations, under whose token the English State developed, the Dutch People freed itself, the North American nation established its independence, France shook off absolutism. The bearers of such hallowed traditions cannot deny this right to the German people, that now for the first time has acquired in its internal polities the possibility of living in harmony with its free will based on law.

---

[4]Danzig was administered by the League of Nations, but its economy would be controlled by Poland.

[5]This concern was well-founded. After the Germans fell behind in their payments in 1923, the French-controlled

Reparations Commission ordered French, Belgian, and Italian technicians into Germany's Ruhr region to collect coal and transport it to the border under military protection.

The Betrayal of Arab Nationalism

◆

26 ◆ *GENERAL SYRIAN CONGRESS OF DAMASCUS, RESOLUTION OF JULY 2, 1919*

Lured by Great Britain's promises of an independent Arab state, Arabs under Sharif Husayn (1856–1931), the ruler of the western lands of the Arabian Peninsula, revolted against the Ottomans in 1916. In 1918, with the end of the war and the defeat of Ottoman Empire, the Arabs looked forward to self-rule.

At the Paris Peace Conference, however, it became apparent that the British and French had no interest in "adjusting colonial claims" or honoring wartime promises to the Arabs. Instead, they planned to divide the Arab Middle East between them, as they had agreed to do during the war. This troubled Woodrow Wilson, who proposed in March 1919 that a commission of inquiry composed of U.S., British, French, and Italian representatives visit the Middle East to gather information so that a settlement could be achieved on the "most scientific basis." The French, British, and Italians refused to cooperate, however, so the commission became a U.S. undertaking, led by educator Henry C. King and industrialist and diplomat Charles R. Crane.

By the time the commission began its inquiry in the summer of 1919, the fate of the region had been sealed by Article 22 of the League of Nations Covenant, which was part of the Versailles Treaty. Article 22 decreed that Germany's former colonies and the Arab regions of the defunct Ottoman Empire were to become League of Nations mandates administered by Great Britain, France, Japan, Australia, and South Africa. The whole system was correctly viewed as a thinly disguised version of old-style colonialism.

Faced with the prospect of French or British rule and in anticipation of the King-Crane Commission's visit, Syrian nationalists called a congress, also attended by Palestinian and Lebanese delegates, and adopted the following resolution on July 2, 1919. The King-Crane Commission included the resolution in its report, but Britain and France ignored it and proceeded with their plans to establish mandates. In March 1920, a second Syrian congress proclaimed Syrian independence, but the new state, which included Palestine and Lebanon, lasted only four months. In July 1920, the French easily crushed the Syrian army, whose ammunition ran out after only a few hours of fighting. On July 25, 1920, the French entered Damascus, ushering in two decades of turbulent French rule.

QUESTIONS FOR ANALYSIS

1. In what ways and for what reasons does the resolution reject the premises of Article 22 of the League of Nations Covenant?
2. How do the delegates envision the mandate system, if forced to accept it?
3. How does the resolution distinguish between Zionists and Jews already residing in Palestine?

4. Why did the delegates prefer the United States as the nation to offer Syria economic and technical aid?

5. All of the resolutions except resolution 5 were accepted unanimously at the congress. Why do you think it was the exception?

We the undersigned members of the General Syrian Congress, meeting in Damascus on Wednesday, July 2nd, 1919 . . . provided with credentials and authorizations by the inhabitants of our various districts, Muslims, Christians, and Jews, have agreed upon the following statement of the desires of the people of the country who have elected us to present them to the American Section of the International Commission; the fifth article was passed by a very large majority; all the other articles were accepted unanimously.

1. We asked absolutely complete political independence for Syria within these boundaries. The Taurus System on the North; Rafah and a line running from Al Jauf to the south of the Syrian and the Hejazian line to Akaba on the south; the Euprates and Khabur Rivers and a line extending east of Abu Kamal to the east of Al Jauf on the east; and the Mediterranean of the west.[1]

2. We ask that the Government of this Syrian country should be a democratic civil constitutional Monarchy on broad decentralization principles, safeguarding the rights of minorities, and that the King be the Emir Feisal, who carried on a glorious struggle in the cause of our liberation and merited our full confidence and entire reliance.[2]

3. Considering the fact that the Arabs inhabiting the Syrian area are not naturally less [capable] than other more advanced races and that they are by no means less developed than the Bulgarians, Serbians, Greeks, and Romanians at the beginning of their independence, we protest against Article 22 of the Covenant

of the League of Nations, placing us among the nations in their middle stage of development which stand in need of a mandatory power.

4. In the event of the rejection by the Peace Conference of this just protest for certain considerations that we may not understand, we, relying on the declarations of President Wilson that his object in waging war was to put an end to the ambition of conquest and colonization, can only regard the mandate mentioned in the Covenant of the League of Nations as equivalent to the rendering of economical and technical assistance that does not prejudice our complete independence. And desiring that our country should not fall a prey to colonization and believing that the American Nation is farthest from any thought of colonization and has no political ambition in our country, we will seek the technical and economical assistance from the United States of America, provided that such assistance does not exceed 20 years.

5. In the event of America not finding herself in a position to accept our desire for assistance, we will seek this assistance from Great Britain, also provided that such assistance does not infringe the complete independence and unity of our country and that the duration of such assistance does not exceed that mentioned in the previous article.

6. We do not acknowledge any right claimed by the French Government in any part whatever of our Syrian country and refuse that she should assist us or have a hand in our country under any circumstances and in any place.

7. We oppose the pretentions of the Zionists to create a Jewish commonwealth in the

---

[1]The region described includes today's states of Syria, Lebanon, Israel, and Jordan.

[2]Prince Feisal (also spelled *Feysel* and *Faysal*), the son of

Sharif Husayn, was an Arab military hero in the Anglo-Arab struggle against the Turks. After the French drove him from Syria in 1920, the British installed him as king of Iraq.

southern part of Syria, known as Palestine, and oppose Zionist migration to any part of our country; for we do not acknowledge their title but consider them a grave peril to our people from the national, economical, and political points of view. Our Jewish compatriots shall enjoy our common rights and assume the common responsibilities.

8. We ask that there should be no separation of the southern part of Syria, known as Palestine, nor of the littoral western zone, which includes Lebanon, from the Syrian country. We desire that the unity of the country should be guaranteed against partition under whatever circumstances.

9. We ask complete independence for emancipated Mesopotamia[3] and that there should be no economic barriers between the two countries.

10. The fundamental principles laid down by President Wilson in condemnation of secret treaties impel us to protest most emphatically against any treaty that stipulates the partition of our Syrian country and against any private engagement aiming at the estab-

lishment of Zionism in the southern part of Syria; therefore we ask the complete annulment of these conventions and agreements.[4]

The noble principles enunciated by President Wilson[5] strengthen our confidence that our desires emanating from the depths of our hearts, shall be the decisive factor in determining our future; and that President Wilson and the free American people will be our supporters for the realization of our hopes, thereby proving their sincerity and noble sympathy with the aspiration of the weaker nations in general and our Arab people in particular.

We also have the fullest confidence that the Peace Conference will realize that we would not have risen against the Turks, with whom we had participated in all civil, political, and representative privileges, but for their violation of our national rights, and so will grant us our desires in full in order that our political rights may not be less after the war than they were before, since we have shed so much blood in the cause of our liberty and independence.

---

[3]The region of modern Iraq.
[4]The passage refers to the Balfour Declaration of 1916, in which Great Britain pledged its support for a Jewish state in Palestine, and the Sykes-Picot Agreement of 1916, in

which Great Britain and France agreed to divide former Ottoman territories between them.
[5]Wilson's Fourteen Points.

The Chinese May Fourth Movement and the Versailles Treaty

◆

27 ◆ *Deng Yingchao, MEMOIRS*

By the mid-1910s, the dreams of Chinese revolutionaries who had toppled the Qing Dynasty and founded a republic in 1911 and 1912 had turned to dust. Sun Yat-sen, the intellectual father of the revolution, resigned his presidency in 1912 after serving only one month. His successor, General Yuan Shikai, undermined the deliberations of the parliament elected to write a constitution, outlawed Sun Yat-sen's political party, the Guomindang, and by late 1915 was preparing to have himself elevated to the position of emperor. With the central government bankrupt and the country falling under the control of local warlords, the Japanese seized German concessions in Shandong province at the beginning of World War I, and in 1915 presented China with the Twenty-One Demands. They demanded that China recognize their political and economic ascendancy in Shandong, Manchuria, and Inner Mongolia; grant a number of economic concessions; and accept Japanese advisors in its ministries of police, the military, and finance. Militarily impotent and dependent on Japanese loans, the government successfully resisted Japanese demands to place advisors in its ministries, but otherwise acquiesced.

Although it had no army or navy capable of fighting, China entered World War I in August 1917 on the Allied side, mainly to gain an advantage in the post-war peace negotiations. In the following months, some one hundred thousand Chinese arrived in Europe after crossing the Pacific to Canada, traveling across Canada by train, and finally shipping across the Atlantic. In France and Belgium they built roads and docks, dug trenches, and worked in factories and munitions dumps. Two thousand Chinese perished in Europe, and another 543 died when their ship was sunk in transit.

When the Chinese delegation left for the Paris Peace Conference, the Chinese had high hopes that China would regain control of Shandong province and perhaps win other concessions. But the treaty writers rejected every Chinese claim and plea. When the news reached China, it sparked the May Fourth Movement, an outburst of public anger, nationalism, and reforming zeal that opened new possibilities for Chinese culture and politics in the 1920s and 1930s.

The following memoir describes the events of May 4, 1919 and their background and their influence on subsequent political and cultural movements. It was written by Deng Yinchao (1904–1992), who at the time was a student in Tianjin, a city in Hebei province some seventy-five miles east of Beijing. She soon joined the Communist Party, married Zhou Enlai, later foreign minister of the Peoples' Republic of China, and remained active in Party affairs until her death in 1992.

QUESTIONS FOR ANALYSIS

1. The students originally demonstrated over the Versailles Treaty, but quickly moved on to other issues. What were these other issues and how were they connected with the treaty?
2. What attitude did the participants in the May Fourth Movement have toward the West?
3. What methods did the students utilize to spread their ideas among the people? How effective were they?
4. What effect did the May Fourth Movement have on Chinese feminism?

On May 4, 1919, the students in Beijing staged a massive demonstration, demanding the punishment of traitors and the rejection of the Versailles Peace Treaty. In a moment of extreme anger, they burned down [a residential building] and beat up many traitors. The news of this demonstration reached Tianjin the next day, shaking the façade of complacency to its very foundation. Students gathered in groups to discuss the Beijing demonstration, and it was decided that we should not hesitate for a moment in rallying behind our Beijing compatriots in this patriotic movement. On May 7 the Tianjin students staged a demonstration of their own, and shortly afterwards such organizations as the Association of Tianjin Students and the Association of Patriotic Women in Tianjin came into existence. Most members of the latter organization were actually women students. . . . Simple and uncomplicated, we relied heavily on our selfless patriotism for our strength. Besides the two slogans previously mentioned, we also called for the abolition of the Twenty-One Demands, the return of Qingdao,[1] the boycott of Japanese goods, the use of Chinese goods only, and, most important of all, "We are determined that we shall not be slaves to any foreigners in our own country."

At that time the government was in the hands of the Peiyang warlords who responded to the students' patriotic movement with suppression and employed such methods as secret informers, bayonets, bullets, high-pressured water hoses, clubs, and massive arrests to carry out their policy of oppression. Like a piece of steel, we were tempered with fire during this period of struggle and gradually raised our own level of political consciousness. Keep in mind that the May Fourth Movement occurred at the end of World War I when new cultures and new ideas rushed into old China like a roaring torrent. These new cultures and new ideas, plus the knowledge of the successful October Revolution in Russia made a deep impression on every youth of China. Not surprisingly, young people played a most important and most progressive role in the May Fourth Movement; it was they who pushed the movement ahead and enabled it to continue to advance. . . .

. . . Nevertheless, our own intuition told us that a patriotic movement, to be effective, had to be more than just a students' movement and that we had to awaken all of our brethren for the attainment of a common goal. We therefore stressed the importance of propaganda work. Many oratorical teams were organized, and I was elected captain of speakers for the Associa-

tion of Patriotic Women as well as head of the oratorical division for the Association of Tianjin Students. My duty was to provide speakers in different areas on a regular basis.

At the beginning we, as female students, did not enjoy the same freedom of movement as our male counterparts, insofar as our speaking tours were concerned. According to the feudal custom of China, women were not supposed to make speeches in the street; we, therefore, had to do our work indoors. We gave speeches in such places as libraries and participated in scheduled debates, all inside a hall or room. The audience was large and responsive in each of these meeting, as we emphasized the duty of everyone to save our country and the necessity of punishing those who sold out our country to the enemy. Many speakers broke down when they spoke of the sufferings of the Koreans under the Japanese rule, the beatings of the Beijing students by the secret police, and our inherent right to assembly for patriotic purposes. Needless to say, the audience was greatly moved by speakers of this kind.

Besides making speeches, we also conducted house-to-house visits which often took us to more remote areas of the city and also to the slums. Some of the families we visited received us warmly, while others slammed their doors in our faces before we could utter a single word. In the latter case we simply moved on to the next house instead of being discouraged. . . .

In addition to speaking tours and house-to-house visits, we also paid great attention to the use of written words as a means of spreading the patriotic sentiments. The Association of Tianjin Students published a journal which started as a half-weekly but became a daily shortly afterwards. . . .

On October 10, 1919, the various patriotic organizations in Tianjin sponsored an all-citizen congress, in which the participants would demand the punishment of [officials who were traitors], the boycott of Japanese goods, and the

---

[1]A port city in the German concession in Shandong province occupied by the Japanese early in World War I.

exercise of such inalienable rights as those of free speech and demonstrations. Before the congress was called into session, we received information that Yang Yide (nicknamed Gangster Yang), the police commissioner of Tianjin, was ready to use force to dissolve the congress if it were held and to disperse any crowd gathered for the purpose of staging a demonstration. . . .

As had been expected, the police, with fixed bayonets, quickly moved in to surround us as soon as the meeting began. . . . Not until the meeting was over and the march began did they clash with us. Steadily they closed in, as our vanguards proceeded to march forward. . . .

We shouted loudly, trying desperately to convert brutal police into compassionate patriots. But the police refused to be converted as they hit us with rifle butts and systematically broke the eyeglasses of many students. In retaliation we hit them with bamboo placards and knocked hats from their heads. When they bent down to pick up their hats, we pushed forward so as to continue our march.

. . . We marched through the city streets until we finally arrived at police headquarters. We demanded to see commissioner Yang and protested against his brutality toward the students. Not until dawn the next day did we finally disperse and proceed home.

Angered by the October Tenth Incident as described above, we female students in Tianjin decided that no longer did we wish to honor the feudal custom of China and that we, female students in Tianjin, had as much right to speak in the street as our male counterparts. The very next day we began to make speeches in the street. From street to street and before one audience after another, we condemned commissioner Yang for having committed brutality against the students.

In the wake of the May Fourth Movement came the feminist movement which was in fact one of its democratic extensions. Among the demands we raised at that time were sexual equality, abolition of arranged marriage, social activities open to women students, freedom of romantic love and marriage, universities open to women students, and employment of women in government institutions. The first step we took toward sexual equality was to merge the associations of male and female students in Tianjin to form a new organization which students of both sexes could join. . . .

As pioneers in the feminist movement who had had the rare opportunity to work side by side with men, we female students in the merged association were conscious of the example we had to set so that no man in the future could deny women the opportunity to work on the ground of alleged incompetence. In short, we worked doubly hard. Fortunately for us, the male students in the association, having been imbued with the new thought of the West, were ready to accept us as equals and judged us according to our performance rather than our sex. . . .

CHAPTER 4

Decades of Crisis in the Western World and the Soviet Union

In May 1920, Warren G. Harding, senator from Ohio and soon to be twenty-ninth president of the United States, told an audience in Boston, "America's present need is not heroics, but healing; not nostrums, but normalcy; not revolution, but restoration, . . . not surgery, but serenity." The term *normalcy* caught the public's attention, and "return to normalcy" became a phrase that expressed the aspirations of millions on both sides of the Atlantic after years of war and postwar conflict. Normalcy had no precise definition, but to most it conjured up vague and not very accurate images of the way things were before 1914 — a time of moral certitudes and political calm, when men and women could lead lives free of turmoil and conflict.

Dreams of normalcy never came close to being realized in the 1920s and 1930s. The war's wounds were too deep, its political and economic consequences too profound, and its psychological impact too devastating. There would be no going back to "normal times," but rather a stumbling forward into a world whose contours were being continually redrawn by political conflict, economic catastrophe, new trends in mass culture, and the transformation of daily life by urbanization, the automobile, and radio. Crisis and conflict were "normal" in the 1920s and 1930s, not the tranquility Harding and so many others yearned for.

For Europe and the rest of the industrialized world, the interwar years fall into three distinct periods. From 1918 through 1923, winners and losers alike faced a host of postwar political and economic problems. The Bolshevik Revolution of 1917 spawned civil war in Russia, inspired communist revolts in Germany and Hungary, and raised fears of revolution throughout Europe and the United States. Border disputes and ethnic conflict embroiled the newly created states of Eastern and Central Europe. Demobilization, the closing of wartime industries, and inflation caused economic hardship and sparked dozens of major strikes in Western Europe and the United States. In 1923 the postwar settlement itself almost collapsed when the Germans defaulted on their reparations payments, and in response, the Belgians and French dispatched one hundred thousand soldiers to the Ruhr region to make sure that they would continue to receive their allocations of German coal. German miners responded with slowdown strikes and sabotage, and the German mark collapsed, its value sinking to 4.2 billion marks to the dollar by the end of 1923.

In another year, however, the Ruhr crisis ended, and the West entered a brief period of economic revival and political calm. A German coalition government under Gustav Stresemann called in the worthless marks and introduced a gold-based currency, and an international commission restructured Germany's reparations payments and helped devise a plan for Germany's economic recovery. The resolution of the 1923 crisis was just one of several hopeful signs between 1923 and 1929. Street fighting and insurrections gave way to political stability, albeit at the expense of democratic institutions in several states. The Locarno Treaty of 1925 was hailed as the first step toward international cooperation and harmony. In it Germany renounced claims to Alsace-Lorraine and its right to remilitarize unilaterally, in return for League of Nations membership and French promises to accelerate troop withdrawals from the Rhineland. Three years later in 1928 almost every country in the world, including all the Great Powers, signed the Kellogg-Briand Pact, in which war was renounced as an instrument of national policy. After 1923 Western economies leaped forward, and as "good times" returned, many hoped that the Roaring Twenties were the start of a better era for a crisis-ridden world.

Such hopes came crashing to the ground with the collapse of the U.S. stock market in October 1929. The ensuing financial crisis laid bare the weaknesses of the brief economic recovery, and soon the world was engulfed in an economic slump of unprecedented severity. Bank failures, boarded-up factories, and unemployment rates as high as 40 percent spelled misery for millions of people in Europe and the United States, and accelerated the collapse of liberal, democratic governments in Europe. To the list of six parliamentary governments that had given way to some form of authoritarianism in the 1920s, nine were added in the 1930s. The most significant failure was the Weimar Republic in Germany, which was crushed into dust by Hitler and the Nazis. As Hitler rearmed Germany and embarked on his plan to overturn the Versailles settlement, one diplomatic crisis followed another until in the fall of 1939, Europe again was at war.

Underlying the ebb and flow of economic shifts and political events were broader, more fundamental changes in Western life and culture. Politics no longer was the exclusive domain of aristocrats and wealthy bourgeoisie. Mass politics was the order of the day, not only in democracies, but also in dictatorships such as Nazi

Germany and Fascist Italy, where propaganda campaigns and political spectacles were carefully orchestrated to ensure popular support. This was also an era of mass culture. Radio programming, popular tabloid newspapers, and the cinema all were geared to mass audiences, as were advertising campaigns to encourage consumption of automobiles, household appliances, golf clubs, phonographs, canned goods, beauty aids, and hundreds of other products. Some intellectuals and social commentators welcomed these changes as positive and liberating; others deplored the debasement of taste and the erosion of standards. All could agree, however, that culture and society were changing in fundamental ways.

Modernism and Mass Culture Between the Wars

Western cultural life between the world wars was intense, spirited, and distinctively "modern," but not particularly innovative. It is difficult to find anything in the music, art, and literature of the 1920s and 1930s that did not have antecedents before World War I. Yet a palpable change in the cultural landscape did take place in the 1920s. Tradition was now in full retreat, and modernism reigned. Before the war, iconoclastic poets, composers, architects, and choreographers were outsiders, an avant-garde of self-conscious rebels issuing manifestos in Paris, St. Petersburg, or Milan on behalf of ideas and movements with a handful of disciples. Elite culture in the 1920s was unabashedly and unequivocally modernistic; the rejection of convention itself became conventional.

The term *modernism* is used to describe the art, music and literature that emerged in Europe and the United States in the 1920s and continued to set the tone for Western culture until the 1950s and beyond. It is difficult to define. If one examines modern literature, modern painting, modern architecture, modern sculpture, modern music, and modern dance to see what characteristics they share in common, modernism is reduced to something broad and general: a rejection of tradition; an abandonment of inherited rules, forms, and themes; and a commitment to experimentation.

The triumph of modernism after World War I can be explained in part by demographics. The prewar avant-garde consisted mainly of young men who, if they survived combat, reached maturity and gained followings after the war. The composer Igor Stravinsky was thirty-two when the war began and lived until 1971; the painter Pablo Picasso founded the cubist movement around 1907 and lived until 1973; the poet T. S. Eliot wrote his first important poems between 1909 and 1911 and lived until 1967. But it was the war itself that consigned the old order to oblivion and affirmed modernism's triumph. It confirmed the bankruptcy of traditional values and the need to create a new culture in keeping with the modern age.

Along with modernism, mass culture was another feature of the 1920s and 1930s. It too had prewar roots. Before 1914, the appearance of mass circulation newspapers, increasing sales of light novels and inexpensive magazines, the popularity of music hall entertainment, and the size of crowds flocking to baseball parks and soccer stadiums all indicated that the "masses" — factory workers, shopkeepers, clerks, stenographers, servants, and laborers — were becoming an important cultural force. They became an even greater force in the 1920s and 1930s.

Mass culture between the wars was a culmination of a century-long process in which urban workers and the lower middle class gradually acquired greater literacy, income, and leisure. By the 1920s the eight-hour workday, paid vacations, and workless weekends had become standard, and incomes had risen to the point that people below the ranks of the bourgeoisie could afford their own entertainment and recreation. The emergence of mass culture also had much to do with three prewar inventions that in the 1920s and 1930s were refined, commercialized, and made affordable to the general public: the radio, the phonograph, and the cinema.

The radio, developed by the Italian Guglielmo Marconi in the 1890s and used on the limited basis by armies during World War I, became fully commercialized in the 1920s. Radios became commonplace in American and European households, and by the end of the decade millions of listeners could gather around their sets and hear the programs transmitted by the BBC or NBC. The phonograph, invented by Edison in 1878, reached a level of quality and affordability in the 1920s that made it a major part of the evolving mass culture. In the United States alone manufacturers turned out more than two million phonographs and one hundred million records annually. The film industry, which in 1908 was already attracting an estimated ten million customers a year in the United States, moved into an era of full-length films, better quality, sound, and sumptuously decorated movie palaces seating as many as five thousand patrons. By the 1930s trips to the movies became routine on both sides of the Atlantic, and Hollywood became synonymous with glamour, adventure, and escape from the drabness of the Great Depression. The age of the masses had arrived, and for better or worse, the soap opera, matinee idol, Hollywood epic, tabloid newspaper, sports hero, and jitterbug were now all part of Western culture.

The Look of Modernity

◆

28 ◆ *Walter Gropius,* *DESSAU BAUHAUS — PRINCIPLES OF BAUHAUS CONSTRUCTION and EXAMPLES OF BAUHAUS DESIGN*

Much of modern art, music, and literature has been geared toward a small, sophisticated audience of individuals who can appreciate and understand its complexities, obscurities, and frequently disturbing messages. Even in the heyday of modernism, only a tiny minority could say honestly that their lives had been much affected by dadaist painting, atonal music, or stream-of-consciousness literature. This is not the case, however, in regard to modern architecture and design. In these two areas, modernism has given a distinctive twentieth-century look to man-made objects that are part of people's daily lives around the world: the buildings where they work, live, and study; the furniture in their homes; the clothes and jewelry they wear; the utensils, plates, and appliances they use in their kitchens; and much else. For this, a German school of art and design that lasted only fourteen years, the Bauhaus, can be given much of the credit.

The Bauhaus — German for House of Construction, or Building School — was the creation of the architect Walter Gropius. Born in 1883 in Berlin and trained in Berlin and Munich, Gropius achieved continentwide prominence for the factories and office buildings he designed before World War I. After the war, he became director of two state-supported schools — one for art and one for crafts — in Weimar. He merged these in 1919 to form the Bauhaus. With some of Central and Eastern Europe's most brilliant architects, painters, and sculptors on its faculty, the Bauhaus integrated crafts and aesthetic training. Its objective was to develop every area of design (architecture, painting, sculpture, furniture, fabrics, jewelry, ceramics, stagecraft, and costume) in ways appropriate to modern industrial society. Forced to move to Dessau in 1925 after the German state of Thuringia cut off funds, and then to Berlin when Nazis took over the Dessau city council, the school was shut down for good after Hitler took power in 1933. The Bauhaus, claimed the Nazis, represented Jewish-Marxist art. Gropius, who had resigned as director of the school in 1927, emigrated to the United States, where as head of Harvard's architecture department he helped train a generation of U.S. architects. He died in 1969.

This section illustrates through writings and examples some of the basic principles of Bauhaus and, by extension, modern design. It begins with a brief statement by Gropius from a pamphlet published in 1927 entitled "Dessau Bauhaus — Principles of Bauhaus Construction." Four examples of Bauhaus design follow: (a) the main Bauhaus building in Dessau, designed by Gropius; (b) a master's (faculty member's) house from the Dessau complex, also designed by Gropius; (c) a chair designed in 1927 by Marcel Breuer (an alumnus of the school who fled Germany and later joined Gropius at Harvard) made of steel tubing and steel thread; and (d) a brass and ebony teapot made in 1924 from a design by Marianne Brandt (a member of the Bauhaus faculty).

QUESTIONS FOR ANALYSIS

1. Why, in Gropius's view, have recent developments dictated the need for a new approach to housing and furnishings design?
2. According to Gropius, what characteristics will a modern dwelling and its furnishings have to put them "in harmony" with the modern world?
3. What views of the modern world are implied or stated by Gropius?
4. What have been the differences between craft production and industrial production in the view of Gropius? What changes in their relationship does he anticipate?

5. **What characteristics do Gropius's Dessau buildings, Breuer's tubular chair, and Brandt's teapot have in common?**
6. **In what ways do these buildings and objects exemplify Gropius's ideals?**

The Bauhaus intends to contribute to the development of housing — from the simplest appliance to the complete dwelling — in a way which is in harmony with the spirit of the age. . . .

Convinced that household appliances and furnishings must relate to each other rationally, the Bauhaus seeks — by means of systematic theoretical and practical research into formal, technical and economic fields — to derive the form of an object from its natural functions and limitations.

Modern man, who wears modern not historical dress, also requires a modern dwelling which is in harmony with himself and with the times in which he lives, and is equipped with all the modern objects in daily use.

The nature of an object is determined by what it does. Before a container, a chair or a house can function properly its nature must first be studied, for it must perfectly serve its purpose; in other words it must function practically, must be cheap, durable and 'beautiful'. Research into the nature of objects leads one to conclude that forms emerge from a determined consideration of all the modern methods of production and construction and of modern materials. These forms diverge from existing models and often seem unfamiliar and surprising. . . .

Only by constant contact with advanced technology, with the diversity of new materials and with new methods of construction, is the creative individual able to bring objects into a vital relationship with the past, and to develop from that a new attitude to design, namely:

Determined acceptance of the living environment of machines and vehicles.

Organic design of objects in terms of their own laws and determined by their contemporaneity, without Romantic beautification and whimsy.

Exclusive use of primary forms and colors comprehensible to everyone.

Simplicity in multiplicity, economical use of space, material, time and money.

The creation of standard types for all objects in daily use is a social necessity.

For most people the necessities of life are the same. The home, its furnishings and equipment are required by everybody, and their design is more a matter of reason than of passion. The machine, which creates standard types, is an effective means of liberating the individual from physical labor through mechanical aids — steam and electricity — and giving him mass-produced products cheaper and better than those made by hand. . . .

The Bauhaus workshops are essentially laboratories in which prototypes suitable for mass production and typical of their time are developed with care and constantly improved. . . .

The Bauhaus believes that the difference between industry and the crafts consists less in the tools each uses than in the division of labor in industry and the unity of labor in the crafts. But the crafts and industry are constantly moving closer. Traditional crafts have changed: the crafts of the future will have a unity of labor in which they will be the medium of experimental work for industrial production. . . .

Bauhaus production is therefore not in competition with industry and craftsmen; it rather provides them with new opportunities for growth. . . .

Dessau Bauhaus Building (1925–1926), Walter Gropius, architect

Master's (faculty member's) House (1926) from the Dessau complex, Walter Gropius, architect

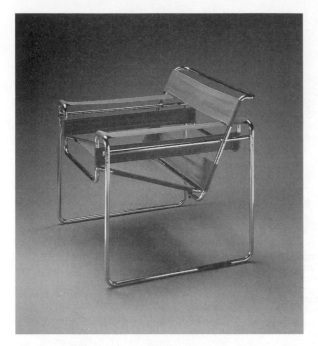

Marcel Breuer, Tubular Steel Chair (1925)

Marianne Brandt, Small Tea-Essence Pot (1924)

Perils of Mass Culture: The Threat to Morality

❖

29 ◆ *Senator Henry L. Myers,*
U.S. SENATE SPEECH, JUNE 29, 1922

Is mass culture dangerous to morals? So it would seem from the persistent out-cries directed toward many of its twentieth-century manifestations: jazz music, rock and roll, pulp fiction, rap lyrics, television violence, dance styles too numerous to count, and more than anything else, films. Early filmmakers knew that sex, violence, and sensationalism sold tickets, and hence produced more than their share of films featuring bawdy comedy, lurid murder scenes, and, by the standards of the day, torrid romance. In 1908, citing moral dangers, the mayor of New York City, George B. McClellan, threatened to close all of the city's cinemas, and during the 1910s state and local censorship boards proliferated. In response, filmmakers in 1909 founded their own self-regulating body, the National Board of Censorship (later named the National Board of Review), which they hoped would head off federal censorship.

The industry's problems with censorship peaked in 1921 and 1922. In their efforts to fill seats in thousands of new theaters built after the war, producers released a spate of films with titles such as *The Blushing Bride, Forbidden Fruit, The Plaything of Broadway, Luring Lips, The Restless Sex,* and *Passion's Playground.* In 1920 scandal rocked Hollywood when one of its biggest stars, Roscoe "Fatty" Arbuckle, was accused (and later acquitted) of raping and murdering a young actress at a wild San Francisco party; a Hollywood producer, William Desmond Taylor, was found dead in a drug-related murder; and a number of prominent actors and actresses, including Rudolph Valentino, became involved in highly publicized divorces.

Against this background several congressmen reintroduced legislation to set up a national board of film censorship. One of its supporters was Senator Henry Myers (1861–1929) of Montana, who presented his observations on the film industry in a Senate speech in June 1922.

The efforts of Myers and other like-minded congressmen failed. Bills calling for federal regulation of films were voted down, in no small part because of the lobbying efforts of Will Hays, recently hired by the film industry to serve as a front man for a new organization, the Motion Picture Producers and Distributors of America. However, Hays did ban Arbuckle, a convenient scapegoat for the industry's problems, from the screen, thereby showing his seriousness of purpose.

QUESTIONS FOR ANALYSIS

1. What is Myer's rationale for involving the federal government in censoring the film industry?
2. What signs of moral deterioration does Myers detect in the United States of his day? To what degree does he believe the film industry can be blamed for this deterioration?

3. Why does Myers believe that industry efforts to regulate itself will fail?
4. What type of regulation of the film industry does he foresee?

The motion picture is a great invention, and it has become a powerful factor for good or bad in our civilization. . . .

Through motion pictures the young and the old may see depicted every good motive, laudable ambition, commendable characteristic, ennobling trait of humanity. They may be taught that honesty is the best policy; that virtue and worth are rewarded; that industry leads to success. . . .

However, from all accounts, the business has been conducted, generally speaking, upon a low plane and in a decidedly sordid manner. Those who own and control the industry seem to have been of the opinion that the sensual, the sordid, the prurient, the phases of fast life, the ways of extravagance, the risqué, the paths of shady life, drew the greatest attendance and coined for them the most money, and apparently they have been out to get the coin, no matter what the effect upon the public, young or old; and when thoughtful people have suggested or advocated official censorship, in the interest of good citizenship and wholesome morals, the owners of the industry have resented it and, in effect, declared that it was nobody's business other than theirs and concerned nobody other than them what kind of shows they produced; that if people did not like their shows they could stay away from them; that it was their business, and they would conduct it as they might please. . . .

In that they are mistaken. The State has an interest in citizenship and a concern in the education of the young. The State has an interest in good morals. It regulates in many ways all of those things. The motion-picture industry vitally concerns all of those things — citizenship, education, morals — and is therefore subject to regulation by the State. It has become a public utility, and is therefore the legitimate subject of State regulation. . . .

The industry has gone so far in defying public sentiment, and has been so flagrant in its abuse of its privileges that a public sentiment for censorship has been aroused which will not be brooked. It may be temporarily checked; it may be temporarily lulled by fair promises, but it is bound to grow, because censorship is needed and would be a good thing. . . .

I believe that a great deal of the extravagance of the day, a great deal of the disposition to live beyond one's means, yea, a great deal of the crime of the day comes from moving pictures. Through them young people gain ideas of fast life, shady ways, laxity of living, loose morals. Crime is freely depicted in alluring colors. Lax morals are held up lightly before them. The sensual is strongly appealed to. Many of the pictures are certainly not elevating; some, at least, are not fit to be seen.

About 18 months ago, in this city, there occurred a foul and most shocking murder. . . . Four youths of this city, in age from 15 to 20 years, as I recollect, stole an automobile, and in it followed an honest, peaceable, industrious barber as he was going to his loving family and quiet home after a day's work, and overtaking him, one of the youths jumped out of the automobile, in a residential section of the city, and murdered him by firing a pistol at him at close range. The victim dropped dead. The youths became panic-stricken on account of close-at-hand pedestrians and fled in the stolen machine. . . .

I have no doubt those young criminals got their ideas of the romance of crime from moving pictures. I believe moving pictures are doing as much harm to-day as saloons did in the days of the open saloon — especially to the young. They are running day and night, Sunday and every other day, the year round, and in most jurisdictions without any regulation by censorship. I would not abolish them. . . . I would close them on Sunday and regulate them week days by judicious censorship. . . .

When we look to the source of the moving pictures, the material for them, the personnel of those who pose for them, we need not wonder that many of the pictures are pernicious. . . .

At Hollywood, Calif., is a colony of these people, where debauchery, riotous living, drunkenness, ribaldry, dissipation, free love, seem to be conspicuous. Many of these "stars," it is reported, were formerly bartenders, butcher boys, sopers, swampers,[1] variety actors and actresses, who may have earned $10 or $20 a week, and some of whom are now paid, it is said, salaries of something like $5,000 a month or more, and they do not know what to do with their wealth, extracted from poor people, in large part, in 25 or 50 cent admission fees, except to spend it in riotous living, dissipation, and "high rolling."

There are some of the characters from whom the young people of to-day are deriving a large part of their education, views of life, and character-forming habits. From these sources our young people gain much of their views of life, inspirations, and education. Rather a poor source, is it not? Looks like there is some need for censorship, does it not? . . .

There was recently some reference in Washington papers to a suggested effort by the Washington Chamber of Commerce or Board of Trade, one or the other, I do not recall which, to induce the Hollywood motion-picture colony to move to this community and establish itself at Great Falls, near this city. I hope it may not be done. From all accounts the Washington Chamber of Commerce or Board of Trade would better invite here a colony of lepers or an institution for the propagation and dissemination of smallpox. . . .

---

[1]In American slang, *butcher boys* were street vendors; *sopers* were drug addicts; *swampers* were truck drivers.

◆

The Impact of the Great Depression

For a few glorious years from 1924 to 1929, people in the industrialized world could believe that postwar economic problems had been solved. Fueled by investments and loans from a booming United States, Europe's economy revived. Inflation seemed under control. Industrialized nations experienced higher employment, increased output, and expanded foreign trade. Despite lagging agricultural prices and pockets of high unemployment, optimism reigned, and the price of stocks, especially on the New York Stock Exchange, skyrocketed. In the summer of 1929, an article in a U.S. magazine touted stock market investing as a sure way to wealth. It was entitled "Everyone Ought to be Rich."

Optimism evaporated in October 1929, when prices on the Exchange began a decline that soon laid bare all the underlying weaknesses of the international economy. As personal fortunes disappeared, banks began to fail by the thousands, investment plummeted, prices and wages fell, and unemployment lines and soup kitchens became features of the urban landscape. The stock market crash caused U.S. bankers to call in short-term loans from European creditors, and in the spring of 1931, major banks in Austria and Germany failed. Worse, the crash stopped the flow of investment dollars to Europe, where the number of boarded-up factories, unemployed workers, and ruined farmers soon reached frightening levels.

More than anything else, the Great Depression was a human tragedy for millions of men and women who lost jobs, farms, investments, homes, savings, personal possessions, health, dignity, and hope. But it also had important political ramifications. In the short run, it undermined parliamentary governments in Germany, Austria, and other Central and Eastern European states, and nearly ended parliamentary governments in Belgium and France. It heightened social tensions and encouraged many of its victims to believe that economic hardship was the fault of Jews, communists, capitalists, or some other convenient scapegoat. International cooperation declined as politicians immersed themselves in domestic issues, raised tariffs, and convinced themselves and their compatriots that their economic problems could be blamed on foreigners or perhaps solved by rearmament or foreign conquests.

The Great Depression also prompted new thinking about the role and purposes of government. It soon became apparent that time-honored governmental responses to recessions — encouraging private charity, slashing government spending, raising tariffs, or just waiting passively for the business cycle to turn upward — were inadequate and perhaps even counterproductive. A new vision of governmental activism, exemplified by Franklin D. Roosevelt's "New Deal" in the United States, emerged. It viewed the state as responsible for society's economic well-being and its citizens' social welfare from "cradle to grave." It utilized economic planning, regulation, and deficit spending to stimulate demand and maintain high employment. It viewed tax policy as a means of redistributing wealth from the rich to the poor. And it envisioned and ultimately created a host of new programs and entitlements to protect people from poverty and ensure decent housing, adequate health care, and "social security" in old age. The trend toward big government and the welfare state was of necessity strengthened and accelerated as a result of the economic catastrophe of the 1930s.

The Victims of the Depression in Germany

30 ◆ H. Hessel Tiltman,
SLUMP! A STUDY OF STRICKEN EUROPE TODAY

H. Hessel Tiltman (1897–1977) was a British author-journalist best known for his coverage of East Asia during the 1930s and 1940s. During 1931 and 1932 as European correspondent for the *Manchester Guardian,* he traveled across Europe to observe the effects of the Great Depression. On his return he recorded his impressions in a widely read book, *Slump! A Study of Stricken Europe Today.* In the following selection he describes the economic and emotional effects of the Depression on three families from Berlin.

QUESTIONS FOR ANALYSIS

1. How has the Great Depression affected the economic situations of the German families?
2. How does the situation of the laborer's family differ from those of the former baker and the former salesman?

3. What does Tiltman's account have to say about the emotional and psychological damage of unemployment?
4. What connection does Tiltman make between Germany's economic woes and the appeal of Nazism?

In the course of those two days beneath the surface of Berlin life I saw overcrowding, because those living on relief can rarely afford more than one room, however large the family. . . . I saw hunger, because, as I have said, these victims cannot escape that horror. I saw rags, because the welfare centers can no longer supply anyone with even secondhand shoes until *both* the soles of the existing pair have been worn to nothing. The mass need is now so great that it has swamped every channel along which relief trickles. . . .

But more painful than any of these things, I saw utter despair. Some of the wives could still hold up their heads and be interested in the life about them, but most of the men were shattered in spirit and breaking in health. They had fought despair for one year, two years, maybe even three years. But it got them in the end. . . .

The first house I entered was still supported by the second category "dole,"[1] the husband, a baker, having been out of work only seven months.

The family comprised husband, wife, and four children, and the total income amounted to 94/-[2] a month, made up of 82/- unemployment benefit, and 12/- a month orphans' pension received for one of the children.

For one room and a kitchen in a large tenement building, with a wall blocking out both view and light, they paid 20/- a month rent, leaving a balance of 74/-.

Electric light and gas cost about 7/- a month, soap 6d. a month, and a burial insurance policy for the family another 1/6 a month. Payments on this policy were being discontinued on the week that I called.

The rest of the income, amounting to 15/- a week, went to buy food for six people, a task made easier by the fact that three of the children were supplied with a midday meal — and a good meal — at the school they attended.

The weekly menus in this home consisted of oatmeal, potato soup, herrings and bread. Only in the case of the husband was there any sign of physical strain, and he was well below the standard of fitness enforced in the German Army in which he had served in what, tragically enough, he spoke of as "happier days." . . .

In another home a family of seven — man, wife, and five children — were living in two rooms. The man, workless since the beginning of 1931, had formerly been employed, first as a clerk, and later as a salesman in a store, his wage in the latter occupation being 42/- a week.

The total income of the family, from the "second category" dole, had amounted to about 30/- a week, but this sum was subject to a cut of 20 percent on June 27, 1932. On the same date the rent of 10/- a week was raised to 12/6, or nearly half their total income, by the reimposition of a rent tax formerly waived in the case of the workless. Thus the relentless march of the crisis forces the living standards of its victims down and down.

Sitting on the only sound chair in that home, in which a sewing machine was the sole article of furniture which would have sold for more than a few pence, I listened while the wife, a woman of twenty-five whose face bore clear marks of strain, explained to me how they managed to feed seven people on 15/- a week.

A loaf of bread a day cast 6d. A pound of dripping[3] a week cost the same sum. They bought

---

[1] The English term for government payments to the unemployed.
[2] Tiltman expresses income and expenditures in units of British money. The number left of the slash represents shillings,

twenty of which make up a pound; the number on the right of the slash represents pence, twelve of which make up a shilling. The symbol of pence is "*d.*"
[3] Animal fat.

one liter . . . of milk a day for the two youngest children, and 1/4 lb. of butter a week for the youngest child. Three lbs. of sugar a week, two tins of condensed milk for the baby, aged nine months, and five cigarettes a day for the man, costing one penny a packet, completed the list of "luxuries." For the rest, they had 8 lbs. of potatoes a day and, twice a week, 3 lbs. of cabbage costing 3d., boiled into a soup to which, on Sundays, was added a penny-worth of bones. Occasionally — not more frequently than once a month — they bought half a pound of pork at the specially reduced prices charged, under government supervision, to those in receipt of "doles." . . .

From that home I went to another near by — two rooms occupied by a builders' laborer, unemployed for over two years. The rooms were in a cellar below the level of the street, and approached through quarters occupied by another family. The income for a family of three was 16/- a week, "a little higher than the average," as the man explained to me. The rent, including the new tax, was 6/- a month. The wife produced the rent book, showing that they owed two months' rent, and in view of the new law, already mentioned, which rendered them liable to eviction at any time upon twelve hours' notice, it worried them. If that happened, they explained, there would be no alternative to a shed somewhere on the outskirts of the city, which would mean living like pigs, and necessitate a long walk for the man every time he had to report to the relief officer.

The husband had just drawn 32/-, two weeks' relief payment, and I went out with the wife to spend it.

The first 9/- went to pay a debt at the grocer's. A cwt.[4] of coal cost another 1/6½; 12/- went to pay the fortnight's rent; 2/6 liquidated a debt for potatoes eaten during the previous week. Seven shillings were left, and the wife spent this on eggs, dripping, bread, potatoes and cabbage — which may be described as the universal diet of the German workless. On that menu, they had to exist for another week at least.

When we returned, the husband was sitting on a box, his head in his hands — gazing fixedly into space. Looking for what? As a trade unionist, he had been a member of the Social Democratic Party[5] the bulwark of the German Republic. Now he was nothing — too broken in spirit to care. Sitting there, a picture of dejection, he might have been looking back to the pre-war days, when the Junkers[6] thundered forth claims to a "place in the sun," and at least found work for their people. If he was, who will blame him? It is one of the misfortunes of these years that troubles have crowded in upon Germany under the republican regime.

A moment later two young men, clad in leather jackets, burst into that cellar-room with a stamp of feet, to provide another glimpse of the curses which afflict Germany today. This time the curse, not of poverty, but of Hitlerism.

It could not truthfully be said that the visitors entered that room. Their domineering manners and assertive attitude somehow preceded them though the door, which they slammed after entering. Compared with the Socialist worker, wearied by waiting for the turn of the tide, these two members of the Nazi "S.A."[7] . . . represented another world — a Germany which has lost its patience and demands the impossible under threat of instant reprisals. . . .

Those two young workless men were walking evidence, seen beside that Socialist, of the fact that whatever else Adolf Hitler has, or has not, done, he has enabled a large number of Germans to keep up their spirits — the great demagogue would himself call it "saving the soul of Germany" — at a time when Germany's spirits were in danger of sinking to zero.

---

[4]Abbreviation for a hundredweight, a unit of weight in the British Imperial System equal to 112 pounds.

[5]The Social Democrats were Marxist, but sought to achieve socialism through legislation, not revolution. The Social Democratic Party was a major supporter of the Weimar Republic.

[6]Aristocrats from the German state of Prussia, who for centuries dominated the Prussian and, after German unification in 1871, the army's officer corps.

[7]Abbreviation for Sturmabteilung, a Nazi paramilitary organization noted for its violence and antisemitism, also known in English as the "Brown Shirts" or "Storm Troopers."

Government Promises a "New Deal"

◆

31 ◆ *Franklin D. Roosevelt,*
ANNUAL ADDRESS TO CONGRESS,
JANUARY 4, 1935

Herbert Hoover, who was just finishing his first year as president when the stock market crashed, was deeply concerned about the human costs of the Depression, but his commitment to volunteerism and a balanced budget doomed to failure his efforts to mitigate its effects. His refusal to commit the federal government to relief or recovery programs infuriated Americans who came to believe he was indifferent to their suffering and interested mainly in protecting business. In 1932 the voters overwhelmingly supported the Democrat Franklin D. Roosevelt, who in the campaign had promised them a new deal.

Franklin D. Roosevelt was born into a wealthy upstate New York family in 1882. A Harvard graduate and a lawyer, he had served as a New York state legislator, assistant secretary of the navy under Wilson, the Democratic vice-presidential candidate in 1920, and governor of New York between 1928 and 1932. Taking office when the Depression was at its worst and promising "bold and persistent experimentation," the new president pushed forward an unprecedented program to resolve the crises of a collapsing banking system, crippling unemployment, and agricultural and industrial breakdown. Two years later, in 1935, with the Depression far from over, Roosevelt shifted his priorities, in what is sometimes called the "Second New Deal," from relief and recovery to basic social and economic reforms.

In the following message to Congress, delivered in January 1935, Roosevelt outlines some of his ideas about the role of government and the nation's economic well-being.

QUESTIONS FOR ANALYSIS

1. How does Roosevelt perceive the "state of the nation" in 1935? What has been accomplished and what still needs to be done by his administration?
2. What evidence does Roosevelt' speech provide that his administration's interests were shifting from relief and recovery to more basic reforms? What groups and regions in U.S. society were most likely to benefit from his proposals?
3. How would you describe Roosevelt's long-term goals for American society?
4. Taken as a whole, how would his proposals result in an expansion of the federal government?

Throughout the world change is the order of the day. In every nation economic problems, long in the making, have brought crises of many kinds for which the masters of old practice and theory were unprepared. In most nations, social justice, no longer a distant ideal, has become a definite goal, and ancient governments are beginning to heed the call. . . .

We find our population suffering from old inequalities, little changed by past sporadic remedies. In spite of our efforts and in spite of our talk, we have not weeded out the overprivileged and we have not effectively lifted up the underprivileged. Both of these manifestations of injustice have retarded happiness. No wise man has any intention of destroying what is known as the "profit motive," because by the profit motive we mean the right by work to earn a decent livelihood for ourselves and for our families.

We have, however, a clear mandate from the people, that Americans must forswear that conception of the acquisition of wealth which, through excessive profits, creates undue private power over private affairs and, to our misfortune, over public affairs as well. In building toward this end we do not destroy ambition, nor do we seek to divide our wealth into equal shares on stated occasions. We continue to recognize the greater ability of some to earn more than others. But we do assert that the ambition of the individual to obtain for him and his a proper security, a reasonable leisure, and a decent living throughout life is an ambition to be preferred to the appetite for great wealth and great power. . . .

In defining immediate factors which enter into our quest, I have spoken to the Congress and the people of three great divisions: first, the security of a livelihood through the better use of the national resources of the land in which we live; second, the security against the major hazards and vicissitudes of life; third, the security of decent homes.

I am now ready to submit to the Congress a broad program designed ultimately to establish all three of these factors of security — a program which because of many lost years will take many future years to fulfill.

A study of our national resources, . . . shows the vast amount of necessary and practicable work which needs to be done for the development and preservation of our national wealth for the enjoyment and advantage of our people

in generations to come. The sound use of land and water is far more comprehensive than the mere planting of trees, building of dams, distributing of electricity, or retirement of submarginal land. It recognizes that stranded populations, either in the country or the city, cannot have security under the conditions that now surround them.

To this end we are ready to begin to meet this problem — the intelligent care of population throughout our nation in accordance with an intelligent distribution of the means of livelihood for that population. A definite program for putting people to work, of which I shall speak in a moment, is a component part of this greater program of security of livelihood through the better use of our national resources.

Closely related to the broad problem of livelihood is that of security against the major hazards of life. Here also a comprehensive survey of what has been attempted or accomplished in many nations and in many states proves to me that the time has come for action by the national government. I shall send to you, in a few days, definite recommendations based on these studies. These recommendations will cover the broad subjects of unemployment insurance and old-age insurance, of benefits for children, for mothers, for the handicapped, for maternity care, and for other aspects of dependency and illness where a beginning can now be made.

The third factor — better homes for our people — has also been the subject of experimentation and study. Here, too, the first practical steps can be made through the proposals which I shall suggest in relation to giving work to the unemployed. . . .

The first objectives of emergency legislation of 1933 were to relieve destitution, to make it possible for industry to operate in a more rational and orderly fashion, and to put behind industrial recovery the impulse of large expenditures in government undertakings. The purpose of the National Industrial Recovery

Act[1] to provide work for more people succeeded in a substantial manner within the first few months of its life, and the act has continued to maintain employment gains and greatly improved working conditions in industry. . . .

But the stark fact before us is that great numbers still remain unemployed. A large proportion of these unemployed and their dependents have been forced on the relief rolls. . . . The lessons of history, confirmed by the evidence immediately before me, show conclusively that continued dependence upon relief induces a spiritual and moral disintegration fundamentally destructive to the national fiber. To dole out relief in this way is to administer a narcotic, a subtle destroyer of the human spirit. . . . Work must be found for able-bodied but destitute workers. . . .

I am not willing that the vitality of our people be further sapped by the giving of cash, of market baskets, of a few hours of weekly work cutting grass, raking leaves, or picking up papers in the public parks. We must preserve not only the bodies of the unemployed from destitution but also their self-respect, their self-reliance, and courage and determination. This decision brings me to the problem of what the government should do with approximately 5 million unemployed now on the relief rolls.

About 1.5 million of these belong to the group which in the past was dependent upon local welfare efforts. Most of them are unable, for one reason or another, to maintain themselves independently — for the most part, through no fault of their own. Such people, in the days before the great depression, were cared for by local efforts — by states, by counties, by towns, by cities, by churches, and by private welfare agencies. . . .

There are, however, an additional 3.5 million employable people who are on relief. With them the problem is different and the responsibility is different. This group was the victim of a nationwide depression caused by conditions which were not local but national. The federal government is the only governmental agency with sufficient power and credit to meet this situation. . . . It is a duty dictated by every intelligent consideration of national policy to ask you to make it possible for the United States to give employment to all of these 3.5 million employable people now on relief, pending their absorption in a rising tide of private employment. . . .

It is my thought that, with the exception of certain of the normal public-building operations of the government, all emergency public works shall be united in a single new and greatly enlarged plan. With the establishment of this new system, we can supersede the Federal Emergency Relief Administration[2] with a coordinated authority which will be charged with the orderly liquidation of our present relief activities and the substitution of a national chart for the giving of work. . . .

The work itself will cover a wide field, including clearance of slums, which for adequate reasons cannot be undertaken by private capital; in rural housing of several kinds, where, again, private capital is unable to function; in rural electrification; in the reforestation of the great watersheds of the nation; in an intensified program to prevent soil erosion and to reclaim blighted areas; in improving existing road systems and in constructing national highways designed to handle modern traffic; in the elimination of grade crossings; in the extension and enlargement of the successful work of the Civilian Conservation Corps;[3] in nonfederal work,

---

[1]The National Industrial Recovery Act established the National Recovery Administration (NRA), which sought to revive U.S. industry by allowing industrial and trade associations to draft codes setting production levels, wages, price policies, and working conditions.
[2]The Federal Emergency Relief Administration (FERA) furnished funds to state and local agencies for relief. It spent close to $3 billion before it was replaced in 1935 by programs that provided work rather than cash payments.
[3]The Civil Conservation Corps (CCC) employed 2.5 million young men to work on reforestation and flood control projects.

mostly self-liquidating and highly useful to local divisions of government; and on many other projects which the nation needs and cannot afford to neglect. . . .

The ledger of the past year shows many more gains than losses. Let us not forget that, in addition to saving millions from utter destitution, child labor has been for the moment outlawed, thousands of homes saved to their owners, and, most important of all, the morale of the nation has been restored. Viewing the year 1934 as a whole, you and I can agree that we have a generous measure of reasons for giving thanks.

◆

Nazism in Theory and Practice

The Nazi movement was born on January 5, 1919, when seven men gathered in a Munich tavern to form the German Workers' Party, renamed a year later the National Socialist German Workers' Party. It died on April 30, 1945, in a bunker beneath the streets of a ravaged and burning Berlin when Adolf Hitler put a gun to his head and committed suicide. The Nazi movement existed for slightly more than twenty-six years, and its leader, Hitler, was Germany's dictator for only thirteen of them, from 1933 to 1945. Yet in this brief time so heinous were the Nazis' deeds, and so great their transgressions, that as long as even the slightest moral sense remains among human beings, Nazism will be remembered as an archsymbol of human depravity and viciousness.

During the 1920s the National Socialists espoused a program of nationalism, anticommunism, opposition to the Weimar Republic, antisemitism, repudiation of the Versailles Treaty, remilitarization, and a return to the old German values of home, hearth, family, and land. Despite the appeal of such ideas to many Germans and Hitler's unquestioned skill as an agitator and orator, the party made little progress in the 1920s. In 1928 it had fewer than one hundred thousand members and won only 2.8 percent of the vote in the national elections held that year. The Nazis' fortunes improved dramatically in 1929 and 1930 as the economy slowed and then crashed, and the Weimar government limped from one crisis to another. In the elections of September 1930, the Nazis won 107 seats in the Reichstag, making them the second largest party after the Social Democrats. They became the largest party in November 1932 when they won 196 seats and approximately one-third of the popular vote. With coalition governments dissolving almost as soon as they were formed and Germany close to political collapse, in January 1933 President von Hindenburg offered Hitler the chancellorship in the hope that as the leader of Germany's largest party Hitler could end the parliamentary crisis. In a way he did just that. On March 23, 1933, with nearly one hundred communist and socialist deputies in jail or in hiding from the secret police, and with Hitler's supporters surrounding the Reichstag and screaming threats against anyone who voted against Hitler, Germany's postwar experiment with democracy ended. Two-thirds of the deputies to the Reichstag voted for the Enabling Act, which gave Hitler dictatorial powers and an opportunity to implement his cruel, fantastic dreams.

The Dreams of the Führer

◆

32 ◆ *Adolf Hitler, MEIN KAMPF*

Born the son of an Austrian customs official and his German wife in 1889, Adolf Hitler moved to Vienna at the age of nineteen to pursue a career as an artist and architect. He failed, however, and lived at the bottom of Viennese society, drifting from one low-paying job to another. In 1912 he moved to Munich, where his life fell into the same purposeless pattern. Enlistment in the German army in World War I gave Hitler comradeship, a sense of direction, and an opportunity to escape his meaningless existence. After the war, a shattered Hitler returned to Munich where he joined the German Workers' Party, which in 1920 changed its name to the National Socialist German Workers' Party, or the Nazi Party.

After becoming leader of the National Socialists, Hitler staged an abortive coup d'état, or putsch, against the government of the German state of Bavaria in 1923. For this he was sentenced to a five-year prison term (serving only nine months), during which he wrote the first volume of his major political work, *Mein Kampf* (My Struggle). To a remarkable degree, this work, completed in 1925, provided the ideas that inspired his millions of followers and guided the National Socialists until their destruction in 1945.

QUESTIONS FOR ANALYSIS

1. What broad purpose does Hitler see in human existence?
2. What, in Hitler's view, are the basic dissimilarities between Aryans and Jews?
3. What is Hitler's view of political leadership?
4. What role do parliaments play in a "folkish" state, according to Hitler?
5. How does Hitler plan to reorient German foreign policy? What goals does he set for Germany, and how are they to be achieved?
6. In what ways are Hitler's ideas reminiscent of those of Nietzsche (see source 16 on p. 62)?
7. Based on these excerpts, what can you guess about Hitler's attitude toward the ideologies of democracy, liberalism, and socialism?

NATION AND RACE

There are some truths that are so plain and obvious that for this very reason the everyday world does not see them or at least does not apprehend them. . . .

So humans invariably wander about the garden of nature, convinced that they know and understand everything, yet with few exceptions are blind to one of the fundamental principles Nature uses in her work: the intrinsic segregation of the species of every living thing on the earth. . . . Each beast mates with only one of its own species: the titmouse with titmouse, finch with finch, stork with stork, field mouse with field mouse, house mouse with house mouse, wolf with wolf. . . . This is only natural.

Any cross-breeding between two not completely equal beings will result in a product that is in between the level of the two parents.

That means that the offspring will be superior to the parent who is at a biologically lower level of being but inferior to the parent at a higher level. This means the offspring will be overcome in the struggle for existence against those at the higher level. Such matings go against the will of Nature for the higher breeding of life.

A precondition for this lies not in the blending of beings of a higher and lower order, but rather the absolute victory of the stronger. The stronger must dominate and must not blend with the weaker orders and sacrifice their powers. Only born weaklings can find this cruel, but after all, they are only weaker and more narrow-minded types of men; unless this law dominated, then any conceivable higher evolution of living organisms would be unthinkable. . . .

Nature looks on this calmly and approvingly. The struggle for daily bread allows all those who are weak, sick, and indecisive to be defeated, while the struggle of the males for females gives to the strongest alone the right or at least the possibility to reproduce. Always this struggle is a means of advancing the health and power of resistance of the species, and thus a means to its higher evolution.

As little as nature approves the mating of higher and lower individuals, she approves even less the blending of higher races with lower ones; for indeed otherwise her previous work toward higher development perhaps over hundreds of thousands of years might be rendered useless with one blow. If this were not the case, progressive development would stop and even deterioration might set in. . . .

All the great civilization of the past died out because contamination of their blood caused them to become decadent. . . . In other words, in order to protect a certain culture, the type of human who created the culture must be preserved. But such preservation is tied to the inalterable law of the necessity and the right of victory of the best and the strongest.

Whoever would live must fight. Whoever will not fight in this world of endless competition does not deserve to live. Whoever ignores or despises these laws of race kills the good fortune that he believes he can attain. He interferes with the victory path of the best race and with it, the precondition for all human progress. . . .

It is an idle undertaking to argue about which race or races were the original standard-bearers of human culture and were therefore the true founders of everything we conceive by the word humanity. It is much simpler to deal with the question as it pertains to the present, and here the answer is simple and clear. What we see before us today as human culture, all the yields of art, science, and technology, are almost exclusively the creative product of the Aryans.[1] Indeed this fact alone leads to the not unfounded conclusion that the Aryan alone is the founder of the higher type of humanity, and further that he represents the prototype of what we understand by the word: MAN. He is the Prometheus[2] from whose brow the bright spark of genius has forever burst forth, time and again rekindling the fire, which as knowledge has illuminated the night full of silent mysteries, and has permitted humans to ascend the path of mastery over the other beings of the earth. Eliminate him — and

---

[1]*Aryan* strictly speaking, is a linguistic term referring to a branch of the Indo-European family of languages known as Indo-Iranian. It is also used to refer to a people who around 2000 B.C.E. began to migrate from their homeland in the steppes of western Asia to Iran, India, Mesopotamia, Asia Minor, and Europe. Their related family of languages, based on an even older language know as *Proto-Indo-European,* is believed to be the ancestor of all Indo-European languages, including Greek, Latin, Celtic, Persian, Sanskrit, and Balto-Slavonic, as well as their derivatives. In the nineteenth century, Aryan was used to refer to the *racial group* that

spoke these languages. According to Hitler and the Nazis, the Aryans provided Europe's original racial stock and stood in contrast to other peoples such as the Jews, who spoke *Semitic* languages.

[2]In Greek mythology Prometheus was the titan (titans were offspring of Uranus, heaven, and Gaiea, earth) who stole fire from the gods and gave it to humans, along with all other arts and civilization. He was also variously regarded as the creator of man (from clay), the first mortal man (along with his brother Epimetheus), and humanity's preserver when Zeus threatened to kill all human beings.

deep darkness will again descend on the earth after a few thousand years; human civilization will die out and the earth will become a desert.

If we were to divide mankind into three categories — the founders of culture, the bearers of culture, and the destroyers of culture, only the Aryans can be considered to be in the first category. From them are built the foundations and walls of all human creations, and only the outward form and colors of these are to be attributed to varying characteristics of the other individual peoples. He provides the mightiest building stones and designs for all human progress. . . .

The Jew provides the greatest contrast to the Aryan. With no other people of the world has the instinct for self-preservation been so developed as by the so-called chosen race.[3] The best proof of this statement rests in the fact that this race still exists. Where can another people be found in the past 2,000 years that has undergone so few changes in its inner qualities, character, etc. as the Jews? What people has undergone upheavals as great as this one — and nonetheless has emerged unchanged from the greatest catastrophes of humanity? What an infinitely tenacious will to live and to preserve one's kind is revealed in this fact. . . .

Since the Jew . . . never had a civilization of his own, others have always provided the foundations of his intellectual labors. His intellect has always developed by the use of those cultural achievements he has found ready at hand around him. Never has it happened the other way around.

For though their drive for self-preservation is not smaller, but larger than that of other people and though their mental capabilities may easily give the impression that their intellectual powers are equal to those of other races, the Jews lack the most basic characteristic of a truly cultured people, namely an idealistic spirit.

It is a remarkable fact that the herd instinct brings people together for mutual protection only so long as there is a common danger that makes mutual assistance necessary or unavoidable. The same pack of wolves that for an instant are combined to overcome their prey will soon after satisfying their hunger again become individual beasts . . . It goes the same way with the Jews. His sense of self sacrifice is only apparent. It lasts only so long as it is strictly necessary. As soon as the common enemy departs, however, as soon as the danger is gone and the booty secured, the superficial harmony among the Jews ends, and original conditions return. Jews act together only when a common danger threatens them or a common prey attracts them. When these two things are lacking, then their characteristic of the crassest egoism returns as a force, and out of this once unified people emerges in a flash a swarm of rats fighting bloodily against one another.

If the Jews existed in the world by themselves, they would wallow in their filth and disasters; they would try to get the best of the other in a hate-filled struggle, and even exterminate one another, that is, if their absolute lack of a sense of self-sacrifice, which is expressed in their venality, did not turn this drama into comedy also. . . .

That is why the Jewish state — which should be the living organism for the maintenance and improvement of the race — has absolutely no borders. For the territorial definition of a state always demands a certain idealism of spirit on the part of the race which forms the state and especially an acceptance of the idea of work. . . . If this attitude is lacking then the prerequisite for civilization is lacking.

◆ Hitler describes the process by which Jews in concert with communists have come close to subverting and controlling the peoples and nations in Europe.

Here he stops at nothing, and his vileness becomes so monstrous that no one should be surprised if among our people the hateful figure of

---

[3]A reference to the Jewish conviction developed in the Hebrew scriptures that God had chosen the Jews to enter into a special relationship or covenant in which God promised to be the God of the Hebrews and favor them in return for true worship and obedience.

the Jew is taken as the personification of the devil and the symbol of evil. . . .

How close they see their approaching victory can be seen in the frightful way that their dealings with members of other races develop.

The black-haired Jewish youth, with satanic joy on his face, lurks in wait for hours for the innocent girls he plans to defile with his blood, and steal the young girl from her people. With every means at hand he seeks to undermine the racial foundations of the people they would subjugate . . . For a people which is racially pure and is conscious of its blood will never be able to be subjugated by the Jews. The Jew in this world will forever only be the masters of bastardized people. . . .

Around those nations which have offered sturdy resistance to their internal attacks, they surround them with a web of enemies; thanks to their international influence, they incite them to war, and when necessary, will plant the flag of revolution, even on the battlefield.

In economics he shakes the foundations of the state long enough so that unprofitable business enterprises are shut down and come under his financial control. In politics he denies the state its means of self-preservation, destroys its means of self-maintenance and defense, annihilates faith in state leadership, insults its history and traditions, and drags everything that is truly great into the gutter.

Culturally, he pollutes art, literature and theater, make a mockery of natural sensibilities, destroys every concept of beauty and nobility, the worthy and the good, and instead drags other men down to the sphere of its own lowly type of existence.

Religion is made an object of mockery, morality and ethics are described as old-fashioned, until finally the last props of a people for maintaining their existence in this world are destroyed.

PERSONALITY AND THE IDEAL OF THE FOLKISH[4] STATE

The folkish world view differs from the Marxist world view fundamentally in that it not only recognizes the value of race, but also that of the individual, and makes these the pillars of its very structure. These are the sustaining factors in its view of the world.

The folkish state must care for the well-being of its citizens by recognizing in everything the worth of the person, and by doing so direct it to the highest level of its productive capability, thus guaranteeing for each the highest level of participation.

Accordingly, the folkish state must free the entire leadership, especially those in political leadership, from the parliamentary principle of majority rule by the multitude, so that the right of personality is guaranteed without any limitation. From this is derived the following realization. *The best state constitution and form is that which with unquestioned certainty raises the best minds from the national community to positions of leading authority and influence.* . . .

There are no majority decisions, rather only responsible individuals, and the word "advice" will once again have its original meaning. Each man will have advisers at his side, *but the decision will be made by one man.*

The principle that made the Prussian army in its time the most splendid instrument of the German people will have to become someday the foundation for the construction of our completed state: *authority of every leader downward and responsibility upward.* . . .

This principle of binding absolute responsibility with absolute authority will gradually bring forth an elite group of leaders which today in an era of irresponsible parliamentarianism is hardly thinkable.

---

[4]The word Hitler uses, *völkisch,* is an adjective derived from *Volk,* meaning "people" or "nation," which Hitler defined in a racial sense; thus a "folkish" state is one that expresses the characteristics of and furthers the interests of a particular race, in this case, the Aryans.

THE DIRECTION AND POLITICS OF EASTERN EUROPE

The foreign policy of the folkish state has as its purpose to guarantee the existence on this planet of the race that it gathers within its borders. With this in mind it must create a natural and healthy ratio between the number and growth of the population and the extent and quality of the land and soil. The balance must be such that it accords with the vital needs of the people. What I call a *healthy* ratio is one in which the support of the people is assured by its own land and soil. Any other condition, even if it lasts centuries or a thousand years, is nevertheless an unhealthy one and will lead sooner or later to damage, if not the total destruction of the affected people. *Only a sufficiently large space on the earth can assure the independent existence of a people....*

If the National Socialist Movement really is to be consecrated in history as fulfilling a great mission for the people, it must, spurred by knowledge and filled with pain over its true situation on this earth, boldly and with a clear sense of direction, take up the battle against the aimlessness and incompetence of our foreign policy. It must, without consideration of "traditions" or preconceived notions, find the courage to gather our people and their forces and advance them on the path from their present restricted living space to new land and soil. This will free the people from the dangers of disappearing from the earth altogether or becoming a slave people in the service of another.

The National Socialist movement must seek to eliminate the disproportion between our people's population and our territory — viewing this as a source of food as well as a basis for national power — and between our historical past and our present hopeless impotence. While doing so it must remain conscious of the fact that we as protectors of the highest humanity on earth are bound also by the highest duty that will be fulfilled only if we inspire the German people with the racial ideal, so that they will occupy themselves not just with the breeding of good dogs, horses, and cats but also show concern about the purity of *their own* blood.

Against everything else we National Socialists must hold unflinchingly to our goal of foreign policy, namely, *to secure for the German people the land on this earth to which they are entitled....*

State boundaries are made by man and can be changed by man.

The fact that a nation has acquired a large amount of land is no mandate that this should be recognized forever. This only goes to prove the strength of the conqueror and the weakness of the conquered. And only in force lies the right of possession. If today the German people are imprisoned within an impossible territorial area and for that reason are face to face with a miserable future, this is not the commandment of fate, any more than a revolt against such a situation would be a violation of the laws of fate; ... the soil on which we now live was not bestowed upon our ancestors by Heaven; rather, they had to conquer it by risking their lives. So with us, in the future we will win soil and with it the means of existence of the people not through some sort of folkish grace but only through the power of the triumphant sword.

But we National Socialists must go further: *The right to land and soil will become an obligation if without further territorial expansion a great people is threatened with its destruction.* And that is particularly true when the people in question is not some little nigger people, but the German mother of life, which has given cultural shape to the modern world. *Germany will either become a world power or will no longer exist.* To achieve world power an expansion in size is needed, which will give the state meaning in today's world and will give life to its citizens....

And so we National Socialists consciously draw a line below the direction of our foreign policy before the war. We take up where we broke off six hundred years ago. We put a stop to the eternal pull of the Germans toward the south and western Europe and turn our gaze to the lands of the east. We put an end to the colonial and commercial policy of the prewar period and shift to the land-oriented policy of the future.

When today we speak of new territory and soil in Europe, we think primarily of *Russia* and her subservient border states.

Motherhood, Duty, and the Nazi Ideal

◆

33 ◆ *Gertrud Scholtz-Klink,*
SPEECH TO THE NATIONAL SOCIALIST WOMEN'S ASSOCIATION, SEPTEMBER, 1935

Along with Judaism and Bolshevism, feminism, according to Hitler, was one of the great afflictions of modern Germany. While all of Weimar Germany's mainline political parties, even the conservative Nationalist Party and People's Party, endorsed women's equality and actively sought women's votes, the Nazis made no secret of their belief that women had no place in their party, politics, or government. Nor did they believe that women belonged in the work force. They should stay at home, bearing children, accepting their husbands' authority, and overseeing their families' happiness and health. Their role in creating a strong Germany was important, but it was distinct from the public lives of men.

Once in power, the Nazis dissolved communist and socialist women's organizations and sought to bring the hundreds of remaining organizations under the umbrella of the National Socialist Women's Association (National Sozialistische Frauenschaft, or NSF). They also created the Frauenwerk (Women's Bureau), an agency to oversee government programs relating to women. In 1934, Gertrud Scholtz-Klink, a thirty-two-year-old widowed mother of four (her husband had died of a heart attack during the excitement of a Nazi Party rally) was appointed National Women's Leader, with the responsibility to oversee all party and state matters relating to women. Despite her imposing title, Scholtz-Klink had no independent power and until the war's end was content to carry out tasks dictated by the all-male party leadership.

In the following speech, delivered at the 1935 Nazi Party Congress in Nuremberg to members of the NSF, Scholtz-Klink outlines some of her strategies for helping women to combine work and motherhood, while encouraging them to become enthusiastic disciples of National Socialism.

QUESTIONS FOR ANALYSIS

1. What is Scholtz-Klink's vision of women's role in the Nazi state?
2. What special tasks do women who are Nazi Party members have in rebuilding Germany?
3. What characteristics and values should the ideal German woman have, according to Scholtz-Klink?
4. What, according to the speaker, are the special problems of working-class women? How is the Party attempting to deal with these problems?
5. What are the reasons, stated and unstated, for the effort to recruit female university students for the Reich Labor Service?
6. On the basis of Scholtz-Klink's speech, what can you conclude about the success of the Nazis in achieving their goal of having women devote their lives to motherhood and family?

A year has passed since the day we met here for the first time as a unified group of German women, to demonstrate our willingness to cooperate in our Führer's work of reconstruction.

This year has been inspired by the desire to mark our times with our best efforts so that our descendants will be able to forget our nation's fourteen years of weakness and sickness. We women knew, quite as well as German men, that we had to teach a people, partially sunk in self-despair, attitudes requiring those very qualities that had been deliberately suppressed in our nation. In order to carry out our intentions to unite and to march shoulder to shoulder, we demanded honor and loyalty, strength and sincerity, humility and respect — such virtues appeal to the soul of a people. In matters of the soul, however, it is no longer the majority who decide, but the strength and inner freedom of upright individuals. Therefore, we could only fulfill our task if it enabled us to penetrate the soul of the individual. . . .

When we came to the point of recognizing that the human eye reflected a nation's soul, we had to reach the women of our nation, once and for all, through our labor on women's behalf. Because as mothers our women have carried the heavy burden of the past fourteen years — and the ruins of the war and post-war period — in their hearts; and as future mothers other women must presently develop an understanding of the demands of our times — to both of these groups we dedicated the first important path that we built to the hearts of German women: our Reichs-Maternity Service.

Urged on by the tired eyes of many over-burdened mothers and the responsibility for the coming generation of mothers, we joined together under the leadership of the National Socialist Women's Association . . . and appealed to the German women especially trained for this work. When I tell you today that, between the 1st of October 1934 and the 1st of April 1935, we enrolled more than 201,700 women in 7,653 maternity school courses in about 2,000 locations throughout the German Reich, it may not seem much at first glance. But we must not forget that we had no funds and met with much opposition, and that we had no patronage since we were quite unknown. But we did have absolute and unshakable faith. None of our traveling teachers asked: How much will I earn? Or, What are my pension rights? We have done this work out of a sense of duty to our nation — and our nation has responded. On Mothers' Day this year we were presented with 3.5 million marks for this work of maternity training. Moreover, on this day of honor for the mothers of Germany, when we all collected money in the streets, we found that our humblest fellow-countrymen were the most generous. This was surely the most wonderful reward for all of us, but it also gave practical evidence of where our major efforts must be directed. And when, only one or two months from now, we open our Reichs-Maternity School in Wedding, formerly one of the most solidly "red"[1] quarters of Berlin, we will be able to congratulate ourselves on having prepared a place, on behalf of our Party and our State, that will reveal to all of you how we are solving our problems.

In this place, mothers of all ages and classes discuss their problems and their needs. Here they will become acquainted with the aims of a National Socialist state and will receive inspiration to pass them on from woman to woman, and thus to recover our national faith in ourselves. If by means of the Reichs-Maternity Service we gradually succeed in brightening the eyes of our mothers and in bringing some joy into their often difficult lives, perhaps even a song to their lips, we may consider that we have accomplished our task, because happy mothers will raise happy children. But our Reichs-Maternity Service must also make a point of teaching our young and future mothers those things that a liberal era did not teach them — for the omission of which our nation has had to pay dearly — namely, that though marriage we consciously become mothers of the nation; that is, we understand and share every national requirement laid upon German

---

[1]Communist.

men, and that, therefore, as wives we must unconditionally become the companions of our men — not merely in personal terms, but in all national requirements.

First we pursued our task by appealing to the mothers of the nation, and then to that generation closest to the mothers, the girls between eighteen and twenty-five years of age. We called upon them to join voluntarily in the chain of helping hands and to create a relationship of unbreakable trust among German women. And they came, our girls of the German Women's Labor Service.[2]

You, my girls, who have now spent two years with me in the struggle for the autonomy of the German people, have learned to carry every responsibility and have become the inspiration of our mothers. No matter whether our girls are cheerfully helping German settlers on the moors in their difficult work of creating new homes; or whether they are working in Rhön, Spessart, or in eastern Bavaria, hand in hand with the National Socialist Welfare Organization in giving help to careworn adults and joyless children, in reawakening a taste for beauty and a belief in themselves; or whether they are helping German peasant women harvest from dawn to dusk — one thing unites them all, for they know: We are needed, we are of some use, and we are playing our parts in the rebirth of our nation. . . .

Since at present we cannot satisfy all these demands [for compulsory labor service], owing to financial and organizational difficulties, we have begun by making only those demands that professional and university women can take the lead in supporting. . . . At one time, it was considered the height of achievement in Germany to know everything and thereby to lose the simple-mindedness of childhood. We wish to impress on our women at the universities that, as university students, they must place the intellectual abilities entrusted to them at the disposal of their na-

tion with the same humility as that with which women workers and mothers fulfill their duties. . . . This summer our women students began to live in this manner and thereby joined the chain of helping hands we have created among ourselves. They went to German factories and replaced working women and mothers, enabling them to have a real vacation in order to regain strength for their hard day-to-day existence. For it is these women, these mothers of families, who are hardest hit by the short working hours or unemployment of their husbands, because at home their children sap their strength. . . .

This brings us to the point where we must consider the millions of German women who perform heavy labor in factories day in and day out. If we consider the human eye as the measure of people's soul, it is here that we find the deepest imprints of that fourteen-year-long attempt to strangle our national soul. We know that a great deal of industrial work must always be done by women, but it is essential that the woman at the machine should feel that she, in her position, represents her nation, in common with all other women. That is to say, we awaken her consciousness so that she will say to herself: "This is my responsibility, my attitude determines the attitude of the nation." . . .

I must deal briefly with a question that is constantly brought to our attention, that is, how our present attitude toward life differs from that of the previous women's movement. First, in principle we permit only Germans to be leaders of German women and to concern themselves with matters of importance to Germans. Second, as a matter of principle we never have demanded, nor shall we ever demand, equal rights for women with the men of our nation. Instead we shall always make women's special interests dependent upon the needs of our entire nation. All further considerations will follow from this unconditional intertwining of the collective fate of the nation.

---

[2]The Reich Labor Service (Reichsarbeitdienst, or RAD) grew out of various government-sponsored programs begun in the Weimar period in which unemployed young men worked on agricultural and construction projects. Under the Nazis, labor service was mandatory for young men between the ages of eighteen and twenty-five, and was brought under Party control. The Women's Labor Service was smaller, and participation was not mandatory until 1939.

The Stalin Revolution in the Soviet Union

After Lenin suffered a debilitating stroke in 1922 and died in January 1924, the Communist Party of the Soviet Union was racked by controversy over its future leadership and direction. Factions led by Leon Trotsky, Lev Kamenev, Gregory Zinoviev, and Nikolai Bukharin fought for Party offices and engaged in highly intellectualized debates about industrial policy, the peasant question, the meaning of socialism, international communism, and party governance. The winner in the power struggle, however, was Joseph Stalin, a man noted more for his political and organizational skills than his intellect. As general secretary of the Party, his control of patronage and his ability to dispense favors to local officials meant that he was able to steadily increase the number of his supporters in party congresses and ultimately the politburo, the Party's central executive committee. One by one, his opponents were voted down, removed from office, expelled from the Party, and frequently exiled to Siberia. When the Fifteenth Party Congress in December 1927 condemned "all deviations from the party line" (then largely decided by Stalin himself), Stalin's control was complete. The stage was set for a new round of earthshaking economic and political changes for the Soviet people.

Joseph Stalin (1879–1953), born Joseph Dzhugashvili, was the son of a shoemaker from the province of Georgia. He was a candidate for the priesthood before he abandoned Christianity for Marxism and joined the Bolshevik wing of the Social Democratic Party in 1903. His position in the party rose steadily, and between periods of exile he attended party congresses in Stockholm and London. Exiled to Siberia, he returned to Petrograd in 1917 after the fall of the tsar and sat on the twelve-member Central Committee that organized the October Revolution. In 1922 he was named general secretary of the Bolshevik Party and, a few years later, commissar of nationalities. Having crushed his opponents in the struggles following Lenin's death, Stalin launched a bold restructuring of the Soviet economy in 1928, setting the Soviet Union on a political and cultural path it would follow in certain respects until the mid-1980s.

The Soviet Model of Economic Planning

34 ◆ Joseph Stalin,
THE RESULTS OF THE FIRST FIVE-YEAR PLAN

In 1928, the New Economic Policy (NEP), which Lenin had adopted in 1921, still guided Soviet economic life. Through the NEP, Lenin had sought to restore agriculture and industry after seven years of war, revolution, and civil strife. Although the state maintained control of banks, foreign trade, and heavy industry, peasants could sell their goods on the open market, and small business owners could hire laborers, operate small factories, and keep their profits. The NEP saved the USSR from economic collapse, but its acceptance of private profit and economic competition troubled Marxist purists and did little to foster large-scale industrialization. Thus in 1928 Stalin abandoned the NEP and replaced it with the first Five-Year Plan, which established a centralized planned economy in which Moscow bureaucrats regulated agriculture, manufacturing, finance, and transportation. In agriculture, the Plan abolished individual peasant holdings and combined them into large collective and state farms. This meant the obliteration of the class of prosperous and successful peasant farmers known as kulaks. In manufacturing, the Plan concentrated on heavy industry and the production of goods such as tractors, trucks, and machinery. Second and third Five-Year Plans were launched in 1933 and 1938.

In the following report, delivered to the Central Committee of the Communist Party of the Soviet Union in January 1933, Stalin outlines the goals and achievements of the first Five-Year Plan.

QUESTIONS FOR ANALYSIS

1. According to Stalin, was socialist theory or the defense of the Soviet Union the more important reason for launching the Five-Year Plans?
2. Why did heavy industry play such an important role in the Five-Year Plans?
3. Why, in Stalin's view, was the collectivization of agriculture such a key component of the Five-Year Plan?
4. What, according to Stalin, were the main obstacles to the success of the Five-Year Plan?
5. In Stalin's view, how have the people of the Soviet Union benefited from the Five-Year Plan? What sacrifices have they been asked to make?
6. How, according to Stalin, does the success of the Five-Year Plan prove communism's superiority to capitalism?

The fundamental task of the Five-Year Plan was to convert the U.S.S.R. from an agrarian and weak country, dependent upon the caprices of the capitalist countries, into an industrial and powerful country, fully self-reliant and independent of the caprices of world capitalism.

The fundamental task of the Five-Year Plan was, in converting the U.S.S.R. into an industrial country, fully to eliminate the capitalist elements, to widen the front of the socialist forms of economy, and to create the economic base for the abolition of classes in the U.S.S.R., for the construction of socialist society.

The fundamental task of the Five-Year Plan was to create such an industry in our country as would be able to re-equip and reorganize, not only the whole of industry, but also transport and agriculture — on the basis of socialism.

The fundamental task of the Five-Year Plan was to transfer small and scattered agriculture onto the lines of large-scale collective farming, so as the ensure the economic base for socialism in the rural districts and thus to eliminate the possibility of the restoration of capitalism in the U.S.S.R.

Finally, the task of the Five-Year Plan was to create in the country all the necessary technical and economic prerequisites for increasing to the utmost the defensive capacity of the country, to enable it to organize determined resistance to any and every attempt at military intervention from outside. . . .

The main link in the Five-Year Plan was heavy industry, with machine building at its core. For only heavy industry is capable of reconstructing industry as a whole, as well as the transport system and agriculture, and of putting them on their feet. . . . Hence, the restoration of heavy industry had to be made on the basis of the fulfillment of the Five-Year Plan. . . .

But the restoration and development of heavy industry, particularly in such a backward and poor country as our country was at the beginning of the Five-Year Plan period, is an extremely difficult task; for, as is well known, heavy industry calls for enormous financial expenditures and the availability of a certain minimum of experienced technical forces, without which, speaking generally, the restoration of heavy industry is impossible. Did the party know this, and did it take this into consideration? Yes, it did. . . . The party declared frankly that this would call for serious sacrifices, and that we must openly and consciously make these sacrifices if we wanted to achieve our goal. . . .

◆ ◆

What are the results of the Five-Year Plan in four years in the sphere of *industry*? . . .

We did not have an iron and steel industry, the foundation for the industrialization of the country. Now we have this industry.

We did not have a tractor industry. Now we have one.

We did not have an automobile industry. Now we have one.

We did not have a machine-tool industry. Now we have one.

We did not have a big and up-to-date chemical industry. Now we have one.

We did not have a real and big industry for the production of modern agricultural machinery. Now we have one.

We did not have an aircraft industry. Now we have one.

In output of electric power we were last on the list. Now we rank among the first.

In the output of oil products and coal we were last on the list. Now we rank among the first. . . .

And as a result of all this the capitalist elements have been completely and [irrevocably] eliminated from industry, and socialist industry has become the sole form of industry in the U.S.S.R.

And as a result of all this our country has been converted from an agrarian into an industrial country; for the proportion of industrial output, as compared with agricultural output, has risen from 48 per cent of the total in the beginning of the Five-Year Plan period (1928) to 70 per cent at the end of the fourth year of the Five-Year Plan period (1932). . . .

Finally, as a result of all this the Soviet Union has been converted from a weak country, unprepared for defense, into a country mighty in defense, a country prepared for every contingency, a country capable of producing on a mass scale all modern weapons of defense and of equipping its army with them in the event of an attack from without. . . .

We are told: This is all very well; but it would have been far better to have abandoned the policy of industrialization, . . . and to have produced more cotton, cloth, shoes, clothing, and other articles of general use. . . .

. . . Of course, out of the 1,500,000,000 rubles in foreign currency that we spent on purchasing equipment for our heavy industries, we could have set apart a half for the purpose of importing raw cotton, hides, wool, rubber, etc. Then we would now have more cotton cloth, shoes and clothing. But we would not have a tractor industry or an automobile industry; we would not have anything like a big iron and steel industry; we would not have metal for the manufacture of machinery — and we would be unarmed, while we are surrounded by capitalist countries which are armed with modern technique. . . . Our position would be more or less analogous to the present position of China, which has no heavy industry and no war industry of her own and which is pecked at by everybody who cares to do so. . . .

◆ ◆

The Five-Year Plan in the sphere of agriculture was a Five-Year Plan of collectivization. What did the party proceed from in carrying out collectivization?

The party proceeded from the fact that in order to consolidate the dictatorship of the proletariat and to build up socialist society it was necessary, in addition to industrialization, to pass from small, individual peasant farming to large-scale collective agriculture equipped with tractors and modern agricultural machinery, as the only firm basis for the Soviet power in the rural districts.

The party proceeded from the fact that without collectivization it would be impossible to lead our country onto the highroad of building the economic foundations of socialism, impossible to free the vast masses of the laboring peasantry from poverty and ignorance. . . .

The party has succeeded, in a matter of three years, in organizing more than 200,000 collective farms and about 5,000 state farms specializing mainly in grain growing and livestock raising, and at the same time it has succeeded, in the course of four years, in enlarging the crop area by 21,000,000 hectares.[1]

The party has succeeded in getting more than 60 per cent of the peasant farms, which account for more than 70 per cent of the land cultivated by peasants to unite into collective farms, which means that we have *fulfilled* the Five-Year Plan *threefold.*

The party has succeeded in creating the possibility of obtaining, not 500,000,000 to 600,000,000 poods[2] of marketable grain, which was the amount purchased in the period when individual peasant farming predominated, but 1,200,000,000 to 1,400,000,000 poods of grain annually.

The party has succeeded in routing the kulaks as a class, although they have not yet been dealt the final blow; the laboring peasants have been emancipated from kulak bondage and exploitation, and a firm economic basis for the Soviet government, the basis of collective farming, has been established in the countryside.

The party has succeeded in converting the U.S.S.R. from a land of small peasant farming into a land where agriculture is run on the largest scale in the world. . . .

Do not all these facts testify to the superiority of the Soviet system of agriculture over the capitalist system? Do not these facts go to show that the collective farms are a more virile form of farming than individual capitalist farms? . . .

. . . Was the party right in pursuing the policy of an accelerated tempo of collectivization? Yes, it was absolutely right, even though certain excesses were committed in the process.[3] In pursuing the policy of eliminating the kulaks as a class, and in destroying the kulak nests, the party could not stop half way. It was necessary to carry this work to completion. . . .

What are the results of these successes as regards the improvement of the material conditions of the workers and peasants? . . .

In our country, in the U.S.S.R., the workers have long forgotten unemployment. Some three years ago we had about one and a half million unemployed. It is already two years now since unemployment has been completely abolished. . . . Look at the capitalist countries: what horrors are taking place there as a result of unemployment! There are now no less than thirty to forty million unemployed in those countries. . . .

---

[1]In the metric system a hectare is slightly less than 2.5 acres.
[2]A Russian measure of weight equal to about thirty-six pounds.
[3]Stalin is understating the case more than a little. It is estimated that as many as fifteen million peasants were deported to labor camps, exiled to Siberia, or sent to work in factories in the late 1920s and early 1930s; of these 15 to 20 percent died or were executed.

Every day they try to get work, seek work, are prepared to accept almost any conditions of work but they are not given work, because they are "superfluous." And this is taking place at a time when vast quantities of goods and products are wasted to satisfy the caprices of the darlings of fate, the scions of capitalists and landlords. The unemployed are refused food because they have no money to pay for the food; they are refused shelter because they have no money to pay rent. How and where do they live? They live on the miserable crumbs from the rich man's table; by raking [searching through] refuse cans, where they find decayed scraps of food; they live in the slums of big cities, and more often in hovels outside of the towns, hastily put up by the unemployed out of packing cases and the bark of trees. . . .

One of the principal achievements of the Five-Year Plan in four years is that we have abolished unemployment and have relieved the workers of the U.S.S.R. of its horrors.

The same thing must be said in regard to the peasants. They, too, have forgotten about the differentiation of the peasants into kulaks and poor peasants, about the exploitation of the poor peasants by the kulaks, about the ruin which, every year, caused hundreds of thousands and millions of poor peasants to go begging. . . .

[The Five-Year Plan] has undermined and smashed the kulaks as a class, thus liberating the poor peasants and a good half of the middle peasants from bondage to the kulaks. . . . It has thus eliminated the possibility of the differentiation of the peasantry into exploiters — kulaks — and exploited — poor peasants. It has raised the poor peasants and the lower stratum of the middle peasants to a position of security in the collective farms, and has thereby put a stop to the process of ruination and impoverishment of the peasantry. . . .

Now there are no more cases of hundreds of thousands and millions of peasants being ruined and forced to hang around the gates of factories and mills. That is what used to happen; but that was long ago. Now the peasant is in a position of security; he is a member of a collective farm which has at its disposal tractors, agricultural machinery, a seed fund, a reserve fund, etc., etc.

Such are the main results of the realization of the Five-Year Plan in industry and agriculture; in the improvement of the conditions of life of the working people and the development of the exchange of goods; in the consolidation of the Soviet power and the development of the class struggle against the remnants and survival of the dying classes.

The Abortion Debate Under Stalin

❖

35 ◆ *LETTERS TO* IZVESTIYA *ON THE ABORTION ISSUE, MAY–JUNE 1936*

On taking power in Russia in 1917, the Bolsheviks, true to the heritage of European socialism, immediately took steps to liberate women from the shackles of religion, ignorance, and male dominance. In its first few months of existence, the Bolshevik government declared marriage a civil, not religious, union, and made divorce more or less available on demand. In 1920 it legalized abortion. After the civil war, women were encouraged to work, and the Ministry of Social Welfare established a system of nationwide day-care centers for children of working mothers. Government schools taught girls how to read and write, and party functionaries from the Zhenotdel, or women's bureau, went into cities, villages, and remote provinces to inform women of their rights, teach literacy, fight prostitution, and explain communism. In 1926 the party reaffirmed its commitment to female equality and women's rights in the revised Family Code adopted by the All Union Council of Soviets.

In the 1930s, however, the Soviet government under Stalin became more authoritarian, and its policies less libertarian and egalitarian. Nationalism, social conservatism, industrialization, and the collectivization of agriculture became its focus. Like many other European leaders, Stalin was disturbed by the Soviet Union's declining birth rate, which fell 50 percent between 1930 and 1935. In response, the government launched a campaign to glorify motherhood and the family, and couples were urged to have larger families. A key step was taken in 1936 when the government proposed legislation to make divorce more difficult and to outlaw abortions except to protect the health of the mother. These issues were never debated in a political forum, but newspapers such as *Pravda* and *Izvestia* were permitted to publish readers' opinions in the form of letters to the editor.

The following excerpts from letters to *Izvestia* provide a sampling of the arguments for and against changing the abortion law. Not surprisingly, despite strong public support for keeping abortion legal, Stalin's government went ahead with its plans. On June 27, 1936, abortion became illegal in the Soviet Union.

QUESTIONS FOR ANALYSIS

1. What arguments for and against abortion are offered by the letter writers?
2. What do the letters reveal about living conditions in the Soviet Union during the 1930s?
3. What views of motherhood are revealed in the letters?
4. What reasons might the government have had for allowing readers' letters to be published?

Letter from a Student [K. B.]

I have read in the press the draft law on the prohibition of abortion, aid to expectant mothers, etc., and cannot remain silent on this matter.

There are thousands of women in the same position as myself. I am a student reading the first course of the second Moscow Medical Institute. My husband is also a student reading the same course at our Institute. Our scholarships amount jointly to 205 rubles. Neither he nor I have a room of our own. Next year we intend to apply for admission to a hostel, but I do not know whether our application will be granted. I love children and shall probably have some in four or five years' time. But can I

have a child now? Having a child now would mean leaving the Institute, lagging behind my husband, forgetting everything I have learnt and probably leaving Moscow because there is nowhere to live.

There is another married couple in our Institute, Mitya and Galya, who live in a hostel. Yesterday Galya said to me: "If I become pregnant I shall have to leave the Institute; one cannot live in a hostel with children."

I consider that the projected law is premature because the housing problem in our towns is a painful one. Very often it is the lack of living quarters that is the reason behind an abortion. If the draft included an article assuring married couples, who are expecting a baby, of a room — that would be a different matter.

In five years' time when I am a doctor and have a job and a room I shall have children. But at present I do not want and cannot undertake such a responsibility. . . .

Letter from an Engineer [E.T.]

. . . I am non-party, married, with a 5-year-old son. I work as an engineer and have been and still am in a responsible position. I regard myself as a good citizen of the U.S.S.R.

I cannot agree with the prohibition of abortions. And I am very glad that this law has not entered into force but has been submitted to the workers for discussion.

The prohibition of abortion means the compulsory birth of a child to a woman who does not want children. The birth of a child ties married people to each other. Not everyone will readily abandon a child, for alimony is not all that children need. Where the parents produce a child of their own free will, all is well. But where a child comes into the family against the will of the parents, a grim personal drama will be enacted which will undoubtedly lower the social value of the parents and leave its mark on the child.

A categorical prohibition of abortion will confront young people with a dilemma: either complete sexual abstinence or the risk of jeopardizing their studies and disrupting their life. To my mind any prohibition of abortion is bound to mutilate many a young life. Apart from this, the result of such a prohibition might be an increase in the death-rate from abortions because they will then be performed illegally.

Answer to the Student K. B. . . .

Your paper recently published a letter from a student, K. B., in which she raised objections to the prohibition of abortions. I think the author of the letter . . . has not grasped the full

significance of the projected law. The difficulties about which K. B. writes and which, according to her, justify abortion are, she thinks, the difficulties of to-day which will have disappeared to-morrow. The writer of that letter completely ignored the fact that the government, by widening the network of child-welfare institutions, is easing the mother's task in looking after the child. The main mistake K. B. makes is, in my view, that she approaches the problem of childbearing as though it were a private matter. This would explain why she writes: "I shall have them (children) in four or five years' time." She hopes by that time to have completed her studies, obtained a medical diploma and found both a job and a room. But one must be logical! If during these years, K. B. intends to have recourse to abortions, who can vouch that by the time when she desires to have children she will still be able to do so? And for a normal woman to be deprived of the possibility of having children is as great a misfortune as the loss of a dear one.

I used to study in a factory and received a very small allowance while bringing up my small son whom I had to bring up on my own. (His father was dead.) It was a hard time. I had to go and unload trains or look for similar work that would bring in some money . . . that was in 1923. Now my son is a good, rough Komsomol[1] and a Red Army soldier in the Far East. How great are my joy and pride that I did not shun the difficulties and that I managed to bring up such a son.

Letter from Professor K. Bogorekov, Leningrad

Abortions are harmful. One cannot disagree with that. But situations in life do exist when this harmful remedy will allow a woman to preserve normal conditions of life.

If a single child already ties a woman down, two, three or four children leave her no possibility

---

[1]A member of the Communist Youth Organization; one could stay in the organization until the age of twenty-five.

at all of participating in social life and having a job. A man suffers less. He gives the family his salary irrespective of the number of children — and the whole burden falls upon the mother.

Sometimes abortion is an extreme but decisive means of averting the disruption of a young woman's life. It may become imperative, through the accident of an unlucky liaison for a young girl-student without means for whom a child would be a heavy penalty, or through bad heredity of the parents or a number of other contingencies which play an important part in life and can often lead to its mutilation. All this must be taken into account.

It must not be thought that the majority of abortions are the result of irresponsible behavior. Experience shows that a woman resorts to abortion as a last resource when other methods of safeguard against pregnancy have failed and the birth of a child threatens to make her life more difficult.

Simple statistics show that in spite of this the birth-rate of our country is increasing rapidly.[2] And what is needed is not pressure, but a stimulation of the birth-rate by means of financial assistance, improved housing conditions, legal action against those who fail to pay alimony, etc. . . .

. . . Abortions will become obsolete by themselves when knowledge of human anatomy spreads, methods of birth-control are more widely used and — last but not least — when housing conditions are improved. . . .

Letter from Professor M. Malinovsky

Performing an abortion is an operation undoubtedly involving great risks. There are few operations so dangerous as the cleaning out of the womb during pregnancy. Under the best of conditions and in the hands of the most experienced specialist this operation still has a "normal" percentage of fatal cases. It is true that the percentage is not very high. Our surgeons have brought the technique of performing abortions to perfection. The foreign doctors who have watched operations in our gynæcological hospitals have unanimously testified that their technique is irreproachable. And yet . . . here are still cases in which it is fatal. This is understandable. The operation is performed in the dark and with instruments which, so far as their effect on so tender an organ as the womb is concerned, remind one of a crowbar. And even the most gifted surgeons, virtuosi at their job, occasionally cause great and serious injuries for which the woman often pays with her life. . . .

The slave-like conditions of hired labor, together with unemployment and poverty, deprive women in capitalist countries of the impulse for childbearing. Their "will to motherhood" is paralyzed. In our country all the conditions for giving birth to and bringing up a healthy generation exist. The "fear of motherhood", the fear of the morrow, the anxiety over the child's future are gone.

The lighthearted attitude towards the family, the feeling of irresponsibility which is still quite strong in men and women, the disgusting disrespect for women and children — all these must come before our guns. Every baseness towards women and every form of profligacy must be considered as serious antisocial acts. . . .

---

[2]From what is known, a false statement.

CHAPTER 5

Latin America in an Era of Economic Challenge and Political Change

A popular slogan among Latin America's politicians and landowners in the late nineteenth and early twentieth centuries was "order and progress," and to an extent that was exceptional in the region's history, they achieved both. Around 1870 Latin America's economy entered a period of export-driven expansion that continued until the 1920s. In an updated version of colonial-era economic relationships, the region became a major supplier of wheat, beef, mutton, coffee, raw rubber, nitrates, copper, tin, and a host of other primary products to Europe and a major market for European manufactured goods. Land prices soared, and English and U.S. capital flowed into Latin America to finance railroads, banks, and food-processing facilities and to lend governments money for the construction of roads, bridges, and public buildings. The defects of this neocolonial economic order soon would be revealed; in the short run, however, it brought riches to the landowners and modernization to the cities.

Latin America's economic boom took place in a climate of relative political stability. In Argentina, Chile, and Brazil this stability was achieved under republican governments controlled by an oligarchy of landowning families, sometimes in alliance with merchants in the import-export trade; in Mexico, Peru, Ecuador, and Venezuela, it resulted from rule by a strong man or dictator (*caudillo*). Dictators and oligarchs alike sought economic growth by maintaining law and order and by encouraging foreign investment, free trade, and land confiscations from the Roman Catholic Church and Native Americans. They faced little opposition. The rural masses were politically apathetic; an urban working class hardly existed; and the small middle class accepted its limited political role as long as prosperity continued.

By the 1930s, however, oligarchic rule and the neocolonial economic order on which it had been based were both in shambles. The turning point was the Great Depression of the 1930s, which exposed the dangers of dependency on industrialized nations for markets, manufactured goods, and capital. Demand for Latin

America's food products and raw materials collapsed, depriving the region of the foreign exchange needed to buy manufactured goods. The collapse of the international financial system shut off the flow of loans and investments from Europe and the United States. Governments faced insolvency, and capital shortages impeded plans to end the economic slump through industrialization. Latin Americans came to resent European and especially U.S. ownership of tin and copper mines, oil fields, railroads, banks, processing plants, and prime agricultural land. Once welcomed as a means of attracting capital and encouraging growth, foreign ownership in the 1930s more frequently was condemned as imperialist plunder.

The oligarchical political order had already begun to disintegrate by the time the Great Depression struck. Economic expansion had generated social changes that undermined the region's two-class system — an elite of wealthy and powerful landowners and a mass of illiterate and impoverished peasants and laborers. Urbanization, fueled by European immigration, modest industrialization, and an influx of people from the countryside, made society more complex and diversified. In Mexico City, Rio de Janeiro, Buenos Aires, and other cities, a factory-based working class emerged, and a middle class made up of professionals, office workers, teachers, writers, and small business owners grew steadily. These groups rejected the oligarchy's economic priorities, and their growing assertiveness undermined the political monopoly of the landowning elite. Their strength was revealed in Argentina in 1912 when the government extended the right to vote to all adult males, and in Mexico in 1910 when middle-class reformers in alliance with rural rebels overthrew the dictatorship of Porfirio Díaz.

Political and social conflict in the 1920s and 1930s was accompanied by the breakdown of the intellectual and cultural assumptions of the era of "order and progress." These assumptions included a faith in science and liberalism, a belief in white racial superiority, and a conviction that things European equaled progress, while things American, or Indian, represented backwardness. The liberalism of the white ruling class faced opposition not only from conservative Catholics, but also from nationalists, communists, anarchists, trade unionists, and fascists who in various contexts and at different times spoke on behalf of the middle class, the proletariat, the military, and the Indians, blacks, and mixed bloods. Modernist artists and writers, like their counterparts in Europe, rejected liberalism, questioned reason and science, and sought to articulate the components of a new cultural identity and of a new society. By the 1920s this quest for self-definition led many intellectuals to discover popular traditions and ethnic, especially Indian, lore, which they regarded as the touchstones of cultural identity.

This current of nativism, or *indigenismo,* strengthened cultural nationalism in states such as Mexico and Peru and prepared the way for the economic nationalism of the Depression years.

Out of this ideological and cultural ferment, no new consensus emerged. In Chile, Uruguay, and Venezuela, oligarchic rule gave way to dominance by new middle-class groups who frequently disagreed about fundamental issues. Mexico became a one-party state controlled by the National Revolutionary Party, which, despite its name, until the mid-1930s was more interested in capitalist development than social reform. A new kind of populist, quasi-fascist leader emerged in the persons of Getúlio Vargas in Brazil and Juan Perón in Argentina. Strong-arm dictators, essentially old-style *caudillos,* held sway in Cuba, the Dominican Republic, El Salvador, Haiti, Honduras, Nicaragua, Paraguay, and Guatemala.

As a result of all these factors, Latin America in the 1920s and 1930s faced a crisis of political legitimacy, as well as deepening fragmentation, instability, and conflict. Old views and institutions were discredited, but no one could agree on what should replace them. A democratic government might come to power briefly, only to be overthrown by the army; populist politicians might institute reforms, only to be replaced by a conservative government that canceled them. There were threats from the left, counterstrikes from the right, divisions in the center — and repeated clashes among them all. A few countries — Mexico, Chile, Uruguay for a time, Costa Rica, Venezuela, and perhaps Colombia — had some success dealing with these competing cross-currents, but in the rest, the conflicts were so deep and the gaps between regions and classes so vast that no government could govern effectively or even hope to survive for long.

New Social and Political Currents: Feminism and *Indigenismo*

Among the issues that confronted Latin American politicians, intellectuals, and civic-minded citizens in the early 1900s, none was more fundamental than the perceived lack of nationhood throughout the region. Their states, many Latin Americans came to believe, lacked not just political consensus but, more fundamentally, any sense of unity or common purpose among their people. Latin American nations were loose amalgams of groups and subgroups differing in speech, ethnic background, economic expectations, and perspectives. Issues were seen through the prisms of class, region, race, gender, and economic self-interest, not the general good. Many became convinced they needed a new type of state with governments committed to serving the interests of all its component groups and drawing on all their energies. This meant breaking the political monopoly of the great landowners and opening up politics to groups who had largely been ignored during the era of oligarchical rule — the bourgeoisie, urban workers, immigrants, and two groups that are the subjects of the documents in this section, women and Native Americans.

The drive for women's rights in Latin America began in the 1870s in the most urbanized and economically advanced states — Argentina, Chile, Uruguay, and Brazil. In all four, liberal governments in the late 1800s established secular schools for girls as part of an effort to end the Roman Catholic Church's monopoly on education. This led to the founding of teacher-training schools for women and the emergence of teaching as an important female profession.

Schoolteachers, along with small numbers of professional women, recent arrivals from Europe, and socialists, provided leadership and energy for Latin American feminism in the early 1900s. They edited journals, attended conferences, and formed societies for the purposes of self-improvement and publicity. Most feminists supported better education for women, access to the professions, improved health care, and greater equality between husbands and wives. There were disagreements, however, on issues of divorce and women's suffrage. Moderates feared liberalized divorce laws would weaken marriage, while socialists and liberals feared that if devout Catholic women were given the right to vote, they would tilt the balance in favor of conservative clerical parties.

Feminists made some gains in the 1920s and 1930s. In 1929 Ecuador, whose conservative leaders hoped women's votes would favor them over their liberal and socialist rivals, was the first Latin American state to grant women the right to vote. In the 1930s women won the right to vote in national elections in Brazil, Uruguay, and Cuba, and in provincial and municipal elections in Mexico, Peru, and Argentina. Progress also was made in education. In Cuba females gained equal access to public schools in 1901, and in several states increasing numbers of women were admitted to universities. In Chile in the 1920s, women received 25 percent of all degrees. Few gains were made in the area of married women's rights; by the late 1930s, only Mexico, Argentina, Chile, and Uruguay had revised their civil codes to limit husbands' authority.

Along with *feminismo, indigenismo* was another word added to Latin America's vocabulary in the early twentieth century. Sometimes translated into English as "Indianism," *indigenismo* became an important movement in states with large Indian populations such as Mexico, Bolivia, Peru, Guatemala, and Ecuador. A term with cultural and political connotations, *indigenismo* meant both an affirmation of the intrinsic value of the Indians' culture and a commitment to improving their economic and social condition. It was part of the general reaction against the assumptions and policies of the late-nineteenth- and early-twentieth-century oligarchies, whose leaders had disdained the Indians' culture and condoned the landowning elite's exploitation of the native population. It also was a result of greater awareness of Indian problems that grew out of Indian revolts in Peru and the demands of Emiliano Zapata and his followers for land reform during the Mexican Revolution.

In the 1920s and 1930s increasing numbers of Latin American writers explored the theme of Indian exploitation, and many intellectuals asserted that Indian culture and values could become a source of national regeneration. Politicians also showed greater interest in Indian problems. The Mexican Constitution of 1917 committed the government to land reform, and during the 1920s and 1930s, millions of acres of land were returned to peasant communities. No one solved the "Indian problem," however, and in Mexico and the Andean states, Indians today remain at the bottom of the economic and social order.

Costs and Benefits of Latin American Feminism

36 ◆ Amanda Labarca, *WHERE IS WOMAN GOING?*

Amanda Labarca was born in 1886 into the family of a successful Chilean merchant in Santiago. Educated in private girls' schools, she attended the University of Chile, where she received a degree in education. After her marriage to Guillermo Hubertson, the couple pursued graduate studies at both Columbia University and the Sorbonne in Paris, and traveled extensively in the United States and Europe. By the time Labarca returned to Chile in 1918, she was a feminist. She became the director of a girls' school in Santiago and in 1919 helped found the National Council of Women of Chile, an organization dedicated to improving women's legal, civil, and educational status. In 1922 she became a professor of education at the University of Chile, and in 1931 was appointed director of secondary education for the entire nation. A well-known figure in international feminist circles, she traveled extensively and published more than twenty books of fiction and social commentary.

The following excerpt is take from an article, "¿Adónde va la mujer?" (Where Is Woman Going?), which first appeared in the 1920s and was republished in an anthology by the same name in 1934. In it she discusses the positive and negative effects of feminism on the region's middle-class women.

QUESTIONS FOR ANALYSIS

1. On the basis of Labarca's essay, how can one characterize views of women and the status of women in Latin American societies before the rise of feminism?
2. In Labarca's view, how have twentieth-century developments eroded traditional views? What were the underlying causes of these developments?
3. According to Labarca, what "losses" have middle-class Latin American women experienced as a result of women's changing social role? Who is largely to blame for these losses?
4. How does Labarca view the essential characteristics of men and women?
5. Is Labarca optimistic about women's future in Latin America? Why or why not?

Has feminism brought gains or losses to the Latin-American middle-class girl of today?

Gains. First of all, the consciousness of her own worth in the totality of human progress. Today's girl knows that there are no insurmountable obstacles to the flight of her intelligence; that the question of whether her entire sex is intelligent will not be raised before she is permitted to engage in any intellectual activity; that in the eyes of the majority her womanhood does not mark her with the stigma of irremediable inferiority, and that if she has talent she will be allowed to display it.

The law codes have returned to her, in large part, control over her life and property. She has well-founded hopes of seeing abolished within her lifetime the laws that still relegate her, in certain aspects, to the position of a second-class citizen, and that accord her unequal legal treatment.

She has made progress in economic liberty, [the] basis of all independence, whether it be a question of a simple individual or one of nations. Today she is gaining admission into fields of labor forbidden to her mother.

Before her extends an unbounded horizon of opportunities. Hopes! She can live her years of illusions imagining — like every adolescent male — that the whole world awaits her, and that only her own limitations can prevent her from ascending the highest peaks of this world.

She has won liberty, including — it may seem ridiculous to mention it — the liberty of going about without papa or the classic brother at her side. . . .

She has lost, in the first place, the respect of the male majority. One might say that formerly consideration for women formed part of good breeding, and it was denied only to one who by her conduct showed that she did not merit it. Today it is the other way around. In general, woman receives no tribute, and she must prove

convincingly that she is a distinguished personage before receiving the homage that once was common.

Which has diminished — the respect or the quality of respectability? . . .

Men used to expect of woman a stainless virtue, perfect submission — after God, thy husband, orders the epistle of St. Paul[1] — and a life-long devotion to the orbit in which her man revolved. A saint in the vaulted niche of her home, saint to the world, mistress of her four walls, and slave to her man. In exchange for this — respect and devotion. True, the father or husband sometimes played the role of sacristan[2] to the saint. They allowed no one to fail to reverence her, but they themselves took liberties and even mistreated her — conduct that the saint had to bear with resignation . . . she had no recourse. . . .

It is unnecessary to refer again to the upheavals that the invention of machinery brought to the world, the sharp rise in the cost of living, and the pauperization of the household, which from producer was reduced to being a simple consumer. It became impossible for a man of average means to satisfy the needs of all his womenfolk, and women had to enter offices, the professions, and other remunerative employment that had been men's traditional source of income. Woman has gone out into the world, and although this fact in itself is an economic imperative and does not essentially imply the abandonment of any virtue, the ordinary man has denied her his respect. . . .

. . . For the ordinary man, woman's freedom is license; her equality, the right to treat her without courtesy.

She has lost in opportunities for marriage, for establishing a household, and for satisfying that yearning for maternity that is her fundamental instinct. The more cultured a woman, the more difficult for her to find a husband, because it is normal for her to seek refuge, understanding,

---

[1]The apostle Paul in I Corinthians 7:39 and other places in his epistles speaks of the need for wives to be obedient to their husbands.

[2]A sacristan is a church official in charge of caring for the vestments and sacred utensils used in religious services, and, in some cases, the entire church building.

and guidance in a person superior to herself. And the latter do not always prefer cultured women. They imagine that knowledge makes them unfeeling — an absurd notion — that it makes them domineering — which concerns not acquired knowledge but character — or that it makes them insufferably pedantic. . . . For their wives men prefer the "old-fashioned" girl.

That is the pathos of the tragedy of middle-class women in the Latin countries. Evolution has taken place in opposition to the fundamental convictions of men, who only tolerate it — in the case of their daughters, for example — because imperious necessity dictates it, and only with profound chagrin. Men — I repeat that I speak of the majority — continue to judge women from the viewpoint of fifty years ago, and if they retain some respect and esteem in their inner beings, they tender it to the woman who remained faithful to the classic type — the woman who has progressed they place very close to those for whom they have no respect.

Men cannot understand that external conditions — culture, profession, liberty — have not radically transformed the classic femininity, the maternal instincts, the impulses of the sweet Samaritan,[3] the yearnings of a noble spirituality. The cases of this kind that he knows about do not convince him; he imagines that they constitute exceptions.

Not are men of more advanced ideas free from this attitude. And it would be amusing — if it did not have tragic implications — to observe what a socialist, a radical, a communist, proclaims on the public platform and what he praises in the intimacy of his home.

Man and woman. Feared and beloved master; slave, sweetly, or tyrannically subjugated; wall and ivy. Today divergent and almost hostile, but not comrades. Woman and man cannot yet be comrades, save in an infinitely small number of cases. The relationship of comrades implies equality, confidence, and the same criteria for judging each other.

"But if she acknowledges her bitter lot, why not turn back?" more than one naive soul asks. Impossible. Time does not turn back. . . . New social theories will solve these problems and create new ones on the way to an inscrutable future that human faith — a flame that wavers but that only death can extinguish — imagines must be a better one.

Meanwhile, sisters, let us not preach feminism to women; let us win over the men, in the hope that our daughters may pay less dearly for their cup of happiness.

---

[3]In the parable of the Good Samaritan (Luke 10:30–37), Jesus tells the story of the Samaritan woman who helped an injured man who had been ignored by others. A samaritan thus came to mean a compassionate person, one willing to help the distressed.

The Indian in Peru: A Marxist Perspective

❖

37 ◆ *José Carlos Mariátegui,* THE PROBLEM OF THE INDIAN AND THE PROBLEM OF THE LAND

Beginning in the 1870s, the economic situation of Peru's Indians, already one of extreme poverty, deteriorated even further. With worldwide demand for Peruvian agricultural products increasing and land prices soaring, wealthy creole landowners (*hacendados*), with the help of lawyers, local officials, and favorable laws passed by the central government, acquired increasing amounts of Indian communal lands. As a result, by the early 1900s Peru's Indians, more than 50 percent of the population, overwhelmingly were landless peasants providing cheap labor for white hacienda owners and bound to the land either through long-term labor contracts or because of debts owed to the landowner. Apathy, illiteracy, and alcoholism marked their lives.

The deterioration of Peruvian Indian life was accompanied by increasing concern for their welfare on the part of some Peruvians. Intellectuals at the University of San Marcos in Lima sought to dispel the notion that Indians were inherently inferior to whites. Some went further to suggest that Indian culture and values could serve as a source for national revival. Educators and clergy recommended programs of education and moral instruction to teach Indians sobriety and good work habits. The radical writer Manuel Gonzalez Prada (1848–1918) went further; he urged the Indians to arm themselves and rebel.

José Carlos Maríategui (1895–1930) was not, therefore, the first Peruvian to speak out on Indian issues. Nor was he Peru's first Marxist. In the 1920s the Peruvian exile Raúl Haya de la Torre founded the Alianza Popular Revolucionaria Americana (APRA), a party with a strong Marxist component, and the author Luís E. Valcarel hailed peasant revolts in the highlands as the first rumblings of a revolution that would usher in true egalitarianism. Maríategui's accomplishment was to provide an analysis of Peruvian society by bringing together a passionate concern for the Indians' welfare and the scientific socialism of Marx.

Maríategui, born in 1895 and raised in poverty by his mother, a seamstress, had only a few years of schooling. At age fourteen he became a printer's apprentice for a newspaper in Lima, Peru's largest city, and continued his self-education. By the age of twenty-one he was writing news stories, poetry, and reviews for his newspaper and other Lima periodicals, and had written a full-length drama performed in a Lima theater. A harsh critic of Peru's politicians for their neglect of the poor, especially the Indians, Maríategui was exiled to Europe in 1919. Returning to Peru in 1923 as a Marxist, he worked to strengthen the labor movement, wrote hundreds of articles, and helped found the Socialist Party of Peru in 1928. His *Seven Interpretative Essays on Peruvian Reality,* his most popular work, appeared in 1928. Before he died at age thirty-five, he participated in discussions leading to the formation of the Peruvian Communist Party, formally organized a month after his death in 1930.

The following selection is made up of excerpts from two essays in *Seven Interpretive Essays on Peruvian Reality,* "The Problem of the Indian," and "The Problem of Land."

QUESTIONS FOR ANALYSIS

1. According to Maríategui, what is at the root of the problems of Indian poverty in Peru?
2. Maríategui rejects previous "solutions" to the problem of Indian poverty. What were they, and why, in his opinion, did they fail?
3. What in Maríategui's view is the only viable solution to the "problem of the Indian"?
4. Does Maríategui indicate how he hopes to accomplish his goals?

[THE PROBLEM OF THE INDIAN]

Any treatment of the problem of the Indian . . . that fails or refuses to recognize it as a socio-economic problem is but a sterile, theoretical exercise destined to be completely discredited. . . . The socialist critic exposes and defines the problem because he looks for its causes in the country's economy and not in its administrative, legal, or ecclesiastic machinery, its racial dualism or pluralism, or its cultural or moral conditions. The problem of the Indian is rooted in the land tenure system of our economy. Any attempt to solve it with administrative . . . measures, through education or by a road building program, is superficial and secondary as long as the feudalism of the *gamonales* [great landowners] continues to exist.

Gamonalismo[1] necessarily invalidates any law or regulation for the protection of the Indian. The hacienda owner, the *latifundista*[2] is a feudal lord. The written law is powerless against his authority, which is supported by custom and habit. Unpaid labor is illegal, yet unpaid and even forced labor survive in the latifundium. The judge, the subprefect, the commissary, the teacher, the tax collector, all are in bondage to the landed estate. The law cannot prevail against the *gamonales*. Any official who insisted on applying it would be abandoned and sacrificed by the central government. . . .

The oldest and most obvious mistake is, unquestionably, that of reducing the protection of the Indian to an ordinary administrative matter. From the days of Spanish colonial legislation, wise and detailed ordinances, worked out after conscientious study, have been quite useless. The republic,[3] since independence, has been prodigal in its decrees, laws, and provisions intended to protect the Indian against exaction and abuse. The *gamonal* of today, . . . however,

has little to fear from administrative theory; he knows that its practice is altogether different.

The individualistic character of the republic's legislation has favored the absorption of Indian property by the latifundium system. . . . The appropriation of most communal and individual Indian property is an accomplished fact. . . .

The assumption that the Indian problem is ethnic is sustained by the most outmoded repertory of imperialist ideas. The concept of inferior races was useful to the white man's West for purposes of expansion and conquest. To expect that the Indian will be emancipated through a steady crossing of the aboriginal race with white immigrants is an anti-sociological naiveté that could only occur to the primitive mentality of an importer of merino sheep. The people of Asia, who are in no way superior to the Indians, have not needed any transfusion of European blood in order to assimilate the most dynamic and creative aspects of Western culture. The degeneration of the Peruvian Indian is a cheap invention of sophists who serve feudal interests. . . .

The tendency to consider the Indian problem as a moral one embodies a liberal, humanitarian, enlightened nineteenth-century attitude. . . . The anti-slavery conferences and societies in Europe that have denounced more or less futilely the crimes of the colonizing nations are born of this tendency, which always has trusted too much in its appeals to the conscience of civilization. . . .

Humanitarian teachings have not halted or hampered European imperialism, nor have they reformed its methods. The struggle against imperialism now relies only on the solidarity and strength of the liberation movement of the colonial masses. . . .

On a moral and intellectual plane, the church took a more energetic or at least a more authoritative stand centuries ago. This crusade, however, achieved only very wise laws and provisions. The

---

[1]A term for the social and political domination of rural Peru by wealthy landowners; sometimes translated as "feudalism."

[2]The owner of a *latifundio,* a large landed estate worked by farm laborers in a state of partial serfdom.
[3]The period after Peruvian independence in 1824.

lot of the Indian remained substantially the same. . . . To wipe out abuses, it would have been necessary to abolish land appropriation and forced labor, in brief, to change the entire colonial regime. Without the toil of the American Indian, the coffers of the Spanish treasury would have been emptied.

But today a religious solution is unquestionably the most outdated and antihistoric of all. . . . If the church could not accomplish its task in a medieval era, when its spiritual and intellectual capacity could be measured by friars like Las Casas,[4] how can it succeed with the elements in commands today? . . . The belief that the Indian problem is one of education does not seem to be supported by even a strictly and independently pedagogical criterion. . . . School and teacher are doomed to be debased under the pressure of the feudal regime, which cannot be reconciled with the most elementary concept of progress and evolution. When this truth becomes partially understood, the saving formula is thought to be discovered in boarding schools for Indians. But the glaring inadequacy of this formula is self-evident in view of the tiny percentage of the indigenous school population that can be boarded in these schools.

The pedagogical solution, advocated by many in good faith, has been discarded officially. . . .

The new approach locates the problem of the Indian in the land tenure system.

[THE PROBLEM OF LAND]

Those of us who approach and define the Indian problem from a Socialist point of view must start out by declaring the complete obsolescence of the humanitarian and philanthropic points of view. . . . We shall try to establish the basically economic character of the problem. First, we protest against the instinctive attempt of the criollo or mestizo[5] to reduce it to an exclusively

administrative, pedagogical, ethnic, or moral problem in order to avoid at all cost recognizing its economic aspect. . . . We are not satisfied to assert the Indian's right to education, culture, progress, love, and heaven. We begin by categorically asserting his right to land. . . .

The agrarian problem is first and foremost the problem of eliminating feudalism in Peru, which should have been done by the democratic-bourgeois regime that followed the War of Independence. But in its one hundred years as a republic, Peru has not had a genuine bourgeois class, a true capitalist class. The old feudal class — camouflaged or disguised as a republican bourgeoisie — has kept its position. . . . During a century of Republican rule, great agricultural property actually has grown stronger and expanded, despite the theoretical liberalism of our constitution and the practical necessities of the development of our capitalist economy. There are two expressions of feudalism that survive: the latifundium and servitude. Inseparable and of the same substance, their analysis leads us to the conclusion that the servitude oppressing the indigenous race cannot be abolished unless the latifundium is abolished. . . .

Everyone knows that the liberal solution for this problem, in conformity with individualist ideology, would be to break up the latifundio in order to create small landed properties. . . .

In conformity with my ideological position, I think that in Peru the hour for trying the liberal method, the individualist formula, has already passed. Leaving doctrinal reasons aside, I regard as fundamental an indisputable and concrete factor that gives a peculiar stamp to our agrarian problem: the survival of the Indian community and of elements of practical socialism in Indian life and agriculture.

In Peru, communal property does not represent a primitive economy that has gradually been replaced by a progressive economy founded on

---

[4]Bartolomé de Las Casas (1474–1566) was a Spanish friar who denounced the exploitation of Amerindians by the Spanish.

[5]A criollo is a Peruvian of European descent; a mestizo is a person of European-Indian descent.

individual property. No; the "communities" have been despoiled of their land for the benefit of the feudal or semi-feudal latifundium, which is constitutionally incapable of technical progress.

The latifundium compares unfavorably with the "community" as an enterprise for agricultural production. . . . Large property seems to be justified by the interests of production, which are identified, at least in theory, with the interests of society. But this is not the case of the latifundium and, therefore, it does not meet an economic need. Except for sugar-cane plantations — which produce *aguardiente* [liquor] to

intoxicate and stupefy the Indian peasant — the latifundium of the sierra generally grows the same crops as the "community," and it produces no more. . . .

The "community," on the one hand, is a system of production that keeps alive in the Indian the moral incentives that stimulate him to do his best work. . . .

By dissolving or abandoning the "community," the system of the feudal latifundium has attacked not only an economic institution but also, and more important, a social institution, one that defends the indigenous tradition [and] maintains the function of the rural family. . . .

◆

Political Responses to the Great Depression

As the Great Depression spread economic misery across Latin America, one government after another fell in an epidemic of election swings, revolts, coups, and countercoups. The military seized power in Argentina and Peru in 1930, and Uruguay's constitutional government collapsed in 1933 when the elected president, Gabriel Terra, established a dictatorship. Dictators also seized power in El Salvador, Guatemala, and Honduras, and, with the help of the U.S. government, in Nicaragua and the Dominican Republic. In Chile, however, the onset of the Depression led in 1931 to the fall of a dictator, Carlos Ibáñez. This was followed by a brief constitutional interlude and more military coups before the establishment of a center-right government under Arturo Alessandri. In Cuba, the dictator Gerardo Machado was forced into exile in 1933, but another dictator, Fulgencio Batista, took his place in 1934. Ecuador had no fewer than fourteen presidents between 1931 and 1940, and Paraguay, four different dictators. Only a few states such as Colombia managed to maintain a measure of political stability.

While most of these regimes had little lasting impact, political changes in Mexico and Brazil had long-term consequences for the two nations themselves and for Latin America as a whole. In Mexico, these changes took place during the presidency of Lázaro Cárdenas, who between 1934 and 1940 revitalized Mexico's revolutionary tradition through educational reform, land redistribution, and nationalization of foreign-owned businesses. In Brazil, they were connected with the career of Getúlio Vargas, who seized power in 1930 and dominated Brazilian politics until 1945 and again from 1951 to 1954. By the end of the 1930s his *Estado Novo* (New State), a mixture of dictatorship, repression, anti-colonialism, economic planning, nationalism, industrialization, and government-sponsored programs for housing, improved wages, and medical care, provided Latin America with an authoritarian model for entry into the era of mass politics.

Economic Nationalism in Mexico

◈

38 ◆ *Lázaro Cárdenas, SPEECH TO THE NATION*

During the 1920s and early 1930s, Mexico's revolution had stalled. Its 1917 constitution called for land reform, granted extensive rights to labor, and proclaimed the state's right to control foreign-owned businesses. But the two dominant politicians of the 1920s and early 1930s, Alvaro Obregón and Plutarco Eliás Calles, had little enthusiasm for social reform despite their revolutionary rhetoric. Their rule mainly benefited generals, businessmen, and landowners, and their modest gestures in the direction of land redistribution were meant to head off rural rebellion. When in 1929 Calles organized Mexico's only national political party, the National Revolutionary Party (PNR), out of dozens of local political machines, his and his henchmen's political domination appeared secure.

Six years later, however, Calles was in exile in the United States, and progressives had taken control of the PNR. The reasons were twofold: the Great Depression and the emergence of a new leader, Lázaro Cárdenas. Born in 1895 to a poor family and with little formal education, Cárdenas achieved prominence in the 1910s as an officer in the revolutionary armies fighting the dictator Victoriano Huerta. In 1920 he was named governor of the state of Michoacan in west central Mexico, where he earned a reputation as a progressive and honest administrator; between 1931 and 1934 he served as Mexico's minister of the interior and of war. In December 1933, Cárdenas, the candidate of the PNR's progressive wing, was nominated for president, and in 1934 he was duly elected. Immediately embarking on a program of land and labor reform, Cárdenas was opposed by Calles, who in 1935 was implicated in a plot to overthrow the new president. Calles was arrested and deported to the United States, while Cárdenas proceeded with his sweeping program of economic and social reform.

Cárdenas confiscated millions of acres of land from large estates for redistribution to peasants, introduced free and compulsory primary education, and sponsored legislation to provide medical and unemployment insurance. His most audacious step, however, was the nationalization of Mexico's oil industry. In 1936 a labor dispute erupted into a strike against U.S.- and British-owned petroleum companies, and in the ensuing legal battle, seventeen oil companies rejected both the prounion ruling of an arbitration board appointed by Cárdenas and the decision of the Mexican Supreme Court, which upheld the board's ruling. In response, in 1938 Cárdenas expropriated the property of the oil companies.

Cárdenas announced this decision in a radio address to the Mexican people on March 18, 1938. In the following excerpt, Cárdenas, after recounting the events of the labor dispute, comments on the oil companies' role in Mexico's economic and social development.

QUESTIONS FOR ANALYSIS

1. In Cárdenas's account, which actions by the foreign oil companies forced him to nationalize their property?
2. According to Cárdenas, what truth is there in the oil companies' claims that their presence has been beneficial to Mexico?
3. Who, according to Cárdenas, is ultimately responsible for the actions of the oil companies?
4. Which political activities of the oil companies does Cárdenas condemn?
5. What hardship does Cárdenas foresee for the Mexican people as a result of nationalization?
6. In what ways does Cárdenas appeal to Mexican nationalism in his speech?

In each and every one of the various attempts of the Executive to arrive at a final solution of the conflict within conciliatory limits . . . the intransigence of the companies was clearly demonstrated.

Their attitude was therefore premeditated and their position deliberately taken, so that the Government, in defense of its own dignity, had to resort to application of the Expropriation Act, as there were no means less drastic or decision less severe that might bring about a solution of the problem.

For additional justification of the measure herein announced, let us trace briefly the history of the oil companies' growth in Mexico and of the resources with which they have developed their activities.

It has been repeated *ad nauseam* that the oil industry has brought additional capital for the development and progress of the country. This assertion is an exaggeration. For many years throughout the major period of their existence, the oil companies have enjoyed great privileges for development and expansion, including customs and tax exemptions and innumerable prerogatives; it is these factors of special privilege, together with the prodigious productivity of the oil deposits granted them by the Nation often against public will and law, that represent almost the total amount of this so-called capital.

Potential wealth of the Nation; miserably underpaid native labor; tax exemptions; economic privileges; governmental tolerance — these are the factors of the boom of the Mexican oil industry.

Let us now examine the social contributions of the companies. In how many of the villages bordering on the oil fields is there a hospital, or school or social center, or a sanitary water supply, or an athletic field, or even an electric plant fed by the millions of cubic meters of natural gas allowed to go to waste?

What center of oil production, on the other hand, does not have its company police force for the protection of private, selfish, and often illegal interests? These organizations, whether authorized by the Government or not, are charged with innumerable outrages, abuses, and murders, always on behalf of the companies that employ them.

Who is not aware of the irritating discrimination governing construction of the company camps? Comfort for the foreign personnel; misery, drabness, and insalubrity for the Mexicans. Refrigeration and protection against tropical insects for the former; indifference and neglect, medical service and supplies always grudgingly provided, for the latter; lower wages and harder more exhausting labor for our people.

The tolerance which the companies have abused was born, it is true, in the shadow of the ignorance, betrayals, and weakness of the country's rulers; but the mechanism was set in motion by investors lacking in the necessary moral resources to give something in exchange for the wealth they have been exploiting.

Another inevitable consequence of the presence of the oil companies, strongly characterized by their anti-social tendencies, and even more harmful than all those already mentioned, has been their persistent and improper intervention in national affairs.

The oil companies' support to strong rebel factions against the constituted government in the Huasteca region of Veracruz and in the Isthmus of Tehuantepec during the years 1917 to 1920 is no longer a matter for discussion by anyone. Nor is anyone ignorant of the fact that in later periods and even at the present time, the oil companies have almost openly encouraged the ambitions of elements discontented with the country's government, every time their interests were affected either by taxation or by the modification of their privileges or the withdrawal of the customary tolerance. They have had money, arms, and munitions for rebellion, money for the anti-patriotic press which defends them, money with which to enrich their unconditional defenders. But for the progress of the country, for establishing an economic equilibrium with their workers through a just compensation of labor, for maintaining hygienic conditions in the districts where they themselves operate, or for conserving the vast riches of the natural petroleum gases from destruction, they have neither money, nor financial possibilities, nor the desire to subtract the necessary funds from the volume of their profits.

Nor is there money with which to meet a responsibility imposed upon them by judicial verdict, for they rely on their pride and their economic power to shield them from the dignity and sovereignty of a Nation which has generously placed in their hands its vast natural resources and now finds itself unable to obtain the satisfaction of the most elementary obligations by ordinary legal means.

As a logical consequence of this brief analysis, it was therefore necessary to adopt a definite and legal measure to end this permanent state of affairs in which the country sees its industrial progress held back by those who hold in their hands the power to erect obstacles as well as the motive power of all activity and who, instead of using it to high and worthy purposes, abuse their economic strength to the point of jeopardizing the very life of a Nation endeavoring to bring about the elevation of its people through its own laws, its own resources, and the free management of its own destinies.

With the only solution to this problem thus placed before it, I ask the entire Nation for moral and material support sufficient to carry out so justified, important, and indispensable a decision.

The Government has already taken suitable steps to maintain the constructive activities now going forward throughout the Republic, and for that purpose it asks the people only for its full confidence and backing in whatever dispositions the Government may be obliged to adopt.

Nevertheless, we shall, if necessary, sacrifice all the constructive projects on which the Nation has embarked during the term of this Administration in order to cope with the financial obligations imposed upon us by the application of the Expropriation Act to such vast interests; and although the subsoil of the country will give us considerable economic resources with which to meet the obligation of indemnization which we have contracted, we must be prepared for the possibility of our individual economy also suffering the indispensable readjustments, even to the point, should the Bank of Mexico deem it necessary, or modifying the present exchange rate of our currency, so that the whole country may be able to count on sufficient currency and resources with which to consolidate this act of profound and essential economic liberation of Mexico.

It is necessary that all groups of the population be imbued with a full optimism and that each citizen, whether in agricultural, industrial, commercial, transportation, or other pursuits, develop a greater activity from this moment on, in order to create new resources which will reveal that the spirit of our people is capable of saving the nation's economy by the efforts of its own citizens.

And, finally, as the fear may arise among the interests now in bitter conflict in the field of international affairs[1] that a deviation of raw materials fundamentally necessary to the struggle in which the most powerful nations are engaged might result from the consummation of this act of national sovereignty and dignity, we wish to state that our petroleum operations will not depart a single inch from the moral solidarity maintained by Mexico with the democratic nations, whom we wish to assure that the expropriation now decreed has as its only purpose the elimination of obstacles erected by groups who do not understand the evolutionary needs of all peoples and who would themselves have no compunction in selling Mexican oil to the highest bidder, without taking into account the consequences of such action to the popular masses and the nations in conflict.

---

[1]World War II in Europe was still more than a year away, but the Japanese invasion of China was in full swing, Spain was in the midst of its civil war, and Nazi Germany had just annexed Austria.

Brazilian Mass Politics and the *Estado Novo*

◈

39 ◆ *Getúlio Vargas,*
EXCERPTS FROM SPEECHES AND
INTERVIEWS, 1937–1940

Not without growing opposition from the middle class and the military, wealthy coffee growers from the states of São Paulo and Minas Gerais maintained their grip on Brazilian politics during the "Old Republic" from 1889 to 1930. In 1930, however, with coffee prices in free fall, a disputed election led to the military overthrow of the government and the installation as president of Getúlio Vargas. The era of the coffee oligarchy was over, and Brazilian politics embarked on a new path.

Born in 1883 into a politically active family of landowners from the state of Rio Grande do Sol, Vargas served in the army, studied law, and was elected as Rio Grande do Sol's congressman and governor before joining the national government as finance minister in 1926 and 1927. In 1930 he ran for president as the candidate of the Liberal Alliance, a coalition of the urban bourgeoisie, intellectuals, some landowners, and reform-minded army officers. He lost the fraud-filled election, and in its wake, his opponents refused to allow his supporters to take their seats in the congress; in all probability these same opponents were behind the murder of his vice-presidential running mate. At this point Vargas's supporters in the army deposed the president, and named Vargas as head of a provisional government.

Having come to power in 1930 with the support of a diverse coalition, Vargas proceeded cautiously at first. He raised tariffs, encouraged industrialization, and sought to prop up the price of coffee. In 1932 he reduced the voting age to eighteen and granted working women the right to vote. In 1934 a new constitution strengthened the executive, gave the government greater control of the economy, and called for the gradual nationalization of foreign-owned businesses.

In 1935 Vargas began to move toward one-man rule. First the communist and fascist Integralist parties were banned, and then in 1937 he canceled elections, promulgated a new constitution, and assumed dictatorial powers. Brazil, he announced, had entered the era of the *Estado Novo,* the New State.

In the following excerpts from interviews and speeches given between 1937 and 1940, Vargas outlines the general philosophy and goals of his New State.

QUESTIONS FOR ANALYSIS

1. According to Vargas, what were the major flaws of Brazilian politics before he took power?
2. What steps did Vargas take or does he plan to take in order to rid Brazil of these flaws?
3. Vargas claims his New State is democratic. Do his comments in his various speeches and interviews support such a claim?
4. Some commentators have discerned elements of fascism in Vargas's political philosophy and policies. Do you agree with such as assessment?
5. What specific policies does Vargas propose in order to appeal to the urban bourgeoisie and working class?

[INTERVIEW, APRIL 1938]

The movement of November 10th[1] was, without doubt, brought about by the national will. We had need of order and security in order to carry on; conspiring against that was the critical state of political decomposition to which we had arrived. Slowly our public life had been transformed into an arena of sterile struggles where plots, clashing interests of the oligarchy, personal competitions, and differences in personal interests were decided. Men of character without ambition to govern drew away from it nauseated, leaving the field open to political professionals and to demagogic and audacious adventurers. It was thus that communism succeeded in infiltrating and came to be at one time a national danger.[2] Defeated in its violent attempt to seize power, it continued, nevertheless, its work of undermining authority by

utilizing as its weapons the other evils that make the situation of the nation so unstable and chaotic: the weakness of political parties, regional jealousies, and dictatorial flights of fancy. Those three evils are in the final analysis simply the result of a single general cause, well formed and known: the sterility and [depletion] of the sources from which the agents of stimulation and renovation of public life ought to come. The political parties had abdicated their social function. . . . Foresight of the danger in which we found ourselves and which was felt by all caused us decisively to favor the political unification of the nation which is precisely why the regime was established on November 10th. The Estado Novo embodies, therefore, the will and ideas which oppose and work against all the factors tending to weaken and dissolve the fatherland — extremism sabotage, and compromise. It is ready to fight

---

[1] On November 10, 1937, Vargas announced in a radio message to the nation that he had canceled the upcoming presidential elections, dissolved the legislature, and assumed dictatorial powers under a new constitution.

[2] In 1937 a wing of the Communist Party took part in an anti-Vargas revolt that was crushed by the government. Later in the year, the government circulated a forged document that supposedly outlined a communist plan to seize power.

against those evils. It will mobilize all the best that we possess in order to make our nation strong, dignified, and happy.

[SPEECH, JULY 1938]

As Chief of Government, I systematically seek to hear those who are informed, to appreciate the word of the technicians, to study and to boldly face the reality of facts. It was thus that, feeling the profound sentiment of the Brazilian people, I did all possible in order to save them from the dangers of extremism, both — from the right as well as from the left — contrary to our sentiments of understanding and Christian tolerance.

I can affirm to you with certainty that the hours of greatest apprehension now have passed. . . .

Through the spirit of good sense and through the persistent intention of conciliating the peace of the people with national dignity, we have given an appreciable example to the world. Thus we proceed . . . trying to assure . . . to all and to each a greater share of well-being and tranquility within the just equilibrium between the duties and prerogatives of the citizen.

[INTERVIEW, MARCH 1938]

Among the profound changes brought about by the new regime are: the [limitation] of direct, universal suffrage, applicable only to specific questions that pertain to all citizens . . . , the municipality as the nuclear base of the political system; the substitution of the principle of the independence of powers[3] by the supremacy of the Executive; the strengthening of the power of the Union; the effective and efficient participation of the economy, through its own organizations, in the constructive and integrating work of the government.

The new system consecrates a government of authority by instituting as law the legislative decree, by giving to the President of the Republic powers to expedite law-decrees when congress is not in session, by attributing to him the [prerogative to] dissolve it in special cases, and by taking from the Judiciary the privilege of supreme interpretation of the constitutionality or unconstitutionality of the laws which involve public interests of great importance. These new powers, placed under the guard of the government, always overcome private interests.

Profoundly nationalistic, the regime insures and consolidates national unity and formally restricts the autonomy of the states[4] by suppressing regional symbols, extending intervention, establishing the supremacy of federal over local laws in the case of concurrent legislation by attributing to the central government the power to requisition at any time the state militias, etc.

The professions are represented in their own and independent chamber with consultative functions in all the projects concerning the national economy, and eventually it will have legislative functions.[5]

Truly we have instituted an essentially democratic regime because it does not base its representation on a system of indications and artificialities but rather on the direct collaboration of the people through their economic forces and their organizations of production and labor. Only thus can our present political structure make known the effective representation of Brazil. . . .

[SPEECH, JULY 1938]

If you would ask me what is the program of the Estado Novo, I would tell you that its program is to crisscross the nation with railroads, highways, and airlines; to increase production; to provide for the laborer and to encourage agricultural

---

[3]The separation of the executive, legislative, and judicial powers within government.
[4]In the Old Republic the states of Brazil had exercised extensive political powers, and politicians from two states, São

Paulo and Minas Gerais, dominated the federal government.
[5]Economic and professional groups would be represented in addition to districts, provinces, etc.

credit; to expand exports; to prepare the armed forces so that they are always ready to face any eventuality; to organize public opinion so that there is, body and soul, one Brazilian thought.

[SPEECH, JANUARY, 1939]

By examining the government's activities, anyone can verify with his own eyes that the basic problems of Brazilian life, without regional distinctions or political preferences, were resolutely attacked: the increase and expansion of industrial and agrarian [nuclei]; the creation of new sources of wealth and the improvement of the processes of exportation . . . ; the measures taken to raise the standard of living of the masses; financial support to the producing classes; economic assistance to the worker by means of social security, . . . a just salary, a good home, and the guarantee of his rights; the increase in the number of centers of technical, physical, and intellectual training; care for public hygiene and rural sanitation by making possible the remunerative utilization of large areas of soil abandoned or sacrificed because of climactic disturbances; the systematic repudiation of extremist ideologies and their . . . followers; the combating of all agents of dissolution or weakening of the national energies by the reinforcement of Brazilian traditions and sentiments and the prohibition from functioning in this country of any organization with anti-national activities or linked to foreign political interests; finally the preparation of internal and external defense by the rearmament of our brave armed forces and the simultaneous education of the new generations inculcating in them the spirit and love of the fatherland, faith in its destinies and the desire to make it strong and respected.

◆

The Mexican Muralists and the Revolution in Mexican Art

After the fall of the dictator Porfirio Díaz in 1910, nationalism intensified in revolutionary Mexico, and *indigenismo* was its most outstanding expression. In 1917 President Alvaro Obregón established a government office of anthropology to study and preserve Indian art, artifacts, and customs, and during the 1920s Mexican anthropology made impressive strides. Obregón also appointed as secretary of education José Vasconcelos (1882–1959), a visionary and enthusiast who foresaw a new race, "a cosmic race," taking root in Spanish America as a result of the blending of Indian and Spanish blood. In his view, the values and cultures of the Indians were not to be scorned and dismissed as they had been under the European-oriented dictator Díaz; instead, they would become a source of national pride and regeneration.

In addition to sponsoring schools and health clinics in thousands of Indian villages, Vasconcelos encouraged composers, choreographers, writers, and artists to explore Mexico's Indian past and incorporate revolutionary themes into their work. In Mexico City he made available to painters walls of public buildings, and in the 1920s they were covered with murals that brought international fame to artists such as Diego Rivera, José Clemente Orozco, and David Alfaro Siqueiros. In bright colors and bold compositions they portrayed the historical experiences of Mexicans and other Latin American peoples as part of the universal human striving to overcome injustice and exploitation.

The Beginnings of the Mexican Muralist Movement

◆

40 ◆ *José Clemente Orozco*, AUTOBIOGRAPHY

José Clemente Orozco (1883–1949) originally intended to become an architect, but at age twenty-six began training as a painter in the Mexican Academy of Fine Arts. As a Marxist and supporter of the Mexican Revolution, he sought to use his artistic talents in the service of the Mexican people. This meant breaking from the style of the officially approved European masters and introducing themes and topics dealing with the struggles of Mexico's Indian and mestizo population. In the following excerpt from his autobiography, first published in the early 1940s, Orozco recalls how in the 1910s and early 1920s he and other painters in Mexico City developed a new vision of Mexican art.

QUESTIONS FOR ANALYSIS

1. According to Orozco, what were the deficiencies of Mexican art before the beginnings of the muralist movement?
2. How did the new school of Mexican art attempt to overcome these deficiencies?
3. What in Orozco's view is the social function of art and the artist?

[In the past, the] Mexican had been a poor colonial servant, incapable of creating or thinking for himself; everything had to be imported ready-made from European centers, for we were an inferior and degenerate race. They let us paint, but we had to paint the way they did in Paris, and it was the Parisian critic who would pass upon the result and pronounce the final verdict.

Architecture was refried chalets and French chateaux. The marbles and carvings in public and private buildings came from Italy.

It was inconceivable that a wretched Mexican should dream of vying with the world abroad, and so he went to that world abroad to "dedicate himself" to art, and if he ever afterward gave a thought to the backward country in which he was born it was only to beg for help in time of need, momentarily swallowing his proud "dedication," which in any case had never protected him from the suspicion of being a vulgar millionaire from the tropics.

Academic criteria held sway: "The ancients long ago reached perfection, they did everything that could be done, and nothing is left for us except to copy them and humbly imitate them. Florentine drawing with Venetian coloring. And if any painter wishes to be a modernist, let him be off to Montparnasse and there take orders."

In the nightly sessions in the Academy . . . , we began to suspect that the whole colonial situation was nothing but a swindle foisted upon us by international traders. We too had a character, which was quite the equal of any other. We would learn what the ancients and the foreigners could teach us, but we could do as much as they, or more. It was not pride but self-confidence that moved us to this belief, a sense of our own being and our destiny.

Now for the first time the painters took stock of the country they lived in. . . .

I set out to explore the wretchedest barrios in the city. On every canvas there began to appear, bit by bit, like a dawn, the Mexican landscape, and familiar forms and the colors. It was only a first and still timid step toward liberation from foreign tyranny, but behind it there was thorough preparation and a rigorous training.

Why must we be eternally on our knees before the Kants and the Hugos? All praise to the masters indeed, but we too could produce a Kant or a Hugo.[1] We too could wrest iron from the bowels of the earth and fashion it into ships and machines. We could raise prodigious cities, and create nations, and explore the universe. Was it not from a mixture of two races that the Titans[2] sprang? . . .

We can summarize Mexican thought about art in the year 1920. . . .

Many people held that pre-Cortesian[3] Art was our true tradition and they even talked of a "renaissance of indigenous art."

Excitement over the [handicrafts] of the contemporary indigenes was at its height. This was the moment when Mexico was first inundated with articles of woven straw, stewpots, huaraches [sandals], dancing figures . . . , serapes, and rebozos,[4] and when the wholesale export of all this began. It was the apogee of the tourist trade in Cuernavaca and Taxco.[5]

There was popular art in all its forms in painting, in sculpture, in the theater, in music, and in literature.

Extreme nationalism put in an appearance. Mexican artists considered themselves the equals or the superiors of foreigners. Their themes had necessarily to be Mexican.

The cult of the Worker was more sharply defined: "Art at the service of the Worker." It was believed that art must be essentially an offensive weapon in the Conflict of the Classes. . . .

Artists were passionately preoccupied with sociology and history. . . .

Later, some of them came to cherish the theme of the painting with such passion that they completely abandoned the field of art and gave themselves over to [revolutionary] activities no longer bearing any relation to their profession.

Mural painting began under good auspices. Even the errors it committed were useful. It broke with the routine into which painting had fallen. It disposed of many prejudices and served to reveal social problems from a new point of view. It liquidated a whole epoch of brutalizing Bohemianism,[6] of frauds who lived the life of a drone in their ivory towers — their fetid dens — where, drunkenly strumming on their guitars, they kept up a pretense of absurd idealism, beggars in a society that was already rotten and close to extinction.

The painters and sculptors of the coming time would be men of action, strong, sound, well trained; ready like a good laborer to work eight or ten hours a day. They found their way into shops, universities, barracks, and schools, eager to learn and understand everything, and as soon as possible to do their part in creating a new world. They wore overalls and mounted the scaffoldings.

---

[1]Immanuel Kant (1724–1804) was a German philosopher; Victor Hugo (1802–1885) was a French novelist, poet, and playwright.

[2]In Greek mythology, the Titans were giants born of Uranus (heaven) and Gaiea (earth).

[3]Cortés was the Spanish adventurer who conquered the Aztecs between 1519 and 1521.

[4]A serape (sarape) is a wool blanket worn as a shawl; a rebozo is a scarf.

[5]Taxco, in southern Mexico, and Cuernavaca, in south central Mexico, were both resort cities.

[6]A Bohemian was a writer or artist who adopted an individualistic, or eccentric, lifestyle with little regard for social conventions.

Political Visions of the Mexican Muralists

❖

41 ◆ *José Clemente Orozco, HISPANIC-AMERICAN SOCIETY, and Diego Rivera, IMPERIALISM*

After completing murals at the National Preparatory School and several other buildings inside and outside of Mexico City, between 1927 and 1934 José Clemente Orozco resided in the United States, where he painted murals at Pomona College in California, the New School for Social Research in New York City, and Dartmouth College in New Hampshire. His theme for the Dartmouth murals was the history of the Americas from the Preconquest Era to the Modern Age. The section from the Dartmouth murals shown on page 164, entitled *Hispano-American Society,* shows an armed Mexican peasant standing against a background filled with crumbling churches, an abandoned factory, politicians, soldiers, and capitalists.

Another great Mexican muralist, Diego Rivera (1886–1957) also was working in the United States when Orozco was painting his Dartmouth murals. Trained in Mexico and Europe, Rivera, like Orozco, painted murals in the 1920s for the National Preparatory School and other public buildings in Mexico City. A visit to the Soviet Union in 1927 reinforced his Marxist views. In 1931 he traveled to the United States to paint murals for the San Francisco Stock Exchange, the Detroit Institute of Art, and Rockefeller Center in New York. The latter work was destroyed by its sponsors because it included a portrait of Lenin.

In 1933, directly after the controversy surrounding the Rockefeller Center murals, Rivera completed a series of twenty-one paintings depicting U.S. history, collectively known as his *Portrait of America.* The paintings covered the walls of the New Workers School, a lecture hall and study center of the Communist Party Opposition, an anti-Stalinist organization that broke with the Communist Party U.S.A. in 1929. The thirteenth painting, *Imperialism,* shown on page 165, is dominated by the guns of U.S. tanks and warships, which emerge from around the portal of the New York Stock Exchange. In the forefront is a mass of Latin American rebels, in whose midst are seen a murdered Caribbean black and a Cuban revolutionary. In the upper right, Augusto Sandino, the Nicaraguan revolutionary executed by the Nicaraguan government in 1934, looks down on the operations of Standard Oil and United Fruit, two U.S. corporations heavily involved in Central and South America.

QUESTIONS FOR ANALYSIS

1. In Orozco's painting, what message is the painter communicating by the crumbling churches, the abandoned factories, the business owners, and the military officers?

2. What message does Orozco convey about the character and qualities of the main central figure, the Mexican peasant?

3. What does Rivera's painting imply about the character, motives, and impact of U.S. imperialism in Latin America?
4. In what specific ways do the paintings reveal the Marxist sympathies of the two Mexican painters?
5. What is the overall message of the two paintings? Is it optimistic about Latin America's prospects?

José Clemente Orozco, Hispano-American Society

Diego Rivera, Imperialism

CHAPTER 6

Africa Under Colonial Rule

By 1920 the preliminaries of European colonialism in Africa were over. Disputes among the colonial powers had been settled, African resistance crushed, and the deck of colonialists reshuffled when Germany lost its "place in the sun" after World War I and had its colonies taken over as League of Nations mandates by France, Britain, Belgium, and South Africa. Africa after World War I consisted of some fifty European-controlled colonies and three independent states. The three independent states were Liberia, with an economy almost completely controlled by a U.S. corporation, the Firestone Rubber Company; Ethiopia, whose independence ended in 1935 and 1936 when it was conquered and turned into a colony by Italy; and South Africa, where whites, who made up slightly less than 20 percent of the population, ruled the 80 percent who were black, Asian, or "colored."

During the 1920s and 1930s Europeans focused on creating an Africa in which they could exploit the continent's mineral wealth and agricultural products in efficiently run colonies populated by submissive, taxpaying natives. Europeans would, so they promised, educate some Africans, teach them moral principles, and gradually give them enough government experience so that someday they could rule themselves. No one had a timetable for independence, but all agreed it would take place far in the future. Some Europeans believed colonialism in Africa would last for centuries, not just for decades.

Although Africa's European masters each had somewhat different philosophies about their role in Africa, colonial administrations were all essentially alike. Authority in each colony was exercised by a governor, who in theory took orders from London, Paris, Brussels, or Lisbon, but in practice decided many matters on the spot. Under the governor was a hierarchy of subgovernors and regional, provincial, and district officers, in addition to officials responsible for education, public works, and public health. The number of European administrators was small. In Nigeria in 1938, approximately forty million Nigerians were governed by fewer than fifteen hundred British officials, whose decisions and policies were carried out by African chiefs, clerks, policemen, and soldiers under the command of British officers. Nowhere did Africans hold positions of responsibility or have a meaningful voice in advisory or legislative councils.

Economic policies of the colonial powers were also broadly similar. All focused on a single goal: to extract maximum wealth and profit from Africa at minimum cost. How this was to be achieved in any given colony depended on climate, mineral deposits, agricultural potential, access to the coast, and the size of the European population. In colonies with good farmland and valuable minerals, white rule meant large-scale land confiscations. In Kenya, Rhodesia, South Africa, Mozambique, Angola, Uganda, and the Belgian Congo, millions of acres of mineral-rich lands and productive farmland were appropriated and sold cheaply or given to Europeans. In 1913, for example, the government of South Africa passed a law that allocated 90 percent of the country's land to whites, who made up under 20 percent of the population. In the 1920s approximately one thousand English settlers controlled almost five million acres of the best farmland in Kenya. In British West Africa and most of French West Africa, where few whites settled, African farmers held on to their land and grew cocoa, peanuts, palm kernels, cotton, and coffee for export. When marketing their products, however, their only option was to sell to European exporters, who offered them prices well below the world market.

To make their economic plans work, Europeans needed African labor. Few Africans, however, had any interest in accepting the Europeans' job offers, since most craftsmen and farmers had no use for European money and could provide adequately for their families by working for themselves. One European solution to this problem was force. Relying on loyal chiefs or colonial police to enforce their mandates, Europeans coerced men to go to work building roads and offices, clearing fields, constructing railroads, carrying goods from place to place, and harvesting crops. Such systems of forced labor continued in the French colonies until 1946 and in Portuguese colonies until the 1960s. Another less blatantly coercive method to pressure African men to accept wage-paying work was government-imposed taxation. Required to pay taxes in cash only, Africans were forced to take wage-paying jobs in mines and fields to earn what they needed to pay the government. Colonial administrations used the taxes to pay their own costs, maintain infrastructure, and, if anything was left, to build schools and medical clinics.

The colonialists' assumption that Africans would endure the injustices of colonial rule for decades or even centuries was a glaring miscalculation. It is true that some Africans — chiefs, petty traders, farmers who grew export crops, and the small number of Africans who had opportunities to study in Europe — welcomed European rule. Most, however, found colonialism oppressive and repugnant. For some, opposition to European rule meant joining new African Christian churches that were run by blacks and preached that God did not want white people to rule over Africans. For others, mainly educated city-dwellers, it meant supporting the Pan-African movement, whose meetings in the interwar years demanded fairness for black people and urged recognition of Africa's achievements and potential. For still others, it meant joining organizations such as the African National Congress, which sought to hold back the racist tide in South Africa, or the National Congress of British West Africa, which sought a greater voice for Africans in colonial administrations. In the 1930s, economic hardship resulting from the Great Depression and outrage over the Italian conquest of Ethiopia in 1935 and 1936 deepened African alienation. African nationalism had taken root, and within fifteen years after World War II, its dreams of freedom and independence would be realized.

European Perspectives on Africa's Future

Having completed the "scramble for Africa" in a scant two decades, Europeans had only sketchy knowledge of African society and culture when they became the continent's colonial masters in the early twentieth century. They also lacked ready answers to many questions about their role in Africa's future. How should Africa be governed? How much should Europeans intervene in colonial affairs? Should they assume responsibility for Africa's economic development or leave it to private capitalists? What part should Africans play in colonial administration? How could the goals and ambitions of missionaries, business interests, and administrators be reconciled? What efforts should be made to introduce Africans to European technology, philosophy, and culture? Should efforts be made to preserve African customs? How long would the colonial order last, and what should Africa look like when it ended?

Answers to these questions differed over time and according to the nationality and interests of the persons providing them, but, broadly speaking, from the late nineteenth century onward, they fell into two general categories. Some Europeans, probably a minority, considered colonialism a form of trusteeship. Such a view inspired nineteenth-century humanitarians who went to Africa to abolish slavery and the slave trade and missionaries who provided schooling and medical care for Africans in addition to instruction in Christianity. After World War I, the ideal of trusteeship found expression in Article 22 of the League of Nations Covenant. In transferring control of Africans in former German colonies to Britain, France, Belgium, and South Africa, it stated that "the well-being and development of such peoples form a sacred trust of civilization." The advanced nations should maintain law and order, guarantee freedom of religion, prohibit abuses such as the slave and liquor trades, and, most importantly, prepare Africans for self-rule.

The competing view saw colonialism as an opportunity to generate wealth for the colonizers. Its proponents had no interest in the Africans except to the degree that they served as miners, farm workers, porters, and minor agents of colonial government. Such a view was represented in the 1890s by men such as Cecil Rhodes, who dreamed of turning Africa into a continent of white settlement, and King Leopold II of Belgium, the professed humanitarian whose agents in the Congo forced thousands of Africans into the rain forest to collect raw rubber, cutting off their hands or feet or shooting them if they failed to meet their quotas. Leopold's atrocious (and short-lived) Congolese regime was an extreme case, but as late as the 1920s, the French forced more than 127,000 Africans to work on constructing a 150-mile railroad line from Pointe Noire, on the Atlantic coast of French Equatorial Africa, to Brazzaville. More than ten thousand Africans died of hunger or disease while working on the project.

For those intent on exploitation, racism provided a convenient rationale for their actions. Was it not the Africans' indolence and backwardness that prevented them from utilizing their continent's riches? Were not Europeans contributing to the good of humanity by making Africa's products and resources available to the world? Nor was racism lacking among the well-meaning Europeans who wanted to improve the Africans' lives. Missionaries taught that all human beings were spiritually equal before God, but this did not mean that black converts could be considered responsible Christians on the European model. The major denominations all excluded blacks from positions as church leaders and administrators. It was a rare European who thought Africans capable of managing their own affairs effectively; rarer still was the European who looked upon an African as his or her equal.

Of the following two sources, one represents the position that Africa's destiny was white settlement, and the other, that Europeans were in Africa to improve the Africans' lot and prepare them for independence. Together, they provide a fair sampling of the opinions and beliefs that shaped European policies in Africa.

Blacks in a White Man's Africa

◆

42 ◆ *Jan Smuts, RHODES MEMORIAL LECTURES*

Jan Smuts, a leading South African statesman, general, and philosopher, was born in 1870. Educated in South Africa and England, where he studied law, Smuts became state attorney for Transvaal in 1898 and fought on the side of the Boers against the British in the South African War (1899–1902). After the war he played a significant role in the founding of the Union of South Africa as a self-governing British dominion in 1910. He served as minister of defense between

1910 and 1919, and during World War I was commander of Allied forces fighting Germany in East Africa. After the war, he represented South Africa at the Paris Peace Conference, and helped plan and organize the League of Nations. As leader of the South Africa Party and later the Union Party, he served as South Africa's prime minister between 1919 and 1924 and between 1939 and 1948. An advocate of racial segregation throughout his life, he nevertheless opposed the extreme Afrikaner nationalists who gained power in 1948 and went on to implement South Africa's apartheid policy.

The following remarks reveal Smuts's views of African affairs in the late 1920s. They are taken from two speeches, "The African and African Settlement" and "Native Policy in Africa," which he delivered as part of the Rhodes Memorial Lectures in November 1929 at Oxford University. A year later they were published in his book, *Africa and Some World Problems*. The selection begins with Smuts's discussion of African employment by whites.

QUESTIONS FOR ANALYSIS

1. What is Smuts's view of the African character and personality? What factors in the Africans' experience have shaped these characteristics?
2. According to Smuts, how does the European personality differ from that of the Africans?
3. How does Smuts view Africa's future? What roles will whites and blacks play in it?
4. What advantages does Smuts see in the practice of maintaining the power of local chiefs?
5. What are the advantages of racial segregation, according to Smuts?

[THE AFRICAN AND AFRICAN SETTLEMENT]

It takes the raw native some time to acquire the habit of going out to work for the white employer. But as his economic needs develop, and they develop rapidly, and as he learns the value of ready money, it soon becomes habitual for him to spend part of his time in white employment. . . .

No inducement is necessary beyond their ordinary growing economic needs. Employment in European industries or with European settlers soon becomes the regular routine, and the natives are quite satisfied and happy to fall into this routine of part-time employment. By temperament they have not much initiative, and if left to themselves and their own tribal routine

they do not respond very well to the stimulus for progress. They are naturally happy-go-lucky, and are not oppressed with the stirrings of that divine discontent which have made the European the most unhappy but the most progressive of all humans. They are easily satisfied and a very little goes a long way with them. As workers they are slow, unintelligent, and essentially imitative. They have little foresight and display little forethought. But these very characteristics make them take readily to a routine which is settled for them by a white employer. And if they are well treated they respond with that good temper and that slow honest toil which makes them so easy to work with and so acceptable to the white employer. For thousands of years they have been accustomed to domination by their chiefs, and therefore they readily accept the firm handling, the lead, and the mastery of the white employer. It fits in with their character and their age-long training. . . .

From all this it follows that the easiest, most natural and obvious way to civilize the African native is to give him decent white employment. White employment is his best school; the gospel of labour is the most salutary gospel for him. The civilization of the African continent will be a vain dream apart from white employment, without the leading hand of the settler and the employer, away from the continuous living contact with the actual example and the actual practice of European industry and agriculture. The civilization of Africa therefore calls for a definite policy, the policy of European settlement, the establishment of a white community inside Africa which will form the steel framework of the whole ambitious structure of African civilization. . . .

. . . It is certainly a very significant fact that in that part of Africa where a great white community exists alongside the natives they have shown the greatest economic progress, the largest increase, and the greatest advance in education and civilization.[1] The fact gives additional force to my argument that the existence of a white community, so far from being contrary to native interests, is indeed a stimulus and guarantee of native progress. . . . [T]he white man's rule in South Africa has on the whole been of immense benefit to the natives, and the economic conditions of the natives in South Africa are far in advance of anything existing anywhere among African natives. . . .

[NATIVE POLICY IN AFRICA]

. . . The negro and the negroid Bantu[2] form a distinct human type which the world would be poorer without. . . . This type has some wonderful characteristics. It has largely remained a child type, with a child psychology and outlook. A child-like human cannot be a bad human, for are we not in spiritual matters bidden to be like unto the little children? Perhaps as a direct result of this temperament the African is the only happy human I have come across. No other race is so easily satisfied, so good-tempered, so care-free. . . . This happy-go-lucky disposition is a great asset, but it has also its drawbacks. There is no inward incentive to improvement, there is no persistent effort in construction, and there is complete absorption in the present, its joys and sorrows. . . . No indigenous religion has been evolved, no literature, no art. . . . These children of nature have not the inner toughness and persistence of the European, nor those social and moral incentives to progress which have built up European civilization in a comparatively short period. But they have a temperament which suits mother Africa, and which brings out the simple joys of life and deadens its pain, such as no other race possesses. . . .

. . . In the interests of the native as well as those of the European administrations responsible for their welfare, we are called upon to retrace our steps, to take all proper measures which are still possible to restore or preserve the authority of the chiefs, and to maintain the bonds of solidarity and discipline which have supported the tribal organization of the natives in the past. This authority or discipline need not be exercised in a barbarous way, and should be shorn of all old-time cruelty and other undesirable features. But in essence it should be maintained, and under the general supervision and check of the European magistrate it should continue to be exercised. . . .

The white administration remains responsible for the larger functions of government, such as the combating of human and animal diseases, the organization of education, the improvement of agriculture, and the construction of public

---

[1]The reference is to South Africa.

[2]The dominant native African group in South Africa.

works, and maintains a staff for these and similar purposes. But all the purely tribal concerns are left to the chief and his counsellors whose actions are supervised by the white officer only in certain cases intended to prevent abuses. . . .

Another important consequence will follow from this system of native institutions. Wherever Europeans and natives live in the same country, it will mean separate parallel institutions for the two. The old practice mixed up black with white in the same institutions; and nothing else was possible, after the native institutions and traditions had been carelessly or deliberately destroyed. But in the new plan these will be what is called in South Africa 'segregation' — separate institutions for the two elements of the population, living in their own separate areas. . . . Institutional segregation carries with it territorial segregation. The new policy therefore gives the native his own

traditional institutions on land which is set aside for his exclusive occupation. For agricultural and pastoral natives, living their tribal life, large areas or reserves are set aside, adequate for their present and future needs. . . . For urbanized natives, on the other hand, who live, not under tribal conditions but as domestic servants or industrial workers in white areas, there are set aside native villages or locations, adjoining to the European towns. . . . Such is the practice now in vogue in South Africa and it is likely to develop still further, and to spread all over Africa where white and black live and work together in the same countries. . . . This separation is imperative, not only in the interests of a native culture, and to prevent native traditions and institutions from being swamped by the more powerful organization of the whites, but also for other important purposes, such as public health, racial purity, and public good order. . . .

Colonialism as Trusteeship

◆

43 ◆ *Sir Frederick Gordon Guggisberg,* THE KEYSTONE

Sir Frederick Gordon Guggisberg (1879–1930) was unusual among Africa's colonial governors in that his background was engineering rather than government administration. Born in Toronto, Canada, he joined the British army, and was named director of surveys in Southern Nigeria in 1910 and acting surveyor general for all of Nigeria in 1913. After serving in World War I, he was named governor of the Gold Coast in 1919, a post he held until 1927. On becoming governor, the idealistic and energetic Guggisberg announced his Ten-Year Plan, a program to bring the Gold Coast new roads and railroads, hospitals, improved harbors, and especially better schools. Improved education, he believed, would encourage the Africanization of the colonial administration, which Guggisberg favored for reasons of economy and justice. With loans and grants from the British government and income from the Gold Coast's healthy cocoa exports, Guggisberg accomplished much of his plan before he was named governor of British Guyana in 1927. Poor health prevented him from taking his new post, and he died in 1930.

In the following excerpt, taken from his book *The Keystone* (1924), Guggisberg sets forth his ideas about education, development, and Africa's future.

QUESTIONS FOR ANALYSIS

1. What is Guggisberg's case for improving and increasing educational opportunities for Africans?
2. What do you suppose Guggisberg means by "character-training," and why does he consider it so necessary?
3. What are Guggisberg's views of the Africans? How do his views differ from those of Smuts?
4. Describe Guggisberg's vision of Africa's future. How does it differ from that of Smuts?

Wherever one turns in the Gold Coast one meets the same demand — a better education for Africans than our present schools are capable of providing. Apart from the fact that the people themselves are clamouring for a better education, the future of the country demands it. In the Government Service alone the need is urgent; the development of the country is progressing so rapidly that we can no longer afford the proportionately larger number of Europeans required to deal with the work, for their long leave, their steamer-passages, and the higher rates of salary due to their employment in what can never be a "White Man's Country" are prohibitive. Government has definitely adopted the policy of employing Africans in appointments hitherto held by Europeans provided that the former are equally qualified in education, ability, *and character*, but progress in carrying out this policy is slow owing to the scarcity of suitably qualified Africans. When, besides the need of Government, that of the Europeans firms — mercantile, banking, and professional — is considered, it is apparent that there is a great field for the employment of well-educated Africans throughout the country.

More important still is the demand of the educated African of the existing literate classes for an education and training that will fit him to take a greater share in the development of his own land. We have not to look far for the reason. To begin with, the southern portions of the Gold Coast have been in closer contact with European civilization for a far longer period than any other of Britain's West African colonies. In

the second place, our great agricultural wealth and trade are far greater in proportion to our size and population than those of almost any other tropical unit of the British Empire. . . . The annual increase of trade has naturally been accompanied by a steady increase of wealth until to-day we are far richer per head of the population than any of our neighbours. Now, prosperity brings a desire for the better things of life, and when this desire is heightened by the knowledge brought by the steady development of elementary education it is not surprising that there is to-day a rapidly increasing demand for better conditions of living, better sanitation, good water supplies, hospitals and dispensaries, and all the other benefits of modern civilization.

To comply with all these demands, to cope with rapidly changing conditions, Government acting by itself will make insufficient progress; its efforts must be supplemented by African enterprise. Government's duty at present is to lay the foundations of development in every direction, to organise the departmental machinery necessary for dealing with each system, and to provide such European staff as the revenue permits; while at the same time it must prepare, organise, and bring into being a system of schools where Africans can obtain the better and higher education that will fit them to enter the various trades and professions, both in the public service and in private enterprise. . . .

Higher education by itself will not solve the problem of the country. It must be accompanied by a better system of training in handicrafts, agriculture, and all those trades that go to provide for the necessities of a community; for although higher education may be the brain of a country, its productive capacity is its heart. Of what use is the brain if the heart ceases to beat? The education of the brain and the training of the hand, *each accompanied by the moulding of the mind*, must proceed together if success is to be sure. . . .

I am well aware of the belief held by some critics — and who has not heard it enunciated? — that the African is not capable of exercising those qualities that will be conferred on him by higher education.

Now, whatever may be my own belief . . . there are two sides to every question, so I am going to examine the contention of these critics dispassionately and ask them four questions.

Firstly, have the critics ever considered that character-training — the essential factor in every branch of education but the all-essential factor in higher education — had hitherto been omitted from the African's curriculum, at any rate in Africa? . . . If they persist in their belief, then they deny that a human being can rise from a lower to a higher plane of development and it does not appear to me that they receive the support of history.

Secondly, are they aware that the African races, in spite of the lack of educational facilities, of character-training, have produced men who have distinguished themselves in various walks of life, many intellectually, a number morally? America, where they have long studied the question of African education, has furnished many examples. . . . Our own African and West Indian colonies furnish others, sufficiently numerous to warrant the belief that, had character-training been in their school curriculum, success would have been wider and more complete.

Thirdly, are the critics aware of the immense field in Africa for the employment of Africans, and if so are they deliberately going to turn men who have an earnest desire for intellectual advancement — and some of whom have shown that they can benefit by it — into a race

of malcontents by confining them to the subordinate work of trades and professions?

And lastly, do the critics honestly believe that we have the right to deny the African the chance of proving that his race is capable of doing what other races have done in the past? If so, they have forgotten that Britain stands where she does to-day by giving her peoples and her opponents alike a "sporting chance." . . .

Other critics have it that, in advocating the provision of a higher education locally for Africans, we are deliberately inviting political troubles in the Gold Coast. Surely the absolute contrary is the case. If politics are to come — and come they must if history is of any value as a guide — surely the safeguards *against* trouble is the local education of the many, accompanied by character-training, rather than the education in Europe of a few, an education that invariably lacks character-training and that more often than not results in bad European habits replacing good African characteristics? If secondary education is not introduced to fill the gap between the English University-trained African and the semi-literate product of our primary schools, we shall be continuing our present system of providing the easy prey of the demagogue. . . .

Another criticism is, that in educating Africans to fill higher appointments in the Government service we shall be deliberately interfering with European employment in the Gold Coast. This is a short-sighted view. I have already pointed out that the development of the country necessitates an annual increase in staff. No Government in the world could afford proportionately the immense financial burden . . . if this increase was to consist of Europeans only. Apart from that, the married European with children has not and never will have a real home life in West Africa, whereas there is a great field of employment for him in the good climates of the Dominions. It will be many long years before Africans are fit to fill the higher appointments in the Government service; in the meantime there is ample room for both. . . .

It has been said that we must go slow, that we must not force education on the people. With regard to the last point there is no question of forcing; one has only to see the crowd of applicants for admission surrounding the primary schools of this country at the beginning of every term. As for going slow, we are going too slow. Although it is perfectly true that the races of the Gold Coast are now in a phase through which every other race has had to pass since time immemorial, yet every century sees a quicker rate of advance made by the primitive peoples of the world. Therefore, although we may draw lessons from the past experience of other nations, it is essential that we should move faster, quicker even than the educational authorities did in the days of our youth. . . .

◆

African Society and Identity Under Colonial Rule

Colonialism in Africa involved more than authoritarian government and economic exploitation. Despite its relative brevity, it profoundly affected every aspect of African life. It fostered population growth, encouraged urbanization, undermined African religions, altered gender relationships, introduced new sports and pastimes, changed how people dressed and what language they spoke, and created new African perspectives on themselves and their place in the world. In the process, much of old Africa — traditional names, music, art, marriage customs, and systems of inheritance — was lost. Africans in the twenty-first century continue to debate whether such changes in the colonial era benefited or harmed Africa in the long run. Unquestionably, however, for most Africans who lived through them in the 1920s and 1930s, these changes were both unsettling and dispiriting.

The Africans' experiences were dispiriting because so much of what took place under colonialism was predicated on the assumption of black inferiority. Colonialism's message, stated or unstated, was that Africans were incapable of governing themselves, or at least incapable of governing themselves effectively; nor were they capable of managing a modern economy or of creating a viable culture and social order. For all these tasks they needed Europeans, who justified their authority by asserting their moral and intellectual superiority. Furthermore, Africans were told that to improve themselves as individuals — to become clerks or civil servants in the colonial administration or to become "assimilated" (for example, to become an *évolué,* or "evolved one" in French Africa) — they would have to shed their Africanness and adopt the ideas, views, work habits, dress, and customs of Europeans. This was the price Africans needed to pay to overcome their backwardness.

Some Africans came to accept their supposed inferiority as a reality, causing them to discard their traditions in the pursuit of "civilization." As the following sources show, however, others resisted colonialism's message. They sought ways to preserve Africa's traditions and strengthen the African's self-respect.

Eagles into Chickens

◆

44 ◆ *James Aggrey, PARABLE OF THE EAGLE*

James Aggrey, an educator and clergyman who was among the most prominent Africans of his day, was born in 1875 in the Gold Coast, a British colony. Educated in a Protestant mission school and a convert to Christianity, at age twenty-three he traveled to the United States to study for the ministry. He remained in the United States for twenty years, studying economics and agriculture, speaking out against racial prejudice, and working among the poor blacks of South Carolina. He returned to Africa in 1918 and died in 1927. His "Parable of the Eagle" was written in the early 1920s.

QUESTIONS FOR ANALYSIS

1. According to the lesson of Aggrey's parable, what psychological damage results from colonialism?
2. What possible implications does the parable have for colonial policies?

A certain man went through a forest seeking any bird of interest he might find. He caught a young eagle, brought it home and put it among his fowls and ducks and turkey, and gave it chickens' food to eat even though it was an eagle, the king of birds.

Five years later a naturalist came to see him and, after passing through his garden, said: "That bird is an eagle, not a chicken."

"Yes," said its owner, "but I have trained it to be a chicken. It is no longer an eagle, it is a chicken, even though it measures fifteen feet from tip to tip of its wings."

"No," said the naturalist, "it is an eagle still; it has the heart of an eagle, and I will make it soar high up to the heavens."

"No," said the owner, "it is a chicken, and it will never fly."

They agreed to test it. The naturalist picked up the eagle, held it up, and said with great intensity: "Eagle, thou art an eagle; thou dost belong to the sky and not to this earth; stretch forth thy wings and fly."

The eagle turned this way and that, and then, looking down, saw the chickens eating their food, and down he jumped.

The owner said: "I told you it was a chicken."

"No," said the naturalist, "it is an eagle. Give it another chance tomorrow."

So the next day he took it to the top of the house and said: "Eagle, thou art an eagle; stretch forth thy wings and fly." But again the eagle, seeing the chickens feeding, jumped down and fed with them.

Then the owner said: "I told you it was a chicken."

"No," asserted the naturalist, "it is an eagle, and it still has the heart of an eagle; only give it one more chance, and I will make it fly tomorrow."

The next morning he rose early and took the eagle outside the city, away from the houses, to the foot of a high mountain. The sun was just rising, gilding the top of the mountain with gold, and every crag was glistening in the joy of that beautiful morning.

He picked up the eagle and said to it: "Eagle, thou art an eagle; thou dost belong to the sky and not to this earth; stretch thy wings and fly!"

The eagle looked around and trembled as if new life were coming to it; but did not fly.

The naturalist then made it look straight at the sun. Suddenly it stretched out its wings and, with the screech of an eagle, it mounted higher and higher and never returned. It was an eagle, though it had been kept and tamed as a chicken!

My people of Africa, we were created in the image of God, but men have made us think that we are chickens, and we still think we are; but we are eagles. Stretch forth your wings and fly! Don't be content with the food of chickens!

The Value of African Religion

◆

45 ◆ *Kabaka Daudi Chwa,* *EDUCATION, CIVILIZATION, AND "FOREIGNIZATION" IN BUGANDA*

The Great Lakes region of east central Africa, dominated by the kingdom of Buganda, was one of the earliest areas of European missionary activity in the nineteenth century. British Protestant missionaries arrived in the region in 1877, and were followed by French Catholic missionaries in 1879. With the traditional Baganda religion already weakened by conversions to Islam, the missionaries made numerous converts, especially among young courtiers in the entourage of the hereditary Baganda ruler, known as the *kabaka*. In the 1880s, Protestant-Catholic rivalries among the chiefs led to civil war, the weakening of the *kabaka*'s power, and the establishment of a British protectorate in 1894. In 1900 British authorities and the Baganda chiefs signed the Buganda Agreement, which recognized Baganda dominance over other peoples in the Uganda protectorate and maintained the chiefs' traditional powers as a means of carrying out British policy. Uganda itself was divided into twenty chieftaincies, of which ten were Protestant, eight were Catholic, and two were Muslim.

Daudi Chwa (1897–1939) as a two-year-old was named *kabaka* of Buganda after his father was deposed and exiled for leading a campaign against the British. A convert to Christianity, Chwa was a figurehead ruler, since the British more or less gave his chiefs a free hand to administer the colony. He did play an active and successful role in opposing the plan to consolidate Uganda, Kenya, and Tanganyika in the 1930s. Toward the end of his life he became disillusioned about the effects of colonial rule, especially on African culture and religion. In 1935 he published his views in a pamphlet, "Education, Civilization, and 'Foreignization' in Buganda." In it, he deplored Christianity's impact on African beliefs and practices.

QUESTIONS FOR ANALYSIS

1. How would you characterize the traditional system of justice of the Baganda? By what means did it try to deter behavior that ran counter to the people's rules and customs?
2. According to the *kabaka*, how and in what ways do traditional Baganda moral values resemble those of Christianity?

3. What have the Baganda gained and lost as a result of European colonialism, according to Chwa?
4. What sort of thinking about the "backwardness" of the Baganda does the *kabaka* try to counter in his letter?
5. In Chwa's view, what should be the proper balance between traditional and European beliefs and practices?

Every one knows that education and civilization were started simultaneously in this country in their respective rudimentary forms by the kind efforts of the members of the various Missionary Societies and have now been enhanced largely due to the assistance rendered by the Protectorate Government.

Naturally education and civilization gained tremendous favour among the Baganda,[1] and as a consequence there are numerous Schools in remote villages in Buganda Kingdom for the education of the young generation; while every facility and luxury which are the outcome of civilization are today being extended to all the Baganda, who can afford to avail themselves of the same, throughout the country.

Now my fears are that instead of the Baganda acquiring proper and legitimate education and civilization there is a possible danger that they may be drifting to 'foreignisation.' . . . To be more explicit, what I mean by the word 'foreignisation' is that instead of the Baganda acquiring proper education at the various Schools and of availing themselves of the legitimate amenities of civilization, I am very much afraid the young generation of this country is merely drifting wholesale towards 'foreignization' of their natural instincts and is discarding its native and traditional customs, habits and good breedings. What is at present popularly termed as education and civilization of a Muganda[2] may be nothing more nor less than mere affectation of the foreign customs and habits of the Western Countries which in some

instances are only injurious to our own inherent morals and ideals of native life.

I am well aware that it has been said more than once that the Baganda have neither morals nor public opinion, but I . . . have always been very strongly opposed to this . . . false accusation brought against the Baganda as a nation. There has always been and shall always be "black sheep" among all nations and tribes throughout the World and naturally I do not wish to be considered in this article to uphold the Baganda as a Nation of Angels — But what I do maintain is that prior to the advent of the Europeans the Baganda had a very strict moral code of their own which was always enforced by a constant and genuine fear of some evil or incurable or even fatal disease being suffered invariably by the breaker of this moral code. In fact I maintain the Baganda observed most strictly the doctrine of the Ten Commandments in spite of the fact that Christianity and the so-called Christian morals were absolutely unknown to the Baganda. For instance there was a very strong public opinion against the following offenses, which are the fundamental principles of the doctrine of the Ten Commandments:

(a) Theft was always punished very severely, invariably by the loss of the right hand of the offender, so as to render him incapable of committing the same offence again.

(b) Adultery was almost unknown among the Baganda and any man found guilty of such offence was always ostracised from Society.

---

[1] The Baganda are the people of the kingdom of Buganda.
[2] *Muganda* is the word (singular) for an individual living in the kingdom of Buganda.

(c) Murder was invariably followed by a very severe vendetta between the members of the family or clan of the victim and those of the offender.

(d) Filial obedience was most honoured among the Baganda and disobedience or disrespect of one's parents was always supposed to be punished by some higher power by the infliction of some horrible or incurable disease upon the offender.

(e) False evidence was looked upon with contempt. The person who bore false evidence and the person against whom it was given were both subjected to a very severe test by forcing them to drink a certain kind of strong drug known as 'Madudu', which was supposed to result in making one of the parties who was in the wrong unconscious.

In this connection I should like to point out that although polygamy was universally recognized among the Baganda and was never considered as immoral yet prostitution was absolutely unheard of. Civilization, education and freedom are the direct causes of the appalling state of affairs as regards prostitution and promiscuous relationships between the Baganda men and women. . . . As [an] illustration of the strictness of the old moral code of the Baganda I should like to point out here one of the most important native custom[s] of looking after the daughters in a Muganda's home. It was one of the worst filial offence[s] for a daughter to become pregnant while living with her parents. As soon as she was discovered in that condition she was at once expelled from her parents' house, and was absolutely cut off from them. She could not eat with them nor would her parents touch her until the child was born and some rites had been gone through which necessitated a great deal of hardship and shame on the part of the girl and her seducer. This custom was intended to stimulate morality among the Baganda girls, since any girl who went astray before she was given in marriage suffered this indignity and was always looked upon with contempt by all her relatives and friends. Furthermore any girl who was given in marriage and was found not to be virgin merited unspeakable disfavour in the eyes of her parents, relations and friends. All this, however, is of course, no longer the case. The present so-called education and civilization prevailing in this country has completely destroyed this moral code by removing the constant fear just referred to above from the minds of the young generation of the Baganda by the freedom and liberty which are the natural consequences of the present World civilization.

I think it would not be out of place to state here definitely that it is my firm belief that prior to the introduction of Christianity in this country the Baganda could not be classified as the worst type of a heathen tribe of Africa since they never indulged in any of the worst heathen customs or rites such as human sacrifice or torture which are found in other parts of Africa. Whilst on the other hand apart from their ignorance of Christianity and their practice of polygamy I am strongly of [the] opinion that most of the traditional customs and etiquette of the Baganda . . . were quite [consistent] with the principles of Christianity. In support of this argument it is only necessary to mention a few customs of the Baganda to show that they unconsciously possessed a sense of modern Christian morality:

(a) It was one of the most important [behaviors] among the Baganda for one's neighbour to be considered as his own relative and to share with him in his happiness or unhappiness. For instance a Muganda would always invite his neighbour if he killed a chicken or goat to share it with him, whilst in case of any danger or misfortune it was always the duty of the nearest neighbour to render every assistance to the party in danger or distress.

(b) It was the recognized etiquette for a Muganda to salute every one that he met on the road, whether he knew him or not.

Chapter 6 *Africa Under Colonial Rule*   *181*

(c) When a Muganda was taking his meal and any one passed by, it was always the custom to invite him to share it with him.

(d) It was always the duty of every one who hears an alarm at any time of day or night or a cry for help to go at once and render assistance to the party in distress or danger. . . .

(e) It was the duty of every Muganda, when requested, to assist any traveller in directing him to his destination, or to give him food or water, and even to give him shelter from rain or for the night. . . .

My intention therefore in this article is to emphasize the fact that while boasting of having acquired Western education and civilization in an amazingly short period, we have entirely and completely ignored our native traditional customs. In other words we have 'foreignised' our native existence by acquiring the worst foreign habits and customs of the Western people. I am only too well aware that this is inevitable in all countries where Western civilization has reached, so I have considered it my duty in this article to warn very strongly all members of the young generation of the Baganda that while they are legitimately entitled to strive to acquire education and civilization they should also take a very great care that acquisition of Western education and civilization does not automatically destroy their best inherent traditions and customs which, in my own opinion, are quite as good as those found among the Western Civilized countries but which only require developing and remodelling where necessary on the lines and ideas of western civilization. . . .

White Rule, African Families

❖

46 ❖ Charlotte Maxeke, SOCIAL CONDITIONS AMONG BANTU WOMEN AND GIRLS

Few groups in Africa were affected more by colonialism than were women. In the precolonial African village, a division of labor between men and women had existed in which women were responsible for planting, weeding, harvesting, food preparation, and child care, while men cleared the land, built houses, herded cattle, and sometimes helped with fieldwork. Such arrangements broke down in West Africa when cash-crop agriculture was introduced. Men took over the farming of cotton or cocoa, leaving responsibility for growing food for domestic consumption exclusively to women. Worse disruption took place in southern and eastern Africa where men left their villages for wage-paying jobs in mines or the cities. This meant long absences of husbands from their families, greater work and domestic responsibilities for women, and frequently the breakdown of family life altogether.

All these issues concerned the South African woman Charlotte Maxeke, the founder of the African National Congress Women's League and a social worker, teacher, and leader in the African Methodist Episcopal Church. Born Charlotte Makgomo in 1874, she received her primary and secondary education in South Africa. While in her early twenties, she toured England, Canada, and the United states with an African choir. She remained in the United States to study at Wilberforce College in Ohio, where she received her bachelor of science degree and met and married another South African, Reverend Marshall Maxeke. On her return to South Africa, she cofounded a secondary school with her husband and remained active in the African National Congress and church affairs until her death in 1939.

In 1930 she presented her views on the plight of black South African women and families in a speech delivered to a rally attended by white and black Christian youth.

QUESTIONS FOR ANALYSIS

1. What, according to Maxeke, are the reasons for the Bantu exodus from the countryside to cities?
2. What special challenges and difficulties confront newly arrived blacks in urban areas?
3. How do the problems of men and women in such circumstances differ?
4. What seems to have been the effect of the changes Maxeke describes on children and young people?
5. What solutions to the problems confronting African women and their families does Maxeke propose? If implemented, are her suggestions likely to be successful?

There are many problems pressing in upon us Bantu,[1] to disturb the peaceful working of our homes. One of the chief is perhaps the stream of Native life into the towns. Men leave their homes, and go into big towns like Johannesburg, where they get a glimpse of a life such as they had never dreamed existed. At the end of their term of employment they receive the wages for which they have worked hard, and which should be used for the sustenance of their families, but the attractive luxuries of civilisation are in many instances too much for them, they waste their hard earned wages, and seem to forget completely the crying need of their family out in the veld.[2]

The wife finds that her husband has apparently forgotten her existence, and she therefore makes her hard and weary way to the town in search of him. When she gets there, and starts looking round for a house of some sort in which to accommodate herself and her children, she meets with the first rebuff. The Location Superintendent[3] informs her that she cannot rent accommodation unless she has a husband. Thus she is driven to the first step on the downward path, for if she would have a roof to cover her children's heads a husband must be found, and so we get these poor women forced by circumstances to consort with men in order to provide shelter for their families. Thus we see that the authorities in enforcing the restrictions in regard to accommodation are often doing Bantu society a grievous harm, for they are forcing its womanhood, its wedded womanhood, to the first step on the downward path of sin and crime.

---

[1]In this context, blacks of South Africa who spoke languages in the Bantu family and who traditionally had been farmers and herders.

[2]Afrikaans (the Dutch-based language spoken by South Africans of Dutch descent) for the grasslands of southern and eastern Africa.

[3]A white official in charge of a black township. Adjacent to white towns or cities, these townships were areas where blacks were by law compelled to live.

Many Bantu women live in the cities at a great price, the price of their children; for these women, even when they live with their husbands, are forced in most cases to go out and work, to bring sufficient [food] into the homes and to keep their children alive. The children of these unfortunate people therefore run wild, and as there are not sufficient schools to house them, it is easy for them to live an aimless existence, learning crime of all sorts. . . .

If these circumstances obtain when husband and wife live together in the towns, imagine the case of the woman, whose husband has gone to town and left her, forgetting apparently all his responsibilities. Here we get young women, the flower of the youth of the Bantu, going up to towns in search of their husbands, and as I have already stated, living as the reputed wives of other men, because of the location requirements, or becoming housekeepers to men in the locations and towns, and eventually their nominal wives.

. . . Thus we see that the European is by his treatment of the Native in these ways which I have mentioned, only pushing him further and further down in the social scale, forgetting that it was he and his kind who brought these conditions about in South Africa, forgetting his responsibilities to those who labour for him and to whom he introduced the benefits, and evils, of civilisation. . . .

Then we come to the *Land Question*. This is very acute in South Africa, especially from the Bantu point of view. South Africa in terms of available land is shrinking daily owing to increased population, and to many other economic and climatic causes. Cattle diseases have crept into the country, ruining many a stock farmer, and thus Bantu wealth is gradually decaying. As a result there are more and more workers making their way to the towns and cities such as Johannesburg to earn a living. And what a living! The majority earn about £3 10s. per month, out of which they must pay 25s. for rent, and 10s. for tram fares, so I leave you to imagine what sort of existence they lead on the remainder.

Here again we come back to the same old problem . . . that of the woman of the home being obliged to find work in order to supplement her husband's wages, with the children growing up undisciplined and uncared for, and the natural following rapid decay of morality among the people. We find that in this state of affairs, the woman in despair very often decides that she cannot leave her children thus uncared for, and she therefore throws up her employment in order to care for them, but is naturally forced into some form of home industry, which, as there is very little choice for her in this direction, more often than not takes the form of the brewing and selling of Skokiaan.[4] Thus the woman starts on a career of crime for herself and her children, a career which often takes her and her children right down the depths of immorality and misery. The woman, poor unfortunate victim of circumstances, goes to prison, and the children are left even more desolate than when their mother left them to earn her living. . . . The children thus become decadent, never having had a chance in life. About ten years ago, there was talk of Industrial schools being started for such unfortunate children, but it was only talk, and we are to-day in the same position, aggravated by the increased numbers steadily streaming in from the rural areas, all undergoing very similar experiences to those I have just outlined. . . .

Many of the Bantu feel and rightly too that the laws of the land are not made for Black and White alike. Take the question of permits for the right to look for work.[5] To look for work, mark you! The poor unfortunate Native, fresh

---

[4]Skokiaan is Afrikaans for Bantu beer, an alcoholic beverage brewed from sorghum.

[5]To prevent too many unemployed blacks from living in towns, the South African government required every black to carry a pass, which showed the name of his or her employer. Those looking for work were required to have temporary passes. Without a valid pass, blacks could be fined, arrested, deported to a rural reserve, or forced to accept a low-paying job for a white employer.

from the country does not know of these rules and regulations, naturally breaks them and is thrown into prison; or if he does happen to know the regulations and obtains a pass for six days, and is obliged to renew it several times, as is of course very often the case, he will find that when he turns up for the third or fourth time for the renewal of his permit, he is put into prison, because he has been unsuccessful in obtaining work. And not only do the Bantu feel that the law for the White and the Black is not similar, but we even find some of them convinced that there are two Gods, one for the White and one for the Black. I had an instance of this in an old Native woman who had suffered much, and could not be convinced that the same God watched over and cared for us all, but felt that the God who gave the Europeans their life of comparative comfort and ease, could not possibly be the same God who allowed his poor Bantu to suffer so. As another instance of the inequalities existing in our social scheme, we have the fact of Natives not being allowed to travel on buses and trams in many towns, except those specially designed for them.

In connection with the difficulty experienced through men being employed almost exclusively in domestic work in the cities, I would mention that this is of course one of the chief reasons for young women, who should rightly be doing that work, going rapidly down in the social life of the community; and it is here that joint service councils of Bantu and White women would be able to do so much for the good of the community. The solution to the problem seems to me to be to get women into service, and to give them proper accommodation, where they know they are safe. Provide hostels, and club-rooms, and rest rooms for these domestic servants, where they may spend their leisure hours, and I think you will find the problem of the employment of female domestic servants will solve itself, and that a better and happier condition of life will come into being for the Bantu.

. . . What we want is more co-operation and friendship between the two races, and more definite display of real Christianity to help us in the solving of these riddles. Let us try to make our Christianity practical.

Nationalism, Pan-Africanism, and Anticolonialism

Although it was clear by the 1920s that efforts to block the European takeover of their continent had failed, Africans in the interwar years did not abandon the fight against colonial rule and its injustices. Not a year passed in which a colonial government somewhere did not use police or troops to quell a tax rebellion, halt demonstrations against forced labor, or forcefully remove individuals from land confiscated by the government. Africans also found legal, nonviolent ways to defend their traditions and resist European rule. They organized political associations, edited journals, wrote books and newspaper editorials, joined independent African Christian churches, attended international meetings, and sent representatives to European capitals to state their grievances.

The short- and long-term goals of African opponents to colonialism varied widely. The Pan-African movement, in which blacks from the United States and the West Indies played important roles, sponsored international meetings to publicize the abuses of colonialism and draw attention to black people's accomplishments; in the 1930s some Pan-Africans concluded that Africans should seek immediate independence from colonial rule. Africans also joined political organizations to protect their rights and advance their interests within colonies and the white-ruled state of South Africa. These organizations included the African National Congress, founded in South Africa in 1912; the National Congress of British West Africa, founded in 1920 by representatives from Nigeria, the Gold Coast, the Gambia, and Sierra Leone; and the Kikuyu Association and the East African Association, founded in Kenya in 1920 and 1921. African workers joined labor unions and went on strike to improve wages and working conditions. Others joined sports and literary associations, singing groups, youth organizations, dance clubs, and African Christian churches that had broken away from mainline European dominations. Although not overtly political, such organizations gave Africans opportunities to express dissatisfaction with European rule in ways not likely to attract the attention of colonial officials. They also enabled Africans to preserve elements of their culture that otherwise might have been eradicated by Europeanization.

African anticolonial movements faced many obstacles in the 1920s and 1930s: the indifference of chiefs, farmers, and petty traders who benefited from European rule; the paucity of Africans with advanced education and political experience; the gap between educated city dwellers and the illiterate villagers; and rivalries between different linguistic and ethnic groups. They also faced active opposition from the colonial governments they sought to change. Despite these barriers, new leaders emerged, political movements multiplied, and critics of colonialism gained followers. After World War II, Africans were ready to demand their independence.

Colonialism and West Africa's Educated Elite

❖

47 ◆ *RESOLUTIONS OF THE NATIONAL CONGRESS OF BRITISH WEST AFRICA, 1920*

Under the leadership of Casely Hayford, a barrister from the Gold Coast, fifty-two delegates from four British West African colonies — the Gambia, Sierra Leone, Nigeria, and the Gold Coast — met in Accra in 1920 to discuss the role of blacks in colonial and municipal government. This was the beginning of the National Congress of British West Africa, an organization that held subsequent meetings at Freetown in 1923, Bathurst in 1925 and 1926, and Lagos in 1929 and 1930. On each occasion the delegates issued demands similar in tone and themes to those of the resolutions adopted in their first meeting in 1920.

The fact that the Congress issued more or less similar demands at each of its meetings is an indication of its failure to achieve most of its goals. Although the Congress took some credit for the decision of British officials in the Gold Coast to institute elections among Africans for positions on the Legislative Council, on the whole the British ignored the Congress's demands, and many rural-based chiefs actively opposed them. The chiefs feared that the authority delegated to them by the British would be undermined if the demands of educated Congress members were met. The National Congress lost direction and leadership after the death of Casely Hayford in 1930, and disbanded in 1933.

Although the Congress achieved few concrete results, it played an important role in the evolution of African nationalism. Its meetings and petitions to London were closely followed in the West African press. It was also one of the first groups to support the idea that colonies could make progress toward independence by turning into nations, and furthermore that these new nations should adopt the British system of government, not the systems formed in Africa's own history.

QUESTIONS FOR ANALYSIS

1. What specific changes in the colonial administration do the resolutions demand? Who would benefit from these proposed changes?
2. How do the resolutions reflect British political and educational views?
3. To what extent are the authors of the resolutions concerned with the preservation of traditional African culture?
4. What demands, if any, in the resolutions would have benefited the colonies' rural population on being implemented?

LEGISLATIVE (INCLUDING MUNICIPAL) REFORMS AND THE GRANTING OF THE FRANCHISE AND ADMINISTRATIVE REFORMS WITH PARTICULAR REFERENCE TO EQUAL RIGHTS AND OPPORTUNITIES

Resolutions

1. That . . . the time has arrived for a change in the Constitutions of the several British West African Colonies, so as to give the people an effective voice in their affairs both in the Legislative and Municipal Governments. . . .
2. That this Conference recommends a Constitution on the following lines: (1) An Executive Council[1] as at present composed.

(2) A Legislative Council[2] composed of representatives of whom one-half shall be nominated by the Crown and the other half elected by the people, to deal with Legislation generally. (3) A House of Assembly, composed of the members of the Legislative Council together with six other financial representatives elected by the people, who shall have the power of imposing all taxes and of discussing freely and without reserve the items on the Annual Estimates of Revenue and Expenditure prepared by the Governor in the Executive Council and approving of them.

3. That each British West African Community[3] shall have the power of electing members to both the Legislative Council and the House of Assembly through such local

---

[1]The Executive Council, an advisory body to the governor, consisted of a small number of British officials named by the governor.

[2]The Legislative Councils in British West African colonies were made up of approximately two dozen individuals named by the governor. They included representatives of the British business community and some Africans, most of whom were chiefs. The councils met annually and were purely advisory.

[3]The peoples who made up the various colonies.

groups as may be found most convenient and expedient, and that where indigenous institutions do not provide a ready means of ascertaining the will of the people, other qualifying methods for voting, such as a property or an Educational standard, shall be resorted to. . . .

5. That this Conference desires to place on record its disapprobation of the invidious distinctions made in the present West African Civil Service by reason of colour, and is of the opinion that all future entries should be based on merit by competitive examinations. . . .

6. That Municipal Corporations[4] with full powers of local self-government be established in each principal town of the British West African Colonies, and that of the members of such Municipal Corporations four-fifths shall be elected by the rate-payers and one-fifth nominated by the Crown, and that such elected and nominated members have the power of electing the Mayor of the Corporation, who however must be an elected member.

EDUCATION WITH PARTICULAR REFERENCE TO A WEST AFRICAN UNIVERSITY

Resolutions

1. That this Conference is of the opinion that the system of Education best suited to the needs and conditions of the various British West African peoples under British influence is one which, whilst enabling the students to attain the highest possible proficiency in the many departments of learning, will least interfere with the development by the student of a proper spirit of reverence for indigenous institutions and modes of life not opposed to equity and good conscience.

2. That in the opinion of this Conference the time has come to found a British West

African University on such lines as would preserve in the students a sense of African Nationality, and therefore recommends that all existing Secondary Schools throughout West Africa, or those about to be formed, should promote a course of training that shall best attain the end in view. . . .

5. That compulsory Education throughout the British West African Colonies be introduced by law, and that the standard of both the Primary and the Secondary Schools be uniformly raised to meet the Standard of the University. . . .

COMMERCIAL ENTERPRISE

Resolutions

1. That this Conference . . . is strongly of the opinion that the natural resources of the British West African Dependencies are not for the exploitation of the Concessionaires[5] under State control. . . .

3. That this Conference, being strongly convinced that the time has come for the co-operation of the peoples of the British West African Dependencies in promoting their economical development, recommends the consideration by the various Committees of the formation of a Corporation, to be known as the British West African Co-operative Association . . . with powers . . . to found Banks, promote shipping facilities, establish Co-operative Stores, and produce buying centres, in such wise as to inspire and maintain a British West African National Economical development.

JUDICIAL REFORMS . . .

Resolutions . . .

3. That the time has come to open definitely to African practitioners of experience all Judicial appointments. . . .

---

[4]Town and city governments.
[5]Businessmen who have received exclusive rights in some economic or commercial activity.

5. That this Conference deplores the gradual modification in successive Ordinances throughout British West Africa of the right of citizens to trial by Jury in Criminal cases, and recommends that the right should be regulated in accordance with English Common and Statute Laws. . . .

12. That this Conference wholly condemns the barbarous practice of flogging African women for any offence whatsoever. . . .

WEST AFRICAN PRESS UNION

Resolutions . . .

3. That this Conference is strongly of the opinion that the liberty of the Press is the birthright of every Community within the British Empire, and deprecates any Legislation that threatens such a right. . . .

THE POLICY OF THE GOVERNMENT IN RELATION TO THE LAND QUESTION

Resolutions

1. That in the opinion of this Conference the principle of Trusteeship with respect of the

lands of the people of British West Africa by Government has been overdone, and that it is proper to declare that the average British West African is quite capable of controlling and looking after his own interests in the land. . . .

THE RIGHT OF THE PEOPLE TO SELF-DETERMINATION

Resolutions

1. That the Conference views with alarm the right assumed by the European powers of exchanging or partitioning Countries between them, without reference to, or regard for, the wishes of the people, and records the opinion that such a course is tantamount to a species of slavery. . . .

4. That this Conference desires to place on record the attachment of the peoples of British West African to the British connection and their unfeigned loyalty and devotion to the throne and person of His Majesty the King-Emperor, and directs that copies of these Resolutions be forwarded in due course to His Majesty's Principal Secretary of State for the Colonies and to each of the Governors of the several Dependencies.

A Plea to the World for Racial Equality

❖

48 ◆ 1921 PAN-AFRICAN CONGRESS, LONDON MANIFESTO

Pan-Africanism, a movement that played a key role in African liberation and in postcolonial politics, was originally inspired by black leaders from the United States and the West Indies in the early 1900s. With the partition of Africa in full swing, color barriers increasing in the West Indies, and lynchings and racial violence growing in the United States, a West Indian lawyer, Henry Sylvester Williams, organized a Pan-African conference in London in 1900. Although most of the thirty-two delegates came from the United States and the West Indies, it caught the attention of Africans. A Nigerian newspaper, *The Lagos Standard,* called the meeting "an event in the history of race movements which for its importance and probable results is perhaps without parallel."

Pan-Africanism was revived in 1919 when the prominent American black W. E. B. Du Bois organized what is recognized as the First Pan-African Conference in Paris to coincide with the Paris Peace Conference. He hoped to demonstrate the solidarity of black people and publicize their needs to the diplomats writing the postwar treaties. In 1921 Du Bois organized a second conference that met sequentially in London, Brussels, and Paris. At the beginning of the 1921 meeting, the 113 delegates from Africa, the United States, England, and the West Indies adopted the following document, known as the London Manifesto. Its demands for racial justice and fair treatment of blacks were widely publicized in Africa, especially in the British colonies of West Africa.

Two more Pan-African conferences were held in the 1920s, but the meeting scheduled for late 1929 had to be canceled as a result of the U.S. stock market crash. Riddled by internal disagreements, the Pan-African movement weakened in the 1930s, but at the Fifth Pan-African Conference at Manchester, England, in 1945, it came alive with a new sense of purpose. With its call for African unity and independence, it was the first step in the post–World War II era toward the realization of African independence.

QUESTIONS FOR ANALYSIS

1. On what grounds does the London Manifesto reject the idea of inequality among the world's races?
2. According to the Manifesto, what is the main obstacle to African advancement in the modern world?
3. What attitude is expressed in the Manifesto toward whites?
4. According to the Manifesto, why should "advanced" people aid Africans?
5. Do the authors of the Manifesto believe Africa is ready for independence? Why or why not?

The absolute equality of races, physical, political and social, is the founding stone of World Peace and human advancement. No one denies great differences of gift, capacity and attainment among individuals of all races, but the voice of Science, Religion and practical Politics is one in denying the God-appointed existence of super races or of races naturally and inevitably and eternally inferior.

That in the vast range of time, one group should in its industrial technique or social organisation or spiritual vision lag a few hundred years behind another or forge fitfully ahead or come to differ decidedly in thought, deed and ideal is proof of the essential richness and variety of human nature, rather than proof of the co-existence of demi-gods and apes in human form. The doctrine of racial equality does not interfere with individual liberty, — rather fulfills it.

And of all the various criteria by which masses of men have in the past been judged and classified that of the color of the skin and texture of the hair is surely the most adventitious [accidental] and idiotic. . . .

The insidious and dishonourable propaganda for which selfish ends so distorts and denies facts as to represent the advancement and development of certain races as impossible and undesirable should be met with wide-spread dissemination of the truth; the experiment of making the Negro slave a free citizen in the

United States is not a failure; the attempts at autonomous government in Haiti and Liberia are not proofs of the impossibility of self-government among black men; the experience of Spanish America does not prove that mulatto democracy will not eventually succeed there; the aspirations of Egypt and India are not successfully to be met by sneers at the capacity of darker races. . . .

If it be proven that absolute world segregation by group, colour or historic affinity is the best thing for the future world, let the white race leave the dark world and the dark races will gladly leave the white. But the proposition is absurd. This is a world of men, — of men whose likenesses far outweigh their differences; who mutually need each other in labour and thought and dream, but who can successfully have each other only on terms of equality, justice and mutual respect. They are the real and only peace-makers who work sincerely and peacefully to this end.

The beginning of Wisdom in inter-racial contact is the establishment of political institutions among suppressed Peoples. The habit of democracy must be made to encircle the earth. Despite the attempt to prove that its practice is the secret and divine Gift of the Few, no habit is more natural and more widely spread among primitive peoples or more easily capable of development among wide masses. Local self-government with a minimum of help and oversight can be established tomorrow in Asia, Africa, America and the Isles of the Sea [the Pacific Islands]. It will in many instances need general control and guidance but it will fail only when that guidance seeks ignorantly and consciously its own selfish ends and not the people's liberty and good.

Surely in the 20th century of the Prince of Peace [Jesus], in the millennium of Buddha and Mahmoud [Muhammad], and in the mightiest era of Human Reason there can be found in the civilised world enough of human altruism, learning and benevolence to develop native institutions for the native's good rather than continuing to allow the majority of mankind to be brutalised and enslaved by ignorant and selfish agents of commercial institutions whose one aim is profit and power for the few.

And this brings us to the crux of the matter; it is to the shame of the world that to-day the relations between the main groups of mankind and their mutual [estimation] and respect is determined chiefly by the degree in which one can subject the other to its service, — enslaving labour, making ignorance compulsory, uprooting ruthlessly religion and custom and destroying government so that the favoured few may luxuriate in the toil of the tortured many. . . .

The day of such world organisation is past and whatever excuse may be made for it in other ages, the 20th century must come to judge men as men and not as merely material and labour. . . .

If we are coming to recognise that the great modern problem is to correct maladjustment in the distribution of wealth, it must be remembered that the basic maladjustment is in the outrageously unjust distribution of the world income between the dominant and suppressed peoples, — in the rape of land and raw material, the monopoly of technique and culture. . . .

What, then, do those demand who see these evils of the colour line and racial discrimination, and who believe in the divine right of Suppressed and Backward Peoples to learn and aspire and be free?

The Suppressed Races through their thinking leaders are demanding:

1. The recognition of civilised men as civilised despite their race and colour.
2. Local self-government for backward groups, deliberately rising as experience and knowledge grow to complete self-government under the limitations of a self-governed world.

3. Education in self-knowledge, in scientific truth and in industrial technique, undivorced from the art of beauty.

4. Freedom in their own religion and customs and with the right to be non-conformist and different.

5. Co-operation with the rest of the world in government, industry and art on the basis of Justice, Freedom and Peace.

6. The ancient common ownership of the Land and its natural fruits and defence against the unrestrained greed of invested capital.

The world must face two eventualities; either the complete assimilation of Africa with two or three of the great world states, with political, civil and social power and privileges absolutely equal for its black and white citizens, or the rise of a great black African State, founded in Peace and Good Will, based on popular education, natural art and industry and freedom of trade, autonomous and sovereign in its internal policy, but from its beginning a part of a great society of peoples in which it takes its place with others as co-rulers of the world. . . .

African Militancy in the 1930s

❖

49 ◆ Gilbert Coka,
THE AFRICAN LIBERATOR, OUR MESSAGE

African nationalism and Pan-Africanism in the 1920s were minority movements, supported mainly by educated city dwellers who sought reforms in the colonial system rather than independence. Because they made moderate demands and had little mass following, colonial officials could afford to ignore them. During the 1930s, however, several developments intensified African opposition to white rule. The calamitous decline in prices for African agricultural products caused economic misery among many black Africans, and forced colonial administrators to cut back on social, educational, and development programs. In South Africa, the removal of blacks from the Cape Province's common voters' roles in 1936 was one of many laws passed in the 1930s to further restrict blacks' rights and freedoms. In 1935 and 1936 African anger exploded when the world stood by and allowed Mussolini's Italian army and air force to conquer Ethiopia, Africa's last remaining truly independent state.

For all these reasons, African nationalists in the 1930s became more defiant, more intent on independence, more willing to use force and economic coercion, and more open to enlisting mass support. The 1930s saw the emergence of new youth movements such as the Gold Coast Youth Conference (1930), the Nigerian Youth Movement (1933), and the West African Youth League (1935). Although all were led by educated city dwellers, they took their message of the need for independence to rural villages. In 1937 cocoa growers in the Gold Coast withheld their cocoa from the market, forcing the British to pay more for their crops. The number of strikes increased in Nigeria, Kenya, and especially South Africa.

In South Africa in 1935, Africans from all parts of the country and all shades of the political spectrum — members of the African National Conference, communists, union leaders, clergy, prominent women, and professionals — met in Bloemfontein at the All-African Convention to denounce recent government actions. The delegates issued the usual list of grievances but also approved a proposal to organize mass meetings to pressure the government. They refused, however, to approve economic boycott as an antigovernment weapon. As a result, when the representatives of the convention met with government officials in 1936, they received a polite reception but no action on their demands.

The lack of response was disappointing to South African militants such as Gilbert Coka. Born in 1910 to the family of a sharecropper in Natal province, Coka attended secondary school, but left in 1927 to work for the black workers' Industrial and Commercial Workers' Union (ICU). Disillusioned with the union's weaknesses and divisions, in the early 1930s he joined the Communist Party of South Africa and went to work for its party newspaper. In 1935 he left the Party and founded his own newspaper, *The African Liberator.* He wrote the following editorial for the newspaper's first issue, which appeared shortly after the Italian invasion of Ethiopia and just weeks before the meeting of the All-African Convention. In it he called on Africans to use their economic strength to break the grip of white racism. After World War II, Coka became active in the African National Congress and died in the 1960s.

QUESTIONS FOR ANALYSIS

1. Why does Coka believe that a new era of African history is about to dawn?
2. What, according to Coka, has held back the liberation of the African people?
3. What strategy does Coka recommend to bring an end to African oppression?
4. What similarities and differences do you see between Coka's editorial and the manifestos of the Pan-African Congress and the National Congress of British West Africa?

War is on. Fascism has let loose the hounds of hell. Greed and envy have their little hour. International conventions and treaties have been treated like a scrap of paper. Wars and rumours of war, are in the air. But the divinity that shapes our ends, has also brought forward the opportunity of liberty to the captive, freedom to the oppressed and opportunity to those who struggle. . . . Africa is opening another era in human history. As she started the era of knowledge, culture, education, civilisation and worship, so today she commences a new era of goodwill, magnanimity and triumph.

The hour of African freedom has struck. That for which Toussaint L'Ouverture[1] suffered and died, that for which Frederick Douglass and Booker [T.] Washington lived and died,[2] that for which Menelik, Shaka, Makana, Lewanika,

---

[1]Toussaint L'Ouverture (1743–1803) led the black rebellion against French rule in Haiti, thus creating the first independent nation in Latin America.
[2]Frederick Douglass (1817–1895), born a slave in Maryland,

was a leading spokesman for abolition and, after the U.S. Civil War, for black political rights. Booker T. Washington (1856–1915), a leading American educator, was the first president of the Tuskegee Institute in Alabama.

Lobengula, Langalibalele and other great sons of Africa, lived, suffered and died. . . .[3] The complete liberty of Africans to shape their own destiny in their own way, has come. . . . Justice will have her way. Africans must be ready to take their great opportunity towards freedom. They must be prepared to act the part of men. The dreams and prophecies of Marcus Garvey,[4] the solidarity of Africans throughout the world, is becoming a fact. And but for a few traitors, Africans had reached the land of Promise — liberty, equality, opportunity and justice.

But this good time coming, will not come of its own volition. It will be brought by Africans themselves when they purge themselves free of envy, jealousies and other manifestations of the inferiority complex which debar them from unity and solidarity. . . . However, the unfortunate thing about us is that we take the monkey apings of our so-called distinguished men for progress. There is no progress in Africans aping Europeans and telling us that they represent the best in the race, for any ordinarily well trained monkey would do the same. The slave mentality still holds our people in chains and they firmly believe that they can only exist through the good graces of their "Masters". Before doing anything worthwhile, they must have the stamp of approval, from some European, otherwise they have no confidence in their work, thoughts and ideas. . . . But in the bottom of their hearts, Europeans as well as other men respect Africans who work out their salvation, [more] than . . . they could ever respect the groups of helpless apes and beggars who make a monopoly of undermining themselves and their people by being

"Good Boys" instead of able men. But such spineless creatures who live by deceit will not forever remain deceiving Africans and therefore cannot permanently impede African progress towards unity, liberty, justice and freedom.

The present war is destroying the Old Africa, which has been undermined for over three centuries. The new Africa is being born. The pangs of suffering attendant upon new birth will follow the bringing forth of a New Africa. But where there is courage there will be a way. Africans must unite and co-operate in their enterprises. They must spend their money where they will get fair returns. As long as they are buyers they will remain despised and powerless, but when they become sellers they will be respected. It is therefore time that Africans reorganized their economic life in order to enter into the new era. They must face the realities of life which are that Nothing can be obtained for nothing and that Money at present is the ruling power of the world. Consequently as workers, they must struggle and obtain higher wages. As buyers they must spend it for tangible returns and that can only be best done by organising consumers cooperatives in every locality. The time has come for Africans to supply themselves with the necessities of life. Our reply to War, oppressive legislation, discrimination, injustice, pauperisation, unemployment and oppression, must be "Let all African money circulate through African friends". An economic boycott against unjust and tyrannical employers, coupled with a persistent struggle for more wages and shorter working conditions [hours], as a part of a national consumers league, supplying all African

---

[3]King Menelik II (1844–1913) led the successful Ethiopian resistance against the attempted Italian takeover in 1896. Shaka (1788–1828) was the Zulu king whose soldiers conquered large parts of southeastern Africa in the early 1800s. Makana was an early-nineteenth-century prophet among the Xhosa people of South Africa whose writings inspired Xhosa resistance to whites from the 1860s through the 1880s. Lewanika was an Ngwato king who converted to Christianity, but was successful for a time in resisting dispossession of his people's lands by Boer settlers. Lobengula (ca. 1828–1894) was king of the Ndebele people during

their rebellion against the British in 1893. Langalibalele (1818–1889) was a chieftain of the AmaHlabi people in Natal who was sentenced to lifetime imprisonment of Robbens Island after three whites were killed in a skirmish with his people over the registration of firearms; on appeal, an English court reversed the sentence, and Langalibalele was released.
[4]Marcus Garvey (1887–1940), born in Jamaica, was a charismatic leader whose pan-Africanism and anticolonialism won him a wide following among Africans.

buyers with the necessities of life, a national liberation movement for equal democratic rights for all South Africans irrespective of colour, creed or race and an independent National newspaper of Africans for Africans by Africans to tell [the] truth about our conditions in the Union, will be worth tons of pious hopes.

Africans! rescue yourselves from degradation, poverty and oppression. . . . African workers unite into your Trade Unions and fight for your rights. African buyers, buy from African traders, put up your cooperatives and get your biggest returns from your monies. Kill envy. Work together. Unite for the greater common good of a free African. . . . But, fellow Africans! Put your house in order. Sink petty selfish jealousies. Organise your consumers cooperatives, Organise your Trades Unions, demand your "Citizen rights," cooperate with all lovers of justice and fair play and make of Africa a land fit for the dwelling of the brave, the just, the humane, the loving, the rich, the powerful, the free and the honest as it was in ancient [times]. Smother internal jealousies, prejudice, injustice and exploitation. To be fit for a new Africa, Unite and cooperate, think and act, struggle and win.

CHAPTER 7

Asia in an Era of Nationalism and Revolution

Asia is the world's largest continent and, in terms of human history, arguably its most important. Asia's river valleys — the Tigris-Euphrates in modern Iran and Iraq, the Indus and Ganges in India, the Yangzi and Hoang He in China — gave rise to humankind's first civilizations some six thousand years ago. Asian sages, prophets, mystics, and teachers developed many of the world's great religions and philosophical traditions — Confucianism, Hinduism, Buddhism, Judaism, Islam, and Christianity. Asian peoples created large and successful states; invented printing, gunpowder, the compass, writing, and metallurgy; made important discoveries in mathematics and astronomy; and had the world's wealthiest and most sophisticated economies during much of human history.

Yet by the 1920s virtually all of Asia consisted of Western colonies, dependencies, or, in the case of Siberia, Central Asia, and Transcaucasia, component parts of a European-based state, the Soviet Union. The beginnings of Asia's subservience to the West can be traced back to the sixteenth century when in their search for trade and converts to Christianity, the Spaniards took over the Philippines and the Portuguese established a line of fortified trading posts stretching from the Red Sea and the Persian Gulf to China and Japan. In the seventeenth century the Dutch, after forcing out the Portuguese, established a commercial and political empire in Sumatra, Java, Borneo, and the Malay Peninsula. More significantly, in the eighteenth century the British East India Company gained control of Bengal in northeast India; from this base the British extended their authority over the whole Indian subcontinent in the nineteenth century.

The British takeover of India was just one example of Western expansion in Asia during the nineteenth and early twentieth centuries. Great Britain and France turned most of Southeast Asia into colonies, the Dutch extended their authority in the East Indies, and the United States replaced Spain as colonial master of the Philippines. In addition, the Western powers established spheres of influence up and down the coast of China, forcefully opened Japan to trade, and took over government finances and much of the economy of the Ottoman Empire and Persia. Except for Japan, which successfully industrialized in the late nineteenth century, Asia became dependent on the West as a market for its raw materials, a supplier of manufactured goods, and a source of capital and technology. Finally, after World War I, Lebanon, Syria, Palestine, Iraq, and Jordan became colonies in all but name when the French and British took them over as parts of League of Nations mandates. In the 1920s only three major Asian states — Turkey, Thailand, and Japan — stood outside the sphere of Western colonialism.

The high point of Western imperialism in Asia, reached after World War I, was followed by its rapid demise after World War II. Of the many factors that contributed to this sudden turnabout, nationalism was the most important. Nationalism in the region first took root in the early twentieth century as Asians came to resent the economic exploitation and political oppression that accompanied colonialism. It gathered strength from the examples of Japan and China. Japan's transformation into a Great Power, exemplified by its victory in the Russo-Japanese War of 1904–1905, awakened Asians to the possibility that they, not just Europeans, were capable of industrialization and military modernization. In addition, China's break with its imperial, Confucian past in the Revolution of 1911 inspired hopes that meaningful political changes also could occur elsewhere in the region.

Events outside of Asia also strengthened nationalist movements. The slaughter of World War I, the failure of the Allies to honor wartime promises to the Arabs and Indians, and the hypocrisy of the League of Nations mandate system undermined the Europeans' claims of moral superiority and further embittered Asians against their colonial masters. The Russian Revolution and its communist ideology also encouraged nationalism, especially in Southeast Asia and China. The new leaders of the Soviet Union denounced colonialism in all its forms and pledged support for political movements and parties working to end the political and economic exploitation of Asia by the capitalist West.

Asian nationalism between the wars meant more than anti-colonialism. It also had social, economic, and cultural implications. Painfully aware of their own societies' shortcomings, nationalist leaders understood that political independence would be meaningless if poverty, illiteracy, and economic underdevelopment continued. Thus with the exception of Gandhi, who venerated manual labor and India's village-based agrarian economy, nationalists were committed to programs of economic and political modernization, and some, such as Mao Zedong in China and Ho Chi Minh in Vietnam, sought revolutionary social changes. As a result, many nationalists found themselves in a dual struggle — against rule by foreigners and also against the social and political conservatism of some of their compatriots.

Nationalists faced other problems as well. With their urban backgrounds and Western educations, many had difficulty drawing the illiterate rural masses into their movements. They also struggled with the concept of nationhood itself. Opposition to Dutch, French, or English rule might bring people together in the short run, but after independence, how would peoples divided by ethnic background, language, and religion stay united?

Despite nationalism's growing strength, only a few colonies — Iraq in 1932 and Egypt in 1936 — became independent between the wars. Elsewhere, the Western powers tenaciously held on to their colonies, and attempted to reassert or maintain their control during and after World War II. This proved beyond their will and capacity, however, and beginning with the independence of Lebanon (1943), Syria (1945), Jordan and the Philippines (1946), and India and Pakistan (1947), colonialism in Asia began to unravel.

◆

Political and Religious Currents in the Middle East

The aftermath of World War I spelled political disaster for the people of the Middle East. The Turks, a defeated ally of Germany, in 1920 were forced to accept the humiliating Treaty of Sèvres, which stripped Turkey of its Arab territories; limited the Turkish army to fifty thousand men; gave France, Britain, and Italy control of its finances; and proposed to cede parts of Turkey itself to Italy, Greece, and the new states of Kurdistan and Armenia. The Arabs, who in 1916 had rebelled against their Turkish overlords in the hope that France and Great Britain would recognize an independent Arab state, soon learned that the British and French had agreed in 1916 to divide the Arab portions of the Ottoman Empire between themselves. This is exactly what happened when, in keeping with Article 22 of the League of Nations Covenant, Iraq, Syria, Palestine, Lebanon, and Jordan became British or French mandates. Farther east, another major Islamic state, Persia, under the decrepit rule of the Qajar Dynasty, was threatened by British plans to turn it into a protectorate.

Efforts to reverse the region's bleak postwar prospects had mixed results. Under the leadership of Mustafa Kemal, between 1919 and 1922 the Turks rallied to drive out Italian and Greek invaders and smash the nascent Armenian state. As a result, in 1923 the European powers agreed to replace the Treaty of Sèvres with the Treaty of Lausanne, which recognized Turkey's integrity and independence. In Iran, another strong military leader, Reza Khan (1878–1944), after engineering an anti-Qajar coup in 1921, reorganized the army and established a government strong enough to discourage the British from pursuing their plan to establish a protectorate.

Arab efforts to attain independence and prevent Jewish immigration to Palestine were less successful. Of the twenty Arab states that stretched from Morocco in the west to Iraq in the east, only relatively backward Saudi Arabia and Yemen were truly independent in the interwar years. Egypt and Iraq attained a measure of self-rule, but continuing British control of foreign policy and military affairs caused resentment in both countries. The drive for independence was even more frustrating in French-controlled Lebanon and Syria. Despite promises to the contrary, the French maintained control of Lebanon until 1943 and Syria until 1945. Arabs also were angered by the British tolerance of Jewish migration to Palestine, which rose dramatically in the 1930s as a result of the Nazi takeover in Germany and immigration restrictions in the United States.

While confronting these immediate postwar problems, the peoples and leaders of the region faced other more fundamental issues. Was the final goal of Arab nationalism the explusion of the British and French and the stifling of Jewish immigration to Palestine? Or was it the attainment of a single united Arab state? What was the best solution to the problem of the region's poverty and illiteracy? How could the teachings and expectations of Islam be reconciled with the realities and demands of modernization? Was modernization itself desirable, and if so, how was it to be achieved? Questions such as these were not new. But in the face of the rapid changes that swept through the region in the first half of the twentieth century, finding answers to them became more urgent and difficult.

Secularism and Nationalism in Republican Turkey

◆

50 ◆ Mustafa Kemal, SPEECH TO THE CONGRESS OF THE PEOPLE'S REPUBLICAN PARTY

The archsymbol of aggressive secularism and nationalism in the Muslim world in the interwar years was Mustafa Kemal (1881–1938), who first achieved prominence as a Turkish military hero during World War I and went on to serve as first president of the Republic of Turkey. Disgusted by the Ottoman sultan's acquiescence to the punitive Treaty of Sèvres and the Greek occupation of the Turkish port of Smyrna in 1919, Kemal assumed leadership of a resistance movement against both the sultan's government and the Allies. He led his supporters to victory over the Greeks and forced the annulment of the Sèvres treaty in 1923.

One year earlier, in 1922, Kemal had convened a National Assembly, which deposed the sultan and set the stage for a decade and a half of revolutionary change. Exercising his broad powers as president, he sought to transform Turkey into a modern secular nation-state. To accomplish this, he broke the power of the Islamic establishment over education and the legal system, encouraged industrialization, accorded women full legal rights, mandated the use of a new Turkish alphabet, and ordered Turks to assume Western-style dress. Directing all Turks to adopt hereditary family names, he took for himself the name Ataturk, or "Great Turk."

Having consolidated his authority, in 1927 Kemal decided to review his accomplishments and impress upon his subjects the need for continued support. He chose as the occasion the meeting of the People's Republican Party, founded by Ataturk and Turkey's only legal political party. Here he delivered an extraordinary speech. Having worked on it for three months (in the process exhausting dozens of secretaries), he delivered it over a period of six days.

In these excerpts, Kemal discusses Turkey's past and future; explains his reasons for abolishing the caliphate, the ancient office by virtue of which Turkish sultans had been the theoretical rulers of all Muslims; and justifies his suppression of the Progressive Republican Party, which despite its name was a party of conservatives who opposed Kemal's plans to modernize Turkey.

QUESTIONS FOR ANALYSIS

1. What, according to Kemal, were the "erroneous ideas" that had guided the Ottoman state in the past?
2. Why does Kemal argue that nation-states, not empires, are the most desirable form of political organization?
3. What is Kemal's view of the West?
4. What are his views of Islam?
5. What arguments does Kemal offer against the continuation of the caliphate?
6. How does Kemal justify his suppression of the Progressive Republicans? What, in his view, were the positive results of this step?

[NATIONALISM AND EMPIRE]

We turn our minds to the times when the Ottoman state in Istanbul . . . was master of the crown and the throne of the East-Roman [Byzantine] Empire. Among the Ottoman rulers there were some who endeavored to form a gigantic empire by seizing Germany and West-Rome [Western Europe]. One of these rulers hoped to unite the whole Islamic world in one body, to lead it and govern it. For this purpose he obtained control of Syria and Egypt and assumed the title of Caliph.[1] Another Sultan pursued the twofold aim, on the one hand of gaining the mastery over Europe, and on the other of subjecting the Islamic world to his authority and government.

The continuous counterattacks from the West, the discontent and insurrections in the Muslim world, as well as the dissensions between the various elements which this policy had artificially brought together within certain limits, had the ultimate result of burying the Ottoman Empire, in the same way as many others, under the pall of history. . . .

To unite different nations under one common name, to give these different elements equal rights, subject them to the same conditions and thus to found a mighty State is a brilliant and attractive political ideal; but it is a misleading one. It is an unrealizable aim to attempt to unite in one tribe the various races existing on the earth, thereby abolishing all boundaries.

---

[1]The reference is to Selim I, who conquered Egypt and Syria in 1515 and 1516; it is doubtful that he actually considered himself caliph.

Herein lies a truth which the centuries that have gone by and the men who have lived during these centuries have clearly shown in dark and sanguinary events.

There is nothing in history to show how the policy of Panislamism[2] could have succeeded or how it could have found a basis for its realization on this earth. As regards the result of the ambition to organize a State which should be governed by the idea of world-supremacy and include the whole of humanity without distinction of race, history does not afford examples of this. For us, there can be no question of the lust of conquest. . . .

The political system which we regard as clear and fully realizable is national policy. . . . This is borne out in history and is the expression of science, reason, and common sense.

In order that our nation should be able [to] live a happy, strenuous, and permanent life, it is necessary that the State should pursue an exclusively national policy and that this policy should be in perfect agreement with our internal organization and be based on it. When I speak of national policy, I mean it in this sense: To work within our national boundaries for the real happiness and welfare of the nation and the country by, above all, relying on our own strength in order to retain our existence. But not to lead the people to follow fictitious aims, of whatever nature, which could only bring them misfortune, and expect from the civilized world civilized human treatment, [and] friendship based on mutuality. . . .

[THE ISSUE OF THE CALIPHATE]

I must call attention to the fact that Hodja Shukri,[3] as well as the politicians who pushed forward his person and signature, had intended to substitute the sovereign bearing the title of Sultan or Padishah by a monarch with the title of Caliph. The only difference was that, instead of speaking of a monarch of this or that country or nation, they now spoke of a monarch whose authority extended over a population of three hundred million souls belonging to manifold nations and dwelling in different continents of the world. Into the hands of this great monarch, whose authority was to extend over the whole of Islam, they placed as the only power that of the Turkish people, that is to say, only from 10 to 15 millions of these three hundred million subjects. The monarch designated under the title of Caliph was to guide the affairs of these Muslim peoples and to secure the execution of the religious prescriptions which would best correspond to their worldly interests. He was to defend the rights of all Muslims and concentrate all the affairs of the Muslim world in his hands with effective authority. . . .

If the Caliph and Caliphate, as they maintained, were to be invested with a dignity embracing the whole of Islam, ought they not to have realized in all justice that a crushing burden would be imposed on Turkey, on her existence; her entire resources and all her forces would be placed at the disposal of the Caliph?

According to their declarations, the Caliph-Monarch would have the right of jurisdiction over all Muslims and all Muslim countries, that is to say, over China, India, Afghanistan, Persia, Iraq, Syria, Palestine, Hijaz,[4] Yemen, Assyria, Egypt, Libya, Tunis, Algeria, Morocco, the Sudan. It is well known that this Utopia has never been realized. . . .

I made statements everywhere, that were necessary to dispel the uncertainty and anxiety of the people concerning this question of the Caliphate. . . . I gave the people to understand

---

[2]The program of uniting all Muslims under one government or ruler.
[3]The events took place in January 1923. After Sultan Mehmed V was deposed as sultan on November 1, 1922, his cousin, Abdul Mejid, was designated caliph. Shukri was

a *hodja* (or *hojja*), a Turkish religious leader; he hoped that the new Turkish state would continue to support the caliphate even after the sultanate was abolished. In 1924, however, Kemal abolished the caliphate.
[4]Western Arabia.

that neither Turkey nor the handful of men she possesses could be placed at the disposal of the Caliph so that he might fulfill the mission attributed to him, namely, to found a State comprising the whole of Islam. The Turkish nation is incapable of undertaking such an irrational mission.

For centuries our nation was guided under the influence of these erroneous ideas. But what has been the result of it? Everywhere they have lost millions of men. "Do you know," I asked, "how many sons of Anatolia have perished in the scorching deserts of the Yemen? Do you know the losses we have suffered in holding Syria and Iraq and Egypt and in maintaining our position in Africa? And do you see what has come out of it? Do you know? "New Turkey, the people of New Turkey, have no reason to think of anything else but their own existence and their own welfare. She has nothing more to give away to others." . . .

[THE SUPPRESSION OF THE PROGRESSIVE REPUBLICANS]

. . . As you know, it was at the time that the members of the opposition had founded a party under the name of "Republican Progressive Party" and published its program. . . .

Could seriousness and sincerity be attributed to the deeds and attitude of people who avoided pronouncing even the word Republic and who tried to suppress the Republic from the very beginning, but who called the party Republican and even Republican Progressive? . . .

Did those who appeared under the same flag, but who wanted to be regarded as progressive Republicans, not follow the deep design of provoking the religious fanaticism of the nation, putting them thus completely against the Republic, progress and reform?

Under the mask of respect for religious ideas and dogmas the new Party addressed itself to the people in the following words:

"We want the re-establishment of the Caliphate; we do not want new laws; we are satisfied with the . . . religious laws . . . ; we shall protect the Medressas, the Tekkes, the pious institutions, the Softahs, the Sheikhs,[5] and their disciples. Be on our side; the party of Mustapha Kemal, having abolished the Caliphate, is breaking Islam into ruins; they will make you into unbelievers. . . ."

Read these sentences, Gentlemen, from a letter written by one of the adherents of this program . . . : "They are attacking the very principles which perpetuate the existence of the Mohamedan [Muslim] world. . . . The assimilation with the Occident means the destruction of our history, our civilisation. . . ."

Gentlemen, facts and events have proved that the program of the Republican Progressive Party has been the work emanating from the brain of traitors. This Party became the refuge and the point of support for reactionary and rebellious elements. . . .

. . . The Government and the Committee found themselves forced to take extraordinary measures. They caused the law regarding the restoration of order to be proclaimed, and the Independence Courts to take action. For a considerable time they kept eight or nine divisions of the army at war strength . . . for the suppression of disorders, and put an end to the injurious organisation which bore the name "Republican Progressive Party."

The result was, of course, the success of the Republic. . . .

There were persons who disseminated and sought to gain credence to the thought that we were making use of the law for Restoration of Order and the Courts of Independence as tools of dictatorship or despotism. . . .

---

[5]A *medressa* is an advanced school of Islamic learning. A *tekke* is a small teaching mosque usually built over the tomb of a saint. A *softah* is a student in an Islamic school. A sheikh, or *shaykh,* is a master of a religious order of Sufis, Muslims who adopted a mystical approach to their religion.

Can anyone be of the opinion that this decision of the High Assembly was intended to hand over to us the means for the carrying on of a dictatorship?

Gentlemen, it was necessary to abolish the fez,[6] which sat on our heads as a sign of ignorance, of fanaticism, of hatred to progress and civilization, and to adopt in its place that hat, the customary headdress of the whole civilised world, thus showing, among other things, that no difference existed in the manner of thought between the Turkish nation and the whole family of civilized mankind. We did that while the law for the Restoration of Order was still in force. If it had not been in force we should have done so all the same; but one can say with complete truth that the existence of this law made the thing much easier for us. As a matter of fact the application of the law for the Restoration of Order prevented the morale of the nation being poisoned to a great extent by reactionaries. . . .

Gentlemen, while the law regarding the Restoration of Order was in force there took place also the closing of the Tekkes, of the convents, and of the mausoleums, as well as the abolition of all sects[7] and all kinds of titles such as Sheikh, Dervish . . . , Occultist, Magician, Mausoleum Guard, etc.[8]

One will be able to imagine how necessary the carrying through of these measures was, in order to prove that our nation as a whole was no primitive nation, filled with superstitions and prejudices.

Could a civilized nation tolerate a mass of people who let themselves be led by the nose by a herd of Sheikhs, Dedes, Seids, Tschelebis, Babas and Emirs;[9] who entrusted their destiny and their lives to chiromancers,[10] magicians, dice-throwers and amulet sellers? Ought one to conserve in the Turkish State, in the Turkish Republic, elements and institutions such as those which had for centuries given the nation the appearance of being other than it really was? Would one not therewith have committed the greatest, most irreparable error to the cause of progress and reawakening?

If we made use of the law for the Restoration of Order in this manner, it was in order to avoid such a historic error; to show the nation's brow pure and luminous, as it is; to prove that our people think neither in a fanatical nor a reactionary manner.

Gentlemen, at the same time the new laws were worked out and decreed which promise the most fruitful results for the nation on the social and economic plane, and in general in all the forms of the expression of human activity . . . the Citizens' Legal Code which ensures the liberty of women and stabilizes the existence of the family.

Accordingly we made use of all circumstances only from one point of view, which consisted therein: to raise the nation on to that step on which it is justified in standing in the civilized world, to stabilize the Turkish Republic more and more on steadfast foundations . . . and in addition to destroy the spirit of despotism for ever.

---

[6]The fez was a brimless hat popular among Turkish men during the nineteenth century. Its lack of a brim allowed the wearer to touch his forehead to the ground while kneeling during prayer without removing the hat.

[7]Islamic religious orders.

[8]A dervish, or *darvish,* was a member of an Islamic sect famous for its whirling dances that symbolized the movement of the heavenly spheres. An Occultist was a Sufi who

achieved a state of withdrawal from the world. A mausoleum guard guarded the tomb of a saint or holy person.

[9]A *dede* was the head of a Sufi order. *Seids,* or *sayyids,* were descendants of the prophet Muhammad through his daughter Fatima. *Baba* was a popular surname among Sufi preachers. In this context, emir is an honorary Turkish title.

[10]People who told the future by reading palms.

The Meaning of Zionism

❖

51 ❖ *Hayyim Nahman Bialik,*
SPEECH AT THE INAUGURATION OF THE
HEBREW UNIVERSITY OF JERUSALEM

After their exile from Palestine by Roman authorities in 70 C.E., Jews resettled in other parts of the Middle East, North Africa, Europe, and years later the Americas. Wherever they went, they were a tiny minority in predominantly Muslim or Christian societies and were often victims of persecution. In all these years, they retained a strong attachment to the "Land of Canaan" in Palestine, which, according to their scriptures, God had given them as their promised land after they had become God's "chosen people." Only in the late nineteenth century, however, in the face of mounting antisemitism in Europe, especially in Russia, where a majority of Europe's Jews lived, did some Jewish intellectuals and religious leaders conclude that Jews could escape persecution and preserve their traditions only if they had their own homeland in Palestine. This Jewish nationalist movement came to be known as Zionism, derived from Mount Zion, one of the two major hills overlooking Jerusalem, the capital of the ancient Jewish kingdom and the site of the temple destroyed by the Romans in 70 C.E.

Although the first advocates of Jewish resettlement in Palestine were Russian Jews reacting to anti-Jewish pogroms in the 1880s, political Zionism, which specifically advocates the foundation of a Jewish state, dates from 1896, when the Vienna-based journalist Theodor Herzl published his book *Der Judenstaat* (The Jewish State), and 1897, when he convened the first international Zionist Congress in Basel, Switzerland. Despite the indifference and outright opposition to Zionism on the part of many assimilated Jews in Western Europe, and despite bitter disputes among Zionists themselves over their visions of a future Jewish state, on the eve of World War I approximately ninety thousand Jews lived in Palestine, almost half of whom were recent immigrants from Europe.

Prospects for Jewish migration to Palestine improved when the British took control of Palestine as a League of Nations mandate after World War I. During the war, Britain's foreign minister, Arthur Balfour, in what came to be known as the Balfour Declaration, committed his government to facilitating "the establishment in Palestine of a national home for the Jewish people." This was a wartime promise the British kept. Under the British mandate, the number of Jews in Palestine increased, especially after the Nazis took control of Germany in 1933. Between 1919 and 1939, the percentage of Jews in Palestine's population grew from slightly under 10 percent to slightly more than 30 percent. These Jews purchased land, established industries, and provided a basis for the growth of Jewish culture in the area through the founding of the Hebrew University of Jerusalem and a technical institute in Haifa in 1925. Despite the opposition of Palestinian Arabs, the Zionists' dreams were becoming a reality. In 1947 the independent state of Israel was born.

The Zionists' hopes and expectations are captured in the following speech delivered by Hayyim Nahman Bialik at the opening of the Hebrew University of Jerusalem in 1925. Born in 1873 in Ukraine, Bialik, after receiving a traditional Jewish education and working briefly as a businessman and as a Hebrew language teacher, became one of the most prominent modern poets and short story writers in Hebrew and Yiddish. In his work he explores the tensions between the Jews' historical experience, especially their persecution, and the modern world. A strong supporter of Zionism, he received permission to leave the Soviet Union in 1921 and settled in Palestine in 1924. He died in 1934 in Vienna, where he had gone for medical treatment, and was buried in Tel Aviv.

In his 1925 speech he describes the Jewish resettlement of Palestine as a historic turning point — not just for the Jews but potentially for all humanity.

QUESTIONS FOR ANALYSIS

1. According to Bialik, why have education and study played such an important role in Jewish history?
2. Why does Bialik feel so strongly about the need of the Jews to have their own state?
3. What in particular does he deplore about the Jews' experience during the diaspora?
4. How does Bialik view the Jews' historic contributions to human culture?
5. What kind of vision does Bialik have for an independent Jewish state? Is his vision shaped primarily by religious or secular concerns?

The solemnity and exaltation of this moment can only be desecrated by any sort of exaggeration. . . . I am sure that the eyes of tens of thousands of Israel that are lifted from all parts of the Diaspora to this hill are shining with hope and comfort; their hearts and their flesh are singing a blessing of thanksgiving unto the Living God Who hath preserved us and sustained us and let us live to see this hour. They all realize that at this moment Israel has kindled . . . the first candle of the renaissance of her intellectual life. . . .

For let people say what they may: This peculiar people called Israel has, despite all the vicissitudes which for two thousand years have daily, yea hourly, attempted to expel it from its own milieu and uproot it from its spiritual climate — this people, I assert, has accepted upon its body and soul the burden of eternal allegiance to the Kingdom of the Spirit. Within that Kingdom it recognizes itself as a creative citizen and in that eternal soil it has planted its feet with all its might for all time. All the sordidness of the accursed Galut[1] and all the pain of our people's poverty did not disfigure its fundamental nature. . . . Within the boundaries of the realm of the Spirit the Jewish nation fashioned the bases of its national heritage and its principal national institutions. These preserved it through millennia of wandering, safeguarded its inner freedom amid outward bondage and have led up to this joyful event. . . . The

---

[1]Hebrew for exile.

national school in all its forms — the *heder,* the *yeshivah,* the *betmidrash*[2] — these have been our securest strongholds throughout our long, hard struggle for existence, and for the right to exist, in the world as a separate and distinct people among the peoples. In times of tempest and wrath we took refuge within the walls of these fortresses, where we polished the only weapon we had left — the Jewish mind — lest it become rusty. . . .

Ladies and Gentlemen! You all know what has become of our old spiritual strongholds in the Diaspora in recent times and I need not dwell upon this theme now. For all their inner strength, and for all the energy the nation had expended upon creating and preserving these centers, they stood not firm on the day of wrath; by the decree of history they are crumbled and razed to the foundations and our people is left standing empty-handed upon their ruins.[3] This is the very curse of the Galut, that our undertakings do not, indeed cannot, prosper. In every land and in every age we have been sowing a bushel and reaping less than a peck. The winds and hurricanes of history always begin by attacking the creating of Israel and, in a moment, uproot and utterly destroy that which hands and minds have produced over a period of generations. Through cruel and bitter trials and tribulations, through blasted hopes and despair of the soul, through innumerable humiliations, we have slowly arrived at the realization that without a tangible homeland, without private national premises that are entirely ours, we can have no sort of a life, either material or spiritual. Without Eretz Israel — Eretz means land, literally land — there is no hope for the rehabilitation of Israel anywhere, ever. . . .

We have come to the conclusion that a people that aspires to a dignified existence must create a culture; it is not enough merely to make use of a culture — a people must create its own, with its own hands and its own implements and materials, and impress it with its own seal. Of course our people in its "diasporas" is creating culture. . . . But as whatever the Jew creates in the Diaspora is always absorbed in the culture of others, it loses its identity and is never accounted to the credit of the Jew. . . . The Jewish people is therefore in a painfully false position: Whereas its true function culturally is that of a proletariat — i.e., it produces with the materials and implements of others for others — it is regarded by others, and at times even by itself, as a cultural parasite, possessing nothing of its own. A self-respecting people will never become reconciled to such a lot; it is bound to arise one day and resolve: No more. Better a little that is undisputedly my own than much that is not definitely either mine or somebody else's. Better a dry crust in my own home and on my own table than a stall-fed ox in the home of others and on the table of others. Better one little university but entirely my own, entirely my handiwork from foundations to coping stones,[4] than thousands of temples of learning from which I derive benefit but in which I have no recognized share. Let my food be little and bitter as the olive, if I may but taste in it the delicious flavor of a gift from myself.

It was in this frame of mind that we took refuge in this land. We are not come here to seek wealth, or dominion, or greatness. How much of these can this poor little country give us? We wish to find here only a domain of our own for our physical and intellectual labor. . . . Already at this early hour we experience cultural needs that cannot be postponed and must be satisfied at once. Besides, we are burdened with heavy cares for the cultural fate of our people in

---

[2]These are schools in the traditional Jewish educational system. *Heder* is an elementary school; *yeshiva* is a higher academy of religious studies; *betmidrash* is a house of learning in which advanced students can pursue studies of sacred literature.

[3]The reference is to the destruction of Jewish schools during pogroms.
[4]Stones having special shapes for use in capping the exposed top of a wall.

the Diaspora. Nations born only yesterday foolishly imagine that through intellectual parching,[5] by means of a *numerus clausus,*[6] they can do to death an old nation with a past of four thousand years of Torah.[7] We must therefore hasten to light here the first lamp of learning and science and of every sort of intellectual activity in Israel, ere the last lamp grows dark for us in foreign lands. . . .

Ladies and Gentlemen! Thousands of our youth, obeying the call of their hearts, are streaming from the four corners of the earth to this land for the purpose of redeeming it from desolation and ruin. They are prepared to pour all their aspirations and longings and to empty all the strength of their youth into the bosom of this wasteland in order to revive it. They are plowing rocks, draining swamps, and building roads amid singing and rejoicing. These young people know how to raise simple and crude labor — physical labor — to the level of highest sanctity, to the level of religion. . . . Let those youths build the Earthly Jerusalem with fire and let them who work within these walls build the Heavenly Jerusalem with fire, and between them let them build and establish our House of Life.

Four thousand years ago there gathered in this land . . . some groups of wandering shepherds divided into a number of tribes. They became in time, in consequence of events of apparently no great importance, a people small and poor in its day — the people Israel. Few and unhappy were the days of this people on its land as "a people dwelling apart, not counted among the nations." But this people produced men . . . like their brethren — who carried the tempest of the spirit of God in their hearts and His earthquakes and thunders in their mouths. Those men . . . dared to turn to eternity, to the Heavens and to

the Earth. And it was they who in the end provided the foundation for the religious and moral culture of the world. . . . After the proclamation of Cyrus,[8] some tens of thousands of exiles rallied again to this poor, waste country and again formed a poor small community, even poorer and smaller than the first. After only some three hundred years, there arose again in this land a man of Israel, the son of an Israelite carpenter,[9] who conveyed the gospel of salvation to the pagan world and cleared the way for the days of the Messiah. Since then two thousand years have elapsed, and we are all witnesses this day that idols have not yet disappeared from the face of the earth; the place of the old has been taken by new ones, no better than the former. And then came the Balfour Declaration. Israel is assembling in Eretz Israel for a third time. Why should not the miracle be repeated again this time? . . .

Who knows but that the task in which great nations have failed amid the tumult of wealth may be achieved by a poor people in its small country? Who knows but in the end of days this doctrine of responsibility for the fate of humanity may go forth from its house of learning and spread to all the people? Surely not for nothing has the hand of God led this people for four thousand years through the pangs of hell and now brought it back unto its land for the third time.

The Books of Chronicles,[10] the last of the Scriptures, are not the last in this history of Israel. To its two small parts there will be added a third, perhaps more important than the first two. And . . . the third will undoubtedly begin with the Proclamation of Balfour and end with a new gospel, the gospel of redemption to the whole of humanity.

---

[5]*Parch* means "to dry up or shrivel."
[6]The reference is to the quota system adopted by universities in Europe to limit Jewish enrollment.
[7]The body of wisdom and law contained in Jewish Scripture, other sacred literature, and oral tradition.
[8]Cyrus the Great, king of Persia (599–530 B.C.E.), after conquering Babylonia in 539 B.C.E., freed the Jewish

captives in Babylonia and allowed them to return to Jerusalem. He also approved the rebuilding of the Jewish temple.
[9]A reference to Jesus.
[10]The two Books of Chronicles, part of the Jewish Bible, recount history from Adam to the time of Cyrus the Great.

A Call for Islamic Social and Political Action

◆

52 ◆ *The Muslim Brotherhood, TOWARD THE LIGHT*

Although the commitment to modernization advocated by Mustafa Kemal had many supporters throughout the Middle East, it also had staunch opponents. Many Muslims — from all classes of society and across all educational levels — were troubled by the prospect of a secularized, Westernized future and sought instead to establish a true Islamic society guided by the Quran and Islamic law. In the inter-war years their hopes were best represented by the Muslim Brotherhood, an organization founded in 1929 by an Egyptian schoolteacher, Hasan al-Banna (1906–1949).

Born in a small town in the Nile Delta, Hasan al-Banna as a student in Cairo after World War I was troubled by the factionalism, social conflict, poverty, and religious indifference he observed in Egypt. He concluded that British colonialism and the widespread acceptance of Western values had caused these ills and that a return to fundamental Islamic teachings would cure them. In 1927 he became a schoolteacher in the Sinai town of Ismailia, where he organized religious study groups and committed himself to Islamic renewal. In 1929 he founded the Muslim Brotherhood, an organization dedicated to the realization of Islamic states in Egypt and other Muslim lands.

In the 1930s the Brotherhood grew into a tightly knit, disciplined organization with approximately a million members. It built mosques, schools, and small hospitals; sponsored youth programs, social clubs, and handicraft industries; and promoted its religious message through preaching, books, and pamphlets. In the 1940s, the organization's increasing political activism led to clashes with British authorities and the Egyptian government itself. Linked to the assassination of several officials, the Brotherhood was outlawed by the Egyptian government in 1949, the same year Hasan al-Banna was assassinated by Egyptian agents.

The Brotherhood was legalized in Egypt in 1950, and since then it has continued to be an important religious and political force in the Arab world. It has branches in Sudan, Syria, and other Arab states; vast financial resources; and an estimated membership of two million. It has accomplished this despite attempts by the Egyptian government to suppress the organization on two occasions in the 1950s and 1960s after members of the Brotherhood were implicated in attempted assassinations and antigovernment conspiracies. The organization also faced internal divisions between militants and moderates. In Egypt, the Brotherhood officially rejected violence in the 1980s and sought to advance its program by winning elected offices and increasing its commitment to social service activities. This official endorsement of moderation caused defections to more militant groups. Islamic Jihad and Hamas, organizations committed to Palestinian liberation and opposed to any compromise with Israel, are both offshoots of the Muslim Brotherhood.

The following excerpt is drawn from a pamphlet issued by the Brotherhood in 1936 and directed to King Faruq of Egypt and other Arab leaders. It summarizes the major goals of the Brotherhood in its first decade of existence.

QUESTIONS FOR ANALYSIS

1. How would you characterize the views of the Brotherhood concerning the purpose and goals of government?
2. According to this document, what is the Brotherhood's conception of the ideal government official?
3. What does the document reveal about the attitude of the Brotherhood toward the West? Are there aspects of Western culture the Brotherhood finds acceptable?
4. What role does the Brotherhood envision for women in Islamic society?
5. According to the Brotherhood, what should be the content and goals of education?
6. What policies does the Brotherhood support to help the poor?
7. What is there in the statement that helps account for the widespread support of the Brotherhood within Middle Eastern Islamic societies?

After having studied the ideals which ought to inspire a renascent nation on the spiritual level, we wish to offer, in conclusion, some practical suggestions. We will list here only the chapter headings because we know very well that each suggestion will require profound study as well as the special attention of experts; we know also that the needs of the nation are enormous; we do not believe that the fulfilling of the needs and the aspirations of the country will be an easy thing; what is more, we do not think that these goals can be reached in one journey or two. We realize the obstacles which these problems must overcome. The task will require a great deal of patience, a great deal of ability, and a willing tenacity.

But one thing is certain: resolve will lead to success. A dedicated nation, working to accomplish the right, will certainly reach, with God's help, the goals toward which it strives.

The following are the chapter headings for a reform based upon the true spirit of Islam:

I. In the political, judicial, and administrative fields:

    1st.   To prohibit political parties and to direct the forces of the nation toward the formation of a united front;

    2nd.   To reform the law in such a way that it will be entirely in accordance with Islamic legal practice;

    3rd.   To build up the army, to increase the number of youth groups; to instill in youth the spirit of holy struggle, faith, and self-sacrifice;

    4th.   To strengthen the ties among Islamic countries and more particularly among Arab countries which is a necessary step toward serious examination of the question of the defunct Caliphate,[1]

    5th.   To propagate an Islamic spirit within the civil administration so that all officials will understand the need for applying the teachings of Islam;

    6th.   To supervise the personal conduct of officials because the private life and the administrative life of these officials forms an indivisible whole;

    7th.   To advance the hours of work in summer and in winter so that the accomplishment of religious obligations will be eased and to prevent all useless staying up late at night;

    8th.   To condemn corruption and influence peddling; to reward only competence and merit;

---

[1] The office of caliph, the successor of Muhammad and head of the Muslim community, had been held by the Ottoman sultans but was abolished by Mustafa Kemal in 1924.

9th.   Government will act in conformity to the law and to Islamic principles; the carrying out of ceremonies, receptions, and official meetings, as well as the administration of prisons and hospitals should not be contrary to Islamic teachings. The scheduling of government services ought to take account of the hours set aside for prayer.

10th.   To train and to use Azharis, that is to say, the graduates of Al-Azhar University,[2] for military and civil roles;

II. In the fields of social and everyday practical life:

1st.   The people should respect public mores: this ought to be the object of special attention — to strongly condemn attacks upon public mores and morality;

2nd.   To find a solution for the problems of women, a solution that will allow her to progress and which will protect her while conforming to Islamic principles. This very important social question should not be ignored because it has become the subject of polemics and of more or less unsupported and exaggerated opinion;

3rd.   To root out clandestine or public prostitution and to consider fornication as a reprehensible crime the authors of which should be punished;

4th.   To prohibit all games of chance (gaming, lotteries, races, golf);

5th.   To stop the use of alcohol and intoxicants — these obliterate the painful consequences of people's evil deeds;

6th.   To stop attacks on modesty, to educate women, to provide quality education for female teachers, school pupils, students, and doctors;

7th.   To prepare instructional programs for girls; to develop an educational program for girls different than the one for boys;

8th.   Male students should not be mixed with female students — any relationship between unmarried men and women is considered to be wrong until it is approved;

9th.   To encourage marriage and procreation — to develop legislation to safeguard the family and to solve marriage problems;

10th.   To close dance halls; to forbid dancing;

11th.   To censor theater productions and films; to be severe in approving films;

12th.   To supervise and approve music;

13th.   To approve programs, songs, and subjects before they are released, to use radio to encourage national education;

14th.   To confiscate malicious articles and books as well as magazines displaying a grotesque character or spreading frivolity;

15th.   To carefully organize vacation centers;

16th.   To change the hours when public cafes are opened or closed, to watch the activities of those who habituate them — to direct these people towards wholesome pursuits, to prevent people from spending too much time in these cafes;

17th.   To use the cafes as centers to teach reading and writing to illiterates, to seek help in this task from primary school teachers and students;

18th.   To combat the bad practices which are prejudicial to the economy and to the morale of the nation, to direct the people toward good customs and

---

[2]An educational institution in Cairo specializing in Islamic studies.

praiseworthy projects such as marriage, orphanages, births, and festivals; the government should provide the example for this;

19th. To bring to trial those who break the laws of Islam, who do not fast, who do not pray, and who insult religion;

20th. To transfer village primary schools to the mosque and to carry on all beneficial activities there (selecting officers, matters of health, interested support for young children learning their religious duties, introducing the old to science);

21st. Religious teaching should constitute the essential subject matter to be taught in all educational establishments and faculties;

22nd. To memorize the Quran in state schools — this condition will be essential in order to obtain diplomas with a religious or philosophical specialty — in every school students should learn part of the Quran;

23rd. To develop a policy designed to raise the level of teaching, to unify the different teaching specialties, to bring together the different branches of culture — emphasis should be put upon teaching morality and physics;

24th. Interested support for teaching the Arabic language in all grades — absolute priority to be given to Arabic over foreign languages (primary teaching);

25th. To study the history of Islam, the nation, and Muslim civilization;

26th. To study the best way to allow people to dress progressively and in an identical manner;

27th. To combat foreign customs (in the realm of vocabulary, customs, dress,

nursing) and to Egyptianize all of these (one finds these customs among the well-to-do members of society);

28th. To orient journalism toward wholesome things, to encourage writers and authors, who should study specifically Muslim and Oriental[3] subjects;

29th. To safeguard public health through every kind of publicity — increasing the number of hospitals, doctors, and out-patient clinics;

30th. To call particular attention to the problems of village life (administration, hygiene, water supply, education, recreation, morality).

III. The economic field:

1st. Organization of the zakat tax[4] according to Islamic precepts, using zakat proceeds for welfare projects such as aiding the indigent, the poor, orphans; the zakat should also be used to strengthen the army;

2nd. To prevent the practice of usury, to direct banks to implement this policy; the government should provide an example by giving up the interest fixed by banks for servicing a personal loan or an industrial loan, etc.;

3rd. To facilitate and to increase the number of economic enterprises and to employ the jobless there, to employ for the nation's benefit the skills possessed by the foreigners in these enterprises;

4th. To protect workers against monopoly companies, to require these companies to obey the law, the public should share in all profits;

5th. Aid for low-ranking employees and enlargement of their pay, lowering the income of high-ranking employees; . . .

---

[3]As opposed to Western studies.
[4]A fixed share of income or property that all Muslims must pay as a tax or as charity for the welfare of the needy.

7th. To encourage agricultural and industrial works, to improve the situation of the peasants and industrial workers;

8th. To give special attention to the technical and social needs of the workers, to raise their level of life and aid their class;

9th. Utilization of certain natural resources (unworked land, neglected mines; etc.);

10th. To give priority to projects whose accomplishment is vital to the country.

◆

Anticolonialism in India and Southeast Asia

During the late nineteenth century, at a time when many Indians were already debating their colonial relationship with Great Britain and some were demanding independence, Southeast Asians were just beginning to experience the full effects of direct European rule. Nevertheless, developments in both areas between the two world wars showed some marked similarities. In India and Southeast Asia alike, nationalism became a potent force, shaking the foundations of Europe's colonial empires.

Indian nationalism in the 1920s and 1930s under the leadership of Mohandas Gandhi was transformed from an ideology of the educated elite into a mass movement. Despite differences in religion, education, and caste status, millions of Indians marched, demonstrated, boycotted British goods, and refused to obey British-imposed laws in an effort to force the British to "quit India" and to achieve Indian self-rule. The British responded with minor concessions but mostly with delaying tactics and armed repression.

Nationalist movements also intensified in Southeast Asia between the wars, but their strength, priorities, and tactics varied widely across a region marked by many ethnic, cultural, and political differences and by dissimilar styles of Western rule. Nationalism was weakest in areas such as the British-controlled Malay States and the French protectorates in Laos and Cambodia, where traditional rulers were retained and little economic modernization or urbanization occurred. Nationalism was strongest in the Dutch East Indies, Burma, and Vietnam, where Western economic penetration and direct rule disrupted traditional economic, political, and social relationships.

Drawing strength and inspiration from both Western ideologies and their own religious and cultural traditions, nationalist leaders formed political parties and attempted to broaden nationalism's appeal by using newspapers, magazines, and the radio. Without exception, however, armed rebellions failed. Communist-inspired uprisings in Indonesia in 1926 and 1927 were crushed by the Dutch; so too was the anti-French mutiny led by the Vietnamese Nationalist Party in 1930.

These failures resulted in part from the colonial powers' superior military strength and in part from divisions within the nationalist movements. Western-educated intellectuals and politicians argued among themselves over political doctrine, and founded a plethora of political parties to represent different ideologies.

Conflicting regional loyalties and disagreements between secularized, European-ized leaders and those with traditional religious views also weakened nationalist movements. Even Gandhi was unable to prevent the splintering of Indian nation-alism into antagonistic Muslim and Hindu camps on the eve of World War II.

Interwar nationalist movements in India and Southeast Asia prepared the groundwork for independence after World War II. They also foretold the conflicts and divisions that would plague the new states of the region once independence had been achieved.

Gandhi's Hopes for India

◆

53 ◆ *Mohandas Gandhi, INDIAN HOME RULE*

Mohandas Gandhi, the outstanding figure in modern Indian history, was born in 1869 in a village north of Bombay on the Arabian Sea. His father was a prominent government official who presided over an extended family devoted to strict Hindu practices. Gandhi studied law in England and, after failing to establish a law practice in Bombay, moved to South Africa in 1893 to serve the Indian population.

In South Africa he became incensed over discriminatory laws against Indian settlers, most of whom were indentured servants, laborers, or small merchants. In his efforts to improve the lot of South Africa's Indians, Gandhi developed his doc-trine of *satyagraha,* usually translated as "soul force." *Satyagraha* sought social justice not through violence but through love, noncompliance to unjust laws, a willingness to suffer, and conversion of the oppressor. Central to its strategy was nonviolent resistance: Gandhi's followers disobeyed unjust laws and accepted the consequences — even beatings and imprisonment — to reach the hearts of the British and change their thinking.

In 1915 Gandhi at the age of forty-five returned to India, where he spent his remaining thirty-three years. By 1920, he was the dominant figure in the Congress Party, which under his leadership launched a noncooperation campaign against British rule between 1920 and 1922. When in 1922 villagers attacked and killed twenty-one policemen and rural watchmen, Gandhi called off the noncooperation campaign, but he continued the tactic of civil disobedience, organizing boycotts of British goods and leading protest marches against unpopular British measures such as the salt tax in 1930. Living a life of self-imposed chastity and poverty, he wrote letters, pamphlets, and books and delivered speeches in every corner of India denouncing British rule and urging Indians to address their own society's ills, especially the treatment of women and untouchables. During the 1930s and the war years, his attacks on British rule intensified, and along with other Con-gress leaders he spent months in jail. As independence approached, he struggled to preserve Hindu-Muslim cooperation and prevent the partition of the nation into a predominantly Muslim Pakistan and a predominantly Hindu India. On Jan-uary 30, 1948, just over four months after Indian and Pakistani independence,

Gandhi was shot and killed by a Hindu zealot who resented Gandhi's commitment to Hindu-Muslim harmony.

The following selection is taken from *Hind Swaraj* (Indian Home Rule), a pamphlet Gandhi wrote in 1908 after meeting with a group of Indian nationalists in England who urged the use of force to oust the British from India. Although written early in his political career and well before he emerged as India's inspirational leader, it contains ideas and principles that guided Gandhi throughout his life. Composed in the form of a dialogue between a reader and an editor (Gandhi), *Indian Home Rule* appeared in hundreds of editions and remains his most widely read work.

QUESTIONS FOR ANALYSIS

1. What does Gandhi see as the major deficiencies of modern civilization?
2. How, according to Gandhi, has modern civilization affected women?
3. What is the basis for Gandhi's faith that Hindus and Muslims will be able to live together in peace in India?
4. What, according to Gandhi, is true civilization, and what is India's role in preserving it?
5. What leads Gandhi to conclude that love is stronger than force?
6. In your view, why did Gandhi's attack on civilization win him support among India's masses?

CIVILIZATION

READER: Now you will have to explain what you mean by civilization. . . .

EDITOR: Let us first consider what state of things is described by the word "civilization." Its true test lies in the fact that people living in it make bodily welfare the object of life. We will take some examples: The people of Europe today live in better-built houses than they did a hundred years ago. This is considered an emblem of civilization, and this is also a matter to promote bodily happiness. Formerly, they wore skins, and used as their weapons spears. Now, they wear long trousers, and for embellishing their bodies they wear a variety of clothing, and, instead of spears, they carry with them revolvers containing five or more chambers. If people of a certain country, who have hitherto not been in the habit of wearing much clothing, boots, etc., adopt European clothing, they are supposed to have become civilized out of savagery. Formerly, in Europe, people plowed their lands mainly by manual labor. Now, one man can plow a vast tract by means of steam-engines, and can thus amass great wealth. This is called a sign of civilization. Formerly, the fewest men wrote books, that were most valuable. Now, anybody writes and prints anything he likes and poisons people's minds. Formerly, men traveled in wagons; now they fly through the air, in trains at the rate of four hundred and more miles per day. This is considered the height of civilization. It has been stated that, as men progress, they shall be able to travel in airships and reach any part of the world in a few hours. Men will not need the use of their hands and feet. They will press a button, and they will have their clothing by their side. They will press another button, and they will have their newspaper. A third, and a motor-car will be in waiting for them. They will have a variety of delicately dished up food. Everything will be done by machinery. Formerly, when people wanted to fight with one another, they measured between them their bodily strength; now it is possible to take away thousands of lives by one man working behind a gun from a hill. This is civilization. Formerly, men worked in the open air only so much as they liked. Now, thousands of workmen meet together and for the sake of maintenance work in factories or mines. Their condition is worse than that of beasts. They are obliged to work, at the risk of their lives, at most dangerous occupations, for the sake of millionaires. Formerly, men were made slaves under physical compulsion, now they are enslaved by temptation of money and of the luxuries that money can buy. There are now diseases of which people never dreamed before, and an army of doctors is engaged in finding out their cures, and so hospitals have increased. This is a test of civilization. Formerly, special messengers were required and much expense was incurred in order to send letters; today, anyone can abuse his fellow by means of a letter for one penny. True, at the same cost, one can send one's thanks also. Formerly, people had two or three meals consisting of homemade bread and vegetables; now, they require something to eat every two hours, so that they have hardly leisure for anything else. What more need I say? . . .

This civilization is irreligion, and it has taken such a hold on the people in Europe that those who are in it appear to be half mad. They lack real physical strength or courage. They keep up their energy by intoxication. They can hardly be happy in solitude. Women, who should be the queens of households, wander in the streets, or they slave away in factories. For the sake of a pittance, half a million women in England alone are laboring under trying circumstances in factories or similar institutions. This awful fact is one of the causes of the daily growing suffragette movement.

This civilization is such that one has only to be patient and it will be destroyed.

THE CONDITION OF INDIA (CONTINUED)

The Hindus and the Muslims

READER: But I am impatient to hear your answer to my question. Has the introduction of Islam not unmade the nation?

EDITOR: India cannot cease to be one nation because people belonging to different religions live in it. The introduction of foreigners does not necessarily destroy the nation, they merge in it. A country is one nation only when such a condition obtains in it. That country must have a faculty for assimilation. India has ever been such a country. In reality, there are as many religions as there are individuals, but those who are conscious of the spirit of nationality do not interfere with one another's religion. If they do, they are not fit to be considered a nation. If the Hindus believe that India should be peopled only by Hindus, they are living in dreamland. The Hindus, the Muslims, the Parsees[1] and the Christians who have made India their country are fellow-countrymen, and they will have to live in unity if only for their own interest. In no part of the world are one nationality and one religion synonymous terms; nor has it ever been so in India.

READER: But what about the inborn enmity between Hindus and Muslims?

EDITOR: That phrase has been invented by our mutual enemy.[2] When the Hindus and Muslims fought against one another, they certainly spoke in that strain. They have long since ceased to fight. How, then, can there be any inborn enmity? Pray remember this too, that we did not cease to fight only after British occupation. The Hindus flourished under Muslim sovereigns and Muslims under the Hindu. Each party recognized that mutual fighting was suicidal, and

---

[1]Disciples of the Zoroastrian religion in India who descended from Persian refugees of the seventh and eighth centuries.

[2]The British.

that neither party would abandon its religion by force of arms. Both parties, therefore, decided to live in peace. With the English advent the quarrels recommenced. . . .

Hindus and Muslims own the same ancestors, and the same blood runs through their veins. Do people become enemies because they change their religion? Is the God of the Muslim different from the God of the Hindu? Religions are different roads converging to the same point. What does it matter that we take different roads, so long as we reach the same goal? . . .

WHAT IS TRUE CIVILIZATION?

READER: You have denounced railways, lawyers and doctors. I can see that you will discard all machinery. What, then, is civilization?

EDITOR: The answer to that question is not difficult. I believe that the civilization India has evolved is not to be beaten in the world. Nothing can equal the seeds sown by our ancestors. Rome went, Greece shared the same fate, the might of the Pharaohs was broken, Japan has become westernized, of China nothing can be said, but India is still, somehow or other, sound at the foundation. . . . India remains immovable, and that is her glory. It is a charge against India that her people are so uncivilized, ignorant, and stolid, that it is not possible to induce them to adopt any changes. It is a charge really against our merit. What we have tested and found true on the anvil of experience, we dare not change. . . .

Civilization is that mode of conduct which points out to man the path of duty. Performance of duty and observance of morality are convertible terms. To observe morality is to attain mastery over our mind and our passions. So doing, we know ourselves. The Gujarati[3] equivalent for civilization means "good conduct."

If this definition be correct, then India, as so many writers have shown, has nothing to learn from anybody else, and this is as it should be.

PASSIVE RESISTANCE

READER: Is there any historical evidence as to the success of what you have called soul-force or truth-force? No instance seems to have happened of any nation having risen through soul-force. I still think that the evil-doers will not cease doing evil without physical punishment.

EDITOR: . . . The force of love is the same as the force of the soul or truth. We have evidence of its working at every step. The universe would disappear without the existence of that force. . . .

Thousands, indeed, tens of thousands, depend for their existence on a very active working of this force. Little quarrels of millions of families in their daily lives disappear before the exercise of this force. Hundreds of nations live in peace. History does not and cannot take note of this fact. History is really a record of every interruption of the even working of the force of love or of the soul. . . . Soul-force, being natural, is not noted in history.

READER: According to what you say, it is plain that instances of the kind of passive resistance are not to be found in history. It is necessary to understand this passive resistance more fully. It will be better, therefore, if you enlarge upon it.

EDITOR: Passive resistance is a method of securing rights by personal suffering; it is the reverse of resistance by arms. When I refuse to do a thing that is repugnant to my conscience, I use soul-force. For instance, the government of the day has passed a law which is applicable to me: I do not like it; if, by using violence, I force the government to repeal the law, I am employing what may be termed body-force. If I do not obey the law and accept the penalty for its breach, I use soul-force. It involves sacrifice of self.

Everybody admits that sacrifice of self is infinitely superior to sacrifice of others. Moreover, if this kind of force is used in a cause that is unjust, only the person using it suffers. He does not make others suffer for his mistakes. . . .

---

[3]An Indian dialect spoken in Gujarat, in northwest India.

READER: From what you say, I deduce that passive resistance is a splendid weapon of the weak but that, when they are strong, they may take up arms.

EDITOR: This is gross ignorance. Passive resistance, that is, soul-force, is matchless. It is superior to the force of arms. How, then, can it be considered only a weapon of the weak? Physical-force men are strangers to the courage that is requisite in a passive resister. . . .

What do you think? Wherein is courage required — in blowing others to pieces from behind a cannon or with a smiling face to approach a cannon and to be blown to pieces? Who is the true warrior — he who keeps death always as a bosom-friend or he who controls the death of others? Believe me that a man devoid of courage and manhood can never be a passive resister.

This, however, I will admit: that even a man, weak in body, is capable of offering this resistance. One man can offer it just as well as millions. Both men and women can indulge in it. It does not require the training of an army; it needs no Jiu-jitsu. Control over the mind is alone necessary, and, when that is attained, man is free like the king of the forest, and his very glance withers the enemy.

Passive resistance is an all-sided sword; it can be used anyhow; it blesses him who uses it and him against whom it is used. Without drawing a drop of blood, it produces far-reaching results.

A Muslim's View of India's Future

◈

54 ◆ *Muhammad Ali Jinnah,*
SPEECH TO THE MUSLIM LEAGUE, 1940

Muhammad Ali Jinnah (1876–1948), the leader of India's Muslims between the wars and the founder of the state of Pakistan, was raised in Lahore in modern Pakistan, where his father was a successful businessman. A brilliant and prosperous lawyer who had studied in London and dressed like an English gentleman, Jinnah joined the Indian National Congress in 1906 and the Muslim League in 1913. For several years he served as a liaison between the two organizations, but in 1920 he resigned from the Congress because of his opposition to Gandhi's civil disobedience campaign and Gandhi's refusal to support the concept of weighted voting rights for India's Muslim minority. Nonetheless, during the 1920s and early 1930s Jinnah continued to work for cooperation between Hindus and Muslims to further the cause of Indian independence.

In the late 1930s, however, chronic disagreements between Hindus and Muslims and mounting communal violence convinced Jinnah that Muslims had no future in an independent India. He lent his support to the founding of an independent Muslim state, Pakistan, meaning "land of the pure." In 1947 his efforts were rewarded when, with the end of British rule in South Asia, not one new state, but two, India and Pakistan, were born. Jinnah served as Pakistan's first governor-general, a post he held for only a year before his death in 1948.

The following selection is from one of this most famous speeches, delivered to a meeting of the Muslim League in Lahore in 1940. On this occasion Jinnah expressed his support for the establishment of independent states in the northwestern and eastern parts of India where Muslims were the majority of the population.

QUESTIONS FOR ANALYSIS

1. What is the basis of Jinnah's objection to the statement he quotes from the London *Times*?
2. Why does Jinnah have so little hope that Hindus and Muslims will ever be able to live together peacefully in a united India?
3. What is the basis of Jinnah's assertion that Islam and Hinduism are "not religions in the strict sense of the word"?
4. How do Jinnah's views of Hindu-Muslim relations differ from those of Gandhi?
5. What is the basis of Jinnah's assertion that Muslims in India are "a nation according to any definition of a nation"?

A leading journal like the London *Times,* commenting on the Government of India Act of 1935, wrote: "Undoubtedly the differences between the Hindus and Muslims are not of religion in the strict sense of the word but also a law and culture, that they may be said, indeed, to represent two entirely distinct and separate civilizations. However, in the course of time, the superstition will die out and India will be molded into a single nation." So, according to the London *Times,* the only difficulties are superstitions. . . . But surely it is a flagrant disregard of the past history of the subcontinent of India as well as the fundamental Islamic conception of society vis-à-vis that of Hinduism to characterize them as mere "superstitions." Notwithstanding a thousand years of close contact, nationalities, which are as divergent today as ever, cannot at any time be expected to transform themselves into one nation merely by means of subjecting them to a democratic constitution and holding them forcibly together by unnatural and artificial methods of British parliamentary statute. What the unitary government of India for one hundred fifty years had failed to achieve cannot be realized by the imposition of a central federal government. . . .

. . . If the British government are really in earnest and sincere to secure [the] peace and happiness of the people of this subcontinent, the only course open to us all is to allow the major nations separate homelands by dividing India into "autonomous national states." There is no reason why these states should be antagonistic to each other. On the other hand, the rivalry and the natural desire and efforts on the part of one to dominate the social order and establish political supremacy over the other in the government of the country will disappear. It will lead more towards natural good will by international pacts between them, and they can live in complete harmony with their neighbors. . . .

It is extremely difficult to appreciate why our Hindu friends fail to understand the real nature of Islam and Hinduism. They are not religions in the strict sense of the word, but are, in fact, different and distinct social orders, and it is a dream that the Hindus and Muslims can ever evolve a common nationality, and this misconception of one Indian nation has gone far beyond the limits and is the cause of most of [our] troubles and will lead India to destruction if we fail to revise our notions in time. The Hindus and Muslims belong to two different religious philosophies, social customs, literatures. They neither intermarry nor interdine together and, indeed, they belong to two different civilizations which are based mainly on conflicting ideas and conceptions. . . . To yoke together two such nations under a single state, one as a numerical minority and the other as a majority, must lead to growing discontent and final destruction of any fabric that may be so built up for the government of such a state.

. . . History has also shown us many geographical tracts, much smaller than the subcontinent of India, which otherwise might have been called one country, but which have been divided into as many states as there are nations inhabiting them. [The] Balkan Peninsula comprises as many as seven or eight sovereign states. Likewise, the Portuguese and the Spanish stand divided in the Iberian Peninsula. Whereas under the plea of the unity of India and one nation, which does not exist, it is sought to pursue here the line of one central government, we know that the history of the last twelve hundred years has failed to achieve unity and has witnessed, during the ages, India always divided into Hindu India and Muslim India. The present artificial unity of India dates back only to the British conquest and is maintained by the British bayonet, but termination of the British regime, which is implicit in the recent declaration of His Majesty's government, will be the herald of the entire break-up with worse disaster than has ever taken place during the last one thousand years under Muslims. . . .

Muslim India cannot accept any constitution which must necessarily result in a Hindu majority government. Hindus and Muslims brought together under a democratic system forced upon the minorities can only mean Hindu rāj [rule]. Democracy of the kind with which the Congress

High Command is enamored would mean the complete destruction of what is most precious in Islam. We have had ample experience of the working of the provincial constitutions during the last two and a half years and any repetition of such a government must lead to civil war and raising of private armies. . . .

Mussalmans [Muslims] are a nation according to any definition of a nation, and they must have their homelands, their territory, and their state. We wish to live in peace and harmony with our neighbors as a free and independent people. We wish our people to develop to the fullest our spiritual, cultural, economic, social, and political life in a way that we think best and in consonance with our own ideals and according to the genius of our people. Honesty demands and the vital interests of millions of our people impose a sacred duty upon us to find an honorable and peaceful solution, which would be just and fair to all. But at the same time we cannot be moved or diverted from our purpose and objective by threats or intimidations. We must be prepared to face all difficulties and consequences, make all the sacrifices that may be required of us to achieve the goal we have set in front of us.

Revolution and Oppression in Vietnam

◆

55 ◆ *Nguyen Thai Hoc,* *LETTER TO THE FRENCH CHAMBER OF DEPUTIES, 1930*

Having seized Vietnam's three southernmost provinces, the region known as Cochin China, in 1862, the French extended their authority over Tongking (northern Vietnam) and Annam (central Vietnam) in the 1880s. Convinced of their civilizing mission, they sought to undermine Vietnam's Confucian culture by creating a French-trained Vietnamese elite willing to cooperate with the colonial regime. Although some members of Vietnam's upper class resisted French rule (including the young emperor Duy-tan, whose plot to overthrow the French was uncovered in 1916), most at first sought some sort of compromise between Western and Vietnamese culture and accepted French rule.

Accommodation and compromise gave way to revolutionary nationalism in the 1920s as a result of Vietnamese anger over continued economic exploitation and political oppression, despite the ninety thousand Vietnamese troops and laborers who had served in Europe during World War I. The leading nationalist organization was the Viet Nam Qoc Dan Dang (Vietnamese Nationalist Party, or VNQDD), founded in 1927 by Nguyen Thai Hoc, a teacher from Hanoi. At first he had moderate goals of more economic and educational opportunities for the Vietnamese, but he soon became disillusioned with French rule and turned to revolution. The VNQDD was modeled on Sun Yat-sen's Chinese Nationalist Party, or Guomindang, and was dedicated to achieving an independent and democratic-socialist Vietnam. In 1929, with its membership at about fifteen hundred and its leaders convinced that the general populace was ready for revolution, the VNQDD plotted an anti-French insurrection. The revolt, known as the Yen Bay uprising, was crushed by the French in 1930, and the VNQDD leaders were arrested and executed.

While awaiting execution, Nguyen Thai Hoc wrote the following letter to France's parliament, the Chamber of Deputies. A defense of his actions and a denunciation of French colonialism, the letter was also released to the Vietnamese public.

QUESTIONS FOR ANALYSIS

1. In Nguyen Thai Hoc's view, what are French intentions in Vietnam and what has been the effect of French occupation?
2. How and why did Nguyen Thai Hoc evolve from a moderate reformer to a revolutionary?
3. If they had been implemented, how would his suggestions to Governor General Varenne have improved the lot of the Vietnamese people?
4. What does the French response to the Yen Bay uprising reveal about the nature of French colonial rule?
5. What do you suppose Nguyen Thai Hoc hoped to accomplish by writing this letter?

Gentlemen: . . .

According to the tenets of justice, everyone has the right to defend his own country when it is invaded by foreigners, and according to the principles of humanity, everyone has the duty to save his compatriots when they are in difficulty or in danger. As for myself, I have assessed the fact that my country has been annexed by you French for more than sixty years. I realize that under your dictatorial yoke, my compatriots have experienced a very hard life, and my people will without doubt be completely annihilated, by the naked principle of natural selection. Therefore, my right and my duty have compelled me to seek every way to defend my country which has been invaded and occupied, and to save my people who are in great danger.

At the beginning, I had thought to cooperate with the French in Indochina in order to serve my compatriots, my country and my people, particularly in the areas of cultural and economic development. As regards economic development, in 1925 I sent a memorandum to

Governor General Varenne,[1] describing to him all our aspirations concerning the protection of local industry and commerce in Indochina. I urged strongly in the same letter the creation of a Superior School of Industrial Development in Tongking. In 1926 I again addressed another letter to the then Governor General of Indochina in which I included some explicit suggestions to relieve the hardships of our poor people. In 1927, for a third time, I sent a letter to the Résident Supérieur[2] in Tongking, requesting permission to publish a weekly magazine with the aim of safeguarding and encouraging local industry and commerce. With regard to the cultural domain, I sent a letter to the Governor General in 1927, requesting (1) the privilege of opening tuition-free schools for the children of the lower classes, particularly children of workers and peasants; (2) freedom to open popular publishing houses and libraries in industrial centers.

It is absolutely ridiculous that every suggestion has been rejected. My letters were without answer; my plans have not been considered; my requests have been ignored; even the articles that I sent to newspapers have been censored and rejected. From the experience of these rejections, I have come to the conclusion that the French have no sincere intention of helping my country or my people. I also concluded that we have to expel France. For this reason, in 1927, I began to organize a revolutionary party, which I named the Vietnamese Nationalist Party, with the aim of overthrowing the dictatorial and oppressive administration in our country. We aspire to create a Republic of Vietnam, composed of persons sincerely concerned with the happiness of the people. My party is a clandestine organization, and in February 1929, it was uncovered by the security police. Among the members of my party, a great number have been arrested. Fifty-two persons have been condemned to forced labor ranging from two to twenty years. Although many have been detained and many others unjustly condemned, my party has not ceased its activity. Under my guidance, the Party continues to operate and progress towards its aim.

During the Yen Bay uprising someone succeeded in killing some French officers. The authorities accused my party of having organized and perpetrated this revolt. They have accused me of having given the orders for the massacre. In truth, I have never given such orders, and I have presented before the Penal Court of Yen Bay all the evidence showing the inanity of this accusation. Even so, some of the members of my party completely ignorant of that event have been accused of participating in it. The French Indochinese government burned and destroyed their houses. They sent French troops to occupy their villages and stole their rice to divide it among the soldiers. Not just members of my party have been suffering from this injustice — we should rather call this cruelty than injustice — but also many simple peasants, interested only in their daily work in the rice fields, living miserable lives like buffaloes and horses, have been compromised in this reprisal. At the present time, in various areas there are tens of thousands of men, women, and children, persons of all ages, who have been massacred.[3] They died either of hunger or exposure because the French Indochinese government burned their homes. I therefore beseech you in tears to redress this injustice which otherwise will annihilate my people, which will stain French honor, and which will belittle all human values.

I have the honor to inform you that I am responsible for all events happening in my country under the leadership of my party from 1927 until the present. You only need to execute me. I beg your indulgence for all the others who at the

---

[1] Alexandre Varenne was governor-general of Indochina from 1925 to 1929.

[2] In the French colonial hierarchy, the *résident-supérieur* of Tongking was the chief administrator of northern Vietnam.

[3] A substantial number of civilian deaths did occur as a result of French actions following the revolt, but Nguyen Thai Hoc's estimate of tens of thousand of deaths is an exaggeration.

present time are imprisoned in various jails. I am the only culprit, all the others are innocent. They are innocent because most of them are indeed members of my party, and have joined it only because I have succeeded in convincing them of their duties as citizens of this country, and of the humiliations of a slave with a lost country. Some of them are not even party members. . . . I have the honor to repeat once again that you need execute only me. If you are not satisfied with killing one man, I advise you to kill also the members of my family, but I strongly beg your indulgence towards those who are innocent.

Finally, I would like to declare in conclusion: if France wants to stay in peace in Indochina, if France does not want to have increasing troubles with revolutionary movements, she should immediately modify the cruel and inhuman policy now practiced in Indochina. The French should behave like friends to the Vietnamese, instead of being cruel and oppressive masters. They should be attentive to the intellectual and material sufferings of the Vietnamese people, instead of being harsh and tough.

Please, Gentlemen, receive my gratitude.

Intellectual Ferment and Revolution in China

The overthrow of the Qing Dynasty in 1911 resulted not in China's long-awaited national revival, but instead in four decades of invasion, civil war, and immense suffering for the Chinese people. In the aftermath of the revolution, Sun Yat-sen and his dreams of a democratic China were pushed aside by General Yuan Shikai, who ruled the Chinese "republic" as a dictator between 1912 and 1916, and was planning to have himself declared emperor when he died in 1916. After his death, China was carved up by dozens of generally unscrupulous and irresponsible warlords, military men whose local authority was based on their control of private armies and whose grip on China was not completely broken until the Communists took power in 1949. With a weak national government, the Chinese endured continuing Western domination of their coastal cities, and offered only feeble resistance when the Japanese conquered Manchuria in 1931 and invaded China itself in 1937. Massive flooding of the Yellow River and widespread famine in north China in the 1920s compounded the people's misery.

The chaos of the 1920s and 1930s prompted an intense debate about China's future. The 1920s in particular were years of intellectual experimentation and inquiry, in which journalists, poets, writers of fiction, academics, and university students scrutinized what it meant to be Chinese and debated what would save China from catastrophe. Most of these intellectuals rejected traditional Chinese values, customs, and philosophical traditions, arguing that only a radical break from the past would allow China to become an equal of Japan and the West. Most turned to the West for inspiration, although they disagreed about what aspects of Western thought and values should be borrowed.

In politics, Chinese who grieved over warlord depredation, Western imperialism, and Japanese aggression had two options. Two revolutionary parties, — the

Nationalist Party, or Guomindang (GMD), and the Chinese Communist Party (CCP) — emerged, each of which sought to unify and govern China. The Guomindang, founded in 1912 by Sun Yat-sen, was theoretically dedicated to Sun's "three principles of the people" — democracy, nationalism, and livelihood — and came to be identified with the educated, Western-oriented bourgeoisie of China's coastal cities. In practice, under General Chiang Kai-shek (1887–1975) the Guomindang showed little enthusiasm for either social reform or democracy and concentrated mainly on fighting the warlords in the 1920s and the Communists in the 1930s. The Chinese Communist Party, founded in 1921, was dedicated to Marxism-Leninism, with its leadership provided by intellectuals and its major support eventually coming from the rural masses.

Aided by agents of the Soviet Union, the Guomindang and Communists formed a coalition in 1923 to rid China of its warlords. With their forces combined into the National Revolutionary Army, the Guomindang and their less numerous Communist allies launched the Northern Expedition against the warlords in 1926. The alliance lasted only until 1927, when Chiang Kai-shek, buoyed by early victories and generous financial support from Chinese businessmen, purged the Communists from the alliance and ordered his troops to kill Communist leaders who were gathered in Shanghai. Communist troops and their commanders fled to the countryside, where under the leadership of Mao Zedong (1893–1975), they rebuilt the party into a formidable military and political force. After a long struggle against the Guomindang and the Japanese, the Communists gained control of China in 1949.

The New Culture Movement and the West

❖

56 ◆ *Hu Shi,*
OUR ATTITUDE TOWARD MODERN CIVILIZATION OF THE WEST

The New Culture Movement, an outburst of literary activity and intellectual inquiry into China's past and future in the 1920s, is traditionally dated from May 4, 1919, when students from thirteen area colleges and universities met in Beijing and demonstrated against provisions of the Paris peace settlement that granted the former German concession in Shandong province to Japan. The events of May 4, however, only served to intensify and accelerate intellectual and literary developments that had begun several years earlier at Beijing University, where a number of young professors had begun to explore new intellectual and cultural paths for China after it jettisoned its Confucian past.

All intellectuals connected with the New Culture Movement looked to the West for guidance and inspiration, but none more so than Hu Shi (1891–1962), a professor of philosophy at Beijing University and one of the movement's leading figures. Born in Shanghai and raised by his mother in poverty after his father, a government official, died when he was four, Hu had an education that included the Confucian classics, English, and Western science. At the age of nineteen he received a scholarship to study at Cornell University, where he earned a bachelor's degree in philosophy, and later at Columbia University, where he worked toward his doctorate. On his return to China in 1917, he joined the Beijing University faculty. In his writings on philosophy, literature, and politics, he espoused Western pragmatism and science, and called on intellectuals to use vernacular Chinese rather than classical Chinese as a written language. After serving as ambassador to the United States between 1938 and 1943, he returned to China in 1946 to serve as chancellor of Beijing University. He fled China after the Communist victory in 1949, and lived in semiretirement in New York City until his death in 1962.

The following excerpt is taken from an essay written in 1926. In it, Hu answers his critics who had argued that traditional Chinese values were more humane and less materialistic than those of the West, and hence more beneficial to humankind's spiritual development.

QUESTIONS FOR ANALYSIS

1. How does Hu explain the attraction of condemning Western civilization for its materialism while praising Eastern civilization for its "spirituality"?
2. On what basis does Hu reject this argument?
3. What does Hu see as the major accomplishments of Western civilization?
4. What does Hu mean when he refers to the "new religion" developing in Western civilization?
5. In what ways do Hu's attitudes toward the West differ from those of Gandhi? How might one explain these differences?

[THE "MATERIALISM" OF WESTERN SOCIETIES]

One of the most baseless, most harmful statements has to do with the condemnation of Western civilization as "materialistic" and the praise of Oriental civilization as "spiritual." . . . In the past it was used to provide some kind of psychological lift, or self-congratulatory consolation, when we, the Oriental people, were cruelly oppressed and badly humiliated by the Occidentals. During the past few years when the Westerners themselves, in reaction to the disastrous World War I, became increasingly disillusioned with a modern civilization based upon the advance of science and technology, we have often heard from their scholars the praise of the so-called spiritual civilization of the East. Though this praise results from an abnormal,

though understandable, mentality of a temporary nature, it is more than welcome to the culturally chauvinistic Orientals. It strengthens the bias about the alleged superiority of Oriental civilization. . . .

. . . While a man in an ocean liner should not look down upon another man sailing a junk, it is ridiculous for the latter to brag about his spiritual superiority simply because his junk is more primitive and less convenient than the ocean liner. Technological backwardness is not synonymous with spiritual advancement. . . .

. . . Throughout history the greatest tragedy has always been man's inability to ward off hunger and cold despite his hard labor. How can we in good conscience lecture a man about to be starved to death on the virtue of contentment, fate, and self-satisfaction? A man who condemns material comfort for no other reason than its unavailability to him can be compared to the fox in a Western fable who announces proudly that it does not like sour grapes when the grapes, ripe and sweet, are too high for it to reach. Poverty is not something to be proud of: those who state otherwise are either indulging in self-deception or too lazy to do something about it. More pathetic still are those who fast, mutilate their bodies, or commit suicide by fire, all in the name of "spiritual civilization." All these people — the self-congratulators, the self-deceivers, the self-mutilators, and the suicides — are mentally ill, really, since their attitude toward life is that of a dying man. . . .

Unlike its Oriental counterpart, the modern civilization of the West takes into full consideration the importance of material enjoyment. It has as its foundation two basic concepts. First, the purpose of life is the pursuit of happiness. Second, poverty is a sin; so is physical weakness or illness. The second concept, logically, is a derivative of the first. The goal of this civilization is, in short, the enrichment of life. As poverty is a sin, the Westerners devote their energy to the opening up of natural resources, the promotion of industry, the improvement of manufactured products, and the expansion of commerce. As physical weakness or illness is also a sin, they spare no effort in the study and improvement of medical care, the promotion of sanitation, hygiene, physical fitness and sports, the prevention of contagious disease, and the improvement of heredity. Since the pursuit of happiness is the purpose of life, they busy themselves with the enhancement of comfort in their living quarters, the improvement of transportation and communication, the beautification of their cities, the promotion of the arts, the assurance of safety in their streets, and finally, the security of incorruptibility in government and among government officials. To be sure, Western civilization contains in it certain elements that sometimes prompt its adherents to commit aggression, pillage, or even mass murder, which has to be condemned, of course. Neither can it be denied that it has brought benefit to those who embrace it.

THE NEW RELIGION

Though modern civilization of the West has not yet dissociated itself from the religion of the past [Christianity], one nevertheless senses that a new religion has been slowly developing. . . . Not surprisingly, the first characteristic of the new religion is its logic and rationality. As modern science enables man to discover new knowledge, to conquer nature for his own benefit, and to do a multitude of things that historically have been regarded as unattainable or even inconceivable, man's confidence in himself has increased enormously, and he believes, for the first time, that he can shape the future in accordance with his own wishes. Not surprisingly, the second characteristic of the new religion is its humanism. The acquisition of more and more knowledge not only enhances man's ability to cope with his environment but also broadens his social perspective, thus increasing his empathy with his fellow men. Not surprisingly, the third characteristic of the new religion is its social ethics.

. . . All the old religions stress salvation on an individual basis, and all the old ethics centers on the civilization of moral worth, again of a personal nature. The adherents of old religions do occasionally speak of the necessity of "saving" others, but they are more than satisfied if they can somehow save themselves. Forever looking inward and, as a result, becoming more and more involved with no one except themselves, they lose contact with the outside world. They do not understand worldly problems, let alone resolve them. . . . What is the use of this so-called self-cultivation of virtues if the net result is a mummy-like parasite, totally ignorant of practical matters and insensitive to the suffering of others? . . .

OCCIDENTAL AND ORIENTAL CIVILIZATIONS COMPARED

As "discontent" characterizes the modern civilization of the West, "content" characterizes the traditional civilization of the East. Being content, we Orientals do not strive for the improvement of our living standard, do not pay much attention to new discoveries and new inventions, and do not, even remotely, contemplate upon such "strange" ideas as the conquest of nature. We relish our ignorance, find satisfaction with the status quo, however unpleasant, and speak resignedly about our "fate." We are not even reformers, let alone revolutionaries. We are, in fact, the obedient servants of our rulers, whomever they happen to be.

Basic Tenets of Chinese Communism

◆

57 ◆ *Mao Zedong,*
REPORT ON AN INVESTIGATION OF THE PEASANT MOVEMENT IN HUNAN and STRATEGIC PROBLEMS OF CHINA'S REVOLUTIONARY WAR

Mao Zedong (1893–1975) was born into a well-to-do peasant family in Hunan province and as a university student participated in the anti-Qing revolution of 1911. During the next several years, while serving as a library assistant at Beijing University, he embraced Marxism and helped organize the Chinese Communist Party, which was officially founded in 1921. Originally given the task of working with urban labor unions, Mao gradually came to believe that peasants, whose capacity for class revolution was discounted by orthodox Marxist-Leninists, would lead China to socialism.

After the break with the Guomindang in 1927, the Communists took their small army to the remote and hilly region on the Hunan-Jiangxi border, where in 1931 they proclaimed the Chinese Soviet Republic. In 1934 Chiang Kai-shek's troops surrounded the Communists' forces, but as they moved in for the kill, more than one hundred thousand Communist troops and officials escaped and embarked on what came to be known as the Long March. This legendary trek lasted more than a year and covered more that six thousand miles before the survivors found safety in the remote mountains around Yan'an in Shaanxi province. Mao, now the party's recognized leader, rebuilt his army and readied himself and his followers for what would be fourteen more years of struggle against the Japanese and Guomindang.

Mao was a prolific writer who from the 1920s until his death in 1976 produced many hundreds of treatises, essays, and even works of poetry. The following excerpts are from two of his most important writings. The first, his *Report on an Investigation of the Peasant Movement in Hunan,* was written in 1927 after he visited Hunan province to study the activities of peasant associations, groups of peasants who with the help of Communist organizers had seized land, humiliated and killed landlords, and taken control of their villages. In it Mao expresses his faith in the poor peasantry as the source of revolution in China. The second excerpt is taken from his *Strategic Problems of China's Revolutionary War,* which was based on a series of lectures presented to the Red Army College in late 1936. In it Mao assesses China's military situation and outlines his strategy for victory through guerrilla warfare.

QUESTIONS FOR ANALYSIS

1. What specific developments in Hunan reinforced Mao's convictions about the peasantry's potential as a revolutionary force?
2. What criticisms have been made of the Hunan peasant movement, and how does Mao attempt to counter these criticisms?
3. What can be learned from these two writings about Mao's view of the role of the Communist Party in China's revolutionary struggle?
4. According to Mao, what have been the sources of oppression for the Chinese people? Once these sources of oppression have been removed, what will China be like?
5. What, according to Mao, are the four unique characteristics of China's revolutionary war, and how do they affect his military strategy?
6. What are the characteristics of Mao's "active defense" as opposed to "passive defense"?

REPORT ON AN INVESTIGATION OF THE PEASANT MOVEMENT IN HUNAN

. . . All talk directed against the peasant movement must be speedily set right. All the wrong measures taken by the revolutionary authorities concerning the peasant movement must be speedily changed. Only thus can the future of the revolution be benefited. For the present upsurge of the peasant movement is a colossal event. In a very short time, in China's central, southern and northern provinces, several hundred million peasants will rise like a mighty storm, like a hurricane, a force so swift and violent that no power, however great, will be able to hold it back. They will smash all the trammels that bind them and rush forward along the road to liberation. They will sweep all the imperialists, warlords, corrupt officials, local tyrants and evil gentry into their graves. Every revolutionary party and every revolutionary comrade will be put to the test, to be accepted or rejected as they decide. There are three alternatives. To march at their head and lead them? To trail behind them, gesticulating and

criticizing? Or to stand in their way and oppose them? Every Chinese is free to choose, but events will force you to make the choice quickly. . . .

"Yes, peasant associations are necessary, but they are going rather too far." This is the opinion of the middle-of-the-roaders. But what is the actual situation? True, the peasants are in a sense "unruly" in the countryside. Supreme in authority, the peasant association allows the landlord no say and sweeps away his prestige. This amounts to striking the landlord down to the dust and keeping him there. . . . People swarm into the houses of local tyrants and evil gentry who are against the peasant association, slaughtering their pigs and consuming their grain. They even loll for a minute or two on the ivory-inlaid beds belonging to the young ladies in the households of the local tyrants and evil gentry. At the slightest provocation they make arrests, crown the arrested with tall paper-hats, and parade them through the villages, saying, "You dirty landlords, now you know who we are!" . . . This is what some people call "going too far," or "exceeding the proper limits in righting a wrong," or "really too much." Such talk may seem plausible, but in fact it is wrong. First, the local tyrants, evil gentry and lawless landlords have themselves driven the peasants to this. For ages they have used their power to tyrannize over the peasants and trample them underfoot; that is why the peasants have reacted so strongly. . . . Secondly, a revolution is not a dinner party, or writing an essay, or painting a picture, or doing embroidery; it cannot be so refined, so leisurely and gentle, so temperate, kind, courteous, restrained and magnanimous. A revolution is an insurrection, an act of violence by which one class overthrows another. A rural revolution is a revolution by which the peasantry overthrows the power of the feudal landlord class. Without using the greatest force, the peasants cannot possibly overthrow the deep-rooted authority of the landlords which has lasted for thousands of years. . . . To put it bluntly, it is necessary to create terror for a while in every rural area, or otherwise it would be impossible to suppress the activities of the counter-revolutionaries in the countryside or overthrow the authority of the gentry.

◆ ◆

A man in China is usually subjected to the domination of three systems of authority: (1) the state system, . . . ranging from the national, provincial and county government down to that of the township; (2) the clan system, . . . ranging from the central ancestral temple and its branch temples down to the head of the household; and (3) the supernatural system (religious authority), ranging from the King of Hell down to the town and village gods belonging to the nether world, and from the Emperor of Heaven down to all the various gods and spirits belonging to the celestial world. As for women, in addition to being dominated by these three systems of authority, they are also dominated by the men (the authority of the husband). These four authorities — political, clan, religious and masculine — are the embodiment of the whole feudal-patriarchal system and ideology, and are the four thick ropes binding the Chinese people, particularly the peasants. . . .

The political authority of the landlords is the backbone of all the other systems of authority.

With that overturned, the clan authority, the religious authority and the authority of the husband all begin to totter. . . . In many places the peasant associations have taken over the temples of the gods as their offices. Everywhere they advocate the appropriation of temple property in order to start peasant schools and to defray the expenses of the associations, calling it "public revenue from superstition." In Liling County, prohibiting superstitious practices and smashing idols have become quite the vogue. . . .

In places where the power of the peasants is predominant, only the older peasants and the women still believe in the gods, the younger peasants no longer doing so. Since the latter control the associations, the overthrow of religious authority and the eradication of superstition are going on everywhere. As to the authority of the husband, this has always been weaker among the poor peasants because, out of economic necessity, their womenfolk have to do more manual labor than the women of the richer classes and therefore have more say and greater power of decision in family matters. With the increasing bankruptcy of the rural economy in recent years, the basis for men's domination over women has already been weakened. With the rise of the peasant movement, the women in many places have now begun to organize rural women's associations; the opportunity has come for them to lift up their heads, and the authority of the husband is getting shakier every day. In a word, the whole feudal-patriarchal system and ideology is tottering with the growth of the peasants' power.

STRATEGIC PROBLEMS OF CHINA'S REVOLUTIONARY WAR

What then are the characteristics of China's revolutionary war?

I think there are four.

The first is that China is a vast semi-colonial country which is unevenly developed both politically and economically. . . .

The unevenness of political and economic development in China — the coexistence of a frail capitalist economy and a preponderant semi-feudal economy; the coexistence of a few modern industrial and commercial cities and the boundless expanses of stagnant rural districts; the coexistence of several millions of industrial workers on the one hand and, on the other, hundreds of millions of peasants and handicraftsmen under the old regime; the coexistence of big warlords controlling the Central government and small warlords controlling the provinces; the coexistence of two kinds of reactionary armies, i.e., the so-called Central army under Chiang Kai-shek and the troops of miscellaneous brands under the warlords in the provinces; and the coexistence of a few railway and steamship lines and motor roads on the one hand and, on the other, the vast number of wheel-barrow paths and trails for pedestrians only, many of which are even difficult for them to negotiate. . . .

The second characteristic is the great strength of the enemy.

What is the situation of the Guomindang, the enemy of the Red Army? It is a party that has seized political power and has relatively stabilized it. It has gained the support of the principal counter-revolutionary countries in the world. It has remodeled its army, which has thus become different from any other army in Chinese history and on the whole similar to the armies of the modern states in the world; its army is supplied much more abundantly with arms and other equipment than the Red Army, and is greater in numerical strength than any army in Chinese history, even than the standing army of any country in the world. . . .

The third characteristic is that the Red Army is weak and small. . . .

Our political power is dispersed and isolated in mountainous or remote regions, and is deprived of any outside help. In economic and cultural conditions the revolutionary base areas are more backward than the Guomindang areas. The revolutionary bases embrace only rural districts and small towns. . . .

The fourth characteristic is the Communist Party's leadership and the agrarian revolution.

This characteristic is the inevitable result of the first one. It gives rise to the following two features. On the one hand, China's revolutionary war, though taking place in a period of reaction in China and throughout the capitalist world, can yet be victorious because it is led by the Communist Party and supported by the peasantry. Because we have secured the support of the peasantry, our base areas, though small, possess great political power and stand firmly opposed to the political power of the Guomindang which encompasses a vast area; in a military sense this creates colossal difficulties for the attacking Guomindang troops. The Red Army, though small, has great fighting capacity, because its men under the leadership of the Communist Party have sprung from the agrarian revolution and are fighting for their own interests, and because officers and men are politically united.

On the other hand, our situation contrasts sharply with that of the Guomindang. Opposed to the agrarian revolution, the Guomindang is deprived of the support of the peasantry. Despite the great size of its army it cannot arouse the bulk of the soldiers or many of the lower-rank officers, who used to be small producers, to risk their lives voluntarily for its sake. Officers and men are politically disunited and this reduces its fighting capacity. . . .

Military experts of new and rapidly developing imperialist countries like Germany and Japan positively boast of the advantages of strategic offensive and condemn strategic defensive. Such an idea is fundamentally unsuitable for China's revolutionary war. Such military experts point out that the great shortcoming of defense lies in the fact that, instead of gingering up {enlivening} the people, it demoralizes them. . . . Our case is different. Under the slogan of safeguarding the revolutionary base areas and safeguarding China, we can rally the greatest majority of the people to fight single-mindedly, because we are the victims of oppression and aggression. . . .

In military terms, our warfare consists in the alternate adoption of the defensive and the offensive. It makes no difference to us whether our offensive is regarded as following the defensive or preceding it, because the turning-point comes when we smash the campaigns of "encirclement and annihilation." It remains a defensive until a campaign of "encirclement and annihilation" is smashed, and then it immediately begins as an offensive; they are but two phases of the same thing, as one campaign of "encirclement and annihilation" of the enemy is closely followed by another. Of the two phases, the defensive phase is more complicated and more important than the offensive phase. It involves numerous problems of how to smash the campaign of "encirclement and annihilation." The basic principle is for active defense and against passive defense.

In the civil war, when the Red Army surpasses the enemy in strength, there will no longer be any use for strategic defensive in general. Then our only directive will be strategic offensive. Such a change depends on an overall change in the relative strength of the enemy and ourselves.

◆

Nationalism and Militarism in Japan

As the experience of modern Japan reveals, nationalism can inspire great achievements, but it can also cause great disasters. In the late nineteenth and early twentieth centuries, cultural pride and a stubborn refusal to succumb to the West united the Japanese behind the Meiji reformers. A national effort that included peasants, business leaders, aristocrats, government officials, soldiers, and workers transformed Japan from an isolated, feudal society into a major industrial and military power within decades. In the 1920s and 1930s nationalism continued to be a major force in Japan. This time, however, it led to a crushing military defeat in World War II.

Japanese nationalism between the wars became increasingly xenophobic, militaristic, and authoritarian. It appealed to generals, right-wing politicians, and millions of peasants who were dissatisfied with parliamentary government, socialism, the Westernization of Japanese culture, and the influence of the *zaibatsu,* or large business conglomerates, on Japanese politics. Nationalists praised Japanese virtues of duty and harmony, sought absolute obedience to the emperor, and idealized warrior values. They demanded military expansion, claiming that only a Japanese empire in Asia would prevent the nation's economic ruin. Nationalists supported the conquest of Manchuria in 1931, the invasion of China in 1937, and the bombing of the U.S. fleet at Pearl Harbor in 1941. They set Japan on a course that ended in August 1945 with nuclear attacks on Hiroshima and Nagasaki, total defeat, and unconditional surrender.

In the 1920s the political balance had shifted from the armed forces and bureaucracy, both subject only to the emperor, to the political parties, whose power base was the elected Diet and whose leaders had close ties with big business. This shift translated into solid gains for democracy, liberalism, social reform, and a foreign policy of international cooperation. But party government lost its appeal once the Great Depression struck Japan in the 1930s. Japanese exports dropped in value by 50 percent between 1929 and 1931, workers' incomes fell, and unemployment reached three million. As a result of the rice crop failure in 1931 in northern Japan, families were reduced to begging, eating bark and roots, and selling daughters to brothel keepers.

The economic crisis broadened support for Japanese ultranationalism, and persuaded its advocates in the military to take bold steps. In 1931 army officers arranged an explosion on the tracks of a Japanese-controlled railroad in Manchuria and, without the approval of the civilian government, used this as an excuse to capture the important cities in the region and establish the puppet state of Manchukuo. In Japan itself, right-wing extremists assassinated business and political leaders, and plotted to overthrow the government. In February 1936 officers and troops of the First Division attacked and briefly occupied government offices in downtown Tokyo. The government suppressed the rebellion and executed its leaders, but to many Japanese the rebels were heroes, not traitors. Constitutional government survived on paper, but when Japanese and Chinese troops clashed outside Beijing in the summer of 1937, the ensuing war between China and Japan put political authority firmly in the hands of militarists and nationalists.

Nationalism continued to inspire the Japanese during World War II. Citizens accepted privation, soldiers fought with fanatical determination, and young pilots sacrificed their lives by crashing their planes into U.S. warships. But this time nationalism was not enough, and defeat came in August 1945.

The Agenda of Ultranationalism

◈

58 ◆ *The Black Dragon Society,* ANNIVERSARY STATEMENT, 1930

In 1881, a group of former samurai (warrior-aristocrats) founded the Genyosha, a secret society dedicated to Japanese expansion in Asia, the preservation of traditional Japanese culture, and absolute dedication to the emperor. In 1901, several of its members broke away and founded the Black Dragon Society, which promoted war with Russia as a means of expanding Japan's influence on the Asian mainland. In the early twentieth century, the Society continued to advocate an aggressive foreign policy to enable Japan to become the dominant force in Asia. It also denounced democracy, capitalism, Americanization, socialism, party politics, and big business, all of which it viewed as threats to Japanese culture or to their plans for Japanese expansionism. Although the membership of the Black Dragon Society and similar organizations was small, their self-promotion, assassinations, and strong-arm tactics kept alive their brand of extreme nationalism, allowing it to flourish in the troubled atmosphere of the 1930s.

In 1930 the Black Dragon Society published the two-volume *Secret History of the Annexation of Korea,* in which it claimed a key role in inspiring early Japanese expansionism. The second volume concluded with the following statement.

QUESTIONS FOR ANALYSIS

1. What is there in the Black Dragon Society's philosophy that explains its interventions in Korea, China, and the Philippines?
2. In what ways, according to the authors of the document, has Japanese foreign policy been thwarted in the years since World War I?
3. According to the Society, how has Japan's domestic situation deteriorated?
4. According to the Society, what is the root of Japan's problems, and what solutions does it offer?
5. What might explain the appeal of such ideas to the Japanese populace?

From the first, we members of the Amur [Black Dragon] Society have worked in accordance with the imperial mission for overseas expansion to solve our overpopulation; at the same time, we have sought to give support and encouragement to the peoples of East Asia. Thus we have sought the spread of humanity and righteousness throughout the world by having the imperial purpose extend to neighboring nations.

Earlier, in order to achieve these principles, we organized the Heavenly Blessing Heroes in Korea in 1894 and helped the Tong Hak rebellion there in order to speed the settlement of the dispute between Japan and China.[1] In 1899 we helped Aguinaldo in his struggle for independence for the Philippines.[2] In 1900 we worked with other comrades in helping Sun Yat-sen start the fires of revolution in South China. In 1901 we organized this Society and became exponents of the punishment of Russia, and thereafter we devoted ourselves to the annexation of Korea while continuing to support the revolutionary movement of China. . . .

During this period we have seen the fulfillment of our national power in the decisive victories in the two major wars against China and Russia,[3] in the annexation of Korea, the acquisition of Formosa [Taiwan] and Sakhalin, and the expulsion of Germany from the Shandong peninsula.[4] Japan's status among the empires of the world has risen until today she ranks as one of the three great powers, and from this eminence she can support other Asiatic nations. . . .

However, in viewing recent international affairs it would seem that the foundation established by the great Meiji emperor is undergoing rapid deterioration. The disposition of the gains of the war with Germany was left to foreign powers, and the government, disregarding the needs of national defense, submitted to unfair demands to limit our naval power.[5] Moreover, the failure of our China policy[6] made the Chinese more and more contemptuous of us, so

---

[1]The Tonghak, or Eastern Learning, movement was a late-nineteenth-century religious movement that drew on Daoist (Taoist), Buddhist, Confucian, and Catholic traditions. In 1894 members of the movement rebelled against the China-oriented government of Korea because of its corruption and indifference to the plight of the poor. Japanese and Chinese troops intervened, leading to the Sino-Japanese War of 1894–1895. The result was the recognition of Korea's independence by China.
[2]Emilio Aguinaldo (1869–1964) led an insurrection against the Spaniards in 1898 and established the Philippine Republic in January 1899. Following the Spanish American War, he resisted the U.S. takeover, but was defeated and retired from politics.

[3]Victory over China in the Sino-Japanese War and over Russia in the Russo-Japanese War (1904–1905).
[4]Japan received Taiwan (Formosa) after the Sino-Japanese War. Its authority over Korea and its claim to the southern half of Sakhalin Island were recognized after the Russo-Japanese War. Japan was granted former German concessions in China's Shandong province after World War I.
[5]The Washington Conference of 1921 set Japan's naval strength at 60 percent of that of the United States and that of Great Britain.
[6]The Twenty-One Demands, submitted by Japan to China in 1915, would have established extensive Japanese influence over the Chinese government. These demands were successfully resisted by China.

much so that they have been brought to demand the surrender of our essential defense lines in Manchuria and Mongolia. Furthermore, in countries like the United States and Australia our immigrants have been deprived of rights which were acquired only after long years of struggle, and we now face a highhanded anti-Japanese expulsion movement which knows no bounds.[7] Men of purpose and of humanity who are at all concerned for their country cannot fail to be upset by the situation.

When we turn our attention to domestic affairs, we feel more than deep concern. There is a great slackening of discipline and order. Men's hearts are becoming corrupt. Look about you! Are not the various government measures and establishments a conglomeration of all sorts of evils and abuses? The laws are confusing, and evil grows apace. The people are overwhelmed by heavy taxes, the confusion in the business world complicates the livelihood of the people, the growth of dangerous thought threatens social order, and our national polity, which has endured for three thousand years, is in danger. This is a critical time for our national destiny; was there ever a more crucial day? What else can we call this time if it is not termed decisive?

And yet, in spite of this our government, instead of pursuing a farsighted policy, casts about for temporary measures. The opposition party simply struggles for political power without any notion of saving our country from this crisis. And even the press, which should devote itself to its duty of guiding and leading society, is the same. For the most part it swims with the current, bows to vulgar opinions, and is chiefly engrossed in money making. Alas! Our empire moves ever closer to rocks which lie before us. . . .

. . . Therefore we of the Amur Society have determined to widen the scope of our activity. Hereafter, besides our interest in foreign affairs, we will give unselfish criticism of internal politics and of social problems, and we will seek to guide public opinion into proper channels. . . . We . . . are resolved to reform the moral corruption of the people, restore social discipline, and ease the insecurity of the people's livelihood by relieving the crises in the financial world, restore national confidence, and increase the national strength, in order to carry out the imperial mission to awaken the countries of Asia. In order to clarify these principles, we here set forth our platform to all our fellow patriots:

◆ ◆

Platform

1. Developing the great plan of the founders of the country, we will widen the great Way [Dao] of Eastern culture, work out a harmony of Eastern and Western cultures, and take the lead among Asian peoples.

2. We will bring to an end many evils, such as formalistic legalism; it restricts the freedom of the people, hampers common sense solutions, prevents efficiency in public and private affairs, and destroys the true meaning of constitutional government. Thereby we will show forth again the essence of the imperial principles.

3. We shall rebuild the present administrative systems. We will develop overseas expansion through the activation of our diplomacy, further the prosperity of the people by reforms in internal government, and solve problems of labor and management by the establishment of new social policies. Thereby we will strengthen the foundations of the empire.

4. We shall carry out the spirit of the Imperial Rescript[8] to Soldiers and Sailors and stimulate a martial spirit by working toward the goal of a nation in arms. Thereby we look toward the perfection of national defense.

5. We plan a fundamental reform of the present educational system, which is copied

---

[7]Both Australia and the United States severely restricted Japanese (and Chinese) immigration in the 1920s.

[8]Issued by the emperor in 1882, the rescript stated that supreme command of the armed forces rested in the hands of the emperor alone, thus strengthening the military's independence from civilian control.

from those of Europe and America; we shall set up a basic study of a national education originating in our national polity. Thereby

we anticipate the further development and heightening of the wisdom and virtue of the Yamato race.[9]

---

[9]According to tradition, Japan's imperial line can be traced back to the state founded by a descendant of the sun goddess on the Yamato plain around 660 B.C.E.

Foreign Policy Priorities on the Eve of the China War

❖

59 ◆ *FUNDAMENTAL PRINCIPLES OF NATIONAL POLICY, 1936*

Despite the failure of the takeover of central Tokyo by nationalist soldiers and officers of the First Division in early 1936, the military retained a strong voice in government. Many politicians bent over backward in support of the military and its right-wing agenda in order to prevent renewed violence. The cabinet of Hirota Koti, in power from March 1936 to February 1937, increased military spending and passed stricter laws against communists and socialists.

In August 1936 the Hirota cabinet approved the following policy statement on foreign and domestic policy. It is an effort to strike a balance between the army's traditional focus on north China and Manchuria as a means of countering the Soviet Union's strength and the navy's new southward policy and its concerns with U.S. naval strength. It also shows the degree to which militarism and expansionism had become the bedrock of Japanese politics on the eve of the war with China.

QUESTIONS FOR ANALYSIS

1. What view of Japan's role in Asian affairs is expressed in this statement?
2. What views of the Soviet Union and the Western powers does the document express?
3. According to the authors of the document, what steps must be taken to prepare Japan for the foreign policy challenges it will meet?
4. What specific statements in the document reveal the militarist priorities of the Hirota government?
5. How do the ideas expressed in this document compare to those of the Black Dragon Society's 1930 anniversary statement?

(1) Japan must strive to eradicate the aggressive policies of the great powers, and share with East Asia the joy which is based on the true principle of co-existence and co-prosperity. This is the realization of the spirit of the Imperial Way which must be accepted as the consistent guiding principle in Japan's policy of foreign expansion.

(2) Japan must complete her national defense and armament to protect her national security

and development. In this way, the position of the Empire as the stabilizing force in East Asia can be secured both in name and in fact.

(3) The policy toward the continent must be based on the following factors: in order to promote Manchukuo's[1] healthy development and to stabilize Japan-Manchukuo national defense, the threat from the north, the Soviet Union, must be eliminated;[2] in order to promote our economic development, we must prepare against Great Britain and the United States and bring about close collaboration between Japan, Manchukuo, and China. In the execution of this policy, Japan must pay due attention to friendly relations with other powers.

(4) Japan plans to promote her racial and economic development in the South Seas, especially in the outerlying South Seas[3] areas. She plans to extend her strength by moderate and peaceful means and without rousing other powers. In this way, concurrently with the firm establishment of Manchukuo, Japan may expect full development and strengthening of her national power.

B. Utilizing the above fundamental principles as the axis, we must unify and coordinate our foreign and domestic policies, and reform our administration thoroughly to reflect the current conditions. The following are the basic outlines.

(1) Japan's national defense and armament must be completed in the following manner:

a. The Army's arms preparations must have as their goal, the ability to withstand the forces which can be deployed by the Soviet Union in the Far East. The Army must expand its Kwantung[4] and Chōsen (Korean) forces to the extent that they can deliver the first decisive blow against the Soviet Far Eastern Army at the outbreak of war.

b. The Navy's arms preparations must have as their goal, creation of forces sufficient to withstand an attack from the U.S. Navy to secure the control of the Western Pacific for Japan.

(2) Our foreign policy must be based on the principle of the smooth execution of the fundamental national policies. It must therefore be coordinated and reformed. In order to facilitate the smooth functioning of activities of diplomatic bureaus, the military must endeavor to give behind-the-scenes assistance, and must avoid overt activities.

(3) In order to conform to the above basic national policies, in effecting reform and improvement in political and administrative organizations, in establishing financial and economic policies, and in administering other agencies, appropriate actions must be taken on the following matters:

a. The domestic public opinion must be led and unified, so as to strengthen the nation's resolve in coping with the present national emergency.

b. Appropriate reforms in administrative agencies and economic organizations must be effected to bring about improvement in industries and important foreign trade necessary for executing national policies.

c. Appropriate measures must be taken to ensure stabilization of national life, strengthening of physical fitness, and development of sound national thought.

d. Appropriate plans must be undertaken to promote rapid growth in aviation and maritime transportation industries.

e. We must promote the establishment of a policy of self-sufficiency with regard to important natural resources and materials required for national defense and industries.

f. Concurrently with the reform of diplomatic bureaus, information and propaganda organizations must be well established to enhance vigorously diplomatic functions and cultural activities overseas.

---

[1]The southern Pacific.
[2]The Japanese name for the puppet government of Manchuria established after the 1931 conquest.
[3]In the mid-1930s the Soviet Union had approximately

240,000 troops in its far eastern provinces, compared to 160,000 Japanese troops in Manchuria.
[4]The Kwantung forces were Japan's army in Manchuria; the Chōsen army was in Korea.

PART THREE

From World War II to the Early 1970s: Decades of Conflict, Decolonization, and Economic Recovery

Inexorably, like blind men without memories approaching an abyss with no one to stop them, the world's Great Powers in the 1930s marched and stumbled into the century's second world war. With the global economy in tatters and no effective response from the League of Nations or individual states, authoritarian, militarist regimes in Italy, Germany, and Japan committed one act of aggression after another: Japan invaded Manchuria in 1931 and China in 1937; Italy conquered Ethiopia in 1935; Nazi Germany, having begun to rearm in 1935, reoccupied the Rhineland in 1936, annexed Austria in 1938, and destroyed Czechoslovakia in March 1939. Then just before dawn on September 1, 1939, assured that its new ally, the Soviet Union, would do nothing, Germany unleashed its troops, tanks, and planes on Poland. Two days later Great Britain and France declared war on Germany, and for the second time in just over two decades, Europe was at war.

In 1941 the European war and the Sino-Japanese War, which had begun in 1937, became parts of a truly global struggle, fully deserving the title World War II. In June 1941 Germany invaded the Soviet Union, and in December Japan attacked the Philippines, the Dutch East Indies, and the British colony of Malaya. Most importantly, Japan bombed the U.S. naval base at Pearl Harbor in Hawaii, thus bringing the United States into the war. For three and a half more years, humanity's most costly and deadly war was fought on and under the world's oceans, on tiny South Pacific islands, in North Africa, and across Eurasia. Only in 1945, with the unconditional surrender of Germany in May and of Japan in August, did the fighting stop.

Unlike the mood following World War I, when victors and vanquished alike failed to comprehend how many things the war had changed and dreamed of a "return to normalcy," the atmosphere after World War II was pervaded by a sense that human affairs had changed irrevocably. When the war ended, much of Europe, the Soviet Union, and Japan had been reduced to rubble; forty, fifty, or sixty million human beings had been killed; and the obliteration of Hiroshima and Nagasaki by atomic bombs in August 1945 presaged a new and even more terrible chapter in the history of warfare. Of the early twentieth century's Great Powers, Germany, Japan, and Italy had been crushed, Great Britain was economically exhausted, and France was haunted by its capitulation to the Germans in 1940 after only six weeks of fighting. World affairs were now dominated by two superpowers, the United States and the

Soviet Union, whose ideological differences, mutual distrust, and clashes over the future of Europe made a third world war seem likely.

In the immediate postwar years, Asia and Africa also seemed on the brink of momentous and unsettling changes. China erupted into civil war, and in dozens of colonies nationalists prepared to renew their struggle for independence. France sent troops to Vietnam to reestablish its authority after the Vietnamese declaration of independence in 1945, and the Dutch did the same in the East Indies after the colony announced its independence in 1945. An era of colonial war seemed imminent. Great Britain, it is true, peacefully granted independence to India and Pakistan in 1947 and to Burma in 1948, but religious and ethnic strife in all three new states did not bode well for their futures.

Soviet-U.S. conflict, the threat of atomic war, daunting economic problems, the full disclosure of Nazi war crimes, the advance of communism in China and Eastern Europe, potential upheaval in colonial Africa and Asia — there were many reasons for pessimism in the late 1940s. Instead, it should have been a time for optimism. The next twenty-five years witnessed unparalleled economic expansion and impressive strides in medicine and public health. The Cold War remained cold, and, despite profound social changes, the political climate in most of the world remained moderate and generally calm. Although vast economic disparities still existed between the world's developed and nondeveloped regions, most human beings in these years were more prosperous and better fed, experienced more material comfort, had more education, and lived longer and healthier lives. After decades of war and economic upheaval, it was possible once more to be hopeful about humanity's prospects.

Although Cold War rhetoric remained shrill and pugnacious, Soviet and U.S. leaders exercised restraint. Confrontations over Berlin (1948 and 1958), Soviet intervention in Hungary (1956) and Czechoslovakia (1968), Egyptian nationalization of the Suez Canal (1956), and the Cuban missile crisis (1962) were all resolved without warfare, and the one hot war between communist and noncommunist forces, in Korea (1950–1953), remained localized. Furthermore, colonialism ended in Asia and Africa in the 1950s and 1960s without the bloody struggles many had anticipated. Of the approximately sixty colonies that became independent between 1947 and 1975, most did so peacefully. Those that did not included Vietnam and the East Indies, where the French and Dutch, respectively, unsuccessfully used force in the late 1940s to prevent independence, and Algeria, Kenya, and Rhodesia, where relatively large European settler populations blocked or complicated independence movements.

The postwar era's most impressive achievement was economic growth. World War I had been followed by currency devaluations, slumping agricultural prices, an international financial crisis caused by war debt and reparation payments, the U.S. stock market crash, and ultimately the Great Depression. World War II, in contrast, was followed by a few years of economic hardship and readjustment and then twenty-five years of expansion. World output of manufactured goods quadrupled between the early 1950s and the 1970s, and world trade in manufactured products increased tenfold. Most of this manufacturing still took place in the capitalist countries of Western Europe, Japan, the United States, Canada, and Australia, where increased rates of automobile and home ownership and a surge in the purchase of televisions, refrigerators, washers and dryers, and a host of new electronic gadgets all indicated a rise in overall prosperity.

The economic boom was not limited to the capitalist West and Japan, however. Economic growth in the Soviet Union and its satellites was even more rapid than in the West, lending substance to Soviet Premier Nikita Khrushchev's boast in 1959 that the Soviet Union would economically "bury" the United States. Even Africans and Asian, who remained poor by Western standards, benefited from strong demand for their nations' minerals and agricultural exports. A dramatic increase in worldwide food production essentially made famines nonexistent in the 1950s and 1960s, except in China during the Great Leap Forward of 1958 to 1960, when government policies led to mass starvation.

By the late 1960s, however, signs of economic decline and political discontent were apparent. Grassroots rebellions in Poland and Czechoslovakia challenged Soviet domination of Eastern Europe. Western Europe experienced turmoil as students and workers rioted in Germany and Italy, protested Francisco Franco's authoritarian government in Spain, and attacked the university system and the DeGaulle regime in France. In the United States, radicalized students protested the Vietnam War, social injustice, and university policies through strikes and demonstrations, and urban black ghettos erupted into violence. Against this backdrop of political turmoil, the revival of feminism and the emergence of a powerful environmental movement added to the atmosphere of protest and disenchantment.

Conflict was not limited to the Western democracies and Eastern Europe. The mid to late 1960s saw a drift toward military rule in much of Africa, civil war in Nigeria, and clashes between right-wing military governments and radical leftist groups in Latin America. Chaos gripped China after Mao Zedong launched the Great Proletarian Cultural Revolution in 1965.

The economic boom was also slowing down. In the West, rates of industrial production began to fall, and inflation and labor-management conflict increased. The delicate balance of international finance was threatened by ballooning government deficits in the United States. In the Soviet bloc, agricultural and industrial output also began to slump despite rosy government reports to the contrary. Then in the wake of the October War between Egypt and Israel in 1973, Arab oil-producing countries embargoed oil shipments to the United States, and in 1974 the Organization of Petroleum Exporting Countries quadrupled the price of oil. Decline and retrenchment struck oil-dependent industrialized states and commodity-producing Third World economies alike. The twentieth century's closest approximation of a golden age was coming to an end.

CHAPTER 8

World War II and Its Aftermath

Whether World War II is dated from July 7, 1937, when Japan declared war on China, or from September 1, 1939, when Germany invaded Poland, by the time it ended in August 1945, it had become the most murderous and costly war in history. It involved no fewer than sixty belligerent states, which together mobilized over ninety million men and women to fight in their armed forces. Costs were enormous. One estimate places the expenditures for World War II at $1,150,000,000,000. Battles were fought by armies of unprecedented size. Hitler attacked the Soviet Union in June 1941 with the largest invasion force in history; it included ten thousand to fifteen thousand tanks, eight thousand planes, and 2.9 million troops, 1.3 million of whom were dead or wounded within a year. Three years later, in June 1944 the Allies launched their cross-Channel invasion of Nazi-held northern Europe, the largest amphibian military operation in history. It involved fifty thousand tanks, armored cars, and trucks; eleven thousand aircraft; and three million troops.

Inevitably, casualties in World War II were enormous. As many as sixty million men, women, and children died, six times more than in World War I, which for a mere twenty-five years had held the distinction of being history's deadliest war. The United States lost three hundred thousand soldiers and civilians; Great Britain, four hundred thousand; Japan, two million; Germany, over four million; Poland, six million; China, fifteen million; and the Soviet Union, between twenty and twenty-five million.

The human losses in World War II were unique in other ways. Over half the victims were civilians. According to the doctrine of "total war" embraced by all belligerents, obliterating the enemies' industries and infrastructure and killing or crushing the spirit of civilians were as important as winning battles. Bombing raids by Japan on Shanghai in 1937 and by Germany on Warsaw in 1939 and on London, Coventry, and Rotterdam in 1940 set a precedent for aerial attacks on enemy population centers throughout the war. In 1942 the British and Americans began bombing major German cities. Among their deadliest raids were the firebombing of Hamburg in 1943, which killed fifty thousand civilians, and the bombing of Dresden only eight weeks before Germany's surrender, which also killed fifty thousand. Allied bombing raids on Germany resulted in Anglo-American losses of fifty thousand pilots, gunners, and navigators, but they killed approximately six hundred thousand German civilians and undoubtedly weakened Germany's capacity to produce armaments. Japan became the target of massive American bombing raids in 1944 and 1945. The firebombing of Tokyo in March 1945, which killed 125,000, was a only a prelude to the dropping of atomic bombs on Hiroshima and Nagasaki in August 1945, which killed two hundred thousand human beings but ended the war.

The brutalization of warfare took other grotesque and atrocious forms. Examples include the Japanese "rape of Nanjing" in October 1937, in which approximately one hundred thousand Chinese were massacred and thousands of Chinese women were raped; the Soviet murder of close to twenty thousand Poles considered unfriendly to the Soviet Union; German treatment of Russian prisoners of war, which led to three million deaths through famine and exposure; the use of slave labor in munitions plants and construction projects by the Japanese and Germans; and the German murders of hostages in response to assassinations and acts of sabotage. Most appalling was the Nazis' war against Europe's Jews. Directed by the German government, tens of thousands of Germans and other European antisemites gassed, shot, tortured, starved to death, worked to death, killed in medical experiments, or murdered in acts of individual cruelty six million Jews, approximately half of the twelve million the Nazis had hoped to exterminate.

Such enormous suffering was not entirely in vain. The war's perpetrators — Italy, Germany, and Japan — were crushed, and the ideologies that had inspired them — radical nationalism, racism, and militarism — were discredited. The war came to symbolize the triumph of good over evil, and fueled hope that human beings might still be capable of creating and living in a just, peaceful, and humane society. At war's end, those who had such hopes put their faith in the newly created United Nations, which in December 1948 approved the Universal Declaration of Human Rights. It condemned tyranny and oppression, and proclaimed as humanity's highest goal the recognition of the inherent dignity of all human beings and their right to peace, justice, and freedom.

How far the human community has fallen short of these goals is clear to anyone familiar with recent history. World War II left behind not only a legacy of achievement and hope but also a host of new and intractable problems, not the least of which was the conflict between the world's two new superpowers, the United States and the Soviet Union. Tensions that first surfaced in the closing

months of the fighting soon blossomed into a full-fledged ideological conflict, with the stakes nothing less than the world's political
and economic future. This legacy of World War II — the Cold War
— would dominate international politics for the next fifty years,
until it, like every other war in human history, came to an end.

Appeasement and the Origins of World War II in Europe

On taking power in January 1933, Hitler immediately set out to overturn the
Treaty of Versailles, the hated "dictated treaty" forced upon Germany after
World War I. He took Germany out of the League of Nations, ordered German
rearmament, reoccupied the Rhineland, and annexed Austria. Then in 1938
Hitler turned his attention to Czechoslovakia, a nation created just twenty years
earlier by the Treaty of Versailles. He demanded the Sudetenland, a swath of
territory on Czechoslovakia's western border that contained some three million
ethnic Germans and much of the nation's industry. The Czechs stood firm, and
in mid September Hitler announced that he would risk world war to unite
the Sudeten Germans with the fatherland. Frantic efforts to preserve peace
came to a climax in late September with the Munich conference, attended by
Hitler, the Italian dictator Benito Mussolini, and the prime ministers of France
and Great Britain, Edouard Daladier and Neville Chamberlain. Czechoslovakia
was not represented.

Daladier and Chamberlain agreed to the immediate German occupation of the
Sudetenland, Polish annexation of Czechoslovakia's coal-rich area of Teschen,
and the transfer of parts of the eastern province of Slovakia to Hungary. Hitler
agreed to "personally guarantee" the boundaries of the shrunken Czechoslovak
state. War was avoided.

With the world breathing a sigh of relief, Chamberlain, the architect of the
Munich agreement, returned home to cheering crowds. For a few months he was
a hero, the savior of the peace, the statesman who had ensured "peace in our
time." History has been less kind to Neville Chamberlain and the Munich agreement he masterminded. "Munich" is remembered not as a triumph but as a
symbol of cowardice, betrayal, capitulation to aggression, and the failure of the
policy of appeasement. In March 1939 Hitler sent troops into Czechoslovakia and
occupied Prague; in September 1939 he invaded Poland. War, as it turned out,
had not been avoided for long.

The Munich agreement was the climax of an appeasement policy pursued
throughout the 1930s by Great Britain and, to a degree, France in their dealings
with Germany, Italy, and Japan, three states that sought to overturn the Versailles settlement. To its advocates, appeasement was a policy based on realism
and pragmatism; it strove to avoid war over peripheral issues while seeking an
overall settlement of diplomatic problems in Europe, the Mediterranean, and

East Asia. This meant a willingness to jettison some aspects of the Versailles Treaty and to tolerate acts of aggression in Manchuria, China, Ethiopia, and Central Europe as long as vital Anglo-French interests were not threatened. Such a policy aimed to placate the dissatisfied nations that threatened the peace, and make them respectable, cooperative members of the international community.

Was appeasement a reasonable and morally justifiable policy to prevent the great powers from stumbling into wars over nonvital issues? Or was it an admission of weakness and an invitation to further aggression? As the following documents show, the merits and limitations of appeasement were topics of intense debate in prewar Britain. They have continued to be so to the present day.

The Search for "Peace in Our Time"

❖

60 ❖ *Neville Chamberlain,* *EXCERPTS FROM CORRESPONDENCE, DIARY, AND SPEECHES*

Neville Chamberlain, the son of the prominent politician Joseph Chamberlain, was born in 1869 in Birmingham, a city where he had a successful business and political career before entering national politics on being elected to Parliament as a Conservative in 1918. Having been chancellor of the exchequer and minister of health in the 1920s, he again served as chancellor of the exchequer during the darkest times of the Great Depression between 1931 and 1937. He succeeded Stanley Baldwin in 1937 as prime minister, an office he held until May 1940, when, in the wake of Britain's failed attempt to take back Norway from the Germans, he was forced to turn over the premiership to Winston Churchill. He served in Churchill's war cabinet until he was struck down with cancer. He died in November 1940.

The following excerpts from Chamberlain's writings and speeches provide insights into his thinking about war and peace, the interests of the British Empire, and the best means of dealing with Hitler. The first excerpt is taken from a letter he wrote to his sister Ida in March 1938. It was written directly after the Anschluss (unification) of Germany and Austria and at a time when the Spanish Civil War was turning in favor of Francisco Franco and the Nationalists, who, with the help of Germany and Italy, were overcoming the republican Loyalists. The second excerpt is from a speech Chamberlain delivered to Parliament on July 26, 1938, when Hitler was pressing his demands for the Sudetenland. The third excerpt is from a diary entry written on September 11, 1938, when the threat of war over the Sudetenland seemed imminent. Four days later, a week of intense diplomacy commenced when Chamberlain flew to Berchtesgaden to meet with Hitler. On September 22 he returned to Germany, informing Hitler in Godesberg that the Sudetenland was his as long as he would guarantee Czechoslovakia's new borders. Believing the crisis had passed, Chamberlain was shocked to learn on September 27 that Hitler was threatening to occupy the

Sudetenland immediately and demanding that Czechoslovakia give up other territories to Poland and Hungary. This new demand provided the background for the fourth excerpt, Chamberlain's radio address to the nation on September 28.

On September 29 Chamberlain flew to Munich, and there with Daladier acquiesced to all of Hitler's demands. For his part, Hitler promised to make no further territorial demands on Czechoslovakia.

QUESTIONS FOR ANALYSIS

1. What views does Chamberlain express about Hitler and the strength of Germany? Is he consistent in his views?
2. Why is Chamberlain convinced that Great Britain can do nothing militarily to help the Czechs in their conflict over the Sudetenland?
3. How would you characterize Chamberlain's attitude toward Czechoslovakia?
4. Were there any circumstances under which Chamberlain would have been willing to take Britain to war in 1938?
5. What role does public opinion seem to play in Chamberlain's foreign policy decisions?
6. Aside from his short-term goal of preventing war over the Sudetenland issue, what was Chamberlain's long-term diplomatic goal?

[LETTER TO HIS SISTER, MARCH 1938]

With Franco in Spain by the aid of German guns and Italian planes, with a French government in which one cannot have the slightest confidence and which I suspect to be in closish [close] touch with our Opposition,[1] with the Russians stealthily and cunningly pulling all the strings behind the scenes to get us involved in war with Germany . . . and finally with a Germany flushed with triumph, and all too conscious of her power, the prospect looked bleak indeed. In face of such problems, to be badgered and pressed to come out and give a clear, decided, bold, and unmistakable lead, show "ordinary courage", and all the rest of the twaddle, is calculated to vex the man who has to take responsibility for the consequences. As a

matter of fact, the plan of the "Grand Alliance", as Winston calls it, had occurred to me long before he mentioned it.[2] . . . It is a very attractive idea; indeed, there is almost everything to be said for it until you come to examine its practicability. From that moment its attraction vanishes. You have only to look at the map to see that nothing that France or we could do could possibly save Czechoslovakia from being overrun by the Germans, if they wanted to do it. The Austrian frontier is practically open; the great Skoda[3] munition works are within easy bombing distance of the German aerodromes, the railways all pass through German territory, Russia is 100 miles away. Therefore we could not help Czechoslovakia — she would simply be a pretext for going to war with Germany. That we could not think of unless we had a reasonable prospect of being able to beat her to her

---

[1] The Labour Party, the main rival to Chamberlain's party, the Conservatives.
[2] Winston Churchill had been demanding a common front among Britain, the Soviet Union, and France against Hitler.

[3] Located in Pilzen, the Skoda works, founded by Emil von Skoda (1839–1900), were a major weapons producer.

knees in a reasonable time, and of that I see no sign. I have therefore abandoned any idea of giving guarantees to Czechoslovakia, or the French in connection with her obligations to that country.

[SPEECH TO PARLIAMENT, JULY 26, 1938]

If only we could find some peaceful solution of this Czechoslovakian question, I should myself feel that the way was open again for a further effort for a general appeasement — an appeasement which cannot be obtained until we can be satisfied that no major cause of difference or dispute remains unsettled. We have already demonstrated the possibility of a complete agreement between a democratic and a totalitarian state, and I do not myself see why that experience should not be repeated. When Herr Hitler made his offer of a naval treaty[4] under which the German fleet was to be restricted to an agreed level bearing a fixed ratio to the size of the British fleet, he made a notable gesture of a most practical kind in the direction of peace, the value of which it seems to me has not ever been fully appreciated as tending toward this general appeasement. . . . Since agreement has already been reached on that point, I do not think that we ought to find it impossible to continue our efforts at understanding, which, if they were successful, would do so much to bring back confidence. . . .

[DIARY ENTRY, SEPTEMBER 11, 1938]

I fully realise that, if eventually things go wrong and the aggression takes place, there will be many, including Winston, who will say that the British government must bear the responsibility, and that if only they had had the courage to tell Hitler now that, if he used force, we should at once declare war, that would have stopped him. By that time it will be impossible to prove the contrary, but I am satisfied that we should be wrong to allow the most vital decision that any country could take, the decision as to peace or war, to pass out of our hands into those of the ruler of another country, and a lunatic at that. I have been fortified in this view by reading a very interesting book on the foreign policy of Canning.[5] . . . Over and over again Canning lays it down that you should never menace unless you are in a position to carry out your threats, and although, if we have to fight I should hope we should be able to give a good account of ourselves, we are certainly not in a position in which our military advisers would feel happy in undertaking to begin hostilities if we were not forced to do so.

[RADIO SPEECH TO THE NATION, SEPTEMBER 28, 1938]

First of all I must say something to those who have written to my wife or myself in these last weeks to tell us of their gratitude for my efforts and to assure us of their prayers for my success. Most of these letters have come from women — mothers or sisters of our own countrymen. But there are countless others besides — from France, from Belgium, from Italy, even from Germany, and it has been heart-breaking to read of the growing anxiety they reveal and their intense relief when they thought, too soon, that the danger of war was past.

If I felt my responsibility heavy before, to read such letters has made it seem almost overwhelming. How horrible, fantastic, incredible it is that we should be digging trenches and trying on gas-masks here because of a quarrel in

---

[4]The Anglo-German Naval Agreement of 1935, by which Great Britain agreed to allow Germany to build a navy 35 percent as large as Britain's.
[5]George Canning (1770–1827) was foreign secretary between 1822 and 1827, and served briefly as prime minister in

1827. The book referred to is probably Harold Temperle, *The Foreign Policy of Canning, 1822–1827* (London: 1925).

a far-away country between people of whom we know nothing. . . .

You know already that I have done all that one man can do to compose this quarrel. After my visits to Germany I have realized vividly how Herr Hitler feels that he must champion other Germans, and his indignation that grievances have not been met before this. He told me privately, and last night he repeated publicly, that after this Sudeten German question is settled, that is the end of Germany's territorial claims in Europe. . . .

However much we may sympathize with a small nation confronted by a big and powerful neighbor, we cannot in all circumstances under-take to involve the whole British Empire in war simply on her account. If we have to fight it must be on larger issues than that. I am myself a man of peace to the depths of my soul. Armed conflict between nations is a nightmare to me; but if I were convinced that any nation had made up its mind to dominate the world by fear of its force, I should feel that it must be resisted. Under such a domination life for people who believe in liberty would not be worth living; but war is a fearful thing, and we must be very clear, before we embark on it, that it is really the great issues that are at stake, and that the call to risk everything in their defense, when all the consequences are weighed, is irresistible.

"A Disaster of the First Magnitude"

◆

61 ◆ *Winston Churchill,*
SPEECH TO PARLIAMENT, OCTOBER 5, 1938

Sir Winston Churchill, one of the twentieth century's most outstanding states-men, was born in 1874 at Blenheim Palace, outside of Oxford, the son of Lord Randolph Churchill and his American wife, Jennie Jerome. An undistinguished student at Harlow School, he attended the Royal Military College at Sandhurst and, after receiving his commission, served in Cuba, the Sudan, and India. While covering the Boer, or South African, War (1899–1902) as a correspondent for the *Morning Post,* his daring escape from captivity made him a celebrity.

In 1900 he was elected to Parliament as a Conservative. He served in Parliament for the next fifty years, in which time he held almost all the high offices of state, including two terms as prime minister. Out of office from 1929 to 1939, he became a vocal critic of Prime Minister Stanley Baldwin's India policy, which seemed to point to independence, and a strong voice in favor of British rearmament and a tough line against Hitler. When war was declared, Churchill was invited to become First Lord of the Admiralty by Chamberlain, whom he succeeded as prime minister in May 1940.

In the following speech — one of his most famous — Churchill denounced the Munich settlement on October 5, 1938. At a time when Chamberlain had over-whelming approval, Churchill's views were unpopular but uncannily prescient.

QUESTIONS FOR ANALYSIS

1. In what specific ways does Churchill view the Munich agreement as a "total and unmitigated defeat"?

2. What, according to Churchill, were the specific mistakes of British diplomacy in their dealings with Hitler?
3. How do Churchill's and Chamberlain's views of Germany differ? How do these views affect their ideas on foreign policy?
4. What, according to Churchill, will be the consequences of appeasement?
5. If given the opportunity, how might Chamberlain have responded to Churchill's speech?

If I do not begin this afternoon by paying the usual, and indeed almost invariable, tributes to the prime minister for his handling of this crisis, it is certainly not from lack of any personal regard. We have always, over a great many years, had very pleasant relations, and I have deeply understood from personal experiences of my own in a similar crisis the stress and strain he has had to bear; but I am sure it is much better to say exactly what we think about public affairs, and this is certainly not the time when it is worth anyone's while to court political popularity. . . .

I will, therefore, begin by saying the most unpopular and most unwelcome thing. I will begin by saying what everybody would like to ignore or forget but which must nevertheless be stated, namely, that we have sustained a total and unmitigated defeat, and that France has suffered even more than we have. . . .

. . . The utmost my right honourable Friend, the prime minister, has been able to secure by all his immense exertions, by all the great efforts and mobilization which took place in this country, and by all the anguish and strain through which we have passed in this country, the utmost he has been able to gain [*Hon. Members: "Is Peace"*]. I thought I might be allowed to make that point in its due place, and I propose to deal with it. The utmost he has been able to gain for Czechoslovakia and in the matters which were in dispute has been that the German dictator, instead of snatching his victuals from the table has been content to have them served to him course by course. . . .

◆   ◆

All is over. Silent, mournful, abandoned, broken, Czechoslovakia recedes into the darkness. She has suffered in every respect by her association with the Western democracies and with the League of Nations, of which she has always been an obedient servant. . . .

I venture to think that in the future the Czechoslovak state cannot be maintained as an independent entity. You will find that in a period of time which may be measured by years, but may be measured only by months, Czechoslovakia will be engulfed in the Nazi regime. . . . It is the most grievous consequence which we have yet experienced of what we have done and of what we have left undone in the last five years: five years of futile good intention, five years of eager search for the line of least resistance, five years of uninterrupted retreat of British power, five years of neglect of our air defenses. . . .

When I think of the fair hopes of a long peace which still lay before Europe at the beginning of 1933 when Herr Hitler first obtained power, and of all the opportunities of arresting the growth of the Nazi power which have been thrown away, when I think of the immense combinations and resources which have been neglected or squandered, I cannot believe that a parallel exists in the whole course of history. So far as this country is concerned the responsibility must rest with those who have the undisputed control of our political affairs. They neither prevented Germany from rearming, nor did they rearm ourselves in time. They quarrelled with Italy without saving Ethiopia. They exploited and discredited the vast institution of the League of Nations and they neglected to make alliances and combinations which might have repaired previous errors, and thus they left us in the hour of trial without adequate national defense or effective international security. . . .

We are in the presence of a disaster of the first magnitude which has befallen Great Britain and France. Do not let us blind ourselves to that. It must now be accepted that all countries of Central and Eastern Europe will make the best terms they can with the triumphant Nazi power. . . . The road down the Danube Valley to the Black Sea, the resources of corn and oil, the road which leads as far as Turkey, has been opened. In fact, if not in form, it seems to me that all those countries of middle Europe, all those Danubian countries, will, one after another, be drawn into this vast system of power politics (not only power military politics but power economic politics) radiating from Berlin, and I believe this can be achieved quite smoothly and swiftly and will not necessarily entail the firing of a single shot. . . . We are talking about countries which are a long way off and of which, as the prime minister might say, we know nothing. (*Interruption*) . . .

. . . What will be the position, I want to know, of France and England this year and the year afterward? What will be the position of that Western Front of which we are in full authority the guarantors? . . . Relieved from all anxiety in the East, and having secured resources which will greatly diminish, if not entirely remove, the deterrent of a naval blockade, the rulers of Nazi Germany will have a free choice open to them in what direction they will turn their eyes. If the Nazi dictator should choose to look westward, as he may, bitterly will France and England regret the loss of that fine army of ancient Bohemia[1] which was estimated last week to require not fewer than thirty German divisions for its destruction. . . . Many people,

no doubt, honestly believe that they are only giving away the interests of Czechoslovakia, whereas I fear we shall find that we have deeply compromised, and perhaps fatally endangered, the safety and even the independence of Great Britain and France. . . . You have to consider the character of the Nazi movement and the rule which it implies. The prime minister desires to see cordial relations between this country and Germany. There is no difficulty at all in having cordial relations with the German people. Our hearts go out to them. But they have no power. You must have diplomatic and correct relations, but there can never be friendship between the British democracy and the Nazi power, that power which spurns Christian ethics, which cheers its onward course by a barbarous paganism, which vaunts the spirit of aggression and conquest, which derives strength and perverted pleasure from persecution, and uses, as we have seen, with pitiless brutality, the threat of murderous force. That power cannot ever be the trusted friend of the British democracy. . . .

We have passed an awful milestone in our history, when the whole equilibrium of Europe has been deranged, and that the terrible words have for the time being been pronounced against the Western democracies:

"Thou art weighed in the balance and found wanting."

And do not suppose that this is the end. This is only the beginning of the reckoning. This is only the first sip, the foretaste of a bitter cup which will be proffered to us year by year unless by a supreme recovery of moral health and martial vigor, we arise again and take our stand for freedom as in the olden times.

---

[1]A centuries-old kingdom of central Europe with its capital in Prague, Bohemia was the major western province of Czechoslovakia.

The Final Solution: Perpetrators and Victims

Antisemitism was not a Nazi invention. In Europe's Middle Ages, Jews were victims of mob violence, forced to live in restricted neighborhoods, or ghettos, subjected to special taxes, and excluded from most professions. By 1500 persecution and expulsions had driven most Jews out of Western Europe to the East, where intolerance, ghettoization, and sporadic massacres continued. In the nineteenth century, anti-Jewish laws were abolished in most Western European states, and Jews were free to attend universities and participate fully in their country's economic, political, and cultural life. But old prejudices persisted, and in an era of social change, nationalism, and new racial doctrines emerging from Charles Darwin's theories of evolution, antisemitism intensified. The Jews fared worst in Russia and the Russian-governed areas of Poland, Ukraine, and Lithuania. In these areas, where millions of Jews lived, Russia's tsarist government enforced and extended anti-Jewish laws and encouraged mob attacks (pogroms) on Jewish communities to deflect attention from its own failures.

As evidenced in *Mein Kampf* (see Chapter 4, source no. 16), Hitler made virulent antisemitism a cornerstone of National Socialism. Millions of Germans were attracted to his racial theories and comforted by his claim that a Jewish-communist conspiracy had caused Germany's defeat in World War I. Their votes carried the Nazis to power in January 1933.

Once in authority, the Nazis began to implement the anti-Jewish policies Hitler had promised. Jewish shops were plundered while police looked the other way; Jewish physicians were excluded from hospitals; Jewish judges lost their posts; Jewish students were denied admission to universities; and Jewish veterans were stripped of their benefits. In 1935 the Nazis promulgated the Nuremberg Laws, which deprived Jews of citizenship and outlawed marriage between Jews and non-Jews. On the night of November 9 to 10, 1938, the Nazis organized nationwide violence against Jewish synagogues and shops in what came to be known as *Kristallnacht,* night of the broken glass.

After the war began, conquests in Eastern Europe provided the Nazis new opportunities to deal with the "Jewish problem." In early 1941, they began to deport Jews from Germany and conquered territories to Poland and Czechoslovakia, where they were used as slave laborers or placed in concentration camps. In June 1941 special units known as *Einsatzgruppe* (special action forces) were organized to exterminate Jews in conquered territories on the Eastern front. In eighteen months, they gunned down over one million Jews. In January 1942 at the Wannsee conference outside Berlin, the Nazi leadership approved the Final Solution to the Jewish problem. Their goal was the extermination of European Jewry, and to reach it they constructed special death camps where their murderous work could be carried out efficiently and quickly.

When World War II ended, the Nazis had not achieved their goal of annihilating all of Europe's Jews. They did, however, slaughter close to six million, thus earning themselves a permanent place in the long history of humankind's inhumanity.

"Führer, You Order, We Obey"

◆

62 ◆ *Rudolf Höss, MEMOIRS*

Born in 1900, Rudolf Höss abandoned plans to become a priest after serving in
World War I, and became active in a number of right-wing political movements,
including the Nazi Party, which he joined in 1922. After serving a jail sentence
for participating in the murder of a teacher suspected of "treason," he became a
farmer and then in 1934, on the urging of Heinrich Himmler, a member of the
Nazi SS, or *Schutzstaffel* (guard detachment). Under Himmler the SS grew from
a small security force whose principal role was to guard Hitler and other high-
ranking Nazis into a powerful organization involved in police work, state security,
intelligence gathering, administration of conquered territories, and management
of the concentration camps. After postings at the Dachau and Sachsenhausen
camps, Höss was appointed commandant of Auschwitz, which began as a camp
for Polish political prisoners but became a huge, sprawling complex where over a
million Jews were gassed or shot and tens of thousands of prisoners served as
slave laborers in nearby factories. In 1943 Höss become overseer of all the Third
Reich's concentration camps, but he returned to Auschwitz in 1944 to oversee the
murder of four hundred thousand Hungarian Jews. After his capture in 1946,
Höss was tried and convicted for crimes against humanity. He was hanged on
April 16, 1947, within sight of the villa where he and his family had lived while
he served at Auschwitz.

While awaiting trial, Höss was encouraged by prosecutors to compose his
memoirs to sharpen his recollection of his experiences. In the following passage
he discusses his views of the Jews and his reaction to the mass killings he
planned and witnessed.

QUESTIONS FOR ANALYSIS

1. According to Höss, what was his attitude toward the Jews and the Final
   Solution?
2. How do his statements about the Jews fit in with his assertion that he
   was a "fanatic National Socialist"?
3. How does Höss characterize his role in the mass extermination of
   the Jews?
4. How did his involvement in the Holocaust affect him personally? How,
   according to Höss, did it affect other German participants?
5. What would you describe as the key components of Höss's personality?
   To what extent was his personality shaped by the Nazi philosophy to which
   he was dedicated?
6. How can one balance Höss's role as a commandant of a killing center and
   his comments about his family life?
7. What insights does this excerpt provide about the extent to which the
   German people knew of and participated in the Holocaust?

Since I was a fanatic National Socialist, I was firmly convinced that our idea would take hold in all countries, modified by the various local customs, and would gradually become dominant. This would then break the dominance of international Jewry. Anti-Semitism was nothing new throughout the whole world. It always made its strongest appearance when the Jews had pushed themselves into positions of power and when their evil actions became known to the general public. . . . I believed that because our ideas were better and stronger, we would prevail in the long run. . . .

I want to emphasize here that I personally never hated the Jews. I considered them to be the enemy of our nation. However, that was precisely the reason to treat them the same way as the other prisoners. I never made a distinction concerning this. Besides, the feeling of hatred is not in me, but I know what hate is, and how it manifests itself. I have seen it and I have felt it.

This original order of 1941 to annihilate all the Jews stated, "All Jews without exception are to be destroyed." . . .

When [Himmler] gave me the order personally in the summer of 1941 to prepare a place for mass killings and then carry it out, I could never have imagined the scale, or what the consequences would be. Of course, this order was something extraordinary, something monstrous. However, the reasoning behind the order of this mass annihilation seemed correct to me. At the time I wasted no thoughts about it. I had received an order; I had to carry it out. I could not allow myself to form an opinion as to whether this mass extermination of the Jews was necessary or not. At the time it was beyond my frame of mind. Since the Führer himself had ordered "The Final Solution of the Jewish Question," there was no second guessing for an old National Socialist, much less an SS officer. "Führer,

you order. We obey" was not just a phrase or a slogan. It was meant to be taken seriously.[1]

Since my arrest I have been told repeatedly that I could have refused to obey this order, and even that I could have shot Himmler dead. I do not believe that among the thousands of SS officers there was even one who would have had even a glimmer of such a thought. . . . Of course, many SS officers moaned and groaned about the many harsh orders. Even then, they carried out every order. . . . As leaders of the SS, Himmler's person was sacred. His fundamental orders in the name of the Führer were holy. There was no reflection, no interpretation, no explanation about these orders. They were carried out ruthlessly, regardless of the final consequences, even if it meant giving your life for them. Quite a few did that during the war.

It was not in vain that the leadership training of the SS officers held up the Japanese as shining examples of those willing to sacrifice their lives for the state and for the emperor, who was also their god. SS education was not just a series of useless high school lectures. It went far deeper, and Himmler knew very well what he could demand of his SS.

Outsiders cannot possibly understand that there was not a single SS officer who would refuse to obey orders from Himmler, or perhaps even try to kill him because of a severely harsh order. Whatever the Führer or Himmler ordered was always right. Even democratic England has its saying, "My country, right or wrong," and every patriotic Englishman follows it.

Before the mass destruction of the Jews began, all the Russian politruks[2] and political commissars were killed in almost every camp during 1941 and 1942. According to the secret order given by Hitler, the Einsatzgruppe searched for

---

[1] All SS members swore the following oath: "I swear to you Adolf Hitler, as Führer and Chancellor of the Reich, loyalty and bravery. I vow to you and to the authorities appointed by you obedience unto death, so help me God."

[2] Communist Party members.

and picked up the Russian politruks and com-missars from all the POW camps. They trans-ferred all they found to the nearest concentration camp for liquidation. . . . The first small trans-ports were shot by firing squads of SS soldiers.

While I was on an official trip, my second in command, Camp Commander Fritzsch, experi-mented with gas for killings. He used a gas called Cyclon B, prussic acid,[3] which was often used as an insecticide in the camp to extermi-nate lice and vermin. There was always a supply on hand. When I returned Fritzsch reported to me about how he had used the gas. We used it again to kill the next transport.

The gassing was carried out in the basement of Block 11. I viewed the killings wearing a gas mask for protection. Death occurred in the crammed-full cells immediately after the gas was thrown in. Only a brief choking outcry and it was all over. . . .

At the time I really didn't waste any thoughts about the killing of the Russian POWs. It was ordered; I had to carry it out. But I must admit openly that the gassings had a calming effect on me, since in the near future the mass annihila-tion of the Jews was to begin. Up to this point it was not clear to me . . . how the killing of the expected masses was to be done. Perhaps by gas? But how, and what kind of gas? Now we had discovered the gas and the procedure. I was al-ways horrified of death by firing squads, espe-cially when I thought of the huge numbers of women and children who would have to be killed. I had had enough of hostage executions,

and the mass killings by firing squad order by Himmler and Heydrich.[4]

Now I was at ease. We were all saved from these bloodbaths, and the victims would be spared until the last moment. That is what I worried about the most when I thought of Eichmann's[5] accounts of the mowing down of the Jews with machine guns and pistols by the Einsatzgruppe. Horrible scenes were supposed to have occurred: people running away even after being shot, the killing of those who were only wounded, especially the women and children. Another thing on my mind was the many sui-cides among the ranks of the SS Special Action Squads who could no longer mentally endure wading in the bloodbaths. Some of them went mad. Most of the members of the Special Action Squads drank a great deal to help get through this horrible work. According to [Captain] Höffle's accounts, the men of Globocnik's[6] ex-termination section drank tremendous quanti-ties of alcohol.

In the spring of 1942 the first transports of Jews arrived from Upper Silesia. All of them were to be exterminated. They were led from the ramp across the meadow, later named sec-tion B-II of Birkenau,[7] to the farmhouse called Bunker I. Aumeier, Palitzsch, and a few other block leaders led them and spoke to them as one would in casual conversation, asking them about their occupations and their schooling in order to fool them. After arriving at the farmhouse they were told to undress. At first they went very quietly into the rooms where they were

---

[3]Cyclon (or Zyclon) B is a blue crystalline substance whose active ingredient, hydrocyanic acid, sublimates into a gas when exposed to air. It causes death by combining with the red blood cells and preventing them from carrying oxygen to the body.
[4]Reinhard Heydrich (1904–1942) was Himmler's chief lieutenant in the SS. He organized the execution of Jews in Eastern Europe in 1941.
[5]Adolf Eichmann (1906–1962) was a Nazi bureaucrat origi-nally involved with Jewish emigration. After the Wannsee conference he was given responsibility for organizing the deportation of approximately three million Jews to death camps. He fled to Argentina in 1946, but was captured by

Israeli agents who took him to Israel, where he was tried and executed in 1962.
[6]Odilio Globocnik (1904–1945) was the officer responsible for organizing and training SS units in Poland for the pur-pose of carrying out the Final Solution. In 1943 he was transferred to Trieste, where he oversaw the annihilation of two thousand Italian Jews in the San Saba death camp. Captured by British troops at the end of the war, he com-mitted suicide in May 1945.
[7]Birkenau was the German name for the town where a large addition to the Auschwitz complex was built in late 1941 and early 1942.

supposed to be disinfected. At that point some of them became suspicious and started talking about suffocation and extermination. Immediately a panic started. Those still standing outside were quickly driven into the chambers, and the doors were bolted shut. In the next transport those who were nervous or upset were identified and watched closely at all times. As soon as unrest was noticed these troublemakers were inconspicuously led behind the farmhouse and killed with a small-caliber pistol, which could not be heard by the others. . . .

I also watched how some women who suspected or knew what was happening, even with the fear of death all over their faces, still managed enough strength to play with their children and to talk to them lovingly. Once a woman with four children, all holding each other by the hand to help the smallest ones over the rough ground, passed by me very slowly. She stepped very close to me and whispered, pointing to her four children, "How can you murder these beautiful, darling children? Don't you have any heart?" . . .

Occasionally some women would suddenly start screaming in a terrible way while undressing. They pulled out their hair and acted as if they had gone crazy. Quickly they were led behind the farmhouse and killed by a bullet in the back of the neck from a small-caliber pistol. . . . As the doors were being shut, I saw a woman trying to shove her children out the chamber, crying out, "Why don't you at least let my precious children live?" There were many heartbreaking scenes like this which affected all who were present. . . .

The mass annihilation with all the accompanying circumstances did not fail to affect those who had to carry it out. They just did not watch what was happening. With very few exceptions all who performed this monstrous "work" had been ordered to this detail. All of us, including myself, were given enough to think about which left a deep impression. Many of the men often approached me during my inspection trips through the killing areas and poured out their depression and anxieties to me, hoping that I could give them some reassurance. During these conversations the question arose again and again, "Is what we have to do here necessary? Is it necessary that hundreds of thousands of women and children have to be annihilated?" And I, who countless times deep inside myself had asked the same question, had to put them off by reminding them that it was Hitler's order. I had to tell them that it was necessary to destroy all the Jews in order to forever free Germany and the future generations from our toughest enemy.

It goes without saying that the Hitler order was a firm fact for all of us, and also that it was the duty of the SS to carry it out. However, secret doubts tormented all of us. Under no circumstances could I reveal my secret doubts to anyone. I had to convince myself to be like a rock when faced with the necessity of carrying out this horrible severe order, and I had to show this in every way, in order to force all those under me to hang on mentally and emotionally. . . .

Hour upon hour I had to witness all that happened. I had to watch day and night, whether it was the dragging and burning of the bodies, the teeth being ripped out, the cutting of the hair,[8] I had to watch all this horror. For hours I had to stand in the horrible, haunting stench while the mass graves were dug open, and the bodies were dragged out and burned. I also had to watch the procession of death itself through the peephole of the gas chamber because the doctors called my attention to it. I had to do all this because I was the one to whom everyone looked, and because I had to

---

[8]Teeth extracted from the corpses were soaked in muriatic acid to remove muscle and bone before the gold fillings were extracted. Some of the gold was distributed to dentists who used it in fillings for SS men and their families; the rest was deposited in the Reichsbank. Hair was used to make felt and thread.

show everybody that I was not only the one who gave the orders and issued the directives, but that I was also willing to be present at whatever task I ordered my men to perform. . . .

And yet, everyone in Auschwitz believed the Kommandant really had a good life. Yes, my family had it good in Auschwitz, every wish that my wife or my children had was fulfilled. The children could live free and easy. My wife had her flower paradise. . . . By the same token no former prisoner can say that he was treated poorly in any way in our house. My wife would have loved to give a present to every prisoner who performed a service for us. The children constantly begged me for cigarettes for the prisoners. The children especially loved the gardeners. In our entire family there was a deep love for farming and especially for animals. Every Sunday I had to drive with them across all the fields, walk them through the stables, and we could never skip visiting the dog kennels.

Their greatest love was for our two horses and our colt. The prisoners who worked in the household were always dragging in some animal the children kept in the garden. Turtles, martens, cats, or lizards; there was always something new and interesting in the garden. The children splashed around in the summertime in the small pool in the garden or the Sola River. Their greatest pleasure was when daddy went into the water with them. But he had only a little time to share all the joys of childhood.

Today I deeply regret that I didn't spend more time with my family. I always believed that I had to be constantly on duty. Through this exaggerated sense of duty I always had made my life more difficult than it actually was. My wife often urged me, "Don't always think of your duty, think of your family too." But what did my wife know about the things that depressed me? She never found out.[9]

---

[9]In an interview with a court-appointed psychiatrist during the Nuremberg trials in 1946, Höss stated that his wife actually did learn of his involvement in the mass executions at the camp, and that afterward they became estranged and ceased having sexual relations.

Evil

63 ◆ *"B.F.," RECOLLECTIONS*

B.F. was a Jew born in Warsaw, Poland, in 1925. In 1935 he and his family moved to Lodz, also in Poland, where he resided at the time of the Nazi conquest in 1939. Sent to the Warsaw ghetto, he escaped, was recaptured, and was finally sent to Sobibor, a Nazi extermination camp at which approximately 250,000 Jews were executed in 1942 and 1943. In the fall of 1943, just before the camp closed, B.F. participated in a breakout in which several hundred Jewish prisoners turned on their captors and escaped. Having survived the war, he recounted his experiences in an interview recorded in 1945.

QUESTIONS FOR ANALYSIS

Readers are encouraged to formulate their own questions about the events described in this source.

After our train moved in, the doors were thrown open and armed Germans and Ukrainians, cracking whips, drove us out of the wagons. We had bloody welts all over our bodies. The day we came to Sobibor was May fifth in the year '42. We were led through a second tower to an assembly point which was ringed by barbed-wire fences, with posts on the wire perimeters capped by some sort of metal hoods. They split us up here — men to one side and women and children to the other. Soon, SS squads came in and led the women with the children away. Where they were being taken to we didn't know, but off in the distance we heard screams of people being beaten and stripped and then we heard the rumblings of motors being started. It was the women and children being killed. We could sense in the air that, locked up like this between the wires, we'd be slaughtered right here. Night fell and we fell into a panic. We'd been told that in Belzec, people were burned alive in pits. We wouldn't believe this while we were in the ghetto, but here, when we saw a fire in the distance, we were sure they were burning people. We were overcome with fear and started saying our *viduyim.*[1]

It was a nightmare. The Ukrainians beat us and wouldn't let us out to relieve ourselves. People evacuated on the spot. . . .

There were thirty men in our group. They divided us up right away. Some were used to sort our belongings. . . . I was taken into the second group and set to work digging a latrine. I never held a shovel in my life and a German who guarded us at work noticed my "skill" and let fly such a blow over my head that he nearly split my skull. That was when I learned how to work.

We worked from daybreak till nine, then they gave us breakfast. Bread and fingerbowls of fat was all we got and afterwards, they put us to work till late evening. As night fell, we were all lined up and an SS man informed us nothing would happen to us if we behaved well. If we

didn't — they'd "make us a gift" of a bullet to the head. . . . Then, simply because he had the urge, he picked two men out — one who had stomach pains and the other who just wasn't to his liking — and led them off into the woods where he shot them. Most of the time, the men returned from work beaten, bloodied, and injured all over the body. . . .

This is what the system of going into the "bath" was like: As soon as a train with a transport of people arrived, everyone was either pulled off violently or made to jump. They were all forced to march into that sealed area. Later, the people were led off in groups of thousands, sometimes groups of hundreds. An SS man addressed them, saying since there was a war on, everyone had to work and they were about to be transported somewhere else for labor. They'd be well taken care of. Children and the old wouldn't have to work, but wouldn't lack food either. So great attention must be paid to cleanliness and we had to take a bath first. Those from the West would always applaud at this point. Later, when the Polish Jews arrived, they knew all this ended in death and screamed and made an uproar. So he said to them: "*Ruhe,*[2] I know you long for death already, but you won't be obliged so easily. First, you must work." And he kept punishing them and demoralizing them like this.

Inside the first barrack, they had their coats, jackets, and pants taken off and in the second barrack, had to strip down completely nude. They were told in that first speech that they wouldn't need any towel or soap — they'd find all that in the bath. All this led to them being brought naked into the third barrack near the bath. There was a special cell there where they were kept on arranged benches, guarded by Germans. Not a sound was permitted. Twenty barbers cut off the women's hair. When the women came in naked and saw the men there, they pulled back, but the Germans dragged them and beat them forward. They had to sit

---

[1]A prayer of confession said by Jews before their death.

[2]German, meaning "Be calm."

naked. I was one of the barbers. To shave someone's head lasted half a minute. We held the
long hair out from the head and snipped it off
all along the scalp so that "stairs" were left —
tufts of hair sticking out from the scalp. The
foreign Jews[3] didn't suspect anything, they
were just sorry about losing their hair. The Germans said it didn't matter — in half a year, the
hair'd grow back. But on the other side, the
Polish Jews screamed and wouldn't let us cut
their hair, and they were beaten, and tortured.
From there, they went straight through a corri-
dor into a chamber. . . .

◆ ◆

I was in the camp eighteen months already. The
next day, a transport of Czech Jews was brought
to the camp. They came at three in the morning
and we were chased out of the bunks in the
dead of night. We hauled the bundles off the
train, running between two rows of Ukrainians
who did nothing but beat us savagely. . . .

That evening, SS man Paul harangued us as
usual. He says he has to have five men for the
Lazarett. What's a *Lazarett*? Well, a *Lazarett* is a
place you don't have to work, you can sleep
without interruption and don't have to bear any
more burdens. But the real *Lazarett*, which
means field hospital, was a small structure with
a cross and icon of Jesus inside — probably
from before the war — and there was a pit there
where he'd lower people down and shoot them.
This was his own *Lazarett*. . . . Every day, that
monster had to have from three to five Jews
in his *Lazarett* and he'd pick them out himself
or just ask, "*Ja*, well, who's sick today? Who
doesn't want to work anymore?" Or he just
grabbed them at random. If he hated someone,
he simply pointed his finger at them and said,
"*Komm, komm,*[4] you look like you don't want to
work anymore," and then led them away. There
were times when some Jews had heard before
what the *Lazarett* meant, and they came forward

to die voluntarily, because this life had driven
them mad with despair. Victims succumbed
like this every day. . . . Death came in many
ways: sometimes by shooting, sometimes being
bludgeoned to death with clubs. Some committed suicide. There were times we got up in
the barrack in the morning, and before our eyes,
saw several Jews hanging from the rafters.

The most cruel death was at the jaws of Paul's
dog, "Bari." Paul would yell at him: "Bari! Be
my deputy!" and the dog tore people into pieces
and devoured them. As soon as he got his jaws
on you, there was no way out. He snapped you
around, whirling you and tearing at you so
long, till there was nothing left for his jaw to
clamp down on. . . .

In the year '43, our group kept growing till
it reached 600 people — 120 women and 480
men.

Paul the murderer fell bewitched of a Czech
Jewish girl. She cleaned up in his barrack and
his attitude to us now became less sadistic. The
other Germans realized this. One time, they
waited till he left for the day, then came and
shot the girl. When he got back, they teased
him: "Well, Paul, where's your Jewish girl
now?" He was so enraged, he persecuted us even
more than before. He'd stand by the barrack
door through which we hauled the packs, with
a hatchet in his hand, and whenever the urge
took him, he just swung away till he hacked
someone down in a pool of blood. When the
new latrines were dug and he came upon some
impurity, he threatened all of us with execution.
Once, he walked into the latrine area and saw
two Jews stooping over the ditch, but there was
a pile nearby so he dragged the two Jews over
and made them eat it. They fell into a swoon,
begging to be shot instead. But he wouldn't
call back his order. They had to keep eating and
then heaved up for the rest of the day. . . .

Sometimes, naked women hid out under the
garbage, under rags. One time, I was about to

---

[3]Jews from outside of Poland.

[4]German for "Come, come."

sort through the rags when I take a look and see a woman lying among them. What do I do? I can't pull the rags away because a German will spot her immediately, so I went off to another pile of rages, but it didn't work — she was found out. She was led off and clubbed to death.

Another time, after one of the disinfections,[5] we found a child, one and a half years old, among the rags. But a Ukrainian immediately ordered me to take the child to the garbage pit, where he said: "*Ach,* a waste of a bullet!" and took a garbage shovel and split open the baby into pieces. The child hardly let out a whipper.

Often, mothers bore children during the night. Whenever found, the babies were thrown straight into the garbage pits or were torn apart down the middle by their legs, or just flung up and shot in the air or wherever they landed.

They made no fuss over children. Finally, the women rebelled. While stripping, they would scream out and attack the Germans, clawing at them and yelling. "You've lost the war anyway! Your death will be a lot crueller than ours! We're defenseless, we have to go to our death — but your women and children will be burned alive!!!" And they screeched and wailed. . . .

While we cut their hair, we stole some conversation with the women — as long as no German was watching, of course. . . .

They asked us how we were still able to work for "them" while everyone else was dead. We answered, "You have it better. You're going to die soon — but we have to keep working, getting beaten all the time, till we're finally exterminated too."

---

[5]Disinfection of clothes.

◆

The Dawn of the Atomic Age

The chain of events and decisions that led to the dropping of atomic bombs on Hiroshima and Nagasaki on August 6 and August 9, 1945, began with a letter to President Franklin D. Roosevelt written in 1939 by Leo Szilard and Albert Einstein, both of whom were distinguished European-born physicists who had immigrated to the United States to escape the scourge of Nazi antisemitism. The letter, signed only by Einstein because of his worldwide fame and because Szilard was considered a security risk, warned that German scientists were pursuing research on nuclear chain reactions with the goal of producing weapons of enormous power. The letter recommended that the U.S. government fund and coordinate similar research. Encouraged by his scientific advisors and by reports on the progress of nuclear research in England, in the early summer of 1941 the president ordered an all-out effort to produce an atomic weapon. A year later the project was placed under the control of the Army and code-named the Manhattan Project.

Under the direction of Brigadier General Leslie Groves, the Manhattan Project became a huge, desperate enterprise, costing approximately two billion dollars and employing over one hundred thousand persons, who worked under the direction of the country's leading nuclear physicists and engineers at thirty-seven installations and a dozen university laboratories. Success was achieved on July 16, 1945, when the first atomic bomb, equal in force to twenty thousand tons of TNT and two thousand times more powerful than the largest conventional bomb, was exploded in the New Mexico desert. In less than a month, atomic bombs reduced Hiroshima and Nagasaki to ashes, and World War II was over.

The Atomic Age had begun, accompanied by an intense debate over the decision to use the bomb. Had it been morally and militarily justified? Had there been ways to have demonstrated the power of the bomb without using it against Japanese cities? Had the bombs been dropped to gain a diplomatic advantage over the Soviet Union in the anticipated postwar competition for power? Had racism played a role in the decision to bomb Japan? Had the military use of atomic bombs made it more difficult to control the postwar development of nuclear weapons? These are just a few of the questions to consider as you read the following sources.

Scientists' Warnings

❖

64 ◆ THE FRANCK REPORT

When it became clear in the spring of 1945 that the testing of the first atomic bomb was near at hand, hard questions were raised about how and where the weapon should be used, if at all. Some scientists, whose primary incentive had been to beat the Nazis in the race to develop nuclear weapons, had misgivings about its military use after Germany had been defeated and ultimate victory over Japan was assured. Beginning in April, several prominent physicists, most of whom had worked at the Chicago Metallurgical Laboratory, sent personal letters and petitions to President Roosevelt and, after his death, to President Truman asking them to refrain from using the bomb militarily. Several, including Leo Szilard, made in-person appeals to presidential advisors and military officials.

Scientific opposition to the military use of the atomic bomb was crystallized in the so-called Franck Report, drawn up in June 1945 by scientists at the Chicago Metallurgical Laboratory who had formed the Committee on the Social and Political Implications of Atomic Energy. Its chairperson was codirector of the laboratory James Franck, a German-born chemist and Nobel laureate (1925) for his work on the bombardment of atoms by electrons. The Committee's recommendations, which were challenged by other leading scientists, were sent to Washington, but ultimately were rejected by the Interim Committee, appointed by President Truman to advise him on the use of atomic weapons.

QUESTIONS FOR ANALYSIS

1. Why, according to the authors of the report, had Germany's defeat changed their thinking about the use of nuclear weapons?
2. According to the report, how would nuclear weapons best be limited and controlled in the postwar era?
3. In the scientists' opinions, would the military use of nuclear weapons undermine any postwar agreement on their control and limitation?

4. What is meant when the report states that "only lack of *trust*" can stand in the way of effective control of nuclear weapons?
5. What kind of future does the report envision in the absence of an agreement to limit nuclear weapons?

Scientists have often before been accused of providing new weapons for the mutual destruction of nations, instead of improving their well-being. It is undoubtedly true that the discovery of flying, for example, has so far brought much more misery than enjoyment and profit to humanity. However, in the past, scientists could disclaim direct responsibility for the use to which mankind had put their disinterested discoveries. We feel compelled to take a more active stand now because the success which we have achieved in the development of nuclear power is fraught with infinitely greater dangers than were all the inventions of the past. All of us, familiar with the present state of nucleonics, live with the vision before our eyes of sudden destruction visited on our own country, of a Pearl Harbor disaster repeated in thousand-fold magnification in every one of our major cities. . . .

. . . The consequences of nuclear warfare, and the type of measures which would have to be taken to protect a country from total destruction by nuclear bombing, must be as abhorrent to other nations as to the United States. England, France, and the smaller nations of the European continent, with their congeries of people and industries, would be in a particularly desperate situation in the face of such a threat. Russia and China are the only great nations at present which could survive a nuclear attack. However, even though these countries may value human life less than the peoples of Western Europe and America, and even though Russia, in particular, has an immense space over which its vital industries could be dispersed and a government which can order this dispersion the day it is convinced that such a measure is necessary — there is no doubt that Russia will shudder at the possibility of a sudden disintegration of

Moscow and Leningrad and of its new industrial cities in the Urals and Siberia. Therefore, only lack of mutual *trust,* and not lack of *desire* for agreement, can stand in the path of an efficient agreement for the preventing of nuclear warfare. The achievement of such an agreement will thus essentially depend on the integrity of intentions and readiness to sacrifice the necessary fraction of one's own sovereignty, by all the parties to the agreement.

From this point of view, the way in which the nuclear weapons now being secretly developed in this country are first revealed to the world appears to be of great, perhaps fateful importance. . . . Although important tactical results undoubtedly can be achieved by a sudden introduction of nuclear weapons, we nevertheless think that the question of the use of the very first available atomic bombs in the Japanese war should be weighed very carefully, not only by military authorities, but by the highest political leadership of this country. If we consider international agreement on total prevention of nuclear warfare as the paramount objective, and believe that it can be achieved, this kind of introduction of atomic weapons to the world may easily destroy all our chances of success. Russia, and even allied countries which bear less mistrust of our ways and intentions, as well as neutral countries may be deeply shocked. It may be very difficult to persuade the world that a nation which was capable of secretly preparing and suddenly releasing a weapon as indiscriminate as the rocket bomb and a million times more destructive is to be trusted in its proclaimed desire of having such weapons abolished by international agreement. . . .

Thus, from the "optimistic" point of view — looking forward to an international agreement on the prevention of nuclear warfare — the military advantages and the saving of American lives achieved by the sudden use of atomic bombs against Japan may be outweighed by the ensuing loss of confidence and by a wave of horror and repulsion sweeping over the rest of the world and perhaps even dividing public opinion at home.

From this point of view, a demonstration of the new weapon might best be made, before the eyes of representatives of all the United Nations, on the desert or a barren island. The best possible atmosphere for the achievement of an international agreement could be achieved if America could say to the world, "You see what sort of a weapon we had but did not use. We are ready to renounce its use in the future if other nations join us in this renunciation and agree to the establishment of an efficient international control."

After such a demonstration the weapon might perhaps be used against Japan if the sanction of the United Nations (and of public opinion at home) were obtained, perhaps after a preliminary ultimatum to Japan to surrender or at least to evacuate certain regions as an alternative to their total destruction. This may sound fantastic, but in nuclear weapons we have something entirely new in order of magnitude of destructive power, and if we want to capitalize fully on the advantage their possession gives us, we must use new and imaginative methods.

It must be stressed that if one takes the pessimistic point of view and discounts the possibility of an effective international control over nuclear weapons at the present time, then the advisability of an early use of nuclear bombs against Japan becomes even more doubtful — quite independently of any humanitarian considerations. If an international agreement is not concluded immediately after the first demonstration, this will mean a flying start toward an unlimited armaments race. If this race is inevitable, we have every reason to delay its beginning as long as possible in order to increase our head start still further. . . .

. . . Thus it is to our interest to delay the beginning of the armaments race. . . . The benefit to the nation, and the saving of American lives in the future, achieved by renouncing an early demonstration of nuclear bombs and letting the other nations come into the race only reluctantly, on the basis of guesswork and without definite knowledge that the "thing does work," may far. outweigh the advantages to be gained by the immediate use of the first and comparatively inefficient bombs in the war against Japan. . . .

Another argument which could be quoted in favor of using atomic bombs as soon as they are available is that so much taxpayers' money has been invested in these Projects that the Congress and the American public will demand a return for their money. The attitude of American public opinion, . . . in the matter of the use of poison gas against Japan, shows that one can expect the American public to understand that it is sometimes desirable to keep a weapon in readiness for use only in extreme emergency; and as soon as the potentialities of nuclear weapons are revealed to the American people, one can be sure that they will support all attempts to make the use of such weapons impossible.

Once this is achieved, the large installations and the accumulation of explosive material at present earmarked for potential military use will become available for important peace time developments, including power production, large engineering undertakings, and mass production of radioactive materials. In this way, the money spent on wartime development of nucleonics may become a boon for the peace time development of [the] national economy.

"The Face of War Is the Face of Death"

◆

65 ◆ *Henry L. Stimson,*
THE DECISION TO USE THE ATOMIC BOMB

President Truman, who did not even know about the Manhattan Project as a senator from Missouri and as vice-president under Roosevelt, learned of the new weapon in a meeting with Secretary of War Henry L. Stimson on April 25, two weeks after President Roosevelt's death. Truman's first response was to appoint a small committee, known as the Interim Committee, to advise him on the use of atomic weapons during and after the war. Its members included Stimson and seven others: George Harrison, an insurance executive who was a special assistant to Stimson; James Byrnes, a presidential advisor and soon secretary of state; Ralph Bard, undersecretary of the navy; William Clayton, assistant secretary of state; Vannevar Bush, president of the Carnegie Institution in Washington; Karl Compton, president of the Massachusetts Institute of Technology; and James Conant, president of Harvard University. They were advised by the Scientific Panel made up of four persons who had played leading roles in the Manhattan Project: Enrico Fermi, of Columbia University; Arthur H. Compton, of the University of Chicago; Ernest Lawrence, of the University of California at Berkeley; and Robert Oppenheimer, director of the atomic energy research project at Los Alamos, New Mexico.

The chair of the Interim Committee, and the author of the following excerpt, was Stimson. Born in 1867 in New York City, and a graduate of Harvard University and Yale Law School, Stimson had a distinguished career as a lawyer and public servant. Having served as secretary of war under President Taft and secretary of state under President Hoover, he was named secretary of war by Roosevelt in 1940, even though he was a Republican. In 1947, after his retirement from public service and less than three years before his death in 1950, he published the article "The Decision to Use the Atomic Bomb" in *Harper's Magazine.* It focused on the work of the Interim Committee and the reasons why Stimson advised President Truman to drop atomic bombs on Japan without warning. Excerpts from the article follow.

QUESTIONS FOR ANALYSIS

1. How did the background and specific purposes of the Manhattan Project affect decision-making in 1945?
2. For those who supported the immediate use of the bombs, what specific goals did they hope to achieve?
3. How was the choice of Hiroshima and Nagasaki as targets related to these goals?
4. How seriously does it appear that the views expressed in the Franck Report were considered by the Interim Committee and Stimson? Why did they ultimately reject the Report's proposals?

5. What were Stimson's views of the nature of war? How did his views affect his decision to support the immediate use of atomic bombs?

GOALS OF THE MANHATTAN PROJECT

The original experimental achievement of atomic fission had occurred in Germany in 1938, and it was known that the Germans had continued their experiments. In 1941 and 1942 they were believed to be ahead of us, and it was vital that they should not be the first to bring atomic weapons into the field of battle. Furthermore, if we should be the first to develop the weapon, we should have a great new instrument for shortening the war and minimizing destruction. At no time, from 1941 to 1945, did I ever hear it suggested by the President, or by any other responsible member of the government, that atomic energy should not be used in the war. All of us of course understood the terrible responsibility involved in our attempt to unlock the doors to such a devastating weapon; President Roosevelt particularly spoke to me many times of his own awareness of the catastrophic potentialities of our work. But we were at war, and the work must be done. . . .

RECOMMENDATION OF THE INTERIM COMMITTEE AND THE SECRETARY OF WAR

The discussions of the committee ranged over the whole field of atomic energy, in its political, military, and scientific aspects. . . . The committee's work included the drafting of the statements which were published immediately after the first bombs were dropped, the drafting of a bill for the domestic control of atomic energy, and recommendations looking toward the international control of atomic energy. . . .

On June 1, after its discussions with the Scientific Panel, the Intermin Committee unanimously adopted the following recommendations:

(1) The bomb should be used against Japan as soon as possible.
(2) It should be used on a dual target — that is, a military installation or war plant surrounded by or adjacent to houses and other buildings most susceptible to damage, and
(3) It should be used without prior warning [of the nature of the weapon]. One member of the committee, Mr. Bard,[1] later changed his view and dissented from recommendation. . . .

In reaching these conclusions the Interim Committee carefully considered such alternatives as a detailed advance warning or a demonstration in some uninhabited area. Both of these suggestions were discarded as impractical. They were not regarded as likely to be effective in compelling a surrender of Japan, and both of them involved serious risks. Even the New Mexico test would not give final proof that any given bomb was certain to explode when dropped from an airplane. Quite apart from the generally unfamiliar nature of atomic explosives, there was the whole problem of exploding a bomb at a predetermined height in the air by a complicated mechanism which could not be tested in the static test of New Mexico. Nothing would have been more damaging to our effort to obtain surrender than a warning or a demonstration followed by a dud — and this was a real possibility. Furthermore, we had no bombs to waste. It was vital that a sufficient effect be quickly obtained with the few we had. . . .

---

[1] Undersecretary of the navy and a member of the Interim Committee. He was the only member of the Committee to oppose its recommendations. In protest, he resigned.

. . . The committee's function was, of course, entirely advisory. The ultimate responsibility for the recommendation to the President rested upon me, and I have no desire to veil it. The conclusions of the committee were similar to my own, although I reached mine independently. I felt that to extract a genuine surrender from the Emperor and his military advisers, they must be administered a tremendous shock which would carry convincing proof of our power to destroy the Empire. Such an effective shock would save many times the number of lives, both American and Japanese, that it would cost.

The facts upon which my reasoning was based and steps taken to carry it out now follow.

The principal political, social, and military objective of the United States in the summer of 1945 was the prompt and complete surrender of Japan. Only the complete destruction of her military power could open the way to lasting peace. . . .

As we understood it in July, there was a very strong possibility that the Japanese government might determine upon resistance to the end, in all the areas of the Far East under its control. In such an event the Allies would be faced with the enormous task of destroying an armed force of five million men and five thousand suicide aircraft, belonging to a race which had already amply demonstrated its ability to fight literally to the death.

The strategic plans of our armed forces for the defeat of Japan, as they stood in July, had been prepared without reliance upon the atomic bomb, which had not yet been tested in New Mexico. We were planning an intensified sea and air blockade, and greatly intensified strategic air bombing, through the summer and early fall, to be followed on November 1 by an invasion of the southern island of Kyushu. This would be followed in turn by an invasion of the main island of Honshu in the spring of 1946. The total U.S. military and naval force involved in this grand design was of the order of 5,000,000 men; if all those indirectly concerned are included, it was larger still.

We estimated that if we should be forced to carry this plan to its conclusion, the major fighting would not end until the latter part of 1946, at the earliest. I was informed that such operations might be expected to cost over a million casualties to American forces alone. Additional large losses might be expected among our allies, and, of course, if our campaign were successful and if we could judge by previous experience, enemy casualties would be much larger than our own. . . .

◆ After Japan on July 28 rejected the Postdam ultimatum, which gave their leaders the choice of immediate surrender or the "utter destruction of the Japanese homeland," plans went forward for using the atomic bombs.

Because of the importance of the atomic mission against Japan, the detailed plans were brought to me by the military staff for approval. With President Truman's warm support I struck off the list of suggested targets the city of Kyoto. Although it was a target of considerable military importance, it had been the ancient capital of Japan and was a shrine of Japanese art and culture. We determined that it should be spared. I approved four other targets including the cities of Hiroshima and Nagasaki.

Hiroshima was bombed on August 6, and Nagasaki on August 9. These two cities were active working parts of the Japanese war effort. One was an army center; the other was naval and industrial. Hiroshima was the headquarters of the Japanese Army defending southern Japan and was a major military storage and assembly point. Nagasaki was a major seaport and it contained several large industrial plants of great wartime importance. We believed that our attacks had struck cities which must certainly be important to the Japanese military leaders, both Army and Navy, and we waited for a result. We waited one day.

FINAL REFLECTIONS

. . . As I look back over the five years of my service as Secretary of War, I see too many stern and heartrending decisions to be willing to pretend that war is anything else than what it is. The face of war is the face of death; death is an inevitable part of every order that a wartime leader gives. The decision to use the atomic bomb was a decision that brought death to over a hundred thousand Japanese. No explanation can change that fact and I do not wish to gloss it over. But this deliberate, premeditated destruction was our least abhorrent choice. The destruction of Hiroshima and Nagasaki put an end to the Japanese war. It stopped the fire raids and the strangling blockade; it ended the ghastly specter of a clash of great land armies.

August 6, 1945

◈

66 ◆ *Iwao Nakamura and Atsuko Tsujioka,* *RECOLLECTIONS*

In 1951 Dr. Arata Osada, a professor of education at the University of Hiroshima, sponsored a project in which Japanese students from primary grades through the university level were asked to write down their memories of the August 6 bombing and its aftermath. Moved by their recollections, he arranged to have published a sample of their compositions in 1951. His stated purpose was to reveal the horrors of nuclear war and thereby encourage nuclear disarmament. An English translation appeared in 1980.

QUESTIONS FOR ANALYSIS

Readers are encouraged to formulate their own questions about the events and experiences described in these sources.

IWAO NAKAMURA

11th Grade Boy (5th Grade at the Time)
Today, as I begin to write an account of my experiences after five years and several months have passed, the wretched scenes of that time float up before my eyes like phantoms. And as these phantoms appear, I can actually hear the pathetic groans, the screams.

In an instant it became dark as night, Hiroshima on that day. Flames shooting up from wrecked houses as if to illuminate this darkness. Amidst this, children aimlessly wandering about, groaning with pain, their burned faces twitching and bloated like balloons. An old man, skin flaking off like the skin of a potato, trying to get away on weak, unsteady legs, praying as

he went. A man frantically calling out the names of his wife and children, both hands to his forehand from which blood trickled down. Just the memory of it makes my blood run cold. This is the real face of war. . . .

I, who cannot forget, was in the fifth year of primary school when it happened. To escape the frequent air raids, I and my sisters had been evacuated to the home of our relatives in the country, but on August 2 returned to my home at Naka Kakomachi (near the former Prefectural Office) during the summer vacation, to recover from the effects of a summer illness that had left me very weak. . . .

It was after eight on August 6 and the midsummer sun was beginning to scorch down on Hiroshima. An all-clear signal had sounded and with relief we sat down for breakfast a little later than usual. Usually by this time, my father had left the house for the office and I would be at the hospital for treatment.

I was just starting on my second bowl of rice. At that moment, a bluish-white ray of light like a magnesium flare hit me in the face, a terrific roar tore at my eardrums and it became so dark I could not see anything. I stood up, dropping my rice bowl and chopsticks. I do not know what happened next or how long I was unconscious. When I came to, I found myself trapped under what seemed like a heavy rock, but my head was free. It was still dark but I finally discovered that I was under a collapsed wall. It was all so sudden that I kept wondering if I was dreaming. I tried very hard to crawl free, but the heavy wall would not budge. A suffocating stench flooded the area and began to choke me. My breathing became short, my ears began to ring, and my heart was pounding as if it were about to burst. "I can't last much longer," I said to myself, and then a draft of cold air flowed past me and some light appeared. The taste of that fresh air is something I shall never forget. I breathed it in with all my might. This fresh air and the brighter surroundings gave me renewed vigor and I somehow managed to struggle out from under the wall. . . .

Nothing was left of the Hiroshima of a few minutes ago. The houses and buildings had been destroyed and the streets transformed into a black desert, with only the flames from burning buildings giving a lurid illumination to the dark sky over Hiroshima. Flames were already shooting out of the wreckage of the house next door. We couldn't see my two brothers. My mother was in tears as she called their names. My father went frantic as he dug among the collapsed walls and scattered tiles. It must have been by the mercy of God that we were able to rescue my brothers from under the wreckage before the flames reached them. They were not hurt, either. The five of us left our burning home and hurried toward Koi. Around us was a sea of flames. The street was filled with flames and

smoke from the burning wreckage of houses and burning power poles which had toppled down blocked our way time after time, almost sending us into the depths of despair. It seems that everyone in the area had already made their escape, for we saw no one but sometimes we heard moans, a sound like a wild beast. . . . As we passed Nakajima Primary School area and approached Sumiyoshi Bridge, I saw a damaged water tank in which a number of people had their heads down, drinking. I was so thirsty and attracted by the sight of people that I left my parents' side without thinking, and approached the tank. But when I got near and was able to see into the tank, I gave an involuntary cry and backed away. What I saw reflected in the blood-stained water were the faces of monsters. They had leaned over the side of the tank and died in that position. From the burned shreds of their sailor uniforms, I knew they were schoolgirls, but they had no hair left and their burned faces were crimson with blood; they no longer appeared human. After we came out on the main road and crossed Sumiyoshi Bridge, we finally came across some living human beings — but maybe it would be more correct to say that we met some people from Hell. They were naked and their skin, burned and bloody, was like red rust and their bodies were bloated up like balloons. . . . The houses on both sides of this street, which was several dozen yards wide, were in flames so that we could only move along a strip in the center about three or four yards wide. This narrow passage was covered with seriously burned and injured people, unable to walk, and with dead bodies, leaving hardly any space for us to get through. At places, we were forced to step over them callously, but we apologized in our hearts as we did this. Among them were old people pleading for water, tiny children seeking help, students unconsciously calling for their parents, brothers, and sisters, and there was a mother prostrate on the ground, moaning with pain but with one arm still tightly embracing her dead baby. But how could we help them when we ourselves did not know our own fate?

When we reached the Koi First Aid Station, we learned that we were among the last to escape from the Sumiyoshi Bridge area. After my father had received some medical treatment, we hurried over Koi Hill to our relatives at Tomo Village in Asa County. When we were crossing the hill late that evening, we could see Hiroshima lying far below, now a mere smoldering desert. After offering a silent prayer for the victims, we descended the hill toward Tomo.

ATSUKO TSUJIOKA

Student, Hiroshima Women's Junior College

It happened instantaneously. I felt as if my back had been struck with a big hammer, and then as if I had been thrown into boiling oil. I was unconscious for a while. When I regained my senses, the whole area was covered with black smoke. . . . I lay on the ground with my arms pressed against my chest, and called for help, again and again: "Mother! Mother! Father!"

But, of course, neither Mother nor Father answered me. . . . I could hear the other girls shouting for their mothers in the hellish darkness, and I sensed that they were getting away. I got up and just ran after them desperately. Near Tsurumi Bridge, a red hot electric wire got wrapped around my ankles. I pulled free of it somehow, without thinking, and ran to the foot of the Tsurumi Bridge. By that time, there was white smoke everywhere. I had been working in a place called Tanaka-cho, about 600 yards from the blast center. I seemed to have been blown quite a bit north and had to take a completely different route to the bridge, which would have been straight ahead of me if I was where I should have been.

There was a large cistern at the foot of the bridge. In the tank were some mothers, one holding her naked, burned baby above her head, and another crying and trying to give her baby milk from her burned breast. Also in the tank were schoolchildren, with only their heads, and their hands clasped in prayer, above the surface

of the water. They were sobbing for their parents, but everyone had been hurt, so there was no one to help them. People's hair was white with dust, and scorched; they did not look human. "Surely not me," I thought, and I looked down at my hands. They were bloody and what looked like rags hung from my arms, and inside was freshlooking flesh, all red, white and black. I was shocked and reached for the handkerchief I carried in the pocket of my trousers, but there was no handkerchief or pocket. The lower part of the trousers had been burned away. I could feel my face swelling up, but there was nothing I could do about it. I and some friends decided to try to get back to our houses in the suburbs. Houses were blazing on both sides of the street as we walked along, and my back started hurting worse.

We heard people calling for help inside wrecked buildings, and then saw the same buildings go up in flames. A boy of about six, covered in blood, was jumping up and down in front of one of the burning houses, holding a cooking pot in is hands and yelling something we could not understand. . . . I wonder what happened to those people? And the ones trapped in the buildings. In our rush to get home quickly, the four of us were proceeding toward the center of the atomic explosion, in the opposite direction from everyone else. However, when we reached Inari-machi, we could not go any further because the bridge had been destroyed, so we headed for Futaba Hill, instead. My legs gave out near Futaba, and I almost crawled the last part of the way to the foot of the hill, saying, "Wait for me! Please wait for me!"

Luckily for us, we met some kind soldiers in white coats there, who took us to a place we could lie down and rest, and treated our wounds. They dug around and told me that they had removed pieces of tile from the back of my head. They bandaged my head for me and tried to console us by saying, "Rest here now. Your teacher is bound to come and get you soon." . . .

That first night ended. There were cries for water from early morning. I was terribly thirsty.

There was a puddle in the middle of the barracks. I realized that the water was filthy, but I scooped up some of it with my shoe and drank it. It looked like coffee with milk. . . . I found out that there was a river just behind the barracks and went out with my shoes and drank to my heart's content. After that, I went back and forth many times to get water for those lying near me, and for the injured soldiers. . . . Mercurochrome had been painted on my burns once, and they got black and sticky. I tried to dry them out in the sun. My friends and the other people were no longer able to move. The skin had peeled off of their burned arms, legs and backs. I wanted to move them, but there was no place on their bodies that I could touch. Some people came around noon on the second day and gave us some rice balls. Our faces were burned and swollen so badly that we could hardly open our mouths, so we got very little of the rice into them. My eyes had swollen up by the third day, and I could not move around. I lay down in the barracks with my friends. I remember being in a kind of dream world, talking on and on with my delirious friends. . . .

Another time, I must have been dreaming: I thought that my father and sister were coming up the hill to get me. I was so glad that I forced my eyes open with my fingers to see, but it was dark and I could not see anything. People who came to the barracks would call out the names and addresses of the people they were looking for. My father and four or five of our neighbors

had been searching for me since the bombing. They found me in a corner of the barracks at the foot of Futaba Hill, on the evening of the third day. They were able to find me because the wooden name tag my father had written for me was on my chest. The writing on the tag had been burned all the way through it, as if it had been etched.

"Atsuko! This is your father!"

I was so happy I couldn't speak. I only nodded my head. My eyes were swollen closed. I could not see my father, but I was saved.

I still have the scars from that day; on my head, face, arms, legs and chest. There are reddish black scars on my arms and the face that I see in the mirror does not look as if it belongs to me. It always saddens me to think that I will never look the way I used to. I lost all hope at first. I was obsessed with the idea that I had become a freak and did not want to be seen by anyone. I cried constantly for my good friends and kind teachers who had died in such terrible way.

My way of thinking became warped and pessimistic. Even my beautiful voice, that my friends had envied, had turned weak and hoarse. When I think of the way it was then, I feel as if I were being strangled. But I have been able to take comfort in the thought that physical beauty is not everything, that a beautiful spirit can do away with physical ugliness. This has given me new hope for the future. I am going to study hard and develop my mind and body, to become someone with culture and inner beauty.

◆

From World War II to the Cold War

In April 1945, the Allies, led by Great Britain, the United States, and the Soviet Union, defeated Hitler and were planning their final victory over Japan. Less than a year later, however, in March 1946, the British wartime leader Winston Churchill warned that an "iron curtain" was descending across Soviet-dominated Eastern Europe, and called for an Anglo-American alliance to halt further Soviet expansion. One year after that, in March 1947, President Harry Truman in an address to Congress denounced the Soviet Union as a menace to world peace and committed the United States to support "free peoples who are resisting attempted subjugation by armed minorities or by outside pressures." Truman's aide, Clark Clifford, described the speech as "the opening gun in a campaign to bring the people up to the realization that the war isn't over by any means." In April 1947 another presidential aide, Bernard Baruch, gave the war a name. It was a "cold war," a war that would dominate international politics until the last decade of the twentieth century.

Historians have minutely explored the causes of the Cold War, and have written a great deal about which side — the Soviet Union or the United States — was to blame for bringing it about. One thing is certain, however: 1946 was a pivotal year in Soviet-U.S. relations. Until then, despite wartime disagreements and postwar conflicts over Iran and Turkey, there were still those on both sides who sought cooperation, not confrontation, between the two emerging super-powers. In 1946, however, attitudes hardened, and moderates such as U.S. Secretary of Commerce Henry Wallace and the Soviet career diplomat Maxim Litinov resigned or were removed from office. When negotiations over nuclear arms control failed in June and the Paris foreign ministers' conference over Eastern Europe ended acrimoniously in August, Soviet-U.S. conflict seemed inevitable.

Two documents written in 1946 illustrate this bleak assessment of U.S.-Soviet relations, and in no small measure contributed to it. The first, composed in February 1946 by the Moscow-based career diplomat George Kennan and known as the Long Telegram, profoundly affected U.S. policy toward the Soviet Union throughout the Cold War. It analyzed the historical and ideological roots of Soviet foreign policy and recommended a policy of "containment" to prevent Soviet expansion. The second document, a telegram written in October 1946 by the Soviet ambassador to the United States, Nikolai Novikov, warned Soviet leaders that the U.S. government was bent on crippling the Soviet Union and achieving world dominance. Although Novikov's cable seems to have had less impact on policy than Kennan's telegram, it nevertheless is a revealing example of Soviet perceptions during these early stages of the Cold War.

The Sources of Soviet Conduct

◆

67 ◆ *George Kennan, THE LONG TELEGRAM*

Born in Milwaukee in 1904 and raised in a strict Protestant household, George Kennan entered the U.S. Foreign Service directly after his graduation from Princeton in 1925. Having mastered the Russian language through studies at the University of Berlin, he had postings in Moscow, Berlin, and Prague before returning to Moscow in 1944 as special advisor to the U.S. ambassador to the Soviet Union, Averill Harriman. In early February 1946 he received a directive from the State Department to analyze the implications of a recent Stalin speech that Washington viewed as confrontational and hostile. Kennan, an advocate of a hard line against the Soviet Union, used the opportunity to write what is arguably the best-known such dispatch in the history of U.S. diplomacy. It was avidly read by State Department officials, cabled to U.S. embassies around the world, and made required reading for hundreds of military officers. In 1947 an edited version of the telegram was published as an article written by "X" in the journal *Foreign Affairs.* Kennan's telegram gave direction and purpose to U.S. foreign policy. Its recommendation to undertake long-term "containment" of Russia's expansionist tendencies through the application of counterforce became the foundation of U.S. Cold War strategy.

In 1947 Kennan was appointed head of the State Department's newly created policy planning staff and given responsibility for long-range planning. His opposition to the formation of the North Atlantic Treaty Organization (NATO), to increased military spending, and to U.S. involvement in the Korean War led to his resignation in 1951. Since then, with the exception of brief ambassadorships to the Soviet Union in 1952 and to Yugoslavia between 1961 and 1963, Kennan has devoted himself to research, writing, and university teaching on foreign policy and Soviet affairs.

QUESTIONS FOR ANALYSIS

1. What views of capitalism and socialism are presented, according to Kennan, in official Soviet propaganda?
2. What does Kennan consider to be the outstanding characteristics of Russia's past?
3. How, according to Kennan, has this past affected the policies and views of the Soviet government since 1917?
4. In Kennan's view, what role does communist ideology play in shaping the policies of the Soviet government?
5. According to Kennan's analysis, what strengths and weaknesses does the Soviet Union bring to the anticipated conflict with the United States?
6. What, in Kennan's view, are the implications of his analysis for U.S. foreign and domestic policy? What must be done to counter the inevitable Soviet threat?

PART 1: BASIC FEATURES OF POSTWAR SOVIET OUTLOOK, AS PUT FORWARD BY OFFICIAL PROPAGANDA MACHINE, ARE AS FOLLOWS

(a) USSR still lives in antagonistic "capitalist encirclement" with which in the long run there can be no permanent peaceful coexistence. . . .

(b) Capitalist world is beset with internal conflicts, inherent in nature of capitalist society. . . . Greatest of them is that between England and US.

(c) Internal conflicts of capitalism inevitably generate wars. Wars thus generated may be of two kinds: intra-capitalist wars between two capitalist states and wars of intervention against socialist world. Smart capitalists, vainly seeking escape from inner conflicts of capitalism, incline toward latter. . . .

PART 2: BACKGROUND OF OUTLOOK

. . . At bottom of Kremlin's neurotic view of world affairs is traditional and instinctive Russian sense of insecurity. Originally, this was insecurity of a peaceful agricultural people trying to live on vast exposed plain in neighborhood of fierce nomadic peoples. To this was added, as Russia came into contact with economically advanced West, fear of more competent, more powerful, more highly organized societies in that area. But this latter type of insecurity was one which afflicted Russian rulers rather than Russian people; for Russian rulers have invariably sensed that their rule was relatively archaic in form, fragile and artificial in its psychological foundations, unable to stand comparison or contact with political systems of Western countries. For this reason they have always feared foreign penetration, feared direct contact between Western world and their own, feared what would happen if Russians learned truth about world without or if foreigners learned truth about world within. And they have learned to seek security only in patient but deadly struggle for total destruction of rival power, never in compacts and compromises with it.

It was no coincidence that Marxism, which had smouldered ineffectively for half a century in Western Europe, caught hold and blazed for the first time in Russia. Only in this land which had never known a friendly neighbor or indeed any tolerant equilibrium of separate powers, either internal or international, could a doctrine thrive which viewed economic conflicts of society as insoluble by peaceful means. After establishment of Bolshevist regime, Marxist dogma, rendered even more truculent and intolerant by Lenin's interpretation, became a perfect vehicle for sense of insecurity with which Bolsheviks, even more than previous Russian rulers, were afflicted. In this dogma, with its basic altruism of purpose, they found justification for their instinctive fear of outside world, for the dictatorship without which they did not know how to rule, for cruelties they did not dare to inflict, for sacrifices they felt bound to demand. In the name of Marxism they sacrificed every single ethical value in their methods and tactics. Today they cannot dispense with it. It is fig leaf of their moral and intellectual respectability. Without it

they would stand before history, at best, as only the last of that long succession of cruel and wasteful Russian rulers who have relentlessly forced country on to ever new heights of military power in order to guarantee external security of their internally weak regimes. . . . Thus Soviet leaders are driven [by] necessities of their own past and present position to put forward a dogma which [apparent omission] outside world as evil, hostile and menacing, but as bearing within itself germs of creeping disease and destined to be wracked with growing internal convulsions until it is given final coup de grace by rising power of socialism and yields to new and better world. . . .

PART 3: PROJECTION OF SOVIET OUTLOOK IN PRACTICAL POLICY ON OFFICIAL LEVEL

We have now seen nature and background of Soviet program. What may we expect by way of its practical implementation? . . .

On official plane we must look for following:

(a) Internal policy devoted to increasing in every way strength and prestige of Soviet state: intensive military-industrialization; maximum development of armed forces; great displays to impress outsiders; continued secretiveness about internal matters, designed to conceal weaknesses and to keep opponents in the dark.

(b) Wherever it is considered timely and promising, efforts will be made to advance official limits of Soviet power. . . .

(c) Russians will participate officially in international organizations where they see opportunity of extending Soviet power or of inhibiting or diluting power of others. . . .

(d) Toward colonial areas and backward or dependent peoples, Soviet policy . . . will be directed toward weakening of power and influence and contacts of advanced Western nations, on theory that insofar as this policy is successful, there will be created a vacuum which will favor Communist-Soviet penetration. . . .

(e) Russians will strive energetically to develop Soviet representation in, and official ties with, countries in which they sense strong possibilities of opposition to Western centers of power. This applies to such widely separated points as Germany, Argentina, Middle Eastern countries, etc.

(f) In international economic matters, Soviet policy will really be dominated by pursuit of autarchy[1] for Soviet Union and Soviet-dominated adjacent areas taken together. . . .

power. Thus, persons who are financially independent — such as individual businessmen, estate owners, successful farmers, artisans — and all those who exercise local leadership or have local prestige — such as popular local clergymen or political figures — are anathema. . . .

(e) Everything possible will be done to set major Western Powers against each other. Anti-British talk will be plugged among Americans, anti-American talk among British. Continentals, including Germans, will be taught to abhor both Anglo-Saxon powers.[2] . . .

PART 4: FOLLOWING MAY BE SAID AS TO WHAT WE MAY EXPECT BY WAY OF IMPLEMENTATION OF BASIC SOVIET POLICIES ON UNOFFICIAL, OR SUBTERRANEAN PLANE . . .

(a) To undermine general political and strategic potential of major Western Powers. Efforts will be made in such countries to disrupt national self-confidence, to hamstring measures of national defense, to increase social and industrial unrest, to stimulate all forms of disunity. All persons with grievances, whether economic or racial, will be urged to seek redress not in mediation and compromise, but in defiant, violent struggle for destruction of other elements of society. Here poor will be set against rich, black against white, young against old, newcomers against established residents, etc. . . .

(d) In foreign countries Communists will, as a rule, work toward destruction of all forms of personal independence — economic, political or moral. Their system can handle only individuals who have been brought into complete dependence on higher

PART 5: PRACTICAL DEDUCTIONS FROM STANDPOINT OF US POLICY

In summary, we have here a political force committed fanatically to the belief that with US there can be no permanent modus vivendi,[3] that it is desirable and necessary that the internal harmony of our society be disrupted, our traditional way of life be destroyed, the international authority of our state be broken, if Soviet power is to be secure. . . . In addition, it has an elaborate and far-flung apparatus for exertion of its influence in other countries, an apparatus of amazing flexibility and versatility, managed by people whose experience and skill in underground methods are presumably without parallel in history. Finally, it is seemingly inaccessible to considerations of reality in its basic reactions. . . . This is admittedly not a pleasant picture. Problem of how to cope with this force [is] undoubtedly greatest task our diplomacy has ever faced and probably greatest it will ever have to face. . . . But I would like to record my conviction that problem is within our power to solve — and that without recourse to any general military conflict. And in support of this conviction

---

[1]Economic self-sufficiency as a national policy; getting along without goods from other countries.
[2]England and the United States.

[3]Latin for manner of living; hence, a temporary agreement in a dispute pending final settlement.

there are certain observations of a more encouraging nature I should like to make:

(1) Soviet power, unlike that of Hitlerite Germany, is neither schematic[4] nor adventuristic. It does not work by fixed plans. It does not take unnecessary risks. Impervious to logic of reason, and it is highly sensitive to logic of force. For this reason it can easily withdraw — and usually does — when strong resistance is encountered at any point. Thus, if the adversary has sufficient force and makes clear his readiness to use it, he rarely has to do so. . . .

(2) Gauged against Western world as a whole, Soviets are still by far the weaker force. Thus, their success will really depend on degree of cohesion, firmness and vigor which Western world can muster. . . .

(3) Success of Soviet system, as form of internal power, is not yet finally proven. . . .

(4) All Soviet propaganda beyond Soviet security sphere is basically negative and destructive. It should therefore be relatively easy to combat it by any intelligent and really constructive program.

For these reasons I think we may approach calmly and with good heart problem of how to deal with Russia. As to how this approach should be made, I only wish to advance, by way of conclusion, following comments:

(1) Our first step must be to apprehend, and recognize for what it is, the nature of the movement with which we are dealing. We must study it with same courage, detachment, objectivity, and same determination not to be emotionally provoked or unseated by it, with which doctor studies unruly and unreasonable individual.

(2) We must see that our public is educated to realities of Russian situation. . . .

(3) Much depends on health and vigor of our own society. World communism is like malignant parasite which feeds only on diseased tissue. This is point at which domestic and foreign policies meet. Every courageous and incisive measure to solve internal problems of our own society, to improve self-confidence, discipline, morale and community spirit of our own people, is a diplomatic victory over Moscow worth a thousand diplomatic notes and joint communiqués. . . .

(4) We must formulate and put forward for other nations a much more positive and constructive picture of sort of world we would like to see than we have put forward in past. . . .

(5) Finally we must have courage and self-confidence to cling to our own methods and conceptions of human society. After all, the greatest danger that can befall us in coping with this problem of Soviet communism is that we shall allow ourselves to become like those with whom we are coping.

---

[4]In this context, having a definite outline or plan to follow.

The U.S. Drive for World Supremacy

◆

68 ◆ *Nikolai Novikov, TELEGRAM, SEPTEMBER 27, 1947*

According to some scholars there is a Soviet version of Kennan's Long Telegram: a cable sent to Moscow from Washington in September 1946 by the recently appointed Soviet ambassador to the United States, Nikolai Novikov. Trained in the early 1930s at Leningrad University in Middle Eastern economies and languages, Novikov hoped to pursue an academic career, but instead was drafted into the foreign service. He was named ambassador to Egypt in 1941 and also served as liaison to the Yugoslav and Greek governments in exile, both of which were located in Cairo. Early in 1945 he was posted to Washington, D.C., where he was named deputy chief of the Soviet mission; in April he became Soviet ambassador to the United States. He resigned from the foreign service in 1947 and returned to the Soviet Union, where he lived in obscurity. He published a memoir of his foreign service career in 1989.

We have little information about the background of Novikov's telegram, which was unknown to scholars until it was distributed by a Soviet official to a group of Soviet and U.S. historians attending a meeting on the origins of the Cold War in Washington in 1990. According to Novikov's memoir, he was requested to write an analysis of U.S. foreign policy goals at the Paris foreign ministers' conference in late summer 1946 by the Soviet foreign minister Viacheslav Molotov (1890–1986). Also according to Novikov, Molotov examined an early outline of the document in Paris and made several suggestions on how it might be improved. This information lends credence to the theory that Molotov, who favored a hard line against the West, wanted Novikov's report to present a dark and perhaps exaggerated picture of U.S. foreign policy goals to strengthen his hand against moderates.

We know that Molotov read Novikov's completed cable. The passages underlined in the following excerpt were passages that Molotov himself underlined on the original document. What happened next is unclear. Did Molotov show the telegram to Stalin and other high-ranking officials? Did the telegram contribute to the atmosphere of confrontation building in 1946? The answer to both questions is probably "yes," but until historians gain complete access to Soviet archives, no one knows exactly what role Novikov's telegram played in the Cold War's murky beginnings.

QUESTIONS FOR ANALYSIS

1. What specific evidence does Novikov cite to prove his assertion that the ultimate goal of U.S. foreign policy is world domination?
2. In Novikov's view, how is the goal to be achieved?
3. What is Novikov's evaluation of U.S. strengths and weaknesses?
4. What point of view does he express concerning Anglo-American cooperation? Is this something the Soviet Union should fear? Why or why not?
5. How does Novikov's analysis compare with Kennan's description in the Long Telegram of the "Basic Features of Postwar Soviet Outlook, as Put Forward by Official Propaganda Machine"? What do your conclusions reveal about the reasons Novikov's memorandum was written?
6. How does Novikov's assessment of U.S. foreign policy compare with Kennan's assessment of Soviet foreign policy goals?

The foreign policy of the United States, which reflects the imperialist tendencies of American monopolistic capital, is characterized in the postwar period by a striving *for world supremacy*. . . . All the forces of American diplomacy — the army, the air force, the navy, industry, and science

— are enlisted in the service of this foreign policy. For this purpose broad plans for expansion have been developed and are being implemented through diplomacy and the establishment of a system of naval and air bases stretching far beyond the boundaries of the United States, through the arms race, and through the creation of ever newer types of weapons.

. . . The foreign policy of the United States is conducted now *in a situation that differs greatly* from the one that existed in the prewar period. This situation does not fully conform to the calculations of those reactionary circles which hoped that during the Second World War they would succeed in avoiding, at least for a long time, the main battles in Europe and Asia. . . .

In this regard, it was thought that the main competitors of the United States would be crushed or greatly weakened in the war, and the United States by virtue of this circumstance would assume *the role of the most powerful factor* in resolving the fundamental questions of the postwar world. These calculations were also based on the assumption . . . that the Soviet Union, which had been subjected to the attack of German Fascism in June 1941, would also be exhausted or even completely destroyed as a result of the war.

Reality did not bear out the calculations of the American imperialists. . . .

In actuality, despite all of the economic difficulties of the postwar period connected with the enormous losses inflicted by the war and the German fascist occupation, the Soviet Union continues to remain economically independent of the outside world and is rebuilding its national economy with its own forces. . . .

The enormous relative weight of the USSR in international affairs in general and in the European countries in particular, the independence of its foreign policy, and the economic and political assistance that it provides to neighboring countries, both allies and former enemies, has led to the growth of the political influence of the Soviet Union in these countries and to the further strengthening of democratic tendencies in them.

Such a situation in Eastern and Southeastern Europe cannot help but be regarded by the American imperialists as an obstacle in the path of the expansionist policy of the United States. . . .

. . . One of the stages in the achievement of dominance over the world by the United States is its *understanding with England concerning the partial division of the world on the basis of mutual concessions.* The basic lines of the secret agreement between the United States and England regarding the division of the world consist, as shown by facts, in their agreement on the inclusion of Japan and China in the sphere of influence of the United States in the Far East, while the United States, for its part, has agreed not to hinder England either in resolving the Indian problem or in strengthening its influence in Siam[1] and Indonesia. . . .

The American policy *in China* is striving for the complete economic and political submission of China to the control of American monopolistic capital. Following this policy, the American government does not shrink even from interference in the internal affairs of China. At the present time in China, there are more than 50,000 American soldiers. . . .

China is gradually being transformed into a bridgehead for the American armed forces. American air bases are located all over its territory. . . . The measures carried out in northern China by the American army show that it intends to stay there for a long time.

In Japan, despite the presence there of only a small contingent of American troops, control is in the hands of the Americans. . . .

Measures taken by the American occupational authorities in the area of domestic policy and intended to support reactionary classes and groups, which the United States plans to use in the struggle against the Soviet Union, also

---

[1]Thailand.

meet with a sympathetic attitude on the part of England. . . .

◆   ◆

Obvious indications of the U.S. effort to establish world dominance are also to be found in the increase in military potential in peacetime and in the establishment of a large number of naval and air bases both in the United States and beyond its borders.

In the summer of 1946, for the first time in the history of the country, Congress passed a law *on the establishment of a peacetime army, not on a volunteer basis but on the basis of universal military service.* The size of the army, which is supposed to amount to about one million persons as of July 1, 1947, was also increased significantly. The size of the navy at the conclusion of the war decreased quite insignificantly in comparison with wartime. At the present time, the American navy occupies first place in the world, leaving England's navy far behind, to say nothing of those of other countries.

Expenditures on the army and navy have risen colossally, amounting to 13 billion dollars according to the budget for 1946–47 (about 40 percent of the total budget of 36 billion dollars). This is more than ten times greater than corresponding expenditures in the budget for 1938, which did not amount to even one billion dollars. . . .

The establishment of American bases on islands that are often 10,000 to 12,000 kilometers from the territory of the United States and are on the other side of the Atlantic and Pacific oceans clearly indicates *the offensive nature of the strategic concepts* of the commands of the U.S. army and navy. This interpretation is also confirmed by the fact that the American navy is intensively studying the naval approaches to the boundaries of Europe. For this purpose, American naval vessels in the course of 1946 visited the ports of Norway, Denmark, Sweden, Turkey, and Greece. In addition, the American navy is constantly operating in the Mediterranean Sea.

All of these facts show clearly that a decisive role in the realization of plans for world dominance by the United States is played by its armed forces.

◆   ◆

. . . In recent years American capital has penetrated very intensively into the economy of the *Near Eastern* countries, in particular into the oil industry. At present there are American oil concessions in all of the Near Eastern countries that have oil deposits (Iraq, Bahrain, Kuwait, Egypt, and Saudi Arabia). American capital, which made its first appearance in the oil industry of the Near East only in 1927, now controls about 42 percent of all proven reserves in the Near East, excluding Iran. . . .

. . . The strengthening of U.S. positions in the Near East and the establishment of conditions for basing the American navy at one or more points on the Mediterranean Sea . . . will therefore signify the emergence of a new threat to the security of the southern regions of the Soviet Union.

. . . The ruling circles of the United States obviously have a sympathetic attitude toward *the idea of a military alliance with England,* but at the present time the matter has not yet culminated in an official alliance. Churchill's speech in Fulton[2] calling for the conclusion of an Anglo-American military alliance for the purpose of establishing joint domination over the world was therefore not supported officially by Truman or Byrnes,[3] although Truman by his presence [during the "Iron Curtain" speech] did indirectly sanction Churchill's appeal.

Even if the United States does not go so far as to conclude a military alliance with England just now, in practice they still maintain very close contact on military questions. The combined

---

[2]A reference to Churchill's Iron Curtain Speech, delivered at Westminster College in Fulton, Missouri, in March 1946.

[3]James Byrnes (1879–1972), secretary of state from 1945 to 1947.

Anglo-American headquarters in Washington continues to exist, despite the fact that over a year has passed since the end of the war. . . .

◆ ◆

. . . One of the most important elements in the general policy of the United States, which is directed toward limiting the international role of the USSR in the postwar world, is the *policy with regard to Germany.* In Germany, the United States is taking measures to strengthen reactionary forces for the purpose of opposing democratic reconstruction. Furthermore, it displays special insistence on accompanying this policy with completely inadequate measures for the demilitarization of Germany. . . .

. . . Instead, the United States is considering the possibility *of terminating the Allied occupation* of German territory before the main tasks of the occupation — the demilitarization and democratization of Germany — have been implemented. This would create the prerequisites for the revival of an imperialist Germany, which the United States plans to use in a future war on its side. One cannot help seeing that such a policy has a clearly outlined *anti-Soviet edge* and constitutes a serious danger to the cause of peace.

. . . The numerous and extremely hostile statements by American government, political, and military figures with regard to the Soviet Union and its foreign policy are very characteristic of the current relationship between the ruling circles of the United States and the USSR. These statements are echoed in an even more unrestrained tone by the overwhelming majority of the American press organs. *Talk about a "third war,"* meaning a war against the Soviet Union, and even a direct call for this war — with the threat of using the atomic bomb — such is the content of the statements on relations with the Soviet Union by reactionaries at public meetings and in the press. . . .

The basic goal of this anti-Soviet campaign of American "public opinion" is to exert political pressure on the Soviet Union and compel it to make concessions. Another, no less important goal of the campaign is the attempt *to create an atmosphere of war psychosis* among the masses, who are weary of war, thus making it easier for the U.S. government to carry out measures for the maintenance of high military potential. . . .

. . . Of course, all of these measures for maintaining a high military potential are not goals in themselves. They are only intended *to prepare the conditions for winning world supremacy* in a new war, the date for which, to be sure, cannot be determined now by anyone, but which is contemplated by the most bellicose circles of American imperialism.

Careful note should be taken of the fact that the preparation by the United States for a future war is being conducted with the prospect of *war against the Soviet Union,* which in the eyes of American imperialists is the main obstacle in the path of the United States to world domination.

CHAPTER 9

The Industrialized West in an Era of Economic Growth and Social Change

In the three decades after World War II, the people and nations of the industrialized West experienced swift and profound changes. Ideologies that before the war had commanded passionate devotion from millions either died, as did fascism, or showed signs of weakening, as did communism. Except for Spain and Portugal, where dictatorships persisted into the 1970s, democratic governments committed to guaranteeing their citizens' well-being through unemployment insurance, state-supported pension systems, public housing, and economic planning gave Western Europe and the United States almost two decades of political tranquility.

Diplomatic relationships were also transformed. European states accepted a diminished role in world affairs, while the United States took its place alongside the Soviet Union as one of the world's superpowers. Such role reversals were difficult for Europeans, who for more than a century had considered it their God-given right to manage world affairs, and Americans, many of whom were uncomfortable with political and military commitments outside the Western hemisphere.

European states lost something else after World War II: their colonies. Between 1947, when India and Pakistan gained their independence from Great Britain, and the early 1970s, by which time some seventy former colonies in Africa and Asia had become sovereign states, the era of European imperialism ended. For the former colonial powers, Asian and African independence was another sign of their dwindling importance in world affairs. For the United States, these regions were a vast new arena in which its ideological and political struggle with the Soviet Union could be played out.

Western economies were also transformed in the postwar era. The 1950s and 1960s were "golden years" of economic expansion, a time when economists, politicians, and journalists routinely used the word *miracle* to describe the transition from wartime devastation to postwar affluence. Between 1950 and 1973, the economies of Great Britain and the United States expanded at an annual rate of 3 percent. In Germany, the growth rate averaged 6 percent a year, and labor shortages required the importation of more than a million and a half workers from Italy, Greece, Turkey, and elsewhere. French and Italian economic growth matched that of Germany. The French gross national product more than doubled in the 1950s and tripled in the 1960s, while in Italy industrial production rose 70% between 1958 and 1963. Europe's smaller nations also participated in the postwar boom. By the 1970s the people of Switzerland and Scandinavia had the highest standards of living in the world.

Social change was the inevitable consequence of economic growth. Urbanization accelerated as million of small farmers, unable to survive economically in an era of mechanized, scientific agriculture, moved to cities. Before World War II, agriculture, fishing, and forestry still employed around 20 percent of the population in Great Britain and Belgium, 25 percent of the population in the United States, and between 35 and 40 percent in France, Austria, and the Scandinavian countries. In the 1950s and 1960s, these percentages decreased by half, and by the 1980s less than 5 percent of the U.S., British, and German populations were farmers.

The makeup of urban populations was also changing. The old middle class, mainly business people and professionals, expanded to include office managers, technicians, teachers, and government officials. Even many factory workers now had enough income and leisure to support the claim that they had entered the ranks of the middle class. Across the socioeconomic spectrum Europeans, Americans, Canadians, and Australians created a new consumer society. They filled their apartments and new suburban homes with refrigerators, televisions, stereos, electric toasters, washing machines, and telephones, products no longer viewed as luxuries but as necessities of modern life. The greatest symbol of postwar affluence was the automobile. In the United States, new car sales jumped from 69,500 in 1945 to 5.1 million in 1949, and to 7.9 million in 1955. In Europe, where car ownership was still rare before World War II, the number of cars on the road increased from 5 million in 1948 to 44 million in 1965.

In politics, liberal democracy triumphed throughout the West. After France granted voting rights to women in 1946, all adult citizens in what came to be known as the "Western democracies" could vote in national elections. These voters mainly supported parties of the moderate right or moderate left, resulting in centrist governments committed to capitalism but supportive of state economic planning and a wide range of state-supported social programs to protect their citizens from misfortunes connected with unemployment, poor health, and old age.

The postwar years were not without conflict. The United States was plagued by racial tensions and bitter divisions over the war in Vietnam. In the late 1950s, France came close to civil war over the issue of Algerian independence. Politicians everywhere continued to argue over taxes, social legislation, and foreign policy. But the wrenching divisions of previous decades — democracy or dictatorship, capitalism or socialism — no longer stirred passionate debate.

This changed in the late 1960s when a wave of protests, demonstrations, and radical movements, driven by young people and inspired mainly by events in the United States, swept across the West from Berlin to Berkeley. The first radical protests took place in the United States in the mid 1960s: Militant blacks challenged moderates such as Martin Luther King, Jr., for leadership of the civil rights movement; student sit-ins and demonstrations connected with the "free-speech movement" convulsed the University of California at Berkeley; and the first protests against U.S. participation in the Vietnam War took place. In 1968 university campuses across Europe and the United States experienced strikes, sit-ins, riots, and demonstrations in which students sought goals that ranged from changing examination policies to ending capitalism. The late 1960s also saw the emergence of movements for women's liberation, homosexual rights, justice for Chicanos and American Indians, and a wide spectrum of environmental causes. More broadly, the youth counterculture rejected old standards of decorum and behavior and replaced them with an ethos of liberation summed up by the motto "If it feels good, do it."

These were heady times, and some radicals excitedly talked of revolution. No revolutions occurred, however, and the political institutions of postwar Western societies remained intact. But the culture and values of the West were indelibly transformed by the ferment of ideas and movements that emerged in the late 1960s and early 1970s.

The End of Empires

In 1939, when World War II began in Europe, a handful of nations — the United States, Belgium, Italy, the Netherlands, Portugal, and especially Great Britain and France — controlled territories in Africa, Asia, Oceania, and Caribbean that contained approximately one-third of the world's population and area. Although the United States, never fully comfortable as an imperialist power, had granted the Philippines self-rule in 1935 with the promise of complete independence ten years later, the other colonial powers during and after World War II were intent on maintaining their colonies. In 1943 British cabinet officials spoke of "many generations" before its colonial subjects were ready for full self-government. And at the Brazzaville Conference on the future of the French empire in Africa, held in 1944 in French Equatorial Africa, the forty French officials who attended declined to even discuss independence for the

African colonies since it was so far in the future. As late as 1948, even after Great Britain had granted independence to India and Pakistan, the British foreign secretary Ernest Bevins recommended that Britain should keep its colonies in Africa to counterbalance the growing world power of the Soviet Union and United States.

Despite such ambitions, by the mid 1970s most African and Asian colonies had become independent states. Although this sweeping change is often referred to by a single word, *decolonization,* it was a complex and variegated process that defies easy generalizations. What caused it, how it unfolded, and what it left behind depended on many variables, including the strength of indigenous nationalist movements, the effects of World War II, the extent of European settlement, differences in colonial policy, and the nature of the colonial societies themselves. Decolonization in India, in which a broadly based, well-organized nationalist movement had existed since the late nineteenth century, was different from decolonization in Africa, where nationalism was just taking root at the time of independence. Decolonization in Africa differed in French, British, Belgian, and Portuguese colonies, and it differed in British colonies such as Rhodesia, where two hundred fifty thousand whites had settled, and the Gold Coast, where essentially the only British residents were administrators.

It is easier to generalize about the broad significance of decolonization. It was, first of all, another symptom of Europe's declining political influence after World War II. It was, in addition, the beginning of a new stage in the Cold War. Having begun as a conflict over the political future of postwar Europe, the Cold War in the 1950s and 1960s expanded to include the new states of Asia and Africa. To win their support, the Soviet Union and the United States extended economic and military aid, sponsored cultural exchanges, and worked behind the scenes to prop up favored politicians. In the case of Vietnam, a former French colony, great power involvement went much further. From the late 1950s until 1973, the United States sent two million troops to Southeast Asia and spent billions of dollars to prevent the unification of Vietnam under communism. The United States failed and, in doing so, learned painful lessons about the limits of power and the strength of nationalism in the postcolonial era.

Great Britain Lets Go of India

◆

69 ◆ *DEBATE IN THE HOUSE OF COMMONS, MARCH 1947*

A turning point in decolonization was the withdrawal of Great Britain from India and the creation of the new states of India and Pakistan in August 1947. After the world's leading imperial power released its hold on its largest colony — the "jewel in the crown" of its empire — nationalist leaders throughout Asia and Africa demanded equal treatment, and European politicians found it more difficult to justify their colonial rule.

British and Indian leaders had debated the timing and framework of Indian independence for decades, but World War II brought the issue to a head. Many Indians, embittered by the meager benefits they had received in return for their sacrifices in World War I, showed little enthusiasm for the British cause in World War II, especially after the British viceroy announced that India was at war with Germany in September 1939 without even consulting Indian leaders. In 1942, after Japan's lightning conquest of Southeast Asia, the British government sent Sir Stafford Cripps to Delhi to offer India full dominion status after the war in return for India's support in the war effort. Negotiations broke down, however, leading Gandhi to launch the "Quit India" movement, his last nationwide passive resistance campaign against British rule. Anti-British feeling intensified in 1943 when a disastrous famine took between one million and three million lives and the pro-Japanese Indian National Army organized by Subhas Bose declared war on Great Britain.

A shift in postwar British politics also affected India's future. Elections in 1945 initiated six years of rule by the Labour Party, which was less committed than the Conservatives to maintaining the empire. In the face of mounting restiveness in India, Prime Minister C. Clement Attlee dispatched a three-person cabinet mission to India in early 1946 charged with preserving Indian unity in the face of Hindu-Muslim enmity and arranging for India's independence as soon as possible. Although Hindus and Muslims could not reconcile their differences, on February 20, 1947, the Labour government went ahead and announced that British rule would end in India no later than June 1948.

This led to an emotional two-day debate in Parliament in which Conservatives and some Liberals argued that independence should be delayed. Labour had a strong majority, however, and in March 1947 Parliament approved its plan. At midnight on August 14 and 15, 1947, predominantly Hindu India and predominantly Muslim Pakistan became independent states.

The following excerpts are from the debates in Parliament on March 4 and 5, 1947. All speakers are in opposition to a proposal of Sir John Anderson, a Liberal from Scotland, that Great Britain should promise independence by June 1948 but withdraw the offer and require further negotiations if a suitable Hindu-Muslim agreement could not be achieved.

QUESTIONS FOR ANALYSIS

1. What disagreement is revealed among the speakers on the subject of the benefits and harm of British colonial rule in India?
2. Several speakers who believed that British rule had benefited India still support independence. Why?
3. The critics of British rule in India also supported immediate independence. What was their line of argument?
4. What view of India and its leaders do the speakers express?
5. According to the speakers, what military and economic realities make it impractical to continue British rule in India?
6. How do the speakers view developments in India as part of broader historical trends?

7. Most of the speakers were members of the Labour Party and thus sympathetic
    to socialism. What examples of a socialist perspective can you find in their
    speeches?

MR. CLEMENT DAVIES[1] (MONTGOMERY) It is an old adage now, that "the order changeth; yielding place to new," but there has been a more rapid change from the old to the new in our time than ever before. We have witnessed great changes in each one of the five Continents, and for many of those changes this country and its people have been directly or indirectly responsible. . . . In all the lands where the British flag flies, we have taught the peoples the rule of law and the value of justice impartially administered. We have extended knowledge, and tried to inculcate understanding and toleration.

Our declared objects were twofold — first, the betterment of the conditions of the people and the improvement of their standard of life; and, second, to teach them the ways of good administration and gradually train them to undertake responsibility so that one day we could hand over to them the full burden of their own self-government. Our teachings and our methods have had widespread effect, and we should rejoice that so many peoples in the world today are awake, and aware of their own individualities, and have a desire to express their own personalities and their traditions, and to live their own mode of life. . . . Our association with India during two centuries has been, on the whole — with mistakes, as we will admit — an honorable one. So far as we were able we brought peace to this great sub-continent; we have introduced not only a system of law and order, but also a system of administration of justice, fair and impartial, which has won their respect. . . . We have tried to inculcate into them the feeling that although they are composed of different races, with different languages,

customs, and religions, they are really part of one great people of India.

The standard of life, pathetically low as it is, has improved so that during the last 30 years there has been an increase in the population of 100 million and they now number 400 million people. We have brought to them schools, universities, and teachers, and we have not only introduced the Indians into the Civil Service but have gradually handed over to them, in the Provinces and even in the Central Government, the administration and government of their own land and their own people. . . . Then in 1946, there was the offer of complete independence, with the right again, if they so chose, of contracting in and coming back within the British Commonwealth of Nations.[2]

I agree that these offers were made subject to the condition that the Indian peoples themselves would co-operate to form a Central Government and draw up not only their own Constitution, but the method of framing it. Unfortunately, the leaders of the two main parties in India have failed to agree upon the formation of even a Constituent Assembly, and have failed, therefore, to agree upon a form of Constitution. . . .

What are the possible courses that could be pursued? . . . The first of the courses would be to restore power into our own hands so that we might not only have a responsibility but the full means of exercising that responsibility. I believe that that is not only impossible but unthinkable at this present stage. . . . Secondly, can we continue, as we do at present, to wait until an agreement is reached for the formation of a Central Government with a full Constitution, capable of acting on behalf of the whole of

---

[1] A London lawyer (1884–1962) who was a Liberal member of Parliament from 1929 until the time of his death.
[2] The British Commonwealth of Nations was founded by Parliament in 1931 through the Statute of Westminster. It is a free association of nations comprised of Great Britain

and a number of its former dependencies which have chosen to maintain ties of friendship and practical cooperation and acknowledge the British monarch as symbolic head of their association. Since 1946 it has been known as the Commonwealth of Nations.

India? The present state of affairs there and the deterioration which has already set in — and which has worsened — have shown us that we cannot long continue on that course.

The third course is the step taken by His Majesty's Government — the declaration made by the Government that we cannot and do not intend in the slightest degree to go back upon our word, that we do not intend to damp the hopes of the Indian peoples but rather to raise them, and that we cannot possibly go on indefinitely as we have been going on during these past months; that not only shall they have the power they now really possess but after June 1948, the full responsibility for government of their own peoples in India. . . .

MR. SORENSEN[3] (LEYTON, WEST) I have considerable sympathy with the hon. and gallant Member for Ayr Burghs (Sir T. Moore),[4] because, politically, he has been dead for some time and does not know it. His ideas were extraordinarily reminiscent of 50 years ago, and I do not propose, therefore, to deal with so unpleasant and decadent a subject. When he drew attention to the service we have rendered to India — and we have undoubtedly rendered service — he overlooked the fact that India has had an existence extending for some thousands of years before the British occupation, and that during that period she managed to run schools, establish a chain of rest houses, preserve an economy, and reach a high level of civilization, when the inhabitants of these islands were in a condition of barbarism and savagery. One has only to discuss such matters with a few representative Indians to realize that they can draw up a fairly powerful indictment of the evil we have taken to India as well as the good. . . .

Whatever may have been the origin of the various problems in India, or the degree of culpability which may be attached to this or that party or person, a situation now confronts us

which demands a decision. . . . That is why, in my estimation, the Government is perfectly right to fix a date for the transference of power. . . . Responsibility is ultimately an Indian matter. Acute problems have existed in India for centuries, and they have not been solved under our domination. Untouchability, the appalling subjugation of women, the division of the castes, the incipient or actual conflict between Muslim and Hindu — all those and many others exist.

I do not forget what is to me the most terrible of all India's problems, the appalling poverty. It has not been solved by us, although we have had our opportunity. On the contrary, in some respects we have increased that problem, because, despite the contributions that we have made to India's welfare, we have taken a great deal of wealth from India in order that we ourselves might enjoy a relatively higher standard of life. Can it be denied that we have benefited in the past substantially by the ignorant, sweated labor of the Indian people? We have not solved those social problems. The Indians may not solve them either. There are many problems that the Western world cannot solve, but at least, those problems are India's responsibility. Indians are more likely, because they are intimate with their own problems, to know how to find their way through those labyrinths than we, who are, to the Indian but aliens and foreigners.

Here I submit a point which surely will receive the endorsement of most hon. Members of this House. It is that even a benevolent autocracy can be no substitute for democracy and liberty. . . .

I would therefore put two points to the House tonight. Are we really asked by hon. Members on the other side to engage in a gamble, first by continuing as we are and trying to control India indefinitely, with the probability that we should not succeed and that all over India there would be rebellion, chaos, and breakdown? Secondly,

---

[3]Richard Sorensen (b. 1884–1971) was a clergyman who served in Parliament as a member of the Labour Party from 1929 to 1931 and from 1939 to 1954.

[4]Lieutenant-Colonel Thomas Moore (1888–1971) was a Conservative member of Parliament from 1929 to 1962. He had just spoken against the government's plan.

are we to try to reconquer India and in doing so, to impose upon ourselves an economic burden which we could not possibly afford? How many men would be required to keep India quiet if the great majority of the Indians were determined to defy our power? I guarantee that the number would not be fewer than a million men, with all the necessary resources and munitions of war. Are we to do this at a time when we are crying out for manpower in this country, when in the mines, the textile industry, and elsewhere we want every man we can possibly secure? There are already 1,500,000 men under arms. To talk about facing the possibility of governing and policing India and keeping India under proper supervision out of our own resources is not only nonsense, but would provide the last straw that breaks the camel's back. . . .

FLIGHT-LIEUTENANT CRAWLEY [5] (BUCKING-HAM) Right hon. and hon. Members opposite, who envisage our staying in India, must have some idea of what type of rule we should maintain. A fact about the Indian Services which they seem to ignore is that they are largely Indianized. Can they really expect the Services, Indianized to the extent of 80 or 90 percent, to carry out their policy any longer? Is it not true that in any situation that is likely to arise in India now, if the British remain without a definite date being given for withdrawal, every single Indian member of the Services, will, in the mind of all politically conscious Indians become a political collaborator? We have seen that in Palestine where Arab hates Arab and Jew hates Jew if they think they are collaborating with the British.[6] How could we get the Indianized part of the Service to carry out a policy which, in the view of all political Indians, is anti-Indian? The only conceivable way in which

we could stay even for seven years in India would be by instituting a type of rule which we in this country abhor more than any other — a purely dictatorial rule based upon all the things we detest most, such as an informative police, not for an emergency measure, but for a long period and imprisonment without trial. . . .

MR. HAROLD DAVIES[7] (LEEK) I believe that India is the pivot of the Pacific Ocean area. All the peoples of Asia are on the move. Can we in this House, by wishful thinking, sweep aside this natural desire for independence, freedom, and nationalism that has grown in Asia from Karachi to Peking, [8] from Karachi to Indonesia and Indo-China? That is all part of that movement, and we must recognize it. I am not a Utopian. I know that the changeover will not be easy. But there is no hon. Member opposite who has given any concrete, practical alternative to the decision, which has been made by my right hon. Friends. What alternative can we give?

This little old country is tottering and wounded as a result of the wars inherent in the capitalist system. Can we, today, carry out vast commitments from one end of the world to another? Is it not time that we said to those for whom we have spoken so long, "The time has come when you shall have your independence. That time has come; the moment is here"? I should like to recall what Macaulay[9] said:

> Many politicians of our times are in the habit of laying it down as a self-evident proposition, that no people ought to be free until they are fit to use their freedom. This maxim is worthy of the fool in the old story who resolved not to go into the water until he had learned to swim.

India must learn now to build up democracy.

---

[5] Aidan Crawley (1908–1992) was an educator and journalist who served in the Royal Air Force during World War II. He was a Labor member of Parliament from 1945 to 1951.
[6] The British were attempting to extricate themselves from Palestine, which they had received as a mandate after World War I and was the scene of bitter Arab-Jewish rivalry.
[7] Harold Davies (1904–1984) was an author and educator

who served in Parliament as a member of the Labor Party from 1959 to 1964.
[8] Karachi, a port city on the Arabian Sea, was soon to become Pakistan's first capital city. *Peking* is a variant spelling of Beijing.
[9] Thomas B. Macaulay (1800–1859) was an English essayist, historian, and statesman.

France Lets Go of Algeria

❖

70 ◆ *Charles de Gaulle,*
COMMENTS ON ALGERIA, APRIL 11, 1961

No other episode in the history of decolonization was as bloody and divisive as Algeria's tortuous path to independence from France in the 1950s and 1960s. A French colony since the 1830s and 1840s, Algeria after World War II had a population of approximately ten million, of which just over one million were French citizens. Known as *pieds noirs* (black feet) after the black boots worn by French soldiers, the Algerian French controlled administrative posts, owned the best land, dominated the economy, and elected representatives to the French National Assembly. Ruled directly by the French Department of the Interior, French Algeria was perceived not as a colony but as an integral part of France. The French who lived in Algeria and those who lived in France itself, regardless of their political views, agreed with the prime minister of the early 1950s, Pierre Mendes-France, when he said, "France without Algeria would not be France."

After World War II, French governments made only token concessions to the demands of moderate Algerian nationalists, and even these were bitterly opposed by the *pieds noirs,* who counted on their own power and that of the French army to maintain the status quo. Inevitably, French intransigence radicalized the Algerian nationalists, and in 1954 the Front de Libération Nationale (FLN), dedicated to achieving complete independence from France, rebelled. French authorities answered with repression, to which the FLN responded with assassinations and indiscriminate terrorism. More French troops were dispatched, and atrocities committed by both sides escalated. By 1958, many French politicians and much of the French public were sickened by the war in Algeria and were prepared to negotiate its end. But this was opposed by the Algerian French and the French generals, who, after defeats in World War II and Vietnam, considered victory in Algeria as the army's last chance to regain its honor. In the spring of 1958, the political deadlock over Algeria led to a constitutional crisis when army units in Algeria revolted against the Paris government and launched a coup d'état.

Civil war was averted by the return to power of General Charles de Gaulle (1890–1970), the hero of the French resistance in World War II and the first president of France's Fourth Republic. The rebellious generals halted their insurrection when de Gaulle agreed to rule for six months with emergency powers while forging a new constitution for France. The generals and the Algerian French were convinced that de Gaulle, a nationalist with an almost mystical sense of France's world mission, would support their struggle against the FLN and Algerian independence.

De Gaulle disappointed and enraged them. Once in power, he gradually came to the conclusion that continuing the struggle in Algeria would irreparably harm his efforts to revive France politically and economically. While the killing and torture continued, de Gaulle vacillated between making concessions to the FLN and the renewed use of force. Then in April 1961 he made what proved to be a definitive statement on Algeria. A referendum would be scheduled, and if, as anticipated, the Algerians voted for independence, France would not stand in their way. De Gaulle had abandoned French Algeria, and in 1962, after the Algerians overwhelmingly voted to sever ties with France, the independent state of Algeria was born.

The following excerpt is from de Gaulle's press conference on April 11, 1961, in which he announced that France would not stand in the way of an independent Algeria.

QUESTIONS FOR ANALYSIS

1. What solution does de Gaulle propose for ending the war in Algeria?
2. What considerations have led de Gaulle to the conclusion that Algerians must determine their own political fate?
3. What, according to de Gaulle, had been the motives of French imperialism in the nineteenth century?
4. How, in de Gaulle's view, does contemporary France's position in regard to colonies differ from that of nineteenth-century France?
5. What views of the Algerians does de Gaulle express in his remarks?
6. De Gaulle claims to have been a long-term advocate of decolonization. Do the content and tone of his remarks confirm this claim?

I should like it to be well understood that in France's policy toward Algeria, the following essential idea must be faced squarely: in the world of today and in the times in which we live, France has no interest whatsoever in maintaining under her jurisdiction and under her dependence an Algeria which would choose another destiny, and it would not be in France's interest to be responsible for the population of an Algeria which would have become master of its own fate and would have nothing to offer in exchange for what it would ask. The fact is that, to say the least, Algeria costs us much more than it is worth to us. Whether in the matter of administrative expenses, economic investments, social welfare, cultural development or the many obligations with regard to the maintenance of law and order — what we furnished to it in effort, money and human ability has no counterpart that anywhere nearly approaches it.

It must in the same way be realized that France's present responsibilities in Algeria constitute heavy military and diplomatic burdens for her. And that is why France would consider today with the greatest calm a solution whereby Algeria would cease to be a part of France — a solution which in former times might have seemed disastrous for us but which, I say it again, we consider with a perfectly calm mind. . . .

. . . There are people who will say: "But it is the rebellion which leads you to think in this way.". . . It is not this that makes me speak as I do; I do not deny that the events which have occurred, which are occurring in Algeria have confirmed what I have thought and demonstrated for more than twenty years, without any joy of course — and you can well understand why — but with the certainty of serving France well.

Since Brazzaville,[1] I have not ceased to affirm that the populations dependent on us should have the right to self-determination. In 1941, I granted independence to the mandated States of Syria and Lebanon. In 1945, I gave all Africans, including Algerian Moslems, the right to vote. In 1947, I approved the Statute of Algeria which, if it had been applied, would probably have led to the progressive institution of an Algerian State Associated with France.[2] . . . I agreed that the protectorate treaties concerning Tunisia and Morocco should be approved. . . . In 1958, having resumed leadership, I, along with my Government, created the Community[3] and later recognized and aided the independence of the young States in Black Africa and Madagascar. Not having returned to power in time to prevent the Algerian insurrection, immediately upon my return I proposed to its leader to conclude the peace of the brave and to open political talks. . . . and I and my government have not ceased to act in order to promote a Moslem leadership in Algeria and to put the Moslems in a position to take local affairs into their own hands, until such time as they are able to take over on the government level. . . .

In conclusion what does this add up to: to decolonization. But if I have undertaken and pursued this task for a long time, it is not only because we could foresee and later because we witnessed the vast movement toward freedom which the world war and its aftermath

unleashed in every corner of the globe, and which the rival bids of the Soviet Union and America did not fail to emphasize. I have done it also, and especially, because it seemed to me contrary to France's present interests and new ambition to remain bound by obligations and burdens which are no longer in keeping with the requirements of her strength and influence.

. . . Moreover, this is true for others as well. It must be recognized that in the great transformation which is taking place from one end of the universe to the other, the itching for independence of erstwhile dominated peoples and also the incitements thrown out by all the demagogues of the world are not the only motivating forces. There is another which is not always very clearly perceived. . . . We French built our empire at a time when our internal activities had reached a sort of ceiling — an industry which was not breaking any new ground, an agriculture which was not making any changes, trade channels which were fixed, salaries and wages unchanged, practically stereotyped budgets, gold currency, interest rates at 3%, etc. On the other hand, our old ambitions of European hegemony and natural frontiers were countered by the treaties of 1815 and, after 1870,[4] by the unity and strength of a threatening Germany. Then we sought in distant extensions a new role for the surplus of our enterprising abilities, a complement to our prestige and soldiers for our defense.

---

[1] The Brazzaville Conference, sponsored by the Free French government and held in French West Africa in 1944, was attended by de Gaulle and some forty colonial administrators. No Africans participated. The conference proposed a number of reforms in the French African colonies, including the abolition of forced labor, increased educational opportunities for Africans, a special form of French citizenship for Africans, and greater African control of African affairs. Independence was not considered as an option.

[2] True, Algerians were given the right to vote for members of the three assemblies that met in 1946 to determine the constitutional framework of postwar Algeria. Voting was weighted in such a way, however, to guarantee French dominance of the assemblies.

[3] The French Community was a plan proposed by de Gaulle in 1958, according to which French colonies, primarily in

Africa, would continue to receive French economic and technical aid and would gain control of their internal affairs; they would still be tied to France diplomatically and politically, however. Although all West African colonies except Guinea approved joining the French Community in 1958, within months they reversed themselves and chose complete independence.

[4] Following the defeat of Napoleon, the treaty approved at the Congress of Vienna (1815) essentially returned France to its borders before the beginning of the French Revolution in 1789. The Treaty of Paris (1870), which followed the French defeat by the Germans in the Franco-Prussian War, resulted in the French loss of the border region of Alsace and most of Lorraine.

France does not have to be at all sorry for what she has achieved overseas in this capacity and in this form. I have said it often and I repeat: it constitutes a great human accomplishment which — notwithstanding certain abuses and errors and despite all the endless spouting of all sorts of worthless demagogues — will forever be a credit to France. But how many things have changed today.

Now our great national ambition is our own national progress, constituting a real source of power and influence. Now the modern era permits us, compels us, to undertake a vast development. Now for this development to succeed we must first of all employ the means and resources at our disposal on our own behalf, in our own country. All the more so as we need these means and resources to ensure our own defense and that of our neighbors against the greatest imperialism that the world has ever known — the imperialism of the Soviet Union. We also need these means to win out in the tremendous economic, technical and social struggle now under way between the forces of humanity and the forces of slavery.[5]

It is a fact: our interest, and consequently our policy, lies in decolonization. Why should we continue to cling to costly, bloody and fruitless domination when our country has to undergo complete renovation, when all the underdeveloped countries, beginning with those which yesterday were our dependencies and which today are our favorite friends, ask for our aid and our assistance? But this aid and this assistance — why should we extend them if it is not worthwhile, if there is no cooperation, if what we give finds no return? Yes, it is a matter of exchange, because of what is due us, but also because of the dignity of those with whom we are dealing. . . .

Some people say, "What would happen to these territories if France withdrew? They would straightaway fall into misery and chaos, until Communism took over." That is, no doubt, what would happen to them; but then we would no longer have any duty toward them other than to pity them.

Some people say also, "Either the Soviet Union or the United States — or both at once — would try to take France's place in the territories from which she withdrew." My answer is: I wish both of them a lot of fun.

But it is also possible that the Algerian populations — through self-determination, while deciding on the institution of a sovereign State — will express their desire to see the new Algeria associated with the new France. In such an event, it would have to be known on both sides what this actually meant. That is why a solution should be submitted to the vote of the Algerian people — pending ratification by the French people — a solution agreed upon beforehand by the Government and the different political elements in Algeria, the rebels in particular. France would undoubtedly be willing to lend her economic, administrative, financial, cultural, military and technical aid to the young Mediterranean State, provided the organic cooperation between the Algerian communities, preferential conditions for economic and cultural exchange, and finally the bases and facilities necessary for our defense, are assured and guaranteed. . . .

Naturally we are anxious that, once peace has been re-established and civil liberties restored, the populations may sincerely choose their destiny. After which, if it is not in vain, France will undoubtedly be led, by her heart and her reason, to give her aid and friendship.

That is what I wanted to say about Algeria.

---

[5] The reference is to the Cold War.

Discontent in the Midst of Prosperity: The United States in the 1950s and Early 1960s

For most white, middle-class Americans, the 1950s and much of the 1960s were the best years in the nation's history. Americans had survived the Great Depression, won World War II, and made the difficult transition from all-out war to peacetime. Confident of their power, secure in their beliefs and values, and trusting of their leaders, Americans were content to enjoy their homes, their automobiles, their television sets, and other consumer goods. In 1954 the General Electric Company launched an advertising campaign with the motto "Progress Is Our Most Important Product." The phrase captured the mood of an optimistic era before assassinations, urban riots, the Vietnam War, oil spills, energy shortages, youth rebellion, and "stagflation" generated the conflict and self-doubt of the late 1960s and 1970s.

For most Americans of the 1950s and early 1960s, progress meant economic progress. Buoyed by cheap energy, large-scale government spending on defense and road-building, little foreign competition, and easy credit, the United States experienced high employment, low inflation, and growing prosperity. With only 6 percent of the world's population, the United States in the mid 1950s produced almost half of the world's manufactured goods and contained within its borders 75 percent of the world's automobiles, 60 percent of its telephones, and 30 percent of its radios and televisions. By 1960 more cars were owned in Los Angeles County than in the whole of Asia or South America. Between 1950 and 1963, the U.S. gross national product (GNP) nearly doubled, and despite the inflation that took place during the Korean War (1951–1953), real wages rose better than 30 percent. In the 1950s and early 1960s, the number of millionaires increased from twenty-seven thousand to almost eighty thousand. Never, so it seemed, had so many Americans had it so good, and never did so many expect it to get even better.

The postwar era was not, however, entirely a time of "happy days," as the popular television show of the same name in the 1970s saw it. Between 1950 and 1953, slightly more than fifty-four thousand U.S. troops died in the Korean War. Although after Korea the Cold War remained cold, Americans practiced civil defense drills and built bomb shelters in their backyards to calm their fears of nuclear attack. Unemployment hovered between 5 and 6 percent even in the midst of the 1950s boom, and reached 7.5 percent in 1958, a year of recession. Old inequalities remained. The wealthiest 5 percent of the population held 33 percent of the national wealth, while the bottom 20 percent held only 5 percent. More than half of all Americans had no savings, and 96 percent owned no corporate stocks. With poverty defined as having an annual income of $3,000 for a family of four and $4,000 for a family of six, 20 to 25 percent of the population lived in poverty and another 10 percent lived on the poverty line. This was a decrease from the dark days of the 1930s, but it still meant that forty million to fifty million Americans lived in poverty or close to it.

Those forty or fifty million poor Americans included people from every region and every ethnic category, but the largest single group within the poor was made up of African-Americans. Almost a century after the end of slavery and only a few years after fighting a war to defeat the Nazi's racist regime, the United States remained a racist society. In the early 1950s, Southern segregation laws required separate but rarely equal facilities for blacks and whites in public transportation, schools, swimming pools, drinking fountains, parking lots, and even cemeteries. Fewer than 5 percent of eligible blacks could vote. Conditions were only marginally better for the many blacks who had migrated to northern cities before and during World War II in search of factory jobs. Incomes were high in comparison to what they had earned in the South, but housing was in short supply, schools were underfunded, and employment opportunities were limited to unskilled, dead-end jobs.

As the United States moved into the 1960s under the presidency of John F. Kennedy, change was in the air. The new president, a young man in his forties, held out the promise of political change and social justice. American businesses were beginning to lose markets to Japanese and German competitors. Civil rights groups and the courts had already launched a full-scale assault on segregation. Women were beginning to question their prescribed roles as wives and mothers. The American public was becoming aware of the dangers of environmental pollution. By 1963, sixteen thousand U.S. troops were in Vietnam to prop up the regime of Ngo Dinh Diem in its struggle against communist insurgency. Then in November 1963 President Kennedy was assassinated in Dallas. His vice-president, Lyndon Baines Johnson, somberly assumed the presidency of a nation on the brink of enormous change.

"The Problem That Has No Name"

71 ◆ Betty Friedan, THE FEMININE MYSTIQUE

During World War II, economic need and the call of patriotism caused millions of women to take office and factory jobs vacated by men inducted into the military. By 1944, 19.4 million women (37 percent of the adult female population) held paying jobs outside the home, including three hundred fifty thousand women who served in the armed forces. After 1954, however, the family-centered ethos of the postwar era consigned women to a domestic role, in which their primary functions were cooking, cleaning, caring for husbands, and raising children. Young women faced strong pressure to marry rather than pursue careers. Popular television comedies of the 1950s and early 1960s, *Leave It to Beaver, The Adventures of Ozzie and Harriet,* and *Father Knows Best,* all centered on "ideal" American families made up of working fathers, stay-at-home mothers, and well-scrubbed children who lived in all-white suburbs in uncluttered homes.

That such a life was financially impossible for many U.S. women is confirmed by the large numbers of women who continued to hold paying jobs in the 1950s.

That such a life was emotionally and intellectually unfulfilling for millions of middle-class women is confirmed by the enormous popularity of a book published in 1963, Betty Friedan's *The Feminine Mystique.*

In the mid 1950s, Betty Friedan, a 1942 graduate of Smith College, was a housewife in a New York City suburb, a mother of three, and a writer for the popular women's magazines, *McCall's, Redbook,* and *Ladies' Home Journal.* By the standards of the day she was successful, yet she was troubled by a "nameless, aching dissatisfaction," and became convinced that "there was something very wrong about the way American women were trying to lead their lives." After five years of research and self-analysis, in 1963 she published *The Feminine Mystique,* in which she rejected the reigning belief that women's lives should revolve around home, husband, and family. The book caused millions of men and women on both sides of the Atlantic to reconsider the place of women in society and was a major inspiration for the emerging "women's liberation" movement. In 1966 Friedan cofounded the National Organization for Women (NOW) and served as its first president.

QUESTIONS FOR ANALYSIS

1. What is the social and educational background of the women whose lives Friedan discusses in *The Feminine Mystique?*
2. What is the problem facing these women, and why does it have no name?
3. Based on her description of the troubles facing women in American society, what solutions do you think Friedan would propose for solving them?

The problem lay buried, unspoken, for many years in the minds of American women. It was a strange stirring, a sense of dissatisfaction, a yearning that women suffered in the middle of the twentieth century in the United States. Each suburban wife struggled with it alone. As she made the beds, shopped for groceries, matched slipcover material, ate peanut butter sandwiches with her children, chauffeured Cub Scouts and Brownies, lay beside her husband at night — she was afraid to ask even of herself the silent question — "Is this all?"

For over fifteen years there was no word of this yearning in the millions of words written about women, for women, in all the columns, books and articles by experts telling women their role was to seek fulfillment as wives and mothers. . . . Experts told them how to catch a man and keep him, how to breastfeed children and handle their toilet training, how to cope with sibling rivalry and adolescent rebellion; how to buy a dishwasher, bake bread, cook gourmet snails, and build a swimming pool with their own hands; how to dress, look, and act more feminine and make marriage more exciting; how to keep their husbands from dying young and their sons from growing into delinquents. They were taught to pity the neurotic, unfeminine, unhappy women who wanted to be poets or physicists or presidents. They learned that truly feminine women do not want careers, higher education, political rights — the independence and the opportunities that the old-fashioned feminists fought for. Some women, in their forties and fifties, still remembered painfully giving up those dreams, but most of the younger women no longer even thought about them. A thousand expert voices applauded their femininity, their adjustment, their new maturity. All they had to do was devote their lives from earliest girlhood to finding a husband and bearing children. . . .

In the fifteen years after World War II, this mystique of feminine fulfillment became the cherished and self-perpetuating core of contemporary American culture. Millions of women lived their lives in the image of those pretty pictures of the American suburban housewife, kissing their husbands goodbye in front of the picture window, depositing their station-wagonsful of children at school, and smiling as they ran the new electric waxer over the spotless kitchen floor. . . . They had no thought for the unfeminine problems of the world outside the home; they wanted the men to make the major decisions. They gloried in their role as women, and wrote proudly on the census blank: "Occupation: housewife." . . .

If a woman had a problem in the 1950's and the 1960's, she knew that something must be wrong with her marriage, or with herself. Other women were satisfied with their lives, she thought. What kind of a woman was she if she did not feel this mysterious fulfillment waxing the kitchen floor? She was so ashamed to admit her dissatisfaction that she never knew how many other women shared it. . . . For over fifteen years women in America found it harder to talk about this problem than about sex. Even the psychoanalysts had no name for it. When a woman went to a psychiatrist for help, as many women did, she would say, "I'm so ashamed," or "I must be hopelessly neurotic." "I don't know what's wrong with women today," a suburban psychiatrist said uneasily. "I only know something is wrong because most of my patients happen to be women. And their problem isn't sexual." . . .

Gradually I came to realize that the problem that has no name was shared by countless women in America. . . . I saw the same signs in suburban ranch houses and split-levels on Long Island and in New Jersey and Westchester County; in colonial houses in a small Massachusetts town; on patios in Memphis; in suburban

and city apartments; in living rooms in the Midwest. Sometimes I sensed the problem, not as a reporter, but as a suburban housewife, for during this time I was also bringing up my own three children in Rockland County, New York. I heard echoes of the problem in college dormitories and semi-private maternity wards, at PTA meetings and luncheons of the League of Women Voters, at suburban cocktail parties, in station wagons waiting for trains, and in snatches of conversation overheard at Schrafft's. The groping words I heard from other women, on quiet afternoons when children were at school or on quiet evenings when husbands worked late, I think I understood first as a woman long before I understood their larger social and psychological implications.

Just what was this problem that has no name? . . . Sometimes a woman would say "I feel empty somehow . . . incomplete." Or she would say, "I feel as if I don't exist." Sometimes she blotted out the feeling with a tranquilizer. Sometimes she thought the problem was with her husband, or her children, or that what she really needed was to redecorate her house, or move to a better neighborhood, or have an affair, or another baby. . . .

Most men, and some women, still did not know that this problem was real. But those who had faced it honestly knew that all the superficial remedies, the sympathetic advice, the scolding words and the cheering words were somehow drowning the problem in unreality. A bitter laugh was beginning to be heard from American women. They were admired, envied, pitied, theorized over until they were sick of it, offered drastic solutions or silly choices that no one could take seriously. They got all kinds of advice from the growing armies of marriage and child-guidance counselors, psychotherapists, and arm-chair psychologists, on how to adjust to their role as housewives. No other road to fulfillment was offered to American women in the middle of the twentieth century. Most adjusted to their role and suffered or ignored the problem that has no name. It can be less painful for a woman, not to hear the strange, dissatisfied voice stirring within her.

It is no longer possible to ignore that voice, to dismiss the desperation of so many American women. This is not what being a woman means, no matter what experts say. . . . The women who suffer this problem have a hunger that food cannot fill. It persists in women whose husbands are struggling interns and law clerks, or prosperous doctors and lawyers; in wives of workers and executives who make $5,000 a year or $50,000. It is not caused by lack of material advantages; it may not even be felt by women preoccupied with desperate problems of hunger, poverty or illness. And women who think it will be solved by more money, a bigger house, a second car, moving to a better suburb, often discover it gets worse. . . .

If I am right, the problem that has no name stirring in the minds of so many American women today is not a matter of loss of femininity or too much education, or the demands of domesticity. It is far more important than anyone recognizes. It is the key to these other new and old problems which have been torturing women and their husbands and children, and puzzling their doctors and educators for years. It may well be the key to our future as a nation and a culture. We can no longer ignore that voice within women that says: "I want something more than my husband and my children and my home."

A Cry for Racial Justice

◆

72 ◆ *Martin Luther King, Jr.,* *LETTER FROM BIRMINGHAM JAIL*

On December 1, 1955, in Montgomery, Alabama, Mrs. Rosa Parks, a Negro seamstress who was sitting in the back of a bus in the "colored section," refused to give up her seat to a white man who had to stand. She was arrested and fined, and in response, a young pastor at the Dexter Avenue Baptist Church organized a citywide boycott by blacks of Montgomery's bus system. The United States civil rights movement had begun in earnest, and with it, the young pastor, Martin Luther King, Jr., achieved national and international fame as its leader. Until his assassination 1968, King's bravery, moral vision, and moving words inspired millions of followers and forced the nation to confront the implications of its long history of racial prejudice and suppression.

Martin Luther King, Jr., was born in Atlanta on January 15, 1929, the son of the Reverend Martin Luther King and Mrs. Alberta Williams King. Educated at Morehouse College, Crozier Theological Seminary, and Boston University, where he received a doctorate in philosophy, King served as pastor in Montgomery and then became copastor with his father of the Ebenezer Baptist Church in Atlanta. After the Montgomery bus boycott he became president of the Southern Christian Leadership Council and organized voter registration drives in Georgia, Alabama, and Virginia. His "I Have a Dream" speech at the March on Washington, D.C., in 1963 provided the civil rights movement with one of its most memorable moments. In the mid 1960s King extended his activities to northern cities and spoke out against the Vietnam War. In 1968 he traveled to Memphis, Tennessee, to support a strike by sanitation workers. There he was assassinated, a crime for which

James Earl Ray, a small-town thief and an escaped prisoner from the Missouri State Prison, was tried and convicted.

King's essay, "Letter from Birmingham Jail," was composed in 1963 while he was serving a jail sentence for participating in civil rights demonstrations in Birmingham, Alabama. It was a response to eight prominent Alabama clergymen who had criticized his leadership in the civil rights movement.

QUESTIONS FOR ANALYSIS

1. What specific criticisms have been leveled against King's campaign in Birmingham? What alternatives do King's critics recommend?
2. In what specific ways does King respond to these criticisms?
3. King describes his method as "nonviolent direct action." What does he mean by this?
4. According to King, what are the main obstacles preventing blacks from achieving their goals in the civil rights movement?
5. King identifies the U.S. civil rights movement with the efforts of Asians and Africans to throw off the bonds of imperialism. Is his analogy valid? Why or why not?

MY DEAR FELLOW CLERGYMEN,

While confined here in the Birmingham city jail, I came across your recent statement calling our present activities "unwise and untimely." Seldom, if ever, do I pause to answer criticism of my work and ideas. If I sought to answer all of the criticisms that cross my desk, my secretaries would be engaged in little else in the course of the day, and I would have no time for constructive work. But since I feel that you are men of genuine good will and your criticisms are sincerely set forth, I would like to answer your statement in what I hope will be patient and reasonable terms. . . .

You may well ask, "Why direct action? Why sit-ins, marches, etc.? Isn't negotiation a better path?" You are exactly right in your call for negotiation. Indeed this is the purpose of direct action. Nonviolent direct action seeks to create such a crisis and establish such creative tension that a community that has constantly refused to

negotiate is forced to confront the issue. It seeks so to dramatize the issue that it can no longer be ignored. . . . Just as Socrates felt that it was necessary to create a tension in the mind so that individuals could rise from the bondage of myths and half-truths to the unfettered realm of creative analysis and objective appraisal, we must see the need of having nonviolent gadflies[1] to create the kind of tension in society that will help men to rise from the dark depths of prejudice and racism to the majestic heights of understanding and brotherhood. . . . Too long has our beloved Southland been bogged down in the tragic attempt to live in monologue rather than dialogue. . . .

We have waited for more than 340 years for our constitutional and God-given rights. The nations of Asia and Africa are moving with jet-like speed toward the goal of political independence, and we still creep at horse and buggy pace toward the gaining of a cup of coffee at a lunch counter. I guess it is easy for those who have

---

[1] A purposely annoying person who stimulates analysis and debate about ideas and behavior through persistent criticism.

never felt the stinging darts of segregation to say, "Wait." But when you have seen vicious mobs lynch your mothers and fathers at will and drown your sisters and brothers at whim; when you have seen hate-filled policemen curse, kick, brutalize and even kill your black brothers and sisters with impunity; when you see the vast majority of your twenty million Negro brothers smothering in an airtight cage of poverty in the midst of an affluent society; when you suddenly find your tongue twisted and your speech stammering as you seek to explain to your six-year-old daughter why she can't go to the public amusement park that has just been advertised on television, and see tears welling up in her little eyes when she is told that Funtown is closed to colored children, and see the depressing clouds of inferiority begin to form in her little mental sky, and see her begin to distort her little personality by unconsciously developing a bitterness toward white people; when you have to concoct an answer for a five-year-old son asking in agonizing pathos: "Daddy, why do white people treat colored people so mean?"; when you take a cross-country drive and find it necessary to sleep night after night in the uncomfortable corners of your automobile because no motel will accept you; when you are humiliated day in and day out by nagging signs reading "white" and "colored"; when your first name becomes "nigger" and your middle name becomes "boy" (however old you are) and your last name becomes "John," and when your wife and mother are never given the respected title "Mrs."; when you are harried by day and haunted by night by the fact that you are a Negro, living constantly at tiptoe stance never quite knowing what to expect next, and plagued with inner fears and outer resentments; when you are forever fighting a degenerating sense of "nobodiness," then you

will understand why we find it difficult to wait. . . . I hope, sirs, you can understand our legitimate and unavoidable impatience.

You express a great deal of anxiety over our willingness to break laws. This is certainly a legitimate concern. Since we so diligently urge people to obey the Supreme Court's decision of 1954[2] outlawing segregation in the public schools, it is rather strange and paradoxical to find us consciously breaking laws. One may well ask, "How can you advocate breaking some laws and obeying others?" The answer if found in the fact that there are two types of laws: there are *just* and there are *unjust* laws. I would agree with Saint Augustine[3] that "Any unjust law is no law at all."

Let me give an explanation. An unjust law is a code inflicted upon a minority which that minority had no part in enacting or creating because they did not have the unhampered right to vote. Who can say that the legislature of Alabama which set up the segregation laws was democratically elected? Throughout the state of Alabama all types of conniving methods are used to prevent Negroes from becoming registered voters and there are some counties without a single Negro registered to vote despite the fact that the Negro constitutes a majority of the population. Can any law set up in such a state be considered democratically structured? . . . .

You spoke of our activity in Birmingham as extreme. At first I was rather disappointed that fellow clergymen would see my nonviolent efforts as those of the extremist. I started thinking about the fact that I stand in the middle of two opposing forces in the Negro community. One is a force of complacency made up of Negroes who, as a result of long years of oppression, have been so completely drained of self-respect and a sense of "somebodiness" that they have adjusted to

---

[2]*Brown vs. Board of Education* is a famous Supreme Court decision which grew out of a suit filed in Kansas by Oliver Brown against the Topeka Board of Education when his daughter was denied permission to attend an all-white school in her neighborhood. The court ruled that segregation at all levels of public schooling is illegal.

[3]St. Augustine of Hippo (354–430 C.E.), a north African bishop and theologian, was a seminal figure in the history of Christian thought.

segregation, and, of a few Negroes in the middle class who, because of a degree of academic and economic security, and because at points they profit by segregation, have unconsciously become insensitive to the problems of the masses. The other force is one of bitterness and hatred, and comes perilously close to advocating violence. It is expressed in the various black nationalist groups that are springing up over the nation, the largest and best known being Elijah Muhammad's Muslim movement.[4] This movement is nourished by the contemporary frustration over the continued existence of racial discrimination. It is made up of people who have lost faith in America, who have absolutely repudiated Christianity, and who have concluded that the white man is an incurable "devil." I have tried to stand between these two forces, saying that we need not follow the "do-nothingism" of the complacent or the hatred and despair of the black nationalist. There is the more excellent way of love and nonviolent protest. I'm grateful to God that, through the Negro church, the dimension of nonviolence entered our struggle. If this philosophy had not emerged, I am convinced that by now many streets of the South would be flowing with floods of blood. . . .

I have no fear about the outcome of our struggle in Birmingham, even if our motives are presently misunderstood. We will reach the goal of freedom in Birmingham and all over the nation, because the goal of America is freedom. Abused and scorned though we may be, our destiny is tied up with the destiny of America. Before the Pilgrims landed at Plymouth we were here. Before the pen of Jefferson etched across the pages of history the majestic words of the Declaration of Independence, we were here. For more than two centuries our foreparents labored in this country without wages; they made cotton king; and they built the homes of their masters in the midst of brutal injustice and shameful humiliation — and yet out of a bottomless vitality they continued to thrive and develop. If the inexpressible cruelties of slavery could not stop us, the opposition we now face will surely fail. We will win our freedom because the sacred heritage of our nation and the eternal will of God are embodied in our echoing demands. . . .

Yours for the cause of Peace and Brotherhood,

MARTIN LUTHER KING, JR.

---

[4]Founded in Detroit in the early 1930s, the Black Muslims in 1934 came under the leadership of Elijah Muhammad, a Georgian originally named Elijah Poole. He moved the organization's headquarters to Chicago, where he preached black self-reliance and separatism from white society. At the time of his death in 1975, Black Muslims numbered between one hundred fifty thousand and two hundred thousand.

The Beginnings of Modern Environmentalism

❖

73 ◆ *Rachel Carson, SILENT SPRING*

American environmentalism can be traced back to the 1890s, when rapid urbanization and the closing of the frontier gave rise to the conservation movement. Its leading advocates were Gifford Pinchot (1865–1946), who sought to protect the nation's forests, rivers, minerals, and grazing lands through scientific planning and regulation, and John Muir (1838–1914), who advocated preserving land as permanent wilderness. Conservation was a priority for President Theodore Roosevelt (1901–1908), who tripled the size of the forest reserves to 150 million acres and established dozens of wildlife refuges. New programs followed in the 1920s and 1930s. Among them was the Civil Conservation Corps, the Depression-era brain-child of President Franklin D. Roosevelt that in 1933 began to provide jobs for millions of young men who worked on reforestation and flood-control projects, built roads and bridges in national forests and parks, and fought forest fires.

For most of the twentieth century, however, environmental issues in the United States truly mattered to only small numbers of government officials and private citizens. This changed dramatically in the 1960s, when millions of Americans became deeply apprehensive about environmental degradation and committed themselves to a wide spectrum of environmental causes. It was easy for Americans to sense that things had gone drastically wrong when they could no longer swim or fish in dying lakes and rivers, listened to daily smog reports on the radio, and watched mountains of garbage pile up in their landfills. To a remarkable degree, however, this new environmental consciousness also resulted from the impact of a single book, *Silent Spring,* whose publication in 1963 can be said to mark the beginning of the modern environmental movement in the United States.

The author of *Silent Spring,* Rachel Carson, was a gifted writer and scientist from Pennsylvania who graduated from the Pennsylvania College for Women in Pittsburgh in 1925 and received further education at the Woods Hole Marine Biology Laboratory in Massachusetts and at Johns Hopkins University. She com-bined careers as a writer and as an official in the U.S. Fish and Wildlife Service until the royalties from her bestseller *The Sea Around Us* allowed her to devote herself completely to research and writing in 1952. Another bestseller, *The Edge of the Sea,* followed in 1955. Then in 1963 she published *Silent Spring* on a topic suggested to her by a friend who was convinced that a spraying program to ex-terminate mosquitoes around her hometown of Duxbury, Massachusetts, was also killing birds. Carson's main target in *Silent Spring* was DDT (dichloro-diphenyl trichlorothane), one of the many synthetic hydrocarbon pesticides that was widely used in the 1950s. Although her book was attacked by the scientific establishment and the chemical industry, its solid research and passionate con-cern for nature struck a responsive chord among the American people. The book challenged scientists, politicians, and corporations to confront the environmental implications of their actions and galvanized citizens to take steps to stem the tide of pollution. Just seven years after the appearance of Carson's book and six years after her death in 1964, on Earth Day in April 1970 nearly every community in the nation and thousands of schools and universities sponsored some type of activity emphasizing the need for action to improve environmental quality.

QUESTIONS FOR ANALYSIS

1. In Carson's assessment, how severe are the environmental problems facing society? What is the basis of her assessment?
2. According to Carson, who is to blame for environmental problems in the United States?
3. How would you describe Carson's attitude toward nature?

4. In Carson's view, what ethical issues are involved in the use of herbicides and insecticides?
5. According to Carson, what fundamental ways of thinking about nature will need to be changed to avert further environmental catastrophe?
6. What are the qualities of Carson's book that account for its popularity and influence?

THE OBLIGATION TO ENDURE

The history of life on earth has been a history of interaction between living things and their surroundings. To a large extent, the physical form and the habits of the earth's vegetation and its animal life have been molded by the environment. Considering the whole span of earthly time, the opposite effect, in which life actually modifies its surroundings, has been relatively slight. Only within the moment of time represented by the present century has one species — man — acquired significant power to alter the nature of his world.

During the past quarter century this power has not only increased to one of disturbing magnitude but it has changed in character. The most alarming of all man's assaults upon the environment is the contamination of air, earth, rivers, and sea with dangerous and even lethal materials. This pollution is for the most part irrecoverable; the chain of evil it initiates not only in the world that must support life but in living tissues is for the most part irreversible. In this now universal contamination of the environment, chemicals are the sinister and little-recognized partners of radiation in changing the very nature of the world — the very nature of its life. . . .

The rapidity of change and the speed with which new situations are created follow the impetuous and heedless pace of man rather than the deliberate pace of nature. Radiation is no longer merely the background radiation of rocks, the bombardment of cosmic rays, the ultraviolet of the sun that have existed before there was any life on earth; radiation is now the unnatural creation of man's tampering with the atom. The chemicals to which life is asked to make its adjustment are no longer merely the calcium and silica and copper and all the rest of the minerals washed out of the rocks and carried in rivers to the sea; they are the synthetic creations of man's inventive mind, brewed in his laboratories, and having no counterparts in nature. . . .

These sprays, dusts, and aerosols are now applied almost universally to farms, gardens, forest, and homes — nonselective chemicals that have the power to kill every insect, the "good" and the "bad," to still the song of birds and the leaping of fish in the streams, to coat the leaves with a deadly film, and to linger on in the soil — all this though the intended target may be only a few weeds or insects. Can anyone believe it is possible to lay down such a barrage of poisons on the surface of the earth without making it unfit for all life? They should not be called "insecticides," but "biocides.". . .

Along with the possibility of the extinction of mankind by nuclear war, the central problem of our age has therefore become the contamination of man's total environment with such substances of incredible potential for harm — substances that accumulate in the tissues of plants and animals and even penetrate the germ cells to shatter or alter the very material of heredity upon which the shape of the future depends. . . .

All this has been risked — for what? Future historians may well be amazed by our distorted sense of proportion. How could intelligent beings seek to control a few unwanted species by a method that contaminated the entire environment and brought the threat of disease and death even to their own kind?

Yet this is precisely what we have done. . . .

EARTH'S GREEN MANTLE

. . . The earth's vegetation is part of a web of life in which there are intimate and essential relations between plants and the earth, between plants and other plants, between plants and animals. Sometimes we have no choice but to disturb these relationships, but we should do so thoughtfully, with full awareness that what we do may have consequences remote in time and place. But no such humility marks the booming "weed killer" business of the present day, in which soaring sales and expanding uses mark the production of plant-killing chemicals. . . .

The chemical weed killers are a bright new toy. They work in a spectacular way; they give a giddy sense of power over nature to those who wield them, and as for the long-range and less obvious effects — these are easily brushed aside as the baseless imaginings of pessimists. . . .

I know well a stretch of road where nature's own landscaping has provided a border of alder, viburnum, sweet fern, and juniper with seasonally changing accents of bright flowers, or of fruits hanging in jeweled clusters in the fall. . . . But the sprayers took over and the miles along that road became something to be traversed quickly, a sight to be endured with one's mind closed to thoughts of the sterile and hideous world we are letting our technicians make. But here and there authority had somehow faltered and by an unaccountable oversight there were oases of beauty in the midst of austere and regimented control — oases that made the desecration of the greater part of the road the more unbearable. In such places my spirit lifted to the sight of the drifts of white clover or the clouds of purple vetch with here and there the flaming cup of a wood lily.

Such plants are "weeds" only to those who make a business of selling and applying chemicals. In a volume of *Proceedings* of one of the weed-control conferences that are now regular institutions, I once read an extraordinary statement of a weed killer's philosophy. The author defended the killing of good plants "simply because they are in bad company." Those who complain about killing wildflowers along roadsides reminded him, he said, of antivivisectionists "to whom, if one were to judge by their actions, the life of a stray dog is more sacred than the lives of children." . . .

NEEDLESS HAVOC

[*Chapter 7 of* Silent Spring *describes the effects of spraying campaigns in Illinois and Michigan to eradicate Japanese beetles.*]

Perhaps no community has suffered more for the sake of a beetleless world than Sheldon, in eastern Illinois, and adjacent areas in Iroquois County. . . . The first "eradication" took place . . . when dieldrin[1] was applied to 1400 acres by air. Another 2600 acres were treated similarly in 1955, and the task was presumably considered complete. But more and more chemical treatments were called for, and by the end of 1961 some 131,000 acres had been covered. Even in the first years of the program it was apparent that heavy losses were occurring among wildlife and domestic animals. The chemical treatments were continued, nevertheless, without consultation with either the United States Fish and Wildlife Service or the Illinois Game Management Division. . . .

Conditions were made to order for poisoning insect-eating birds, both in the poisons used and in the events set in motion by their application. In the early programs at Sheldon, dieldrin was applied at the rate of 3 pounds to the acre. To understand its effect on birds one need only remember that in laboratory experiments on

---

[1]Dieldrin is an insecticide used in the 1950s and 1960s for mothproofing, termite control, and the extermination of mosquitoes, Japanese beetles, and tsetse flies. It was banned by the U.S. Environmental Protection Agency in 1974 except for use against termites.

quail dieldrin has proved to be about 50 times as poisonous as DDT. . . .

As the chemical penetrated the soil, poisoned beetle grubs crawled out on the surface of the ground, where they remained for some time before they died, attractive to insect-eating birds. Dead and dying insects of various species were conspicuous for about two weeks after the treatment. The effect on the bird populations could easily have been foretold. Brown thrashers, starlings, meadowlarks, grackles, and pheasants were virtually wiped out. Robins were "almost annihilated," according to the biologists' report. . . .

Incidents like the eastern Illinois spraying raise a question that is not only scientific but moral. The question is whether any civilization can wage relentless war on life without destroying itself, and without losing the right to be called civilized.

These insecticides are not selective poisons; they do not single out the one species of which we desire to be rid. Each of them is used for the simple reason that it is a deadly poison. It therefore poisons all life with which it comes in contact: the cat beloved of some family, the farmer's cattle, the rabbit in the field, and the horned lark out of the sky. These creatures are innocent of any harm to man. Indeed, by their very existence they and their fellows make his life more pleasant. Yet he rewards them with a death that is not only sudden but horrible. Scientific observers at Sheldon described the symptoms of a meadowlark found near death: "Although it lacked muscular coordination and could not fly or stand, it continued to beat its wings and clutch with its toes while lying on its side. Its beak was held open and breathing was labored." Even more pitiful was the mute testimony of the dead ground squirrels, which "exhibited a characteristic attitude in death. The back was bowed, and the forelegs with the toes of the feet tightly clenched were drawn close to the thorax . . . The head and neck were outstretched and the mouth often contained dirt, suggesting that the dying animal had been biting at the ground."

By acquiescing in an act that can cause such suffering to a living creature, who among us is not diminished as human being?

AND NO BIRDS SING

[*This is the concluding paragraph from Chapter 8, which describes the effects of insecticides on birds.*]

In each of these situations, one turns away to ponder the question: Who has made the decision that sets in motion these chains of poisonings, this ever-widening wave of death that spreads out, like ripples when a pebble is dropped into a still pond? Who has placed in one pan of the scales the leaves that might have been eaten by the beetles and in the other the pitiful heaps of many-hued feathers, the lifeless remains of the birds that fell before the unselective bludgeon of insecticidal poisons? Who has decided — who has the *right* to decide — for the countless legions of people who were not consulted that the supreme value is a world without insects, even though it be also a sterile world ungraced by the curving wing of a bird in flight? The decision is that of the authoritarian temporarily entrusted with power; he has made it during a moment of inattention by millions to whom beauty and the ordered world of nature still have a meaning that is deep and imperative.

THE OTHER ROAD

[*In the book's final Chapter, Carson makes a plea for the development and use of biological controls for insects populations. The book ends with the following words.*]

. . . As crude a weapon as the cave man's club, the chemical barrage has been hurled against the fabric of life — a fabric on the one hand delicate and destructible, on the other miraculously tough and resilient, and capable of striking back in unexpected ways. These extraordinary capacities of life have been ignored by the practitioners of chemical control who have brought to their task no "high-minded orientation," no humility before the vast forces with which they tamper.

The "control of nature" is a phrase conceived in arrogance, born of the Neanderthal age of biology and philosophy, when it was supposed that nature exists for the convenience of man. The concepts and practices of applied entomology for the most part date from the Stone Age of science. It is our alarming misfortune that so primitive a science has armed itself with the most modern and terrible weapons, and that in turning them against the insects it has also turned them against the earth.

The Late 1960s: Years of Protest and Polarization

In 1960 the Student League for Industrial Democracy had chapters on three campuses — Michigan, Columbia, and Yale — and fewer than one hundred members. In that same year, however, with a new name — Students for Democratic Society (SDS) — and an increasingly radical agenda, the organization began to grow. By 1962 it had one thousand members, by 1964, twenty-five hundred members, and by 1968, more than one hundred thousand members on some three hundred campuses. In 1968 and 1969 the SDS played a key role in organizing demonstrations, sit-ins, teach-ins, student strikes, and building takeovers at Columbia, Harvard, Cornell, Berkeley, and other campuses across the country. With its radical critique of American higher education, its denunciations of corporate and bureaucratic power, and its opposition to the war in Vietnam, the SDS became a symbol of youthful political rebellion and a leading representative of the New Left.

The meteoric rise of the SDS from a fringe organization to a major, though ephemeral, force in American politics is just one example of the swift and bewildering changes that took place in the United States and Europe in the late 1960s and the early 1970s. Large numbers of previously apathetic young people, galvanized by their opposition to the war in Vietnam, rejected the values of consumerism, capitalism, imperialism, and the Cold War; rebelled against the authority of parents, teachers, politicians, corporations, and university administrators; and sought to "change the system" through campus activism and antiwar demonstrations. In 1968 student strikes and building takeovers took place at dozens of universities in Europe and the United States; militants viewed these actions as the first steps toward the destruction of capitalism and the end of bureaucratic oppression.

While many thousands of young people were drawn to radical politics, others rebelled against traditional values by becoming part of the counterculture. For a small minority this meant joining a rural commune or moving to a neighborhood such as Haight-Ashbury in San Francisco, where "hippies" embraced an alternative lifestyle based on sharing, free love, peace, and the copious use of marijuana and psychedelic drugs. Those not ready to "drop out," stayed in school or kept their jobs, joined the youth rebellion by wearing long hair and tie-dyed shirts, listening to acid rock, smoking pot, denouncing war, and ridiculing the values of their parents' generation.

Feminism also underwent far-reaching changes in the late 1960s. The moderate feminism that had grown in Europe and the United States after the publication of Simone de Beauvoir's *The Second Sex* in 1949 and Betty Friedan's *The Feminine Mystique* in 1963 gave way to the women's liberation movement. Many feminists became radical and confrontational, with an agenda that went beyond better pay, easier divorces, legalized abortions, and equal opportunities in jobs, schools, and athletics. Radical feminists questioned marriage, saw men as the enemy, and sought nothing less than the complete liberation of women from the weight of sexual taboos, archaic stereotypes, and male authority.

The struggle for civil rights in the United States also became more radical and confrontational. Beginning with the Watts riots in Los Angeles in 1965 and continuing for three more "long, hot summers," blacks in the nation's inner cities expressed their rage through a series of destructive riots. Leadership in the civil rights movement shifted from moderate organizations such as the National Association for the Advancement of Colored People (NAACP) and the Southern Christian Leadership Council (SCLC) to groups that rejected white members, appealed to black pride, and repudiated Martin Luther King, Jr.'s gospel of nonviolence. They included the Congress for Racial Equality (CORE), the Black Muslims, the Black Panthers, and the Student Nonviolent Coordinating Committee (SNCC). The Black Panthers donned menacing paramilitary outfits and carried rifles, while H. Rap Brown of SNCC announced that "if America don't come around, we're going to burn it down."

The storm of youthful protest and rebellion in the late 1960s was intense but brief. In Europe, the university strikes of May and June 1968 were never repeated. In the United States, campus demonstrations continued for a time, with the largest protests taking place in May 1970 after the shooting by National Guard troops of four Kent State University students who were protesting the U.S. invasion of Cambodia. Within two years after the Kent State protests, however, the SDS had broken apart; Haight-Ashbury had become a neighborhood of hard drugs, crime, and derelicts; "Black Power" was a forgotten motto; and radical feminism had lost much of its appeal.

Despite the brevity of the youth rebellion, neither Europe nor the United States would ever be the same after the assault of the 1960s on hierarchy, privilege, and tradition. Black violence and militancy forced white Americans to confront their racist past and made them appreciate the depth of black anger. Similarly, radical feminism alerted the European and American public to the full range of women's grievances, leading to expanded opportunities for women in schools, professions, marriage, and athletics. The counterculture did not inspire widespread acceptance of free love, but it did help dissolve the repressive sexual atmosphere of the 1950s. Campus protests helped end American involvement in Vietnam, brought about important changes in higher education, and created a culture of campus activism whose idealism and spirit were later redirected to causes such as environmentalism. Although no governments were toppled and no new utopias were achieved, the radical protests of the late 1960s had a permanent, perhaps even revolutionary impact on Western culture, values, and politics.

From Civil Rights to Black Power

◆

74 ◆ *Student Nonviolent Coordinating Committee,* *WE WANT BLACK POWER*

By the mid 1960s the civil rights movement in the United States had made impressive gains. Legal segregation in the South had been eliminated through Supreme Court decisions and legislation such as the Civil Rights Act of 1964 and the Voting Rights Act of 1965. But legal and legislative victories did not translate into jobs, higher standards of living, or the end of de facto segregation and prejudice. Millions of blacks, both those in the South and those who had migrated to northern cities, lived in poverty, a fact highlighted by the efforts of the Johnson administration in 1964 and 1965 to eliminate poverty through its War on Poverty and Great Society programs. Rising expectations frustrated by poverty and prejudice stoked African-American anger, an anger that changed the nature of the civil rights movement and translated into riots in more than three hundred cities between 1964 and 1968.

The radicalization of the civil rights movement is epitomized by the history of the Student Nonviolent Coordinating Committee (SNCC), an organization mainly of college students founded in 1960 as a spinoff of Martin Luther King, Jr.'s Southern Christian Leadership Council. SNCC members led the fight for the integration of stores and restaurants in the South through sit-ins, and in 1964 organized a Freedom Summer in Mississippi to register black voters and teach literacy and black history in Freedom Schools. Nearly sixty thousand black Mississippians were registered to vote, but at great cost. Thirty buildings were bombed, hundreds of SNCC members were beaten and arrested, and seven members were murdered.

In 1966 a militant faction won control of the organization when it elected as chairman Stokely Carmichael, a recent graduate of Howard University in Washington, D.C. In 1966 Carmichael first began the chant "Black Power! Black Power!" in a speech during a civil rights march from Memphis, Tennessee, to Jackson, Mississippi. Soon "Black Power" replaced "We Shall Overcome" and "Freedom Now" as the slogan for the civil rights movement.

The Black Power movement had antecedents in Marcus Garvey's back-to-Africa crusade of the 1920s and organizations such as the Nation of Islam, founded in the 1930s, which called for a separate black nation. In the late 1960s Black Power became a rallying cry for black militancy and was embraced by the Congress for Racial Equality (CORE), the Black Panthers, and SNCC. A nebulous term, Black Power could mean black pride, black control of black communities, and resistance to assimilation into a totally integrated society. To some, however, it also meant hatred and an endorsement of violence, as is clear from the following pamphlet issued by SNCC in 1967, the year in which urban violence in the United States peaked.

QUESTIONS FOR ANALYSIS

1. What goals are defined in this document for the Black Power movement?
2. Why do the authors of the pamphlet believe that creating a black culture is so important to their goals?
3. According to the leaflet, why are ghetto blacks most suited to leading the Black Power movement?
4. What views of whites are contained in the pamphlet?
5. In what specific ways do the ideas expressed in this leaflet differ from those of Martin Luther King, Jr., in his Letter from Birmingham Jail (source 72)?

The black man in America is in a perpetual state of slavery no matter what the white man's propaganda tells us.

The black man in America is exploited and oppressed the same as his black brothers are all over the face of the earth by the same white man. We will never be free until we are all free and that means all black oppressed people all over the earth.

We are not alone in this fight, we are a part of the struggle for self-determination of all black men everywhere. We here in America must unite ourselves to be ready to help our brothers elsewhere.

We must first gain BLACK POWER here in America. Living inside the camp of the leaders of the enemy forces, it is our duty to our Brothers to revolt against the system and create our own system so that we can live as MEN.

We must take over the political and economic systems where we are in the majority in the heart of every major city in this country as well as in the rural areas. We must create our own black culture to erase the lies the white man has fed our minds from the day we were born. . . .

The black Brother in the ghetto will lead the Black Power Movement and make changes that are necessary for its success.

The black man in the ghetto has one big advantage that the bourgeois Negro does not have despite his "superior" education. He is already living outside the value system white society imposes on all black Americans.

He has to look at things from another direction in order to survive. He is ready. He received his training in the streets, in the jails, from the ADC[1] check his mother did not receive in time and the head-beatings he got from the cop on the corner. . . .

Once he makes that first important discovery about the great pride you feel inside as a BLACK MAN and the great heritage of the mother country, Africa, there is no stopping him from dedicating himself to fight the white man's system. . . .

The bourgeois Negro has been force-fed the white man's propaganda and has lived too long in the half-world between white and phony black bourgeois society. He cannot think for himself because he is a shell of a man full of

---

[1]ADC stands for Aid to Dependent Children, a form of welfare payment.

contradictions he cannot resolve. He is not to be trusted under any circumstances until he has proved himself to be "cured." There are a minute handful of these "cured" bourgeois Negroes in the Black Power Movement and they are most valuable but they must not be allowed to take control. . . .

We have to all learn to become leaders for ourselves and remove all white values from our minds. When we see a Brother using a white value through error, it is our duty to the Movement to point it out to him. We must thank our Brothers who show us our own errors. . . .

As a part of our education, we must travel to other cities and make contacts with the Brothers in all the ghettos in America so that when the time is right we can unite as one under the banner of BLACK POWER. . . .

We have to learn that black is so much better than belonging to the white race with the blood of millions dripping from their hands that it goes far beyond any prejudice or resentment. We must fill ourselves with hate for all white things. This is not vengeance or trying to take the white oppressors' place to become new black oppressors but is a oneness with a worldwide black brotherhood.

We must regain respect for the lost religion of our fathers, the spirits of the black earth of Africa. The white man has so poisoned our minds that if a Brother told you he practiced Voodoo, you would roll around on the floor laughing at how stupid and superstitious he was.

We have to learn to roll around on the floor laughing at the black man who says he worships the white Jesus. He is truly sick. . . .

We must infiltrate all government agencies. This will not be hard because black clerks work in all agencies in poor-paying jobs and have a natural resentment of the white men who run these jobs.

People must be assigned to seek out these dissatisfied black men and women and put pressure on them to give us the information we need. Any man in overalls, carrying a tool box, can enter a building if he looks like he knows what he is doing.

Modern America depends on many complex systems such as electricity, water, gas, sewerage, and transportation, and all are vulnerable. Much of the government is run by computers that must operate in air conditioning. Cut off the air conditioning and they cannot function.

We must begin to investigate and learn all these things so that we can use them if it becomes necessary. We cannot train an army in the local park, but we can be ready for the final confrontation with the white man's system.

Remember your Brothers in South Africa and do not delude yourselves that it could not happen here. . . .

We must stop fighting a "fair game." We must do whatever is necessary to win BLACK POWER. We must have to hate and disrupt and destroy and blackmail and lie and steal and become blood-brothers like the Mau-Mau.[2]

We must eliminate or render ineffective all traitors. We must make them fear to stand up like puppets for the white men, and we must make the world understand that these so-called men do not represent us or even belong to the same black race because they sold out their birthright for a mess of white society pottage.[3] Let them choke on it. . . .

The political system, economic system, military system, educational system, religious system, and anything else you name is used to

---

[2]Mau-Mau refers to a militant nationalist movement directed against British rule that originated among the Kikuyu people of Kenya in the 1950s. In 1952 the British government launched a military operation against the Mau-Mau movement that lasted until 1956 and cost tens of thousands of lives.

[3]Genesis 25 and 27 tell the story of how Esau, the other son of the patriarch Isaac, sold his birthright to his younger brother, Jacob, for a "mess of pottage" is a moment of hunger.

preserve the status quo of white America getting fatter and fatter while the black man gets more and more hungry.

We must spend our time telling our Brothers the truth.

We must tell them that any black woman who wears a diamond on her finger is wearing the blood of her Brothers and Sisters in slavery in South Africa, where one out of every three black babies dies before the age of one, from starvation, to make the white man rich.

We must stop wearing the symbols of slavery on our fingers.

We must stop going to other countries to exterminate our Brothers and Sisters for the white man's greed.

We must ask our Brothers which side they are on.

Once you know the truth for yourself, it is your duty to dedicate your life to recruiting your Brothers and to counteract the white man's propaganda.

We must disrupt the white man's system to create our own. We must publish newspapers and get radio stations. Black Unity is strength — let's use it now to get BLACK POWER.

The Emergence of Militant Feminism

◆

75 ◆ *FEMINIST MANIFESTOES FROM THE LATE 1960S*

After having won the right to vote in most Western democracies by the 1920s, the powerful feminist movements of the nineteenth and early twentieth centuries lost momentum. In the 1930s and 1940s women diverted their energies to surviving the Great Depression and winning World War II. In the immediate postwar years, with a return of prosperity, women in the United States and Europe were content to accept the domestic role prescribed for them by the family-centered ethos of the postwar era.

Beginning in the 1960s, feminism reemerged as a powerful force, with its impetus and energy derived from ideas and movements originating in the United States. The revival of feminism began in the early 1960s with the appointment of President Kennedy of the Presidential Commission on the Status of Women in 1961, the publication of Betty Friedan's *The Feminine Mystique* in 1963, and the inclusion of gender as one of the categories protected by the Civil Rights Act of 1964. The National Organization for Women (NOW), which concentrated on redressing gender-based vocational and educational inequalities, seemed ready after its founding in 1966 to assume leadership of a new feminist movement that was moderate and liberal.

Within only a few years, however, calls for legal equality gave way to angry demands for women's liberation, as the feminist movement, like the civil rights movement, became increasingly radical and militant. Radical feminists of the late 1960s were young, and, like the black militants, were angered by the huge disparity between American rhetoric about equality and the reality of their lives. Beginning in 1967 and 1968 the first radical feminist groups formed in Chicago, New York, and San Francisco, and the first radical feminist journals began to appear. In 1968 the New York Radical Women pioneered the technique of consciousness-raising, in which women met to participate in open-ended discussions of how societal oppression affected their personal lives.

Then in September 1968 an event took place that catapulted radical feminism into the headlines and made "women's liberation" a household phrase. On September 7, several hundred women, organized by the New York Radical Feminists, converged on Atlantic City, New Jersey, to protest the Miss America Pageant. Convinced that the Pageant epitomized the evils of gender stereotyping, the women picketed, tossed symbols of female enslavement and torture (high heels, girdles, bras, and kitchen detergents) into a trash can, briefly interrupted the nationally televised closing ceremony, and crowned a sheep as Miss America. While picketing, they handed out the ten-point manifesto included below.

Lavishly covered by the media, the Atlantic City demonstration brought the new feminist agenda into the limelight and was a catalyst for a half-decade of intense activity on behalf of women's liberation. Women demanded legalized abortion, denounced sexism in language and advertising, produced a huge quantity of feminist literature and scholarships, and founded hundreds of feminist organizations. Among them was the Westchester Radical Feminists, organized by suburban New York women in 1972. Their manifesto, printed below, offers an opportunity to compare their views with those of another suburban New York woman, Betty Friedan, whose *The Feminine Mystique* had appeared just nine years earlier.

QUESTIONS FOR ANALYSIS

1. According to the Atlantic City protesters, what qualities are rewarded in the Miss America Pageant? How is this a disservice to American women in general?
2. What does the document reveal about links between the Miss America Pageant protest and other protest movements of the late 1960s?
3. According to the Atlantic City protesters, what flaws in American life other than sexism does the Miss America Pageant reveal?
4. According to the Westchester manifesto, what is the underlying cause of female oppression?
5. What, according to the Westchester feminists, must be changed in U.S. society to achieve "women's liberation"?
6. How do the issues and tone of these two manifestoes differ from those of Friedan's *The Feminine Mystique*?

NO MORE MISS AMERICA

On September 7th in Atlantic City, the Annual Miss America Pageant will again crown "your ideal." But this year, reality will liberate the contest auction-block in the guise of "genyooine" de-plasticized, breathing women. Women's Liberation Groups, black women, high-school and college women, women's peace groups, women's welfare and social-work groups, women's job-equality groups, pro-birth control and pro-abortion groups — women of every political persuasion — all are invited to join us in a day-long boardwalk-theater event, starting at 1:00 p.m. on the boardwalk in front of Atlantic City's Convention Hall. . . .

Male reporters will be refused interviews. We reject patronizing reportage. *Only newswomen will be recognized.*

The Ten Points
We Protest:

1. The *Degrading Mindless-Boob-Girlie Symbol.* The Pageant contestants epitomize the roles we are all forced to play as women. The parade down the runway blares the metaphor of the 4-H Club county fair, where the nervous animals are judged for teeth, fleece, etc., and where the best "specimen" gets the blue ribbon. So are women in our society forced daily to compete for male approval, enslaved by ludicrous "beauty" standards we ourselves are conditioned to take seriously.

2. *Racism with Roses.* Since its inception in 1921, the Pageant has not had one Black finalist, and this has not been for a lack of test-case contestants. There has never been a Puerto Rican, Alaskan, Hawaiian, or Mexican-American winner. Nor has there ever been a *true* Miss America — an American Indian.

3. *Miss America as Military Death Mascot.* The highlight of her reign each year is a cheerleader-tour of American troops abroad — last year she went to Vietnam to pep-talk our husbands, fathers, sons and boyfriends into dying and killing with a better spirit. She personifies the "unstained patriotic American womanhood our boys are fighting for." The Living Bra and the Dead Soldier. We refuse to be used as Mascots for Murder.

4. *The Consumer Con-Game.* Miss America is a walking commercial for the Pageant's sponsors. Wind her up and she plugs your product on promotion tours and TV — all in an "honest, objective" endorsement. What a shill.

5. *Competition Rigged and Unrigged.* We deplore the encouragement of an American

myth that oppresses men as well as women: the win-or-you're-worthless competitive disease. The "beauty contest" creates only one winner to be "used" and forty-nine losers who are "useless."

6. *The Woman As Pop Culture Obsolescent Theme.* Spindle, mutilate, and then discard tomorrow. What is so ignored as last year's Miss America? This only reflects the gospel of our society, according to Saint Male: women must be young, juicy, malleable — hence age discrimination and the cult of youth. And we women are brainwashed into believing this ourselves!

7. *The Unbeatable Madonna-Whore Combination.* Miss America and Playboy's centerfold are sisters over the skin. To win approval, we must be both sexy and wholesome, delicate but able to cope, demure yet titillatingly bitchy. Deviation of any sort brings, we are told, disaster: "You won't get a man!!"

8. *The Irrelevant Crown on the Throne of Mediocrity.* Miss America represents what women are supposed to be: unoffensive, bland, apolitical. If you are tall, short, over or under what weight The Man prescribes you should be, forget it. Personality, articulateness, intelligence, commitment — unwise. Conformity is the key to the crown — and, by extension, to success in our society.

9. *Miss America as Dream Equivalent To — ?* In this reputedly democratic society, where every little boy supposedly can grow up to be President, what can every little girl hope to grow up to be? Miss America. That's where it's at. Real power to control our own lives is restricted to men, while women get patronizing pseudopower, an ermine cloak and a bunch of flowers; men are judged by their actions, women by their appearance.

10. *Miss America as Big Sister Watching You.* The Pageant exercises Thought Control, attempts to sear the Image onto our minds,

to further make women oppressed and men oppressors; to enslave us all the more in high-heeled, low-status roles; to inculate false values in young girls; to use women as beasts of buying; to seduce us to prostitute ourselves before our own oppression.

WESTCHESTER RADICAL FEMINISTS' MANIFESTO

Suburban women, in common with all women, have lived in intimacy with and dependence on our oppressor. In isolation and tightly bound to our families, we have viewed the world and our condition from the level of patriarchal ideas of money and power. We now recognize that these patriarchal concepts have and still do dominate and control our lives, but our thinking, hopes and aspirations are changing. . . .

As suburban women, we recognize that many of us live in more economic and material comfort than our urban sisters, but we have come to realize through the woman's movement, feminist ideas and consciousness raising, that this comfort only hides our essential powerlessness and oppression. . . . Like dogs on a leash, our own status and power will reach as far as our husbands and their income and prestige will allow. As human beings, as individuals, we, in fact, own very little and should our husbands leave us or us them, we will find ourselves with the care and responsibility of children and without money, jobs, credit or power. For this questionable condition, we have paid the price of isolation and exploitation by the institutions of marriage, motherhood, psychiatry and consumerism. Although our life styles may appear materially better, we are, as all women, dominated by men at home, in bed and on the job; emotionally, sexually, domestically and financially. . . .

We believe that:

1. The notion of fixed sex roles is arbitrary and unjust.

2. That suburbia is a wasteland; a human ghetto for women minimizing their opportunity for growth.

3. That diverse forms of sexual relationships based on mutual consent are a matter of individual choice and right.

4. The institution of marriage presumes and establishes the lifelong servitude of women.

5. All economic institutions subject and deprive the suburban women, as well as all women, of economic power; even her power as a consumer is a myth since she spends and buys no more than her husband will allow.

6. Women are no more inherently suited to child rearing than men and men must be held responsible also for the emotional, educational and physical development of children.

7. The mutual dependence of mothers and children is in essence an act of tyranny which serves to thwart, retard and immobilize both mother and children.

8. The adjustment theories adhered to by most psychologists and psychiatrists and their institutions perpetuate destructive attitudes towards women, undermine their self value and self esteem and are generally harmful to the wholesome development and welfare of women.

9. The fact that we live with and even support some of these institutions which are sexist does not in any way alter our basic beliefs. We presently live the way we do because there are no good alternatives.

10. Women's liberation is not human liberation and we place the cause of women above all other causes.

11. We are committed to the understanding of our condition as women so that we may create and invent new ways to live and to find both collective and individual realization and strength.

Campus Outrage

❖

76 ◆ *THREE STUDENT PAMPHLETS FROM THE UNIVERSITY OF PARIS*

During the 1960s, the number of students enrolled in universities in Europe and the United States had never been higher. In prewar Germany, Great Britain, and France, with a combined population of 150,000,000, only 150,000 attended universities — approximately one-tenth of 1 percent of the total population. Between 1960 and 1970, however, the number of French university students increased more than threefold, from 211,000 to 651,000, while in Great Britain, West Germany, and Italy, the student population doubled. In the United States, which had pioneered mass college education, the 1960s began with 3,789,000 university students and ended with 7,850,000. For the first time in the history of the United States, or of any nation, there were more university students than farmers.

As the numbers of university students grew, so did their political activism. In 1964 the Berkeley campus of the University of California was disrupted by student strikes, demonstrations, and clashes with police when the Free Speech Movement challenged the university's decision to ban political and civil rights groups from using a strip of land at the edge of the campus. In 1965 the first teach-in protesting the Vietnam War took place at the University of Michigan, and by 1967 student-led campaigns against draft boards, ROTC programs, university research for the Defense Department, and campus recruitment by corporations such as the Dow Chemical Company (the maker of napalm) made college campuses the core of the antiwar movement. In Europe in the mid 1960s, the Socialist German Student League organized demonstrations against the Vietnam War, imperialism, and right-wing politicians, and Italian students occupied buildings and clashed with police to show their disgust with university policies and practices.

None of this prepared the world for the eruptions on European and American campuses in 1968, however. With a fury no one could have predicted, hundreds of thousands of students across Europe and the United States violently challenged the established order in campus takeovers, riots, and street clashes. Although opposition to U.S. involvement in Vietnam was a common theme — indeed, the dominant theme in the United States — no single cause or issue was at stake in the youth rebellion. In Berlin, student ire focused on the Springer Press, a chain of right-wing newspapers and publishing outlets that students blamed for inspiring the attempted assassination of the student radical Rudi Dutschke. In Italy, the issue was an authoritarian and impersonal university system characterized by decaying buildings and indifferent professors. At Nanterre, a branch campus of the University of Paris, it was sexual segregation in the dormitories. At Columbia, it was the university's plan to build a new gymnasium on land that included a neighborhood playground.

Although student rebellions shocked the public and unsettled authorities in the United States, Germany, and Italy, in France they came close to launching a revolution. The student rebellion began at the Nanterre campus, a new branch of the University of Paris built in the midst of one of France's worst slums. Agitation over teaching issues, examinations, and the right of males to visit females in their dormitories caused the dean to suspend classes on May 2. Nanterre student leaders then joined forces with radicals at the University of Paris, where demonstrations involving tens of thousands of students led to arrests, further demonstrations, and bloody clashes with riot police. In mid May, industrial workers, who were concerned with rising unemployment and stagnant wages, threw in their lot with the students and joined them in a march through Paris with six hundred fifty thousand to seven hundred thousand participants. In the following days, students reoccupied the university district, the Sorbonne, and approximately ten million workers, about 60 percent of the work force, went on strike. Revolution seemed imminent.

In late May and early June, however, the movement lost momentum in the face of a tough speech by President de Gaulle, a promised wage increase for workers, counterdemonstrations organized by the government, and ideological fissures among the students. After a final clash between police and students on June 12, 1968, students abandoned control of the Sorbonne, and workers ended their general strike. In parliamentary elections held in late June, de Gaulle's party, the Union for the Defense of the Republic, won a resounding victory. The student revolution in Paris was over, leaving a legacy of modest reforms in the French university system and the memory of idealistic young people who thought they could change the world.

The weeks of protest in France produced a mountain of pamphlets, manifestoes, editorials, speeches, and proclamations. The following three selections provide a sample of the profusion of ideas that was generated. The first, "How to Train a Stuffed Goose," is from a pamphlet, *Stuffed Geese,* circulated in February or March 1968 on the Nanterre campus. The second, "Why We Are Fighting," is an editorial printed on May 7 in *Action,* a pro-student newspaper. The third, "Your Struggle Is Our Struggle," is a proclamation issued on May 24 by the Movement of March 22, a student organization that had originated at Nanterre.

QUESTIONS FOR ANALYSIS

1. What image of French student life is portrayed in the pamphlet *Stuffed Geese*?
2. How do the views of the remaining two selections resemble and differ from those expressed in *Stuffed Geese*?
3. What do the three selections reveal about students' concerns and worries about their futures?
4. What are the students' views of the role that universities have played in French society? How do the students want to change that role?
5. Why, according to the last selection, is the students' struggle similar to that of the workers?
6. If the students had been given the opportunity of completely reshaping the French universities according to their ideas, what would these universities have looked like?

"HOW TO TRAIN A STUFFED GOOSE"

Lethargy, disappointment, and disgust compose the daily atmosphere of all lecture halls, nor is this peculiar to the first year. Collapse of any real vocation, dearth of professional openings and esteem, a specialty that boils down to making children count red balls and blue balls, these are the ultimate results for psychologists and sociologists of years of "study," during which all real value, all intellectual dynamism has been nibbled away. . . . Actually what the [faculty] offers us, when what we are looking for are possibilities of extending our mental horizons, is a crude paternalism which, by promoting the breeding of "stuffed geese". . . maintains us in a state of intellectual sterility. . . .

Teaching Methods

Existing To begin with, this type of teaching bores us even before we become disgusted by its mechanical, deadly aspects, as also by the banality and extremely insipid way it is presented. The student, being unconcerned by its insipidness, and maintained in a state of mental passivity, becomes a mere scribe who copies the teacher's lifeless words; later, these copies will be useful to him, since he will reproduce them, without omitting a comma, on his examination paper, as he is required to do by the teacher.

Demanded . . . We demand the introduction of genuine dialogue, of real student-professor cooperation. We demand that the insipidness and lethargy of the lecture halls be replaced by an atmosphere of life, enthusiasm, research, and real work in common. We demand that the courses . . . contain an incitement to original thought and research in the form of bibliographical information that corresponds to precise problems. Then the students will be able to work intelligently on real problems, analyze bibliographic relationships, and discuss among themselves, during their "work group" meetings, all the results of their individual research. In this way they will be glad to attend classes, since these

classes will finally be discussion meetings in which a dialogue will be set up between the professor and the students. . . .

Examinations

Existing Copying: obviously, any eighth grader would exult in such tests as these, which would recall his easiest written interrogations. He would excel in these exams because he would lend himself perfectly to these checkups merely of the student's faculty of memory. . . . He would act in this way just as lots of us have acted because they had understood how to meet the requirements of an examination and how to get the approval of the teaching body, or at least of the assistants. Because quite evidently, for the latter, who give the validity of correction as alibi, the "value" of an answer is proportionate to the degree of perfection with which the lecture is copied, harking back to methods formerly used by primary school teachers for correcting their famous "*copy books.*"

Demanded Open books, justice: we demand that examinations be held with our books open, and should take into consideration, above all, the student's capacity for intellectual initiative and his powers of analysis and in-depth reflection and not, as now, merely the sterile feat of memory.

Doubtless this genuine examination by its very nature would challenge the competence of certain assistants today who, in their hasty, superficial correcting, are too accustomed not to see this capacity for intellectual initiative, and only understand the premise through the exactness of the copy. . . .

These basic demands are vital of us, and must be presented immediately to the faculty members.

"WHY WE ARE FIGHTING"

For years students have been protesting the authoritarian methods that the government wanted to force upon them. . . . For years, calmly, but also in an atmosphere of general indifference, the government ignored their protests just as it ignored the workers' protests. For years these protests remained vain and without response.

Today, the students are resisting.

Their only crime is to reject a University the sole goal of which is to train future bosses and docile tools for the economy. Their only crime is to reject an authoritarian and hierarchical social system which rejects any radical opposition; this means refusing to be the servants of this system.

For this crime alone, they are being rewarded by blackjacks and prison sentences. . . . In Paris and in Nanterre they are not fighting alone; they are not fighting only for themselves. In Germany, on May first, tens of thousands of students and workers were *together,* on the initiative of the SDS,[1] in the first anti-capitalist demonstration that has taken place in Berlin since [Nazism]. The "handful of agitators" became a mass movement. Those who are combating the capitalist University stood shoulder to shoulder with those who are combating capitalist exploitation.

In France we also know that our fight has only begun; we know that youth is sensitive to the capitalist crisis and to the crisis of imperialism oppressing people in Vietnam, in Latin America, everywhere in the Third World. In Redon, in Caen,[2] young workers are revolting violently, more violently than we are. . . . In spite of the government, in spite of the silence and the manipulations of its servile press, our struggle and theirs will converge.

Today students are becoming aware of what they are being trained for: to be managers for the existing economic system, paid to make it function in the best possible way. Their fight concerns all workers because it is also the workers' fight: they refuse to become professors in the service of an educational system which chooses the sons of the bourgeoisie and eliminates the others; sociologists who manufacture slogans for governmental election campaigns; psychologists responsible for making "worker teams function"

in the best interest of the employers; managers responsible for applying against the workers a system to which they themselves are subjected.

Young people in the high schools, universities, and from the working class reject the future offered them by today's society; they reject unemployment, which is becoming a growing threat; they reject today's University, which gives them only worthless, ultra-specialized training and which, under the pretext of "selection," reserves know-how for sons of the bourgeoisie, and is but a tool for repression of all non-conformist ideas in the interest of the ruling class.

"YOUR STRUGGLE IS OUR STRUGGLE"

We are occupying the [colleges]; you are occupying the factories. Are we both fighting for the same thing?

Ten percent of the students in higher education are sons of workers. Are we fighting so that there will be a higher percentage, for a democratic reform of the University? It would be better, but it is not the most important thing. These sons of workers will become students like any others. That a son of a worker might become a director is not in our program. We want to do away with the separation between workers, laborers, and managers. . . .

We refuse to be scholars cut off from social reality. We refuse to be used for the benefit of the ruling class. We want to do away with the separation between carrying out work and planning and organizing it. We want to construct a classless society; the goal of your struggle is the same.

You demand a minimum salary of 1,000 francs . . . in the Paris area, retirement at 60, and a 40-hour week at the same salary now paid for a 48-hour week.

---

[1]Sozialistische Deutsche Studentenbund, a Marxist student organization active in Germany during the 1960s. Not to be confused with the American Students for a Democratic Society.

[2]Caen and Redon were two of several cities in which wildcat strikes and workers' demonstrations led to violence in March and April 1968.

These demands are fair and they are not new. Nevertheless, they seem to have no connection with our goals. But in fact, you are occupying the factories, you are taking the employers as hostages, you are striking without previous notice. . . .

These struggles are more radical than your legitimate demands because they do not only seek the betterment of the workers' lot within the capitalist system, they imply the destruction of this system. They are political in the true sense of the word; you are not fighting to have the Prime Minister replaced, but so the employer will no longer be in power, either in the factory or in society. The form of your struggle presents us, students, with a model of truly socialist action: appropriation of the means of production and the power of decision by the workers.

Your fight and our fight are convergent. All that separates one from the other must be destroyed.

CHAPTER 10

Worlds Apart: The USSR, the Soviet Bloc, and China

For three decades after the Russian Revolution of 1917, the Union of Soviet Socialist Republics (USSR) stood alone as the world's only Marxist state. Then in the decade following World War II, it was joined by twelve others. In Europe, Albania, Yugoslavia, Poland, Hungary, Bulgaria, Romania, Czechoslovakia, and East Germany became communist states between 1945 and 1948, while in Asia, communist regimes were established in North Korea in 1945, China and Mongolia in 1949, and North Vietnam in 1954. Although a handful of states, most notably Cuba in 1959, later became communist, they were small and relatively insignificant. In large measure, the era of communist expansion was over by the mid 1950s. By then, approximately one-third of the world's people lived under communist rule.

Until the closing years of the twentieth century, these states existed in a largely self-contained universe separated economically and culturally from the rest of the world. This separation began in the 1920s and 1930s when most nations refused to have dealings with the Soviet Union and Stalin concentrated on building "socialism in one country." It widened after World War II when the mutual fears and hostilities generated by the Cold War created innumerable figurative and real barriers to trade, tourism, and cultural exchange.

During the 1950s and 1960s, self-contained development, not foreign trade, was the goal of communist economies, and what little foreign trade did take place was largely among the communist states themselves. Currencies of communist countries, such as the Soviet ruble and Chinese yuan, were not traded on international markets, and communist states did not participate in the International Monetary Fund or the General Agreement on Tariffs and Trade. Tourism between communist and noncommunist states was discouraged, and when journalists or scholars from one bloc visited a nation in the other ideological camp, their activities were closely monitored by police and intelligence officials. Government censorship guaranteed that people under communism had little accurate information about the outside world, while propaganda in capitalist states created distorted images of life under communism. The most powerful symbol of the division between the communist and noncommunist worlds was the Berlin Wall, a twenty-five mile barrier through Berlin constructed in 1961 on order of the East German government to stop the flight of its citizens to the West.

The world's communist states shared a number of common characteristics. Most, out of choice or coercion, at first modeled their political systems and economies on those of Stalin's Soviet Union. This meant control of the government by the Communist Party, and control of the Party by a dictator or a small handful of officials. It also meant abolition of rival political parties; eradication of opponents; the suppression of civil liberties; censorship; state control of newspapers, radio, and television; and the lavish use of propaganda. These states' economic policies also followed the Stalinist model of central planning, nationalization of major industries and businesses, and the collectivization of agriculture. The goal was rapid industrialization, with an emphasis on iron and steel, heavy machinery, and power generation rather than consumer goods. Most communist regimes were aggressively secular and sought to undermine established religions.

The communist states' allegiance to Marxist socialism and their shared hostility to the United States and its allies encouraged diplomatic and economic collaboration. In 1949 the Soviet Union and its European satellites formed the Council of Mutual Economic Assistance (COMECON) to coordinate economic planning, and in 1955 they ratified the Warsaw Pact, by which they pledged to come to one another's defense if attacked. The Soviet Union and China signed a pact of friendship and cooperation in 1950, and during the 1950s the Soviet Union provided China with financial and technical aid for economic development.

But there were fissures within the socialist camp from the start, and they widened with time. Yugoslavia's Marshal Tito gradually broke with Stalin in 1947 and 1948, and later refused to join COMECON or the Warsaw Pact. Albania at first aligned itself with the Soviet Union, then switched to China, and in the early 1970s embarked on an independent course. China and the Soviet Union became bitter antagonists in the 1960s, and in the 1970s many world leaders anticipated a full-scale war between the two communist powers.

Furthermore, many communist states sought to develop their own variety of socialism distinct from the Soviet model. China under Mao Zedong abandoned central planning during the Great Leap Forward between 1958 and 1960; Tito's Yugoslavia fashioned a mixed economy in the 1950s, as did Hungary on a lesser scale in the 1960s. Poland resisted both agricultural collectivization and suppression of the Roman Catholic Church. East Germany in 1953, Hungary in 1956, and Czechoslovakia in 1968 all experienced broad-based movements for democratization only to have them crushed by military force. Even the Soviet Union itself experimented with liberalization and economic reform after Stalin's death in 1953.

The new socialist family of nations was neither static nor lacking in disagreements. It was composed of states that struggled with issues of economic development, dissent, and the exercise of state power, and sought their own paths toward socialism within the constraints of Marxist /Leninist ideology. Given their unique histories, distinct cultures, and differing needs, this could hardly have been otherwise.

Dissent and Repression in the Soviet Union

The issue of whether political dissent should be tolerated in the Soviet Union was settled in 1921 when the Tenth Communist Party Conference banned all opposing political parties and outlawed factions within the Bolshevik Party itself. The issue of how much freedom of expression should be accorded to writers and artists was decided some years later. Under the tightening screws of Stalin's dictatorship, Soviet thought and culture were brought under control of the state in the 1930s, and scientists, writers, and artists were all required to serve Stalin and the Communist Party unequivocally. In 1934, 590 delegates to the First All-Union Congress of Soviet Writers approve the doctrine of "socialist realism," which required that all literature must promote the Party's goals and strengthen the masses' allegiance to socialism. During Stalin's purges between 1936 and 1938, writers who failed to pass the Party's test of ideological conformity were branded "enemies of the people." Hundreds disappeared without a trace. Temporarily relaxed during World Was II, rigid controls were revived after 1945.

Following Stalin's death in 1953, socialist realism continued to be the guiding principle of art and literature; but the dictator's demise ushered in a series of thaws and freezes in Soviet cultural and intellectual life that continued until the glasnost era of the mid 1980s. Nikita Khrushchev, Party secretary after Stalin's death and head of state after 1957, at first seemed sympathetic to greater artistic and intellectual freedom. As a member of the ruling collective that took power in 1953, he tolerated the outburst of literary creativity that followed Stalin's death. In 1956 he launched a campaign of destalinization after denouncing Stalin in a "secret speech" to the Twentieth Party Congress as a cruel, irrational tyrant. But destalinization under Khrushchev had its limits. Tugged and pulled between intellectuals who wanted more freedom and unrepentant Stalinists who yearned for the old controls, Khrushchev zigged and zagged between thaws and freezes. Before he fell from power in October 1964, he was tilting toward repression.

Tight controls and censorship continued under Khrushchev's cautious successors, Leonid Brezhnev and Alexis Kosygin. Nonconforming writers continued to produce literary works in great quantities, but with no publishing opportunities in the Soviet Union, they circulated them in handwritten, typed, or mimeographed version or had them published abroad. In 1966, however, the government sought to intimidate writers by bringing to trial and sentencing to hard labor two authors, Andrei Siniavsky and Juli Daniel, who had arranged to have their works smuggled into the Soviet Union after publication in the West. When outraged intellectuals campaigned to overturn the sentences, the government arrested four of their spokesmen in 1967, and gave them harsher punishments than those imposed on Siniavsky and Daniel.

The government's crackdown had unexpected results. Rather than silencing the intellectuals, it galvanized many of them to fight harder for their basic freedoms. In 1970 the physicist Andrei Sakharov organized the Human Rights Movement, and between 1968 and 1972, the underground journal *The Chronicle of Current Events* regularly published reports on human rights abuses. Other intellectuals were even bolder, addressing high government officials with demands for democratic reforms and criticism of policies such as the invasion of Czechoslovakia in 1968. The government responded by sending some of its more outspoken critics into exile or to psychiatric hospitals to cure their "insanity." But sensitivity to world opinion prevented harsher measures, and by the early 1970s, the Soviet secret police estimated that there were approximately three hundred thousand dissidents in the USSR, compared to just a few dozen a decade earlier. The tense standoff continued between intellectuals and their government as the Soviet Union drifted deeper into stagnation during the 1970s and early 1980s.

A Plea for Democratic Reform

❖

77 ❖ *Andrei Sakharov, Roy Medvedev, and Valentin Turchin,* LETTER TO COMRADES BREZHNEV, KOSYGIN, AND PODGORNY

By the late 1960s dissidents were no longer content to circulate their views in foreign publications or among themselves in "self-published' versions. They now addressed their leaders directly. One of the most important such appeals was a letter sent in 1970 to the three most powerful men in the Soviet government: Leonid Brezhnev, the Party secretary; Alexis Kosygin, premier; and Nicholas Podgorny, first secretary of the politburo. It was drafted by Andrei Sakharov, an internationally known thermonuclear physicist and three-time recipient of the Hero of Socialist Labor medal. In the late 1960s he became a critic of Soviet nuclear weapons testing and an advocate of civil liberties. He was awarded the Nobel Peace Prize in 1975 for his crusades advocating disarmament and democratization in the Soviet Union. The government refused him permission to leave the Soviet Union to receive the award, and in 1980 sent him into internal exile in the city of Gorky. Sakharov was released in 1986 and died three years later.

Sakharov's 1970 letter was sent to the Soviet leaders after it had been revised in minor ways and signed by two other dissidents, Roy Medvedev, a historian, and Valentin Turchin, a physicist. Although their call for the democratization of the Soviet Union was radical, they recommended a gradualist approach that would be implemented from above by the Party.

QUESTION FOR ANALYSIS

1. How would you characterize the three authors' attitude toward socialism and Marxism?
2. What, according to the authors, are the main problems facing the Soviet Union, and what has caused these problems?
3. How do the authors view the West?
4. What do the authors seem to mean by the term *democracy*?
5. How, in the authors' opinion, will democratic reforms help solve the Soviet Union's economic and political problems?

RESPECTED COMRADES:

Over the past decade, menacing signs of breakdown and stagnation have begun to show themselves in the economy of our country, the roots of which go back to an earlier period and are very deep-seated. . . . A great mass of data is available showing mistakes in the determination of technical and economic policy in industry and agriculture and an intolerable procrastination about finding solutions to urgent problems. Defects in the system of planning, accounting, and incentives often cause contradictions between local and departmental interests and those of the state and nation. As a result, new means of developing production potential are not being discovered or properly put to use, and technical progress has slowed down abruptly. For these very reasons, the natural wealth of the country is often destroyed with impunity and without any supervision or controls: forests are leveled, reservoirs polluted, valuable agricultural land flooded, soil eroded or salinized, and so on. The chronically difficult situation in agriculture, particularly in regard to livestock, is well known. The population's real income in recent years has hardly grown at all; food supply and medical and consumer services are improving very slowly,

and with unevenness between regions. The number of goods in short supply continues to grow. There are clear signs of inflation.

Of particular concern regarding our country's future is the lag in the development of education: our total expenditures for education in all forms are three times below what they are in the United States, and are rising at a slower rate. Alcoholism is growing in a tragic way, and drug addiction is beginning to surface. In many regions of the country, the crime rate is climbing systematically. Signs of corruption are becoming more and more noticeable in a number of places. In the work of scientific and scientific-technical organizations, bureaucratism, departmentalism, a formal attitude toward one's tasks, and lack of initiative are becoming more and more pronounced. . . .

In comparing our economy with that of the United States, we see that ours lags behind not only in quantitative but also — most regrettable of all — in qualitative terms. . . . We outstrip America in coal production, but we lag behind in the output of oil, gas, and electric power; we lag behind tenfold in the field of chemistry, and we are infinitely outstripped in computer technology. The latter is especially crucial, because the introduction of electronic computers into the economy is a phenomenon of decisive importance that radically changes the outlines of the production system and of the entire culture. . . . Nevertheless, our stock of computers is *1 percent* of that of the United States. . . . We simply live in another age.

Things are no better in the sphere of scientific and technological breakthroughs. Our role in this area has not advanced either. Rather, the contrary has been true. . . .

The source of our difficulties does not lie in the socialist system; on the contrary, it lies in those peculiarities and conditions of our life that run counter to socialism and are hostile to it. The source lies in the antidemocratic traditions and norms of public life established in the Stalin era, which have not been decisively eliminated to this day.

Noneconomic coercion, limitations on the exchange of information, restrictions on intellectual freedom, and other examples of the antidemocratic distortion of socialism that took place under Stalin were accepted in our country as an overhead expense of the industrialization process. . . . But there is no doubt that since the beginning of the second industrial revolution these phenomena have become a decisive economic factor; they have become the main brake on the development of the productive forces in this country. As a consequence of the increased size and complexity of economic systems, the problems of management and organization have moved to the forefront. . . . These problems demand the creative participation of millions of people on all levels of the economic system. They demand the broad exchange of information and ideas. . . .

However, we encounter certain insurmountable obstacles on the road toward the free exchange of ideas and information. Truthful information about our shortcomings and negative manifestations is hushed up on the grounds that it "may be used by enemy propaganda." Exchange of information with foreign countries is restricted for fear of "penetration by an enemy ideology." Theoretical generalizations and practical proposals, if they seem too bold to some individuals, are nipped in the bud without any discussion, because of the fear that they might "undermine our foundations." . . . Under such circumstances, the conditions are created for the advancement up the rungs of the official ladder not of those who distinguish themselves by their professional qualities and commitment to principles but of those who verbally proclaim their devotion to the Party but in practice are only concerned with their own narrow personal interests or are passive timeservers. . . .

The overwhelming majority of the intelligentsia and the youth recognize the need for democratization, and the need for it to be cautious and gradual, but they cannot understand or condone measures of a patently antidemocratic nature. And, indeed, how can one justify the confinement in prisons, camps, and insane asylums of people who hold oppositionist views but whose opposition stands on legal ground, in the area of ideas and convictions? In many instances, no opposition was involved, but only a striving for information, or simply a courageous and unprejudiced discussion of important social questions. . . .

. . . Democratization, with its fullness of information and clash of ideas, must restore to our ideological life its dynamism and creativity — in the social sciences, arts, and propaganda — and eliminate the bureaucratic, ritualistic, dogmatic, openly hypocritical, and mediocre style that reigns in these areas today. . . .

What is in store for our nation if it does not take the course toward democratization? The fate of lagging behind the capitalist countries and gradually becoming a second-rate provincial power . . .; the growth of economic difficulties; increasingly tense relations between the Party and government apparatus, on the one hand, and the intelligentsia, on the other; the danger of ill-considered moves to the left or right; exacerbation of national problems, because the movement for democratization emanating from below in the national republics inevitably assumes a nationalistic character. . . .

Respected comrades! There is no way out of the difficulties now facing our country except a course toward democratization, carried out by the Soviet Communist Party in accordance with a carefully worked-out plan. A turn to the right — that is, a victory for the forces that advocate a stronger administration, a "tightening of the screws" — would not only fail to solve any of the problems but, on the contrary, aggravate them to an extreme point and lead our country into a tragic impasse. The tactic of waiting passively would ultimately have the same result. Today, we still have the chance to take the right road and to carry out the necessary reforms. In a few years, it may be too late.

The Dissidents' Adversary

78 ◆ SECRET KGB REPORT, DECEMBER 21, 1970

With responsibility for domestic and foreign security, the KGB (*Komitét Gosudárstvennoĭ Bezopásnosti*), or the Committee on State Security, was both the Federal Bureau of Investigation and Central Intelligence Agency of the Soviet Union. Under Yuri Andropov, who was named director in 1967, the KGB established in 1969 a special division, the Fifth Main Directorate, to combat political opposition and to tighten control over the general population in the face of the emerging dissident movement. Dominated by hard-liners, the KGB submitted the following report on the dissident movement to Soviet leaders in December 1970.

QUESTION FOR ANALYSIS

1. According to the KGB report, what are the presuppositions of the democratic socialist movement concerning the Soviet Union's future?
2. What are the short-term goals of the democratic socialists, according to the KGB?
3. What does the report suggest about the strength of the democratic socialist movement?

TOP SECRET

Among the scientific, technical and part of the creative intelligentsia documents are being passed around in which various forms of 'democratic socialism' are being propounded. According to one of these schemes of 'democratic socialism', whose author is Academician Sakharov, the evolutionary path of internal political development of the USSR will inevitably lead to the creation in the country of a 'truly democratic system'. As part of this, mathematicians and economists should in good time develop its model so that it could be a synthesis of what is positive in existing socio-political systems.

In a number of projects for the 'democratization' of the USSR the 'restriction or liquidation of the monopoly power of the CPSU[1] and the national development of an opposition loyal to socialism' is envisaged. Their authors and

---

[1]Communist Party of the Soviet Union.

distributors consider that the current level of development of socialist democracy should allow opposition views to exist, and demand legal opportunities to express views that disagree with the official course to be made available. From this perspective they declare that criminal legislation that prosecutes anti-Soviet agitation and propaganda or the distribution of obviously false fabrications, smearing the Soviet state and its social system, it unconstitutional.

On the basis of the preparation and distribution of 'samizdat'[2] literature there is taking place a noticeable consolidation of like-minded persons, and there are marked indications of attempts to create something like an opposition.

Approximately towards the end of 1968–early 1969 there emerged out of oppositionally

minded elements a political core, called the 'democratic movement', which in their view has the three characteristics of an opposition: they 'have leaders, activists and are based on a significant number of sympathizers, not taking on the clear shape of an organisation, but set themselves clear aims and choose a suitable tactic, to gain legality'.

The main aims of the 'movement', as formulated in the thirteenth issue of *The Chronicle of Current Events* issued by the Moscow group of the 'democratic movement' headed by Yakir,[3] is 'the democratization of the country by developing in people democratic and scientific convictions, resistance to Stalinism, self-defence from repression, the struggle against extremism of whatever sort'.

---

[2]Literally, "self-publication." The term refers to the hand-copied, typed, or mimeographed writings circulated by dissidents whose work was denied publication by the government.
[3]Peter Yakir (1923–1986) was a historian imprisoned between 1937 and 1954 for being the son of Iona Yakir, a general who had been executed as an enemy of the people during

Stalin's purges. On his release, he studied at the Moscow State Historical Archive Institute, where he collected material on the abuse of psychiatry for political ends. After joining the dissident movement in 1966, he was arrested in 1972 and suffered a breakdown under interrogation. Freed in 1974, he lived in isolation in Moscow until his death.

◆

Unrest in Eastern Europe and Soviet Response

In February 1948, with communist trade unionists organized into armed "action units" and the Soviet army mobilized on his nation's borders, the president of Czechoslovakia, Eduard Beneš, agreed to an all-communist administration, and the Soviet Empire in Eastern Europe was complete. East Germany, Poland, Romania, Bulgaria, Hungary, and now Czechoslovakia were all one-party communist states that had been installed with the help of the Soviet army and were controlled by men willing to follow Moscow's line and turn their countries into small-scale replicas of the USSR. This meant the collectivization of agriculture, the nationalization of major industries, central planning, and an emphasis on heavy industry rather than consumer goods. It also meant the suppression of political opposition, the surveillance of intellectuals, attacks on the churches, censorship, show trials, and the imprisonment or execution of dissidents.

Despite strict state controls, protest and rebellion marked the forty-year history of the Soviet Empire. Soviet troops had to intervene in East Germany in

1953, when after Stalin's death, strikes in Berlin sparked nationwide demonstrations for better pay and free elections. Peace was restored, but several thousand civilians were killed and twenty thousand were arrested.

Serious disturbances took place in Poland and Hungary in 1956 after expectations for change were heightened by Khrushchev's destalinization campaign and his efforts to patch up differences with Yugoslavia, a communist state that had pursued an independent path toward socialism outside of the Soviet orbit. In Poland, nationwide demonstrations and strikes calling for economic reform, protection of the Catholic Church, and the removal of Soviet troops ended in a compromise between Khrushchev and Poland's new leader, Wladyslaw Gomulka: Poland would remain a one-party communist state and a member of the Warsaw Pact, but it would have more control over its domestic affairs.

In Hungary, protesters had a more ambitious agenda. They demanded free elections, the reinstatement of banned political parties, and Hungary's withdrawal from the Warsaw Pact. They also provoked a harsher Soviet response. In November, with the Hungarian security police disbanded, noncommunist political parties reorganizing, and free elections planned, Soviet leaders sent in troops. They crushed the revolt at the cost of three thousand Hungarians killed and thirteen thousand injured. In the crackdown that followed, two thousand to twenty-five hundred insurgents were executed, twenty thousand imprisoned, and thousands more were sent to Soviet prison camps.

History repeated itself in 1968 in Czechoslovakia, where moderate economic reforms in the mid 1960s raised hopes for political liberalization. The premier, Antonin Novotny, resisted further change, however, and in the face of demonstrations in Prague and mounting criticism from intellectuals, he resigned in favor of Alexander Dubček in January 1968. Dubček presided over the so-called Prague Spring, in which censorship was loosened, restrictions on travel were lifted, and a reduction of Party control over all aspects of society was promised. By summer, Soviet leaders were convinced that Czechoslovakia was about to become another Hungary. In August they ordered an invasion by a force of mainly Soviet troops, which faced only passive resistance and easily snuffed out the reform movement. Dubček was removed from office, and all communists who had supported reform — about one-third of the membership — were expelled or given menial jobs. For the next twenty years Czechoslovakia had the Soviet bloc's most oppressive regime.

Although the suppression of the Czechoslovakian reform movement resulted in only a few casualties, it had a greater psychological and political impact on Eastern Europe than the Soviet invasion of Hungary in 1956. Unlike the Hungarians, the Czechs had not sought the end of communist rule or withdrawal from the Warsaw Pact. Theirs was a program of moderate reform with broad support from Party members. Its destruction by military force crushed hopes for the liberalization of Eastern Europe's communist regimes, which now were revealed as lacking both political legitimacy and a capacity to change.

Socialism with a Human Face

❖

79 ◆ *Ludvik Vačulík,*
TWO THOUSAND WORDS TO WORKERS,
FARMERS, SCIENTISTS, ARTISTS,
AND EVERYONE

The climax of the Prague Spring came in April 1968, when after months of debate, the Czechoslovakian Communist Party issued its Action Program. A plan for achieving a less oppressive form of socialism, "socialism with a human face," it called for a reduction in state power, more freedom for farmers and factory managers, strengthening of the courts and parliament, and the recognition of civil liberties. The Communist Party would retain power, but it would be more responsive to the needs of farmers, consumers, students, workers, and other interest groups.

While Party leaders debated how to implement their program, and progressives called for more rapid and thoroughgoing reforms, pressure on Czechoslovakia from the Soviet Union and other Warsaw Pact countries intensified. In May the Soviet Union ordered twenty-five thousand troops to the Czech-Polish border and announced that military exercises would be held in Czechoslovakia in June. State-controlled newspapers throughout the Soviet bloc denounced the reform movement, especially after Dubček angered Moscow by welcoming to Prague Yugoslavia's Marshal Tito, who symbolized national independence within the communist movement.

Then on June 27, with special party elections about to begin, there appeared in four Prague newspapers an essay, "Two Thousand Words," written by Ludvik Vačulík, (pronounced Vaht-*soo*-leek), a prominent novelist and journalist. The essay, signed by many public figures, denounced the Communist Party and called on the people to maintain pressure on their leaders to press on with reform. It warned that unless the democratic movement kept moving forward, conservatives would reassert their authority and roll back the reforms.

Vačulík's essay elicited a strong positive response within the general population. Thousands of supporting letters, resolutions, and telegrams were sent to members of the National Assembly and leaders of the Czechoslovakian Communist Party. Vačulík's essay also elicited a response in Moscow and other Warsaw Pact capitals. By giving the impression that the Czech reform movement was about to spin out of control, it strengthened the hand of politicians who favored military intervention.

Intervention came on the night of August 20 to 21 1968, when Warsaw Pact troops invaded Czechoslovakia and occupied its major cities. Within weeks political conditions were "normalized," and strict Party rule was reimposed. Vačulík lost his job with the Writers' Union and, as an unemployed author, remained under police scrutiny until the collapse of Czechoslovakian communism in 1989.

QUESTIONS FOR ANALYSIS

1. What are Vačulík's views of the failings of the Czechoslovakian Communist Party? What role, if any, should the Party play in the process of reforming Czechoslovakian society?
2. According to Vačulík, what have been the results of communist rule of Czechoslovakian politics and society?
3. What strategy does Vačulík envision for saving the Czechoslovakian reform movement and pushing it forward?
4. If the reform movement had succeeded as Vačulík had hoped, what would Czechoslovakian government and society have looked like?
5. How do Vačulík's views compare to those expressed two years later by Sakharov, Medvedev, and Turchin in their letter to the Soviet leadership (source 77)?

After the war people had great confidence in the Communist party, but it gradually preferred to have official positions instead of the people's trust, until it had only official positions and nothing else. . . . The incorrect line of the leadership turned the party from a political party and ideological grouping into a power organization which became very attractive to power-hungry egotists, reproachful cowards, and people with bad consciences. When they came into the party, its character and behavior began to be affected. Its internal organization was such that good people, who might have maintained its development for it to have fitted into the modern world, could not wield any influence at all without shameful incidents occurring. Many communists opposed this decline, but not in one single case did they have any success in preventing what happened.

The conditions in the Communist party were the model for and the cause of an identical situation in the state. . . . There was no criticism of the activity of the state and economic organizations. Parliament forgot how to debate: The government forgot how to govern and the directors how to direct. Elections had no significance, and the laws lost their weight. We could not trust representatives on any committee, and even if we did, we could not ask them to do anything, because they could accomplish nothing. What was still worse was that we could hardly trust each other anymore. There was a decline of individual and communal honor. You didn't get anywhere by being honest, and it was useless expecting ability to be appreciated. Most people, therefore, lost interest in public affairs; they worried only about themselves and about their money. . . . To sum up, the country reached a point where its spiritual health and character were both threatened. . . .

In the future, we shall have to display personal initiative and determination of our own.

Above all, we shall have to oppose the view, should it arise, that it is possible to conduct some sort of a democratic revival without the communists or possibly against them. This would be both unjust and unreasonable. The communists have well-constructed organizations, and we should support the progressive wing within them. They have experienced officials, and last but not least, they also have in their hands the decisive levers and buttons. Their Action Program has been presented to the public. It is a program for the initial adjustment of the greatest inequalities, and no one else has any similarly concrete program. We must demand that local Action Programs be submitted to the public in each district and each community. By doing so, we shall have suddenly taken very ordinary and long-expected steps in the right direction. . . .

The practical quality of the future democracy depends on what becomes of the [factories] and what will happen in them. . . . We have to find good managers and back them up. It is true that, in comparison with the developed countries, we are all badly paid, and some are worse off than others.

We can demand more money — but although it can be printed, it will be worth less. We should instead demand that directors and chairmen explain to us the nature and extent of the capital they want for production, to whom they want to sell their products and for how much, what profit they can expect to make, and the percentage of this profit that is to be invested in the modernization of production and the percentage to be shared out.

Under quite superficially boring headlines, a very fierce struggle is going on in the press about democracy and who leads the country. Workers can intervene in this struggle by means of the people they elect to [factory] administrations and councils.[1] As employees, they can do what is best for themselves by electing as their representatives on trade union organs their natural leaders, capable and honest people no matter what their party affiliation is.

If at the moment we cannot expect any more from the central political organs, we must achieve more in the districts and smaller communities. We should demand the resignation of people who have misused their power, who have damaged public property, or who have acted in a dishonest or brutal way. We have to find ways and means to persuade them to resign, through public criticism, for instance, through resolutions, demonstrations, demonstration work brigades, collections for retirement gifts for them, strikes, and picketing their houses. . . . And let us set up special citizens' committees and commissions to deal with subjects that nobody is yet interested in. It's quite simple, a few people get together, elect a chairman, keep regular minutes, publish their findings, demand a solution, and do not allow themselves to be intimidated.

We must turn the district and local press, which has degenerated into a mouthpiece for official views, into a platform for all the positive political forces. . . . Let us establish committees for the defence of the freedom of the press. Let us organize our own monitoring services at meetings. If we hear strange news, let's check on it ourselves, and let's send delegations to the people concerned and, if need be, publish their replies . . .

This spring, as after the war, we have been given a great chance. We have once again the opportunity to take a firm grip on a common cause, which has the working title of socialism, and to give it a form which will much better suit the once good reputation that we had and the relatively good opinion that we once had of ourselves. The spring has now come to an end, and it will never return. By winter we will know everything.

---

[1]In the late spring, workers at many factories had formed councils to protect their interests during the anticipated process of economic reform.

The Brezhnev Doctrine

❖

80 ◆ Leonid Brezhnev, *SPEECH TO THE FIFTH CONGRESS OF THE POLISH UNITED WORKERS' PARTY*

After the invasion of Czechoslovakia, the Soviet leader Leonid Brezhnev sought to justify what many perceived to have been an overreaction to a program of moderate reform that sought neither the end of communism nor independence form the Soviet bloc. In what became known as the Brezhnev Doctrine, Brezhnev claimed that socialist states have the right to intervene in the domestic affairs of another socialist state if communism is threatened. Such is his theme in the following selection, taken from a speech delivered to a Polish Communist Party congress in November 1968.

Although Soviet leaders denied that a Brezhnev Doctrine ever was official Soviet policy, the Soviet leader Mikhail Gorbachev formally repudiated it in 1989. The Brezhnev Doctrine, he said, was to be replaced by the "Sinatra Doctrine." Just as the American singer proudly proclaimed in his popular song that "I did things my way," the European satellites would not be allowed to do things "their way" in ordering their affairs.

QUESTION FOR ANALYSIS

1. What, or whom, does Brezhnev blame for the increased activity of forces hostile to socialism in Czechoslovakia?
2. What, according to Brezhnev, are the "common natural laws of socialist construction" that justify outside intervention in the affairs of socialist states?
3. How, according to Brezhnev, do socialist and "imperialist" nations view the issue of nations' "sovereign rights" differently?
4. Reduced to its basics, what is the definition of the Brezhnev Doctrine as spelled out in this speech?

The might of the socialist camp today is such that the imperialists fear military defeat in the event of a direct clash with the chief forces of socialism. . . . However, it is a fact that in the new conditions the imperialists are making increasingly frequent use of different and more insidious tactics. They are seeking out the weak links in the socialist front, pursuing a course of subversive ideological work inside the socialist countries, trying to influence the economic development of these countries, attempting to sow dissension, drive wedges between them and encourage and inflame nationalist feelings and tendencies, and are seeking to isolate individual socialist states so that they can then seize them by the throat one by one. In short, imperialism is trying to undermine socialism's solidarity precisely as a world system. . . .

Socialist states stand for strict respect for the sovereignty of all countries. We resolutely oppose interference in the affairs of any states and the violation of their sovereignty.

At the same time, affirmation and defense of the sovereignty of states that have taken the path of socialist construction are of special significance to us communists. The forces of imperialism and reaction are seeking to deprive the people first in one, then another socialist country of the sovereign right they have earned to ensure prosperity for their country and well-being and happiness for the broad working masses by building a society free from all oppression and exploitation. And when encroachments on this right receive a joint rebuff from the socialist camp, the bourgeois propagandists raise the cry of "defense of sovereignty" and "noninterference." It is clear that this is the sheerest deceit and demagoguery on their part. In reality these loudmouths are concerned not about preserving socialist sovereignty but about destroying it.

It is common knowledge that the Soviet Union has really done a good deal to strengthen the sovereignty and autonomy of the socialist countries. . . . But it is well known, comrades, that there are common natural laws of socialist construction, deviation from which could lead to deviation from socialism as such. And when external and internal forces hostile to socialism try to turn the development of a given socialist country in the direction of restoration of the capitalist system, when a threat arises to the cause of socialism in that country — a threat to the security of the socialist commonwealth as a whole — this is no longer merely a problem for that country's people, but a common problem, the concern of all socialist countries. *(Applause.)*

It is quite clear that an action such as military assistance to a fraternal country to end a threat to the socialist system is an extraordinary measure, dictated by necessity; it can be called forth only by the overt actions of enemies of socialism within the country and beyond its boundaries, actions that create a threat to the common interests of the socialist camp.

Experience bears witness that in present conditions the triumph of the socialist system in a country can be regarded as final, but the restoration of capitalism can be considered ruled out only if the Communist party, as the leading force in society, steadfastly pursues a Marxist–Leninist policy in the development of all spheres of society's life; only if the party indefatigably strengthens the country's defense and the protection of its revolutionary gains, and if it itself is vigilant and instills in the people vigilance with respect to the class enemy and implacability toward bourgeois ideology; only if the principle of socialist internationalism is held sacred, and unity and fraternal solidarity with the other socialist countries are strengthened. *(Prolonged applause.)*

◆

Utopian Dreams in Mao's China

On October 1, 1949, with the armies of Chiang Kai-shek in full retreat in the south, Mao Zedong, the leader of the Chinese Communist Party, stood above the Gate of Heavenly Peace in Beijing and proclaimed the People's Republic of China. China's civil war had ended, and the fate of 540 million Chinese lay in the hands of Mao Zedong and a small number of followers who for twenty-five years had struggled to unify China under communist rule.

China's new leaders had ambitious, even grandiose, plans for their country. They envisioned a strong, independent China, no longer vulnerable to imperialism and its attendant humiliations. They envisioned a China in which poverty would be eradicated through agricultural modernization, industrialization, and a program of road-building, railroad construction, and energy development. They envisioned a China in which ancient inequalities — between men and women, landlords and peasants, the learned and the illiterate, bureaucrats and subjects — would no longer exist.

But was it possible to achieve rapid economic development in a truly egalitarian society? Finding an answer to this question became the great challenge for China's policymakers. Mao, whose opinion mattered most, believed that both goals could be achieved simultaneously by tapping the potential of the Chinese people, who, under the guidance of the Party, would dedicate themselves to achieving a modernized, communist China, not self-enrichment. Their energy and willpower, not the planning of bureaucrats, the research of scientists, or the know-how of engineers, would create a prosperous and egalitarian China.

Mao never realized his dreams. His economic and political experiments proved disastrous, and after his death in 1976, China's leaders abandoned revolutionary egalitarianism in favor of a development strategy based on a principle that Mao had despised — that the interests of society were best served when individuals were free to pursue their own personal gain.

Industrial Heroism in the Great Leap Forward

❖

81 ◆ *Tan Manni, LUSHAN'S PIG-IRON "SPUTNIK"*

In its first decade, communist China experienced profound changes. Between 1949 and 1953, large-scale businesses were nationalized, and land was seized from rich landowners and redistributed to peasants. In 1953, in imitation of Stalin's Soviet Union, China instituted its first Five-Year Plan. Its key components were centralized economic planning, the collectivization of agriculture, and rapid industrialization, with emphasis on steel, industrial equipment, chemicals, and electric power.

Despite an average annual growth rate of 18 percent in the 1950s, Mao was unhappy with the Soviet model of economic development. Farm output registered only minor gains, and what increases had occurred largely came from privately owned plots rather than common lands. The Soviet model, he believed, had other dangers. Central planning meant larger and more powerful bureaucracies, while rapid industrialization brought disproportionate wealth and status to elite managers and engineers. Thus by late 1957, Mao was prepared to take China into a new stage of its socialist development — the Great Leap Forward.

The Great Leap Forward shifted the focus of China's economic development from cities to the countryside, where millions of peasants, in the selfless pursuit of socialism, would dedicate themselves to road construction, farming, stock-raising, iron-making, and other enterprises to transform China into a modern socialist society in just a few years. It began in late 1957 when million of peasants were put to work on hundreds of water control and irrigation projects that supposedly opened up eight hundred million acres to cultivation in a few months. It was thought that equally impressive gains could be achieved by consolidating China's 740,000 cooperative farms into giant communes. By the end of 1958, 120 million households, or 99 percent of the rural population, had joined 26,000 communes, which Party officials ran according to strict egalitarian principles: private plots were abolished; commune members all received the same pay and food ration irrespective of their work; families were organized collectively, with meals and child care provided by the commune. Commune members did more than farm. They also joined militias, built and operated backyard iron foundries and factories, worked on construction projects, and prospected for uranium. Those with talent were encouraged to write inspirational poetry and songs.

The Great Leap Forward had its share of achievements, but overall it was a disaster. People were worked to exhaustion; the backyard iron foundries produced millions of iron pots and tools, but most were unusable; worst of all, farm output failed to reach unrealistically high production targets, and as the communes' grain, vegetables, and meat were handed over to the state to feed city dwellers, famine swept through rural China. It claimed twenty million lives between 1959 and 1962.

Why did the Great Leap Forward fail? Some answers are provided by the following article, even though the author, Tan Manni, wrote it to impress his readers with its great achievements. In the article, which appeared in the journal *China Reconstructs* in 1959, Tan describes how a commune in Lushan county, a region in Jianxi Province, reached a "sputnik" in iron production. *Sputnik* was the name of the first man-made satellite sent into orbit by the USSR in 1957. During the Great Leap Forward, the term was used for high production goals in agriculture and manufacturing.

QUESTIONS FOR ANALYSIS

1. What does the selection reveal about the level of economic and technological development in Lushan county at the time of the Great Leap Forward?
2. According to the author, how do the workers view their labors? What methods have been used to motivate them?
3. What does the article reveal about the reason for the poor quality of pig iron produced in the Lushan county foundries?
4. How does the article help explain the reasons for the fall in agricultural production during the Great Leap Forward?
5. What changes in social and family relationships accompanied the Great Leap Forward? Why were they necessary?

Furnace fields are everywhere . . . plots of hundreds of small earthen furnaces were "growing," in late autumn when I was there, alongside fields of sweet potatoes and tobacco. . . .

Small red flags fly overhead indicating the sections belonging to the various companies and squads of farmer-steelworkers, who are organized like militia units. . . .

At one of the ten-foot-high furnaces, a man climbs a wooden ladder to dump coke and firewood through the top. After a few minutes beside the 1,000-degree heat, he descends and another worker goes up to tamp the fuel down with his rake. A third man follows to pull the hot rake away from the blast of the fire. Beside the furnace another crew is pushing the handle of the huge homemade wooden bellows. With all his might one of them pulls the handle, half as tall as himself, and pushes it back with the weight of his body. Three other men standing by to take their turns jokingly cheer him on. . . .

The river a few miles away from the county town is another scene of activity. Undaunted by cold north wind, 25,000 students, women, and local government workers are ankle-deep in the water, washing for the iron-bearing sand that has been carried down from the nearby mountains. On the banks, groups of students off their working shift hold classes, and a crew of older women minds the children for the mothers beside the temporary living quarters made for workers from distant parts of the county. . . .

The office of the county Communist Party committee where I stayed in the county town of Lushan is like the headquarters of an army, for the party had undertaken direct leadership of the iron campaign. Any time of the day or night, one can hear someone shouting into the telephone, "Long distance . . . urgent . . . coal . . . tons."

This is the verve which enabled Lushan, the small mountainous county which six months ago possessed neither a blast furnace nor an engineer, or even an automobile, to startle the entire country by proving it could turn out 1,000 tons of iron a day. That record on last August 28 opened a new page in the nation-wide campaign for iron and steel, for it did away with the belief that smelting by local methods does not add up to much.

Lushan's achievement was called a "sputnik," and within the next month it inspired seventy-three more counties to reach that level. Now the record has been surpassed hundreds of times, but the county's 430,000 people are still seized by the iron and steel fever. Each day 100,000 of them work directly in its production, and many thousands more "at the rear" help transport ore after a day's work in the fields.

The people of Lushan began making small amounts of iron early in the summer, in line with the country's policy of developing small local industry as well as large plants, and to meet their own needs in making labor-saving farm machinery. . . . In Lushan, local materials and simple homemade tools were used to cut down initial investment and half of the funds were contributed by the people themselves. A dozen blacksmiths who at the beginning did not know how to smelt ore, led by the party vice-secretary, studied and experimented until they found a suitable process, and then passed the technique on to 600 other farmer-steelworkers. . . .

. . . The farming had to be done with as few people as possible so as to free as many workers as possible to build and operate more furnaces, and mine and transport ore and coal. . . .

As the work could not go ahead without full mass support and understanding, the meetings to discuss the proposal [to set higher production goals] became hot debates — a struggle of ideas. It was through this that the farmers came to realize their real power to produce. Party leaders put the need for iron in terms of the county's own needs — it could bring hydroelectric power

stations on every one of the 600 reservoirs the people had built in the spring, better farm tools and machines, multi-storied buildings. They also pointed out that more iron for national construction would mean more tractors, rail lines and other improvements for all.

The way [to proceed], most people agreed, was large-scale organization. Lushan's mountains had ore but few people to do the mining. On the plains, on the other hand, there was manpower to spare. So their coops[1] decided that only by merging could they better deploy the working force. This later formed the basis for the people's commune which now embraces all of Lushan county.

Suggestions for nurseries and canteens to release more women were also adopted. In one large village alone, these measures freed 2,100 women for productive work. . . .

When the time came to sign up for iron work, 95 percent of the county's able-bodied persons applied, and 65,000 were soon actually making iron. Shock teams were organized to man the furnaces, mine the ore, mold crucibles, and repair roads to facilitate transport. They built 500 new furnaces, and methods were developed to make the older ones yield twenty times as much iron per heat.

In the fortnight which preceded the target date of August 28, few people got a full night's sleep. It was just in those weeks that news came of the aggressive military build-up by the United States in the Taiwan Straits area and of provocations against the mainland.[2] Determination became even greater. On August 27, just as the furnaces were being lit, word arrived about the nation-wide call to raise the 1958 national production of steel to 10.7 million tons, twice as much as the year before. On August 28, Lushan's furnaces yielded 1,068 tons of pig iron. The "sputnik" had succeeded and Lushan had set a new standard for local iron production.

---

[1]Cooperative farms.

[2]In August 1958 China demanded the withdrawal of U.S. forces from Taiwan after Chinese forces began bombing raids against Quemoy, an offshore island near the port of Amoy controlled by the Nationalist government of Taiwan. A standoff ensued. China continued the bombardment until December but made no attacks on the supply ships sent to Quemoy under U.S. navy escort.

Soon the daily average was far surpassing this one-time figure. In the autumn, 40,000 more workers came from neighboring counties. By early November 150,000 tons were being produced in one day — as much as had been planned for the whole year.

Creating a New China in the Great Proletarian Cultural Revolution

❖

82 ❖ *ONE HUNDRED ITEMS FOR DESTROYING THE OLD AND ESTABLISHING THE NEW*

By mid 1959, it was clear to millions of Chinese that the Great Leap Forward had failed. It was no less clear to members of the Central Committee of the Communist Party, who removed Mao from the day-to-day control of the Party and shifted power to Deng Xiaoping and Liu Shaoqi, who sought to revive China's economy by dismantling Mao's experiment. Communes were reduced in size, and hundreds of thousands of failed rural industrial enterprises were scrapped. Peasants once more were allowed to farm private plots and sell their products for profit. Central planning was reinstated, and material incentives for successful managers and productive workers were revived. As a result, between 1960 and 1965 industrial production grew by 11 percent a year, and grain production grew from 195 million tons in 1961 to 240 million tons in 1965.

Despite China's recovery, the Party leadership remained bitterly divided. On one side were the moderate supporters of Deng and Liu, who believed that China's most pressing need was economic development and that this goal could best be achieved through central planning; reliance on the contributions of university-trained engineers, managers, and scientists; and acceptance of incentives as a means of boosting production. On the other side were Chairman Mao and his disciples, who wanted economic development, but not at the expense of social equality, ongoing revolution, and ideological purity.

During the early 1960s, Mao gained support within the army and from a small but influential group of radical intellectuals. By late spring of 1966, Mao felt strong enough to launch what came to be known as the Great Proletarian Cultural Revolution. He and his supporters purged opponents from the Ministry of Culture and encouraged demonstrations by high school and university students against administrators and moderate Party members. Given red arm bands and copies of the "little red book," *Quotations from Chairman Mao*, students throughout China were released from classes to crusade against the "four olds" of Chinese society — old customs, old habits, old culture, and old thinking. These vague guidelines, along with Mao's directive to "destroy the old and construct the new," gave the student Red Guards many potential targets — as is demonstrated by the following document.

This list of demands was drawn up by Red Guards between the ages of fifteen and eighteen from the Maoism School, formerly known as Beijing Middle School Number 26. The students' list, compiled in August 1966, offers insights into the goals, opinions, and motives of the Red Guards, who, along with radicalized workers, kept China in an extraordinary state of turmoil between 1966 and 1969.

QUESTIONS FOR ANALYSIS

1. What view of Mao Zedong is presented in the students' list of proposals?
2. How do the authors of the manifesto characterize the bourgeoisie? What concrete steps are proposed to limit the wealth and status of the bourgeoisie?
3. What economic proposals are contained in the students' list? In what ways will their proposed changes benefit the peasants and workers?
4. According to the manifesto, what changes are necessary in Chinese family life and education in order to bring them into conformity with Mao Zedong thought?
5. The authors of the manifesto express an interest in ridding China of gambling, swearing, "decadent" music, drinking, smoking, and "weird" clothing. What may explain the students' strong views on these matters?

The onrushing tide of the Great Proletarian Cultural Revolution is just now crashing down on the remnant strength of the bourgeoisie with the might of a thunderbolt, washing the old ideology, the old culture, the old customs, and the old habits of the bourgeoisie down the stream. Chairman Mao tell us: "In the last analysis, all the truths of Marxism can be summed up in one sentence. 'To rebel is justified.'" The present Great Proletarian Cultural Revolution must overthrow the old ideology, the old culture, the old customs, and the old habits; to rebel all out against the bourgeoisie is to completely smash the bourgeoisie, to establish the proletariat on a grand scale, to make the radiance of great Mao Zedong Thought illuminate the entire capital, the entire nation, the entire world. Armed with great Mao Zedong Thought we are the most militant troops, the mortal enemy of the "four olds"; we are the destroyers of the old world; we are the creators of the new world. . . . We must thoroughly clear the books of the utterly illogical capitalist system. . . .

◆ ◆

. . . Under the charge of residential committees, every street must set up a quotation plaque; every household must have on its walls a picture of the Chairman plus quotations by Chairman Mao.

. . . More quotations by Chairman Mao must be put up in the parks. Ticket takers on buses and conductors on trains should make the propagation of Mao Zedong Thought and the reading of Chairman Mao's quotations their primary task. . . .

. . . Printing companies must print quotations by the Chairman in large numbers; they must be sold in every bookstore until there is a copy of the *Quotations from Chairman Mao* in the hands of everyone in the whole country.

. . . With a copy of the *Quotations from Chairman Mao* in the hands of everyone, each must carry it with him, constantly study it, and do everything in accord with it. . . .

. . . Neighborhood work must put Mao Zedong Thought in first place, must set up small groups for the study of Chairman Mao's works, and must revolutionize housewives. . . .

. . . Broadcasting units must be set up in every park and at every major intersection, and, under the organizational responsibility of such organs as the Red Guards, propagate Mao Zedong Thought and current international and national events. . . .

. . . Letters and stamps must never have bourgeois things printed on them (such as cats, dogs, or other artistic things). Politics must be predominant. A quotation by Chairman Mao or a militant utterance by a hero must be printed on every envelope. . . .

. . . Shop windows cannot be dominated by displays of scents and perfumes. They must be decorated with simplicity and dignity and must put Mao Zedong Thought first.

. . . Theaters must have a strong political atmosphere. Before the movie starts, quotations from Chairman Mao must be shown. Don't let the bourgeoisie rule our stages. Cut the superfluous hooligan scenes, and reduce the price of tickets on behalf of the workers, peasants, and soldiers.

. . . Literary and art workers must energetically model in clay heroic images of workers, peasants and soldiers engaged in living study and living application of chairman Mao's works. Their works must be pervaded by the one red line of Mao Zedong Thought. . . .

. . . In a proletarian society, private enterprise cannot be allowed to exist. We propose to take all firms using joint state and private management and change them to state management and change joint state and private management enterprises into state-owned enterprises.

. . . Our socialist society absolutely cannot allow any hoodlums or juvenile delinquents to exist. We order you right this minute to get rid of your blue jeans, shave off your slick hairdos, take off your rocket shoes, and quit your black[1] organizations. Beijing is the heart of world revolution. . . . We warn you: You are not allowed to go on recklessly doing your evil deeds — if you do, you will be responsible for the consequences.

. . . All who are in service trades are not permitted to serve the bourgeoisie. Clothing stores are firmly prohibited from making tight pants, Hong Kong–style suits, weird women's outfits, and grotesque men's suits. . . .

. . . All daily necessities (perfume, snowflake cream,[2] etc.) that do not serve the broad worker, peasant, and soldier masses must be prohibited from sale right away. . . .

. . . All the landlords, rich-peasants, counterrevolutionaries, hooligans, Rightists, and other members of the bourgeois class are not permitted to collect pornographic books and decadent records. Whoever violates this rule will, when discovered, be treated as guilty of attempting to restore the old order, and his collections will be destroyed.

. . . Children must sing revolutionary songs. Those rotten tunes of the cat and dog variety must never again waft in the air of our socialist state. In this great socialist state of ours, absolutely no one is allowed to play games of chance.

. . . The bastards of the bourgeoisie are not allowed to hire governesses. Whoever dares to violate or resist this rule and thus continues to ride on the heads of the laboring people will be severely punished. . . .

. . . Every industrial enterprise must abolish the bourgeois bonus award system. In this great socialist nation of ours, the broad worker, peasant, soldier masses, armed with the great Mao Zedong Thought, have no need for material incentives.

. . . Heads of families are not allowed to educate their children with bourgeois ideology. The feudal family-head system[3] will be abolished.

. . . You old bastards of the bourgeoisie who receive high salaries, listen well: Before Liberation you rode on the heads of the people, sometimes severe, sometimes lenient. Now you still receive salaries many times more than ten times higher than those of the workers. You are thus drinking the blood of the people — you are

---

[1]Black was associated with reactionary politics.
[2]Facial cream.
[3]In the traditional Chinese family the father was the center of authority. In theory, he controlled the family's property and arranged marriages for his children and grandchildren. In en-

couraging young people to reject the values of their parents and elders — indeed, to denounce them to authorities for erroneous thinking — the Cultural Revolution rejected the age-old doctrine of filial piety, according to which children owed their parents unquestioned reverence and obedience.

guilty. Starting in September, you are ordered to lower your high salaries to the level of those of the workers. . . .

. . . Landlords, rich-peasants, counter-revolutionaries, hooligans, Rightists, and capitalists, when they go out, must wear plaques as monsters and freaks under the supervision of the masses. . . .

. . . All circus and theater programs must be changed. They must put on meaningful things. Actors are not allowed to dress up in strange fashions, because we don't need those filthy things. . . .

. . . Nobody may address letters to 'Sir" so and so. The whole range of feudal practices must be abolished and new customs advocated. . . .

. . . All those athletic activities that don't correspond with practical significance will be appropriately reduced. Physical education for national defense, such as swimming, mountain climbing, shooting, etc., will be greatly developed so that gradually every youth or adult over fifteen years of age will have a range of enemy-killing abilities. All the people are soldiers, always prepared to annihilate the invading enemy. . . .

. . . We order those under thirty-five to quit drinking and smoking immediately. Bad habits of this sort absolutely may not be cultivated.

. . . Telling jokes, uttering profanities, and doing vulgar things are strictly forbidden. . . .

. . . The responsible organizations must do their best to find ways to establish public toilets in the various alleys so as to reduce the heavy work of the sanitation workers. . . .

. . . From now on, all universities, high schools, and vocational schools will be run as communist schools with part-time work and part-time study and part-time farming and part-time study.

. . . We students must respond to Chairman Mao's appeal. Students must also learn from the workers, the peasants, and the soldiers, and each year during their vacations they must go to factories, farms, and military camps to train themselves. . . .

. . . Schools must use Mao's works as textbooks and educate the youth in Mao Zedong Thought. . . .

. . . Schools must destroy the feudal teacher-student etiquette and establish an equal relationship between teacher and student.

Visualizing the New China

◆

83 ◆ *POSTER ART FROM THE CULTURAL REVOLUTION*

At a conference of artists and writers held in 1942, Mao Zedong spelled out the principles of socialist art and literature. Art and literature existed for one purpose only — to advance the revolution by bringing the Party's message to workers, peasants, and soldiers. This was never more the case than during the Cultural Revolution, when graphic designers, artists, and printers, under close supervision from Party officials, produced literally millions of political posters. Pasted or tacked to public buildings, doors, bridges, buses, trucks, and the walls of schools, government offices, factories, army barracks, and private homes, these posters were the preferred method of publicizing the goals of the Cultural Revolution, glorifying Mao, and demonizing the regime's enemies.

Three representative posters follow. The first, from 1966, shows a crowd of people in Beijing's Tiananmen Square holding up Mao's "little red book," and proclaiming their wish that Mao might live many "ten thousands" of years.

The second, "Fully Criticize the Stinking Chinese Khrushchev," probably dates from 1967. It shows the obliteration of Liu Shaoqi, one of the earliest and most prominent victims of the Cultural Revolution. He is being painted over by a group of Mao's supporters. A long-time associate of Mao, head of state, and Mao's heir apparent, Liu, along with Deng Xiaoping, had dominated the Party after the failure of the Great Leap Forward. He was stripped of his office in 1966 and sent to prison, where he died in 1969 of probable neglect and abuse. The Soviet leader Khrushchev, out of power since 1964, was still considered a villain by the Chinese for his supposed perversion of Marxism-Leninism and his criticisms of the Great Leap Forward.

The third poster, from 1969, shows a struggle session in progress. A struggle session was an emotion-charged assembly in which "enemies of the people" were questioned, accused, and badgered until they confessed their crimes. The setting of this particular session is a Shanghai ink-manufacturing plant, where pictures of the individual being denounce and lists of his crimes are posted on the wall.

QUESTIONS FOR ANALYSIS

1. What different groups in Chinese society are featured in the posters? What generalizations can be made about their ages?
2. What generalizations can you make about the emotions of the most prominent figures and their physical appearance?
3. What do the posters reveal about attitudes toward Mao that inspired the Great Proletarian Cultural Revolution?
4. Compare the visual message of the three posters with the list of demands made by the students at the Maoism School (see source 82). To what extent do they present similar messages and themes?
5. What is your assessment of the strengths and weaknesses of these posters as a source for understanding the Cultural Revolution?

Chairman Mao Ten Thousand Years! Ten Thousand! Ten Thousand Years!

Fully Criticize the Stinking Chinese Khrushchev from a Political, Ideological, and Theoretical Perspective

Firmly Grasp Large-Scale Revolutionary Criticism

CHAPTER 11

The Emergence of a Third World

In an article titled "Three Worlds, One Planet," published in the French magazine *L'Observateur* in 1952, the demographer Alfred Sauvy coined the phrase *Third World* to describe the regions of Africa, Asia, and Latin America that were just beginning to emerge from colonialism after World War II. He sought to draw a distinction between these areas and the First World, made up of the Western capitalist states, and the Second World, made up of the Soviet Union and its Eastern European satellites. He also wanted to draw an analogy between the role of the *Third World* in the era of decolonization and that of the *Third Estate* in the French Revolution of the 1790s. Just as in France the oppressed Third Estate, made up of the bourgeoisie and peasants, had wrested power from the privileged first two estates, the clergy and nobility, the people of the Third World, "ignored, exploited, and despised," were seeking equality and justice in the postcolonial era.

Although the concept of three worlds is firmly entrenched in common usage and in the vocabulary of journalists, historians, and politicians, it continues to have many critics. These critics, who consider the concept imprecise and politically incorrect, have proposed a number of alternatives. The United Nations and the World Bank have opted for cold, analytical terms such as "developed countries" versus "developing countries," "less developed countries," or "countries of low human development." Others have suggested neutral geographical terminology of "North" versus "South" or the notion of "core" nations versus the "periphery." Still others have abandoned the search for appropriate descriptive terminology altogether. Why not avoid controversy and simply refer to the regions of Africa, Latin America, Asia, and the Caribbean as . . . the regions of Africa, Latin America, Asia, and the Caribbean? Each of these suggestions has its shortcomings, however, and none has come close to replacing the Third World as a term of description and analysis.

What then is meant by the Third World? As Sauvy emphasized in his article, all Third World societies (except Thailand and perhaps Iran) had once been colonies. In Africa and Asia this had meant the loss of political independence and the subordination of both regions' economic interests to those of the colonizers. In Latin America, where political independence from Spain and Portugal had been won in the early 1800s, it had meant foreign control of banks, railroads, mines, large-scale agricultural operations, and the petroleum industry and sporadic foreign intervention in domestic politics. It had also meant dependency on the United States and Europe as a source of capital, as a market for exports, and as the region's principal supplier of machinery and manufactured products.

General poverty was another characteristic of Third World societies in the postcolonial era. Poverty, in turn, was a result of their lack of industrialization, reliance on agriculture, rudimentary communications and transportation systems, and inadequate schools. In the optimistic atmosphere following the end of colonialism, it was an article of faith that Third World poverty would disappear once Asia, Africa, and Latin America experienced economic development and modernization. Development meant industrialization, accompanied ideally by the formation of stable, democratic governments, while modernization meant the transition from traditional customs and attitudes to the scientific and secular values of developed nations, primarily those in the West.

For a time, such optimism seemed well grounded. In the 1950s and 1960s, food production increased in Africa, Asia, and Latin America, and the worldwide economic boom ensured healthy prices for these regions' agricultural and mineral exports. Governments embarked on ambitious economic development plans, and in the 1960s, despite population increases, real per capita income grew. Only in the 1970s, with its spiraling oil prices and worldwide economic downturn, did Third World economic prospects darken.

Another characteristic of the emerging Third World was nonalignment, that is, neutrality in the Cold War between capitalism and communism. The concept of nonalignment first gained attention as a result of the African-Asian Conference held in the Indonesian city Bandung in 1955. Hosted by Indonesia's Premier Sukarno and attended by representatives of twenty-nine African and Asian countries, the Conference denounced colonialism, condemned runaway military spending by the superpowers, and called for increased economic aid from rich to poor nations. As the Cold War continued, many Asian and African countries found it expedient or necessary to abandon nonalignment, but during the 1950s and 1960s their commitment to an independent diplomatic course strengthened the idea that there really was a Third World with interests and ambitions different from those of the First and Second Worlds.

Since the 1970s the Third World has undergone many changes. South Korea, Taiwan, Singapore, and Hong Kong became industrial and financial powers and ceased being considered part of the Third World. Saudi Arabia, Kuwait, Bahrain, and other Middle Eastern oil producers became fabulously rich as a result of the spike in oil prices during the 1970s, and they too have been moved out of the Third World category or placed in a subcategory of their own. Post-Soviet Russia, on the other hand, with its collapsing economy, decaying infrastructure, and demoralized population, has, according to some, moved from the Second World to the Third.

The greatest change in our thinking about the Third World has been the loss of optimism. Economic development has proved infinitely more difficult than imagined, and for every success like South Korea there have been dozens of failures. Fifty years after Sauvy introduced the concept, the Third World still exists, but dreams of orderly government and economic progress have given way to nightmare visions of political breakdown, environmental catastrophe, and deepening human misery.

◆

New Sources of Conflict in the Middle East

For thousands of years geography ordained that the Middle East would play a central role in human affairs. As the western terminus of overland trade routes from East Asia and as the link between the Mediterranean Sea and the Indian Ocean via the Red Sea and the Persian Gulf, it was a center of international trade. At the juncture of Asia, Africa, and Europe, it was a place that attracted recurring waves of invaders and migrants who intermingled, competed, and shared ideas with one another. This explains in part why human beings made some of their greatest achievements in the Middle East. Here they developed agriculture, the alphabet, and metallurgy; established some of their most important religions — Judaism, Christianity, and Islam; and built some of their most impressive cities — Cairo, Baghdad, Damascus, and Isfahan.

After World War II, the Middle East continued to play a central role in human affairs, but for reasons more geological than geographical. Millions of years earlier, enormous quantities of one-celled marine plants and animals fell to the floor of the ocean that covered the region and, finding the right temperatures and rock formations, were slowly transformed into huge fields of oil and natural gas. These fields, which were discovered in Iran in 1908, Iraq in 1927, and Kuwait and Saudi Arabia in 1938, contain high-quality oil that is close to the surface and easy to extract. European and American companies soon were pumping millions of barrels of oil a day out of the earth, transporting it through pipelines to refineries, and supplying the world with fuel oil, heating oil, and gasoline. By the early 1970s Middle Eastern oil had become the life-blood of the world's economy, and maintaining political stability in the region became a priority of world leaders.

Achieving stability proved difficult, in part because all of the states in the region were new. Republican Turkey had emerged from the ruins of the Ottoman Empire in 1922 to 1923; Egypt gained control of its domestic affairs from Britain only in 1936; Iran, though technically independent, rid itself of Soviet and British occupying troops only after World War II; Saudi Arabia was created in the 1920s. Iraq, Transjordan (renamed Jordan in 1948), Syria, and Lebanon became fully independent when the British and French mandates ended after World War II.

Politics in the region was complicated further by ethnic rivalries, religious divisions, and fundamental political disagreements. Maronite Christians, Sunni Muslims, and Shiite Muslims shared power in Lebanon; Kurds made up a substantial minority in Turkey, Iran, and Iraq; Shiite Muslims and smaller sects such the Druze and the Aalawites (whom the orthodox do not even consider to be Muslim) lived in largely Sunni Syria; Shiites made up 20 percent of the population in Iraq. On political issues, nationalists, liberals, socialists, communists, and supporters of traditional monarchy competed for power and public support, as did secularists, who admired the West, and Muslim fundamentalists, who considered the West satanic.

By far the greatest destabilizing force in the region was the existence of Israel. The founding of Israel in 1948 was the culmination of events that go back to the 1890s, when European Zionists proclaimed as their goal the creation of a national Jewish homeland in Palestine, a region on the eastern Mediterranean which then was part of the Ottoman Empire. Jewish migration to the region, which became a British mandate after World War I, accelerated after the Nazis seized power in Germany in 1933, and resulted in a postwar Palestine populated by six hundred thousand Jews and 1.8 million Muslim Arabs. Both groups wanted an end to the British mandate, but the Arabs demanded a unified state ruled by the Arab majority, while the Jews demanded the partition of Palestine and their own Jewish state. With compromise impossible and violence mounting, the British handed over the Palestinian issue to the United Nations, which in November 1947 voted in favor of separate Jewish and Arab states. On May 14, 1948, Jewish leaders formally established the state of Israel, and on the same day Egypt, Iraq, Syria, and Jordan declared war on the new state, vowing its destruction.

Palestine as an Arab Homeland

❖

84 ◆ THE PALESTINE NATIONAL CHARTER

Arab armies were defeated in the Arab-Israel War of 1948 to 1949, but the real losers were Palestinian Arabs. Approximately one hundred fifty thousand Palestinians remained in Israel during and after the war and became Israeli citizens, who, though subject to numerous restrictions, had political rights, economic benefits, and educational opportunities. Some four hundred thousand Palestinians who lived in the West Bank, a region of Palestine not conquered by Israel, became subjects of the king of Jordan, who annexed the territory in 1949.

Anywhere from five hundred thousand to eight hundred thousand Palestinians who had fled their homes in Israel during the war became refugees in squalid camps on the borders of Israel in the Gaza region, the West Bank, Syria, and Lebanon. In 1967, after the third Arab-Israeli war, the Six-Day War, the number of Palestinian refugees swelled by another two hundred thousand when the West Bank was conquered by the Israelis and incorporated into Israel.

During the 1950s, numerous welfare agencies, social organizations, and paramilitary groups were founded to serve the needs of refugees and keep alive the goal of Palestinian statehood. At a summit meeting in 1964, Arab leaders approved the founding of the Palestine Liberation Organization (PLO), with responsibility for overseeing and coordinating all these Palestinian organizations. Later in the year representatives of the organizations met in Jerusalem and formed a PLO executive board, laid plans for the formation of a Palestinian army, and began work on a national charter. The Palestine National Charter, after several revisions, was approved at a meeting of the Fourth Palestine National Council in 1968.

Excerpts from this document follow.

QUESTIONS FOR ANALYSIS

1. How does the Charter define a Palestinian?
2. Why does the Charter equate Zionism with imperialism? Why does it equate Zionism with racism?
3. How valid are these comparisons in your view?
4. On what grounds does the Charter reject the validity of the UN decision to partition Palestine in 1947?
5. How do the authors of the Charter propose to achieve liberation from Israel?

1. Palestine, the homeland of the Palestinian Arab people, is an inseparable part of the greater Arab homeland, and the Palestinian people are a part of the Arab Nation.

2. Palestine, within the frontiers that existed under the British Mandate, is an indivisible territorial unit.

3. The Palestinian Arab people alone have legitimate rights to their homeland, and shall exercise the right of self-determination after the liberation of their homeland, in keeping with their wishes and entirely of their own accord.

4. The Palestinian identity is an authentic, intrinsic and indissoluble quality that is transmitted from father to son. Neither the Zionist occupation nor the dispersal of the Palestinian

Arab people as a result of the afflictions they have suffered can efface this Palestinian identity.

5. Palestinians are Arab citizens who were normally resident in Palestine until 1947. This includes both those who were forced to leave or who stayed in Palestine. Anyone born to a Palestinian father after that date, whether inside or outside Palestine, is a Palestinian.

6. Jews who were normally resident in Palestine up to the beginning of the Zionist invasion are Palestinians.

7. Palestinian identity, and material, spiritual and historical links with Palestine are immutable realities. It is a national obligation to provide every Palestinian with a revolutionary Arab upbringing, and to instill in him a

profound spiritual and material familiarity with his homeland and a readiness for armed struggle and for the sacrifice of his material possessions and his life, for the recovery of his homeland. . . .

8. The Palestinian people is at the stage of national struggle for the liberation of its homeland. For that reason, differences between Palestinian national forces must give way to the fundamental difference that exists between Zionism and imperialism on the one hand and the Palestinian Arab people on the other. On that basis, the Palestinian masses, both as organizations and as individuals, whether in the homeland or in such places as they now live as refugees, constitute a single national front working for the recovery and liberation of Palestine through armed struggle.

9. The Palestinian Arab people hereby affirm their unwavering determination to carry on the armed struggle and to press on towards popular revolution for the liberation of and return to their homeland. They also affirm their right to a normal life in their homeland, to the exercise of their right of self-determination therein and to sovereignty over it.

10. Commando action[1] constitutes the nucleus of the Palestinian popular war of liberation. This requires that commando action should be escalated, expanded and protected, and that all the resources of the Palestinian masses and all scientific potentials available to them should be mobilized and organized to play their part in the armed Palestinian revolution. . . .

12. The Palestinian Arab people believe in Arab unity. To fulfill their role in the achievement of that objective, they must, at the present stage in their national struggle, retain their Palestinian identity and all that it involves, work for increased awareness of it and oppose all measures liable to weaken or dissolve it. . . .

14. The destiny of the Arab nation, indeed the continued existence of the Arabs, depends on the fate of the Palestinian cause. This interrelationship is the point of departure of the Arab endeavor to liberate Palestine. The Palestinian people are the vanguard of the movement to achieve this sacred national objective.

15. The liberation of Palestine is a national obligation for the Arabs. It is their duty to repel the Zionist and imperialist invasion of the greater Arab homeland and to liquidate the Zionist presence in Palestine. . . .

16. On the spiritual plane, the liberation of Palestine will establish in the Holy Land an atmosphere of peace and tranquility in which all religious institutions will be safeguarded and freedom of worship and the right of visit guaranteed to all without discrimination or distinction of race, color, language or creed. For this reason the people of Palestine look to all spiritual forces in the world for support.

17. On the human plane, the liberation of Palestine will restore to the Palestinians their dignity, integrity and freedom. For this reason, the Palestinian Arab people look at all those who believe in the dignity and freedom of man for support. . . .

19. The partition of Palestine, which took place in 1947, and the establishment of Israel, are fundamentally invalid, however long they last, for they contravene the will of the people of Palestine and their natural right to their homeland and contradict the principles of the United Nations Charter, foremost among which is the right of self-determination.

20. The Balfour Declaration, the Mandate Instrument, and all their consequences, are hereby declared null and void.[2] The claim of historical or spiritual links between the Jews and Palestine is neither in conformity with historical fact nor does it satisfy the requirements for statehood. Judaism is a revealed religion; it is not a separate nationality, nor are the Jews a single people with a separate identity; they are citizens of their respective countries. . . .

---

[1]Commandos are highly trained soldiers who operate in small units usually inside enemy territory.

[2]The Balfour Declaration of 1917 pledged Great Britain to support the establishment of a Jewish state in Palestine.

22. Zionism is a political movement that is organically linked with world imperialism and is opposed to all liberation movements or movements for progress in the world. The Zionist movement is essentially fanatical and racialist; its objectives involve aggression, expansion and the establishment of colonial settlements, and its methods are those of the Fascists and the Nazis. Israel acts as cat's paw[3] for the Zionist movement, a geographic and manpower base for world imperialism and a springboard for its thrust into the Arab homeland to frustrate the aspirations of the Arab nation to liberation, unity and progress. Israel is a constant threat to peace in the Middle East and the whole world. Inasmuch as the liberation of Palestine will eliminate the Zionist and imperialist presence in that country and bring peace to the Middle East, the Palestinian people look for support to all liberals and to all forces of good, peace and progress in the world, and call on them, whatever their political convictions, for all possible aid and support in their just and legitimate struggle to liberate their homeland.

---

[3]Someone or something used by another as a tool.

Palestine as a Jewish Homeland

❖

85 ◆ Chaim Herzog, SPEECH TO THE UNITED NATIONS GENERAL ASSEMBLY

In the mid 1970s the Palestine Liberation Organization, with the support of most Arab states, began a campaign to discredit Israel in international forums. In the summer of 1975, at the urging of the PLO, the Organization of African Unity and the Conference of Non-aligned Nations both condemned Zionism as racist and imperialist and grouped Israel with the white racist regimes of Rhodesia and South Africa. Several months later an anti-Israel resolution was proposed in the General Assembly of the United Nations.

Chaim Herzog, Israeli ambassador to the UN, denounced the resolution in the following speech delivered on November 10, 1975. Just hours later a coalition of Muslim, Arab, Third World, and Soviet-bloc nations approved the resolution which states that "Zionism is a form of racism and racial discrimination."

QUESTIONS FOR ANALYSIS

1. What does Herzog mean when he says, "Zionism is to the Jewish people what the liberation movements of Africa and Asia have been to their own people"?
2. How does Herzog's historical perspective on Palestine differ from that of the 1968 Palestine National Charter?
3. What is at stake in the debate on the resolution, other than the existence of Israel?

It is symbolic that this debate, which may well prove to be a turning point in the fortunes of the United Nations and a decisive factor in the possible continued existence of this organization, should take place on November 10. Tonight, thirty-seven years ago, has gone down in history as Kristallnacht, the Night of the Crystals. This was the night in 1938 when Hitler's Nazi storm-troopers launched a coordinated attack on the Jewish community in Germany, burned the synagogues in all its cities and made bonfires in the streets of the Holy Books and the Scrolls of the Holy Law and Bible. It was the night when Jewish homes were attacked and heads of families taken away, many of them never to return. It was the night when the windows of all Jewish businesses and stores were smashed, covering the streets in the cities of Germany with a film of broken glass which dissolved into the millions of crystals which gave the night its name. It was the night which led eventually to the crematoria and the gas chambers, Auschwitz, Birkenau, Dachau, Buchenwald, Teresienstadt and others. It was the night which led to the most terrifying holocaust in the history of man.

It is indeed befitting, Mr. President, that this debate, conceived in the desire to deflect the Middle East from its moves towards peace and born of a deep pervading feeling of anti-Semitism, should take place on the anniversary of this day. It is indeed befitting, Mr. President, that the United Nations, which began its life as an anti-Nazi alliance, should thirty years later find itself on its way to becoming the world center of anti-Semitism. Hitler would have felt at home on a number of occasions during the past year, listening to the proceedings in this forum, and above all to the proceedings during the debate on Zionism.

It is sobering to consider to what level this body has been dragged down if we are obliged today to contemplate an attack on Zionism. For this attack constitutes not only an anti-Israeli attack of the foulest type, but also an assault in the United Nations on Judaism — one of the oldest established religions in the world, a religion which has given the world the human values of the Bible, and from which two other great religions, Christianity and Islam, sprang. Is it not tragic to consider that we here at this meeting in the year 1975 are contemplating what is a scurrilous attack on a great and established religion which has given to the world the Bible with its Ten Commandments, the great prophets of old, Moses, Isaiah, Amos; the great thinkers of history, Maimonides, Spinoza, Marx, Einstein,[1] many of the masters of the arts and as high a percentage of Nobel Prize–winners in the world, in sciences, in the arts and in the humanities as has been achieved by any people on earth? . . .

I do not come to this rostrum to defend the moral and historical values of the Jewish people. They do not need to be defended. They speak for themselves. They have given to mankind much of what is great and eternal. They have done for the spirit of man more than can readily be appreciated by a forum such as this one.

I come here to denounce the two great evils which menace society in general and a society of nations in particular. These two evils are hatred and ignorance. These two evils are the motivating force behind the proponents of this resolution and their supporters. These two evils characterize those who would drag this world organization, the ideals of which were first conceived by the prophets of Israel, to the depths to which it has been dragged today.

The key to understanding Zionism is in its name. The eastern-most of the two hills of ancient Jerusalem during the tenth century B.C. was called Zion. In fact, the name Zion, referring to Jerusalem, appears 152 times in the Old Testament. The name is overwhelmingly a poetic and prophetic designation. The religious

---

[1]Maimonides (1135–1204) and Baruch Spinoza (1632–1677) were prominent philosophers. Einstein (1879–1955) was of course a giant of modern physics. There is some irony in Herzog's mention of Karl Marx; every communist state in the UN voted for the anti-Zionist resolution.

and emotional qualities of the name arise from the importance of Jerusalem as the Royal City and the City of the Temple. "Mount Zion" is the place where God dwells. Jerusalem, or Zion, is a place where the Lord is King, and where He has installed His King, David.

King David made Jerusalem the capital of Israel almost three thousand years ago, and Jerusalem has remained the capital ever since. During the centuries the term "Zion" grew and expanded to mean the whole of Israel. The Israelites in exile could not forget Zion. The Hebrew Psalmist sat by the waters of Babylon and swore: "If I forget thee, O Jerusalem, let my right hand forget her cunning." This oath has been repeated for thousands of years by Jews throughout the world. It is an oath which was made over seven hundred years before the advent of Christianity and over twelve hundred years before the advent of Islam, and Zion came to mean the Jewish homeland, symbolic of Judaism, of Jewish national aspirations.

While praying to his God every Jew, wherever he is in the world, faces towards Jerusalem. For over two thousand years of exile these prayers have expressed the yearning of the Jewish people to return to their ancient homeland, Israel. . . .

Zionism is the name of the national movement of the Jewish people and is the modern expression of the ancient Jewish heritage. The Zionist ideal, as set out in the Bible, has been, and is, an integral part of the Jewish religion.

Zionism is to the Jewish people what the liberation movements of Africa and Asia have been to their own people. . . .

In modern times, in the late nineteenth century, spurred by the twin forces of anti-Semitic persecution and of nationalism, the Jewish people organized the Zionist movement in order to transform their dream into reality. Zionism as a political movement was the revolt of an oppressed nation against the depredation and wicked discrimination and oppression of the countries in which anti-Semitism flourished. It is no coincidence that the co-sponsors and supporters of this resolution include countries who are guilty of the horrible crimes of anti-Semitism and discrimination to this very day.

Support for the aim of Zionism was written into the League of Nations Mandate for Palestine and was again endorsed by the United Nations in 1947, when the General Assembly voted by overwhelming majority for the restoration of Jewish independence in our ancient land.

The re-establishment of Jewish independence in Israel, after centuries of struggle to overcome foreign conquest and exile, is a vindication of the fundamental concepts of the equality of nations and of self-determination. To question the Jewish people's right to national existence and freedom is not only to deny to the Jewish people the right accorded to every other people on this globe, but it is also to deny the central precepts of the United Nations.

◆

Revolution and Reaction in Latin America

In August 1961 delegates to a meeting of the Organization of America States in Punta del Este, Uruguay, approved a set of goals for the Alliance for Progress, a new program proposed by U.S. President John F. Kennedy to foster Latin American economic development and social reform with the help of billions of American dollars. Their list of goals, known as the Charter of Punta del Este, was ambitious. Within a decade participants hope to achieve economic growth of 2.5 percent per year, more equitable distribution of national income, greater industrialization, agrarian reform, elimination of adult illiteracy, price stability, improved health care, reduced infant mortality, increased life expectancy by at least five years, and much more. The result would be "maximum levels of well-being, with equal opportunities for all, in democratic societies adapted to their own needs and desires."

Viewed against the record of Latin American states in the 1960s and 1970s, the Punta del Este Charter makes depressing reading. The Alliance for Progress poured billions of dollars into hastily conceived programs that did little to advance economic development or democracy. Latin America floundered politically and economically; if anything, the problems the Alliance for Progress sought to eradicate in ten years became worse, not better.

By the early 1970s Latin America was experiencing widening trade deficits, weakened commodity prices, and double- and even triple-digit inflation. Some states, such as Brazil, had achieved growth in manufacturing, but this mainly benefited foreign corporations, mostly from the United States. With the aid of tax breaks and other government favors, these corporations swallowed up or bankrupted smaller national firms, and took approximately three dollars out of the region for each dollar invested. Most governments ignored the problem of mass poverty, which worsened as a result of population growth, depressed wages, and urbanization. Serious programs for social reform, adopted in Guatemala and Bolivia in the early 1950s, Peru in 1968, and Chile in the early 1970s, either languished or were quashed by right-wing coups.

One state that experienced major social reforms was Fidel Castro's Cuba. After the overthrow of the dictator Batista in 1959, Castro's socialist revolution carried out land reform, nationalized industries, provided universal health care and education, and succeeded in raising standards of living. Paradoxically, it also dimmed the prospects for social reform in the rest of the region. Although it raised hopes among the poor and inspired dozens of revolutionary movements, Castro's Cuba frightened Latin America's elites, who rallied behind military dictatorships that promised to halt the spread of communism.

Such military regimes were supported by the U.S. government, whose political involvement in Latin America reached new heights with the onset of the Cold War and after the Cuban Revolution. The Eisenhower administration sought to limit social and economic reform in Bolivia after a revolution in 1952; cooperated with Great Britain to overthrow a left-leaning administration in British Guiana; and trained and outfitted rebels who overthrew Guatemala's democratically elected government in 1954 after its plans for land reform threatened the Boston-based banana conglomerate, the United Fruit Company.

Similar efforts to overthrow Castro failed. Assassination plots came to nothing, and the CIA-planned invasion of Cuba by anti-Castro exiles was crushed in April 1961. The United States also attempted to counter communism with the Alliance for Progress, the program of social reform and economic development that failed, and support for right-wing governments, a program that in the short run succeeded. During the 1970s, repressive authoritarian regimes proliferated in Central and South America. They used death squads, assassins, torturers, and U.S.-equipped armies against leftist politicians, social reformers, and Marxist revolutionaries. Communism was contained, but rural poverty, inflation, foreign debt, and rampant urbanization became worse than ever.

"Create Two, Three, or Many Vietnams"

◆

86 ◆ Ernesto "Che" Guevara, *MESSAGE TO THE TRICONTINENTAL CONFERENCE*

Ernesto Guevara (nicknamed "Che" by Cubans after the colloquial Argentinean term for mate) was born into a well-to-do Argentinean family in 1928 and was trained as a doctor. After traveling through much of Latin America, including a stop in Guatemala where he fought against the CIA-sponsored invasion in 1954, he was introduced to Fidel Castro, a young Cuban, in Mexico City in 1955. Castro, who had been fighting to overthrow the Cuban dictator Fulgencio Batista since 1953, convinced Guevara to join the band of fighters he was organizing to land in Cuba and renew the struggle. After the expeditionary force reached Cuba in 1956, Guevara proved his mastery of guerrilla warfare and became Castro's second in command. He led the troops that took Havana in January 1959.

Once Castro was in power, Guevara served as head of the national bank and minister of industry. But he dedicated most of his efforts to the cause of Third World revolution, something he believed could be achieved by following the Cuban model of rural insurrection and guerrilla warfare. In 1966 he helped organize the first Tricontinental Conference in Havana, attended by Castro supporters from Asia, Africa, and Latin America. In 1967 his message to this conference was published in the journal *Tricontinental.*

By the time the article appeared, Guevara had left Cuba for Bolivia, where he sought to organize guerrillas fighting against the right-wing generals who had seized power in 1964. Hunted down and captured by government troops, he was executed by a firing squad in October 1967. Che lived on, however, as a revolutionary hero for student radicals around the world, who chanted "Che lives!" and carried posters with his image as they marched and demonstrated in the late 1960s.

QUESTIONS FOR ANALYSIS

1. According to Guevara, how is U.S. imperialism manifested in Latin America?
2. What factors, according to Guevara, make Latin America a promising area for revolutionary activity?
3. How does Guevara view the future of the revolutionary movement in Latin America?
4. What does Guevara specifically mean when he envisions "two, three, or many Viet Nams"?
5. What are Guevara's hopes for the future of Latin America and the world?

U.S. imperialism is guilty of aggression — its crimes are enormous and cover the whole world. We already know all that, gentlemen! . . . But imperialism is bogging down in Viet Nam, is unable to find a way out and desperately seeks one that will overcome with dignity this dangerous situation in which it now finds itself. . . .

What role shall we, the exploited people of the world, play? The peoples of the three continents focus their attention on Viet Nam and learn their lesson. Since imperialists blackmail humanity by threatening it with war, the wise reaction is not to fear war. The general tactics of the people should be to launch a constant and a firm attack on all fronts where the confrontation is taking place.

In those places where the meager peace we have has been violated, what is our duty? To liberate ourselves at any price. . . .

The fundamental field of imperialist exploitation comprises the three underdeveloped continents: America, Asia, and Africa. Every country has its own characteristics, but each continent, as a whole, also presents its own characteristics. America constitutes a group of more or less homogeneous countries and in most parts of its territory U.S. monopoly capital maintains an absolute supremacy. Puppet governments or, in the best of cases, weak and fearful local rulers, are incapable of contradicting orders from their Yankee master. . . . Its policy is to maintain that which has already been conquered. The line of action, at the present time, is limited to the brutal use of force with the purpose of thwarting the liberation movements, no matter of what type they might happen to be.

The slogan "we will not allow another Cuba" hides the possibility of perpetrating aggressions without fear of reprisal, such as the one carried out against the Dominican Republic, or before that, the massacre in Panama[1] — and the clear warning stating that Yankee troops are ready to intervene anywhere in America where the established order may be altered, thus endangering their interests. . . . But almost every country of this continent is ripe for a type of struggle that, in order to achieve victory, cannot be content with anything less than establishing a government of a socialist nature. . . .

. . . There is also such a great similarity among the classes of the different countries, that an identification exists among them, as an "international American" type, much more complete than that of other continents. Language, customs, religion, a common foreign master, unite them. The degree and forms of exploitation are similar in their effects for both the exploiters and the exploited in many of the countries of our America. And rebellion is ripening swiftly here.

We may ask ourselves: how will this rebellion come to fruition? What type will it be? We have maintained for quite some time now that, owing to the similarity of characteristics, the struggle in America will achieve, in due course, continental proportions. It will be the scene of many great battles fought for the liberation of humanity. . . . But if the foci of war are developed with sufficient political and military wisdom, they will become practically invincible, obliging the Yankees to send reinforcements. . . . Little by little, the obsolete weapons which are sufficient for the repression of small armed bands will be exchanged for modern armaments and the U.S. military "advisers" will be replaced by U.S. soldiers until, at a given moment, they will be forced to send increasingly greater numbers of regular troops to ensure the relative stability of a government whose national puppet army is disintegrating before the attacks of the guerrillas. It is the road of Viet Nam; it is the road that should be followed by the peoples; it is the road that will be followed in America. . . .

America, forgotten continent in the world's more recent liberation struggles, now beginning to make itself heard through the Tricontinental in the voice of the vanguard of its peoples, the

---

[1]In 1965 President Lyndon Johnson dispatched Marines to the Dominican Republic to suppress a rebellion against the military dictatorship that had taken power by a coup d'état two years earlier. In 1959 one hundred would-be revolutionaries who landed in Panama were trapped and annihilated by Panamanian and U.S. troops.

Cuban Revolution, will have a task of much greater relevance: to create a Second or a Third Viet Nam, or the Second and Third Viet Nam of the world. . . .

. . . The struggle will be long, harsh, and its battle fronts will be the guerrilla's refuge, the cities, the homes of the fighters — where the repressive forces will go seeking easy victims among their families — among the massacred rural population, in the villages or cities destroyed by the bombardments of the enemy. . . . The great lesson of the invincibility of the guerrillas will take root in the dispossessed masses. The galvanizing of national spirit, preparation for harder tasks, for resisting even more violent repressions. Hatred as an element of struggle; relentless hatred of the enemy that impels us over and beyond the natural limitations of man and transforms us into effective, violent, selective and cold killing machines. Our soldiers must be thus; a people without hatred cannot vanquish a brutal enemy.

We must carry the war as far as the enemy carries it: to his home, to his centers of entertainment, make it a total war. It is necessary to prevent him from having a moment of peace, a quiet moment outside his barracks or even inside; we must attack him wherever he may be, make him feel like a cornered beast wherever he may move. Then his morale will begin to fall. . . .

What a luminous, near future would be visible to us if two, three or many Viet Nams flourished throughout the world with their share of death and their immense tragedies, their everyday heroism and their repeated blows against imperialism obliging it to disperse its forces under the attack of the increasing hatred of all the peoples of the earth!

And if we were all capable of uniting to make our blows more solid and more infallible so that the effectiveness of every kind of support given to the struggling peoples were increased — how great and how near that future would be!

. . . Our very action is a battle cry against imperialism, and a call for the peoples' unity against the great enemy of mankind: the United States of America. Wherever death may surprise us, it will be welcome, provided that this, our battle cry, has reached a receptive ear and that another hand be extended to take up our weapons, and that other men come forward to intone the funeral dirge with the staccato of machine guns and new cries of battle and victory.

The Fall of Allende and the CIA

87 ◆ *CHURCH COMMITTEE REPORT ON COVERT ACTIONS IN CHILE, 1963–1973*

Established by the National Security Act of 1947, the Central Intelligence Agency was in the vanguard of the U.S. campaign against international communism for the next forty years. CIA experts, researchers, and agents advised U.S. presidents on international developments; provided information on political and economic conditions in other countries; carried on counterintelligence activities; monitored foreign broadcasts, newspapers, and government communiqués; and engaged in more direct forms of espionage. As the following selection reveals, the goals of espionage included weakening or removing from power politicians perceived as threats to U.S. interests.

Chile, a country with a long democratic tradition and rich copper deposits, was the scene of intense CIA activity in the 1960s and early 1970s. In the 1964 presidential elections, the CIA helped undermine the candidacy of Salvador Allende, the physician turned politician who led a socialist-communist coalition on a platform of anti-imperialism, anticapitalism, land reform, and the nationalization of industry. Allende received 39 percent of the vote, but was handily defeated by Eduardo Frei, the leader of the centrist Christian Democrats. By the next presidential election in 1970, the political situation had changed. Frei's Christian Democrats had run out of ideas, inflation was surging, and, most importantly, the rightist parties were running their own candidate rather than backing the Christian Democrats. Allende received 36 percent of the vote — less than in 1964, but enough to win a plurality. In October 1970, after a military coup failed to overturn the election, Allende became president.

Despite his narrow victory, Allende boldly proceeded with his socialist program. The government froze prices and raised wages, nationalized the copper industry and dozens of other sectors of the economy, and liquidated large estates as part of its land reform program. But Allende faced formidable obstacles. Radicals in his coalition demanded faster change, while conservatives and moderates remained inalterably opposed to his policies. Furthermore, the cessation of U.S. aid and the halt in loans and foreign investments crippled a Chilean economy already weakened by the transition from private to government ownership. In September 1973 Allende's opponents within the military mounted a coup d'état that resulted in the death of Allende and five thousand other Chileans and the end of Chile's socialist experiment. It also resulted in the beginning of military rule under General Augusto Pinochet, who remained Chile's dictator until 1990.

Historians still debate the reasons for Allende's fall, but all agree his chances of survival were weakened by the campaign to destabilize his government orchestrated by the CIA and other U.S. government agencies. The full extent of this campaign was revealed in a report issued in 1975 by the Select Committee to Study Governmental Operations in Respect to Intelligence Activities. Better known as the Church Committee, after its chair, Senator Frank Church of Idaho, it had been charged by the Senate to investigate "illegal, improper, or unethical" operations by the CIA. The committee's findings, along with those of a House of Representatives committee, led to executive orders under Presidents Ford and Carter to increase presidential control over the CIA's covert operations and the passing by Congress of the Intelligence Oversight Act in 1980.

QUESTIONS FOR ANALYSIS

1. What does the Church Committee report reveal about U.S. Cold War attitudes and goals?
2. How much did the CIA destabilization efforts described in this document depend on the cooperation of Chileans?
3. What does the document reveal about the control and oversight of CIA operations by the executive branch?
4. The Church Committee was charged with judging whether CIA activities in Chile were "improper and immoral." What is your own judgment on this issue?

[THE 1964 ELECTION]

The United States was involved on a massive scale in the 1964 presidential election in Chile. . . . A total of nearly four million dollars was spent on some fifteen covert action projects, ranging from organizing slum dwellers to passing funds to political parties.

The goal, broadly, was to prevent or minimize the influence of Chilean Communists or Marxists in the government that would emerge from the 1964 election. Consequently, the U.S. sought the most effective way of opposing FRAP[1] (Popular Action Front), an alliance of Chilean Socialists, Communists, and several miniscule non-Marxist parties of the left which backed the candidacy of Salvador Allende. Specifically, the policy called for support of the Christian Democratic Party, the Democratic Front (a coalition of rightist parties), and a variety of anti-communist propaganda and organizing activities. . . .

Covert action during the 1964 campaign was composed of two major elements. One was direct financial support of the Christian Democratic campaign. The CIA underwrote slightly more than half of the total cost of that campaign. After debate, the Special Group[2] decided not to inform the Christian Democratic candidate, Eduardo Frei, of American covert support of his campaign. A number of intermediaries were therefore mobilized to pass the money to the Christian Democrats. . . .

In addition to support for political parties, the CIA mounted a massive anti-communist propaganda campaign. Extensive use was made of the press, radio, films, pamphlets, posters, leaflets, direct mailings, paper streamers, and wall painting. It was a "scare campaign," which relied heavily on images of Soviet tanks and Cuban firing squads and was directed especially to women. Hundreds of thousands of copies of the anti-communist pastoral letter of Pope Pius XI[3] were distributed by Christian Democratic organizations. They carried the designation, "printed privately by citizens without political affiliation, in order more broadly to disseminate its content." "Disinformation" and — "black propaganda" — material which purported to originate from another source, such as the Chilean Communist Party — were used as well.

The propaganda campaign was enormous. During the first week of intensive propaganda activity . . ., a CIA-funded propaganda group produced twenty radio spots per day in Santiago and on 44 provincial stations; twelve-minute news broadcasts five times daily on three Santiago stations and 24 provincial outlets; thousands of cartoons, and much paid press advertising. By the end of June, the group produced 24 daily newscasts in Santiago and the provinces, 26 weekly "commentary" programs, and distributed 3,000 posters daily. . . .

[COVERT ACTION: 1964–1969]

Covert action efforts were conducted during this period to influence the political development of various sectors of Chilean society. One project, conducted prior to the 1964 elections to strengthen Christian Democratic support among peasants and slum dwellers, continued to help train and organize "anti-communists" in these and other sectors until public exposure of CIA funding in 1967 forced its termination. A project to compete organizationally with the Marxists among the urban poor of Santiago was initiated shortly after the 1964 election, and was terminated in mid-1969 because the principal agent was unwilling to prejudice the independent posture of the organization by using it on a large scale to deliver votes in the 1969 and 1970 presidential elections. In the mid-1960s, the CIA

---

[1]FRAP stands for Frente de Action Popular, a coalition of leftist parties that competed in elections in the 1950s and 1960s.
[2]The CIA operatives responsible for activities relating to the election.

[3]Pius XI was pope from 1922 until 1939. A staunch anti-Marxist, in 1931 he issued the encyclical *Quadragesimo anno,* in which he stressed the need for Christian social action to deal with poverty.

supported an anti-communist women's group active in Chilean political and intellectual life. . . .

[THE 1970 ELECTION]

. . . In March 1970, the 40 Committee[4] decided that the United States should not support any single candidate in the election but should instead wage "spoiling" operations against the Popular Unity[5] coalition which supported the Marxist candidate, Salvador Allende. In all, the CIA spent from $800,000 to $1,000,000 on convert action to affect the outcome of the 1970 Presidential election. . . .

There was a wide variety of propaganda products: a newsletter mailed to approximately two thousand journalists, academicians, politicians, and other opinion makers; a booklet showing what life would be like if Allende won the presidential election; translation and distribution of chronicles of opposition to the Soviet regime; poster distribution and sign-painting teams. The sign-painting teams had instructions to paint the slogan "*su paredón*" (your wall) on 2,000 walls, evoking an image of communist firing squads. The "scare campaign" . . . exploited the violence of the invasion of Czechoslovakia[6] with large photographs of Prague and of tanks in downtown Santiago. Other posters, resembling those used in 1964, portrayed Cuban political prisoners before the firing squad, and warned that an Allende victory would mean the end of religion and family life in Chile. . . .

[BETWEEN SEPTEMBER 4 AND OCTOBER 24, 1970]

On September 4, 1970, Allende won a plurality in Chile's presidential election. Since no candidate had received a majority of the popular vote, the Chilean Constitution required that a joint session of its Congress decide between the first- and second-place finishers. The date set for the congressional session was October 24, 1970.

The reaction in Washington to Allende's plurality victory was immediate. The 40 Committee met on September 8 and 14 to discuss what action should be taken prior to the October 24 congressional vote. On September 15, President Nixon informed CIA Director Richard Helms that an Allende regime in Chile would not be acceptable to the United States and instructed the CIA to play a direct role in organizing a military *coup d'etat* in Chile to prevent Allende's accession to the Presidency. . . .

. . . U.S. Government efforts to prevent Allende from assuming office proceeded on two tracks. Track I comprised all covert activities approved by the 40 Committee, including political, economic and propaganda activities. . . . Track II activities in Chile were undertaken in response to President Nixon's September 15 order and were directed toward actively promoting and encouraging the Chilean military to move against Allende. . . .

On October 24, 1970, Salvador Allende was confirmed as President by Chilean Congress. On November 3, he was inaugurated. U.S. efforts, both overt and covert, to prevent his assumption of office had failed.

[COVERT ACTION DURING THE ALLENDE YEARS, 1970–1973]

United States foreign economic policy toward Allende's government was articulated at the highest levels of the U.S. government, and coordinated by interagency task forces. . . . Richard Helms'[7] notes from his September 15, 1970, meeting with President Nixon, the meeting

---

[4]The 40 Committee was a subcabinet-level body of the executive branch with a mandate to review and approve major covert actions by the CIA. It was chaired by the president's assistant for national security affairs, and included the undersecretary of state for political affairs, the deputy secretary of defense, the chairman of the joint chiefs of staff, and the CIA director.

[5]Popular Unity (Unidad Popular) replaced FRAP as the coalition of the left in the 1970 election.
[6]A reference to the Soviet invasion of Czechoslovakia in 1968 to halt the reform movement in the Czechoslovakian Communist Party (see Chapter 10, source 79).
[7]Director of the CIA from 1965 to 1973.

which initiated Track II, contain the indication: "Make the economy scream." A week later Ambassador Korry[8] reported telling Frei, through his Defense Minister, that "not a nut or bolt would be allowed to reach Chile under Allende." . . .

The policy of economic pressure . . . was to be implemented through several means. All new bilateral foreign assistance was to be stopped. . . . The U.S. would use its predominant position in international financial institutions to dry up the flow of new multilateral credit or other financial assistance. To the extent possible, financial assistance or guarantees to U.S. private investment in Chile would be ended, and U.S. businesses would be made aware of the government's concern and its restrictive policies. . . .

After the failure of Track II, the CIA rebuilt its network of contacts and remained close to Chilean military officers in order to monitor developments within the armed forces. For their part, Chilean officers who were aware that the United States once had sought a coup to prevent Allende from becoming president must have been sensitive to indications of continuing U.S. support for a coup.

By September 1971 a new network of agents was in place and the Station was receiving almost daily reports of new coup plotting. The Station and Headquarters[9] began to explore ways to use this network. At the same time, and in parallel, the Station and Headquarters discussed a "deception operation" designed to alert Chilean officers to real or purported Cuban involvement in the Chilean army. . . .

The CIA's information-gathering efforts with regard to the Chilean military included activity which went beyond the mere collection of information. More generally, those efforts must be viewed in the context of United States opposition, overt and covert, to the Allende government. They put the United States Government in contact with those Chileans who sought a military alternative to the Allende presidency. . . .

[AFTER THE COUP D'ÉTAT]

Following the September 11, 1973, coup, the military Junta, led by General Augusto Pinochet, moved quickly to consolidate its newly acquired power. Political parties were banned, Congress was put in indefinite recess, press censorship was instituted, supporters of Allende and others deemed opponents of the new regime were jailed, and elections were put off indefinitely. . . .

In addition, charges concerning the violation of human rights in Chile continue to be directed to the Junta. Most recently, a United Nations report on Chile charged that "torture centers" are being operated in Santiago and other parts of the country. The lengthy document, issued October 14, 1975, listed 11 centers where it says prisoners are being questioned "by methods amounting to torture." . . .

The goal of covert action immediately following the coup was to assist the Junta in gaining a more positive image, both at home and abroad, and to maintain access to the command levels of the Chilean government. Another goal, achieved in part through work done at the opposition research organization before the coup, was to help the new government organize and implement new policies. Project files record that CIA collaborators were involved in preparing an initial overall economic plan which has served as the basis for the Junta's most important economic decisions.

---

[8]Edward Korry, U.S. ambassador to Chile.
[9]*Station* refers to the headquarters of agents in place in Chile; *Headquarters* refers to CIA headquarters in Langley, Virginia.

Racism and Ethnic Conflict in Independent Africa

Once the scramble for Africa began in the late nineteenth century, it took the European powers only two decades to impose their authority on the continent. After World War II, it took them even less time to leave. In the late 1940s European colonial administrators viewed African independence as an event so far off in the future that to discuss even the vaguest of timetables was premature. Actual events were far different from expectations. After the Gold Coast gained independence from Great Britain in 1957 and became Ghana, decolonization proceeded in a rush. Between 1957 and 1975 forty-six former African colonies became sovereign states. Zimbabwe (formerly Rhodesia) became independent in 1980 as did Namibia (occupied by South Africa since the 1920s) in 1990. The last vestige of white political rule in Africa ended when South Africa abandoned apartheid in 1994 and granted blacks full political rights.

At first the new African states made progress toward reaching one of their primary goals, improving their people's standard of living. Through the 1960s annual growth rates were between 3 percent and 4 percent, and inflation was kept to reasonable levels. Between 1960 and 1972, the number of African students attending schools at the primary, secondary, and university levels increased from 17.8 million to 37.6 million. Such accomplishments were short-lived, however. In a catastrophe no one could have anticipated in the 1960s, a host of problems, including rapid population growth, drought, falling commodity prices, increased energy costs, mismanagement, and government corruption soon sent the African economy into free fall.

Another goal of the new states, stable government, proved difficult from the start. Africa's new leaders were soon overwhelmed by a host of intractable problems: poor communications, low literacy levels, resistance of peasant societies to taxation by distant governments, widespread poverty, arbitrarily drawn national boundaries, foreign interference, and the persistence of local and ethnic loyalties. Some new states began to fall apart at the moment of independence. In the Congo Republic, the former Belgian Congo and now the Democratic Republic of Congo, civil war broke out in June 1960, within hours after Belgian rule ended. Nigeria, which became independent in 1960, also fell victim to civil war when its eastern province rebelled and declared itself the independent state of Biafra in 1967.

Most African states held together but quickly abandoned parliamentary government. The experience of Ghana, which won its independence in 1957, was not untypical. Kwame Nkrumah, the leader of the independence movement and Ghana's first prime minister, soon scuttled the Ghanaian constitution, had political opponents jailed without trial, and abolished competing political parties. Even his own party, the Convention People's Party, withered away, having been made superfluous by Nkrumah's dictatorship. While the economy suffered from plummeting cocoa prices, Nkrumah shifted from capitalism to socialism and sponsored massive public works projects, one of which was turning his ancestral hut into a national shrine. In 1966 while visiting China, he was overthrown by the military, whose seizure of power set a pattern of military coups interspersed by periods of civilian government. An exile, Nkrumah died in a Romanian sanatorium in 1973.

Blacks in South Africa faced a different kind of political challenge. Ever since South Africa had gained its independence from Great Britain in 1910, blacks, along with Indians and coloreds (people of mixed blood), had steadily lost ground politically and economically as a result of discriminatory laws imposed by the white minority. In the 1950s and early 1960s, a barrage of legislation sponsored by the Nationalist Party turned South African discrimination policies into something much harsher, the apartheid system. Nonwhites lost their remaining political rights; mixed marriages and interracial sex were outlawed; racial segregation was decreed for schools, technical colleges, universities, public transportation, restaurants, theaters, and sports facilities. Apartheid also demanded residential segregation, requiring blacks to live in urban townships or rural homelands known as bantustans. Unlike European colonialism, which melted away at the first sign of black nationalism, apartheid persisted despite black resistance and pressure from the international community. It ended only in 1994 when blacks received the right to vote for members of a parliament that would serve for five years and write a new constitution. The era of white rule in sub-Saharan Africa was finally over.

The Onset of Military Rule in Uganda

❖

88 ❖ *STATEMENTS FROM GENERAL IDI AMIN AND THE UGANDAN ARMY*

While cultural and ethnic divisions led to civil wars in newly independent Zaire and Nigeria, in Uganda they led to a military coup engineered by generals who promised order and constructive change but whose legacy was ineptitude, brutality, and deepening chaos. Like other former colonies, ethnic and religious divisions made colonial Uganda an unpromising candidate for nationhood. Northerners were mainly Muslims, while southerners were mostly Christians — some Catholics and some Protestants. In addition, under British rule a special arrangement had been struck between colonial authorities and the Bagandans (residents of Buganda), an ethnic group from the south who in return for their cooperation received preferential treatment in education, commerce, and the colonial administration.

Such differences were papered over by British authorities and Ugandan nationalists, and in 1962 Uganda became independent. The first prime minister was Milton Obote, a member of the northern Langi tribe and head of the Uganda People's Congress; the president was Mutesa II, Kabaka (hereditary ruler) of Buganda, which enjoyed a special and separate position within the republic.

Obote sought to overcome Uganda's divisions through authoritarian rule and reliance on the army. In 1966 he proclaimed a new constitution under the slogan "one country, one parliament, one government, one people," and then drove the Kabaka out of the country when Bagandans resisted their loss of privileges. In 1969 he issued "The Common Man's Charter," which outlined his plans for a socialist Uganda. After an attempt on Obote's life, his opponents were jailed, and all political parties were banned except his own. In 1971 he ordered the arrest and execution of his enemies in the army, but before the command could be carried out, army leaders under Idi Amin executed a successful coup d'état while Obote was attending a meeting of British Commonwealth leaders in Singapore.

Uganda's new leader, Idi Amin, was a northerner and a self-described Muslim. Having risen through the ranks of the army under the British, he became Uganda's commander-in-chief after independence. Despite promises of free elections, on seizing power he suspended all political activity and introduced detention without trial. Before he was overthrown in 1978, Uganda experienced both a reign of terror, in which as many as three hundred thousand Ugandans were murdered or disappeared, and economic catastrophe, caused in part by Amin's expulsion of Uganda's seven thousand Asian residents. He fell from power in 1978 when Tanzanian troops conquered most of Uganda after Amin had invaded Tanzania over a border dispute.

In the following selection, Amin himself and a spokesperson for the Ugandan army explain their reasons for overthrowing Obote in January 1971. The first part is from a press statement issued by Amin two days after the insurrection; the second part is from a manifesto issued by the army a short time later.

QUESTIONS FOR ANALYSIS

1. According to Amin, what were Obote's major deficiencies as a ruler?
2. According to Amin, how had Obote kept himself in power?
3. How does the emphasis of the army's manifesto differ from that of Amin's statement?
4. How prominently do matters of political principle, as opposed to self-interest, figure in the two anti-Obote statements?

[COMMANDER IDI AMIN'S PRESS STATEMENT]

What can be said without any doubt whatsoever is that Obote's regime was one of great hypocrites. Obote himself always claimed that he was a great socialist and yet there were very many things that he did that showed that he way anything but a socialist.

Obote had two palaces in Entebbe, three in Kampala, one in Jinja (fifty miles away), one in Tororo, one in Mbale (twenty eight miles from Tororo), one in Lira and elsewhere. All these palaces had to be furnished and maintained at great public expense, and yet all but one remained idle and unused almost all the time! It is no wonder that the people in Jinja, in their great joy attacked and damaged the so-called President's Palace at Jinja, total destruction of the place only being prevented by the Army.

Obote's mode of living was also anything but socialist. He heavily indulged in drink, smoking and women, and carried a big retinue (including bodyguards) wherever he went. This idle living was maintained at public expense and was also indulged in by Obote's Ministers and close advisers. . . .

Obote talked lofty words and wrote high-sounding pamphlets about socialism and yet his actions never matched his words. The endless taxes and high prices of basic commodities also showed that socialist Obote never cared anything about the people. As an example, the price of sugar, salt, rice, meat and many other foods doubled when Uganda changed over from the imperial to the metric systems of weights and measures, and yet Obote never enquired why this was so.

Corruption in Obote's regime was so widespread that it was almost being taken for granted. Ministers, Chairmen of parastatal bodies[1] and top public servants owned fleets of cars, buses, scores of houses for renting, bars, petrol stations etc. and Obote never in one single instance questioned any of his men as to the way they had acquired this wealth. . . . The worst aspect of the financial greed of Obote's men was that most of them ran the very businesses that ought to have been left to the common people, e.g. the taxi business and butcheries.

When it came to proposals for National Service it was obvious that Obote did not have the interest of the Common Man[1] at heart. Obote proposed that 'all able bodied persons' should spend at least two years in a National Service Camp, far away from their home districts, digging and learning all about agriculture. The people were not to be paid for their work on the National Service Camps. In making his National Service proposals, 'socialist' Obote totally ignored the social problems that would inevitably arise if his proposals were put into effect, especially those relating to the split family. . . .

Regardless of public feeling and popular opinion, Obote was determined to stay in power,

together with his whole bunch of corrupt Ministers. The last elections were held in Uganda in 1962, and Parliament was given a five year mandate expiring in 1967. . . .

In 1970 Obote solemnly declared that elections would be held in Uganda by April 1971, and he appointed an Electoral Commission to demarcate the electoral boundaries. He declared that candidates, all of whom would be nominated by the President's Election Commission, would have to stand in 4 widely scattered Constituencies.

This 4-Constituency idea was a trick by Obote to keep his henchmen in power since it obviously favoured the well known, and those who had funds to campaign in 4 scattered parts of the country. Obote's men obviously had funds, and moreover they all had embarked on intensive campaigns everywhere on Government expenses (under the guise of official tours) long before any official campaign period had been announced. . . .

Despite the fact that these confused electoral proposals were hedged around with safeguards and safety valves for Obote and his bunch of corrupt henchmen, Obote could never bring himself to announcing the date for a General Election. With most of the heavy pre-election programme not even started on by January 1971 . . . it was obvious to everybody that Obote's elections would not he held by April 1971 as he had solemnly promised. In fact he had already decided to 'postpone' the elections until October 1971, and no doubt . . . when that date arrived he would happily have 'postponed' the elections to some other date. . . .

Obote's actions in recent times showed that he hated and distrusted the Army which had kept him in power right from the day of Independence in 1962. He also greatly distrusted the people he ruled. For that reason Obote amassed hordes of weapons . . . and they have already been shown to the local and international press.

[1]Organizations that take on some roles of government through which the government operates indirectly.

[2]A sarcastic reference to Obote's "Common Man's Charter."

[MANIFESTO OF THE UGANDAN ARMY]

- Economic policies have left many people unemployed and even more insecure and lacking in the basic needs of life like food, clothing, medicine and shelter.
- High taxes have left the common man of this country poorer than ever before. Here are some of the taxes which the common man has to bear: Development Tax, Graduated Tax, Sales Tax, Social Security Fund Tax. The big men can always escape these taxes or pass them on to the common man.
- The prices which the common man gets for his crops like cotton and coffee have not gone up and sometimes they have gone down, whereas the cost of food, education, etc., has always gone up. . . .
- The creation of a wealthy class of leaders who are always talking of socialism while they grow richer and the common man poorer. . . .
- The Cabinet Office, by training large numbers of people (largely from the Akokoro County in Lango District where Obote and Akena Adoko, the Chief General Service Officer, came from) in armed warfare, has turned into a second army. Uganda therefore has had two armies, one in the Cabinet, the other Regular.
- The Lango development master plan written in 1967 decided that all key positions in Uganda's political, commercial, army and industrial life have to be occupied and controlled by people from Akokoro County, Lango District. Emphasis was put on development of Akokoro County in Lango District at the expense of other areas of Uganda.
- Obote . . . has sought to divide the Uganda Armed Forces and the rest of Uganda by picking out his own tribesmen and putting them in key positions in the Army and elsewhere. Examples: the Chief General Service Office, the Export and Import Corporation, Uganda Meat Packers, the Public Service Commission, Nyanza Textiles and a Russian textile factory to be situated in Lango.
- From the time Obote took over power in 1962 his greatest and most loyal supporter has been the Army. The Army has always tried to be an example to the whole of Africa by not taking over the Government and we have always followed that principle. It is, therefore, now a shock to us to see that Obote wants to divide and downgrade the Army by turning the Cabinet Office into another army. In doing this, Obote and Akena Adoko have bribed and used some senior officers who have turned against their fellow soldiers.

We all want only unity in Uganda and we do not want bloodshed. Everybody in Uganda knows that. The matters mentioned above appear to us to lead to bloodshed only.

Apartheid's Bitter Fruits

❖

89 ◆ *Nelson Mandela,* THE RIVONIA TRIAL SPEECH TO THE COURT

In 1912, two years after South Africa had been granted independence from Great Britain, blacks formed the African National Congress (ANC) to foster black unity and win political rights. At first the ANC sought to reach its goals through petitions and appeals to white politicians, but following the implementation of apartheid after World War II, it sponsored campaigns of passive resistance and supported strikes by black labor unions. The result was more government repression.

Predictably, some blacks abandoned moderation for sabotage and terrorism. Among them was Nelson Mandela (b. 1918), the son of a tribal chieftain, who became a lawyer and an ANC activist in the 1940s. After the ANC was outlawed in 1960, and after he organized a three-day stay-at-home protest in 1961, Mandela went into hiding. While avoiding a nationwide manhunt, he helped found Umkonto we Sizwe (Spear of the Nation), a branch of the ANC that carried out bombings in several cities. Arrested in 1963, he was convicted of treason and sent to the notorious prison on Robben Island, forty miles off South Africa's southern coast. He remained a prisoner until 1990, when he was released by President F. W. de Klerk as one of the first steps toward the abolition of the apartheid system.

The following excerpt comes from a speech delivered by Nelson Mandela on April 20, 1964, in which he opened his defense against charges of treason before an all-white court.

QUESTIONS FOR ANALYSIS

1. Why did Mandela decide that the ANC must resort to violence to achieve its goals?
2. What distinction does Mandela draw between sabotage and terrorism?
3. What attractions did Mandela and other ANC leaders see in communism?
4. What aspects of apartheid does Mandela find most degrading?
5. According to Mandela, how does apartheid affect the daily lives of the blacks?
6. How does Mandela's description of life in the black townships compare with Charlotte Maxeke's description of South African urban life in the 1930s (see Chapter 6, source 46)?

In my youth . . . I listened to the elders of my tribe telling stories of the old days. Amongst the tales they related to me were those of wars fought by our ancestors in defense of the fatherland. . . . I hoped then that life might offer me the opportunity to serve my people and make my own humble contribution to their freedom struggle. This is what has motivated me in all that I have done in relation to the charges made against me in this case. . . .

I have already mentioned that I was one of the persons who helped to form Umkonto. I, and the others who started the organization, did so for two reasons. Firstly, we believed that as a result of Government policy, violence by the African people had become inevitable, and that

unless responsible leadership was given to canalize and control the feelings of our people, there would be outbreaks of terrorism which would produce an intensity of bitterness and hostility between the various races of this country which is not produced even by war. Secondly, we felt that without violence there would be no way open to the African people to succeed in their struggle against the principle of White supremacy. All lawful modes of expressing opposition to this principle had been closed by legislation, and we were placed in a position in which we had either to accept a permanent state of inferiority, or to defy the Government. . . .

But the violence which we chose to adopt was not terrorism. We who formed Umkonto were all members of the African National Congress, and had behind us the ANC tradition of non-violence and negotiation as a means of solving political disputes. We believed that South Africa belonged to all the people who lived in it, and not to one group, be it Black or White. We did not want an interracial war, and tried to avoid it to the last minute. . . .

The African National Congress was formed in 1912 to defend the rights of the African people. . . . For thirty-seven years — that is until 1949 — it adhered strictly to a constitutional struggle. It put forward demands and resolutions; it sent delegations to the Government in the belief that African grievances could be settled through peaceful discussion and that Africans could advance gradually to full political rights. But White Governments remained unmoved, and the rights of Africans became less instead of becoming greater. . . .

Even after 1949, the ANC remained determined to avoid violence. At this time, however, there was a change from the strictly constitutional means of protest which had been employed in the past. The change was embodied in a decision which was taken to protest against apartheid legislation by peaceful, but unlawful, demonstrations against certain laws. Pursuant to this policy the ANC launched the Defiance Campaign, in which I was placed in charge of volunteers. This campaign was based on the principles of passive resistance. More than 8,500 people defied apartheid laws and went to jail. Yet there was not a single instance of violence in the course of this campaign on the part of any defier. . . .

In 1960 there was the shooting at Sharpeville,[1] which resulted in the proclamation of a state of emergency and the declaration of the ANC as an unlawful organization. My colleagues and I, after careful consideration, decided that we would not obey this decree. The African people were not part of the Government and did not make the laws by which they were governed. We believed in the words of the Universal Declaration of Human Rights,[2] that "the will of the people shall be the basis of authority of the Government," and for us to accept the banning was equivalent to accepting the silencing of the Africans for all time. The ANC refused to dissolve, but instead went underground. . . .

. . . Each disturbance pointed clearly to the inevitable growth among Africans of the belief that violence was the only way out — it showed that a Government which uses force to maintain its rule teaches the oppressed to use force to oppose it. . . .

The avoidance of civil war had dominated our thinking for many years, but when we decided to adopt violence as part of our policy, we realized that we might one day have to face the prospect of such a war. . . . We did not want to be committed to civil war, but we wanted to be ready if it became inevitable.

Four forms of violence were possible. There is sabotage, there is guerrilla warfare, there is terrorism, and there is open revolution. We chose to adopt the first method and to exhaust it before taking any other decision.

In the light of our political background the choice was a logical one. Sabotage did not involve loss of life, and it offered the best hope for future race relations. Bitterness would be kept to a minimum and, if the policy bore fruit, democratic government could become a reality. . . .

Attacks on the economic life lines of the country were to be linked with sabotage on Government buildings and other symbols of apartheid. These attacks would serve as a source of inspiration to our people. In addition, they would provide an outlet for those people who were urging the adoption of violent methods and would enable us to give concrete proof to our followers that we had adopted a stronger line and were fighting back against Government violence. . . .

---

[1]The Sharpeville Massacre took place in 1960 when police killed 69 and wounded 178 anti-apartheid demonstrators.

[2]The Universal Declaration of Human Rights was adopted by the United Nations on December 10, 1948.

Another of the allegations made by the State is that the aims and objects of the ANC and the Communist Party are the same. . . .

It is true that there has often been close co-operation between the ANC and the Communist Party. But cooperation is merely proof of a common goal — in this case the removal of White supremacy — and is not proof of a complete community of interests. . . .

It is perhaps difficult for White South Africans, with an ingrained prejudice against communism, to understand why experienced African politicians so readily accept communists as their friends. But to us the reason is obvious. Theoretical differences amongst those fighting against oppression is a luxury we cannot afford at this stage. What is more, for many decades communists were the only political group in South Africa who were prepared to treat Africans as human beings and their equals; who were prepared to eat with us, talk with us, live with us, and work with us. They were the only political group which was prepared to work with the Africans for the attainment of political rights and a stake in society. Because of this, there are many Africans who, today, tend to equate freedom with communism. . . .

Our fight is against real, and not imaginary, hardships or, to use the language of the State prosecutor, "so-called hardships." Basically, we fight against two features which are the hallmarks of African life in South Africa and which are entrenched by legislation which we seek to have repealed. These features are poverty and lack of human dignity. . . .

South Africa is the richest country in Africa, and could be one of the richest countries in the world. But it is a land of extremes and remarkable contrasts. The Whites enjoy what may well be the highest standard of living in the world, whilst Africans live in poverty and misery. Forty percent of the Africans live in hopelessly overcrowded and, in some cases, drought-stricken Reserves, where soil erosion and the overworking of the soil make it impossible for them to live properly off the land. Thirty

percent are laborers, labor tenants, and squatters on White farms and work and live under conditions similar to those of the serfs of the Middle Ages. The other 30 percent live in towns where they have developed economic and social habits which bring them closer in many respects to White standards. Yet most Africans, even in this group, are impoverished by low incomes and [the] high cost of living. . . .

The lack of human dignity experienced by Africans is the direct result of the policy of White supremacy. White supremacy implies Black inferiority. Legislation designed to preserve White supremacy entrenches this notion. Menial tasks in South Africa are invariably performed by Africans. When anything has to be carried or cleaned the White man will look around for an African to do it for him, whether the African is employed by him or not. Because of this sort of attitude, Whites tend to regard Africans as a separate breed. They do not look upon them as people with families of their own; they do not realize that they have emotions — that they fall in love like White people do; that they want to be with their wives and children like White people want to be with theirs; that they want to earn enough money to support their families properly, to feed and clothe them and send them to school. And what "house-boy" or "garden-boy" or laborer can ever hope to do this? . . .

Poverty and the breakdown of family life have secondary effects. Children wander about the streets of the townships because they have no schools to go to, or no money to enable them to go to school, or no parents at home to see that they go to school, because both parents (if there be two) have to work to keep the family alive. This leads to a breakdown in moral standards, to an alarming rise in illegitimacy, and to growing violence which erupts, not only politically, but everywhere. Life in the townships is dangerous. There is not a day that goes by without somebody being stabbed or assaulted. And violence is carried out of the townships in the White living areas. People are afraid to walk alone in the streets after dark. House-breakings and robberies are increasing, despite the fact that the death sentence can now be imposed for such offenses. Death sentences cannot cure the festering sore. . . .

During my lifetime I have dedicated myself to this struggle of the African people. I have fought against White domination, and I have fought against Black domination. I have cherished the ideal of a democratic and free society in which all persons live together in harmony and with equal opportunities. It is an ideal which I hope to live for and to achieve. But if needs be, it is an ideal for which I am prepared to die.

◆

South and Southeast Asia
After Colonialism

In the two decades after World War II, the peoples of South and Southeast Asia achieved independence from foreign rule, though how they achieved it varied widely. In the Philippines, it was the culmination of a long-standing U.S. plan to prepare the Filipinos for self-government. In India, it was the result of a protracted struggle on the part of the Indian people against British rule. In the Dutch East Indies, French Indochina, and British-controlled Burma, Singapore, and Malaya, Western imperialism effectively ended with the Japanese conquests of 1942, but in the case of Indochina and the East Indies, it took several years of fighting after World War II before the Dutch and French realized this and relinquished control of their colonies.

After achieving independence, the new nations of South and Southeast Asia faced many similar problems. All had high levels of poverty, widespread illiteracy, and little industry. All but a few had populations divided by race, language, and ethnic background. India was predominantly Hindu, but had large Sikh and Muslim minorities; so great was its linguistic diversity that its parliament approved no less than fourteen official languages in the 1950s. Burma had a population in which approximately one-third of its people practiced different religions and spoke different languages from those of the Buddhist majority. In Malaysia, the Malays, mainly farmers, and the Chinese, mainly businesspeople, viewed each other with distrust, as did the Tamils and Sinhalese in Ceylon (Sri Lanka) and the Muslims and Catholics in the Philippines. Pakistan was divided into two sections, two thousand miles apart, in which the people of West Pakistan spoke Urdu, grew wheat, and worried about drought while those in East Pakistan spoke Hindi, grew rice, and worried about floods. Indonesia was a nation of seventy-six million people who spoke two hundred fifty different languages and lived on thousands of islands that stretched across a distance equal to that between Boston and Ireland.

The region's new states all faced formidable political challenges. Although most started out as parliamentary democracies, democracy soon gave way to authoritarian regimes installed by the military in Burma, Pakistan, Thailand, and Indonesia. Vietnam, which was divided into a communist north and a noncommunist south after the French departed in 1954, became the scene of major U.S. military intervention to prevent the unification of the country under communist rule. The number of U.S. troops fighting in Vietnam grew slowly under Presidents Eisenhower and Kennedy, peaked at over five hundred thousand under President Johnson, and then rapidly declined under President Nixon, whose policy of Vietnamization resulted in U.S. troop withdrawals but continued support for the army of South Vietnam. Laos and Cambodia were also drawn into the struggle. The Ho Chi Minh Trail, by which North Vietnam sent troops and supplies to the south, ran through both countries, and this led to U.S. bombings, intervention to prop up anticommunist rulers, and the invasion of Cambodia by U.S. and South Vietnamese troops in 1970.

The U.S. mission in Southeast Asia failed on all fronts. Although the United States lost fifty-eight thousand troops, dropped more bombs on North Vietnam than it had dropped in all of World War II, and spent billions of dollars, in April 1975 South Vietnamese resistance collapsed, and Vietnam was united under communist rule. Later in 1975 communist regimes also gained control of Cambodia and Laos.

For Cambodians, the horror was not quite over. During the rule of the communist dictator Pol Pot, forced labor, starvation, systematic torture, and massacres of intellectuals, political opponents, and resident Vietnamese resulted in an estimated 1.7 million deaths. Only the invasion and occupation of Cambodia by North Vietnam in 1979 brought this chapter in the history of Southeast Asia to a close.

Nehru's Blueprint for India

❖

90 ◆ *Jawaharlal Nehru,* *SPEECHES AND WRITINGS, 1952–1955*

Born into a prestigious upper-class family in 1889, Jawaharlal Nehru was educated in England at Harrow School and at Cambridge University before studying law in London. On his return to India in 1912, he joined the Congress Party, which since 1885 had worked for increased Indian participation in the colonial administration and ultimately Indian independence. In 1919 Nehru decided to devote himself completely to the cause of Indian independence, after troops, on orders from a British officer, fired into a crowd of unarmed demonstrators in Amritsar, killing several hundred. He was elected president of the Congress Party in 1929. Repeatedly arrested by the British for participation in civil disobedience strikes and other political actions, he spent half of his next eighteen years in prison. After World War II, he took part in the negotiations that led to the creation of the separate states in India and Pakistan; after independece he helped craft India's constitution.

After Indian independence in 1947, Nehru served as head of the Congress Party and prime minister until his death in 1964. More so than any other individual, he shaped India's economic and political development. In the following excerpts from speeches and writings of the 1950s, he discusses his basic ideas.

QUESTIONS FOR ANALYSIS

1. What kind of society does Nehru envision for India, and how is it to be achieved? What role will capitalism play in India's future?
2. What does Nehru mean by "planning"?
3. Does Nehru seem to anticipate any difficulties that would prevent Indian planning from achieving its goals? What timetable does Nehru seem to have for achieving his economic goals for India?
4. What role should religion and the caste system play in modern India, according to Nehru?

[PLANNING AND THE WELFARE STATE]

As you all know, planning is essential, and without it there would be anarchy in our economic development. About five years ago, planning was not acceptable to many people in high places but today it has come to be recognized as essential even by the man in the street. . . .

. . . We cannot have a welfare state in India with all the socialism or even communism in the world unless our national income goes up greatly. Socialism or communism might help you to divide your existing wealth, if you like, but in India, there is no existing wealth for you to divide; there is only poverty to divide. It is not a question of distributing the wealth of the few rich men here and there. That is not going to make any difference in our national income. . . . We must produce wealth, and then divide it equitably. How can we have a welfare state without wealth? Wealth need not mean gold and silver but wealth in goods and services. Our economic policy must therefore aim at plenty. . . .

. . . The conception of planning today is not to think of the money we have and then to divide it up in the various schemes but to measure the physical needs, that is to say, how much of food the people want, how much of clothes they want, how much of housing they want, how much of education they want, how much of health services they want, how much of work

and employment they want, and so on. We calculate all these and then decide what everyone in India should have of these things. Once we do that, we can set about increasing production and fulfilling these needs. It is not a simple matter because in calculating the needs of the people, we have to calculate on the basis not only of an increasing population but of increasing needs. . . . Therefore, in making calculations, we have to keep in mind that the extra money that goes into circulation because of the higher salaries and wages, affects consumption. So we find out what in five years' time will be the needs of our people, including even items needed by our Defence Services. Then we decide how to produce those things in India. In order to meet a particular variety of needs we have now to put up a factory which will produce the goods that we need five years hence. Thus, planning is a much more complicated process than merely drawing up some schemes and fixing a system of priorities. . . .

But production is not all. . . . Mass production inevitably involves mass consumption, which in turn involves many other factors, chiefly the purchasing power of the consumer. Therefore planning must take note of the need to provide more purchasing power by way of wages, salaries and so on. Enough money should be thrown in to provide this purchasing power and to complete the circle of production and consumption. You will then produce more and consume more, and as a result your standard of living will go up. . . .

[SOCIALISM VS. CAPITALISM]

The whole of the capitalist structure is based on some kind of an acquisitive society. It may be that, to some extent, the tendency to acquisitiveness is inherent in us. A socialist society must try to get rid of this tendency to acquisitiveness and replace it by co-operation. You cannot bring about this change by a sudden law. There have to be long processes of training the people; without this you cannot wholly succeed. Even from the very limited point of view of changing your economic structure, apart from your minds and hearts, it takes time to build a socialist society. The countries that have gone fastest have also taken time. I would like you to consider that the Soviet Union, which has gone fast in industrialization, has taken thirty-five years or more over it. Chairman Mao of the People's Republic of China — which is more or less a communist state — said, about three or four years ago, that it would take China twenty years to achieve some kind of socialism. Mind you, this [is] in spite of the fact that theirs is an authoritarian state, and the people are exceedingly disciplined and industrious. Chairman Mao was speaking as a practical idealist. We must realize that the process of bringing socialism to India, especially in the way we are doing it, that is, the democratic way, will inevitably take time. . . .

[A SECULAR STATE]

Where the great majority of the people in a state belong to one religion, this fact alone may colour, to some extent, the cultural climate of that state. But nevertheless the state, as a state, can remain independent of any particular religion.

In a sense, this is a more or less modern conception. India has a long history of religious tolerance. That is one aspect of a secular state, but it is not the whole of it. In a country like India, which has many faiths and religions, no real nationalism can be built up except on the basis of secularity. Any narrower approach must necessarily exclude a section of the population, and then nationalism itself will have a much more restricted meaning than it should possess. In India we would have then to consider Hindu nationalism, Muslim nationalism, Sikh nationalism or Christian nationalism and not Indian nationalism.

As a matter of fact, these narrow religious nationalisms are relics of a past age and are no longer relevant today. They represent a backward and out-of-date society. In the measure we have even today so-called communal troubles, we display our backwardness as social groups. . . .

. . . The word 'secular' perhaps is not a very happy one. And yet, for want of a better word, we have used it. What exactly does it mean? It does not obviously mean a state where religion as such is discouraged. It means freedom of religion and conscience, including freedom for those who may have no religion. . . .

The word 'secular', however, conveys something much more to me, although that might not be its dictionary meaning. It conveys the idea of social and political equality. Thus, a caste-ridden society[1] is not properly secular. I have no desire to interfere with any person's belief, but when those beliefs become petrified in caste divisions, undoubtedly they affect the social structure of the state. They prevent us from realizing the idea of equality which we claim to place before ourselves. They interfere in political matters, just as communalism interferes.

---

[1]The Indian caste system, which dates from 1000–800 B.C.E., is a rigid form of social differentiation in which groups, traditionally linked to occupational specialties, are ranked on a hierarchical scale. Each caste has its own code of appropriate behavior, and marriage is generally restricted to members of the same caste.

Two Perspectives on the War in Vietnam

◆

91 ◆ *HO CHI MINH–JOHNSON CORRESPONDENCE, FEBRUARY 1967*

By early 1967 it was clear that there would be no quick American victory in Vietnam. Despite the commitment of approximately four hundred thousand U.S. troops and devastating bombing attacks on North Vietnam, the war had become a deadly stalemate and had bitterly divided the American people. Faced with these realities, President Johnson and his advisors renewed their efforts to end the war through negotiation. In February 1967 Johnson wrote directly to the North Vietnamese leader, Ho Chi Minh, spelling out the U.S. negotiating stance. Ho rejected Johnson's proposal, and formal negotiations between the two sides did not begin until May 1968. By then another one hundred thousand U.S. troops had been committed to Vietnam.

It is not surprising that Ho Chi Minh, an ardent nationalist and communist, was reluctant to negotiate an agreement that fell short of his goal of a united, communist Vietnam. Born in 1890, Ho, then known as Nguyen Sinh Cung, left French Indochina at the age of twenty-one to work on a French oceangoing ship and then at a hotel in London. Toward the end of World War I he moved to France, where he became a socialist and tried to convince the negotiators at the Paris Peace Conference to accept a plan for Vietnamese independence. In 1920 he joined the French Communist Party and became a student of Lenin's writings. In 1923 he went to the Soviet Union, and after a year of training was sent by the Communist International to Indochina. There he organized the Indochinese Communist Party in 1930. Forced to flee during the 1930s, he returned to Vietnam in 1943 and founded the communist-controlled League for the Independence of Vietnam, or Viet Minh, which led resistance campaigns against the occupying Japanese while building a base for a postwar independence movement. Only then did Nguyen adopt the name Ho Chi Minh, meaning "one who enlightens." With the defeat of the Japanese in 1945, he proclaimed the independent Democratic Republic of Vietnam and became its first president. Until his death in 1969, he led his country during eight years of warfare against the French and fifteen years of warfare against the anticommunist South Vietnamese regime established in 1954 at the Geneva Conference.

The following selection includes a brief excerpt from President Johnson's letter to Ho Chi Minh written in 1967 and the entire text of Ho's response. The exchange reveals the broad differences in the thinking of the two statesmen.

QUESTIONS FOR ANALYSIS

1. According to Johnson's letter, what had the Vietnamese proposed as conditions for beginning "direct bilateral talks"?
2. Why does Johnson reject the Vietnamese proposal, and what does he propose instead?

3. In the last paragraph of his letter, Ho Chi Minh states, "Our cause is absolutely just." What is the basis of his assertion?
4. Why does Ho reject President Johnson's proposal for negotiations? What counterproposal does he make?

His Excellency Ho Chi Minh
President, Democratic Republic of Vietnam

Dear Mr. President,

I am writing to you in the hope that the conflict in Vietnam can be brought to an end. The conflict has already taken a heavy toll — in lives lost, in wounds inflicted, in property destroyed, and in simple human misery. If we fail to find a just and peaceful solution, history will judge us harshly. . . .

In the past two weeks, I have noted public statements by representatives of your government suggesting that you would be prepared to enter into direct bilateral talks with representatives of the U.S. Government, provided that we ceased "unconditionally" and permanently our bombing operations against your country and all military actions against it. In the last days, serious and responsible parties have assured us indirectly that this is in fact your proposal.

Let me frankly state that I see two great difficulties with this proposal. In view of your public position, such action on our part would inevitably produce worldwide speculation that discussions were under way and would impair the privacy and secrecy of those discussions. Secondly, there would inevitably be grave concern on our part whether your government would make use of such action by us to improve its military position.

With these problems in mind, I am prepared to move even further toward an ending of the hostilities than your government has proposed in either public statements or through private diplomatic channels. I am prepared to order a cessation of bombing against your country and the stopping of further augmentation of U.S. forces in South Vietnam as soon as I am assured that infiltration into South Vietnam by land and by sea has stopped. These acts of restraint on both sides would, I believe, make it possible for us to conduct serious and private discussions leading toward an early peace. . . .

As to the site of the bilateral discussions I propose, there are several possibilities. We could, for example, have our representatives meet in Moscow where contacts have already occurred. They could meet in some other country such as Burma. You may have other arrangements or sites in mind, and I would try to meet your suggestions. . . .

Sincerely,

LYNDON B. JOHNSON

To His Excellency Mr. Lyndon B. Johnson
President
United States of America

Your Excellency,

On February 10, 1967, I received your message. This is my reply.

Vietnam is thousands of miles away from the United States. The Vietnamese people have never done any harm to the United States. But contrary to the pledges made by its representative at the 1954 Geneva Conference, the U.S. Government has ceaselessly intervened in Vietnam, it has unleashed and intensified the war of aggression in South Vietnam with a view to prolonging the partition of Vietnam and turning South Vietnam into a neo-colony and a military base of the United States. For over two years now, the U.S. Government has, with its air and naval forces, carried the war to the Democratic Republic of Vietnam, an independent and sovereign country.

The U.S. Government has committed war crimes, crimes against peace and against mankind. In South Vietnam, half a million U.S. and satellite troops have resorted to the most inhuman weapons and the most barbarous methods of warfare, such as napalm,[1] toxic chemicals and gases, to massacre our compatriots, destroy crops, and raze villages to the ground. In North Vietnam, thousands of U.S. aircraft have dropped hundreds of thousands of tons of bombs, destroying towns, villages, factories, roads, bridges, dikes, dams, and even churches, pagodas, hospitals, schools. In your message, you apparently deplored the sufferings and destructions in Vietnam. May I ask you: Who has perpetrated these monstrous crimes? It is the U.S. and satellite troops. The U.S. Government is entirely responsible for the extremely serious situation in Vietnam.

The U.S. war of aggression against the Vietnamese people constitutes a challenge to the countries of the socialist camp, a threat to the national independence movement, and a serious danger to peace in Asia and the world.

The Vietnamese people deeply love independence, freedom and peace. But in the face of the U.S. aggression, they have risen up, united as one man, fearless of sacrifices and hardships; they are determined to carry on their Resistance until they have won genuine independence and freedom and true peace. Our just cause enjoys strong sympathy and support from the peoples of the whole world including broad sections of the American people.

The U.S. Government has unleashed the war of aggression in Vietnam. It must cease this aggression. This is the only way to the restoration of peace. The U.S. Government must stop definitively and unconditionally its bombing raids and all other acts of war against the Democratic Republic of Vietnam, withdraw from South Vietnam all U.S. and satellite troops, recognize the South Vietnam National Front for Liberation,[2] and let the Vietnamese people settle [for] themselves their own affairs. Such is the basic content of the four-point stand of the Government of the Democratic Republic of Vietnam, which embodies the essential principles and provisions of the 1954 Geneva Agreements on Vietnam. It is the basis of a correct political solution to the Vietnam problem.

In your message, you suggested direct talks between the Democratic Republic of Vietnam and the United States. If the U.S. Government really wants these talks, it must first of all stop unconditionally its bombing raids and all other acts of war against the Democratic Republic of Vietnam. It is only after the unconditional cessation of the U.S. bombing raids and all other acts of war against the Democratic Republic of Vietnam that the Democratic Republic of Vietnam and the United States could enter into talks and discuss questions concerning the two sides.

The Vietnamese people will never submit to force; they will never accept talks under the threat of bombs.

Our cause is absolutely just. It is to be hoped that the U.S. Government will act in accordance with reason.

Sincerely,

HO CHI MINH

---

[1]Napalm is a military incendiary substance made up of gasoline, other fuels, and a gelling agent (made up of naphthenic and palmitic acids from which is derived the acronym *napalm*). A napalm-armed bomb or flamethrower broadcasts the substance over a wide area where it burns with intense heat. Its use to destroy villages and defoliate jungles to reveal enemy camps was bitterly protested by antiwar activists.

[2]The National Front for Liberation, or NLF, was founded in 1960 by supporters of Ho Chi Minh of South Vietnam. It became the umbrella organization under which guerrilla warfare was waged against the South Vietnamese government.

PART FOUR

Century's Close: From Cold War to Globalization

Writing contemporary history — the history of events that have just occurred — presents unique difficulties. The historian's most basic task — getting the facts right and determining "what happened" — is relatively easy. Historians of the recent past have lived through the events they are describing, can interview eyewitnesses and participants, and in the modern era have access not only to information contained in books, newspapers, and government documents, but also to visual evidence from films, video recordings, and photographs. Writing history, however, requires more than factual accuracy and telling "what happened." It also involves making interpretations, judging what's important and what's trivial, and determining how events and developments fit into long-term patterns and trends. To do these tasks well, historians need a perspective that includes knowledge of what preceded and what followed the events they are describing. Contemporary historians, with no knowledge of the future, will always lack this perspective, and can make only educated guesses about the meaning of events that have just taken place.

Consider, for example, the disintegration of the Soviet Union in the late 1980s and early 1990s. Soon after it occurred, politicians, journalists, and historians — indeed, everyone who had anything to say about it — characterized it as a historic turning point in human affairs. The demise of the Soviet Union, they argued, ended the Cold War, lifted the shadow of nuclear holocaust, revealed fatal flaws in communism, confirmed the superiority of capitalism, and opened up new possibilities for world peace and cooperation. U.S. political scientist Francis Fukuyama went even further; to him it meant the "end of history." Liberal democracy and capitalism had cleared the field of all competitors and would dominate human societies around the globe forever.

Events of the twenty-first century, however, may reveal that all of these assumptions about the breakup of the Soviet Union were incorrect. The Russians might abandon their not very successful experiment with capitalism and reinstate a communist dictatorship or something close to it. They might come under control of authoritarian nationalists who will, as the Nazis did in Germany, revive and remilitarize a weak and demoralized people and lead them on a path of military conquest and expansion. Such scenarios are unlikely, but if either were to occur, the "demise of Soviet communism" and "the humbling of Russia" that took place in the late 1980s and 1990s would no longer be viewed as a turning point, but rather as a temporary interruption of long-term patterns.

What is true about the fall of the Soviet Union also applies to any number of other events and trends of the late twentieth century. Is the recent intensification of Islamic fundamentalism a prelude to a "battle of civilizations" between the West and Islam or a passing phase in Islam's history? Are the recent gains made by Western women in education, job opportunities, and legal status the first stage of a movement toward greater gender equality worldwide or an early indication that feminism will remain a uniquely Western phenomenon? Will late-twentieth-century environmentalism be hailed as a triumph of human foresight or mourned as a movement that came too late and accomplished too little? Will China's recent economic growth be considered the first step in its emergence as a new superpower or the prelude to some unforeseen economic or political upheaval? Will recent population increases result in sustainability or catastrophe? No one will be able to answer these and countless other questions for another fifty years or more, and until then histories of the late twentieth century must remain tentative and provisional.

Perhaps the greatest challenge for contemporary historians is making sense of the combination of recent economic, political, technological, and cultural changes described by the word *globalization*. Variously defined, globalization refers to a world of free trade, open markets, and capitalist competition in which goods, services, and capital flow across seamless international borders. It also refers to a world in which a remarkable series of technological breakthroughs — computers, communications satellites, fiber-optic cable, jet aircraft, and the Internet — have destroyed the barriers of time and space. It refers, finally, to a world of cultural homogeneity in which tastes in music, art, architecture, personal dress, and countless other areas have becoming increasingly standardized and, for better or worse, Americanized.

Historians can agree that globalization represents an acceleration and intensification of a trend that has been a key feature of world history ever since the European overseas expansion of the 1500s and 1600s — greater interdependency and interaction among the world's peoples. Where globalization will take us, however, is impossible to predict. Its supporters see universal benefits from worldwide economic growth, strengthened democracies through better-informed citizenry, increased capacity to deal with global environmental problems, and even a heightened sense of human community. Its detractors, of which there are many, see a widening divide between haves and have-nots, dangerous political transitions, the triumph of an ethos of corporate greed, and a bland uniformity in world culture. Whichever side is correct, understanding the roots and meaning of globalization will be a primary challenge for future historians.

CHAPTER 12

The 1970s and 1980s: Years of Challenge and Change

After two decades of economic depression and war, the 1950s and 1960s were marked by optimism and high expectations in much of the world. By contrast, the 1970s and 1980s were years of self-doubt, lowered expectations, and disillusionment with once promising political formulas. Several factors contributed to this change, but the most important was the halt of postwar economic expansion. In the early 1970s the world entered an era in which inflation accompanied stagnation, periods of sluggish growth were interrupted by three major recessions, some areas of the world flourished while others languished, and an oil shortage in the 1970s was followed by an oil glut in the 1980s.

Why and how the world economy became so erratic is still unclear. Undoubtedly, a major factor was the steep increase in oil prices between October 1973, when a barrel of oil sold by members of the Organization of Petroleum Exporting Countries cost $2.59, and late 1980, when a barrel cost just over $30. Prices fell to under $20 a barrel by the mid 1980s, but by then higher energy costs had done their damage: inflation, shrunken corporate profits, trade deficits for oil-importing nations, and the erosion of consumer spending. Oil costs were not the only culprit, however. Currency fluctuations, inflationary wage settlements in the late 1960s and early 1970s, decreased state spending in the face of rising deficits, declining productivity and investments, and a failure of oil-producing states to recycle their immense profits through loans and investments all played a role.

The effects of the "Great Slowdown" varied enormously. Oil producers at first reaped huge profits, but they faced a crisis in the mid 1980s when oil prices plummeted by 30 to 40 percent. Japan, Hong Kong, South Korea, Taiwan, and Singapore, continued to find new markets for their cars, electronic goods, and textiles, and experienced only slight increases in unemployment and inflation. In the United States, however, the average unemployment rate between 1973 and 1989 was 7.1 percent, compared to 4.8 percent between 1960 and 1973; in Europe unemployment grew from less than 3 percent in 1970 to more than 10 percent in 1986. Inflation also was a severe problem. The inflation rate in Europe and the United States rose to 13 percent in 1974, fell back to 8 percent by 1976, and returned to 13 percent in 1979 before gradually falling in the 1980s.

For sub-Saharan Africa, Latin America, and much of Asia, the 1970s and 1980s were catastrophic. Rising energy costs and declining growth rates among the industrialized countries reduced demand and undercut prices for their agricultural and mineral exports, while their own energy bills went up like everyone else's. In these regions economic growth virtually stopped, and in a few cases ran into negative territory. Governments borrowed extravagantly, inflation soared, and poverty worsened.

Political change accompanied economic uncertainty. China, having survived the Great Leap Forward and the Cultural Revolution, abandoned Mao's effort to combine economic development and egalitarianism when new leaders after Mao's death made economic growth rather than ideological purity their priority. Events in Iran revealed the power of religious fundamentalism when Iranians overthrew the shah in 1979 and instituted a government led by clerics determined to rule according to Islamic law. Conservative governments in Great Britain under Margaret Thatcher and in the United States under Ronald Reagan cut taxes, fought union demands for higher wages, and sought to eliminate or at least slow the growth of entitlement programs established in the 1960s and 1970s. Throughout much of Latin America and Africa, dozens of democratic governments gave way to dictatorships.

Meanwhile the Cold War continued. Despite U.S. involvement in Vietnam, Soviet-U.S. relations improved during the 1970s. The two superpowers settled disputes over Berlin in 1971, agreed to limit the production of antiballistic missiles in 1972, and along with other European states accepted existing national boundaries in Europe and promised to protect human rights by signing the Helsinki Accords in 1975. By the early 1980s, however, détente, or accommodation, between the Soviet Union and the United States was in shambles, the victim of Soviet meddling in Africa and the Soviet invasion of Afghanistan in 1979. It was dealt a further blow by the policies of President Reagan, who, after taking office in 1981, boosted military spending, funded research on the "Star Wars" antimissile system, and denounced the Soviet Union with a vehemence not heard since the 1950s.

Then in 1985 the new premier of the Soviet Union, Mikhail Gorbachev, announced plans to rejuvenate Soviet communism by introducing policies based on glasnost, or openness, and perestroika, or restructuring. To the world's shock, this step led

not to communism's revival but its demise. By 1991, communist
regimes had disappeared throughout Eastern Europe, the Soviet
Union had collapsed, and the Cold War, which had dominated international diplomacy for over four decades, had ended.

◆

New Forces in the International Economy

Two developments in the 1970s and 1980s provide evidence of fundamental
changes in the world economy. The first was the emergence of the Organization
of Petroleum Exporting Countries (OPEC) as a major economic force. During the
1970s, OPEC's twelve Asian, African, and Latin American members, whose
economies had been largely controlled and manipulated by Western powers,
shocked the world when they orchestrated a quadrupling of the price of oil
in 1974 and then quadrupled it again in 1979. The second was the "economic
miracle" that took place first in Japan and somewhat later in South Korea,
Taiwan, Hong Kong, and Singapore. These "Asian Tigers" suddenly emerged as
centers of international finance and leading exporters of steel, automobiles, electronic goods, and consumer items. The Pacific Rim took its place alongside the
United States and Western Europe as a major force in the world economy.

The emergence of OPEC took place against a background of soaring demand
for oil during the postwar boom. World oil consumption grew from approximately 3.9 billion barrels in 1953 to 20.4 billion barrels in 1973. Nonetheless,
prices stayed low, mainly because they were set by huge oil companies, such as
Texaco, Mobil, Standard Oil of California, British Petroleum, and the Royal
Dutch/Shell Group, that were interested in keeping demand high and paying the
oil producers as little as possible. Oil-producing nations sought higher prices,
and in 1960 five of them, Iran, Iraq, Saudi Arabia, Venezuela, and Kuwait,
founded OPEC to achieve this goal. Although membership in the 1960s and early
1970s expanded to include Qatar, Libya, Indonesia, Abu Dhabi, Ecuador, Gabon,
and Nigeria, in 1973 the price of oil measured against inflation was still only half
of what it had been in the early 1950s.

This changed dramatically in late 1973 and 1974 when a group of Arab oil
producers — Saudi Arabia, Iraq, Kuwait, and the United Arab Emirates —
decided to use oil as a political weapon after the outbreak in October 1973 of the
fourth Arab-Israeli war, known as the Yom Kippur War in Israel and the
Ramadan War in Muslim countries. To support Egypt and Syria, these Arab
states voted to stop oil deliveries to the United States, which was sending the
Israelis weapons, and the Netherlands, which had made available its airfields to
Israel-bound U.S. supply planes. This step, combined with across-the-board cuts
in production, drove up the price of oil to $10 a barrel, a level that OPEC nations
were able to maintain throughout the 1970s and push even higher after the outbreak of the Iran-Iraq war in 1979.

As gasoline prices soared in the United States during the 1970s, many Americans traded in their gas-guzzling Detroit-made Fords, Chevrolets, and Chryslers for fuel-efficient Japanese Toyotas, Datsuns, and Hondas. The fact that twenty years earlier the Japanese auto industry had hardly existed underscores the rapid transformation of postwar Japan's economy. After their nation's defeat in World War II, Japanese business and government leaders perceived that Japan's economic recovery depended on producing manufactured goods not just for domestic and Asian markets, but for export throughout the world. With a probusiness government, an industrious and well-educated work force, high rates of savings, a talented entrepreneurial class, and an intense competitive spirit, the Japanese succeeded spectacularly. They moved from steel and shipbuilding in the 1950s to electronics, computers, consumer goods, and automobiles in the 1960s and 1970s. By the mid 1980s Japan had trade surpluses of more than $80 billion a year and one of the world's highest standards of living. By then South Korea, Taiwan, Singapore, and Hong Kong also had emerged as financial and industrial powers, and many commentators began to speak of the late twentieth century as the dawn of the Pacific Era in the world's economy.

Middle Eastern Politics and the Price of Oil

❖

92 ◆ *Mana Saeed al-Otaiba,* THE ARAB OIL WEAPON

Abu Dhabi and Dabai, two small Arab sheikhdoms on the Persian Gulf that were for most of the nineteenth and twentieth centuries part of the British protectorate known as the Trucial States, joined five other sheikhdoms in 1971 to form the United Arab Emirates (UAE). Once the center of a thriving pearl industry, the sparsely populated sheikhdoms had fallen on hard times after cultured pearls were introduced into the world market in the 1920s. In the 1950s, however, British and French firms discovered oil in Abu Dhabi and Dabai, and within a decade annual exports totaled approximately seven hundred thousand barrels. By the late 1960s Abu Dhabi had joined OPEC, and its ruler, Sheikh Shakhbut ibn Sultan al Nahyan, whose annual income in the 1930s had amounted to $150,000, was receiving oil royalties in the range of $84 million per year. That was nothing compared to the $8 billion in annual royalties received by his successor, Sheikh Zaid, in the early 1980s.

With its founding in 1971, the United Arab Emirates assumed Abu Dhabi's place in OPEC and generally sided with Saudi Arabia in disputes over production and pricing. Along with Saudi Arabia's long-time oil minister, Ahmad Zaki Yamani, the UAE's director of petroleum affairs Mana Saeed al-Otaiba became a spokesperson for the Arab oil-producing states, especially during and after the oil crisis of 1973 to 1974. In the following comments from speeches in 1974 and early 1975, Mana Saeed al-Otaiba describes the Arabs' use of the "oil weapon" in the wake of the Arab-Israeli war of 1973.

QUESTIONS FOR ANALYSIS

1. How does Mana Saeed al-Otaiba interpret the strategy of the major oil companies in their dealings with OPEC after the outbreak of the fourth Arab-Israeli war?
2. According to Mana Saeed al-Otaiba, who actually made the decision to limit oil production and halt the sale of oil to the United States and the Netherlands?
3. What did the Arab oil producers hope to accomplish by the steps they took in late 1973 and 1974? According to Mana Saeed al-Otaiba, how successful were they?
4. What does Mana Saeed al-Otaiba see as the main deficiency of the international economy? How, in his view, will the steps taken by the oil-producing nations help eliminate it?

On 6 October 1973 the Holy Ramadan war broke out. . . .

By coincidence, on that day OPEC met in Vienna to consider the question of oil prices. . . . After a meeting between the Arabian Gulf oil ministers and the oil companies' delegation at which the ministers set out their countries' stand on the price issue, the oil company representatives asked for time to consult their principals and promised to return to the negotiations after two days. After this deadline elapsed and the companies had asked for another one-day delay, their negotiators finally came back late bringing with them a new request for a further adjournment of 15 days. When they were asked to meet the ministers to discuss the third request for postponement, they refused to attend and left Vienna suddenly without informing their fellow-negotiators. Faced with this improper conduct the Arabian Gulf oil ministers had no alternative but to settle their business themselves. They agreed to meet in Kuwait on 16 October to solve the oil price problem. . . .

All this happened in the blazing heat of the Ramadan war. What happened in Vienna was not far away from what was happening in Sinai and Golan. The oil companies grasped this organic link between what was happening in the two arenas, the arena of war in the Middle East and the arena of oil in Vienna. So the companies' trickery and repeated requests for delays

had something behind it — temporising and waiting until the result of the war going on in the Middle East would be clear. The oil companies were waiting for the war to end as wars had ended in the past, with an Arab defeat, so that the Arab negotiating position would be weak and they could be beaten in the oil arena as they were beaten in the arena of war. . . .

16 October arrived and the . . . Arabian Gulf oil ministers met in Kuwait and decided to fix oil prices themselves.

Since that day a new principle has been established in the oil industry: oil pricing must be decided upon by the legal owners of the oil.

On the following day 17 October, the Arab oil ministers met in Kuwait to employ the full weight of the oil weapon in the service of the battle. . . .

After a long debate lasting more than seven hours continuously, agreement was reached among the Arab oil producers — except for Iraq which withdrew from the meeting — on adopting . . . a comprehensive production cut by at least five per cent. The Abu Dhabi delegation had its own view of this decision but agreed to it so as to preserve an Arab consensus. Abu Dhabi felt that it was essential to take a more effective measure against those states which showed open hostility to the Arab nation, especially the USA which had opened its war arsenal to Israel and provided it with the most modern weapons, as well as with military experts and with volunteers. . . .

Shortly after the meeting broke up we called a press conference at which we announced Abu Dhabi's decision to cut off oil supplies to the US in line with special instructions from His Highness Shaikh Zayed bin Sultan Al Nahayan. . . . This initiative taken by Abu Dhabi elicited a big reaction both in the Arab world and on the international scene. In the event the rest of the Arab states followed Abu Dhabi's example three days later and cut off oil supplies to the US. . . .

In taking this decision Abu Dhabi was motivated by its belief that the Arabs must win this battle, and that if they were defeated this time they would have nothing left to count on for the future. All Abu Dhabi's actions sprang from its belief in Arab rights, and its belief that justice must prevail in the world. This step was truly a pioneering move, surprising enemies as much as it surprised friends. It was the embodiment of the fortitude of the right, however small, against the wrong, however great, in a world where the powerful rule. . . .

◆   ◆

. . . I shall try here to summarise the effects which followed from the Arab use of the oil weapon and which led to the revelation of reality to many in the world who had been blinded and deceived by lying Zionist propaganda.

(1) The Arabs discovered themselves through their use of the oil weapon and realised the extent of the power represented by this weapon in their possession if it is well used.

(2) The whole world understood the extent of the economic power which lies in the hands of the Arabs. If they act together, which they actually did in using the oil weapon, they can influence the world balance of power and oblige the world to understand their problems and respect their feelings. This led many states to seek to win the friendship of the Arabs.

(3) There is no doubt the consensus among the Arab states in using the oil weapon hastened

their advent as a major economic and political force in the world, because they are the major source of crude oil and gas, both as regards production and reserves, and an emerging repository of financial power.

(4) Through oil the Arabs were able to isolate Israel politically from the world, win more friends and influence a number of other states which used to side with Israel. This has revealed the falsehood of the lies with which Israel used to deceive a large number of small peace-loving states, lies which kept repeating that it was the Arabs who were calling for war and who were striving to exterminate the Israelis and throw them into the sea. These lies did not last long; it soon became clear that this artificial ministate represented the cancer which was spreading and expanding at every opportunity at the expense of the neighbouring Arab states.

(5) More than 30 African states broke off diplomatic relations with Israel when it became clear to them that the Arab cause was the cause of right and justice. Here it was up to the Arab oil-exporting states to give freely in order to reward friendly African states collectively and individually. The sum of $150 million was allotted in 1974 for aid to African states which were affected by the rise in oil prices. . . .

(6) A number of oil-exporting countries have gained great material benefits as a result of the Arab use of the oil weapon. The output cutback and embargo measures have resulted in a world oil supply shortage and a feeling on the part of many consumer states that they must try to obtain sufficient crude oil to assure their needs for a reasonable period of time. . . . In these circumstances industrial states vied with each other to pay high prices for non-Arab oil. . . . We find it necessary to mention this, to point out the positive role of the Arab oil weapon in respect of non-Arab oil-exporting states, which we Arabs affect and are affected by. . . .

(8) As for the USA, they were exposed to the power of the Arab oil weapon from the first moment because of the unlimited support

they gave to Israel during the Ramadan war. After the embargo on Arab oil exports to the USA had been imposed, American public opinion, which had been deceived by Zionist propaganda, began to shift from an anti-Arab position to one of understanding for the Arab position. . . .

◆ ◆

The economic problems the world faces today, under whose weight the world economy is groaning and which are undermining the development of the Third World . . ., go far beyond the subject of oil. This is the contrary of what is alleged by some industrial states which lay the whole blame for the current economic crisis on oil and oil prices. . . .

The faulty structure of the world economy has rested for long centuries on a division of the world into two — a rich world and a poor world, a world which enjoys everything and a world deprived of everything, a world which plunders wealth to build civilisation, industry and progress, and another which is oppressed. . . . This is the situation that the OPEC states

have grasped and refused to accept, and are now endeavouring to correct. . . .

Some of the industrial countries, the main oil consumers, reacted by spreading much propaganda to the effect that the oil-exporting countries were undermining the world economies, forgetting that they had previously exploited these states and blocked their development, and also forgetting that we also are part of that world economy and belong to the international family. . . . The state of the world economy is like a man who has broken his leg, and the bone has been set in a crooked position; all the doctor can do is break the crooked bone again and set it true, despite the pain the new break caused, this being undoubtedly best for the patient. That is the story of the world economy. The industrial countries were alarmed in case another group of primary producers might also organise their ranks in a club like OPEC and call for fair prices for the resources and raw materials they produce. This state of affairs would not, of course, please some of the industrial countries which have grown used to getting these primary products cheap. . . .

Japan's Economic Miracle

◆

93 ◆ *Akio Morita, MADE IN JAPAN*

After World War II, a former Japanese naval lieutenant, Akio Morita, and a defense contractor, Masaru Ibuka, borrowed $500 to form the Tokyo Telecommunications Engineering Corporation. With plans to produce consumer goods for the domestic market, they built a small factory in Tokyo and began to manufacture electric rice cookers. In their first year they had sales of $7500 and a profit of $300. With an infusion of capital from Morita's father, the head of a family-owned sake brewery, the firm moved into consumer electronics with the marketing of a tape recorder in Japan in the early 1950s. Later in the decade the firm burst into the international market with a miniaturized radio that used transistors, tiny new capacitors developed by Bell Laboratories in the United States, rather than electronic tubes. Named Sony from the Latin word *sonus* for sound, the radios became so popular that Morita and Ibuka changed their company's name to the Sony Corporation in 1958. Beginning in the 1960s, the corporation branched out into chemicals, insurance, the recording industry, and real estate while introducing a stream of successful new products, including transistorized tape recorders, videotape cameras and recorders, and color televisions. Although growth slowed in the 1970s, Sony rebounded in the 1980s and 1990s with new products such as the Walkman, digital audiotape, and compact disks and with acquisitions such as the purchase of Columbia Films from Coca-Cola in 1989 for $3.4 billion.

During the 1980s Morita, having presided over one of Japan's most spectacular economic success stories, relinquished some of his duties to younger men. This gave him time to write his memoirs, which were published in English in 1986 with the title *Made in Japan.* In the book Morita discusses the unique features of Japanese business philosophy, underscoring the differences between Japanese and American attitudes and practices. It became required reading in many U.S. business schools before the Japanese economy entered a prolonged slump in the early 1990s. Morita died of pneumonia in 1999 at the age of seventy-eight.

QUESTIONS FOR ANALYSIS

1. According to Morita, what were some of the obstacles Japan had to overcome to build its economy in the postwar years?
2. Why does Morita believe that good employee-employer relations are the key to business success?
3. What are some of the steps taken by the Sony Corporation to ensure good employee relations?
4. According to Morita, what are some of the differences between business executives in Japan and in the United States?
5. Why does Morita believe that Japanese business methods and philosophy are superior to those of Americans?

SELLING TO THE WORLD

Although our company was still small and we saw Japan as quite a large and potentially active market, it was the consensus among Japanese industrialists that a Japanese company must export goods in order to survive. With no natural resources except our people's energy, Japan had no alternative. And so it was natural for us to look to foreign markets. Besides, as business prospered, it became obvious to me that if we did not set our sights on marketing abroad, we would not grow to be the kind of company Ibuka and I had envisioned. We wanted to change the image of Japanese goods as poor in quality, and, we reasoned, if you are going to sell a high-quality, expensive product, you need an affluent market, and that means a rich, sophisticated country. Today, over 99 percent of all Japanese homes have color TV; more than 98 percent have electric refrigerators and washing machines; and the penetration rate for tape recorders and stereo systems is between 60 and 70 percent. But in 1958, the year after we produced our "pocketable" transistorized radio, only 1 percent of Japanese homes had a TV set, only 5 percent had a washing machine, and only two-tenths of 1 percent had an electric refrigerator. Fortunately, the Japanese economy began to grow vigorously from the mid-fifties onward.

Double-digit increases in the gross national product and low inflation gave a great boost to consumer spending. Many people say Japan's true postwar era really began in 1955, the year we introduced the first transistorized radio in Japan. The country's GNP grew, amazingly, by 10.8 percent. Japanese households needed everything, and because of the high savings rate, which in those days was over 20 percent, the people could afford to buy. So with good and growing markets at home and potential markets abroad, the world was beginning to look bright to us. . . .

We were doing well, although we still had tough competition getting our name known in Japan, where brand consciousness and brand loyalty are very high. Overseas we were all on an even footing. And perhaps we were in a better position abroad than anybody. Quality Japanese consumer goods were virtually unknown before the war. The image of anything marked "Made in Japan" that had been shipped abroad before the war was very low. Most people in the United States and Europe, I learned, associated Japan with paper umbrellas, kimonos, toys, and cheap trinkets. In choosing our name we did not purposely try to hide our national identity — after all, international rules require you to state the country of origin on your product — but we certainly did not want to emphasize it and run the risk of being rejected before we could demonstrate the quality of our products. But I must confess that in the early days we printed the line "Made in Japan" as small as possible, once too small for U.S. Customs, which made us make it bigger on one product.

ON MANAGEMENT

There is no secret ingredient or hidden formula responsible for the success of the best Japanese companies. No theory or plan or government policy will make a business a success; that can only be done by people. The most important mission for a Japanese manager is to develop a healthy relationship with his employees, to create a familylike feeling within the corporation, a feeling that employees and managers share the same fate. Those companies that are most successful in Japan are those that have managed to create a shared sense of fate among all employees, what Americans call labor and management, and the shareholders.

I have not found this simple management system applied anywhere else in the world, and yet we have demonstrated convincingly, I believe, that it works. For others to adopt the Japanese system may not be possible because they may be too tradition-bound, or too timid. The emphasis on people must be genuine and sometimes very bold and daring, and it can even be quite risky. But in the long run — and I emphasize this — no matter how good or successful you are or how clever or crafty, your business and its future are in the hands of the people you hire. To put it a bit more dramatically, the fate of your business is actually in the hands of the youngest recruit on the staff.

That is why I make it a point personally to address all of our incoming college graduates each year. The Japanese school year ends in March, and companies recruit employees in their last semester, so that before the end of the school year they know where they are going. They take up their new jobs in April. I always gather these new recruits together at headquarters in Tokyo, where we have an introductory or orientation ceremony. This year I looked out at more than seven hundred young, eager faces and gave them a lecture, as I have been doing for almost forty years. . . .

The new employees are getting their first direct and sobering view of what it will be like in the business world. I tell them what I think is important for them to know about the company and about themselves. I put it this way to the last class of entering employees:

"We did not draft you. This is not the army, so that means you have voluntarily chosen Sony. This is your responsibility, and normally if you join this company we expect that you will stay for the next twenty or thirty years.

"Nobody can live twice, and the next twenty or thirty years is the brightest period of your life. You only get it once.

"When you leave the company thirty years from now or when your life is finished, I do not want you to regret that you spent all those years here. That would be a tragedy. I cannot stress the point too much that this is your responsibility to yourself. So I say to you, the most important thing in the next few months is for you to decide whether you will be happy or unhappy here. So even though we recruited you, we cannot, as management, or a third party, make other people happy; happiness must be created yourself." . . .

The concept of lifetime employment arose when Japanese managers and employees both realized that they had much in common and that they had to make some long-range plans. The laws made it difficult legally, and expensive, to fire anybody, but that didn't seem like such a bad idea, since workers were badly in need of work, and struggling businesses needed employees who would remain loyal. Without class disputes, despite the Communist and Socialist party propaganda, the Japanese, who are a homogeneous people, were able to cooperate to provide for their common welfare. I have often said that the Japanese company has become very much a social security organization.

In the postwar era, the tax laws make it useless for a company to pay an executive a lot of money, because the graduated tax rises sharply very quickly, and you are very soon in the highest bracket. Company-paid amenities such as worker dormitories and allowances for commuting, for example, help workers make up for the tax system. Tax shelters and tax avoidance are virtually unknown in Japan. Today, the salary for a top management official is rarely more than seven or eight times that of an entry-level junior executive trainee. This means Japan has no multimillion-dollar brass, and companies give no huge executive bonuses, no stock options, no deferred income, no golden parachutes, and therefore the psychological, as well as the

real, gap between employees is narrower than in other countries. There may be some exceptions to the general rule, but I am sure they are few.

What we in industry learned in dealing with people is that people do not work just for money and that if you are trying to motivate, money is not the most effective tool. To motivate people, you must bring them into the family and treat them like respected members of it. Granted, in our one-race nation this might be easier to do than elsewhere, but it is still possible if you have an educated population. . . .

AMERICAN AND JAPANESE STYLES

But the differences between U.S. and Japanese companies go beyond the cultural. If you ask a Japanese executive, "What is your most important responsibility?" he will invariably say that continued employment and improving the livelihood of the workers is at or near the top of the list. In order to do that, the company must make a profit. Making a profit will never be at the top of the list. Most of the American business executives I know put the highest priority on return to the investors or this year's profit. They have the responsibility because the investors gave it to them, and to stay in their jobs they have to continue to keep the investors happy. The board of directors represents the investors, and if top management fails to give the return the investors feel they need, he will be fired. For that reason he is entitled to use the factory and the machinery of the company, and also the workers, as tools to accomplish his aim. This can be detrimental.

Visiting an American television plant in the Midwest a few years ago, I commented to the manager that I thought he really needed to buy some more modern equipment in order to improve the company's productivity. He shocked me when he told me that his compensation was based on the company's financial performance and that he was not going to do anything, like making long-range investments, that might cut his compensation for the sake of the next manager who would be along in a year or so. . . .

Generally, in the United States, management's attitude toward the labor force and even the lower-level executives is very hierarchical, much more so than in Japan, an Oriental country where Westerners always expect to see such hierarchies. When I visited the Illinois television assembly plant of Motorola, one of the first things I noticed was that the offices were air-conditioned, but out on the shop floor it was stifling, people were dripping with sweat, and big noisy fans were blowing the hot air around. The workers were plainly uncomfortable, and I thought, "How can you get quality work from people laboring under such conditions? And what kind of loyalty can they be expected to show to the big bosses in their cool offices!" In Japan people often used to say that the shop floor where the goods were made was always more comfortable than the workers' homes. That has changed as the Japanese workers have become more affluent, and air-conditioning has become more common at home. By the middle of 1984, more than half of Japan's homes and apartments had it. But back in the late fifties, we air-conditioned our factories before the offices.

Amenities are not of great concern to management in Japan. The struggle for an office with a carpet, a water carafe, and an original oil painting on the wall is not common. Just recently a U.S. company, the maker of highly complex computerized graphics equipment, formed a joint venture with a Japanese company and the Japanese partner said to his foreign associate: "We would like you to design the showroom, but please allow us to design the office space upstairs." It seemed reasonable enough. The showroom was beautifully appointed, with soft lighting and comfortable chairs for visitors and clients. The equipment was highlighted using modern display techniques, and there were video demonstrations and elegant four-color brochures on the company and its equipment. Upstairs, the entire office staff was housed in one big open room without partitions, just a grid of desks with telephones, filing cabinets and other necessary furniture in a simple, very Spartan arrangement. The U.S. partner raised his eyebrows, and his Japanese colleague explained, "If Japanese clients come into the office of a new and struggling company and see plush carpet and private offices and too much comfort, they become suspicious that this company is not serious, that it is devoting too much thought and company resources to management's comfort, and perhaps not enough to the product or to potential customers. If we are successful after one year, we might put up low partitions. After two or three years, we might give the top executive a closed office. But for now we have to all be reminded that we are struggling together to make this company a success."

Environmentalism, Economic Development, and Social Justice

By the early 1990s, it was estimated that five million British, five million Germans, and close to fourteen million Americans, about one in every seven adults, were members of some sort of environmental organization. Such statistics are one indicator of the broad support for environmental causes that emerged in Western industrialized nations during the 1970s and 1980s. Further evidence is provided by the emergence in the United States and Western Europe of proenvironment "green" political parties that in France, Sweden, Austria, and especially West Germany have had success in national elections. In the U.S. presidential election of 2000, Green Party candidate Ralph Nader received only 3 percent of the vote, but by attracting the support of voters who might otherwise have voted for Democrat Al Gore, may well have tipped the election in favor of the Republican candidate, George W. Bush.

The strongest indication of environmentalism's strength in the 1970s and 1980s was its impact on legislation and public policy. In the United States in the early 1970s, President Nixon signed laws on clean air and water, pesticides, hazardous chemicals, and endangered species, and created the Environmental Protection Agency to enforce them. Many European states in the 1970s also established agencies and passed laws that made environmental management and protection part of their governments' responsibilities. Despite internal divisions and organized opposition to many of its programs, the environmental movement became an important cultural and political force in the Western democracies during the 1970s and 1980s.

Nothing comparable happened outside the West. The environmental record of communist states, for example, was abysmal. With the Soviet Union providing a model, communist governments sought economic development at all costs, with an emphasis on huge public works projects, mammoth factories, and giant agricultural collectives. China experimented with small-scale rural factories during the Great Leap Forward, but the initiative failed disastrously, and in any case was inspired by political ideology, not environmental awareness. Year after year communist plant managers struggled to meet state-imposed production goals, oblivious to the environmental calamities they were causing. The explosion of the Soviet Union's Chernobyl nuclear reactor in 1986 was only the most notorious of literally thousands of environmental missteps that made the Soviet Union and Eastern Europe a land of dying forests, noxious air, polluted rivers, and high rates of cancer, lung disease, and infections.

Economic development also took precedence over the environment in the less developed regions of Africa, Latin America, and Asia. For countries desperately trying to modernize their economies, curbing development to preserve energy supplies, protect rain forests, or meet environmental standards set by experts from affluent societies had little appeal. At the environmental conference sponsored by the United Nations in Stockholm in 1972, the Indian prime minister Indira Gandhi told the delegates that if pollution was the price of progress, then India wanted pollution.

Despite the prodevelopment stance of most governments, environmentalism had some backing in developing countries during the 1970s and 1980s. These movements often found support among poor people whose livelihoods were threatened by polluting factories, commercial logging, oil drilling, or large dams. Examples include efforts in the mid 1980s by the Penan people of Malaysia to halt commercial logging in their homeland through blockades and demonstrations; peasant protests in Thailand in the late 1970s to put an end to the conversion of natural forest into plantations; numerous grassroots campaigns in India to stop large-scale dam projects, protect forests, and limit pollution from factories and mines; and efforts by Brazilian rubber tappers and indigenous peoples to block and reverse the destruction of the Amazon rain forest.

Such movements on behalf of environmental protection and social justice received worldwide publicity and support from European and U.S. environmental groups. But they also encountered resistance in their own countries from state officials, developers, and foreign corporations. It was an unequal struggle, in which proponents of "environmentalism of the poor" won occasional battles but had little success changing their leaders' convictions that economic development was more important than preserving the environment.

Saving the Rain Forest in Brazil

◆

94 ◆ *Chico Mendes, FIGHT FOR THE FOREST*

With its headwaters in the Peruvian Andes just one hundred miles from South America's Pacific coast, the Amazon River stretches four thousand miles across Brazil before it flows into the Atlantic Ocean. Along with its tributaries, it drains 1.2 billion acres of land and contains the world's largest tropical forest area. Beginning in the 1960s, when the Brazilian government began to construct thousands of miles of roads in the region, the Amazon territory became a magnet for landless peasants and, more importantly, for loggers, miners, land speculators, and cattle ranchers. As a result, deforestation occurred at a staggering rate. In thirty years almost 10 percent of the rain forest, approximately 150 million acres, was destroyed.

The devastation of the Amazon rain forest has become a major concern of environmentalists around the globe, who are convinced that it has grave implications for problems of global warming and species extinction, among others. At first, however, the struggle to limit development in the region was carried on by poor people who lived in the region itself and made their living by harvesting forest products such as rubber, Brazil nuts, jute, and various palm tree products. Although many of these people had been living in the region for generations, they lacked legal titles to their lands and were expelled when ranchers arrived and turned forest into pasture.

Resistance by rubber tappers (individuals who tap rubber trees to collect latex for sale) was organized by Chico Mendes (1944–1988), a rubber tapper himself from the westernmost Brazilian state of Acre. In 1975 he helped found the Federation of Rural Workers of Acre, whose members sought to block the destruction of the forest through *empates*, or "standoffs," in which they formed nonviolent human blockades around forest areas threatened with clearing. The movement spread to other parts of Brazil, and in 1985 rubber tappers from the entire Amazon region formed the National Council of Rubber Tappers. With the support of the region's indigenous peoples, they demanded the establishment of "extractive reserves," lands protected from development on which rural workers could continue to tap rubber trees and gather fruits, nuts, and fibers. Mendes's campaign also attracted international support. Between 1985 and 1988 he made several trips to the United States, where, with the backing of environmental and human rights organizations, he lobbied Congress and the World Bank to withhold funds for Amazon development projects and support his proposals for extractive reserves. He was now a figure of international prominence, and also a target of numerous death threats from ranchers. On December 22, 1988, he momentarily left the protection of his bodyguards to step out on his back porch, where he was assassinated by the son of a local rancher.

Just weeks before his murder, Mendes granted an extensive interview to an English friend and supporter Tony Gross, who published the interview as a book, *Fight for the Forest*, in mid 1989. In the following passages Mendes discusses the sources of support and opposition for his movement.

During the 1990s the Brazilian government, with support from the World Bank, established extractive reserves in part of the rain forest. But deforestation continues.

QUESTIONS FOR ANALYSIS

1. According to Mendes, who are the allies of the rubber tappers in their campaign to halt deforestation in the Amazon?
2. What are the main sources of opposition to the rubber tappers' campaign against deforestation?
3. How does Mendes view his opponents' arguments and tactics? How does Mendes respond to these arguments? How did he and supporters respond to their opponents' tactics?
4. What vision does Mendes have for the future of the Amazon region?
5. In your opinion, was the environment or social justice Mendes's major concern?

[EXTRACTIVE RESERVES]

We accepted that the Amazon could not be turned into some kind of sanctuary that nobody could touch. On the other hand, we knew it was important to stop the deforestation that is threatening the Amazon and all human life on the planet. We felt our alternative should involve preserving the forest, but it should also include a plan to develop the economy. So we came up with the idea of extractive reserves.

What do we mean by an extractive reserve? We mean the land is under public ownership but the rubber tappers and other workers that live on that land should have the right to live and work there. I say 'other workers' because there are not only rubber tappers in the forest. In our area, rubber tappers also harvest brazil nuts, but in other parts of the Amazon there are people who earn a living solely from harvesting nuts, while there are others who harvest babacu[1] and jute. . . .

. . . A sustainable fishing industry could be developed, exploiting the resource in a rational way. The enormous variety of plants with medicinal properties in this forest could prove very important to the country, if only some research was done. . . . I believe if this happened,

---

[1] A species of palm tree. Its nuts are a source of palm oil. The husks are used as fuel, its leaves are made into fiber for making hats and baskets, and the juice from its stalks is used to make a fermented drink.

and if the government took it all seriously, then in ten years the Amazon region could be very rich and have an important role in the national economy. . . .

[EMPATES — "STANDOFFS"]

. . . The *empates* are organised in the following way. When a community is threatened by deforestation it gets in touch with other communities in the area. They all get together in a mass meeting in the middle of the forest and organise teams of people to take the lead in confronting the workers cutting down the trees with their chainsaws and so on — all this in a peaceful but organised way. These teams try and convince the workers employed by the landowners to leave the area. The rubber tappers also dismantle the camps used by those workers to force them out. We are often attacked by the police because the landowners always apply to the courts for police protection. The judicial system has always done what the landowners wanted and sent in the police and there have been a lot of arrests.

One important point is that the whole community — men, women and children — takes part in the *empate*. The women stay at the front to prevent the police from shooting us. The police know if they open fire, they will kill women and children. . . .

[SUPPORTERS AND ENEMIES]

We . . . wanted to seek out the leaders of the Indian peoples in Acre and discuss how to unite our resistance movements, especially since Indians and rubber tappers have been at odds with each other for centuries. In Acre the leaders of the rubber tappers and Indian peoples met and concluded that neither of us was to blame for this. The real culprits were the rubber estate owners, the bankers and all the other powerful interest groups that had exploited us both.

People understood this very quickly, and from the beginning of 1986 the alliance of the peoples of the forest got stronger and stronger. . . .

. . . Our biggest assets are the international environmental lobby and the international press. I'm afraid we have had more support from abroad than from people in Brazil, and the opposite should be the case. It was only after international recognition and pressure that we started to get support from the rest of Brazil. . . .

. . . We have had a lot to do with the Church but there have been clashes at times, because although the Church has an important role in our struggle, it is only prepared to go so far. For example it has been very difficult about our interest in linking up with political parties. . . . We have good links with the Prelacy[2] of Acre-Purus, but things are much worse in the Juruá Valley where the Church is very conservative. We have a good relationship with the Church at Carauari, another region in the state of the Amazonas. I think the links we've had with the Church have been positive and we've been able to build up a working relationship which benefits both the Church and the rubber tappers. . . .

. . . People in the cities have always ignored us. However, since the CNS[3] was set up we have begun to get some support, for example from Acre University, which is quite an important political institution. We know the great majority of professors in the university either support the UDR[4] or are very conservative, but we hope to get some support from the new Rector there. Student support has been a bit unsteady but it's increasing now the Greens[5] are getting organised in Acre.

We have found it very difficult to get proper legal assistance. . . .

---

[2]The bishop and other churchmen who administer a diocese.
[3]Conselho Nacional dos Seringueiros (National Rubber Tappers' Council), founded in 1985.
[4]Uniao Democratica Ruralistica (Democratic Rural Union), an organization of landowners founded in 1985, originally

to oppose land reform legislation being considered by the National Congress.
[5]Partido Verde (Green Party), a political party dedicated to progressive and environmental causes.

Our union doesn't have enough money to employ a lawyer, but in July 1988 the Institute of Amazon Studies helped us obtain the services of a lawyer from Paraná, Genésio Felipe. . . . He covers the whole of Acre, so he's got a big job on!

I'm afraid we don't get much help from the lawyers round here. There are dozens of lawyers in Acre but they are all the children of landowners and other sectors of society that are against the workers' movement.

. . . We know we face powerful opposition. As well as the landowners and businessmen who dominate the Amazon region, we are up against the power of those who voted against land reform in the Constituent Assembly.[6] The voting power of these people in Congress has been a problem for us and has encouraged the growth of the right-wing landowners' movement, the Rural Democratic Union. . . . The defeat of the land reform proposal was a big victory for the landowners and land speculators. Now, since the establishment of the UDR in Acre, we've got a real fight on our hands. . . .

. . . We know, through people who have been to UDR meetings here, that their aim is to destroy the Xapuri[7] union by striking at the grassroots organisations of the Xapuri rubber tappers. They think if they can defeat Xapuri they can impose their terms on the whole state and further afield in the Amazon region as well. . . . In this fight, our only defence is the pressure put on the authorities by Brazilian society and the international scientific community. . . . There was a time when the state government seemed to be paying a lot of attention to environmental problems and to the rubber tappers. But we soon realised it was just putting on a show of defending the environment so the international

banks and other international organisations would approve its development projects.

We can't see how the authorities can say they defend the ecological system while at the same time deploying police to protect those who are destroying the forest. That happened, for example, in the case of the Ecuador rubber estate where there were many nut and rubber trees. . . .

. . . People have used all kind of arguments against us. The landowners say we're holding back progress and harming the country's economy. They say rubber is not important to the economy and the future lies with cattle raising. Others say the Amazon is a vast expanse of uninhabited territory and that it should be developed. . . .

The landowners use all the economic power at their disposal. They bribe the authorities; it's common knowledge that they've bought off the IBDF[8] staff in the Amazon region. They also use the law. They request police protection for the workers hired to cut down the trees, saying it is their land so they can do whatever they like with it. They accuse the rubber tappers of trespassing when we try and stop the deforestation. They turn to the courts for support and protection, claiming the land is private property. But the rubber tappers have been here for centuries! . . .

The other tactic the landowners use, and it's a very effective one, is to use hired guns to intimidate us. Our movement's leaders, not just myself but quite a few others as well, have been threatened a lot this year. We are all on the death list of the UDR's assassination squads. . . .

We are sure this will be the landowners' main tactic from now on. They are going to fight our movement with violence and intimidation. There's no doubt in our minds about that.

---

[6]A land reform program that would have redistributed approximately 170,000 square miles of land to small farmers was proposed in 1985; after intense lobbying by land-owning and business interests, only a watered-down version was passed.

[7]Xapuri is a city in the Brazilian state of Acre, where Mendes helped found a local chapter of the Rural Workers' Union in the 1970s.

[8]Instituto Brasiliero de Desenvolvimento Florestal (Brazilian Forestry Development Institute), an agency of the federal government with responsibility for enforcing laws relating to forest use.

Yangzi! Yangzi!

◆━◆

95 ◆ *Li Boning and Hou Xueyu,*
VIEWS OF CHINA'S THREE GORGES PROJECT

The Yangzi, which flows 3,700 miles from the mountains of Tibet to the East China Sea, is the longest river in Asia and the fourth longest river in the world. The source of 70 percent of China's rice crop, the site of five cities with populations of two million or more, and a key component of China's transportation system, the Yangzi Valley provides a home for more than three hundred million people. But the river also has been the cause of much devastation and suffering. Despite efforts to control its waters, the Yangzi regularly floods, frequently with catastrophic results. In the twentieth century alone, major floods occurred in 1910, 1911, 1931, 1935, 1949, and 1954. Though none equaled the devastation caused by the inundation of 1870, the flood of 1931 caused approximately thirty thousand deaths, created millions of refugees, and covered an area larger than the state of New York.

To end Yangzi flooding and produce hydroelectric power, Chinese politicians and engineers had eyed the scenic Three Gorges area, some 240 miles west of the city of Wuhan, as a potential dam site ever since Sun Yat-sen first mentioned it in his "Plan to Develop Industry" in 1919. Having been considered and dropped by the Nationalist government of Chiang Kai-shek, the idea was revived by the communists in 1953, just one year before a flood destroyed sections of the cities of Wuhan and Nanjing and killed thousands. For thirty years experts debated the feasibility of the project, the dam's size and placement, the desired depth of the water level above the dam, and plans to relocate displaced people. Many of these issues were still unresolved even as the government in the 1980s developed designs and arranged financing from the World Bank and investors from Sweden, Japan, Canada, and the United States. In 1988 the State Planning Commission approved building a milewide dam that would create a reservoir stretching 350 miles upstream and displacing 1.9 million people. All that was needed was approval from the National People's Congress, the rubber-stamp parliament scheduled to meet in March 1989.

Shockingly, when the congress met, more than two hundred delegates expressed opposition to the project, and once more it was put on hold. A major factor in these developments was the appearance in February 1989 of *Yangzi! Yangzi!*, a collection of letters, essays, and interviews by scientists, hydrologists, and engineers who opposed the dam. The publication of *Yangzi! Yangzi!*, edited by a female journalist, Dai Qing, was an extraordinary event in a society where dissent was rare and the government closely controlled the media. But it derailed the Three Gorges project only temporarily. Once the government had suppressed the prodemocracy movement that crested in the spring of 1989 but was abruptly halted by the Tiananmen Square Massacre in June, it silenced critics of the Three Gorges project. In October 1989, *Yangzi! Yangzi!* was officially banned, and its editor, Dai Qing, was jailed for close to a year. In 1991 the government decided to proceed with the project, which was proposed for approval by the People's National Congress in April 1992. Although 177 delegates voted against the project and 649 abstained, 1,767 delegates voted to approve it. Construction began in 1994.

Both of the following selections appeared in the 1989 edition of *Yangzi! Yangzi!* The first excerpt is from a 1988 speech of Li Boning, a government official who had served as deputy minister of the Ministry of Water Resources and Electric Power. The editor, Dai Qing, included his pro-dam speech to give balance to her book. The second excerpt is from an interview of a distinguished botanist, Hou Xueyu, who opposed the dam, by the journalist Zhu Jianhong.

QUESTIONS FOR ANALYSIS

1. According to Li Boning, what are the potential advantages of going forward with the Three Gorges Dam project?
2. According to Li, what are the weaknesses of the alternative proposals suggested by the opponents of Three Gorges?
3. According to Hou Xueyu, what are the potential environmental dangers of the project?
4. According to Hou, what are the weaknesses of the "solutions" proposed by the dam's advocates to alleviate environmental damage?
5. How does Hou explain the fact that only ten "experts" refused to approve the plan for the Three Gorges Dam project?
6. What are the grounds of the basic disagreement between Li and Hou on the subjects of economic development and the environment?

[LI BONING, "OPINIONS AND RECOMMENDATIONS"]

As a result of numerous experiments and comparisons along with the urgency of the realization of the four modernizations, it is clear that there is no alternative to the Three Gorges project for flood control, electricity, navigation, economic development in the reservoir area, and extensive economic benefits. . . . Thus, harnessing the Yangzi River floods for the economic development of the lower and middle reaches can ensure the security of hundreds of thousands of human lives and millions of *yuan*[1]

worth of property. In addition, it can relieve acute electricity shortages and strains on the coal supply for the thermal power plants in central and eastern China. It can also realize the image of the Yangzi River as a golden waterway by permitting a fleet of 10,000-ton ships to sail directly from Wuhan to Chongqing.[2] . . .

Some comrades favor the idea of "tributaries first and the mainstream of the river second" with regard to the construction of reservoirs and hydro-electric power plants along the Yangzi River. They contend that the tributary reservoirs require less investment and offer quicker results than the Three Gorges project, which would

---

[1]The basic unit (Y) of Chinese currency.
[2]Chongqing is approximately six hundred miles from Wuhan.

therefore make the Three Gorges unnecessary. This assumption has no scientific basis at all. . . .

Even if every possible effort is made in this respect, it would not be possible to start construction within a few years' time. In comparison with thermal plants of the same scale, the Three Gorges project could save 40 million tons of coal per year. . . . Given the present overload on railway transportation, relying on thermal plants to meet the demands for electricity in central and eastern China would necessitate laying more than 1,000 kilometers of additional track and opening up of several large-scale coal mines to ensure the supply for the thermal plants. This is not an economical use of time or money. Furthermore, the thermal plants create considerable pollution and coal is a valuable but non-renewable source of energy. . . .

Although nuclear power is a very promising energy source, we need some time to accumulate our own experience in this field, because of its belated development in our country. . . . Besides, the nuclear plants cannot control flooding or improve navigation. . . .

. . . The safety of the Yangzi and Yellow rivers has an important bearing on the nation as a whole. Catastrophic floods could disrupt our overall national economic planning and delay implementation of the four modernizations. At the present time, when the whole nation is working heart and soul to overcome economic difficulties, we could not sustain such a devastating blow. . . .

. . . As for the debate on the Three Gorges project, is it democratic and scientific to listen to the opinions held by the minority alone — to reject the project — without any sound scientific evidence? . . . [Those who oppose the project] simply repeat old slogans of the 1950s, inventing more and more accusatory labels for the achievements made by the scientists and experts, and arbitrarily dismiss them with many irrelevant accusations. It does not conform with

the values we have been promoting, that is, respect for knowledge, respect for science and respect for intellectuals.

[HOU XUEYU, "AN ENORMOUS ENVIRONMENTAL DISASTER"]

Zhu Jianhong: Once the Three Gorges dam is built, it will be the largest hydro-electric project in the world. . . . Could you tell us something more about its impact?

Hou Xueyu: The project will submerge 19 counties and more than 400,000 *mu*[3] of cultivated land, including some of the richest soil along the river basin. Along with the well-known mustard tuber, medicinal herbs and grain, 73,900 *mu* of orange groves, which produce a net profit of Y1,500 per *mu*, will be lost. The losses would be at least Y100 million per year, Y1 billion in a decade.

Zhu Jianhong: It has been suggested that, in order to make up for the losses caused by the project, new land for orange groves be opened up on terraced fields.

Hou Xueyu: This is an irresponsible suggestion. After the rich plains are gone, only rocky hills with thin layers of poor topsoil would be left. Those terraced fields could easily be washed away by heavy rainfall in the area. . . .

Zhu Jianhong: However, after the completion of the reservoir, the newly developed water resources could be used as fish ponds, even if the soil were destroyed. So the losses can still be made up. What do you think of this?

Hou Xueyu: I don't think it could be made up in this way. Water and soil are not interchangeable. The rich arable land destroyed by the reservoir could never be reclaimed. Of course, fish could be raised; but, as you know, reservoir construction will destroy some existing fish ponds. . . .

Apart from irreparable damage to the soil, the natural beauty and cultural heritage of the

---

[3]One *mu* equals approximately one eighth of an acre.

area would be permanently damaged as well. I think the Three Gorges is the most beautiful of all the world's gorges. The surrounding areas have many national treasures, some more than 5,000 years old. These include the famous ruins of the ancient Daxi culture,[4] and tombs from the Warring States period [475–221 B.C.], the Eastern Han [25 B.C.–200 A.D.], and the Ming [1368–1622] and Qing [1662–1912] dynasties, most of which are scattered below 180 meters. . . . All of this would be inundated if the reservoir were built, and tourism would suffer incalculable economic losses.

Zhu Jianhong: But some have suggested that these historical relics could always be moved to safer places.

Hou Xueyu: They have, and one even recommended building a museum to display these relics. Even if they could be moved, their authenticity would be destroyed, together with the unique value and cultural significance of the original context. For instance, how would it strike you to compare the on-site remains of a 5,000 year-old tombs with museum reconstructions? . . .

Zhu Jianhong: You mentioned that the construction of the project could destroy fish ponds. Can you elaborate on this point?

Hou Xueyu: The middle reaches of the Yangzi River . . . is one of the major breeding grounds for black, silver, grass and variegated carp. . . .

Breeding requires a water temperature of 18 degrees centigrade. However, with the discharge of reservoir water, that temperature cannot be retained, thereby reducing the breeding period by 20 days. Because of changes in the river-bed after the completion of the reservoir, the quantities of fish would be reduced, eventually resulting in decreased output. Some rare species would be affected too, including Lipotesvexillifer, Chinese paddlefish, and sturgeon. In danger of extinction, these species have been given priority protection by the state. . . .

Furthermore, reservoir construction would bring about changes in water quality and temperature at the mouth of the Yangzi River, and consequently reduce fish production. For instance, anchovies, white bait, hilsa herring, and prawns — all found in semi-salty water — will probably diminish in quantity. . . .

Zhu Jianhong: What other serious effects would the Three Gorges project cause?

Hou Xueyu: Tremendous losses would be inflicted on industry and mining. The plan to set the high-water level at 180 meters would submerge 624 factories, including six major factories in Chongqing. Some mineral resources would also be lost since the mining areas would be below water level after construction of the reservoir. . . .

Zhu Jianhong: Some have said that a new environmental balance can be reached if the programs for population relocation and development of new towns and cities are carefully formulated and properly carried out.

Hou Xueyu: I think the destruction would outweigh a new balance. The saying "man can conquer nature" is unrealistic. . . . Nature will not allow it. If one doesn't consider natural conditions, it is impossible to work out a program beneficial to the people. . . .

Zhu Jianhong: Some feel it inevitable that the environment pay some price for the economic benefits the project will produce. What do you think?

Hou Xueyu: Environmental interests and economic benefits go hand in hand. A better environment will enhance economic benefits. Otherwise, the economic benefits, no matter how high, will have to pay for the environmental damage. In the end, it is the common people who will suffer these losses. It is one-sided and unscientific to consider only the benefits, such as the production of electric power, without counting the cost to the environment and natural resources. . . .

---

[4]In 1959 excavations in Daxi, a village at the east entrance of Qutang Gorge, one of the Three Gorges, revealed ruins of villages estimated to be between 4000 and 6000 years old along with pottery and stone, jade, and bone wares.

Zhu Jianhong: Among the 412 experts who participated in the leading group's assessment, only 10 refused to sign the assessment report, and you are one of the 10.[5]

Hou Xueyu: I was invited only to show the public that people of different opinions were included. There were many others who possess valuable knowledge and insight with regard to this project who were not invited. . . . As far as I know, some experts who were not in agreement with the report, signed it, for various reasons.

Zhu Jianhong: What are the "various reasons"?

Hou Xueyu: That's very complicated. For example, some experts were persuaded by their leaders, who went to their houses to ask their approval. How could they refuse? Some were told that it was already finalized by the Party Central Committee. What was the use of opposing it? So on and so forth.

Zhu Jianhong: Will you still insist on your position?

Hou Xueyu: Certainly yes. . . . Our generation will have made an irrevocable mistake if navigation on the golden waterway is severed.

---

[5]Thirteen "experts' groups" on topics ranging from seismology to ecology to construction had been appointed to evaluate aspects of the project and report to the Leading Group for the Assessment of the Three Gorges Project. Hou had been a member of the Experts' Group on Ecology and Environment.

◆

Religion and Politics in the 1970s and 1980s

During much of the twentieth century, it would not have been unreasonable to conclude that religion was a dying force among the world's peoples. The Islamic Brotherhood's popularity in the Arab world during the 1930s and 1940s and the Hindu-Muslim strife accompanying Indian independence are examples of religion's continuing vigor, but in general organized religion was on the defensive. Avowedly atheist regimes in the Soviet Union and communist China sought to obliterate religious belief and practice altogether. In the West, mainline Protestant churches experienced declining membership and attendance, and the Roman Catholic Church found it increasingly difficult to attract young men to the priesthood. In Turkey, Iran, India, and Indonesia, governments embraced aggressively secularist policies as part of campaigns to modernize their economies, educational systems, and culture.

For all of these reasons, when the people of Iran in 1979 rose up against the Western-oriented, secularist government of Shah Muhammad Reza Pahlavi and instituted an Islamic republic guided by religious values and laws, many considered it an aberration or a sign of a defect within Islam. It is now clear, however, that Iran's revolution was neither. It was one of many examples of religion's continuing vitality and growing political importance in the 1970s and 1980s.

The most striking sign of religion's vigor in the late twentieth century was the phenomenon of religious fundamentalism. Fundamentalists, irrespective of their confessional allegiance, share two basic beliefs. First, they reject modernism, secularism, and all other intellectual and religious tendencies that challenge or belittle religious truths passed down by tradition or set forth in sacred texts. Second, they believe that these religious truths should regulate and inspire all aspects of public and private life.

In the late twentieth century, fundamentalist movements appeared in every major faith and in states at every level of economic development. The religious right in the United States flexed its political muscle at the local, state, and national levels during the 1980s and 1990s; conservative religious Jews in Israel increased their influence on foreign and domestic policy. Fundamentalism was strongest, however, in the Middle East, North Africa, India, and Southeast Asia, where affirmation of traditional religious values provided a way to strengthen cultural identity and limit the influence of foreign, Western-inspired values.

Most fundamentalists are conservative in that they oppose social, political, and cultural changes that threaten practices sanctioned by their religion. But deeply religious individuals also have promoted progressive social and political movements in many parts of the world. A Baptist minister, Martin Luther King, Jr., with broad support from the nation's clergy, led the civil rights movement in the United States. Religious people also played important roles in the struggle against apartheid in South Africa, in various movements on behalf of nuclear disarmament, and even in the events that led to the downfall of communism in Eastern Europe in the 1980s. In Latin America during the 1970s and 1980s, while poverty worsened and much of the region groaned under harsh authoritarian rule, Catholic clergy committed themselves to serving the poor, called for social justice and democracy, and denounced dictatorship. They did so at great risk. No fewer than 850 priests, nuns, and bishops were murdered by right-wing death squads or individual assassins in the 1970s and 1980s. Their martyrdom is convincing evidence of religion's enduring power in the late twentieth century.

Latin American Catholicism and the Theology of Liberation

◆

96 ◆ *FINAL DOCUMENT OF THE THIRD GENERAL CONFERENCE OF THE LATIN AMERICAN EPISCOPATE*

When some six hundred bishops gathered in Puebla, Mexico, in 1979 for the Third General Conference of the Latin American Episcopate, they sensed that the Latin American Church, with 35 percent of the world's Catholics, was at a crossroads. In the 1960s reformist and even revolutionary currents had emerged among the clergy. This was in part a response to the liberal atmosphere in the broader church after the Second Vatican Council of 1962 and in part an expression of the growing conviction that the Church's indifference to social injustice distorted Christ's teachings and threatened to lose the masses to Marxism or religious apathy. During the 1960s bishops spoke out in favor of land reform; young priests went into urban slums to establish clinics, schools, and self-help organizations; and Catholic intellectuals developed a new "theology of liberation," which centered the Church's mission on ministering to the poor. Their efforts culminated in decisions made at the second conference of Latin American bishops in Medellin, Columbia, in 1968, by which bishops committed the Church to the task of liberating Latin America's poor from economic and social injustice.

This leftward shift provoked a counterreaction in the 1970s. Conservative bishops denounced reformers as more Marxist than Christian, and many Catholics expressed reservations about the clergy's political activism. Conservatives hoped to regain control of the Church at the third Catholic bishops' conference in Puebla in 1979. Well-known liberation theologians were excluded, and conservative bishops drafted a policy statement that, if accepted, would have endorsed capitalism and rejected the clergy's involvement in politics. Remarks by Pope John Paul II, who addressed the opening of the conference, seemed to support the progressives, however, and after two weeks of discussion, the delegates approved a generally progressive statement from which the following excerpts are drawn.

After Puebla, the Latin American Church remained divided. Churchmen in Chile and Brazil continued to speak out against military regimes, and clergy in Central America were still in the forefront of the struggle for social change. Overall, however, conservatives made gains, especially in Argentina and Columbia. This trend was supported by an increasingly conservative Pope John Paul II, who named conservatives as bishops and approved the disciplining of Leonardo Boff, the popular Brazilian liberation theologian, in the mid 1980s. While the Catholic Church struggled to clarify its mission, more Latin Americans abandoned religion or joined one of the many Pentecostal Protestant sects spreading through the region.

QUESTIONS FOR ANALYSIS

1. What is the document's overall assessment of the economic and political state of Latin America?
2. What can be gleaned from the document about the bishops' views of the underlying causes of Latin American poverty?
3. Why, according to the Puebla statement, should Latin American poverty be especially intolerable to Catholics?
4. What statements in the document seem to confirm the view that it was a compromise between progressives and conservatives?
5. Critics of the Puebla statement contend that it was essentially worthless because it lacked concrete proposals to deal with Latin America's problems. Do you agree with such criticisms?

Viewing it in the light of faith, we see the growing gap between rich and poor as a scandal and a contradiction to Christian existence. . . . The luxury of a few becomes an insult to the wretched poverty of the vast masses. . . . This is contrary to the plan of the Creator and to the honor that is due him. In this anxiety and sorrow the Church sees a situation of social sinfulness, all the more serious because it exists in countries that call themselves Catholic and are capable of changing the situation. . . .

This situation of pervasive extreme poverty takes on very concrete faces in real life. In these faces we ought to recognize the suffering features of Christ the Lord, who questions and challenges us. They include:

- the faces of young children, struck down by poverty before they are born, their chance for self-development blocked by irreparable mental and physical deficiencies; and of the vagrant children in our cities who are so often exploited, products of poverty and the moral disorganization of the family;
- the faces of young people, who are disoriented because they cannot find their place in society, and who are frustrated, particularly in marginal rural and urban areas, by the lack of opportunity to obtain training and work;
- the faces of the indigenous peoples, and frequently of the Afro-Americans as well; living marginalized lives in inhuman situations, they can be considered the poorest of the poor;
- the faces of the peasants; as a social group, they live in exile almost everywhere on our continent, deprived of land, caught in a situation of internal and external dependence, and subjected to systems of commercialization that exploit them;
- the faces of laborers, who frequently are ill-paid and who have difficulty in organizing themselves and defending their rights;

- the faces of the underemployed and the unemployed, who are dismissed because of the harsh exigencies of economic crises, and often because of development-models that subject workers and their families to cold economic calculations;
- the faces of marginalized and overcrowded urban dwellers, whose lack of material goods is matched by the ostentatious display of wealth by other segments of society;
- the faces of old people, who are growing more numerous every day, and who are frequently marginalized in a progress-oriented society that totally disregards people not engaged in production.

We share other anxieties of our people that stem from a lack of respect for their dignity as human beings, made in the image and likeness of God, and for their inalienable rights as children of God.

. . . Our mission to bring God to human beings, and human beings to God, also entails the task of fashioning a more fraternal society here. And the unjust social situation has not failed to produce tensions within the Church itself. On the one hand they are provoked by groups that stress the "spiritual" side of the Church's mission and resent active efforts at societal improvement. On the other hand they are provoked by people who want to make the Church's mission nothing more than an effort at human betterment.

There are other novel and disturbing phenomena. We refer to the partisan political activity of priests — not as individuals, as some had acted in the past . . ., but as organized pressure groups. And we also refer to the fact that some of them are applying social analyses with strong political connotations to pastoral work.

The Church's awareness of its evangelizing mission[1] has led it in the past ten years to publish numerous pastoral documents about social

---

[1]*Evangelization* means "preaching Christianity with the view of bringing about conversion or rededication to the faith."

justice; to create [organizations] designed to express solidarity with the afflicted, to denounce outrages, and to defend human rights; . . . and to endure the persecution and at times death of its members in witness to its prophetic mission. Much remains to be done, of course, if the Church is to display greater oneness and solidarity. Fear of Marxism keeps many from facing up to the oppressive reality of liberal capitalism. One could say that some people, faced with the danger of one clearly sinful system, forgot to denounce and combat the established reality of another equally sinful system. . . . We must give full attention to the latter system, without overlooking the violent and atheistic historical forms of Marxism. . . .

To this are added other anxieties that stem from abuses of power, which are typical of regimes based on force. There are the anxieties based on systematic or selective repression; it is accompanied by accusations, violations of privacy, improper pressures, tortures, and exiles. There are the anxieties produced in many families by the disappearance of their loved ones, about whom they cannot get any news. There is the total insecurity bound up with arrest and detention without judicial consent. There are the anxieties felt in the face of a system of justice that has been suborned or cowed. As the Supreme Pontiffs point out, the Church . . . must raise its voice to denounce and condemn these situations, particularly when the responsible officials or rulers call themselves Christians.

Then there are the anxieties raised by guerrilla violence, by terrorism, and by the kidnappings carried out by various brands of extremists. They, too, pose a threat to life together in society. . . .

The free-market economy, in its most rigid expression, is still the prevailing system on our continent. Legitimated by liberal ideologies, it has increased the gap between the rich and the poor by giving priority to capital over labor, economics over the social realm. Small groups in our nations, who are often tied in with foreign interests, have taken advantage of the opportunities provided by these older forms of the free market to profit for themselves while the interests of the vast majority of the people suffer.

Marxist ideologies have also spread among workers, students, teachers, and others, promising greater social justice. In practice their strategies have sacrificed many Christian, and hence human, values; or else they have fallen prey to utopian forms of unrealism. Finding their inspiration in policies that use force as a basic tool, they have only intensified the spiral of violence.

A Platform for the Religious Right in the United States

❖

97 ◆ *Jerry Falwell, AN AGENDA FOR THE 1980s*

In the late 1970s proudly fundamentalist religious leaders and their followers, mainly Protestant, emerged as a powerful force in U.S. political life. Claiming to represent the views of the "moral majority," they rejected what they perceived as the disastrous legacy of the late 1960s and the 1970s: crime, drugs, illegitimacy, sexual permissiveness, pornography, failed schools, and soaring divorce rates. They sought to reverse America's moral decline by affirming the traditional values, religious and otherwise, they believed had made the United States great but now were threatened.

Among the stars of the religious right was the Virginia-based pastor and televangelist, Jerry Falwell. Born in 1933 into the family of a Lynchburg, Virginia, businessman, Falwell dreamed of becoming a professional baseball player or engineer before he experienced a religious conversion as a sophomore at

Lynchburg College and decided to become a minister. After graduating from the Baptist Bible College of Missouri, he founded the Thomas Road Baptist Church in Lynchburg in 1956. He gained a national following in the 1970s when his radio program, *The Old Time Gospel Hour,* began to be televised nationally. Having expanded his mission to include Liberty University in Lynchburg, a home for unwed mothers, and a treatment center for alcoholics, in 1979 he assumed leadership of the Moral Majority Incorporated, a religious special-interest group whose main tenets are described in his "An Agenda for the 1980s."

After registering (by its own count) four million new conservative voters in the early 1980s, the Moral Majority gradually began to lose support and was disbanded by Falwell in 1989. Falwell continues to be an important figure in contemporary American politics and religious life. His Liberty Baptist Church in Lynchburg has twenty-two thousand members, twelve thousand of whom can worship at one time in the church's giant sanctuary. In 2000 Falwell agreed to become director of People of Faith, an organization that sought to raise $15 million and register ten million new voters in support of conservative candidates.

QUESTIONS FOR ANALYSIS

1. According to Falwell, what are the manifestations of America's moral decline?
2. What has been the cause of this decline?
3. How does Falwell define morality? How does his definition differ from one that would likely have been offered by the authors of the Puebla Declaration? (See source 96.)
4. In what ways is the platform of the Moral Majority a specific repudiation of the legacy of the 1960s and 1970s?

The 1980s are certainly a decade of destiny for America. The rising tide of secularism threatens to obliterate the Judeo-Christian influence on American society. In the realm of religion, liberal clergy have seduced the average American away from the Bible and the kind of simple faith on which this country was built. We need to call America back to God, back to the Bible, and back to moral sanity. . . . During the 1960s and 1970s, people felt confused and began to turn away from the liberalized institutional church that was not meeting their spiritual needs. As attendance drastically declined in the mainline denominations, it dramatically increased in conservative denominations. Liberalism is obviously losing its influence on America. The time has come for Fundamentalists and Evangelicals to return our nation to its spiritual and moral roots. . . .

. . . Something had to be done. The federal government was encroaching upon the sovereignty of both the church and the family. The U.S. Supreme Court had legalized abortion-on-demand. The Equal Rights Amendment,[1] with its vague language, threatened to do further damage to the traditional family, as did the rising sentiment toward so-called homosexual rights. Most Americans were shocked, but kept

[1]The Equal Rights Amendment (ERA) was a proposed amendment to the Constitution approved by Congress and submitted to the states for approval in 1972. It provided that "Equality of Rights under the law shall not be denied or abridged . . . on account of sex." Having been ratified by only thirty-five states (three short of the necessary two-thirds), efforts to pass the amendment ended in 1982 when the time limit expired.

hoping someone would do something about all this moral chaos.

Facing the desperate need in the impending crisis of the hour, several concerned pastors urge me to put together a political organization that could provide a vehicle to address these crucial issues. . . . They urged that we formulate a non-partisan political organization to promote morality in public life and combat legislation that favored the legalization of immorality. Together we formulated the Moral Majority, Inc. . . .

Here is how Moral Majority stands on today's vital issues:

1. *We believe in the separation of Church and State.* Moral Majority, Inc., is a political organization that provides a platform for religious and nonreligious Americans who share moral values to address their concerns. . . . We are Americans who are proud to be conservative in our approach to moral, social, and political concerns.

2. *We are pro-life.* We believe that life begins at fertilization. We strongly oppose the massive "biological holocaust" that is resulting in the abortion of one-and-a-half-million babies each year in America. We believe that unborn babies have the right to life as much as babies who have been born. . . .

3. *We are pro-traditional family.* We believe that the only acceptable family form begins with a legal marriage of a man and woman. We feel that homosexual relationships and common-law relationships should not be accepted as traditional families. We oppose legislation that favors these kinds of "diverse family form," thereby penalizing the traditional family. We do not oppose civil rights for homosexuals. We do oppose "special rights" for homosexuals who have chosen a perverted lifestyle rather than a traditional way-of-life.

4. *We oppose the illegal drug traffic in America.* The youth of America are in the midst of a drug epidemic. Through education, legislation, and other means, we want to do our part to save our young people from death on the installment plan through illegal drug addiction.

5. *We oppose pornography.* While we do not advocate censorship, we do believe that education and legislation can help stem the tide of pornography and obscenity that is poisoning the American spirit today. Economic boycotts are a proper way in America's free enterprise system to help persuade the media to move back to a sensible and reasonable moral stand. . . .

6. *We support the state of Israel and Jewish people everywhere.* It is impossible to separate the state of Israel from the Jewish family internationally. Many Moral Majority members, because of their theological convictions, are committed to the Jewish people. Others stand upon the human and civil rights of all persons as a premise for support of the state of Israel. Support of Israel is one of the essential commitments of Moral Majority. No anti-Semitic influence is allowed in Moral Majority, Inc.

7. *We believe that a strong national defense is the best deterrent to war.* . . . The only way America can remain free is to remain strong. Therefore we support Reagan administration efforts to regain our position of military preparedness — with a sincere hope that we will never need to use any of our weapons against any people anywhere.

8. *We support equal rights for women.* We agree with President Reagan's commitment to help every governor and every state legislature to move quickly to ensure that, during the 1980s, every American woman will earn as much money and enjoy the same opportunities for advancement as her male counterpart in the same vocation.

9. *We believe ERA is the wrong vehicle to obtain equal rights for women.* We feel that the ambiguous and simplistic language of the proposed amendment could lead to court interpretations that might put women in combat, sanction homosexual relationships, and financially penalize widows and deserted wives. . . .

This is how Moral Majority, Inc., is contributing to bringing America back to moral sanity:

1. *By educating millions of Americans concerning the vital moral issues of our day.* . . .

2. *By mobilizing millions of previously "inactive" Americans.* We have registered millions of voters and reactivated more millions of frustrated citizens into a special-interest group who are effectively making themselves heard in the halls of Congress, in the White House, and in every state legislature.

3. *By lobbying intensively in Congress to defeat any legislation that would further erode our constitutionally guaranteed freedom*, and by introducing and/or supporting legislation that promotes traditional family and moral values, followed by the goal of passage of a Human Life Amendment, which is a top priority of the Moral Majority agenda. . . .

4. *By informing all Americans about the voting records of their representatives so that every American,*

with full information available, can vote intelligently following his or her own convictions. . . .

5. *By organizing and training millions of Americans who can become moral activists.* . . .

6. *By encouraging and promoting private schools in their attempt to excel in academics while simultaneously teaching traditional family and moral values.* . . .

Moral Majority, Inc., does not advocate the abolition of public schools. Public schools will always be needed in our pluralistic society. We are committed to helping public schools regain excellence. That is why we support the return of voluntary prayer to public schools and strongly oppose the teaching of the "religion" of secular humanism in the public classroom.

The Place of Hinduism in Modern India

◈

98 ◆ Girilal Jain, EDITORIALS

Independent India has never been free of religious tensions. Even after Muslims were given their own state of Pakistan in 1947, religious pluralism characterized India's population: today it is composed of approximately 83 percent Hindus, 11 percent Muslims, 2.6 percent Christians, slightly over 1 percent Sikhs, and smaller numbers of Jains, Parsis, and Buddhists. None of these groups has been completely satisfied with India's constitution, which proclaims India to be a secular state with partiality toward no religious group. Many Hindus, however, believe that the government bends over backwards to protect Muslims and Sikhs; Muslims and Sikhs, conversely, are convinced that the government panders to Hindus. In the early 1980s religious tensions intensified as Muslims began to make converts among low-caste Hindus in the south, Sikhs agitated for an independent Punjab, and Hindus organized their own political party, the Bharatiya Janata (Indian People's Party), or BJP, whose goal was the "Hinduization" of India. Founded in 1982, BJP representation in parliament rose from two members in 1984 to 185 in 1996, fifty more than that of the Congress Party, which had enjoyed a parliamentary majority in all but four years since independence.

An important spokesman for Hindu nationalism and the BJP before his death in 1993 was the journalist Girilal Jain, who was editor-in-chief of the New Delhi *Times of India* between 1978 and 1988. Born into a poor rural family in 1922 and educated at Delhi University, Jain was jailed by the British during the 1942 Quit India campaign. As a journalist he was best known for his impassioned support of Indira Gandhi, prime minister between 1966 and 1970 and 1980 and 1984. During the 1980s he was drawn to Hindu nationalism and the BJP.

The following editorials were written in 1990, when Hindu-Muslim tensions were peaking over the Babri mosque in the city of Ayodhya built in the sixteenth century on the site of a Hindu temple believed to be the birthplace of the Hindu god-king Ram. Hindus demanded the destruction of the mosque, which was no longer used, so a temple in honor of Ram could be built. In December 1992, Hindus stormed the mosque and destroyed it, precipitating a government crisis and causing violence that took the lives of thousands. The government, with its commitment to religious pluralism and democracy, survived, but religious tensions remained high.

QUESTIONS FOR ANALYSIS

1. What are the reasons for Jain's disenchantment with India's government?
2. What does Jain mean when he says that the issues that concern the BJP have to do with "civilization," not religion?
3. How does Jain define "the West"? How does he view the West's role in Indian history?
4. Why, according to Jain, is the controversy over the Ayodhya mosque so significant for India's future?
5. In Jain's viewpoint, why have the Muslims been satisfied to go along with the secularist policies of the Indian state?
6. What is Jain's vision of India's future?

A specter haunts dominant sections of India's political and intellectual elites — the specter of a growing Hindu self-awareness and self-assertion. Till recently these elites had used the bogey of Hindu "communalism"[1] and revivalism as a convenient device to keep themselves in power and to "legitimize" their slavish imitation of the West. Unfortunately for them, the ghost has now materialized.

Millions of Hindus have stood up. It will not be easy to trick them back into acquiescing in an order which has been characterized not so much by its "appeasement of Muslims" as by its alienness, rootlessness and contempt for the land's unique cultural past. Secularism, a euphemism for irreligion and repudiation of the Hindu ethos, and socialism, a euphemism for denigration and humiliation of the business community to the benefit of ever expanding rapacious bureaucracy, . . . have been major planks of this order. Both have lost much of their old glitter and, therefore, capacity to dazzle and mislead. . . .

The Hindu fight is not at all with Muslims; the fight is between Hindus anxious to renew themselves in the spirit of their civilization, and the state, Indian in name and not in spirit and the political and intellectual class trapped in the debris the British managed to bury us under before they left. The proponents of the Western ideology are using Muslims as auxiliaries and it is a pity Muslim "leaders" are allowing themselves to be so used. . . .

Secularist-versus-Hindu-Rashtra[2] controversy is, of course, not new. In fact, it has been with us since the twenties when some of our forebears

---

[1]Communalism is a system in which rival minority groups are devoted to their own interests rather than those of the whole society; in the context of Indian politics the term refers to loyalties of religious communities.

[2]*Rashtra* is Hindi for state, or polity.

began to search for a definition of nationalism which could transcend at once the Hindu-Muslim divide and the aggregationist approach whereby India was regarded as a Hindu-Muslim-Sikh-Christian land. But it has acquired an intensity it has not had since partition. . . .

India, to put the matter brusquely, has been a battleground between two civilizations (Hindu and Islamic) for well over a thousand years, and three (Hindu, Muslim and Western) for over two hundred years. None of them has ever won a decisive enough and durable enough victory to oblige the other two to assimilate themselves fully into it. So the battle continues. This stalemate lies at the root of the crisis of identity the intelligentsia has faced since the beginning of the freedom movement in the last quarter of the nineteenth century. . . .

The more resilient and upwardly mobile section of the intelligentsia must, by definition, seek to come to terms with the ruling power and its mores, and the less successful part of it to look for its roots and seek comfort in its cultural past. This was so during the Muslim period; this was the case during the British Raj;[3] and this rule has not ceased to operate since independence.

Thus in the medieval period of our history there grew up a class of Hindus in and around centers of Muslim power who took to the Persian-Arabic culture and ways of the rulers; similarly under the more securely founded and far better organized and managed Raj there arose a vast number of Hindus who took to the English language, Western ideas, ideals, dress and eating habits; . . . they, their progeny and other recruits to their class have continued to dominate independent India.

They are the self-proclaimed secularists who have sought, and continue to seek, to remake India in the Western image. The image has, of course, been an eclectic one; if they have stuck to the institutional framework inherited from the British, they have been more than willing to take up not only the Soviet model of economic development,[4] but also the Soviet theories on a variety of issues such as the nationalities problem and the nature of imperialism and neo-colonialism.

Behind them has stood, and continues to stand, the awesome intellectual might of the West, which may or may not be anti-India, depending on the exigencies of its interests, but which has to be antipathetic to Hinduism. . . .

Some secularists may be genuinely pro-Muslim. . . . But, by and large, that is not the motivating force in their lives. They are driven, above all, by the fear of what they call regression into their own past which they hate and dread. Most of the exponents of this viewpoint have come and continue to come understandably from the Left, understandably because no other group of Indians can possibly be so alienated from the country's cultural past as the followers of Lenin, Stalin and Mao, who have spared little effort to turn their own countries into cultural wastelands. . . .

The state in independent India has, it is true, sought, broadly speaking, to be neutral in the matter of religion. But this is a surface view of the reality. The Indian state has been far from neutral in civilizational terms. It has been an agency, and a powerful agency, for the spread of Western values and mores. It has willfully sought to replicate Western institutions, the Soviet Union too being essentially part of Western civilization. It could not be otherwise in view of the orientation and aspirations of the dominant elite of which Nehru[5] remains the guiding spirit.

Muslims have found such a state acceptable principally on three counts. First, it has agreed to leave them alone in respect of their personal

---

[3]*Raj* is Hindi for reign, or rule; often used to refer to the British colonial administration.

[4]In 1951 the government adopted a series of five-year plans for the nation's economic development in imitation of the Five-Year Plans initiated by Stalin in 1928. The plans featured central planning and state ownership of major enterprises.

[5]Jawaharlal Nehru (1899–1964), India's first prime minister, was a major target of Jain because of his commitment to socialism and secularism (see Chapter 11, source 90).

law. . . . Secondly, it has allowed them to expand their traditional . . . educational system in madrasahs[6] attached to mosques. Above all, it has helped them avoid the necessity to come to terms with Hindu civilization in a predominantly Hindu India. This last count is the crux of the matter. . . .

In the past up to the sixteenth century, great temples have been built in our country by rulers to mark the rise of a new dynasty or to mark a triumph. . . . In the present case, the proposal to build the Rama temple[7] has also to help produce an "army" which can in the first instance achieve the victory the construction can proclaim.

The raising of such an "army" in our democracy, however flawed, involves not only a body of disciplined cadres, which is available in the shape of the RSS,[8] a political oganization, which too is available in the Bharatiya Janata Party, but also an aroused citizenry. . . . The Vishwa Hindu Parishad[9] and its allies have fulfilled this need in a manner which is truly spectacular.

The BJP-VHP-RSS leaders have rendered the country another great service. They have brought Hindu interests, if not the Hindu ethos, into the public domain where they legitimately belong. . . .

The Nehru order is as much in the throes of death as its progenitor, the Marxist-Leninist-Stalinist order. A new order is waiting to be conceived and born. It needs a mother as well as a mid-wife.

---

[6]Madrasahs were advanced schools of learning, or colleges, devoted to Islamic studies.

[7]This refers to the controversy about the Babri mosque in Ayodhya; see source introduction.

[8]RSS stands for Rashtriya Swayamsevak Sangh, a militant Hindu organization founded in 1925 and dedicated to the strengthening of Hindu culture.

[9]The Vishwa Hindu Parishad (VHP), or World Hindu Society, was founded in 1964. It is dedicated to demolishing mosques built on Hindu holy sites.

◆

Third World Women Between Tradition and Change

During the twentieth century, political leaders of industrialized nations, revolutionaries such as Lenin and Mao, and nationalist heroes as different as Ataturk and Gandhi all supported the ideal of women's equality with men. The United Nations Charter of 1945 commits the organization to the same ideal, and the UN Universal Declaration of Human Rights of 1948 reaffirms the goal of ending all forms of gender-based discrimination. Beginning in the 1960s powerful feminist movements with agendas ranging from equal educational access to legalized abortion took root in the Western industrialized nations and to a lesser degree in Asia, Latin America, and Africa.

Despite this broad support for gender equality, progress for women worldwide was uneven in the 1970s and 1980s. In developed industrial societies, women undoubtedly made great strides. Large numbers of women entered professions such as law, medicine, and university teaching; contraception and legal abortions were made available in most nations; laws forbidding gender-based discrimination were passed. Nonetheless, even in developed countries women still earned less than men for doing the same job, were underrepresented in managerial positions, and played a less significant role in politics than did men. Furthermore, movements for gender equality met strong opposition from individuals and groups who were convinced that women's liberation threatened the family, undermined morality, and would leave women unhappy and unfulfilled.

In less economically developed parts of the world, attainment of gender equality faced even more obstacles. Being small, the pool of educated women was less able to promote the development of feminist movements, and advocates for women's rights were few. Supporters of feminism were mainly middle-class, urban women whose concerns had little appeal or even meaning for millions of women in urban slums or rural villages whose lives were a daily struggle against poverty. Religious fundamentalists in the Islamic world and elsewhere also sought to keep women in traditional roles. Even in China and India, both of which adopted strong antidiscrimination laws, it proved difficult to modify, let alone eradicate, centuries-old educational patterns, work stereotypes, marriage customs, and attitudes. More so than in almost any other area of modern life, tradition has held its own against those movements and ideologies that have sought to liberate Third World women from the burdens of patriarchy and inequality.

Women and Iran's Islamic Revolution

❖

99 ◆ *Zand Dokht,*
THE REVOLUTION THAT FAILED WOMEN

Although the Pahlavi rulers of Iran, Reza Shah (1925–1941) and Muhammad Reza Shah (1941–1979), gave women political rights, allowed them to abandon the veil for Western-style dress, and encouraged female literacy and higher education, in the 1970s millions of Iranian women shared in the growing disgust with their government's autocracy, corruption, and secularism. Women played an important role in the massive demonstrations that preceded Muhammad Reza Shah's downfall in 1979 and led to his replacement by a government led by an Islamic fundamentalist, Ayatollah Ruhulla Khomeini (1902–1989). True to its Islamic principles, Khomeini's government revoked Pahlavi legislation on women and the family and reinstated traditional Islamic practices.

Iranian women who had taken advantage of educational opportunities and had benefited professionally during the Pahlavi years opposed the Islamic republic's effort to turn back the clock. In 1979 representatives from various women's organizations founded the Women's Solidarity Committee, an organization dedicated to the protection of women's rights in Iran. Although later banned in Iran itself, Iranian women living in England maintained a branch of the organization in London. Known as the Iranian Woman's Solidarity Group, in the 1980s it published pamphlets and newsletters on issues pertaining to women in Iran. The following selection, written by a Solidarity Committee member, Zand Dokht, appeared in one of its publications in 1981.

QUESTIONS FOR ANALYSIS

1. In what specific ways did the Islamic Revolution in Iran affect women?
2. According to the author, how do Iran's new leaders envision woman's role in society?
3. How does the author explain the fact that so many Iranian women supported the revolution that toppled the shah?
4. Why, in the author's view, did the shahs' reforms fail to satisfy large numbers of Iranian women?

When Khomeini created his Islamic Republic in 1979, he relied on the institution of the family, on support from the women, the merchants, and the private system of landownership. The new Islamic constitution declared women's primary position as mothers. The black veil, symbol of the position of women under Islam, was made compulsory. Guards were posted outside government offices to enforce it, and women were sacked from their jobs without compensation for refusing to wear the veil. The chairman of the Employment Office, in an interview with the government's women's magazine said, "We can account for 100,000 women government employees being sacked as they resisted the order of the revolutionary government when it was demanded of them to put the veil on."

Schools were segregated, which meant that women were barred from some technical schools, even some religious schools, and young girls' education in the villages was halted. Lowering the marriage age for girls to 13, reinstating polygamy and *Sighen* [temporary wives] . . . meant that women did not need education and jobs, they only needed to find husbands.

The Ayatollahs[1] in their numerous public prayers, which grew to be the only possible national activity, continuously gave sermons on the advantages of marriage, family, and children being brought up on their mother's lap. They preached that society would be pure, trouble free, criminal-less (look at the youth problem in the West) if everybody married young, and if men married as many times as possible (to save

the unprotected women who might otherwise become prostitutes). The government created a marriage bank at a time when half the working population was unemployed, whereby men were given huge sums — around £3,500 — to get married. Another *masterpiece* of the revolutionary Islamic government was to create a system of arranged marriages in prisons, between men and women prisoners, to "protect" women after they leave prison.

Because abortion and contraception are now unobtainable, marriage means frequent pregnancy. If you are 13 when you get married, it is likely that you will have six children by the time you are 20. This, in a country where half the total population are already under 16, is a tragedy for future generations.

Religious morality demands that all pleasures and entertainments be banned. Wine, music, dancing, chess, women's parts in theater, cinema and television — you name it, Khomeini banned it. He even segregated the mountains and the seas, for male and female climbers and swimmers.

But compulsory morality, compulsory marriage, and the compulsory wearing of the veil did not create the Holy Society that Khomeini was after; but public lashings, stonings, chopping of hands and daily group executions sank Iran into the age of Barbarism.

Perhaps nowhere else in the world have women been murdered for walking in the street open-faced. The question of the veil is the most important issue of women's liberation in Muslim

---

[1]*Ayatollah* is a title of respect for a high Shiite Muslim religious leader.

countries. The veil, a long engulfing black robe, is the extension of the four walls of the home, where women belong. The veil is the historical symbol of woman's oppression, seclusion, denial of her social participation and equal rights with men. It is a cover which defaces and objectifies women. To wear or not to wear the veil, for Muslim women is "the right to choose." . . .

Why do women, workers and unemployed, support this regime which has done everything in its power to attack their rights and interests? The power of Islam in our culture and tradition has been seriously underestimated . . . and it was through this ideology that Khomeini directed his revolutionary government. The clergy dealt with everyday problems and spoke out on human relationships, sexuality, security and protection of the family and the spiritual needs of human beings. It was easy for people to identify with these issues and support the clergy, although nobody knew what they were later to do. When Khomeini asked for sacrifices — "we haven't made the Revolution in order to eat chicken or dress better" — women (so great in the art of sacrifice) and workers accepted these anti-materialist ideas. . . .

Women's attraction to Khomeini's ideas was not based simply on his Islamic politics, but also on the way he criticized the treatment of women — as secretaries and media sex objects — under the Shah's regime. Women were genuinely unsatisfied and looking for change. Some educated Iranian women went back to Iran from America and Europe to aid the clergy with the same messages, and became the government's spokeswomen. They put on the veil willingly, defended Islamic virtues and spiritual values while drawing from their own experiences in the West. They said it was cold and lonely, Western women were only in pursuit of careers and self-sufficiency, and that their polygamous sexual relationships had not brought them liberation, but confusion and exploitation. These women joined ranks with an already growing force of Muslim women, to retrieve the tradition of true/happy Muslim women — in defense of patriarchy.

The mosque is not just a place of prayer, it is also a social club for women. It provides a warm, safe room for women to meet, chat or listen to a sermon, and there are traditional women-only parties and picnics in gardens or holy places. Take away these traditional and religious customs from women which the Shah — with his capitalist and imperialist reforms, irrelevant to women's needs — tried to do and a huge vacuum is left. Khomeini stepped in to fill that vacuum. The reason why Khomeini won was that the Shah's social-economic program for women was dictatorial, bureaucratic, inadequate (especially in terms of health education) and therefore irrelevant to women's needs. What little the Shah's reform brought to women was just a token gesture. Women dissatisfied with the Shah's reform felt that they had benefited little from him and would not miss it if it was taken away.

An African Perspective on Female Circumcision

❖

100 ◆ Association of African Women for Research and Development,
A STATEMENT ON GENITAL MUTILATION

Female circumcision is a general term describing a variety of ritual procedures ranging from the drawing of blood, to clitoridectomy (the removal of the clitoris), to infibulation (the removal of the clitoris, the labia minora, and most of the labia majora, the remaining sides of which are joined together to leave a small opening). The operation, which in different regions takes place anytime from shortly after birth to the onset of puberty, is usually performed by midwives or

village women without benefit of anesthesia or antibiotics. No accurate statistics on the prevalence of the practice exists. It is most common in sub-Saharan Africa, especially in the Sudan region, but it is also practiced in New Guinea, Australia, Malaysia, Brazil, Mexico, Peru, India, Egypt, and the southern and eastern parts of the Arabian Peninsula. Presumably instituted to encourage chastity by dulling a woman's sexual desire, the practice has come under harsh criticism both from within the societies in which it exists and from outsiders, especially from the West. Efforts to suppress the practice have had, however, little effect among peoples who consider the custom part of their ethnic and religious heritage and a rite of passage into adulthood.

Denunciations of female circumcision by Westerners and Western-inspired campaigns to end the practice have frequently backfired, especially in Africa, where the custom is most deeply rooted. The following statement, issued in 1980 by the Association of African Women for Research and Development (AAWORD), which was founded in 1977 in Dakar, Senegal, reveals that even Africans who oppose the practice resent Western interference.

QUESTIONS FOR ANALYSIS

1. What is the basis of the authors' assertion that critics of female circumcision are guilty of "latent racism"?
2. How have Western criticisms of female circumcision hindered the efforts of African critics to limit the practice?
3. In the view of the authors, what would be an appropriate Western approach to the issue of female circumcision?
4. How might an ardent Western critic of African female circumcision counter the arguments contained in the AAWORD statement?

In the past few years, Western public opinion has been shocked to find out that in the middle of the 20th century thousands of women and children have been "savagely mutilated" because of "barbarous customs from another age." The good conscience of Western society has once again been shaken. Something must be done to help these people, to show public disapproval of such acts.

There have been press conferences, documentary files, headlines in the newspapers, information days, open letters, action groups — all this to mobilize public opinion and put pressure on governments of the countries where genital mutilation is still practiced. . . .

. . . In trying to reach their own public, the new crusaders have fallen back on sensational-

ism, and have become insensitive to the dignity of the very women they want to "save." They are totally unconscious of the latent racism which such a campaign evokes in countries where ethnocentric prejudice is so deep-rooted. And in their conviction that this is a "just cause," they have forgotten that these women from a different race and different culture are also *human beings*, and that solidarity can only exist alongside self-affirmation and mutual respect.

This campaign has aroused three kinds of reaction in Africa:

1. the highly conservative, which stresses the right of cultural difference and the defence of traditional values and practices whose supposed aim is to protect and elevate

women; this view denies Westerners the right to interfere in problems related to culture;

2. which, while condemning genital mutilation for health reasons, considers it premature to open the issue to public debate;

3. which concentrates on the aggressive nature of the campaign and considers that the fanaticism of the new crusaders only serves to draw attention away from the fundamental problems of the economic exploitation and oppression of developing countries, which contribute to the continuation of such practices.

Although all these reactions rightly criticize the campaign against genital mutilation as imperialist and paternalist, they remain passive and defensive. As is the case with many other issues, we refuse here to confront our cultural heritage and to criticize it constructively. We seem to prefer to draw a veil of modesty over certain traditional practices, whatever the consequences may be. However, it is time that Africans realized they must take a position on all problems which concern their society, and to take steps to end any practice which debases human beings.

AAWORD, whose aim is to carry out research which leads to the liberation of African people and women in particular, *firmly condemns* genital mutilation and all other practices — traditional or modern — which oppress women and justify exploiting them economically or socially, as a serious violation of the fundamental rights of women. . . .

However, as far as AAWORD is concerned, the fight against genital mutilation, although necessary, should not take on such proportions that the wood cannot be seen for the trees. Young girls and women who are mutilated in Africa are usually among those who cannot even satisfy their basic needs and who have to struggle daily for survival. This is due to the exploitation of developing countries, manifested especially through the impoverishment of the poorest social classes. In the context of the present world economic crisis, tradition, with all of its constraints, becomes more than ever a form of security for the peoples of the Third World, and especially for the "wretched of the earth." For these people, the modern world, which is primarily Western and bourgeois, can only represent aggression at all levels — political, economic, social and cultural. It is unable to propose viable alternatives for them.

Moreover, to fight against genital mutilation without placing it in the context of ignorance, obscurantism, exploitation, poverty, etc., without questioning the structures and social relations which perpetuate this situation, is like "refusing to see the sun in the middle of the day." This, however, is precisely the approach taken by many Westerners, and is highly suspect, especially since Westerners necessarily profit from the exploitation of the peoples and women of Africa, whether directly or indirectly.

Feminists from developed countries — at least those who are sincerely concerned about this situation rather than those who use it only for their personal prestige — should understand this other aspect of the problem. They must accept that it is a problem for *African women*, and that no change is possible without the conscious participation of African women. They must avoid ill-timed interference, maternalism, ethnocentrism and misuse of power. These are attitudes which can only widen the gap between the Western feminist movement and that of the Third World. . . .

On the question of such traditional practices as genital mutilation, African women must no longer equivocate or react only to Western interference. They must speak out in favour of the total eradication of all these practices, and they must lead information and education campaigns to this end within their own countries and on a continental level.

The Impact of the Indian Dowry System

101 ◆ *EDITORIAL AGAINST DOWRY*

Although some improvement in the status of Hindu women took place under British rule, major steps toward gender equality were taken only after Indian independence in 1947. Women received the right to vote, hold political office, own property, and divorce their husbands; in addition, the government outlawed child marriage and polygamy, and eased restrictions against intercaste marriages. In 1961, the government also outlawed dowries, the gifts of property a new bride's family was expected to make to the husband or the husband's family. It was hoped that such a step would lessen the financial burdens of families with daughters and encourage men from higher castes to marry women from lower castes.

As the following editorial shows, however, the practice of dowries continued, often with tragic results for young married women. This anonymous editorial was originally published in 1979 in *Manushi*, an Indian magazine for women.

QUESTIONS FOR ANALYSIS

1. According to the author of this editorial, is the giving and taking of dowries the result of recent developments or of long-standing Indian traditions?
2. According to the author, why have efforts to end the practice of dowries failed?
3. What does the author see as the solution to the problem?
4. According to the author, to what degree do dowry murders fit into a general pattern of mistreatment of women in Indian society?

Most people are not even aware that the giving and taking of dowry is a legal offense. Since the Prohibition of Dowry Act was passed in 1961, the custom has flowered and flourished, invading castes and communities among whom it was hitherto unknown — sprouting new forms and varieties. It is percolating downwards and becoming so widespread even among the working classes that it is no longer possible to consider it a problem of the middle class alone.

With the entire bourgeois mass media oriented towards viciously promoting the religion of mindless consumerism, demands for dowry are becoming more and more "modernized."

Marriages are made and broken for such items as cars, scooters, TVs, refrigerators and washing machines, wedding receptions in five-star hotels or an air ticket plus the promise of a job for the son-in-law in a foreign country.

In India, we have a glorious heritage of systematic violence on women in the family itself, sati[1] and female infanticide being the two better-known forms. Today, we do not kill girl-babies at birth. We let them die through systematic neglect — the mortality rate among female children is 30-60% higher than among male children. Today, we do not wait till a woman is widowed before we burn her to death.

---

[1]Sati is the custom in which a Hindu widow is willingly cremated on the funeral pyre of her dead husband as a sign of devotion to him.

We burn her in the lifetime of her husband so that he can get a new bride with a fatter dowry.

"Woman burnt to death. A case of suicide has been registered. The police are enquiring into the matter." For years, such three-line news items have appeared almost every day in the newspapers and gone unnoticed. It is only lately that dowry deaths are being given detailed coverage. It is not by accident that fuller reporting of such cases has coincided with a spurt of protest demonstrations.

We, as women, have too long been silent spectators, often willing participants in the degrading drama of matrimony — when girls are advertised, displayed, bargained over, and disposed of with the pious injunction: "Daughter, we are sending you to your husband's home. You are not to leave it till your corpse emerges from its doors." It is significant that in all the cases of dowry murders recently reported, the girls had on previous occasions left the in-laws' houses where they were being tortured and felt insecure. Their parents had insisted on their going back and "adjusting" there.

Death may be slow in coming — a long process of killing the girl's spirit by harassment, taunts, torture. It may be only too quick — fiery and sudden. Dousing the woman with kerosene and setting her on fire seems to have become the most popular way of murdering a daughter-in-law because with police connivance it is the easiest to make out as a case of suicide or accident.

And for every one reported murder, hundreds go unreported, especially in rural areas where it is almost impossible to get redress unless one is rich and influential. . . .

Why is it that gifts have to be given with the daughter? Hindu scriptures proclaim that the girl herself is the most precious of gifts "presented" by her father to her husband. Thus the money transaction between families is bound up with the marriage transaction whereby the girl becomes a piece of transferrable property. So little is a woman worth that a man has literally to be paid to take her off her father's hands.

The dramatic increase in dowry-giving in the post-independence period reflects the declining value of women in our society. Their only worth is as reproducers who provide "legitimate" heirs for their husbands' property.

Most people opposing dowry feel that the problem can be solved by giving girls an equal share in their fathers' property. This was one of the reasons why daughters were given near-equal rights in the Hindu Succession Act, 1956. And yet the law has been reduced to a farce because in most cases, daughters are pressured to, or even willingly sign away their rights in favor of their brothers. In any case, it is the woman's husband who usually controls any property she inherits. So the property transaction remains between men, women acting only as vehicles for this transaction.

This will continue to be so as long as the majority of women remain economically dependent on men and as long as this dependence is reinforced by our social values and institutions so that even those women who earn seldom have the right to control their own income. . . .

. . . We appeal, therefore, to all the women's organizations to undertake a broad-based united action on this issue and launch an intensive, concerted campaign instead of the isolated, sporadic protests which have so far been organized, and which can have only a short-term, limited impact.

Perhaps even more urgent is the need to begin the movement from our own homes. Are we sure that none of us who participated so vociferously in these demonstrations will take dowry from our parents or give it to our daughters in however veiled a form? That we will rather say "No" to marriage than live a life of humiliations and compromises? Do we have the courage to boycott marriages where dowry is given? Even the marriage of a brother or sister or of a dear friend? Will we socially ostracize such people, no matter how close they are to us? All the protest demonstrations will be only so much hot air unless we are prepared to create pressures against dowry beginning from our own homes.

Communism's Reform, Communism's Retreat

After World War II, global politics entered an era of moral and ideological absolutes. On one side was the communist world composed of the Soviet Union, its Eastern European satellites, and China. With authoritarian, one-party governments and centralized economic planning, these states proclaimed their commitment to Marxism and the worldwide demise of capitalism. On the other side was a bloc of states led by the United States that claimed it represented the "free world"; its goal was the defense of capitalism and the spread of liberal democracy. For more than forty years these two blocs organized themselves into military alliances, built up huge nuclear arsenals, supported giant intelligence establishments, and competed for support among the world's nonaligned nations. For both sides the dualisms of the Cold War — communism versus capitalism, the United States versus the Soviet Union, NATO versus the Warsaw Pact — gave clarity, direction, and meaning to international politics.

By the end of the twentieth century, however, communism was no longer a significant force in world affairs. Only four marginal states, Cuba, Laos, Vietnam, and North Korea, were still officially communist and maintained socioeconomic systems that for much of the twentieth century defined what it meant to be communist — one-party rule, tight censorship, collectivized agriculture, and state-controlled economies. China still called itself communist, but in practice had enthusiastically embraced the capitalist road that Mao had so passionately abhorred.

Although communism collapsed in Eastern Europe and the Soviet Union in a brief two-year period between 1989 and 1991, it had been losing ground for more than a decade. Despite the crushing of the Czech reform movement by Soviet troops in 1968, communist orthodoxy was weakening in Eastern Europe. Hungary developed a mixed socialist-capitalist economy that became the strongest in the region, and in 1980 and 1981 Poland was rocked by strikes and demonstrations for political and economic reform sponsored by Solidarity, a new, independent organization of labor unions that was forced to go underground in December 1981 after the communist regime outlawed it and declared martial law.

Chinese communism also underwent significant changes in the late 1970s and 1980s. After Mao Zedong's death in 1976, his successor, the pragmatic Deng Xiaoping, deemphasized ideology and egalitarianism in favor of rapid economic development. He approved the opening of small private businesses, fostered a market economy in agriculture, opened China to foreign investment, supported scientific and technological education, and encouraged Chinese exports of manufactured goods. The results were spectacular, with annual growth rates of 12 percent achieved by the early 1990s. China remained authoritarian and officially communist, but with its commitment to entrepreneurialism and the free market, it was worlds apart from the isolated, ideology-driven China of previous decades.

Within the Soviet Union the era of reform began in 1985 when General Secretary Mikhail Gorbachev introduced policies of glasnost (openness) and perestroika (restructuring) to rejuvenate the Soviet communist system. But his efforts to save communism by democratization and economic liberalization released forces he could not control, and by the end of 1991, communist rule had disappeared throughout Eastern Europe, the Soviet Union had broken apart, and the Cold War was over. No one doubted that a new era of world politics had dawned.

China's New Course

102 ◆ Deng Xiaoping, *SPEECHES AND WRITINGS*

After emerging as a unified empire in the third century B.C.E., China had been the world's most successful state in terms of size, wealth, technological sophistication, and the continuity of its political institutions. This was easy to forget in the nineteenth and twentieth centuries when China became a pawn of the Western powers and a victim of political breakdown, military defeat, and economic decline. In the 1980s, however, China's leaders set a new course for their country, which, if successful, might restore China to preeminence in Asia, if not primacy among the world's powers.

The man responsible for China's change of direction was Deng Xiaoping, the victor in the struggle for power that followed Mao Zedong's death in 1976. Born into the family of a well-off landowner in 1904, Deng was sent to France after World War I to continue his education. Having spent all his money, he worked in a factory before returning to China by way of the Soviet Union, where he studied in 1925 and 1926. On his return to China he joined the Communist Party and became one of Mao's loyal followers in the long struggle against the Guomindang and the Japanese. After 1949 he became a member of the politburo, with responsibilities for overseeing economic development in south China. Following the Party line, he supported the Stalinist model for China's economic development through investment in heavy industry, agricultural collectivization, and central planning. This was scrapped in 1958 when Mao instituted the Great Leap Forward. In the wake of its failure, Deng and other moderates dismantled the communes and reintroduced centralized planning.

This made Deng a prime candidate for vilification during the Cultural Revolution. Having fallen from power, he was paraded through the streets in a dunce cap and put to work in a mess hall and a tractor repair shop. As the intensity of the Cultural Revolution diminished, Deng was reinstated as a Party official, and after Mao's death he led the moderates in their struggle with the radicals led by Mao's widow, Jiang Qing. Deng's faction won, and in December 1978, the Communist Party's Central Committee officially abandoned Mao's emphasis on ideology and class struggle in favor of a moderate, pragmatic policy designed to achieve the "four modernizations" in science and technology, agriculture, industry, and the military. To encourage economic growth, the government fostered free markets, competition, and private incentives. Although Deng claimed that China had entered its "second revolution," it was an economic revolution only. Reformers who demanded the "fifth modernization" — democracy — were arrested and silenced in 1979. A decade later when hundreds of thousands of Chinese demonstrated for democratic reform in 1989 in Beijing, the government crushed the demonstrators with soldiers and tanks, thus assuring the continuation of the Party dictatorship. Deng withdrew from public life in the 1990s, and died in early 1997.

The following excerpts are from speeches and interviews given by Deng between 1983 and 1986.

QUESTIONS FOR ANALYSIS

1. According to Deng, what had been the shortcomings of China's economic development planning under Mao Zedong?
2. According to Deng, how is China's new economic policy truly Marxist and truly socialist?
3. How does Deng view China's role in the world? What implications, in his view, will China's new economic priorities have for its foreign policy?
4. What is Deng's rationale for opposing democracy in China?
5. What similarities and differences do you see between Deng's economic program for China and Stalin's plans for the Soviet Union in the late 1920s and the 1930s (see Chapter 4, source 34)?

MAOISM'S FLAWS

After the founding of the People's Republic, in the rural areas we initiated agrarian reform and launched a movement for the co-operative transformation of agriculture,[1] while in the cities we conducted the socialist transformation of capitalist industry and commerce.[2] We were successful in both. However, from 1957 on, China was plagued by "Left" ideology, which gradually became dominant. During the Great Leap Forward in 1958, people rushed headlong into mass action to establish people's communes. They placed lopsided emphasis on making the communes large in size and collective in nature, urging everyone to "eat from the same big pot," and by so doing brought disaster upon the nation. We won't even mention the "cultural revolution." . . . During the 20 years from 1958 to 1978 the income of peasants and workers rose only a little, and consequently their standard of living remained very low. The development of the productive forces was sluggish during those years. In 1978 per capita GNP was less than $250. . . .

Comrade Mao Zedong was a great leader, and it was under his leadership that the Chinese revolution triumphed. But he made the grave mistake of neglecting the development of the productive forces. . . .

[1]Following the communist victory in 1949, large estates were confiscated from landlords and redistributed to the peasantry. But in the early 1950s agriculture became collectivized under state control, and peasants essentially became paid agricultural laborers who turned over their crops to the government in return for wages.

[2]During the 1950s private businesses involved in manufacturing and finance were phased out and became state enterprises subject to centralized state control.

The fundamental principle of Marxism is that the productive forces must be developed. The goal for Marxists is to realize communism, which must be built on the basis of highly developed productive forces. What is a communist society? It is a society in which there is vast material wealth and in which the principle of from each according to his ability, to each according to his needs is applied. . . .

Our experience in the 20 years from 1958 to 1978 teaches us that poverty is not socialism, that socialism means eliminating poverty. Unless you are developing the productive forces and raising people's living standards, you cannot say that you are building socialism.

After the Third Plenary Session[3] we proceeded to explore ways of building socialism in China. Finally we decided to develop the productive forces and gradually expand the economy. The first goal we set was to achieve comparative prosperity by the end of the century. . . . So taking population increase into consideration, we planned to quadruple our GNP, which meant that per capita GNP would grow from $250 to $800 or $1,000. We shall lead a much better life when we reach this level, although it is still much lower than that of the developed countries. That is why we call it comparative prosperity. When we attain that level, China's GNP will have reached $1,000 billion, representing increased national strength. And the most populous nation in the world will have shaken off poverty and be able to make a greater contribution to mankind. With a GNP of $1,000 billion as a springboard, within 30 or 50 more years — 50, to be more accurate — China may reach its second goal, to approach the level of the developed countries. . . . We began our reform in the countryside. The main point of the rural reform has been to bring the peasants' initiative into full play by introducing the responsibility system and discarding the

system whereby everybody ate from the same big pot. . . . After three years of practice the rural reform has proved successful. I can say with assurance it is a good policy. The countryside has assumed a new look. The living standards of 90 per cent of the rural population have been raised. . . .

. . . Urban reform is more complicated and risky. This is especially true in China, because we have no expertise in this regard. Also, China has traditionally been a very closed society, so that people lack information about what's going on elsewhere. . . .

It is our hope that businessmen and economists in other countries will appreciate that to help China develop will benefit the world. China's foreign trade volume makes up a very small portion of the world's total. If we succeed in quadrupling the GNP, the volume of our foreign trade will increase considerably, promoting China's economic relations with other countries and expanding its market. Therefore, judged from the perspective of world politics and economics, China's development will benefit world peace and the world economy. . . .

TRUE SOCIALISM

Our modernization programme is a socialist programme, not anything else. All our policies for carrying out reform, opening to the outside world and invigorating the domestic economy are designed to develop the socialist economy. We allow the development of individual economy, of joint ventures with both Chinese and foreign investment and of enterprises wholly owned by foreign businessmen, but socialist public ownership will always remain predominant. The aim of socialism is to make all our people prosperous, not to create polarization. If our policies led to polarization, it would mean that we had failed; if a new bourgoisie emerged,

---

[3]The Third Plenary Session of the Eleventh Central Committee of the Chinese Communist Party, held in December 1978, approved the "four modernizations" program favored by Deng.

it would mean that we had strayed from the right path. In encouraging some regions to become prosperous first, we intend that they should help the economically backward ones to develop. Similarly, in encouraging some people to become prosperous first, we intend that they should help others who are still in poverty to become better off, so that there will be common prosperity rather than polarization. A limit should be placed on the wealth of people who become prosperous first, through the income tax, for example. In addition, we should encourage them to contribute money to run schools and build roads, although we definitely shouldn't set quotas for them. . . .

In short, predominance of public ownership and common prosperity are the two fundamental socialist principles that we must adhere to. . . .

SPECIAL ECONOMIC ZONES

In establishing special economic zones[4] and implementing an open policy, we must make it clear that our guideline is just that — to open and not to close.

I was impressed by the prosperity of the Shenzhen[5] Special Economic Zone during my stay there. The pace of construction in Shenzhen is rapid. It is particularly fast in Shekou, because the authorities there are permitted to make their own spending decisions up to a limit of U.S. $5 million. Their slogan is "time is money, efficiency is life." In Shenzhen, it doesn't take long to erect a tall building; the workers complete a storey in a couple of days. The construction workers there are from inland cities. Their high efficiency is due to the "contracted responsibility system," under which they are paid according to their performance, and to a fair system of rewards and penalties.

A special economic zone is a medium for introducing technology, management and knowledge. It is also a window for our foreign policy. Through the special economic zone we can import foreign technology, obtain knowledge and learn management, which is also a kind of knowledge. . . . Public order in Shenzhen is reportedly better than before, and people who slipped off to Hong Kong have begun to return. One reason is that there are more job opportunities and people's incomes and living standards are rising, all of which proves that cultural and ideological progress is based on material progress.

CHINA'S FOREIGN RELATIONS

While invigorating the domestic economy, we have also formulated a policy of opening to the outside world. Reviewing our history, we have concluded that one of the most important reasons for China's long years of stagnation and backwardness was its policy of closing the country to outside contact. Our experience shows that China cannot rebuild itself with its doors closed to the outside and that it cannot develop in isolation from the rest of the world. It goes without saying that a large country like China . . . must depend mainly on itself, on its own efforts. Nevertheless, while holding to self-reliance, we should open our country to the outside world to obtain such aid as foreign investment capital and technology. . . .

CHINA'S POLITICAL FUTURE

The recent student unrest[6] is not going to lead to any major disturbances. But because of its nature it must be taken very seriously. Firm measures must be taken against any student who creates trouble at Tiananmen Square. . . .

---

[4]Special economic zones (SEZ) were restricted areas in which foreign firms could establish plants and house foreign personnel.
[5]A district next to Hong Kong.

[6]Deng made these remarks in December 1986, when student demonstrations and speechmaking on behalf of the prodemocracy movement had been going on in Tiananmen Square in Beijing for several years.

In the beginning, we mainly used persuasion, which is as it should be in dealing with student demonstrators. But if any of them disturb public order or violate the law, they must be dealt with unhesitatingly. Persuasion includes application of the law. . . . It is essential to adhere firmly to the Four Cardinal Principles;[7] otherwise bourgeois liberalization will spread unchecked — and that has been the root cause of the problem. . . .

Without leadership by the Communist Party and without socialism, there is no future for China. This truth has been demonstrated in the past, and it will be demonstrated again in future. When we succeed in raising China's per capita GNP to $4,000 and everyone is prosperous, that will better demonstrate the superiority of socialism over capitalism, it will point the way for three quarters of the world's population and it will provide further proof of the correctness of Marxism. Therefore, we must confidently keep to the socialist road and uphold the Four Cardinal Principles.

We cannot do without dictatorship. We must not only affirm the need for it but exercise it when necessary. Of course, we must be cautious about resorting to dictatorial means and make as few arrests as possible. But if some people attempt to provoke bloodshed, what are we going to do about it? We should first expose their plot and then do our best to avoid shedding blood, even if that means some of our own people get hurt. However, ringleaders who have violated the law must be sentenced according to law. . . . If we take no action and back down, we shall only have more trouble down the road.

---

[7]Issued by Deng in 1979, the Four Cardinal Principles were (1) the socialist path, (2) the dictatorship of the proletariat, (3) party leadership, (4) Marxism–Leninism–Mao Zedong thought.

Visualizing China in the Modernization Era

103 ◆ *CHINESE POSTER ART FROM THE 1980s*

Although China's leaders in the 1980s rejected much of Mao Zedong's legacy, they continued the practice of using posters to convey their political message. Not surprisingly, however, as is shown in the following posters, their message was dramatically different. The first poster, *Advance Bravely Along the Road of Socialism with Chinese Characteristics* (1989) shows a group of Chinese advancing toward the future against a dramatic background of construction projects, doves, and unfurled banners. The second poster, *The Age of Smiling* (1988), shows an attractive young woman, brimming with courtesy and polite behavior, who is selling two brands of cola that were popular in China in the 1980s but were swept away by Pepsi-Cola and Coca-Cola in the 1990s.

QUESTIONS FOR ANALYSIS

1. Consider the backgrounds to *Advance Bravely* and *The Age of Smiling*. What do they communicate about the government's vision of China's future?
2. What are the social backgrounds of the people depicted in *Advance Bravely*? How do their backgrounds differ from those of the individuals who are featured in the posters from Mao's era (see Chapter 10, source 83)?

3. Consider the outward appearance and demeanor of the individuals in
   Advance Bravely and *The Age of Smiling*. How do they differ from those of
   the individuals depicted in the posters from the 1960s and 1970s? What
   explains these differences?

Advance bravely along the road of socialism with Chinese characteristics (1989)

The Age of Smiling (1988)

A Plan to Save Communism in the Soviet Union

104 ◆ *Mikhail Gorbachev, PERESTROIKA*

The Soviet Union in the 1970s and 1980s was still one of the world's two super-powers. It had an enormous army, what was perceived as an impressive indus-trial establishment, a solid record of technological achievement, and a seemingly unshakable authoritarian government. No one saw any reason why it would not continue to be the United States's great rival in international affairs. In reality, industrial and agricultural production was stagnating, the people's morale was plummeting, and a fossilized bureaucracy — the nomenklatura — was mired in old policies and theories that no longer worked. Against this background Mikhail Gorbachev became general secretary of the Communist Party in March 1985 and began the task of reviving Soviet communism by introducing reforms based on glasnost, or openness, and perestroika, or restructuring.

Gorbachev, the son of peasants and with training in law and agricultural economics, joined the Communist Party and steadily advanced in the Party hierarchy. In 1979 he became a member of the politburo, the ultimate power in the Soviet state, and in 1985 was elevated to the position of general secretary at the age of fifty-four. After serving as the Soviet leader for two years, he published a book, *Perestroika*, from which the following excerpts are taken. In them Gorbachev outlines his goals for communism in the Soviet Union.

QUESTIONS FOR ANALYSIS

1. What conditions in the Soviet Union convinced Gorbachev that Soviet society and government were in need of reform?
2. In Gorbachev's analysis, what caused Soviet society to lose its momentum?
3. How, in Gorbachev's view, will the individual in Soviet society be affected by his reforms?
4. To what extent is Gorbachev's idea of perestroika democratic?
5. What similarities and differences do you see between Gorbachev's statements about perestroika and Deng Xiaoping's plans for China (see source 103)?
6. Compare and contrast Gorbachev's views of Soviet society with those of Soviet and Eastern European dissidents from the 1960s and early 1970s (see Chapter 10, sources 77 and 79).

Over the past seven decades — a short span in the history of human civilization — our country has traveled a path equal to centuries. One of the mightiest powers in the world rose up to replace the backward semi-colonial and semi-feudal Russian Empire. . . .

At some stage — this became particularly clear in the latter half of the seventies — something happened that was at first sight inexplicable. The country began to lose momentum. Economic failures became more frequent. . . . Elements of what we call stagnation and other phenomena alien to socialism began to appear in the life of society. A kind of "braking mechanism" affecting social and economic development formed. And all this happened at a time when scientific and technological revolution opened up new prospects for economic and social progress. . . .

. . . In the last fifteen years the national income growth rates had declined by more than a half and by the beginning of the eighties had fallen to a level close to economic stagnation. A country that was once quickly closing on the world's advanced nations began to lose one position after another. . . .

It became typical of many of our economic executives to think not of how to build up the national assets, but of how to put more material, labor, and working time into an item to sell it at a higher price. Consequently, for all our "gross output," there was a shortage of goods. We spent, in fact we are still spending, far more on raw materials, energy, and other resources per unit of output than other developed nations. Our country's wealth in terms of natural and manpower resources has spoilt, one may even say corrupted, us. . . .

The presentation of a "problem-free" reality backfired: a breach had formed between word and deed, which bred public passivity and disbelief in the slogans being proclaimed. It was only natural that this situation resulted in a credibility gap: everything that was proclaimed from the rostrums and printed in newspapers and textbooks was put in question. Decay began in public morals; the great feeling of solidarity with each other that was forged during the heroic times of the Revolution, the first five-year plans, the Great Patriotic War,[1] and postwar rehabilitation was weakening; alcoholism, drug addiction, and crime were growing; and the penetration of the stereotypes of mass culture alien to us, which bred vulgarity and low tastes and brought about ideological barrenness, increased.

Political flirtation and mass distribution of awards, titles, and bonuses often replaced genuine concern for the people, for their living and working conditions, for a favorable social atmosphere. An atmosphere emerged of "everything goes," and fewer and fewer demands were made on discipline and responsibility. Attempts were made to cover it all up with pompous campaigns and undertakings and celebrations. . . . The world of day-to-day realities and the world of feigned prosperity were diverging more and more. . . .

By saying all this I want to make the reader understand that the energy for revolutionary change has been accumulating amid our people and in the Party for some time. And the ideas of perestroika have been prompted not just by pragmatic interests and considerations but also by our troubled conscience, by the indomitable commitment to ideals which we inherited from the Revolution and as a result of a theoretical quest which gave us a better knowledge of society and reinforced our determination to go ahead. . . .

. . . Here I think it is appropriate to draw your attention to one specific feature of socialism. I have in mind the high degree of social protection in our society. On the one hand, it is, doubtless, a benefit and a major achievement of ours. On the other, it makes some people spongers.

There is virtually no unemployment. The state has assumed concern for ensuring employment. Even a person dismissed for laziness or a breach of labor discipline must be given another job. Also, wage-leveling has become a regular feature of our everyday life: even if a person is a bad worker, he gets enough to live fairly comfortably. The children of an outright parasite will not be left to the mercy of fate. We have enormous sums of money concentrated in the social funds from which people receive financial assistance. The same funds provide subsidies for the upkeep of kindergartens, orphanages, Young Pioneer[2] houses, and other institutions related to children's creativity and sport. Health care is free, and so is education. People are protected from the vicissitudes of life, and we are proud of this.

But we also see that dishonest people try to exploit these advantages of socialism; they know only their rights, but they do not want to know their duties: they work poorly, shirk, and drink hard. . . . They give little to society, but nevertheless managed to get from it all that is possible and what even seems impossible; they have lived on unearned incomes.

The policy of restructuring puts everything in its place. We are fully restoring the principle of socialism. "From each according to his ability, to each according to his work," and we seek to affirm social justice for all, equal rights for all, one law for all, one kind of discipline for all, and high responsibilities for each. Perestroika raises the level of social responsibility and expectation. . . .

It is essential to learn to adjust policy in keeping with the way it is received by the masses, and to ensure feedback, absorbing the ideas, opinions, and advice coming from the people. The masses suggest a lot of useful and interesting things which are not always clearly perceived "from the top." That is why we must prevent at all costs an arrogant attitude to what people are saying. In the final account the most important thing for the success of perestroika is the people's attitude to it.

---

[1] The name for World War II in the Soviet Union.

[2] A youth organization sponsored by the Soviet regime.

Thus, not only theory but the reality of the processes under way made us embark on the program for all-around democratic changes in public life which we presented at the January 1987 Plenary Meeting of the CPSU[3] Central Committee.

The Plenary Meeting encouraged extensive efforts to strengthen the democratic basis of Soviet society, to develop self-government and extend glasnost, that is openness, in the entire management network. We see now how stimulating that impulse was for the nation. Democratic changes have been taking place at every work collective, at every state and public organization, and within the Party. More glasnost, genuine control from "below," and greater initiative and enterprise at work are now part and parcel of our life. . . .

Perestroika means overcoming the stagnation process, breaking down the braking mechanism, creating a dependable and effective mechanism for the acceleration of social and economic progress and giving it greater dynamism.

Perestroika means mass initiative. It is the comprehensive development of democracy, socialist self-government, encouraging of initiative and creative endeavor, improved order and discipline, more glasnost, criticism, and self-criticism in all spheres of our society. It is utmost respect for the individual and consideration for personal dignity.

Perestroika is the all-around intensification of the Soviet economy, the revival and develop-ment of the principles of democratic centralism in running the national economy, the universal introduction of economic methods, the renunciation of management by injunction and by administrative methods, and the over-all encouragement of innovation and socialist enterprise. . . .

Perestroika means priority development of the social sphere aimed at ever better satisfaction of the Soviet people's requirements for good living and working conditions, for good rest and recreation, education, and health care. It means unceasing concern for cultural and spiritual wealth, for the culture of every individual and society as a whole.

Perestroika means the elimination from society of the distortions of socialist ethics, the consistent implementation of the principles of social justice. It means the unity of words and deeds, rights and duties. It is the elevation of honest, highly-qualified labor, the overcoming of leveling tendencies in pay and consumerism. . . .

. . . The essence of perestroika lies in the fact that it *unites socialism with democracy* and revives the Leninist concept of socialist construction both in theory and in practice. Such is the essence of perestroika, which accounts for its genuine revolutionary spirit and its all-embracing scope.

The goal is worth the effort. And we are sure that our effort will be a worthy contribution to humanity's social progress.

---

[3]Communist Party of the Soviet Union.

CHAPTER 13

The Century's Last Decade

The twentieth century's last decade had a promising start. After forty years of international tension, ideological conflict, and the threat of nuclear holocaust, the Cold War was over, and according to the U.S. president George Bush a "new world order" had dawned. No one claimed to know exactly what the new order would be like. All but the most cynical, however, hoped that the end of Soviet totalitarianism marked the beginning of a more peaceful and promising era for humanity. Such dreams may yet be realized, but the 1990s were anything but peaceful and harmonious. By decade's end optimism was tempered by a realization that a world without a cold war did not mean a world without conflict and danger.

The 1990s did have their share of impressive, even inspiring, achievements. The inauguration of Nelson Mandela, a black man, as president of South Africa in 1994 definitively ended that nation's apartheid system, one of the century's cruelest expressions of racial bigotry, and inspired hope that human beings elsewhere could resolve conflicts and end injustices. In Eastern Europe new democracies took root, and in Africa, a continent of dictators in the 1970s and 1980s, thirty-six of its fifty-four countries held free elections. Human beings in the 1990s lived longer, and educated more of their children. Population growth slowed, with the mean number of births per woman in Asia, Africa, and Latin America declining to half of what it had been two decades earlier. Scientific and technological advances continued. The mapping of the human genetic code and advancements in computer technology and global communications reconfirmed the awesome power of the human mind.

Other developments in the 1990s were less encouraging. Long-festering conflicts between Protestants and Catholics in Northern Ireland and between Palestinian Arabs and Israelis in the Middle East seemed on the verge of resolution, only to have painstakingly achieved compromises blasted away by renewed violence. Wars — anywhere from twenty-five to thirty-five in each year of the decade — continued to be fought, and nuclear war and nuclear accidents were still possibilities. At decade's end, the five acknowledged nuclear powers, the United States, the Russian Federation, France, Great Britain, and China, had thirty thousand nuclear weapons in their arsenals, and Israel, India, and Pakistan had an undetermined number. The United States continued to plan for a "Star Wars" defensive shield against nuclear attack, and Iraq, North Korea, and Libya all reputedly supported research programs for developing nuclear arms.

Environmental problems persisted. Nothing as traumatic as the Chernobyl nuclear disaster took place, but in 1998 land clearing efforts started fires in the Indonesian rain forest that caused a toxic haze to settle over much of Indonesia and Southeast Asia, closing schools and offices, sickening thousands, and causing the death of 234 passengers on an Indonesian airliner that crashed in the smoke.

The decade's most disturbing events took place in Bosnia, Rwanda, Kosovo, and East Timor, where ethnic and religious hatreds gave rise to unspeakable atrocities that raised troubling questions about our very nature as human beings.

Facing new and old problems, the international community showed little unanimity about how to respond. International conferences sponsored by the United Nations on the environment (Rio de Janeiro, 1992), human rights (Vienna, 1993), population growth (Cairo, 1994), women's rights (Beijing, 1995), and global warming (Kyoto, 1997) revealed wide disagreements on fundamental issues, especially between developed and developing countries. In 1990 and 1991, when the flow of oil to the industrialized world was threatened by Iraq's invasion of Kuwait, the United States and its allies acted decisively to defeat the armies of Saddam Hussein in the Persian Gulf War. But when faced with other crises — ethnic cleansing in Bosnia, famine and AIDs in Africa, mass murder in Rwanda — the response was slow, tentative, and, in the case of Rwanda, so slight as to be useless.

Optimism at the end of the 1990s was also tempered by an acknowledgment that none of the century's major ideologies was likely to make good its promises for humanity. At various points in the twentieth century, advocates of fascism, communism, nationalism, the welfare state, and free market capitalism all claimed to have discovered in their particular ideology a blueprint for a better, perhaps even utopian, future. By century's end, fascism and communism had been discarded, the survival of the nation-state was being called into question, social programs in welfare states were being scaled back, and free market capitalism had proved its ability to produce wealth but not the capacity to provide justice or security.

The twentieth century, so it seemed, destroyed or discredited every ideology that claimed to have a formula for a radically new society and a radically different future. It did not, however, destroy hope. True, it was a century of genocides, wars, and injustices. It was also a century in which many wrongs were righted, many illusions were dispelled, and many human beings proved themselves capable of great vision and courage.

◆

The Debate on Free Trade and Economic Globalization

In July 1944 economists and officials from forty-four nations met in the New Hampshire resort town of Bretton Woods to lay the foundations for the world economy after World War II. Their goal was to create an institutional framework for trade, investment, and finance that would foster economic expansion and strengthen global capitalism, and by doing so would contribute to political stability and peace. The institutions that grew out of the Bretton Woods meeting remained the core of the world economy for the rest of the twentieth century: the International Monetary Fund (IMF), which promotes monetary cooperation and exchange; the World Bank, which makes loans for economic development projects; and the General Agreement on Tariffs and Trade (GATT), which, until it was replaced by the World Trade Organization (WTO) in 1995, provided rules for settling trade disputes and negotiating reductions in trade barriers and tariffs.

All three Bretton Woods institutions, especially GATT, were dedicated to the principles of liberalizing international commerce and free market capitalism. Protectionism, universally practiced in the first half of the twentieth century, had, so the planners believed, hindered growth, inflated prices, sharpened national rivalries through trade wars, and contributed to the collapse of international trade during the Great Depression. Liberalizing world trade would unleash capitalism's full potential and bring about worldwide economic growth. Not incidentally, it also would open markets for the agricultural and manufactured goods of the United States, whose representatives played a preponderant role in framing the Bretton Woods agreements and in administering the organizations they created.

To encourage free trade, GATT sponsored seven sets of negotiations, or "rounds," in the 1960s and 1970s in which member nations negotiated reductions in tariffs and other trade barriers. After the seventh round, the Tokyo Round, in 1979, worldwide tariff levels had fallen from about 40 percent to 5 percent, with tariff duties eliminated completely for some commodities. Despite GATT's accomplishments, the world was still not a free trade utopia. In every country free trade had its critics among economists, consumers, union members, and politicians, and powerful economic interests — Japanese rice farmers, U.S. automakers, and French winemakers, among others — clamored for protection from foreign competitors. Even after having lowered tariffs, therefore, many governments found ways to limit imports through nontariff barriers (NTBs) such as quotas, special labeling and packaging requirements, and complex customs procedures and rules. By the late 1970s, with global recession setting in, more governments took steps to keep foreign products out of their domestic markets, and the prospects for free trade looked dim.

Beginning in the mid 1980s, however, with the backing of multinational corporations eager to tap into new markets and the support of newly elected European and U.S. politicians dedicated to free market principles, free trade made a comeback. By the mid 1980s the European Community, which had begun as the European Common Market in 1957 with six members, had expanded to twelve nations, creating a powerful free trade zone in Europe. In addition, in 1986 the eighth round of GATT-sponsored tariff discussions, the Uruguay Round, got under way. After eight years of bargaining, the final protocol, twenty-two thousand pages in length, was a breakthrough for international free trade. Agricultural products and services such as engineering, accounting, and advertising were included for the first time, and steps were taken to eliminate NTBs. Most importantly, the Uruguay Round established the World Trade Organization, a body that would replace GATT and, from its headquarters in Geneva, Switzerland, have authority to investigate grievances, settle trade disputes, and enforce rules. Finally, in 1990 the leaders of Mexico, Canada, and the United States announced their intention to establish a free trade zone in North America. Three years later in 1993, the North American Free Trade Agreement (NAFTA), with strong support from the Clinton administration, gained congressional approval, and in 1995 so did the provisions of the Uruguay Round.

Free trade was once more ascendant, and its supporters were confident that a new era of capitalist expansion was at hand. But free trade still had many opponents, and as the twentieth century closed, the debate about its benefits and liabilities continued.

The Dangers of NAFTA, GATT, and Free Trade

◆

105 ◆ *Ralph Nader,*
FREE TRADE AND THE DECLINE
OF DEMOCRACY

During the nationwide debate preceding the congressional vote on the North American Free Trade Agreement in December 1993, opponents denounced the treaty's economic, political, and environmental implications. A leading critic was Ralph Nader, a lawyer from Connecticut who in the 1960s emerged as a prominent consumer advocate when he published a book, *Unsafe at Any Speed,* about the dangers of flawed automobile design. In the 1970s and 1980s Nader rallied support for a wide range of consumer and environmental causes, and helped found organizations such as the Center for the Study for Responsive Law, the Public Interest Research Group, Congress Watch, and the Tax Reform Group. In 2000 he ran for president on the Green Party ticket, receiving 3 percent of the popular vote. The following article was published in 1993 in an anthology, *The Case Against "Free Trade."*

QUESTIONS FOR ANALYSIS

1. According to Nader, why are multinational corporations so supportive of NAFTA and the new GATT proposals?
2. What will be the economic implications of NAFTA for the U.S. economy, according to Nader?
3. What, in Nader's view, are the potential political dangers of free trade?
4. Why is Nader convinced that there are "no winners" in free trade?
5. What is Nader's alternative to an international economy based on free trade?

Citizens beware. An unprecedented corporate power grab is underway in global negotiations over International trade.

Operating under the deceptive banner of "free" trade, multinational corporations are working hard to expand their control over the international economy and to undo vital health, safety, and environmental protections won by citizen movements across the globe in recent decades.

The megacorporations are not expecting these victories to be gained in town halls, state offices, the U.S. Capitol, or even at the United Nations. They are looking to circumvent the democratic process altogether, in a bold and brazen drive to achieve an autocratic far-reaching agenda through two trade agreements, the U.S.-Mexico-Canada free trade deal (formally known as NAFTA, the North American Free Trade Agreement) and an expansion of the General Agreement on Tariffs and Trade (GATT), called the Uruguay Round.

The Fortune 200's GATT and NAFTA agenda would make the air you breathe dirtier and the water you drink more polluted. It would cost jobs, depress wage levels, and make workplaces less safe. It would destroy family farms and undermine consumer protections such as those ensuring that the food you eat is not compromised by unsanitary conditions or higher levels of pesticides and preservatives.

And that's only for the industrialized countries. The large global companies have an even more ambitious set of goals for the Third World. They hope to use GATT and NAFTA to capitalize on the poverty of Third World countries and exploit their generally low environmental, safety, and wage standards. At the same time, these corporations plan to displace locally owned businesses and solidify their control over developing countries' economies and natural resources. . . .

U.S. corporations long ago learned how to pit states against each other in "a race to the bottom" — to profit from the lower wages, pollution standards, and taxes. Now, through their NAFTA and GATT campaigns, multinational corporations are directing their efforts to the international arena, where desperately poor countries are willing and able to offer standards at 19th century American levels and below.

It's an old game: when fifty years ago the textile workers of Massachusetts demanded higher wages and safer working conditions, the industry moved its factories to the Carolinas and Georgia. If California considers enacting environmental standards in order to make it safer for people to breathe, business threatens to shut down and move to another state.

The trade agreements are crafted to enable corporations to play this game at the global level, to pit country against country in a race to see who can set the lowest wage levels, the lowest environmental standards, the lowest consumer safety standards. . . .

Enactment of the free trade deals virtually ensures that any local, state, or even national effort in the United States to demand that corporations pay their fair share of taxes, provide a decent standard of living to their employees, or limit their pollution of the air, water, and land will be met with the refrain, "You can't burden us like that. If you do, we won't be able to compete. We'll have to close down and move to a country that offers us a more hospitable business climate." This sort of threat is extremely powerful — communities already devastated by plant closures and a declining manufacturing base are desperate not to lose more jobs, and they know all too well from experience that threats of this sort are often carried out.

Want a small-scale preview of the post-GATT and NAFTA free trade world? Check out the U.S.-Mexico border region, where hundreds of U.S. companies have opened up shop during the last two decades in a special free trade zone made up of factories known as *maquiladoras*. . . . Here are some examples of conditions that prevail in the U.S.-Mexico border region:

- In Brownsville, Texas, just across the border from Matamoros, a *maquiladora* town, babies are being born without brains in record numbers; public health officials in the area believe there is a link between anencephaly (the name of this horrendous birth defect) and exposure of pregnant women to certain toxic chemicals dumped in streams and on the ground in the *maquiladoras* across the border. Imagine the effect on fetal health in Matamoros itself.
- U.S. companies in Mexico dump xylene, an industrial solvent, at levels up to 50,000 times

what is allowed in the United States, and some companies dump methylene chloride at levels up to 215,000 times the U.S. standards, according to test results of a U.S. Environmental Protection Agency certified laboratory. . . .
- Working conditions inside the *maquiladora* plants are deplorable. The National Safe Workplace Institute reports that "most experts are in agreement that *maquila* workers suffer much higher levels of injuries than U.S. workers," and notes that "an alarming number of mentally retarded infants have been born to mothers who worked in *maquila* plants during pregnancies."

In many instances, large corporations are already forcing U.S. workers and communities to compete against this Dickensian[1] industrialization — but the situation will become much worse with NAFTA and Uruguay Round expansion of GATT. . . .

Worst of all, the corporate-induced race to the bottom is a game that no country or community can win. There is always some place in the world that is a little worse off, where the living conditions are a little bit more wretched. . . .

. . . "Non-tariff trade barriers," in fact, has become a code phrase to undermine all sorts of citizen-protection standards and regulations. Literally, the term means any measure that is not a tariff and that inhibits trade — for instance restrictions on trade in food containing too much pesticide residue or products that don't meet safety standards. Corporate interests focus on a safety, health, or environmental regulation that they don't like, develop an argument about how it violates the rules of a trade agreement, and then demand that the regulation be revoked. . . .

. . . Already, a Dutch and several U.S. states' recycling programs, the U.S. asbestos ban, the U.S. Delaney clause prohibiting carcinogenic additives to food, a Canadian reforestation program, U.S., Indonesian, and other countries'

---

[1]Many of the novels of the famous English writer Charles Dickens (1812–1879) focused on the bleakness of early factory life.

restrictions on exports of unprocessed logs . . ., the gas guzzler tax, driftnet fishing and whaling restrictions, U.S. laws designed to protect dolphins, smoking and smokeless tobacco restrictions, and a European ban on beef tainted with growth hormones have either been attacked as non-tariff barriers under existing free trade agreements or threatened with future challenges under the Uruguay Round when it is completed. . . .

U.S. citizen groups already have enough problems dealing in Washington with corporate lobbyists and indentured politicians without being told that decisions are going to be made in other countries, by other officials, and by other lobbies that have no accountability or disclosure requirements in the country. . . .

To compound the autocracy, disputes about non-tariff trade barriers are decided not by elected officials or their appointees, but by secretive panels of foreign trade bureaucrats. Only national government representatives are allowed to participate in the trade agreement dispute resolution; citizen organizations are locked out.

. . . As the world prepares to enter the twenty-first century, GATT and NAFTA would lead the planet in exactly the wrong direction. . . . No one denies the usefulness of international trade and commerce. But societies need to focus their attention on fostering community-oriented production. Such smaller-scale operations are more flexible and adaptable to local needs and environmentally sustainable production methods, and more susceptible to democratic controls. They are less likely to threaten to migrate, and they may perceive their interests as more overlapping with general community interests.

Similarly, allocating power to lower level governmental bodies tends to increase citizen power. Concentrating power in international organizations, as the trade pacts do, tends to remove critical decisions from citizen influence — it's a lot easier to get ahold of your city council representative than international trade bureaucrats.

Formulas for Economic Success and Failure

❖

106 ◆ *David R. Henderson, ECONOMIC MIRACLES*

David R. Henderson, a Canadian by birth, received his B.A. from the University of Winnipeg and Ph.D. in economics from the University of California at Los Angeles. He has had academic appointments at the University of Rochester, the University of Santa Clara, and Washington University of St. Louis. During the Reagan administration he served as a senior economist on energy and health policy for the President's Council of Economic Advisers. Since the mid 1990s he has held appointments as a research fellow with the Hoover Institution in Palo Alto, California, and as an associate professor of economics at the Naval Postgraduate School in Monterey, California. In his numerous writings he has strongly criticized government spending while promoting the benefits of freedom and free markets. In his article, "Economic Miracles," published in the journal *Society* in 1995, he offers his views on the benefits of free trade and economic deregulation.

QUESTIONS FOR ANALYSIS

1. According to Henderson, what explains the contrasting economic experiences of South Korea and India in the post–World War II era? What economic lessons does he draw from the experiences of Chile?

2. How, according to Henderson, does government regulation hamper economic performance?
3. Why does Henderson believe that high marginal tax rates so negatively affect economic performance?
4. How would Nader have responded to Henderson's arguments for free trade and economic deregulation?

Our adventure in looking at economic "miracles" begins with a tale of two countries. Their names are withheld to increase the suspense. For now, they will be called country A and country B. In 1950, these two nations are similar in many ways. Measured in 1990 dollars, country A has a per capita income of $240; country B's is $550. Both countries are so far behind the industrialized world that most observers think neither can ever attain a comfortable standard of living, let alone narrow the gap.

Country A has a number of things going for it: ample natural resources, a huge domestic market, railways and other infrastructure that are good by Third-World standards, and competent judges and civil servants. Country B lacks all of these. Country A's savings rate is 12 percent of its gross national product . . ., while country B's in an anemic 8 percent.

In the early 1950s, country A's government begins a policy of heavy government intervention in both international trade and domestic business. Not only does the government impose tariffs in excess of a hundred percent, but it also requires all importers to get permission to import, often refusing to give that permission. Moreover, country A's government imposed detailed regulation on each industry. Let's say that you run a company in country A and you decide that you want to increase production. You cannot just do so without a license from the government. You want to enter an industry, but you cannot do so without a license. You cannot even diversify your product line without a government-granted license. And often the government refuses to grant these licenses.

"Why?," you might ask.

In 1967, one of the bureaucrats answers why. He says that, without the industrial licensing regime, this country would fritter away its resources producing lipstick. . . .

Country A's government also owns and runs entire industries: atomic energy, iron and steel, heavy machinery, coal, railways, airlines, telecommunications, and electricity generation and transmission.

What are the results of all this government intervention? By 1990, country A's income per capita is up from $240 to $350.

Country B's government, with fewer natural resources, less infrastructure, and a lower savings rate, pursues a different policy. It allows much freer trade. And, although it regulates industries, by comparison with country A, it is a model of laissez faire. The result? By 1990, country B's per capita GNP is $5,400, and country B did well in spite of a major war conducted there between 1950 and 1953.

Country A is India. Country B is South Korea. . . .

ECONOMIC POLICIES TO AVOID

. . . By the mid-1950s, Indian firms had to get permission to import components or capital goods, and the government imposed massive tariff rates on those imports that it did allow. These restrictions, combined with many others, caused massive inefficiency. The Indian Tariff Commission complained that everything made a noise in Indian-made cars except the horn. India's economy stagnated.

Then, in June 1991, in the midst of a foreign-debt crisis, newly elected Prime Minister Narasimha Rao and his finance minister, Dr. Manmohan Singh, an economist who had argued in favor of opening India's economy to the rest of the world, began to free the economy. Import controls, except for those on consumer goods, were dismantled, and in three years the highest tariff rates fell by almost half, to 65 percent. The government planned to lower tariffs to 25 percent within four years. . . .

The results of these and other reforms have already been dramatic. Per capita gross domestic product (GDP) is growing at 2.5 percent a year. Exports in 1993 rose by more than 20 percent, to over $22 billion, and are expected to increase another 20 percent in 1994. . . . India's middle class, now numbering 150 million, and with incomes of 30,000 rupees ($20,000 in U.S. purchasing power), is growing by 5 to 10 percent a year. . . .

In the 1950s and 1960s, Chile was highly protectionist, with tariffs averaging over 100 percent. By 1972, socialist president Salvador Allende damaged trade by having the government take it over. Between 1961 and 1972, real GDP grew moderately, averaging 4.2 percent. In 1973, the year of the coup that toppled Allende, economic growth was –5.6 percent.

In desperation, the Pinochet regime turned to the so-called "Chicago boys," native Chileans who had studied economics at the University of Chicago. . . . From 1974 to 1979, trade was liberalized, with average tariffs falling to 10 percent. After two years of adjustment, 1974 and 1975, in which real GDP grew by 1 percent and 12.9 percent respectively, economic growth took off, averaging 7.2 percent a year between 1976 and 1981. . . .

A new round of trade liberalization began in 1985, bringing average tariff levels down to 11 percent by 1991. Between 1986 and 1991, Chilean economic growth averaged 6.7 percent. Economists Rudiger Dornbusch of MIT and Sebastian Edwards of UCLA, both experts on Chile's economy, wrote, "For the second time in two decades, one speaks of a Chilean "miracle.""

What India and Chile learned the hard way is that protectionism stunts growth. Its opposite, an open economy, allows each country to specialize in producing the goods and services in which it has a comparative advantage, and

protectionism removes some of the incentive to specialize. . . .

Avoid Price Controls

Virtually the whole economics profession rejects price controls. . . . The reason is simple: If governments keep prices well below their free-market competitive level, suppliers have much less incentive to supply; demanders have an artificial incentive to demand more. The result is a shortage that gets worse the bigger the gap between controlled prices and the price that would have existed in a free market.

A student of mine from Indonesia, when asked what were the major things he learned in my public policy course, focused on one. He said that he had always wondered why so many rice fields in his country were no longer being used to grow rice and why Indonesia had switched from rice exporter to importer. He now knew the answer: price controls on rice. Indonesia's case is familiar in Third World countries. Many of those countries governments, dominated by urban dweller, impose price controls on agricultural crops and cause huge shortages, and then subsidize imports.

Avoid High Marginal Tax Rates at All Income Levels

In 1979, newly elected Prime Minister Margaret Thatcher cut the United Kingdom's top tax rate on earned income from 83 percent to 60 percent and on so-called "unearned" income (income from interest and dividends) from 98 percent to 60 percent. President Ronald Reagan in 1981, along with Congress, cut marginal tax rates by 23 percent of three years and cut the top tax rate from 70 percent to 50 percent immediately. Following their example, many countries around the world cut marginal tax rates at all income levels. . . .

These tax cuts led to economic booms virtually everywhere they were tried. . . .

Why did such cuts in marginal tax rates lead to economic booms? The reason is that the marginal tax rate is the price people pay to the government for earning income. When the price falls, people will find ways of earning more — by working harder, working smarter, working longer, and moving from the underground economy to the above-ground economy. Similarly, a reduction in the marginal tax rate raises the cost of taking deductions, causing people to take fewer deductions. . . .

Deregulate

. . . One factor that is surprisingly unimportant for economic growth is natural resources. There is little relationship between a country's natural resource base and its degree of economic development. Two of the most resource-rich countries in the world are Russia and Brazil. Both countries, especially Russia, are in terrible economic shape. Hong Kong, on the other hand, which is nothing but a rock at the edge of the ocean — and not even a large rock — is doing quite well economically. . . .

The basic lesson to be learned from the postwar evidence on countries' economic growth is that growth's major enemy is heavy government intervention — whether through tariffs, price controls, high taxes, lavish government spending, or detailed regulation. Therefore, the way to increase economic well-being is to scale back government dramatically. This does not mean that government should do nothing. It has a crucial — role to protect its citizens from foreign invasion, to protect them from each other, to maintain and enforce property rights, and to enforce contracts. But most functions that it performs beyond those few hamper not only freedom but also economic well-being.

◆

The New Immigration and Its Critics

An Indian software designer working in Silicon Valley . . . a Korean shopkeeper in Los Angeles . . . a Haitian cutting sugar cane in the Dominican Republic . . . a Thai girl working as a prostitute in Berlin . . . a Bosnian Muslim forced to flee his homeland to escape ethnic cleansing . . . victims of drought in Mali . . . a Chinese man working fourteen-hour days in New York to pay off the "skinhead" who smuggled him into the United States . . . a Russian playing professional hockey in Detroit. All of these and millions of other human beings from every corner of the globe were part of the changing patterns of international migration at the close of the twentieth century.

Migration has always been a part of human history, but never has it played so prominent a role as in the last forty years of the twentieth century, a time when more human beings chose or were forced to migrate than ever before. In a report issued in 2000, the International Organization for Migration, a Geneva-based agency advocating immigrants' rights, estimated that the number of international migrants, legal and illegal, reached 90 million in 1990, grew to 150 million in 2000, and would continue to grow for at least two more decades. In the 1990s, approximately three in every one hundred human beings were international migrants, and, in contrast to earlier periods when two-thirds of all migrants were males, almost half of these migrants were women.

The geography of migration also changed. Europe, for example, was transformed from a land of emigrants to a land of immigrants. Between 1500 and the mid twentieth century, Europe provided most of the millions of immigrants who populated the Americas, Australia, New Zealand, and parts of Africa. In the late twentieth century, however, this outflow virtually stopped, and Europe became a destination for migrants from the Middle East, the Caribbean, Africa, and Eastern Europe. Migration also changed for the United States, Canada, and Australia, the world's major immigration destinations; during the late twentieth century, all three nations abandoned quota systems that had discriminated against non-Europeans. As a result, Asians in Australia, Asians and West Indians in Canada, and Asians, West Indians, and Latin Americans in the United States became the dominant immigrant groups.

Many factors contributed to these changes: growing economic disparities between rich and poor nations; changing demographic patterns, resulting in slow-growing, aging populations in industrialized states, and younger, fast-growing populations in Africa, Latin America, and Asia; the intensification of ethnic strife and political conflict in many parts of the world; cheaper and faster means of transportation; new technologies that make possible instant communication between immigrants and family and friends at home; the creation of free trade areas that encourage movements of labor; the liberalization of immigration laws in Canada, Australia, and the United States; and, in developing nations, the weakening of restraints on women's independence and freedom of movement. In other words, migration is one part of the transnational revolution that is re-shaping societies around the globe.

Migration can be disruptive, even traumatic, for the migrants themselves, for the countries they are leaving, and for the countries of their destination. This certainly was the case in the late twentieth century, when the number of migrants swelled and most immigrants practiced religions, spoke languages, and came from racial stock different from the majority of those in their new country's population. Thus, as the number of immigrants rose, so too did the number of individuals and organizations demanding immigration restrictions. Opponents of immigration worried about immigration's economic effects, the difficulty of assimilating newcomers, pressures on government services, and, on a deeper level, the dilution and erosion of distinct national cultures in an era of globalization.

The Failure of Multiculturalism

107 ◆ *Jörg Haider, THE FREEDOM I MEAN*

In the second half of the twentieth century Austria became a land of immigration. Between 1945 and 1990 approximately 2.6 million people came to Austria as immigrants or refugees. Most either returned home or moved on to some other country, but approximately 650,000, most of them non-German speakers, stayed and became Austrian citizens. Many of these immigrants were refugees from the Soviet bloc, who, for example, fled Hungary after the Soviet repression of the Hungarian Revolution of 1956 or Czechoslovakia after the crushing of the Prague Spring in 1968. Between 1992 and 1994 Austria also accepted many thousands of Bosnian Muslims fleeing persecution during the Yugoslavian civil war. In addition, beginning in the 1950s Austria became the home of numerous guest workers, mainly unskilled Yugoslavs or Turks who took menial jobs with low salaries. In 1991 there were 260,000 registered guest workers in Austria, and they and their families made up approximately 80 percent of the 550,000 legally registered foreigners in the country.

Unease over immigration to Austria played into the hands of right-wing politicians whose xenophobia and thinly veiled racism echoed discredited Nazi doctrines of the 1930s and 1940s. The leading critic of Austria's immigration policies in the 1980s and 1990s was Jörg Haider (b. 1952), a lawyer who took control of the Austrian Freedom Party in the mid 1980s. Under Haider's leadership, with a platform of nationalism and opposition to immigration, the Freedom Party regularly polled 20 percent in national elections, making it the third-largest party after the Social Democrats and the Austrian People's Party. Following a strong showing in parliamentary elections in late 1999, the Freedom Party joined a coalition government with the People's Party in early 2000. Haider remained on the sidelines, but six members of his party received ministerial posts. Appalled that a European state should empower a party whose doctrines evoked the racism of Nazism, the United States and Israel withdrew their ambassadors from Austria, and the European Union imposed economic and diplomatic sanctions. Haider resigned as head of the Freedom Party in February 2000, but he continued to serve as governor of the Austrian state of Carinthia. In September the European Union, despite protests from France and Germany, ended its sanctions against Austria. Public opinion polls showed continuing strong support for the Freedom Party, and Haider has affirmed his ambition to serve one day as Austrian chancellor.

In 1992 Haider published a collection of speeches and writings entitled *The Freedom I Mean.* In the essay "Multiculturalism and the Love of One's Country," he presents his views on immigration.

QUESTIONS FOR ANALYSIS

1. According to Haider, what has been the cause of the recent upsurge of immigration to Austria?
2. How would Haider define "nation"?
3. According to Haider, why is multiculturalism doomed to failure?
4. In Haider's view, how has the increase in immigration disrupted Austrian society?
5. According to Haider, why do political parties of the left oppose immigration restrictions?
6. What are Haider's short- and long-term solutions to Austria's immigration "problem"?

Of course no country alone can solve the global problem of migration. The discrepancies in wealth between East and West have triggered monumental migration movements, which challenge all the states in Europe. Mass poverty in the Third World, a population explosion and dramatic destruction of the environment, mean that in Africa alone more than 40 million people cannot live in their home countries, but are in search of some other place to survive. . . .

Our job is to tackle the reasons behind migration. Whoever in his own country has no hope for the future will naturally look to go somewhere else. Those who do this, however, should recognize that they come as guests and should behave as such, respecting their host country accordingly.

All the states in the West should try to help people in need so that it is possible for them to stay in their Home Lands and encourage them to rebuild their countries. Let us not forget the generation of our parents, who amidst the ruins and rubble of bombed Germany and Austria did not run away in search of the golden West. With guts, hard work and grit, they rebuilt their countries. They could serve as an example for the youth of Eastern Europe. Or should they all run away, leaving a generation behind whose lives have been ruined by Communism to face further misery?

. . . Since the Left failed to convert people to Marxist Socialism it has been in search of a new ideology, and new enemies. They found their new ideology in the idea of a multi-cultural society which to some has the same appeal as a classless society. But the experiment of a multi-cultural society has never worked anywhere in practice. Wherever and whenever it was tried, immense social problems, ghettos, slums, crime and social unrest ensued. The USA is the best example of this. In the American "melting pot" neither a social nor a cultural balance has been successful. The disturbances in Los Angeles[1] are just an example of many. . . .

Order in a state requires a minimal consensus on basic values. This is endangered when incompatible norms meet each other in an enclosed area. This is the crux of the problem of a multi-cultural society. . . . In many European cities this is best illustrated by immigrants of Islamic faith. In France there are over three million Muslims, in Britain about a million, in Germany roughly 1.7 million. The social order of Islam is diametrically opposed to Western values. . . .

However one assesses the danger of Islamic fundamentalism, the problems posed by the encounter of two very different cultural spheres remain. This is not easy to overcome as we could see from the dispute in France over whether Islamic schoolgirls should wear headscarves. In Austria there was an outcry when Islamic parents demanded that the crucifix be removed from schoolrooms because it offended the religious feelings of their children!

This is the kernel of the problem of a would-be multi-cultural society. It is not the immigrants who integrate into the society and culture they find themselves in; instead they expect from the natives that they should accept their customs. Peaceful integration on these terms is not likely.

A society which does not rest on a shared value system leads inexorably into chaos and the breakup of law and order. This may be [all right] for the fans of leftist teaching with its anarchist tendencies. For citizens who want to live in peace in their country, such "utopian" dreams quickly turn into a nightmare. The arguments of the advocates of multi-cultural society are not only naive and divorced from the real world but for the most part are plain cynical. This is especially true for the argument that we need large immigration to offset the decline in the birth rate. The same people who are for abortion on demand and constantly devalue the family justify unrestricted immigration to compensate for the results. . . .

The question is, who should decide which path to take? In my opinion: the people. Whoever doubts the role of the people as the highest sovereign questions the very essence of democracy. People have the right not just to go to the polls every four years but are entitled to have a say in questions which are decisive for the future of

---

[1]In 1992 Los Angeles experienced widespread street-fighting and looting in which blacks clashed with Latinos and Koreans.

their country. For this reason I and my party introduced at the beginning of 1993 the popular initiative "Austria first", which included the following 12 points:

1. *A constitutional provision: "Austria is no country of immigration".*

On account of its size and density of population, Austria is no country of immigration. Whereas on average in Europe there are 100 inhabitants per square kilometer of settled land, this amounts to 230 inhabitants in Austria.

2. *An end to immigration until a satisfactory solution to the problem of illegal foreigners has been found, until the {housing} shortage has been resolved and until unemployment goes down to 5%.*

In Vienna about 100,000 foreigners live illegally. This puts extra pressure on the labor market and {housing}. Only through an end to immigration can further social conflicts between the indigenous population and foreigners be prevented.

3. *An ID requirement for foreign employees at the work place which should be presented for the work permit and for registration for health insurance.*

Only controls can put a stop to the illegal hiring of foreigners, which has meant not only tax evasion and the bypassing of compulsory social insurance contributions, but has also led to a decline in wage levels. . . .

4. *An expansion of the police-force (aliens and criminal branches) as well as better pay and resources to trace illegal foreigners and to effectively combat crime, especially organized crime.*

To be effective, it is necessary to increase manpower. This can only be achieved through making the profession more attractive. In the first instance this includes an increase in pay.

5. *Immediate creation of permanent border controls (customs-police) in place of the army.*

The auxiliary employment of the army on Austria's border has become a long-term feature. The creation of a separate border patrol from the police and customs officials is absolutely vital.

6. *A reduction of tension in schools by limiting the percentage of pupils with a foreign mother tongue in elementary and vocational schools to a maximum of 30%; in case of more than 30% of foreign speaking children, special classes for foreigners should be set up.*

The preservation of our cultural identity, the achievement of educational goals and the need for integration all make a limitation on the percentage of foreign-speaking children in classes indispensable.

7. *Reduction of tension in schools through participation in regular education by those with only adequate knowledge of German.*

In preparatory classes children of school age with a foreign mother tongue should be taught German in order to enable them to take part in education in the regular school classes.

8. *No right to vote for foreigners in general elections.*

The opposite demand of the government coalition and the Greens[2] is primarily aimed at new votes, gaining to compensate for recent losses.

9. *No premature granting of Austrian citizenship.*

We demand that the 10 year period laid down in the law should be kept and exceptions should be kept to a minimum.

---

[2]The Social Democrats and the Austrian People's Party had ruled Austria as coalition partners since the 1960s. The Green Party, founded in the early 1980s with a proenvironment, progressive agenda, was supported by approximately 5 percent of the electorate in national elections.

10. *Rigorous measures against illegal business activities of foreigners and the abuse of social benefits.*

Many associations of foreigners run restaurants and clubs which do not meet commercial, health or legal requirements. Some serve as centres for the black market.

11. *Immediate deportation and residence ban for foreign offenders of the law.*

The crime rate among foreigners, especially in Vienna, has soared, making it necessary to provide extra detention cells. In practice deportees cannot be detained because of the acute lack of cells.

12. *The establishment of an Eastern Europe Foundation to prevent migration.*

The lasting improvement of conditions of life in Eastern European countries should be provided by specially targeted economic help to prevent emigration for economic reasons.

Too Many Immigrants

◈

108 ◆ *Roy H. Beck,* THE CASE AGAINST IMMIGRATION

The United States is a nation of immigrants, but the number of immigrants diminished dramatically from the 1920s through the 1960s, largely due to restrictive legislation passed in the 1920s. Immigration averaged 185,000 persons a year between 1925 and 1965, and around 250,000 a year in the 1950s and early 1960s. This was a far cry from the average of 880,000 immigrants a year between 1901 and 1910. A major change took place in 1965 with the passage of the Immigration and Nationality Act. This law abolished the quota system adopted in 1924 that favored immigrants from western Europe, limited those from southern and eastern Europe, and totally excluded Asians. The new law made family reunification and the nation's need for skills more important determinants of who would be admitted than nationality. The provision for family reunification meant that if a single family member could gain legal immigrant status, it opened the door to his or her spouse, dependent children, adult children, parents, brothers and sisters. Thus a single immigrant could begin a chain reaction that enabled a large extended family to immigrate.

After the new legislation, legal immigration, mainly from Asia, Latin America, and the Caribbean, rose from an average of 450,000 immigrants per year in the 1970s, to 730,000 in the 1980s, and to over a million in the 1990s. These figures do not include illegal immigrants, who may have numbered as many as three million to five million by the mid 1980s. By the early 1990s more than twenty million Americans had been born in other countries, and legal immigration accounted for almost 40 percent of American population growth.

Against a backdrop of economic recession, a movement to curb legal and illegal immigration into the United States gathered strength in the early 1990s. A leading spokesperson for immigration reform was the journalist Roy H. Beck, who in 1996 published a widely read book, *The Case Against Immigration.* Though trained as a lawyer, Beck became a journalist with jobs at newspapers in Cincinnati; Grand Rapids, Michigan; and Dallas. An active member of the United Methodist Church, he edited the denomination's newsletter in the 1980s. Deeply concerned about environmental issues and poverty, he became convinced that population growth and high immigration were at the root of many social and economic problems in the United States. Since 1991 Beck has edited the quarterly journal *The Social Contract,* which publishes material on population, the environment, and immigration.

QUESTIONS FOR ANALYSIS

1. According to Beck, what have been the most damaging effects of high immigration on U.S. society?
2. In Beck's view, which groups have been most adversely affected by high immigration? Which groups have benefited?
3. Why, according to Beck, has Congress been slow to react to the "immigration crisis," despite widespread support among the general populace for immigration reform?
4. In what ways are Beck's and Haider's views of immigration similar? How are they different?
5. How do the views of Haider and Beck compare to the ideas expressed by the U.S. senator, Henry Cabot Lodge, at the end of the nineteenth century (see Chaper 1, source 9)?

Although we often hear that the United States is a nation of immigrants, we seldom ask just what that means. It can be difficult to ask tough questions about immigration when we see nostalgic images of Ellis Island, recall our own families' coming to America, or encounter a new immigrant who is striving admirably to achieve the American dream.

But tough questions about immigration can no longer be avoided as we enter a fourth decade of unprecedentedly high immigration and struggle with its impact on job markets, on the quality of life and social fabric of our communities, and on the state of the environment. . . .

Until recently, policymakers and politicians of every stripe had ignored what public opinion polls found to be the public's growing dissatisfaction with the abnormally high level of immigration. Majority public opinion can be shallow, fleeting, and wrong, but an honest look at major trends during the recent mass immigration shows that ordinary Americans'

concerns can hardly be dismissed as narrow and unenlightened:

- Whole industries in the 1970s and 1980s reorganized to exploit compliant foreign labor, with the result that conditions have deteriorated for all workers in those industries.
- Long trends of rising U.S. wages have been reversed.
- Poverty has increased.
- The middle-class way of life has come under siege; income disparities have widened disturbingly.
- Aggressive civil rights programs to benefit the descendants of slavery have been watered down, co-opted, and undermined because of the unanticipated volume of new immigration. A nearly half-century march of economic progress for black Americans has been halted and turned back.
- The culture — and even — language — of many local communities has been transformed

against the wishes of their native inhabitants. Instead of spawning healthy diversity, immigration has turned many cities into caldrons of increased ethnic tension and divisiveness.

- A stabilizing U.S. population with low birth rates (like other advanced nations) has become the most rapidly congesting industrialized nation in the world (resembling trends in Third World countries). Vast tracts of remaining farmland, natural habitat, and ecosystems have been destroyed to accommodate the growing population. . . .
- Numerous organized crime syndicates headquartered in the new immigrants' home countries have gained solid beachheads of operations. Law enforcement agencies have been confounded just as they thought they were near victory over the crime organizations that other ethnic groups had brought with them. . . .

. . . Some observers fear that the volume of non-European immigration threatens to swamp America's cultural heritage; others welcome an ever more multicultural society. Nonetheless, the chief difficulties that America faces because of current immigration are not triggered by *who* the immigrants are but by *how many* they are. . . . It is time to confront the true costs and benefits of immigration numbers, which have skyrocketed beyond our society's ability to handle them successfully. . . .

Who wins and who loses? A glance through the roster of immigration winners quickly finds business owners who have followed a low-wage labor strategy. Land developers, real estate agents, home mortgage officials, and others who tend to profit from population growth are winners. Owners of high-tech industries have lowered their costs by importing skilled immigrants who will work at lower wages than college-educated Americans. People who can afford nannies, gardeners, and housekeepers have benefitted from lower costs. . . . Others have won by having the security, prestige, or pay of

their jobs enhanced by the high immigrant flow. That would include immigration lawyers, refugee resettlement agency personnel, officials of immigrant-advocacy groups, and educators and other social services employees who work the immigrants.

Unfortunately, the roster of immigration losers is much larger and includes some of America's most vulnerable citizens: poor children, lower-skilled workers, residents of declining urban communities, large numbers of African Americans, the unskilled immigrants who already are here and face the most severe competition from new immigrants, and even some of America's brightest young people, who lose opportunities to pursue science-based careers because of some corporations' and universities' preferences for foreign scientists and engineers. . . .

. . . Finally, it is the local community as a whole that is forced to assume the costs of immigration. . . . Some of the subsidy is monetary: social services to foreign workers who do not earn enough money to rise above poverty; issuance of new school bonds to educate the foreign workers' children; additional infrastructure to handle an expanding population that cannot pay enough taxes to cover the costs; social services to American workers who lose jobs or drop into poverty wages because of the foreign job competition.

. . . We cannot deny that cutting immigration will hurt some citizens. Most immigration lawyers might lose their livelihood and have to enter other specialties. Not surprisingly, they and their organization, the American Immigration Lawyers Association, have been the most aggressive in fighting any reductions whatsoever. . . . Also suffering from the change — at least temporarily — would be the businesses which the lawyers represent and which have decided to rely heavily on foreign labor. . . . A number of national church bureaucracies and other private refugee organizations might have to cut their staffs. On the other hand, the charitable organizations should be able to find plenty of humanitarian work to do overseas — where nearly all refugees are, anyway — as well as among the black underclass and other impoverished citizens here in America. . . . Then there are the ethnic immigrant organizations that had counted on a continuing flow of their countrymen to boost the power of their budding political machines. . . .

Those few groups that stand to lose money, power, or prestige with a cut in immigration wield tremendous power on Capitol Hill. People representing the broad public interest will have to speak very loudly to be heard. The majority of members of Congress previously earned their living in self-employed occupations or as executives; they think like employers who love a labor surplus instead of like most Americans who depend on paychecks and benefit from tight-labor markets. . . .

Immigration is so high now that the cuts proposed in Congress reduce the numbers only back to the level of the Great Wave.[1] In fighting that slight reduction, the National Association of Manufacturers[2] proclaimed the great myth about immigration: "Legal immigration strengthens and energizes America. Throughout America's history, legally admitted immigrants have been a source of strength and vitality to our nation. Our current legal immigration policies are specifically designed to reflect American values and serve national interests."

Nothing could be further from the truth, if "national interest" is defined by what is good for the majority of the public. High immigration almost always has reflected the values and served the interest of a small elite at the *expense* of the national interest.

---

[1]The "Great Wave" of immigration to the United States from the 1890s to the 1910s.
[2]The National Association of Manufacturers, founded in 1895, is an organization of U.S. industrial and business

firms joined together to further their trade, business, and financial interests, and to publicize the advantages of free enterprise. Its headquarters is in Washington, D.C., where it carries on extensive lobbying activity.

◆

Ethnic Hatreds and Racial Reconciliation

More so than at any other time in human history, racism was a source of oppression and suffering in the twentieth century. Modern racism in the West, with its belief in the superiority of white people of European descent and the inferiority of people of color, took shape in the nineteenth century out of a mix of misapplied Darwinian theory, nationalism, slavery in the Americas, and the growing disparity between "advanced" Europeans and "backward" Africans, Asians, native Australians, and native Americans. Twentieth-century racism gave comfort to imperialists; justified segregation in the United States and South Africa; inspired restrictive immigration laws directed against Asians, southern Europeans, blacks, and Latinos; provided the Nazis with their core beliefs; and was a source of injustice and inequality in many societies.

To the credit of millions of human beings who stood up against racial bigotry and fought to change the institutions it sustained, racism weakened in the second half of the twentieth century. The Nazis were defeated and Nazism totally discredited, colonialism came to an end, segregation laws were eliminated in the United States, and immigration quotas directed against Asians, African, and Latin Americans were discarded. Between 1990 and 1994, the world's last avowedly racist regime ended when the white leaders of South Africa bowed to pressures from their own people and the international community and dismantled the apartheid system. By century's end, racists still existed, and many societies, none more so than the United States, struggled to deal with the legacy of their racist pasts. But at least for the moment, racism was losing its hold.

The same cannot be said for ethnic conflict. Rivalries based on differences in language, religion, and culture have existed throughout history, but as long as most human beings lived in large empires or stateless societies, the destructive potential of such rivalries was limited. In empires ethnic conflicts could be adjudiated or forcefully suppressed by a higher government authority, and in stateless societies conflicts with a neighboring people could be avoided by migration. In the twentieth century — an era of nation-states — neither option was possible. With the end of colonialism in Africa and Asia and the breakup of the Soviet Empire at century's end, many newly created nations had populations consisting of different ethnic groups that became bitter rivals for political power, economic favors, and cultural ascendancy. In a few cases ethnic rivalries were resolved through compromise, and in many more instances they were restrained by authoritarian governments. As the 1990s amply revealed, however, they also led to civil wars, the disintegration of states, and cruelty of the worst kind.

Serbs, Bosnians, and Ethnic Cleansing

❖

109 ◆ *T. D. Allman, SERBIA'S BLOOD WAR*

Created after World War I, multiethnic, religiously divided Yugoslavia was held together tenuously by an authoritarian monarchy in the 1920s and 1930s, and more firmly by the communist government of Marshal Josip Tito from 1945 until Tito's death in 1980. Communist rule continued in the 1980s, with the presidency rotating among representatives of the nation's eight provinces, but it failed to contain destructive nationalist rivalries that between 1990 and 1995 led to the secession of four provinces, a brutal civil war, and the ultimate ruination of the state.

After festering in the 1980s, Yugoslavia's ethnic tensions burst into open conflict in 1991 when the largely Catholic provinces in Slovenia and Croatia declared their independence. Serbs living in Croatia, who were Orthodox, rather than Catholic, Christians, refused to accept Croatian independence, and the government of Serbia, Yugoslavia's most populous state, backed Croatian Serb militias and sent in regular Yugoslavian troops to aid their rebellion. Serbia's rabidly nationalist dictator, Slobodon Milošević, hoped to blocked Croatian independence, or, failing in that goal, sought to conquer as much Croatian territory as possible and include it in an expanded Greater Serbia. Within a few months the Serbs held almost 40 percent of Croatia, and had driven many thousands of Croats from their homes to create ethnically pure Serb enclaves.

In 1992 another Yugoslavian province, Bosnia-Herzegovina, which was mainly Muslim but had large Croat and Serb minorities, also voted for independence. Bosnian Serbs refused to accept the vote, and a complex civil war involving Bosnian Croats, Bosnian Muslims, Bosnian Serbs, Serbia, and newly independent Croatia soon erupted. While Croatia helped itself to Bosnian territory in the west, the Bosnian Serbs, with the aid of the Yugoslavian (essentially Serbian) army took control of most of the province and began a brutal campaign to kill or drive out Bosnia's Muslims through a policy that came to be known as "ethnic cleansing."

Ethnic cleansing was a euphemism for acts of cruelty not visited upon Europe since the Nazi era. Men gang-raped girls barely beyond puberty, slit the throats of neighbors, blew up Muslim homes and mosques, and sent thousands of Bosnian Muslims to concentration camps where they were starved, beaten, tortured, mutilated, taunted, humiliated, and murdered. The Bosnian city of Sarajevo, host of the Winter Olympics in 1984, was reduced to rubble after three years of sniping and artillery fire. The United Nations sent in peacekeepers to enforce cease-fires and protect Muslim enclaves, but the Serbs snubbed their noses at the UN and continued to "cleanse" Muslim villages and neighborhoods. The fighting and murdering ended only in 1995 after the United States arranged the Dayton Peace Agreement, by which Bosnia was to remain a single state that included a Bosnian-Croat federation and a Serb republic.

In 1993 the prominent American journalist T. D. Allman toured the Bosnian countryside, visited concentration camps, and interviewed Serb leaders, including President Milošovíc. He wrote about his visit in an article, "Serbia's Blood War," which was published in the American magazine *Vanity Fair.* In the following excerpts, Allman describes his experiences in Prijedor, a Muslim town taken over by the Serbs; at a concentration camp; and at a dinner hosted by the police chiefs of the cities of Prijedor and Banja Luka, which was also attended by an American writer for *Newsday,* Roy Gutman.

QUESTIONS FOR ANALYSIS

1. What, according to Allman's account, were the methods used by the Serbs to carry out ethnic cleansing?
2. How were the methods of ethnic cleansing related to its ultimate goals?
3. What evidence does Allman's account provide about Serbian attitudes toward the Bosnian Muslims?
4. On the basis of Allman's encounters and conversations with various Serbs, how would you characterize the Serbs' view of themselves, their role in history, and their future? Whom do they blame for the deaths of the Bosnian Muslims?
5. What do the Banja Luka police chief's comments about Jews reveal about his beliefs?

[DEATH IN PRIJEDOR]

The shiny glass teacups and spotless, ironed tea towels are still on their shelves in the kitchen, next to the downstairs bedroom, where the explosion crushed the couple to death. The TV sits in the living room, its vacant glass eye somehow intact, and the little red Lada station wagon waits in the garage, its finish still gleaming.

This town is called Prijedor. It's in northeastern Bosnia, a region paradigmatic of what the world has come to call "ethnic cleansing." . . .

"The Serbs came in the night," a neighbor whispers in German. "The explosion was at one." They put dynamite in the sanctuary of the mosque and around the minaret. When the minaret collapsed, the explosion blew out the back wall of their house. The mother and father were killed instantly. "The children were sleeping upstairs with their grandmother," he adds, "and survived. They fled. No one knows where." . . .

After inspecting the debris of the mosque, which was really just a neighborhood chapel, we drive over to see the Roman Catholic church the Serbs blew up. . . . The church is a tangle of cement and iron girders now, but the steeple stands — or rather it leans — twisted, pock-marked, scorched by the explosion. . . .

It's getting late now, and people scurry past us into their houses, refusing to answer questions. I knock on several doors. Finally, a Serb opens his door. His house faces the side of the church. Windows in his house were shattered. "Blowing up the church was a bad thing to do," he says. He explains why: "Serbs live around here. Serb property was damaged. Serb people were hurt." . . .

[LIFE IN A CONCENTRATION CAMP]

. . . Some 1,200 men are packed into this cattle shed, located on an unprotected mountainside. They are arranged in six long lines, and each man has only the space of a folded blanket where he can sit or lie down on the floor, which is not really a floor, only gravel. The gravel slopes downward, so when it rains or snows the thin blankets are soaked, chilling the emaciated men, none of whom have coats. There is no heating in this shed, or in any of the other sheds in this camp, where some 5,000 people face winter in the same conditions. . . .

Here, as in the intellectual salons of Belgrade, one encounters the lack of shame or guilt that normally characterizes pathological behavior. To the contrary, the Serbs are proud of this camp. They believe it proves they are treating their "prisoners of war" decently. But aside from the fact that conditions here do not comply with the Geneva Convention,[1] there's another note-worthy aspect to these "prisoners of war": none of them are soldiers. They are all still wearing the same light summer civilian clothing they had on when they were apprehended months ago. When I ask the Serb authorities about weapons captured from these "prisoners of war," they say there are none.

Another curiosity: there are no wounded here, or in the camp hospital, which is actually just a small dispensary. They do have men who are suffering, but from disease or malnutrition, not wounds. This raises the question of what the Serbs in Bosnia do with real POWs. "They kill them all," an international relief official who has investigated these matters explains later.

The camp hospital is manned by imprisoned Croat and Bosnian Muslim doctors. . . .

The doctors are terrified . . . and later I learn why. In Bosnia it is Serb practice when they "cleanse" a town like Prijedor to terrorize average people, especially women and children, into fleeing after signing over their houses and other property to what is called "the Serbian Republic of Bosnia and Hercegovina." Men capable — even though not culpable — or armed resistance are imprisoned, like the prisoners in this camp. Then they kill the non-Serb elite: the doctors, lawyers, engineers, rich businessmen, and elected officials, like the mayor of Prijedor, who, along with 48 other of the town's notables, was never seen alive again after being seized by Serb gunmen. . . .

I try to compose a purely technical line of inquiry: "Given the physical circumstances of this camp — the mountain exposure, lack of shelter from the cold, and limited sanitary

---

[1]The Geneva Convention is one of a series of international agreements to provide for humane treatment of the wounded, prisoners of war, and civilians in time of war. The first Convention was signed in 1864, the most recent in 1949.

facilities — what will be the public-health implications of the onset of winter?"

"Forty percent of the people here will die," the doctor answers. . . .

[SUPPING WITH THE DEVIL]

At Banja Luka's Bosna Hotel, which looks like a Ramada Inn, I sup with the Devil, and it occurs to me that I have neglected to bring a long spoon. Actually, the police chief of Prijedor, seated on my right, is amiable, though didactic. Over cocktails he delivers a long discourse on his specialty, which he describes as "ethnic warfare." By his own account he played a major role in "cleansing" Prijedor, and helped run the notorious Omarska camp.

As the first course arrives he opines that it's "very mean" of the media to say Serbs have committed war crimes. "You Americans do not understand ethnic warfare," he says, "because you fight only clean wars, like Kuwait and Vietnam. We do not have that luxury. We Serbs are fighting to save ourselves from genocide." He explains, almost pedantically: "In ethnic warfare the enemy doesn't wear a uniform or carry a gun. Everyone is the enemy." . . .

Our host, the Banja Luka police chief, plays good cop; the Prijedor police chief is the bad cop. . . .

. . . Like nearly all the Serbs I meet, [the Prijedor police chief] believes that Serbia is a great nation, chosen to play a special role in history, and that the world is destined to pay dearly for the folly of not recognizing this fact. "We Serbs forgive, but we don't forget," he says more in sorrow than anger. "We won't forget the West sided with the Muslims and Croats."

"Yes, the world will pay a big price for opposing us," another official agrees.

"What price?" I ask.

"World War I began here," he answers matter-of-factly. "World War III will begin here, too."

This prospect seems to alarm none of our Serb dinner companions. To the contrary, they see it as proof they are right and "the world" is wrong.

"You come from a decadent civilization," the Prijedor police chief elaborates. "You have forgotten who your real enemies are."

At this point the Banja Luka police chief, the good cop, breaks in. "Mr. Gutman," he says amiably, "I think you are Jewish."

"Yes," Roy answers.

"We like Jews!" he says, beaming. "Jews understand Muslims. They know how to deal with them."

Roy resumes his questioning without comment. Is it true, he asks, that Serbs killed all the male children in the village of Verbanći? Can our Serb dinner companions enlighten us on the reports that 167 people were crushed to death trying to escape through an air-conditioning duct because they were suffocating in the room where they were being held? And what about the ravine story: how, after a bus full of Muslims was stopped and the passengers killed, the bodies were thrown down a ravine?

There are three official responses to all such questions, punctuated by smiles and toasts to Serb-American understanding: "Muslim lies." "Croat lies." And: "We are investigating."

Still, even in the good cop's smile, there is puzzlement. Why should this Jew care about Muslim bodies thrown down a ravine? Can't he understand we are all fighting the same enemy — or at least should be? . . .

After a few hours, the debris of the meal lies around us. "A number of the prisoners we saw are starving," I say.

"Because they are Muslims," the official who predicted World War III interjects. "We do everything for them, but sometimes we have only pork grease for cooking, so they refuse to eat." . . .

I begin again. "What did you do to your mayor?" I ask the police chief of Prijedor. "He was freely elected. He was your boss, wasn't he?"

"He was elected by Muslims."

"They say you killed him."

"He escaped."

"Along with the 48 other officials and civic leaders?"

"Yes. Same night. We never saw them again."

"More slivovitz!"[2] the good cop says.

I take another sip and ask, "Do you want your children to be killers or computer salesmen?"

At this point the police chief of Prijedor stands up, looks at me, and says, "I am leaving." There's no anger or hatred in his look, only the realization he's been wasting his time. First he had to be polite to the Jew. . .: Now he's squandered the whole dinner trying to talk sense into the American.

Our dinner party goes on for another hour. The good cop wants his sons to be computer salesmen. "When the war is over," he assures us, "American investment will be welcome in Banja Luka."

---

[2]A plum brandy popular in Balkan countries.

Genocide in Rwanda: 1994

❖

110 ◆ *Fergal Keane, SEASON OF BLOOD*

Their weapons were primitive: Iron bars, nail-studded clubs, and machetes were all they had. Nonetheless, in less than three months government-trained terrorists, with the help of thousands of their countrymen, carried out the twentieth century's most intense and efficient genocide. The place was Rwanda, a landlocked country in east central Africa about the size of Maryland; the time was April, May, and June 1994. In less than ninety days Hutus killed between five hundred thousand and eight hundred thousand Tutsis, as much as 10 percent of their country's population, at a rate three times faster than the Nazi murder of Jews in World War II.

The Rwandan tragedy was grounded in long-standing ethnic rivalries, fears, and resentments, fanned to the point of mass murder by fanatics and desperate politicians. The region of modern Rwanda and Burundi was settled by Bantu-speaking Hutus around the eleventh century. After 1500 they gradually succumbed to the political authority of the Tutsis, pastoralists who moved into the region from the north and, despite making up only 15 percent of the population, reduced the Hutus to semiservile status. When the region became part of German East Africa in the late 1800s, the Germans relied on Tutsi chieftains to administer their colony, and the Belgians did the same after they took over the colony following World War I. Under Belgian rule, Tutsis monopolized administrative posts, army commissions, and places in Rwanda's schools. The Belgians also instituted a pass system in 1933, which classified every Rwandan as a Hutu, Tutsi, or Twa, a pygmoid people that made up only 1 percent of the population. "Race" had little to do with whether one was a Hutu or Tutsi. The Belgians decided that anyone with ten head of cattle or more was a Tutsi, anyone with less was a Hutu, and that a newborn's "ethnicity" would be inherited from his or her father.

In the late 1950s, with independence approaching, the Hutus, fearing future Tutsi domination, rebelled. With Belgian authorities doing little to halt the violence, the Hutus killed thousands of Tutsis and forced many thousands more into exile. The Belgians, believing Tutsi power had been destroyed, replaced Tutsi administrators with Hutus, and when independence came, Hutus dominated the new state. Under the dictatorial rule of Grégoire Habyarimana, Rwanda remained stable in the 1970s and 1980s despite widespread graft, poverty, AIDS, and population pressures. This changed in 1990 when Rwanda was invaded by the army of the Rwandan Patriotic Front (RPF), an organization of Tutsi refugees supported by Uganda, which proclaimed as its goal a multiethnic, democratic state to which Tutsi exiles could return. After three years of fighting, the RPF and Habyarimana signed an agreement that provided for power sharing and future free elections. The compromise enraged Hutu extremists, who launched a hate-filled propaganda campaign against the Tutsis and began to train killing squads (*interahamwe*) made up largely of unemployed young men who were promised the land of Tutsis they killed. Then on April 6, 1994, President Habyarimana was killed after his plane was shot down, probably by Hutu extremists. Claiming the crash had been the work of Tutsi "cockroaches," these same extremists launched their killing squads against Rwanda's Tutsis.

As the killings, rapes, and maimings continued, and the RPF army once more took the field, the world expressed shock but did little, until a small contingent of French troops arrived in late June. By then the RPF had conquered the country, declared a cease-fire, and instituted a coalition government that included Hutu moderates. With more than a million killed or forced into exile, the Rwandan genocide was over.

When the killing began, Fergal Keane, a young Irish-born television reporter for the British Broadcasting Company (BBC), was dispatched to Rwanda to cover the story. With a Ugandan driver, Moses, another BBC reporter, David, two South African cameramen, Glenn and Tony, and Frank, a soldier from the RPF, Keane made his way across Rwanda, preparing a series of award-winning news reports and recording the material for the book he published in 1995, *Season of Blood.*

In the first part of the following excerpt, Keane recounts his visits to an orphanage, to a Rwandan river where thousands drowned, and to a church in Nyarubuye where three thousand Tutsis were slaughtered. In the second part he describes his encounter with two Hutu academics, the rector of the National University of Rwanda at Butare and vice-rector, Dr. Birchmans.

QUESTIONS FOR ANALYSIS

1. What aspects of the Rwandan massacre particularly disturb Keane?
2. How do the actions he describes differ from those of the Serbs in Bosnia?
3. On the basis of Keane's account, what can you conclude about the ultimate goals of the Hutu extremists?
4. How does Dr. Birchmans view the events in Rwanda? How do his views resemble those of the Serbian police chiefs interviewed by Allman?
5. What is the meaning of the episode when Keane was invited to the rector's home to view the World Cup soccer match on television?

[CHILDREN'S STORIES]

A group of children gathered around us. Among them was another girl whose head and right arm were heavily bandaged. I cannot remember her name but her story left me wordless. 'The Interahamwe came to our house and they asked all who are *inyenzi* (cockroaches) to step outside. They knew that we were Tutsis, these people, because some of them are our neighbours. When we did not come out they broke down the door. We were inside and could hear them shouting. And then they came through the front door and I followed my parents and brothers and sisters out into the fields at the back and we ran. But they ran fast and caught us and they killed my family members and they thought they had killed me too. They hit me with the machetes and clubs and then threw all the bodies together so that I was lying under my mother who was dead. But I was not dead and at night I crawled away and hid in the fields where the grass was very high. Then after a time the soldiers of the RPF came and they helped me and brought me here.' . . .

. . . The militias were always on the alert for the exclamations of small frightened voices. Once caught, children were much easier to kill. The little body frames were clubbed and hacked down within minutes. Some, however, survived their appalling injuries. There were many accounts of children who hid under mounds of bodies until they felt it was safe to crawl out. Rose [the director of the orphanage] said that many of the children called out at night in their sleep. Some called for dead parents; others screamed out in the grip of some nightmare whose depth of terror even she, with her experience of war, could not begin to contemplate. For some children the destruction of their entire family groups had robbed them of the will to live. Frequently as we journeyed through Rwanda, we would hear of little boys and girls who had literally died of sorrow, withdrawing from everyone and refusing to eat or drink, until they finally wasted away. . . .

[DEATH AT THE RIVER]

The Kagera River flows from the highlands of Rwanda, down through the country until it crosses the border into Tanzania and then Uganda, finally filtering out into the vastness of Lake Victoria. The river therefore became an ideal carriageway for the dispersal of evidence of Rwanda's genocide. People were routinely lined up beside the river for execution and then pushed into the flood. An alternative method of killing was to force people to jump into the fast running water. Most drowned within a few minutes. The Interahamwe gangs noted that this was a particularly efficient way of killing small children, who were more easily carried off in the current. . . . There were so many bodies it seemed the earth could not hold them. When the dead finally reached Lake Victoria, Ugandan fishermen went out in their boats to recover them and give them a decent burial. Moses and Edward had heard of many men going out day after day without being paid, to gather in the corpses. Colleagues had seen the bodies of mothers and children who had been tied together and thrown into the water. There were thousands of corpses.

[THE SLAUGHTER AT NYARUBUYE]

. . . As I walk towards the gate, I must make a detour to avoid the bodies of several people. There is a child who has been decapitated and there are three other corpses splayed on the ground. . . . I must walk on, stepping over the corpse of a tall man who lies directly across the path, and, feeling the grass brush against my legs, I look down to my left and see a child who has been hacked almost into two pieces. . . .

. . . I begin to pray to myself. 'Our father who art in heaven . . .' These are prayers I have not said since my childhood but I need them now. . . .

. . . We pass a classroom and inside a mother is lying in the corner surrounded by four children.

The chalk marks from the last lesson in mathematics are still on the board. But the desks have been upturned by the killers. It looks as if the woman and her children had tried to hide underneath the desks. We pass around the corner and I step over the remains of a small boy. Again he has been decapitated. To my immediate left is a large room filled with bodies. There is blood, rust coloured now with the passing weeks, smeared on the walls. . . .

. . . While we are waiting for Glenn and Tony to pack the equipment away, we hear a noise coming from one of the rooms of the dead. . . . 'What is that? Did you hear that?' I ask. Edward notices the edge of fear in my voice and strains his ear to listen. But there is no more sound. 'It is only rats, only rats,' says Moses. As we turn to go I look back and in the darkness see the form of the marble Christ gazing down on the dead. The rats scuttle in the classrooms again.

[ENCOUNTERS IN BUTARE]

. . . It is a beautiful evening. The sun is dipping below the thick garden of trees that surrounds the university. Long, slanting rays of golden light come through the window, illuminating the round face of Mr Birchmans and the full glass of whisky he holds in his chubby fingers. Birchmans is a fat man. He has a moon face and big eyes that bulge when he makes one of his frequent denunciations of RPF. . . .

I fill the glasses again and ask Birchmans what has happened to the Tutsis who lived in Butare. They have all left, he says. But surely he must have know about the massacres? No, he has seen nothing like that. Yes, he knows that people have been killed, but in a war people are killed. . . .

'But did the Tutsis deserve to die?'. . .

He pauses. He exhales. 'Killing is a terrible thing, but in war people are killed. That is how it happens.' . . .

◆ ◆

The following night the rector [of the university] comes again to our door. 'Come with me,' he says. 'You are Irish, are you not?'

'Yes, I am,' I reply.

'You will like this, then,' he says, opening the door to his sitting-room, where his wife and several children of all ages are sitting in front of a large television screen. The reception is hazy but I can easily make out the green of the Irish football jerseys. I had forgotten that on the other side of the world, in the middle of the American summer, men were playing in the World Cup. 'Rwanda has no team in this tournament so we will cheer for you,' says the rector.

I am given the most comfortable seat in the room. A deep leather armchair. I notice several family photographs on the wall. There is a portrait of the Pope. When Ireland scores the room explodes into wild cheering. I smile inanely and express my gratitude. While I am sitting watching the game, in a town that has become a citadel of killers, there are thousands of my fellow countrymen cheering and drinking the night away in New York. I wish I was there. I wish I was anywhere but here. 'Goodnight, Monsieur Rector, but you will understand. I have a headache. I am not well and must sleep.' He gives me a puzzled look. There is an element of hurt in his expression. The rector cannot understand why I would reject the friendship of his family. But he says nothing about it. He only shrugs and bids me goodnight.

◆ ◆

. . . I am not an especially religious person but I went to Rwanda believing in a spiritual world in which evil was kept at bay by a powerful force for good. Sometimes the battle was close but I felt there was enough decency and love around to nourish the gift of hope. There will be many who say that I was foolish, naïve to ever have had such faith in man. Maybe they are right. In any event after Rwanda I lost that optimism. I am not sure that it will ever return. For now I can only promise to remember the victims: the dead of Nyarubuye, the wounded and the traumatized, the orphans and the refugees, all of the lost ones whose hands reach out through the ever lengthening distance. At

the very outset I asked what it was that dreams asked of us.[1] Perhaps they request something very ordinary: simply that we do not forget.

---

[1]Keane began the book by describing the nightmares he experienced in the months after leaving Rwanda. In these terrifying dreams, "the brothers and sisters, the mothers and fathers and children, all the great wailing families of the night are back, holding fast with their withering hands, demanding my attention."

Let There Be Justice and Peace for All

111 ◆ Nelson Mandela,
PRESIDENTIAL INAUGURATION SPEECH,
MAY 10, 1994

During the 1980s, as the South African system of apartheid entered its fourth decade, the Nationalist government under P. W. Botha sought to diffuse black resentment by introducing what the government perceived as major social and political reforms. In 1979 it legalized black labor unions, and in the mid 1980s it granted blacks greater property rights in cities, established black town councils with limited control over local affairs, revoked the ban on multiracial political parties, ended the prohibition against interracial marriage, and repealed the hated pass laws that had prohibited the movement of blacks into cities. With most of the nation's apartheid laws unchanged, however, and with blacks still excluded from participation in national politics, blacks responded with rent strikes, school boycotts, demonstrations, and strikes. The government declared a state of emergency, arrested thousands of government opponents, deployed the army in the townships to maintain law and order, and looked the other way when vigilantes attacked black activists.

Faced with a deteriorating economy, almost universal condemnation from the international community, and imminent civil war, President Botha was forced to step down as prime minister in 1989 and was replaced by F. W. de Klerk. Convinced that South Africa's only hope lay in abandoning apartheid, de Klerk in February 1990 lifted the ban on the African National Congress (ANC) and released Nelson Mandela, the leader of the ANC, from a twenty-seven-year prison sentence (see Chapter 11, source 89). In 1991 major apartheid laws were repealed, and ANC leaders and de Klerk's government began negotiations on a new constitution. Overcoming opposition from white rightists, radical black organizations, and the Inkatha Freedom Party, which represented the interests of the Zulus, the two sides drew up a constitution that went into effect in 1994.

In the first election, Nelson Mandela, the heroic black leader who had spent half his adult life in prison for opposing South Africa's white supremacist government, was chosen as the nation's first democratically elected president. His inauguration on May 10, 1994, with representatives of 150 countries in attendance, was a joyful celebration of a new beginning for South Africa. Coming at the end of a century that often showed humanity at its worst, it was also a reminder of the human capacity to right wrongs and overcome even the most extreme forms of injustice.

QUESTIONS FOR ANALYSIS

1. According to Mandela, who should be credited for bringing about the series of events that led to his inauguration?
2. When Mandela uses the phrase "the people of South Africa," to whom is he referring?
3. According to Mandela, what is the significance of his inauguration as president of South Africa?

Today, all of us do, by our presence here, and by our celebrations in other parts of our country and the world, confer glory and hope to newborn liberty. Out of the experience of an extraordinary human disaster that lasted too long, must be born a society of which all humanity will be proud. Our daily deeds as ordinary South Africans must produce an actual South African reality that will reinforce humanity's belief in justice, strengthen its confidence in the nobility of the human soul and sustain all our hopes for a glorious life for all.

All this we owe both to ourselves and to the peoples of the world who are so well represented here today. To my compatriots, I have no hesitation in saying that each one of us is as intimately attached to the soil of this beautiful country as are the famous jacaranda trees of Pretoria and the mimosa trees of the bushveld.

Each time one of us touches the soil of this land, we feel a sense of personal renewal. The national mood changes as the seasons change. We are moved by a sense of joy and exhilaration when the grass turns green and the flowers bloom.

That spiritual and physical oneness we all share with this common homeland explains the depth of the pain we all carried in our hearts as we saw our country tear itself apart in a terrible conflict, and as we saw it spurned, outlawed and isolated by the peoples of the world, precisely because it has become the universal base of the pernicious ideology and practice of racism and racial oppression.

We, the people of South Africa, feel fulfilled that humanity has taken us back into its bosom, that we, who were outlaws not so long ago, have today been given the rare privilege to be host to the nations of the world on our own soil.

We thank all our distinguished international guests for having come to take possession with the people of our country of what is, after all, a common victory for justice, for peace, for human dignity. We trust that you will continue to stand by us as we tackle the challenges of building peace, prosperity, non-sexism, non-racialism and democracy.

We deeply appreciate the role that the masses of our people and their political mass democratic, religious, women, youth, business, traditional and other leaders have played to bring about this conclusion. Not least among them is my Second Deputy President, the Honorable F. W. de Klerk.

We would also like to pay tribute to our security forces, in all their ranks, for the distinguished role they have played in securing our first democratic elections and the transition to democracy, from blood-thirsty forces which still refuse to see the light.

The time for the healing of the wounds has come.

The moment to bridge the chasms that divide us has come.

The time to build is upon us.

We have, at last, achieved our political emancipation. We pledge ourselves to liberate all our people from the continuing bondage of poverty, deprivation, suffering, gender and other discrimination.

We succeeded to take our last steps to freedom in conditions of relative peace. We commit ourselves to the construction of a complete, just and lasting peace.

We have triumphed in the effort to implant hope in the breasts of the millions of our people. We enter into a covenant that we shall build the society in which all South Africans, both black and white, will be able to walk tall, without any fear in their hearts, assured of their inalienable right to human dignity — a rainbow nation at peace with itself and the world.

As a token of its commitment to the renewal of our country, the new Interim Government of National Unity will, as a matter of urgency, address the issue of amnesty for various categories of our people who are currently serving terms of imprisonment.

We dedicate this day to all the heroes and heroines in this country and the rest of the world, who sacrificed in many ways and surrendered their lives so that we could be free.

Their dreams have become reality. Freedom is their reward.

We are both humbled and elevated by the honor and privilege that you, the people of South Africa, have bestowed on us, as the first President of a united, democratic, non-racial and non-sexist South Africa, to lead our country out of the valley of darkness.

We understand it still that there is no easy road to freedom. We know it well that none of us acting alone can achieve success. We must therefore act together as a united people, for national reconciliation, for nation building, for the birth of a new world.

Let there be justice for all.

Let there be peace for all.

Let there be work, bread, water and salt for all.

Let each know that for each the body, the mind and the soul have been freed to fulfill themselves.

Never, never and never again shall it be that this beautiful land will again experience the oppression of one by another and suffer the indignity of being the skunk of the world.

Let freedom reign.

The sun shall never set on so glorious a human achievement!

God bless Africa!

Sources

PART ONE ◆ The World in an Era of Transformation and Western Dominance, 1880–1914

Chapter 1

Source 3: From C. G. K. Gwasa and John Iliffe, *Records of the Maji Maji Rising* (Nairobi: East African Publishing House, 1967), 4–8 (Historical Association of Tanzania, Paper Number 4).

Source 7: David J. Lu, *Japan: A Documentary History.* Copyright © 1997. Reprinted by permission from M. E. Sharpe, Inc., Armonk, NY 10504.

Source 8: Abdool Rehman, "Memorandum to Lord Selborne, High Commissioner of Transvaal, October 1905," from *Collected Works of Mahatma Gandhi,* Vol. V, pp. 96–98. Reprinted with permission.

Chapter 2

Source 10: From *Prescriptions for Saving China: Selected Writings of Sun Yat-sen,* edited by Julie Lee Wei, Ramon H. Myers, and Donald G. Gillin, with the permission of the publisher, Hoover Institution Press. Translation copyright © 1994 by the Board of Trustees of the Lelands Stanford Junior University.

Source 11: From Basil Dmytryshyn, *Imperial Russia: A Source Book, 1700–1917, Third Edition.* Copyright © Academic International Press (Gulf Breeze, Fla. 1999). Reprinted by permission.

Source 12: From *Zapata and the Mexican Revolution* by John Womack Jr. Copyright © 1968 by John Womack Jr. Used by permission of Alfred A. Knopf, a division of Random House, Inc.

Source 13: Bahithat al-Badiya, "A Lecture in the Club of the Umma Party, 1909," as appeared in Margot Badran and Miriam Cooke, *Opening the Gates.* Copyright © 1990. Reprinted by permission of the publisher, Indiana University Press.

Source 15: Reprinted with the permission of The Free Press, a Division of Simon & Schuster, Inc., from *Chinese Civilization: A Source Book* by Patricia Buckley Ebrey. Copyright © 1993 by Patricia Buckley Ebrey.

Source 17: From *Futurist Manifestos* by Umbro Apollonio, translated by F. T. Marinetti and R. W. Flint, copyright © 1970 by Verlag M. Dumont Schauberg and Gabriele Mazzotta editore. English translation © 1973 by Thames & Hudson Ltd. Used by permission of Viking Penguin, a division of Penguin Putnam, Inc.

PART TWO ◆ Decades of War, Economic Upheaval, and Revolution, 1914–1939

Chapter 3

Source 19: By Wilfred Owen, from *The Collected Poems of Wilfred Owen.* Copyright © 1963 by Chatto & Windus, Ltd. Reprinted by permission of New Directions Publishing Corp.

Source 23: V. I. Lenin, *Collected Works,* Vol. 24, pp. 21–25. Copyright © 1964 by Progress Publishers, Moscow, Russia. Reprinted by permission.

Source 24: V. I. Lenin, *Selected Works,* Vol. II, Book I, pp. 382–384. Copyright © 1964 by Progress Publishers, Moscow, Russia. Reprinted by permission.

Source 25: "Comments of the German Delegation to the Paris Peace Conference on the Conditions of Peace, October 1919," in *International Conciliation,* October 1919 (no. 143), pp. 1208, 1210–1213, 1215–1222.

Source 27: Reprinted and edited with the permission of The Free Press, a Division of Simon & Schuster, Inc., from *Chinese Civilization: A Source Book* by Patricia Buckley Ebrey. Copyright © 1993 by Patricia Buckley Ebrey.

Chapter 4

Source 28: From Frank Whitford, *Bauhaus,* Copyright © 1984, pp. 205–207.

Source 30: From H. Hessel Tiltman, *Slump! A Study of Stricken Europe Today,* © 1932, pp. 39–41.

Source 33: From Bell, Susan Groag and Karen M. Offen, eds., *Women, The Family, and Freedom: The Debate in Documents,* Vol. II, 1750–1880. Copyright © 1983 by the Board of Trustees of the Leland Stanford Junior University.

Source 35: From Rudolf Schlesinger, ed., *The Family in the U.S.S.R.* Copyright © 1949. Reprinted by permission of Taylor & Francis Books, Ltd.

Chapter 5

Source 36: Reprinted by permission of the editor from Benjamin Keen, ed., *Latin American Civilization.* Copyright © 1955, pp. 427–429.

Source 37: From *Seven Interpretive Essays on Peruvian Reality* by José Carlos Mariátegui, translated by Marjory Urquidi, Copyright © 1971. Reprinted by permission of the University of Texas Press.

Source 40: Jose Clemente Orozco, *An Autobiography,* trans. Robert Stephenson, © 1962, pp. 19–22. Published by the University of Texas Press.

Chapter 6

Source 42: J. C. Smuts, *Africa and Some World Problems,* © 1930, pp. 46–49, 59–60, 74–76, 90–93. Reprinted by permission of Oxford University Press.

Source 44: "Parable of the Eagle," from Edward W. Smith. From *Aggrey of Africa.* Copyright © 1929 by SCM Press.

Source 45: Donald Low, *The Mind of Buganda.* Copyright © 1971 D. A. Low. Reprinted by permission of the publisher, the University of California Press.

Source 46: Thomas Karis and Gwendolen M. Carter, eds., *From Protest to Challenge. A Documentary History of South Africa,* 1882–1964, vol. 1 (Stanford, Cal.: Hoover Institution Press, 1972), 344–346.

Source 49: Thomas Karis and Gwendolen M. Carter, eds., *From Protest to Challenge: A Documentary History of South Africa,* 1882–1964, vol. 1 (Stanford, Cal.: Hoover Institution Press, 1972), 16–18.

Chapter 7

Source 51: From *The Zionist Idea* by Arthur Hertzberg, copyright © 1959 by Arthur Hertzberg. Used by permission of Doubleday, a division of Random House, Inc.

Source 52: From *The Emergence of the Middle East* by Robert Langdon. © 1970. Reprinted with permission of Wadsworth, a division of Thomson Learning. Fax 800 730-2215.

Source 53: Mohandas Gandhi, *Indian Home Rule* (Madras, India: Ganesh & Co., 1922), pp. 30–35, 47–50, 63–64, 85–86, 90–91. Copyright © 1922. Used by permission of Ganesh & Co.

Source 55: Reprinted by permission of the author from Harry Benda and John Larkin, *The World of Southeast Asia.* Copyright © 1967.

Source 56: Reprinted with the permission of Scribner, a Division of Simon & Schuster from *Modern China from Mandarin to Commissar,* by Dun J. Li. Copyright © 1978 by Dun J. Li.

Source 57: From Mao Zedong, *Selected Works of Ma Tse-Tung.* Copyright © 1965. Reprinted by permission of International Publishers Co.

Source 58: From *Sources of Japanese Tradition, Vol. II,* by Tsunada, de Bary, and Keene. © 1964 Columbia University Press.

Source 59: David J. Lu, *Japan: A Documentary History* (Armonk, NY: M. E. Sharpe, 1997). Reprinted by permission of the author.

PART THREE ◆ From World War II to the Early 1970s: Decades of Conflict, Decolonization, and Economic Recovery

Chapter 8

Source 60: From Neville Chamberlain, *The Struggle for Peace.* Copyright © 1939 Hutchinson Publishing.

Source 62: From Rudolph Höss, edited by Steven Paskuly, *Death Dealer: The Memoirs of The SS Kommandant at Auschwitz,* pp. 141, 142, 156–159, 161–164 (Amherst, NY: Prometheus Books), copyright © 1992. Reprinted by permission of the publisher.

Source 63: Isaiah Trunk, *Jewish Responses to Nazi Persecution* (New York: Stein & Day, 1978), pp. 268–277, passim. Copyright © 1978 by Isaiah Trunk. Reprinted with permission of Scarborough House Publishers.

Source 65: Copyright © 1947 by *Harper's Magazine.* All rights reserved. Reproduced from the February issue by special permission.

Source 66: Arata Osada, *Children of Hiroshima* (London: Taylor and Francis, 1981), pp. 173–177, 265–269; original published in 1980 by Publishing Committee for "Children of Hiroshima."

Source 67: From *Origins of the Cold War: The Novikov, Kennan, and Roberts 'Long' Telegrams of 1946.* Copyright © by the Endowment of the United States Institute of Peace, 1993. Used with permission by the United States Institute of Peace, Washington, D.C.

Source 68: From *Origins of the Cold War: The Novikov, Kennan, and Roberts 'Long' Telegrams of 1946.* Copyright © by the Endowment of the United States Institute of Peace, 1993. Used with permission by the United States Institute of Peace, Washington, D.C.

Chapter 9

Source 70: "Fourth Press Conference Held by General Charles de Gaulle as President of the French Republic in Paris and the Elysee Palace on April 11, 1961," from *Major Addresses, Statements, and Press Conferences of General Charles de Gaulle, May 19, 1958–January 31, 1964* (New York: French Embassy Press and Information Division, 1964), pp. 113–118. Reprinted with permission of the French Embassy in the United States.

Source 71: From *The Feminine Mystique* by Betty Friedan. Copyright © 1983, 1974, 1973, 1963 by Betty Friedan. Used by permission of W. W. Norton & Company, Inc.

Source 72: "Letter from a Birmingham Jail," From Martin Luther King, Jr., *Why We Can't Wait* (New York: Harper and Row, 1963). Reprinted by arrangement with the Heirs to the Estate of Martin Luther King, Jr., c/o Writers House, Inc. as agent for the proprietor. Copyright 1963 by Martin Luther King, Jr., copyright renewed 1991 by Coretta Scott King.

Source 73: "The Obligation to Endure," from *Silent Spring.* Copyright © 1962 by Rachel L. Carson. Copyright © renewed 1990 by Roger Christie. Reprinted by permission of Houghton Mifflin Co. All rights reserved.

Source 74: From *The Times Were A Changin'* by Irwin Unger and Debi Unger. Copyright © 1998 by Irwin Unger. Used by permission of Three Rivers Press, a division of Random House, Inc.

Source 75: "No More Miss Amerca," by Robin Morgan from *Sisterhood is Powerful: An Anthology of Writings from the Women's Liberation Movement,* edited by Robin Morgan. Copyright © Robin Morgan, 1970. Reprinted by permission of Edite Kroll Literary Agency, Inc.

Source 75: From Anne Koedt, Ellen Levine, Anita Rapaone, *Radical Feminist,* Quadrangel Books. Copyright © 1973, pp. 385, 386.

Source 76: *The French Student Uprisings,* by Alain Schnapp and Pierre Vidal-Naquet. Translation by Maria Jolas, copyright © 1971 by Beacon Press. Originally published in French as *Journal de la Commune Etudiante: Textes et Documents Novembre 1967–Juin 1968,* copyright © 1969 by Editions du Seuil. Reprinted by permission of Georges Borchardt, Inc., Literary Agency.

Chapter 10

Source 77: From *An End to Silence: Uncensored Opinion in the Soviet Union* by Stephen F. Cohen, editor, translated by George Saunders. Copyright © 1982 by W. W. Norton & Company, Inc. Used by permission of W. W. Norton & Company, Inc.

Source 78: Richard Sakwa, *The Rise and Fall of the Soviet Union,* © 1999. Reprinted by permission of Routledge UK.

Source 79: Gale Stokes, ed., *From Stalinism to Pluralism* © 1996, pp. 126–127. Reprinted by permission of Oxford University Press.

Source 80: Translation copyright © 1968 by *The Current Digest of the Soviet Press,* published weekly at Columbus, Ohio. Reprinted by permission of the digest.

Source 82: Copyright © 1979 by Monthly Review Press. Reprinted by permission of Monthly Review Foundation.

Chapter 11

Source 84: From Yeyoshafat Herkabi, *The Palestine Convenant and Its Meaning.* Copyright © 1979. Reprinted with permission from Vallentine Mitchell Publishing.

Source 85: From *Who Stands Accused?* by Chaim Herzog. Copyright © 1978 by the State of Israel. Used by permission of Random House, Inc.

Source 86: Guerva, from "Message to the Tricontinental: Create Two, Three, Many Vietnams." Published in English by the Executive Secretariat of the Organization of the Solidarity of the Peoples of Africa, Asia, and Latin America, Havannah, Cuba, April 16, 1967.

Source 88: From General Idi Amin and the Ugandan Army, as found in Martin Mingue and Judith Molloy, *African Aims and Attitudes,* © 1974, pp. 361–365.

Source 89: Nelson Mandela, *No Easy Walk to Freedom,* ed. Ruth First (New York: Basic Books, 1965), pp. 163–168. Copyright © 1965. Used by permission of Heinemann Educational Books, Ltd.

Source 90: From Jawaharlal Nehru, *An Anthology,* Sarvepalli Gopal, ed., pp. 311, 312, 315, 327, 328, 330.

Source 91: From *President Ho Chi Minh Answers President L. B. Johnson.* Copyright © 1967, pp. 9–12, 27–29.

PART FOUR ◆ Century's Close: From Cold War to Globalization

Chapter 12

Source 92: Mana Saeed Al-Otaiba, *Essays on Petroleum.* Copyright © 1982 Croom Helm, pp. 46–47; 50–55; 75–76.

Source 93: From *Made in Japan* by Akio Morita and Edwin M. Reingold, and Mitsuko Shimomura, copyright © 1986 by E. P. Dutton. Used by permission of Dutton, a division of Penguin Putnam, Inc.

Source 94: "Fighting for the Forest," by Chico Mendes, from *Fight for the Forest,* © 1989 Latin America Bureau, London. Reprinted with permission.

Source 95: From Dai Qing, *Yangtze! Yangtze!* Copyright © 1994. Reprinted by permission of the publisher, Kogan Page Ltd.

Source 96: From the English translation of the final document of the Third General Conference of the Latin American Episcopate. Copyright © United States Catholic Conference, Inc., Washington D.C. Reprinted with permission. All rights reserved.

Source 97: Reprinted with permission from Ed Dobson, Jerry Falwell, and Ed Hindson, *The Fundamentalist Phenomenon: The Resurgence of Conservative Christianity.* Copyright © 1981.

Source 98: Girilal Jain, "On Hindu Rashtra," from Koenrad Elst, *Ayodya and After* (New Delhi: Crescent Printing Works, 1991). Reprinted by permission of the author.

Source 99: From Miranda Davies, *Third World, Second Sex.* Copyright © 1983. Reprinted by permission of Zed Books Ltd.

Source 100: From Miranda Davies, *Third World, Second Sex.* Copyright © 1983. Reprinted by permission of Zed Books Ltd.

Source 101: From Madhu Kishwar and Ruth Vanitar, *In Search of Answers: Indian Voices from Manusha.* Copyright © 1984. Reprinted by permission of Zed Books Ltd.

Source 102: Deng Xiaoping, *Fundamental Issues in Present-Day China* (Beijing: Foreign Languages Press, 1987), pp. 105–109; 42–44; 69–72; 101–102; 162–163. Pergamon Press.

Source 104: Pages 18, 19, 21–25, 30–36 from *Perestroika* by Mikhail Gorbachev. Copyright © 1987 by Mikhail Gorbachev. Reprinted by permission of HarperCollins Publishers, Inc.

Chapter 13

Source 105: Ralph Nader et al., *The Case Against Free Trade,* Earth Island Press, © 1993 North Atlantic Books.

Source 106: Reprinted by permission of Transaction Publishers, "Economic Miracles," by David R. Henderson, *Society,* Vol. 32, No. 59, September 1, 1995. Copyright © 1995 by Transaction Publishers; all rights reserved.

Source 107: Reprinted with permission by Swan Books, Pine Plains, New York.

Source 108: From *The Case Against Immigration* by Roy Beck. Copyright © 1996 by Roy Beck. Used by permission of W. W. Norton & Company, Inc.

Source 109: From T. D. Allman, *Why Bosnia?.* Copyright © 1993. Published by The Pamphleteer's Press. Reprinted by permission.

Source 110: Fergal Keene, *A Season of Blood,* (London: Penguin Books Ltd.), pp. 69–72, 74–75, 78–81, 171–174, 190–191. Copyright © 1995. Reproduced by permission of Penguin Books Ltd.

Source 111: Nelson Mandela, "Presidential Inauguration Speech, May 10, 1994," as appeared in *Historic Documents of 1994,* © 1995, pp. 249–251.

Photo Credits

Chapter 3

77 (left): B. Hennerberg, *The Departure.* From *World War I and European Society: A Sourcebook* by Marilyn Shevin-Coetzee and Frans Coetzee (Lexington, MA: D. C. Heath, 1995) p. 6. Copyright 1995. Used by permission of D. C. Heath & Co.

77 (right): Advertisement card from Golden Dawn Cigarettes. Courtesy of Imperial War Museum, London.

78 (left): Australian recruitment poster from 1915. Courtesy of Imperial War Museum, London.

78 (right): French poster encouraging purchase of war bonds, 1916. Courtesy of Imperial War Museum, London.

82: C. R. W. Nevinson, *The Harvest of Battle.* Courtesy of Imperial War Museum, London.

83: Otto Dix, *The War II/2: Storm Troop Advancing Under Gas Attack* (1924). Etching, aquatint and drypoint, printed in black, plate: 7-9/16 × 11-5/16: (19.3 × 28.2 cm.). Courtesy of The Museum of Modern Art, New York. Gift of Abby Aldrich Rockefeller. Photograph Copyright 1997 The Museum of Modern Art, New York.

Chapter 4

115 (top): Main Bauhaus building, designed by architect Walter Gropius in 1926, c. 1930. Hulton Archive. Liaison Agency.

115 (bottom): Master's house from Dessau. Bauhaus-Archiv Museum fur Gestaltung, Klingelhofestrasse. 14, 1 Berlin30.

116 (top): Bauhaus chair, designed by Marcel Breuer in 1927. Cooper-Hewitt Museum, Smithsonian Institution/Art Resource, NY.

116 (bottom): Bauhaus teapot, designed by Marianne Brandt in 1924. Copyright 2001 Artists Rights Society (ARS), New York/VG Gild-Kunst, Bonn.

Chapter 5

164: José Clemente Orozco, *Hispano-American Society.* Copyright 2001 Trustees of Dartmouth College, Hanover, New Hampshire. Not to be produced without permission of the Hood Museum of Art.

165: Diego Rivera, *Imperialism.* Banco de México, Fiduciario en el Fidelicomiso Relativo a los Museos Diego Rivera y Frida Kahlo.

Chapter 10

337 (top): *Chairman Mao Ten Thousand Years! Ten Thousand! Ten Thousand Years!* Internationaal Instituut voor Sociale Geschiedenis.

337 (bottom): *Fully Criticize the Stinking Chinese Khrushchev from a Political, Ideological, and Theoretical Perspective.* Internationaal Instituut voor Sociale Geschiedenis.

338: *Firmly Grasp Large-Scale Revolutionary Criticism.* Internationaal Instituut voor Sociale Geschiedenis.

Chapter 12

417: *Advance Bravely Along the Road of Socialism with Chinese Characteristics* (1989). Internationaal Instituut voor Sociale Geschiedenis.

418: *The Age of Smiling* (1988). Internationaal Instituut voor Sociale Geschiedenis.